from cloisters
to
cup finals

Peter May in stripes (second left) and John Tanner (nearest camera). David Roy and Replay Publishing

from cloisters
to
cup finals

A History of Charterhouse Football

Malcolm Bailey

Dedicated to Angela, Sarah and Matthew for their support,
and to all Carthusian footballers and Brooke Hall coaches.

ISBN 978-1-899163-87-8
Copyright © 2009 Malcolm Bailey
First published 2009

Published by
JJG Publishing
Sparrow Hall
Hindrigham
Norfolk NR21 0DP

Designed by Graham Hiles
Printed in China through Colorcraft Ltd., Hong Kong

contents

aknowleogements

Bob Noble, especially for his statistics

Ann Wheeler, Sue Cole, Shirley Corke and
  Margaret Mardall in Charterhouse's archives

Roger Smeeton for his many photographs

David Miller, President OCFC

David Barber of the Football Association

David Downes, Reading FC

Peter Holme, National Football Museum

Bryan Horsnell

Jason Leggett, Wolverhampton Wanderers FC

John Little, CUAFC

Brian Pearce and all our referees

Colin Weir, David Roy and Replay Publishing

Louis Adomakoh

Richard Balkwill

Dick Crawford

Mike Doggart

Keith Ellis

Peter Godby

Peter Goodliffe

John Peters

Jerry Schofield

The Tetley family

Paul Williams

Archivists at our various competing schools

Corinthian Casuals FC and Rob Cavallini

The Carthusian Society

Publication of this book has been made possible by a generous grant
from the Carthusian Society

Abbreviations

ADC = Arthur Dunn Cup;
LCC = London Charity Cup;
LSC = London Senior Cup;

OCFC = Old Carthusian Football Club;
CUAFC = Cambridge University FC etc.
OQ = school terms (R, g) = House names.

Academic awards and military honours are abbreviated also.

Houses (in order of foundation)

S = Saunderites	g = Girdlestoneites	H = Hodgsonites	P = Pageites
V = Verites	L = Lockites	D = Daviesites	R = Robinites
G = Gownboys	W = Weekites	B = Bodeites	U = Uskites

FOREWORD

As this commendable history went to press, the Old Carthusian Football Club had just won the Arthur Dunn Cup for the twenty-first time, having narrowly defeated ancient rivals from Shrewsbury by the only goal in the semi-final and then, equally narrowly, Brentwood in the final. Not solely on account of this latest success, the contribution of OCFC to the game in England has, without exaggeration, in its modest way been unique. It continues to be so, along with rival schools in League and Cup contests, for being exclusively amateur, the more precious at a time when the professional game, though marvellous in the exhilaration it brings in spectacle from time to time, is increasingly mired by misconduct in many forms. The amateur ethic, in which the game is played for fun, for camaraderie with both colleagues and opponents, is something especially valuable at a time when even the lower levels of football are subjected to financial considerations: where even once-famous Corinthian-Casuals are undermined by the poaching of promising young players for a fee by opponents from relatively lowly minor leagues. In this sense, old-boy football retains a particular distinction. Moreover, current success by OCFC runs in parallel with the School, which recently won, for the first time in four finals, the Independent Schools FA final, defeating Millfield. On both fronts, some of this success is attributable to Malcolm Bailey, for many years the master in charge of the game at Charterhouse, who has helped generate many

years of achievement, comparable to those by other distinguished schoolmaster coaches such as Denis Saunders and Ken Shearwood – both members of the FA Amateur Cup winning teams of Pegasus in the fifties – with respectively Malvern and Lancing, also Robin Trimby with Shrewsbury and Howard Fabian, legendary Corinthian, with Highgate.

It has been my privilege to be associated with Charterhouse football for almost half the 132 years of existence of OCFC, founded in 1876, coming under the influence as a boy of Anthony Wreford Brown, son of Corinthian stalwart centre-half Charles, then later getting to know AG Bower, Carthusian, Corinthian and the last of the amateurs to play for the full England international team, and also to witness the fluctuating successes by OCFC.

The contribution by the School goes back to the foundation of the Football Association in 1863 when BF Hartshorne, the School Captain, was present at the formation meeting by eleven clubs, though abstaining from a vote on account of the uncertainty of action by other schools. In 1882, RL Escombe, member of the School XI two years earlier, was a founding member of the Corinthians. His contemporary WN Cobbold gained with Corinthians the title of "Prince of Dribblers", earning with Carthusian full-backs AM and PM Walters – inevitably "Morning and Afternoon" – lofty international reputation. Then followed in the nineties legendary GO Smith, his dexterity with the ball for England

and Corinthians – scoring ninety goals in 102 appearances for the latter – said to have been a triumph of mind over matter. Early OCFC triumphs in the twenties in the augural years of the Arthur Dunn Cup have punctuated that competition's history, notably again in several seasons following World War II and the advent of another mercurial centre-forward, John Tanner, the last Carthusian to win an amateur cap as well as appearing for a whole season with Huddersfield in the old Football League First Division.

As a player of modest contribution, my four seasons with Pegasus immediately following their second Wembley victory, were an experience of rare physical and mental intoxication: a collective pursuit of excellence which, however humble and ragged it looked on those less successful, sometimes grotty afternoons in all too earthy surroundings far from Wembley, carried a special feeling of crusade, a responsibility beyond oneself and the club to that intangible concept of the game which for over a century has stirred the minds and imaginations of millions. I confess that in my early post-university playing days I yearned for what I thought was

the greater efficiency of the professional to be established in the amateur game, to eliminate much of the dead-wood dogma, the *amateurish* attitude. Yet today, after watching the professional game intimately for fifty years, it is clear that, for all the technical shortcomings of amateur football, it has much to commend it. What is missing in all but a handful of outstanding professional clubs is that premise, drummed into us sixty years ago before school matches by Tony Wreford Brown: the game is always more important than the players.

The lesson not just of Arthur Dunn football but of any sport is that it takes two to make a game. So much of professional sport has been corrupted by an eleventh commandment: that no-one shall be denied the right to earn his or her living by any of the other ten. Too many professionals forget that the quality of the winner is established, in part, by the quality of the loser. Today, as 132 years ago, the amateur still has something worthwhile to teach the pro.

David Miller
President OCFC

David Miller in action in the Centenary Match 1976

ancient roots and the mob game

"Thank God for the public schools," wrote Melvyn Bragg in the *Daily Telegraph* on 15 April 2006, as his television series "12 books that changed the world" was reviewed in the newspaper's sports section. He argued that the group of Oxford undergraduates who sat down in a pub in Lincoln's Inn Fields in 1863 changed the world as much as any scientist or politician, as they devised the Rules of Association Football. The brevity of the rules was a "stroke of organisational genius".

Football or a similar form of the game was played by ancient civilisations in China, with documented evidence found in a Chinese military manual during the Warring States period, around the 4th century BC. This game was known as "cuju" which involved kicking a leather ball through a hole in a silk cloth strung between two poles. This is also known as "tsu'chu" which translated meant kick with feet and leather stuffed ball. In Japan the game was called "kemari" and this eight-a-side activity, played on a court, 14 square metres in size, was simply "keepie uppie" and was performed as part of a religious ceremony within the Japanese imperial court from 600 AD. This has been revived as a tourist attraction. In Greece a game was known as "episkryos" or "pheninda" mentioned by the Greek playwright, Antiphanes (388-311 BC) was probably brought to England by the Romans, who witnessed the game during their invasion of Greece in 146 BC. This game was included in the ancient Olympics. The Romans' game "harpastum" involved two teams, a rectangular pitch and a ball. The idea was to cross the opponent's goal line with the ball as in rugby. Most of these games were violent, as was the game brought to us through the Norman Conquest known as "La Soule" or "Choule". William Fitzstephen in his *History of London*, c.1175, refers to the young men of the city going to the field after dinner to play the well-known game of "ball of the day". "After dinner all the youth of the city goes out into the fields for the very popular game of ball. The scholars from each school have their own ball, and most of the workers of each trade have theirs also in their hands …"

Elsewhere, games of football were played at festivals, notably on Shrove Tuesday and Ash Wednesday, in villages throughout the land from the Orkneys to St Bee's and Ashbourne in Derbyshire to Dorking. Dating as far back as 217 AD, in these settlements, the entire community took part in a mass game in which the ball had to be moved from one part of the village to another by hundreds of people – some "up town" and some "down town". Before the penitential season of Lent, this was a good excuse to let off a bit of noise, to feast and fight. From Medieval times the folk of Seascale, Cumbria went to Laking How (The Hill of Playing) on the third Sunday of Lent. One mob defended The How and the other mob had to prevent the ball from going into the sea. Linkside football was played until the west coast railway cut the "pitch" in half.

Without doubt the game was popular which did not always help crowd control.

Adam Eyre in 1646 discovered that when he went "to Bordhill to see the match played at football between Penistone and Thurlston (South Yorkshire) . . . the crowd hindered and nothing was done".

Married men took on single men at Scone in Scotland and wives played spinsters in Midlothian. Youths chased a ball in the market squares of big cities such as London in Smithfield, Covent Garden and Lincoln Inn fields. From as early as 1280, records show that as a result of deaths from stabbings during the game, weapons were banned. It is thought that the ball represented the sun and it passed over as many fields as possible, to help improve the harvest.

Edward II banned the game in 1314 because of the "rageries" and congestion it caused, whilst Edward III insisted that his people practised archery rather than waste their time with the game of idle practices. Even after the Second World War, midweek football was banned for two seasons to allow "undistracted" industrial production to take place and aid the recovery.

Richard III showed concern for the distractions of games such as football, quoits and dice, as did James I in Scotland. Henry VIII, 1548, and Elizabeth I, in 1572, had to act against it on grounds of disorder. Research has revealed that Henry did actually play himself. Even William Shakespeare makes reference to the game in *The Comedy of Errors*: "That like a football you do spurn me" (Act II; scene I) and he makes use of the word football in King Lear (Act I; scene IV). Cromwell was a keen player at Cambridge and Pepys's diary mentions despite the great frost in the January 1665, "the streets were full of footballs".

Games were reported by travellers as far afield as Greenland, their game called "Aqsaqtuk", and Victoria, Australia where the aborigines played "Marn Grook", which simply means ball game.

In Italy, of course, "calcio", meaning "I kick", was a well-established game at this time. The young aristocratic Italians who played 21-a-side in the Piazza della Signoria in Florence celebrated the feast of St John the Baptist, the city's patron saint. Players could punch, shoulder charge and kick opponents in a game that was thought to be originally a military training exercise. Mussolini insisted that his nation's game retained its name of calcio and did not adopt the

The mob game

universal name of football.

Considering the ancient roots of the game, one wonders, therefore, why England is regarded as the "birthplace of football". However it must be considered the home of the organised global football as we know it today.

Richard Mulcaster, an Old Etonian, headmaster of Merchant Taylors' School and later St Paul's School, was a pioneer in education, who had published a volume in 1581 that announced the many benefits of football in schools. He agreed with the 16th century humanism that was found in the Italian game of calcio with little violence and highly disciplined and controlled, excellent for recreation and spectating.

The game, in its various forms, survived the centuries, although it appeared to decay under puritan influences. Samuel Butler, the head of Shrewsbury School, saw the game as "only fit for farm boys and labourers", whilst an Etonian was heard to say in 1831 that "I cannot consider the game at all gentlemanly; after all, the Yorkshire common folk play it". The public schools showed many signs of social neglect and the living conditions were squalid. Charterhouse, founded in 1611 in central London, gradually declined in numbers and by 1835 only had a hundred pupils. As Dickens advised in his novels, the schools needed to fight back and education became revolutionised, as did the art of football. The game that had been regarded by many as plebeian was civilised by the public schools. A new breed of headmaster, a modernising society and demanding parents wanted discipline in the schools. The Eton Wall Game was a response to this, in which the law of "offside" is insisted upon. Thomas Arnold encouraged a game of football at Rugby School and in Charterhouse, Harrow, Winchester and Shrewsbury similar games became traditional. The great public schools played the manly game of football and civilised it.

In the 16th and 17th centuries the game was securely based amidst the students at Oxford and Cambridge. Records make reference to its popularity amongst the undergraduates, but regulations were needed to control the disorder that often occurred, even in these civilised establishments. Games would have two halves to allow the Etonians to play by their rules in the first half and the old boys from Rugby played by their code in the second.

It took until the middle of the 19th century for the game to be standardised and accepted further afield. At the "public schools" and probably in the militia, universities and hospitals, games developed depending very much on the local environs. It was at the old Charterhouse that its own game developed, a very different affair, compared to the game at Westminster, Harrow or Eton.

The Charterhouse Song, this version first sung in 1794 to the tune of Ally Coker, made reference to football:

> "I challenge all the men alive to say they e're
>   were gladder,
> Than boys all striving should kick most
>   wind out of the bladder."

In 1891 an Old Carthusian Theatrical, contained a line that said:

> "Or when in Autumn's soberer tints of grey,
> We long to join in football's mimic fray."

Again in 1892 a verse referred to the much loved game:

> "Here flourish still our well-lov'd games,
>   designed
> To brace the limbs and discipline minds;
> Witness the brilliant skill, which all confess.
> And gentle manliness of G.O.S" (GO Smith)

At Cambridge, JC Thring and H. de Winton, both Salopians, gathered friends from their old school and Eton on Parker's Piece to play. From this point they decided on some common laws which were posted at the ground in 1848. The Old Harrovians were responsible for setting up the Sheffield Club (1855), the oldest in the land. They also had a hand in the Forest Club in Essex (1859) and more Harrovians inspired the Wanderers and of course the Old Harrovian Football Club. Ten signatories from Shrewsbury, Eton, Rugby, Harrow and Cambridge University put their names to a further set of regulations in 1856 as they founded the Cambridge University Football Club, however the first varsity match with Oxford was not played until 1874. The 1856 version stated that the ball could be touched with the hands but that there should be no tripping, holding or pushing. Thring, when he was the headmaster of Uppingham School, published some rules under the heading of "The Simplest Game" in 1862. In October 1863, nine Cambridge men from Shrewsbury, Eton, Harrow, Rugby, Marlborough and Westminster gave the Cambridge football laws a new look and Rule 14 read that "all charging is fair, but holding, pushing with the hands, tripping and shinning are forbidden." In London, where undergraduates ended up playing for clubs, these new rules were passed on and nine days after the Cambridge publication, on 26th Octo-

ber 1863, the proposed Football Association first met.

After the development of the game in these various institutions, the professionals took over and from the late 19th century, the amateurs quietly took a back seat. The game spread far and wide from its "birthplace", Britain, and it grew into the huge multinational business that it is now, in the 21st century.

When Thomas Sutton died in 1611 with his will beside him on his death bed, he had completed a significant philanthropic act by stating his desire to found a school and an almshouse confirmed by Act of Parliament. Located in the green Smith Field which had once been occupied by a Carthusian Monastery, between 1371 and 1535, the land was in the hands of the Earl of Suffolk after Henry VIII abolished the monasteries. Sutton bought it for £13,000. As London grew the

Drawing of runabout at the Old Charterhouse. The game was played with a single football and any number could participate, coming and going as they pleased.

school became engulfed in what could only be described as a "morally insalubrious environment" (James McConnell – *The English Public Schools*), so the Public Schools Commission (known as the Clarendon Commission) recommended that it should move and Haig Brown, the headmaster of the time, removed the school in 1872 to the airy sandstone plateau located north-east of Godalming and the River Wey valley. The almshouse remained in London and is now the Old Charterhouse where 40 "brothers" can live their later years in comfort and safety.

Today, Carthusian influences are still felt in the game of football, such as Brian Glanville and David Miller who are leading sports' writers in our national press, but it was in the last part of the 19th century that Charterhouse was a major force, not just in schools' football but on the international stage. In these pages, I hope to explain how this happened by referring to the many archives available in the school and outside. The main sources have been from the Captains' Books (first written in 1862), the *Carthusian*, the OC Newsletter and many historic documents kept so carefully in the school's archives. The earlier records are very clear and detailed, even during the war years. As the 1960s and 1970s passed, I am afraid that records were less well kept and results have gone astray, until the Captain's Book was re-established in 1979.

I hope that this book of football history will be of value to others in their quest to find out more about the game and that it will serve as a small monument to the many Carthusians, OCs

Earliest page from 1862 Captain's Book

and members of Brooke Hall who have devoted their time to playing and administration. I would also pay tribute to our archivists, Ann Wheeler, Sue Cole and Shirley Corke who have a hunger for details of all matters related to Charterhouse. Bob Noble has worked parallel to me in his quest to find out every result ever gained by any sports' team or individual from Charterhouse!

As I see new footballers arrive at Charterhouse, especially as new hops (13-year-olds), I know that they will get a firm grounding in the way the game is played. I also hope that they learn to appreciate the history of the game and the important part that Charterhouse and Carthusians have played in its evolution.

the original game at the old charterhouse

Ye boarders camme downe from ye boarders
  base
with victorie gleaminge in evverie face;
For they had likkeddeye gowneboye foe,
of whom fulle maine hadde been laide low.
But a day of vengeance cometh at last,
ye game it waxeth fierce and faste;
'Go itte, ye cripples!' is ye shoute,
'let's putte ye boarders to ye route.'
Ye boardere championne rushed with
  mighte,
into ye thickeste of the fighte;

Ye gowneboye hereo like a rocke;
stands firme to meete ye comminge shocke.
'Now shove ye gowneboyes shove, I praye!
Perchance your valour winnes ye day.'
'Squash oute!' shoutes evverie boardere
  fagge,
'Nor lette your droppinge courage lagge.'
But now through cloisteres comes ye crye,
'Ye fagges!' ye fagges come rushing bye;
And now ye bateile's loste and wonne
and now ye hurley-burlkey's donee.

(*CRB Barrett and GE Smythe*)

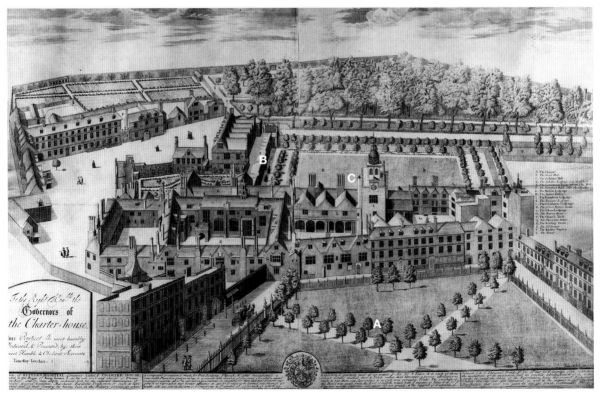

Plan of old Charterhouse. A is Charterhouse Square, B is the terrace over the Cloisters, C is the Bowling Green.
School archive

Cloisters, Charter-House.

Top. Picture of Old Charterhouse cloisters
Bottom. New view taken 2007. School archive

At Charterhouse and Westminster the cloisters, "which echoed to the tread of running feet", are where the beginnings of football are to be found. The history of the game is "shrouded in mystery" but it was originally a kind of battle in a street or some other convenient space.

The Cloister game was the most interesting affair played "indoors" at the Old Charterhouse where there was a brick covered passage, part of the extensive Cloisters surrounding Green. This section of the cloisters was paved with smooth flag-stones, it was some 70 yards long, 9 feet wide and 12 feet high, stretching from Gownboys to the Gownboy Dining Hall. This long, brick barrel-vaulted arcade was built by the fourth Duke of Norfolk in the 1560s, so that he could walk from his mansion to the tennis court. It was built upon the site of a monastic cloister and later the Merchant Taylors' Hall was sited at one end. On top of these cloisters ran a terrace with a splendid view of the Green which in due course was to become the site of the next scene in the evolution of Charterhouse football.

There was a blind wall on the west side of the cloisters (the front of the old line of monastic cells). The east walls were jagged with flints supported by iron bars and buttresses between the windows that were 3 feet 6 inches from the ground facing out towards Upper Green. There was a middle square area that opened out east-west called Middle Briars. This was a good place for a "scrimmage" and the game started here in a central position. The northern end had a narrow door, about six feet wide, that lead to the Gownboys boarding house and a southern door, about three feet wide that went out on to

SCHOLARS' HALL, OR GOWN BOYS' DINING HALL; VIEW OF CLOISTERS THROUGH DOORWAY

View from Gownboys dining room into cloisters. School archive

Green. These doors were at right-angles to the passage and served as goals. The designated team goalkeeper blocked each goal, there was one back and the rest were forwards in the pack. Six to nine players each side was ideal but numbers were often larger and "fags" (younger boys) were the pawns in the game, being part of the scrimmage, preventing the ball from getting loose.

No one could throw the ball or pick it off the ground, but if it was caught on the first bounce or above the knee, a punt or drop kick could be taken. These kicks required skill to keep the ball above the heads of the players but below the iron bars supporting the roof. There were no penalties, nor hacking, for the site had enough potential for injury. The ball was kept inside this passage but if it went out through a window the nearest players vaulted out and the first to "touch" it threw it back in, hence the use of the phrase "in touch".

When a goal was scored the teams changed ends and kick-offs were taken from the end of the pitch by the team conceding the goal. When the ball got in behind a buttress there would be sixty bodies trying to extricate it. A skilful player feeling the ball between his legs would bide his time and wait for an opportunity to work the ball out of the scrum and run it down towards the opponents' goal. The squash would then dissolve and the packs would give chase. One fag would come from the defending door to slow down the dribbling opponent. This allowed the others to catch up and sometimes if the defender did his job well, then another scrimmage would ensue. This might last 45 minutes or so and all kinds of damage would be done to clothes and bodies. The best dribblers were often the smallest and dexterous players who could out-run and skip past larger opponents.

Old Carthusians WL Southwell (S 1868-73), RM Hewett (S 1871-6) and HA Erskine (G 1867-74), who played the game at the Old Charterhouse and migrated with the school to

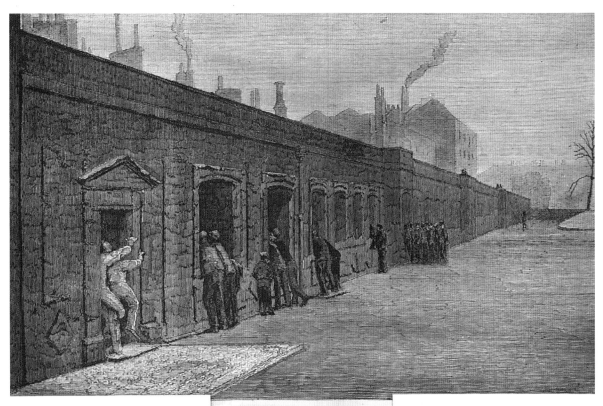

CLOISTERS; FOOTBALL WITHIN

Top. Boys watching a game in the old Charterhouse cloisters. School archive
Below. Photo taken 2007 by MJB

Godalming, gave an impression of how the game was played in their day, comparing it to the new buildings:

Imagine then a Cloister about the size of the South African War Memorial Cloister in Godalming; only rather longer and with no ornamentation, just plain brick walls and vaulting, on the East unglazed windows, looking out on to Green; in the middle a bay with seats, called Middle Briars; two narrow doorways leading, the one to Green and the other Gownboys; these were in the sides, but a few feet from each end. So that the game often surged past them and ebbed back; they formed the goals.

Whereas in the field game the sides were limited in number, generally eleven, in the cloister game it was not always so; for instance, sometimes, when Saunderites played Gownboys, the whole house took part, the fags being off to "keep the ball close". In the field game there was much rushing and dribbling, practically no passing. The other game consisted of "squashes" often so prolonged that the players were refreshed, so it is said, with lemons through the windows. There was no carrying the ball, but handling was permitted, whenever a player could work the ball knee high by the use of his foot, he then called "up" and was allowed to throw the ball. The toughest squashes were in Middle Briars. You could jump out of one of the windows and come in at another, and thus get behind the ball and stem the rush. The ball was not so much kicked through the goal as driven by the weight of human bodies. All agree that it was a rough game, at times even dangerous; but it seems to have been popular. Sometimes a school match that had begun on Under Green was continued in the Cloister, sometimes the other way round. But most of the matches were internal affairs and sometimes a boy was good enough to play for the school in this game but not in the field game.

(*Carthusiana XVII* EM Jameson)

Football in Cloisters was an invention unrivalled among games for joyous severity of scuffle, and muscular contempt of science. Was there anything equal in these respects to a hustle in Middle Briar?

(Rev HW Phillott)

Joseph Addison, essayist, poet and statesman, admitted that "I have played in many a match myself" in his young days at Charterhouse (1685-7) when there was talk of the rough and tumble of the "mob".

The curious code of rules was adopted at the London site in 1861 and it was in that year that a Charterhouse eleven was selected and the blue cap with red piping for players was first worn. Matches against Dingley Dell were recorded. The blazer was white with red-and-blue piping with white trousers. In the Long Room above the cricket pavilion at the Godalming site, in what was called Crown, now known as the Peter May Pavilion, there are colours' boards listing the XIs from 1862 up to the present day.

When games were played in the Cloisters, experience told and the "many mysteries of Middle Briars – the windows – the bars – the rough projecting stones in the walls which at times had a singularly unpleasant affect on the inexperienced player". The elements also played their part, especially as games continued towards dusk – the "darkness was considerably augmented by the London fog". In the next chapter it is recorded that Mr Cardale's XI found themselves returning to the Cloisters to finish their game. Along with Cardale were "prestigious players" such as HC Malkin (G 1848-55), FP Evans, WGH Shaw and the Mowbray brothers, both of whom "gave so much individual exertion that resulted in them sustaining injuries". The captain at the time, GJ Cookson, and BF Hartshorne were in the school team and they would soon be present at the first meeting of the Football Association.

The first existing Captain's Book was begun in 1862, the year the first national Football Association was formed.

In 1865 the Oration Quarter matches were played in Cloisters and in the Long Quarter the game went outside "into the field", which became known as the "Green game". "Foreign" or away matches took place and a team of "Owls" in 1868

. . . though professing to play Rugby rule, they were in a most wretched dilemma after the first ten minutes during which time the boys had obtained four games i.e. goals. Twenty minutes later CEB Nepean asked them if they wanted to continue but they found the task too difficult in Cloisters and they resigned from the game being 0-7 down in games.

Playing on Under Green made the game more open and eventually led to the development of soccer. When the weather was inclement the game went indoors.

On Wednesday at 2.30 pm a notice announced that all "fags should be in Cloisters". Twenty or so fags from Gownboys would guard their end of the Cloister and twenty or so from the Rest of the School would guard the other end. The older groups would arrange themselves in between. Inevitably the ball would get behind a buttress and there would be "squashes" with fifty or sixty boys packing into the space. This led to a dead block with the ball not emerging for half an hour or so. The ball was not allowed to be carried so dribbling took its place . The skill was to get the ball in front of your legs just as occurs in a rugby scrum today and wait for an opportunity to wriggle one's way out and round the scrum, running to the other end of the cloister. To defend the goal a leading fag would leave the bulk and run towards the dribbling forward. If he got past that then the next obstacle was the pack! Long kicking was excluded, presumably because possession was given away.

(EP Eardley Wilmot and EC Streatfeild: *Charterhouse Old and New* 1895)

From these descriptions it is plain to see how the Charterhouse game came to be.

The peculiarities of the local environment dictated what could be played and how games evolved. Space was limited and a game developed which depended on dribbling since the ball could not be kicked high or punted long distances as it could at Eton.

(James Walvin – *The People's Game* 1975)

The boys were delighted to find another "Cloister" at the new site, running between Gownboys and Verites. It is now blocked up. The internal buttresses provided extra hazards but the boys' attempts to play there were soon frustrated because the entrance to Brooke Hall (located there until 1916) was in that passage. There was a scheme to build a special cloister in the grounds since funds had been collected for the building of a Rackets court but nothing emerged. It does show that even in the late 1870s the game had a hold over the boys.

The outdoor game was transferred to Godalming and was known as "Runabout". The cloister game was eventually suppressed, being considered too dangerous. Playing outside the Cloisters had its dangers as well, as this passage reveals:

Green had recently been gravelled and thus we played cricket on stones ... and Under Green lately added from the monastic Wilderness, the ancient grass had forced its way through the stony covering...There were several trees, some of them fine ones. One of the trees was an ash and in football time it was a cherished feat to kick a ball over the great ash.

I passed briefly by football, of which one characteristic was that Upper Gownboys, in the days when all Gownboys wore knee-breeches, protected their legs with a second pair of house stockings, if they could persuade the matron to let them have a pair for this purpose.

The Rev HW Phillott (G July 1827 – August 1834) in the *Greyfriar* volume II No 8 August 1892.

Sir Ronald Storrs in *Orientations* wrote that "Association Football dominated our life not only in the football season but in the summer indirectly when any member of the eleven would be seen wearing his colours in mid-July".

The old game was re-inacted on 7th March 1972 between the school and the OCs. In 2000 the 1st XI played a Godalming AFC XI on Big Ground for charity as part of the Millennium celebrations. Ray Lewis the retired FIFA referee (he also refereed the fateful Hillsborough FA Cup semi-final) officiated following the 1867 laws for the first half of the game. In front of a sizeable crowd of about 200, the teams played halves of both old and present laws. The school won the old game and the town the new!

Town v Gown. A millennium celebration match on Big Ground between the 1st XI and Godalming AFC. Matthew Bailey and Jon Jackson pursue Godalming players. Ray Lewis is the referee.

the outdoor game at the old charterhouse

BISHOP EDGAR CS GIBSON, writing in the *Carthusian*, June 1922, recounted his time at school from 1859. The game of football was in a rudimentary state at that time and the rules were uncertain and unwritten. They were simply a matter of tradition. The captain of the Cricket Eleven was, he believed, the ipso facto captain of Football and there was no regular eleven and no colours awarded. It was not until the early 1860s that things became organised.

Bishop Gibson was born on 23rd January 1848 and died on 8th March 1924. He was a Gownboy from February 1859 until April 1867 and he captained the XI in 1867. He went up to Trinity College, Oxford in 1870 and after various posts in Theology and "service", he became Hon. Chaplain to Queen Victoria in 1901 and was made Bishop of Gloucester from 1905-22.

The Reverend Gerald S. Davies in *Charterhouse in London* reported that at the Freemason's Tavern meeting in London to discuss the formation of rules for football, the newly printed Charterhouse rules were taken by our two representatives as a guideline. Davies was born on 24th October 1845 and was at Charterhouse and in Gownboys from January 1856 until December 1864. He played for the XI at cricket and for the 1st XI football in 1863-4, then went to Christ's College, Cambridge and returned to Charterhouse to be an assistant master in 1873. He was Housemaster of Daviesites 1874-90 and then Verites until 1905. After this he became Master of the Old Charterhouse in 1908 until 1927.

Under Green, at the Old Charterhouse, proved to be a very fast ground. This was still the case when the school moved to Godalming where the light sandy soils provided dry, quick ground.

Matches were "internal" to begin with, between the Sixth (sixth form) and the Twenty (best twenty players), or singers versus non-singers.

Charterhouse and Westminster both allowed the forward pass and offside was a different rule to the one that developed in rugby, so players became more spread out on the pitch. Being "off his side" was when a player had fewer than three opponents in front of him when the ball was passed forward. This distinctive feature of the Charterhouse-Westminster game formed the basis of Association Football. There was no referee in the first games and each captain held a copy of the laws in his pocket. By the time the FA Cup began, two linesmen would be in charge of the game and they would refer any disputes to the "referee" on the sidelines.

There is evidence of a school XI being picked in 1861 but in October 1862 the first football XI was organised and printed rules were drawn up for the game to be played on Under Green at the London Charterhouse.

The first foreign match was played on 29th October 1862 against a team called "Dingley Dell" and the two teams kicked off at 2.45pm and played for about an hour and a half. Mr LP Evans was captain of the opposition so it is possible that this was a team made up by his associates. The two teams met in a return game on

School from the Green, 1842 and ...

... present view 2007. School archive

Wednesday 12th November. There was no Old Carthusian football, as such, being played at this time and Mr George Cardale's XI appeared twice in the term, firstly on 5th November when his team known as the "Grand Amalgamated Mediocrities" awaited the start of an outdoor game on Under Green. However "the elements under the leadership of Jupitus Pluvius, appeared to have combined with a view to thwart the execution of the designs of those who were to retrieve the reputation of their prowess...". The state of the pitch forced the decision to play the game in Cloisters. On 19th November, "the new rules which the eleven have drawn up were now used for the second time and appeared to be well adapted..."

GEORGE CARDALE was born on 18th December 1839 and died on 1st December 1884. He lived in Albury, Surrey but was a day boy in London from June 1854 until August 1858. Presumably he lived with somebody near the school. He played school cricket in 1858. He went up to Oriel College, Oxford in 1862.

The final match of Oration Quarter was played on 3rd December against Mr Shaw's XI (he was an old Weekite) and as is always the case at the end of the Oration Quarter "the ground was totally devoid of any verdure". The last game of any sort was a week later when Gownboys, the Scholars, played the rest of the school in Cloisters. There were a number of internal games played during the term when teams made up from groups of boys in the school, the Choir, the Sixth, the XI or just friends pitt their skills against each other.

In the Long Quarter 1863 against the Crusaders, **KENNETH A MUIR MACKENZIE** (G), for Charterhouse, "kicked the ball through the required limits only to see that the cord was hanging slack and therefore the ball went over". Later, Sir Kenneth A Muir Mackenzie became Permanent Secretary to the Lord Chancellor and a member of the Governing Body. He regularly brought teams to play the school. Born on 26th June 1845, he became a Saunderite in March 1857 and then was a Gownboy from June 1860 until August 1864. He was in the football XI 1862-3 and was the captain in 1863. He also

played cricket for the school from 1861 until 1864, being made captain in his final year. He went up to Balliol College, Oxford getting his BA in 1868 and MA 1873. He held many legal posts, being involved with the Governing Body and becoming Warden of Winchester College 1904-15. He married Amy, daughter of William Graham, MP for Glasgow. He died in London on 22nd May 1930.

Also in Muir MacKenzie's 1863 team was **JAMES T HODGSON** (G), son of the Provost of Eton and grandson of the Rev. James Hodgson OC. He originally went to Eton but joined Charterhouse in February 1857 until May 1864. He played cricket and football in 1862-3 before going up to University College, Oxford. He was an assistant master at Charterhouse from 1872 and gave his name to Hodgsonites when he was housemaster from 1872-80. He married Marie Blanchard 1872 and died in Brighton 3rd September 1880.

This XI also contained **SIR COURTENAY BOYLE**, who later became the Permanent Secretary to the Board of Trade. Born on 21st October 1845, he was a Gownboy from September 1857 until December 1863, ending up as Captain of the School. He was also captain of cricket and played in the XI 1862-3. He went up to Christ Church, Oxford getting an MA in 1867. He was in the OUCC 1865-7, played tennis for Oxford and was involved in business and politics. Married Lady Muriel Sarah Campbell 1876 and died on 19th May 1901.

Mention was made of HI Steward of the Crusaders, originally known as Brentwood (possibly the school team, possibly a town team), who "in second base was unequalled". This suggests that he was a second defender of the base line, a sort of goalkeeper. Substitutes had to be provided for many visiting teams especially when the weather was bad or perhaps when there was some apathy about travelling. In these circumstances the game lost some of its interest since the Carthusians played against too many of their own kind! There was a Brentwood team on the fixture card at this time.

On 18th March, Herbert C Malkin's XI (an Old Gownboy) had "great preponderance in

Photo of 1863 team. l to r: JT Hodgson, CE Boyle, KA Muir Mackenzie, HH Cameron, BF Hartshorne (capt.), GE Smythe, FS O'Grady, AC Seymour, EL Pearson, LH Stevenson, M Muir Mackenzie. School archive

weight" and this seemed to be most important in deciding matches, obviously having an advantage in the scrimmage. Born on 21st September 1836, he was in school from September 1848 until August 1855. He was Captain of the School, played cricket XI 1854-5, went on to be a scholar at Trinity College, Cambridge MA 1862 and played Surrey cricket 1859. Clerk in Parliament office, House of Lords 1861. He spent 1862-3 as an assistant master, entered Lincoln's Inn 1873, called to the Bar 1876, Clerk of Public Bills 1871-1901. He was first president of the Greyfriar Cricket Club (1874-9) which later became the Old Carthusian Club. He married Elizabeth in 1879 and died 18th August 1913.

There was also a game against Herbert H Gilbert's XI. Herbert was born on 17th June 1840 and died 2nd March 1932. Gilbert was in

Saunderites from 1853 until the summer of 1859. He was in the cricket XI 1858-9, at Magdalen College, Oxford with a BA in 1863, serving in the army until 1901.

The games would start after 2.30pm usually and sometimes later, due to the late arrival of the opposition, going on to 4.50pm or beyond in this case, until everyone had apparently had enough exercise. Reference was made to a lack of practice by the XI and the tactics of keeping three players "in base" was decidedly questionable. This suggests a lack of fitness or just a very defensive strategy.

On Monday 26th October 1863 eleven clubs from the London area met in the Freemason's Tavern in Queen Street, Lincoln's Inn Fields, London in order to form an association to decide what rules should apply between them.

Those clubs were: NN (the No Names of Kilburn), Barnes, The War Office, Forest (later to be Leytonstone), Perceval House (Blackheath), Crusaders (formerly Brentwood), Crystal Palace, Blackheath, Kennington School (or Kensington School possibly), Surbiton, Blackheath Proprietory School and an observer from Charterhouse.

The Football Association was formed and Bertram F Hartshorne, the Hon. Secretary of football, and George J Cookson, the 18-year-old school captain in 1862-3, represented Charterhouse. As captain, Cookson would carry his "rules" in a pocket book during games and if a dispute occurred he would draw forth his document and read it out loud to the dismay of the foreign opposition. GS Davies reported that he invariably read the word "goal" as "gaol".

GJ COOKSON was born 26th October 1840 and died 22nd February 1913. He was a Saunderite from June 1855-August 1863, played cricket in 1862-3 and football in 1862, as captain.

BF HARTSHORNE, his successor, was born on 26th October 1844 and died 31st December 1921. He was a Gownboy from February 1857 until December 1863 and he also played cricket for the XI, before going up to Pembroke College, Oxford.

The forming members of the FA present paid a guinea subscription each, but Hartshorne did not. After some arguments over the laws, especially hacking, the Blackheath members chose not to join the Association. In the proposed FA laws, Rule 9 specifically mentions that the ball may be carried, if a fair catch was made, and Rule 10 said that anyone doing so may be charged, held, tripped or hacked. Eventually the new association expunged these two rules and football and rugby went in different directions. When the Rugby Association was formed in 1871 at the instigation of the Blackheath Club, ironically, hacking was removed from the game.

On 29th October 1863, Hartshorne wrote to the Hon Secretary of this newly formed association, EC Morley, to say that:

> I beg to acknowledge the receipt of your communication yesterday, and to inform you that I am directed to state that Charterhouse

cannot as yet be included amongst the clubs who form the Football Association.

AC Pember, the President, observed that he had recently read the laws in use at Charterhouse and had found them very simple, and he felt that if two other schools joined, so would Charterhouse. Harrow and Westminster also declined but at least they had the courtesy to reply. Rugby, Winchester and Eton had no answer. The association did replace the hitherto stringent offside law with the one adopted by Charterhouse and Westminster, involving three defenders.

So, Charterhouse initially remained independent, seeking advice from other Public Schools. It may have been that the school was biding its time before making such a big commitment. It is later recorded that the school joined the Association in 1868.

One of the moving forces behind this organisation was Charles W Alcock (an Old Harrovian of Druries House recently run in the 1990s through to the new millennium by the well-known referee David Elleray) aided by his brother James. Charles was not at the meeting but evidence reveals that he was involved in the arrangements. When Charterhouse played Westminster the rules were modified to secure the adherence of both sets of players.

In the Oration Quarter 1863, the Tunbridge Wells Club came to Charterhouse and then St Bartholomew's Hospital as more foreign matches were played. St Bart's of course was sited next to Charterhouse in London.

In the original Captain's Book, it was recorded that on Wednesday December 3rd the school played Westminster at Vincent Square for the first time "for many years". This fixture is regarded as the oldest known schools' fixture. "The day had rained as much as it possibly could have and the ground was wet and sloppy making dribbling no easy task."

Basil Verely's account of The Westminster Match in the book, *A Study in Charterhouse Life* by Archibald K Ingram (George Allen & Co Ltd) gives numerous references to the oldest schools' fixture.

Against the Civil Service a goal was scored in

First report from Captain's book of Westminster game 1863

the most peculiar way when the Carthusians, having dribbled the ball up to their goalposts, Malkin and Voules from the opponents "managed to lie on the ball and aided by their side for a time resisted every effort of the Carthusians to push the ball through. At length the ball and those lying on it were pushed inch by inch inside the goalposts". This is described as "winning a game", i.e. scoring a goal. In some reports, teams won "points". This scrimmage helped Charterhouse to victory 3-2. At this time, "ends" were changed after each "game" and it was not until 1875 that the FA Cup final eventually had halves without the teams swapping ends after each goal was scored.

The weather was often reported by the captain in his write up of a game and "on a rainy and snowy day" in February 1864 the game against the St Bart's team was discontinued after a discussion about the "propriety of taking the ball to Cloisters". Some matches appeared to be played partly on Under Green and partly in Cloisters where a hard stony floor was uninviting. Obviously St Bart's objected to playing on paving. KA Muir Mackenzie also brought a side to play during this Lent Quarter.

GS Davies observed that the game of Association Football had not taken shape prior to 1865 but that the games of Charterhouse and Westminster came perhaps nearest to the Association that was created afterwards. The distribution of the field as we know it now had no existence and the goalkeeper was the only person on the field who had a designated post. Some games allowed any player to handle the ball with no designation. The aim of any player was to get the ball and keep it – and passing was scarcely heeded.

In the Oration Quarter 1865, the first match against the Civil Service was played but not until October 16th as a result of the "long summer", suggesting hard grounds prevented safe play. There was also a game against a Mr Wearne's XI which may well have included players from the Civil Service team since his name is linked with that office.

By 1866 all vestiges of rugby had disappeared from the game and though hacking and tripping were defined and forbidden, there was no mention of the "penalty" in the original code.

At Charterhouse the shape of the team changed from one goalkeeper (base man) and ten outfield players to backs, sides and forwards. The code of rules that AH Tod said "could only be given from memory" stated that in the case of an infringement of the rules the opposite side shall have the option to consider the ball dead, in which case it shall be kicked off from the middle of the ground.

It was not possible to pick the ball off the ground, nor throw, carry or handle it but it was possible to catch it on its first bound (bounce) or above the knees and then take a drop kick or punt. There were no free kicks, the goalkeeper could catch the ball or stop it with his hands but he could not knock or throw it away. If the ball went out of play, the first person to touch it had a throw or kick in (hence the use of the word touchline) between two lines of players as in rugby; there were no corner kicks but the ball was restarted from the goal line on the "die" it went out from. Ends were changed whenever there was a goal (known as a base or game) scored. So a match might be won by two games to one. "Hacking" was not allowed and in some "codes" this was quite an important part of the game plan as was "shinning". Players would serrate their leather soles to make the boot a dangerous weapon.

Disputes were held over until the end of the game but there would be questions asked by the captains whenever any infringement occurred.

The Hon. FG Pownall's XI visiting that term probably came from Exeter College, Oxford and **J BUTTER**'s XI also had Oxford origins. James Butter was born on 28th May 1843 and became a Gownboy in June 1853 to December 1861. He played school cricket in 1860-1 went up to Balliol College, Oxford gaining an MA in 1871. He was the Gownboy master 1866-7 then held various clerical posts before dying on 7th January 1898. He is described as the organiser of the Charterhouse Mission.

On Saturday 2nd November 1867 at Battersea Park these new rules were tested in a match arranged between Middlesex County and a combined Kent and Surrey team. Nepean played in the Middlesex team. On 25th January 1868 FG Paulson was a Carthusian representative for Kent in another trial 12-a-side game at the West London running ground, Brompton.

A newspaper in 1867, the year before Charterhouse joined the Football Association, stated that "there was a match between the school and the Public Schools of Oxford". The school won 4-0 and "the Oxonians strove hard to equal the honours, but their base referee was not fully alive to his office, and allowed, after a short contest, the victorious Carthusians to score a second base. The play of the Carthusians was excellent; there can be no question that it is the best football team which could be produced about London." This team included many eminent men, including ECS Gibson and Reginald **W MACAN**, afterwards Master of University College, Oxford. Macan was born 2nd April

1848, died 23rd March 1941. He was in Verites between September 1864 until August 1867, playing cricket 1864-7 and football 1865-6. He went to Christ Church, Oxford 1868-72 and was Master of University College 1906-23.

In Long Quarter 1868 **CHARLES W ALCOCK**'s team played in Cloisters as an experimental contest losing 2-0. From "their ignorance of the Cloister war and their want of practice on the hard pavement they were placed at a great disadvantage." Alcock's name appears many times in the register and he was obviously keen to play football at every opportunity. The Wanderers, with Alcock as the captain, was made up from Old Harrovians and other public school players (see chapter 5 *The FA Cup*). Alcock later became secretary to the FA, and was regarded as the father of the Football Association. He also played for Kinnaird's XI, Crystal Palace and captained Upton Park FC. The Old Etonians team included the Right Honorable Alfred F Kinnaird who was described as the best player of his day, football's first superstar and the FA's first President. Lord Kinnaird's teams are to be found in the fixture card in the late 1860s. He played in nine FA Cup Finals with the Wanderers and the Old Etonians from 1873 until 1883, winning five times. He had a flaming red beard and his physique allowed him to tackle ferociously. A description of the 1881 final between the OCs and Old Etonians mentions Kinnaird's robust play. In 1911 after over fifty years of serving football he was awarded the FA Cup in use and a new cup was made for 1912.

The Wanderers emerged from near Forest School, Snaresbrook, a school that Charterhouse plays today. Set in Epping Forest, it is the only school team to have taken part in the FA Cup and this happened between 1875 and 1879. In the last two years the Old Foresters also competed, making a unique double. The old boys' team still plays in the Arthurian League and Arthur Dunn Cup. Forest Football Club was founded in 1857 and might be regarded as the

Charterhouse football rules of 1863

1. Before the commencement of the game, the Captain of each side, or his representative, shall toss up for choice of goals, which shall be changed at the end of each game, and fix a time for leaving off playing.

2. The ball may not be carried or thrown by the hands, or knocked out of the hands of any player who has caught it, either out of the air or after it has bounded from the ground above his knees.

3. Players shall be allowed to stop the ball with their hands, and also necessary, to stoop to do so; but no player may strike the ball with his hand in any way, either when in the air or when upon the ground.

4. In order to win the game, the ball must go between the two flags and underneath the cord of the goal of the opposite side, provided that it is not hit or otherwise impelled through by the hands of any of the side who are not defending the goal; if hit, or in any way impelled through by any of the side who are defending the goal, the game is counted.

5. No player may hold, push with the hands, purposely kick or trip up any player of the opposite side, or in any way push him behind his back.

6. When the ball is kicked out of bounds at the side of the ground, it must immediately be taken in three yards from the place where it left the ground, and thrown or kicked in at right angles to that side, and along the ground.

7. When the ball is kicked behind the goal, it must be kicked off by the side behind whose goal it went, within six yards from the limit of their goal. The side who thus kicked the ball are entitled to a fair kick off in whatever way they please, without obstruction, the opposite side not being allowed to approach within six yards of the ball.

8. Any player is "off his side", or "behind" when only three or less than three of the opposite side are between him and the opposite goal. Any player off his side is not to stop or kick the ball until it has been kicked or otherwise moved by one of the opposite side. This does not include the case of a player who is fairly following up the ball.

9. If any player violate any clause of the above rules, the side which has not violated the rule may, at its option, consider the ball dead; in which case it shall be kicked off by that side from the middle of the ground, provided that no player belonging to the side which has not violated the rule has kicked or otherwise touched the ball. And if any disagreement arise concerning any one of the above rules, or any clause therein contained, the matter shall stand over for discussion until the conclusion of the game in which the players are then engaged.

FA rules of 1863

1. The winner of the toss shall have choice of goals. The game shall commence by a place kick from the centre of the ground by the side losing the toss, the other side shall not approach within 10 yards of the ball until it is kicked.

3. After a goal is won the losing side shall kick off and the goals shall be changed.

9. No player shall carry the ball.
11. A player shall not throw the ball or pass it to another.
12. No player shall take the ball from the ground with his hands while it is in play under any pretence whatever.

8. If a player makes a fair catch he shall be entitled to a free kick, provided he claims it by making a mark with his heel at once; and in order to take such kick he may go as far back as he pleases, and no player on the opposite side shall advance beyond his mark until he has kicked.

4. A goal shall be won when the ball passes between the goal posts (at whatever height), not being thrown, knocked on, or carried.

10. Neither tripping nor hacking shall be allowed and no player shall use his hands to hold or push his adversary.

5. When the ball is in touch the first player who touches it shall throw it from the point on the boundary line where it left the ground, in a direction at right angles with the boundary line.

7. In case the ball goes behind the goal line, if a player on the side to whom the goal belongs first touches the ball, one of his side shall be entitled to a free kick from the goal line at the point opposite the place where the ball shall be touched. If a player of the opposite side first touches the ball, one of his die shall be entitled to a free kick (but at the goal only) from a point 15 yards from the goal line opposite the place where the ball is touched. The opposing side shall stand behind their goal line until he has had his kick.

6. When a player has kicked the ball any one of the same side who is nearer to the opponent's goal line is out of play and may not touch the ball himself nor in any way whatever prevent any other player from doing so until the ball has been played; but no player is out of play when the ball is kicked from behind the goal line.

1. The maximum length of the ground shall be 200 yards, the maximum breadth shall be 100 yards, the length and breadth shall be marked with flags; the goals shall be defined by two upright posts, 8 yards apart, without any tape or bar across them.
13. No player shall wear projecting nails, iron plates, or gutta percha on the soles or heels of his boots.

oldest club. Various histories report that the club changed its name to the Wanderers in 1863. Forest School magazines however record matches between the school and Forest Club annually until 1874. The Wanderers earliest match was against the Army at Aldershot on 5th November 1864. The home matches for the Wanderers were played at Battersea Park, although their name suggest that they had no home base.

24th February 1868 saw the first match between the school and the Old Carthusians. This resulted in the school "getting two games to none in front on Under Green and then three more games were added by the school in the Cloisters" although it was thought that the OCs would have an advantage of weight in the tighter area of play. The second goal was described as a good exhibition of the "species squash" which is the scrimmage, where a large number of players manoeuvre the ball through the goal.

On 11th March the weather was "worse than it had ever been before" and the snow was falling. The Civil Service arrived intending to play on Under Green. It was useless to advise Cloisters to them, for the Civil Service would not trust themselves to play at the mercy of the Charterhouse XI, whom they declared would "break all their bones".

In this period as well as foreign matches there were home matches and these were played, often as practice, between "Church v State", the XI v School, Gownboys (the Scholars) v School and the Sixth v School.

Mr J Butter's team seemed to take to the Charterhouse rules quite naturally and in another school match against a Cambridge XI at the Middlesex County ground, Islington, the word "flukey" was used to describe a kick by Thompson from the opposition.

Other games in this year, 1868, were against Kilburn (written as NN meaning no names), the Royal Engineers at Islington, the Old Harrovians and the Harrow Chequers, described as "a celebrated club". The Civil Service match was played away at Battersea Park but most fixtures were played at Charterhouse. The OCs train in Battersea Park weekly in modern times, on astro turf!

In 1870 CF Reid's XI may well have contained some of the Wanderers because he also played for them and in Oration Quarter 1870 the Royal Engineers, at the Oval, beat the school 5-0, "owing to the much larger space of the ground". Some grounds may well have been 200 yards long as allowed in the 1863 rules. In February 1871 the XI played Barnes away and in the game with Clapham Rovers, Under Green was "paved with broken bits of brick, rendering a fall decidedly unpleasant".

On 1st March, the Wanderers game, a 3-3 draw, was marred by disputes by a team who appeared to think it derogatory to be beaten by Charterhouse – perhaps this was the first record of football anarchy.

In this period, between 1867-8, **HENRY JOHN ALMOND** (G) was in the XI. He was born on 17th April 1850 and died at sea on 12th March 1910. He was the son of William of Westminster and joined the school in April 1863 staying until 1868, after which he became a civil engineer in Costa Rica, working for the La Guayra and Caracas Railway Company of Venezuela. He married Lucy.

Stoke City (granted city status in 1926) has long been considered the second-oldest Football League club, although uncertainty clouds the actual date of formation. In 1863 the story goes that former pupils of the Charterhouse School formed a football club while serving as apprentices at the North Staffordshire Railway works in Stoke. But little evidence exists of any matches taking place, even though at that time some form of soccer may have already existed in the area as the headmaster of Stoke St Peter's School, J Thomas, was an active sportsman and secretary of the local Victoria Athletic Club.

Five years later a report in *The Field* magazine of September 1868 made things much clearer. It stated that a new Association Football club had been formed in Stoke-on-Trent and its founder

Photos of 1868 cricket team with Nepean, seated with pads, and Hooman, back left. School archive

PHYLLIS COURT,
22, ROSECROFT AVENUE,
HAMPSTEAD, N.W.3.

30th December, 1950.

Dear Sir,

Thank you for your letter of 13th December and for the interest you have shown in my Father's old medal.

In view of what you say some of my Fathers recollections and views on the Game, as it is, and as it was, may be of interest.

He felt that the masses have been given a fine and manly sport by the Great Public Schools which they have degraded to the level of a moneymaking racket. Though the Football Association every year of the latter days of his life always sent him tickets for a Box at the Final Tie he always refused for the above reasons.

For many years he was the only survivor of the First Final, for which his medal was given, and he was always the subject of Press interviews. The Press-men concerned were, I know, the recepients of his very outspoken views on the low level to which the game has fallen. The buying and selling of players, particularly, met with his wholehearted condemnation. He regarded the present game as no longer worthy of the name of "sport".

He deplored the way in which the ball is, today, so much in the air. In his day it was kept along the ground and dribbling was a fine art. The high "balooning" of the ball was regarded as an heinous crime.

In that first Final there was no Referee: only Linesmen, and the Captains jointly decided on such matters as "fouls" and "off side".

The game was very fast and robust and all players were expected to be tough. Hard shoulder charging was an accomplishment which no first class player of his day could be without. He often told me that he broke the collar-bone of one of the Engineers, Von Donop, in a fair charge during that game. Von Donop never turned an hair but played the rest of the game with little or no sign of the injury he had sustained.

These facts are interesting in view of the development of our own "Run About" and the strong, robust "Bricking" which was always "Carthusian" pride, at any rate while I was at school. We were, after all, perhaps the greatest of the originators of the Association Game. Though in my Father's time Eton and Westminster played a very large part.

That first Wanderer winning team, so far as I remember, contained among their number:- Lord Kinnaird, Carter and Preston of Eton, Quentin Hogg, Sealy-Vidal of Westminster, C.W. Allcock and my Father.

Yours sincerely,

P.S. In view of my Father's views, as outlined above, the School Museum is the only place for his old medal, though I know the Football Association would very much like to have it.

Letter from Hooman's relative. School archive

member was an ex-Charterhouse School pupil. So it's possible that soccer had been played in the area during the previous five years, although in terms of official records the first game played by Almond's team, known as Stoke Ramblers and consisting largely of railway employees, was in October 1868. The historic match, against an EW May XV, ended in a 1-1 draw and was played at the Victoria Cricket Club ground, near to Lonsdale Street and Church Street. Almond, the skipper, scored the first-ever goal by a Stoke player, although he was soon to leave the club and the area to pursue his career as a civil engineer.

Also in the school team at this time was **THOMAS CHARLES HOOMAN** (g) who was the oldest member of the 1872 Cup winning team at 31 years old and he was in school between 1863 and 1868. He was born at The Copse, Hoo Lane, Kidderminster, on 28th December 1850 and died at Marine Parade, Hythe, Kent on 22nd September 1938.

Hooman was in the Charterhouse XI 1867-8 and became an F.A.Cup winner with the Wanderers 1872, the first Cup Final. He also played for Middlesex and London FA (for example against Sheffield at Bramall Lane on 2nd November 1872 under the "Sheffield Rules") the North and performed in four pre-official internationals v Scotland in 1871 and 1872 and was chosen for the first full matches in 1872-3 but was unavailable. He was a highly-rated forward of his day and among first choice for big matches. He was "the fastest dribbler of his day and an accomplished player; can play back and kick well". Hooman was an excellent cricketer, heading the averages at school between 1867-8. He ran the sprint for England in 1872, rowed in the Grand Final at Henley for Kingston, was a good boxer, marksman and golfer. He was the father of Charles VL Hooman, the Walker Cup golfer, a Racquets champion and Kent cricketer. At Brasenose, Oxford, Charles got a Blue for racquets, golf and cricket. He played in the Kent championship side in 1910, for the Gentleman v Players and appeared in golf internationals against Scotland and the USA in 1922-3. Thomas was a carpet manufacturer, but he went into London business as a merchant ship broker and then a manufacturer of Portland cement. His death followed an operation and his obitu-

ary mentioned a recent interview with him in which he claimed to have scored the winning goal in the Cup Final, but no contemporary report agrees with him. He also claimed that the final was played with no referee or umpires and again reports do not support this. Hooman was 87 at this time and it was suggested that his memory was failing him!

The Reverend **CHARLES EDWARD BURROUGHS NEPEAN** (G) was born in Mayfair, 5th February 1851 and died at Lenham Vicarage, near Maidstone, Kent on 26th March 1903. After Charterhouse where he played in the XI from 1865 to 1870 (captain 1868), he went to University College, Oxford in 1870; getting a BA from St Alban Hall 1873 and an MA in 1880. He won the FA Cup with Oxford University in 1874, when he got his Blue. He also represented Middlesex and played in pre-official internationals in 1871 and 1872 for Scotland against England in both matches, having had Scottish ancestry. He was the goalkeeper in the Cup Final but more often would play as a forward where he was eulogised as "may be fairly classed as the best player of the day, works the ball with surprising skill, and never misses a shot at goal; can take any position with credit to himself." He was "hard working, energetic, and conspicuous". He was selected to play in the 1873 final but could not free himself to play. He was the founder member of the Oxford University FA which was formed on 9th November 1871. He was a good wicketkeeper, playing in the school XI between 1866-9 (captain in 1868-9), appearing for Oxford 1870-3 (Blue in 1873), Middlesex 1873-4 and Dorset and in 1873 he played for the Gentlemen v Players. In his ten first class matches he caught seven and stumped six and in 1873 he was ninth in the national batting averages. He later served on the Kent CCC Committee. He was the son of a clergyman and he was ordained deacon in 1874 and a priest a year later. He was curate of Hartley Wintney, Hampshire 1874-6, then Vicar of Lenham, Kent 1876-1903. His brother, AA St JM, played for

Middlesex and his uncle, EA, also represented this county.

The following teams on the Charterhouse fixture card in this period were included in the first FA Cup draw in 1871: Barnes, Civil Service, Clapham Rovers, Crystal Palace, Harrow Chequers, Reigate Priory, Royal Engineers (Chatham) and the Wanderers. The other competitors came from Donington (near Spalding, Lincolnshire) Grammar School, Hampstead Heath(ens), Hitchin, Maidenhead, Marlow, Queen's Park (Glasgow) and Upton Park.

The Wanderers, won the first Cup Final with a goal scored by Morton Peto Betts sometimes reported as AH Chequer (A Harrow Chequer). There was nothing to stop a player representing more than one club and indeed Betts was picked to play for the Harrow Chequers in their first-round match against the Wanderers but the Harrow team scratched. Betts was Headmaster at Harrow between 1862 and 1865.

A poem was written to commemorate the Charterhouse v Civil Service match in February 1872 before the move to Godalming:

Sing a song of sixpence,
Listen to my lay,
Two and twenty mudlarks,
In a pudding play.
When the game was opened
The birds began to kick,
They staggered in the pudding
So sticky, rich and thick.
Giffard was in goal
Looking for the squalls,

The rest were playing forward
In scrimmages and mauls.
Carter stood in the centre
Resisting all attacks,
Tho' Hamilton and Lindsay
Were anything but lax.
Carthusians made a grand rush
Upon the Service line,
And shouts of joy go ringing
At Parry's kick so fine.
The change of end makes no change,
Again C.S. gives way,
Again the school's triumphant,
Again, again! I say.
And so on till half past four,
When "no side" is called out,
And mudlarks splashed with pudding,
Leave off and right about.
The game may be amusing
To those who're looking on;
But not to those mudlarks,
Whose play they look upon.
For it is not pleasant
To be upset in the cream,
And stick there, till on rising,
Like a scavenger you seem.
But difficulties lessen
Where there's friendship and goodwill,
And so it is at Charterhouse,
And I'd like to play there still.
And now that they are going
On Surrey's hills to stay,
Let's give them three times, three cheers,
And hope football there to play.

This was recorded as a 6-0 win to the school.

The final match at the old Charterhouse was played against the Wanderers with Alcock, Bonsor, Vidal, Crake, Welch and AH Chequer in their eleven. Each side "obtained a goal".

CHAPTER 4

the outdoor game at godalming from 1872-82

When the school moved to Godalming, Charterhouse football, as it was known, changed when the Cloisters game died as a tradition, the last official game being played on 7th March 1872 against the Old Boys. Some people wanted Cloisters to be reconstructed at the new site, but on 19th September, when the new football season began at Godalming, there was a pitch established running across Green, west to east, 120 yards by 60 yards – an enormous change from the London site. It was regarded as likely to help the school play against foreign teams who also had bigger pitches. When it was wet the game was played on the "practice ground" to the west end of Green (near Big Ground).

The "Runabout" developed with one ball, dozens of players with no sides, no hard kicking, with dribbling in any direction. Anthony Quick in his book *Charterhouse – A History of the School* wrote: "At 12.30 the boys rushed out of school and dumped their books and portfolios under the 'Tree of Knowledge' and joined their 'club' in a runabout with over a hundred pursuing a single ball." The Tree of Knowledge stood on the north side of where the Memorial Chapel is sited, on the edge of Green in line with Crown. Runabout rarely took place on Big Ground unless there were special circumstances such as when snow needed shifting in the winter to allow a more formal match to take place. Runabout developed two-footed players who were more likely to be picked for official teams because of their skills.

EP Wilmot and EC Streatfeild described in winter the various football grounds at the new site presenting "an animated appearance as each is occupied with 30 to 50 boys busily engaged in runabout". Jameson described how "a newcomer to the game, let out late by a keen master, would join the side on the defensive to redress the balance. It was a most exhilarating game and not as rough as it sounds, though it gave opportunities to settle old scores. It was a magnificent preparation for soccer."

W Veale in *From a New Angle* describes Big Ground as a "road with grass verges on either side". All First XI, Under School Club and House matches were played on it, with practices and "shootabouts" at 12.30. There were four other grounds known as Club grounds; three on Green and one on Wilderness; one in front of Crown (the main cricket pavilion, now known as the Peter May Pavilion) running parallel to it, one "lower down" (south) running east-west from the Verites' garden on Promontory and another running east-west at the Godalming end of Big Ground towards the Gownboy garden. This gave Green a "most lively appearance". Each Club had time allotted on the pitch and there was usually a second game later in the afternoon. The Clubs replaced what was known as "compulsory football" and gave the Under School organised games. This was regarded to be an important period in school history, helping to promote better players for the elevens.

These grounds had no attention given to them and were constantly used for "runabout" after morning school. There were no groundstaff and the boys were responsible for preparing and mending pitches. AH Tod noted that the game was "made up by any number playing. It went on between school and dinner; the players do not change for it and they join and leave it when they please. There was no handling, no hard kicking, no long shots at goal, everyone must play forward, no one may change his side. If the ball goes out it is returned anyhow. It is the most vigorous of games. This taught the individual to keep the ball and thereby develop his dribbling skills." Some groups were occupied in more leisurely pursuits such a "puntabout" which formed in 1875 and was less instructive. Good backs patronised the puntabout which was simply kicking the ball as high and as far as possible. This led to a lazy "hand in pocket habit". "Shootabout" was regarded by some as a means of training the first eleven forwards in the art of shooting but the detractors saw it as very leisurely – several balls were used and players hung around the goal until a ball came to their feet, at which they shot and did not even have to dodge a half back or even go and get the ball. It was of little value for the goalkeeper either because shots did not come to him as they would in a game.

There was also "sixes" played – used as a method of getting fit. Small sided games certainly do that and help develop techniques.

To be in the Charterhouse Football Eleven was a sort of passport to the athletic world and the school and the sport were inseparable. There was discussion about the incentive of prizes for sports, especially in athletics and cricket. It was believed that this fostered a selfish spirit but not in football where there "were no such inducements set before the players but the school's reputation."

By the time the school moved to Godalming, with Big Ground eventually the official pitch to play on, although it was regarded as still narrow, the shape of the team developed. There was a goalkeeper, not selected on merit, who often changed with outfield players, one back and nine forwards, who were split into two sides of four or five players, with no central division.

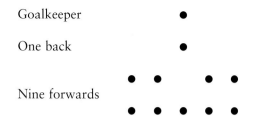

Goalkeeper	●
One back	●
Nine forwards	● ● ● ●
	● ● ● ● ●

Andrew Amos (OC) said that the "fame of Charterhouse at football is due largely to the character of the ground, and the efforts made to adjust to its peculiarities. Strictly speaking it is not turf at all, but rather a plain, as hard and as bare as a road. The forwards had to have exceptional control and the backs had to kick cleanly and quickly while as the ground was so narrow it had to be accurate. Westminster (school) was nearly up to Charterhouse level as a nursery of Association Football."

The FA Challenge Cup competition was also first played in this season and the arrangements were fairly chaotic. An early player for the Crystal Palace cup team was Charles Eastlake Smith, an international footballer, cousin to GO Smith. A description of the 1872 FA Cup final between the Royal Engineers and the Wanderers mentioned many features of the Charterhouse game. The cord strung across the goal between two posts, a marked pitch perimeter but no lines inside the playing area. There was little heading, only one handed throw-ins by the team that "touched" the ball first when it went out of play and it was a robust dribbling game with men "backing up" the player in possession. Defence seemed to be largely ignored although Charterhouse did have "base men". The passing game evolved in the north and especially in Scotland with the Queen's Park club. When the Wanderers came to Charterhouse to play on 11th December they only brought seven men with them. Substitutes from the school had to be provided for the visitors, epitomising the casual approach that many teams showed to the game at this time.

School v OCs 1882. The hedge in the distance marks what was then the end of the school's property and the house behind is Lessington House.
Players named are: In the distance in front of the house; Eddis, Vintcent, Cobbold, AM Walters, Sugden.
On right in distance: Tod, Hanwell, Henley. On left: Hatchard. Taking kick: Escombe. School archive

Match on Green 1883. School archive

In Oration Quarter 1872 the school abolished handling, except for the goalkeeper, and visiting teams still had to conform to the school's local rules. The main differences were that when there was "behind", Charterhouse insisted on "more than three" opposition players being assigned instead of "at least three" as in the rules of the Association. There was a difference in "throw-ing in" when the ball was kicked outside the limits of the ground. "There is a little too much eagerness to touch the ball before it reaches the ground and consequently fouls are frequent." There were no free kicks or corners in the Char-terhouse game. During the season with games in the cup, the free-kick for handling was intro-duced. Previously the law had been left to the

School 1st XI team 1873-4. Standing: AW Corrie, E Williams, WW Drew, A Orford, HD Verelst. Sitting: NJ Abdy, HG Jeaffreson, EH Parry, FJ Synge. School archive

respective captains, assuming that no gentleman would deliberately break the laws. If he did, the player would back away from the ball. The laws became more complex and therefore a third party was necessary. Soon the school also had to conform to Association rules and this happened in August 1875.

At Cambridge the university sports club was founded, gathering on Parker's Piece. At Oxford the venue for the non-rugby schools to play football was the Parks. By 1872-3 Oxford University Football Club had reached the final of the FA Cup (losing to the Wanderers) and the next year there was a Varsity Match (30th March 1874), which Oxford won 1-0. CEB Nepean, a half back, was the lone Carthusian to play for Oxford in that game. The Oxford formation was:

1 goalie-1 back-2 halves-7 forwards.

The first game on the new ground at Charterhouse was played against the Civil Service on Wednesday 16th October 1872 at 4pm. The late kick off was caused by the arrangements of the local train timetable. Having the luxury of more space and more pupils, House matches began on November 9th, the first ever contest being between Gownboys and Verites. This was part of a triangular tournament involving Saunderites also. No cup was awarded, just pride prevailed. There was the first OCs match in Godalming (14 a side) and even more home matches such as the Cricket XI v School and contests between the Odd Initials v Even Initials.

In OQ 1873 three matches were accommodated against the OCs on 13th November. Brooke Hall played its first game against the XI (there is no record of the result) and the "north" side of Chapel took on the "south" side. In those days the pupils did not sit by house, so the teams would be a rare mixture of boys from several houses.

During the winter of 1873-4 Cloister football was called for due to the wet weather conditions. It was hoped that a building to suit the needs of the game would be built alongside Green, but this was not a priority.

FT Swan merged Gownboys, Girdlestoneites and Bodeites to form, appropriately, the Cygnets in 1874. Swallows (Saunderites, Pageites and Robinites) followed with Verites and Lockites forming Nomads – and finally Weekites, Daviesites and Hodgsonites made up Harpies later. Each club was made up from Under school members (Unders) to give them organisation and they looked after a pitch; organised matches took place between clubs. Later, Uppers joined in, except for the best players who played for the school teams. So it was possible to get club colours. Uppers tended to join the better club games and the less able or younger members were designated to an unruly fourth game or were left out altogether. The house captains were responsible for organising several games every day for over a hundred boys, many of whom they did not know, and there would be shirkers who could avoid the exercise. The system did not run as smoothly as they hoped, so by 1894 a league was developed. WAE Austin was the captain who was responsible for the detail of the scheme.

Each club had its own song and made reference to the various skills of each club – particularly football. For instance:

> "...a swallow is a merry soul
> As he cheerily dribbles the ball on the green,
> With a mind firm fixed on the enemy's goal,
> Now passing – now charging – now dodging
>   between."

> The Cygnet "in the struggle
> Maintains his credit whole
> And defends with equal prowess
> The wicket and the goal."

> "And the Harpy on Carthusian ground
> By many a deed of prowess renowned
> And shines with lustre all unknown before
> In football triumph and in cricket score."

> The Nomads mention "at cricket and
>   football he makes a good show."

Club colours were awarded in more modern times for playing in lesser teams such as the U16 XI. The colour system was reformed in 2000 when club ties disappeared.

At this early time, an attempt to organise house matches was banned on the grounds that nothing could be more destructive to the general interests of the school than these conflicts.

So an Unders league was found to be valuable and indeed eventually led to the formation of an Uppers' competition also – hence the formation of "Turning Up" competitions. The Captain of Football did all the administration and the senior boys refereed. Turning Up games often took place after dinner so it is difficult to imagine what the light was like in the winter. Peripatetics, etceteras (the less talented players) and yearlings (in their first year at the school) were provided for and these competitions were first mentioned in 1876, when there was also a rise in the interest in hockey. Peripatetics were abolished in 1878, giving way to clubs again.

Usually the worst player was put in goal, although Robert Baden-Powell (Gg), a goalie, might have disagreed with this as he had an admirable influence on the game and even had time to amuse his friends on the touchline by doing handstands when the ball was at the other end of the ground. It was also recorded in August 1876 "that anyone who has the idea that a goalkeeper holds an inferior position to the rest of the eleven should see the captain of the Royal Engineers play". Lord Baden-Powell "took a very liberal view of the goalkeeper's function, his voice enabled him to direct the forwards at the other end of the ground and his agility enabled him to cheer the spectators with impromptu dances when he had nothing too pressing to do".

ROBERT SS BADEN-POWELL (Gg) was born on 22nd February 1857 as the seventh son of the Rev B-P, FRS, Savilian Professor of Geometry at Oxford. He joined Gownboys in OQ 1870 and went to Girdlestoneites in 1874 when it was founded. He played for the XI in 1876, leaving school in LQ 1876. He joined the 13th Hussars serving in South Africa, Zululand as well as other posts, becoming the CO 5th Dragoon Guards, 1897 and the Defender of Mafeking,

Baden-Powell in shooting team with AH Tod (third from left). RSS Baden Powell (sixth from left). School archive

FKW Girdlestone. Long-serving Carthusian, OC, member of Brooke Hall and housemaster

1899-1900. Promoted to Major-General, raising the S.African constabulary, becoming Inspector General and then officer commanding Northumbrian Division, 1908; KVCO, KCB, 1909 retiring a year later. He instituted the Boy Scout Movement in 1908.

Baden-Powell transferred houses when FKW Girdlestone started his new boarding house in 1874 and Baden-Powell's name adorns the original honours board on boys' side. Frederick Girdlestone was a visionary Housemaster of Girdlestoneites from 1874 until 1912, who had Duck's Ground constructed so that his boys could practise their sports. He also helped initiate the Turning Up leagues in the school, ensuring that all boys took exercise in healthy competition. He even hired the local hero, Julius Caesar of Surrey and England, to coach the boys cricket on Duck's Ground.

On 30th January 1939, Baden-Powell wrote to the Editor of the *Carthusian* from Paxtu, Nyeri in the Kenyan Colony. He was critical of the way that the crowd at an XI match depressed him by singing a "doleful sing-song dirge which goes around the

Jan ary 30th 1939   *Paxtu*
                                           Nyeri
        ♛   *Kenya Colony.*

Dear Editor

    I say! I hope you won't mind if I write a letter which I
expect will be very distasteful to Carthusians . If you don't
like it, you know you always have the   W.P.B. available.

            If you publish it your readers will at once say
" It is one of these old generals again, who tells you how much
better things were in the good old days ,begad, and what rotters
these modern fellows are " .

    Well, as a matter of fact, I think the modern fellows are
pretty nearly jolly good ,and far more knowledgeable than we were
in my time -   but that is another story .

            I have at any rate this excuse for being critical .
I was in the Football Eleven myself; so may I say that we did not
in those days need to have a claque to encourage us to play
up and do our -   well , you know what - to win .

        Last time I wnnt to see a match at Charterhouse I got
depressed by the doleful sing-song dirge which goes on round the
ground,(presumably by order) ◛ " Char- ter- house - - ,
Char- ter-house " with monotonous re-iteration .

            It reminded me rather of the applause in the Greek
play as rendered in a certain school where the waving by
monitors of their canes to the right means " Everybody applaud" ,
and when waved to the left it means " All laugh" .

    Totalitarian States are not in it for ordered applause .

    Since the idea comes from America , why not go the whole hog,
and brighten up the game   by having a Yell Leader ,jumping
around and putting "pep" into it with his "Ra-ra-ra" .

        No. Better let the players alone, to concentrate all their
power on their job,and when they show an exceptionally piece of
play then let your applause spring spontaneously ,with a
full throated cheer from the heart ,whether it's for yourown
side or for the visitors .

        The play's the thing. Floreat .

        Yours sincerely

        Baden-Powell

Baden-Powell. Copy of letter sent to school 1939

ground (presumably by order) Char-ter-house, Char-ter-house" with monotonous re-iteration. In his day, he wrote, "We did not need to have a

claque to encourage us to play." He mischievously suggested having an American style Yell Leader, but in the end plumped for advising the school to: "Better let the players alone, to concentrate all their power on their job and when they show an exceptional piece of play, then let your applause spring spontaneously with a full-throated cheer from the heart, whether it's for your own side or for the visitors."

Baden-Powell recognised as early as 1908 in *Scouting for Boys* that, "Football is a grand game for developing a lad physically and morally...But it is a vicious game when it draws crowds of lads away from playing the game themselves to be merely onlookers at a few paid performers...boys and young men, pale, narrow chested, hunched up, miserable specimens, smoking endless cigarettes, betting, all of them learning to be hysterical as they groan and cheer in panic unison with their neighbours..."

EH PARRY (G), school captain of 1873-4, then playing for Oxford University, brought an Oxford team to the school in OQ 1874. He played in the Varsity match, later that year, on 28th November 1874, at the Kennington Oval.

The shape of the team was beginning to change and in 1874 there were seven attackers out of eleven men with three centre forwards. In the late 1870s this number changed to six forwards and in 1883 the Cambridge team went to only five forwards with the spare man becoming

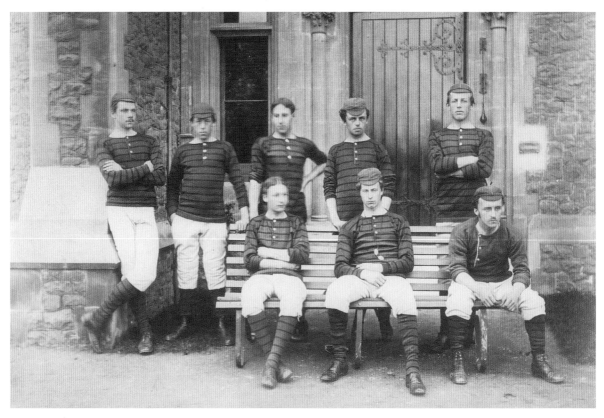

School team 1874-5. Standing: HB Southwell, AF Wilson, EM Short, AH Todd, RE Hulton. Sitting: WR Page, NJ Abdy, HG Jeaffreson. School archive

a centre half. 1874 also saw the introduction of shin guards.

In September 1875, the Association Rules were adopted at school "to save many disputes which occurred in foreign matches under our rules". Nationally the free kick and corner kick had been introduced in 1871, a wooden cross-bar added to the goal in 1875, replacing the tape, so that the Cup Final finally had a rigid goal.

The school game in 1875 against Westminster had two tactically different formations and Westminster "kept constantly on the ball with an apparent disregard of sides". Later two half backs emerged with a second back, with forwards in mutually supportive pairs one behind the other. Eventually one of the deeper forwards became a centre half back and the WM formation developed from there.

Backs

Half backs

Forwards supporting each other

Would soon change to

Full backs

Half backs

Inside forwards

Wingers and centre forward

At Oxford and Cambridge the game was undergoing some changes also – there was much passing and forwards kept to definite places in the field. These changes did not suit everyone as after one game the match was described by one famous player as a "mere dawdle". There was not "a single run made of even average merit".

W. Veale describes the Westminster match as "the biggest match of the season with hundreds from the school, town and London coming to watch. Tea was provided in Hall. The team players were men with moustaches and side whiskers, wearing jerseys with coloured hoops that made them look beefy. They certainly had a man's drink after matches, a jack of beer and twenty-four mugs (two for the umpires) brought from Saunderites which was put on one of the iron seats on the terrace from which to help themselves".

NJ ABDY (g) the school captain in 1875, went to Cambridge, gaining a Blue in 1878. As with most Blues, he returned with an XI to play against the school.

The autumn of 1876 saw the season open with the first "foreign" eleven-a-side game against Brooke Hall on 4th October, but prior to this various practice matches had been played such as the VII playing XI and the XI playing the XXII. The school team did not lose a single match in that year.

On Saturday 25th November 1876 the Old Carthusians, having initially amalgamated with the OC Cricket Club, played their first official game against the school on "a wet day". EM Short (Gg) captained the XI in 1876 and also later brought his own team to play in OQ 1876. EH Parry captained Oxford to another 1-0 win, in February 1877.

The *Carthusian*, introducing the 1877-8 season, said that the team was in "rather worse condition than last year with only two team members remaining". There was the loss of the captain, WR Page (VGg), whose dribbling skills were wonderful, and those returning were EF Growse (G) and JFM Prinsep (RW). Back play was wanton and the remaining colours were halves as there was plenty of scope for new

School team 1876-7. Standing: EG Wynyard, HW Devenish, EF Growse, JFM Prinsep, SF Smith, A Keightley Sitting: JE Eddis, WR Page, WTB Hayter, GD Keightley. School archive

blood amongst the backs and the forwards. They also needed a goalkeeper, described as a "much abused personage, but of great importance". The house captains were encouraged to seek out likely candidates and "not be slack about the rules about 'Hands' and 'Throwing In'." Puntabout was regarded as a "capital institution, but it may be made too much of – especially if the hands are used too much". There was also concern shown for the damage done to the grass by such activity; play was to be restricted to the lower part of Under Green "as often no game is played there". The fixtures arranged for the term were against Clapham Rovers on 20th October, WR Page's XI, the Old Harrovians and a Cambridge XI, with Westminster at Vincent Square and the Old Harrovians again after Christmas.

WW Drew (G) and TE Page (Brooke Hall) arranged teams to play the school in 1877. AWF Wilson (a goalie) and WR Page (a forward) played for Oxford – losing 1-5 to Cambridge on 23rd February 1878. WTB Hayter's (LW) XI played the school in OQ 1878.

The whistle to control play in a football match was first blown in 1878. Prior to that in some games the players played to the "handkerchief" rather like the yellow flag used in American Gridiron Football. Also this year, Bramall Lane, Sheffield staged the first floodlit game.

In 1878 house matches were revived after some five years and the final has been contested every year since – although in 1882 the final was not completed due to bad light and weather conditions. The *Carthusian* in February 1883, reluctant "to revive a painful controversy", left it as this: "we cannot but think that the captain of the Eleven acted throughout strictly within his rights…though for the future we should advise an earlier start to be made, considering the uncertainty of the weather for that period of the year."

A Challenge Cup was purchased by general subscription. It was sincerely hoped that this would generate "no ill-will on the part of rival

School team 1877-8. Standing: CJ Stubbs, O Evan Thomas, HM Hull, WE Hansell, S Medlicott.
Seated: CE Keith Falconer, CM Burdon, EF Growse, WEC Frith, EJ Wilson. School archive

Gownboys house cup winners 1884. Earliest team photo with cup.

houses". The incentive was to make a stimulus for the end of OQ and to act as an incentive to some of the smaller fellows so that they might represent their houses. These matches were not to interfere with house clubs, which was "too good an institution to be meddled with", so Club matches would be played off as usual. It was noted that Mr Girdlestone's House competed under that name. Saunderites beat Lockites on a snow-covered pitch 4-2 on 14th December 1878. The first round of matches were L *v* g, H *v* D, G *v* V and S *v* W. Then H played L and S played V.

WALTER KW JENNER (S) scored a goal in the first house match final (1878), helping Saunderites win the cup. He was born on 12th October 1860 and died on the same day, 12th October 1948 at Lytes Cary, Somerset. At school he was a Junior and Senior Scholar. He was in the football XI in 1878, leaving school OQ78. He then joined the 9th Lancers in 1880 retiring as a major 1902. In the Great War, Staff, DSO Bt-Lt-Col 1919. JP Somerset. He married Flora in 1893 and he succeeded his father as second Baronet. He played for the London FA on 27th December 1879 against Sheffield at the Oval, as well as composing an opera that was performed on the BBC. He left his compositions to the school.

In the school XI at this time was **LIEU-TENANT-COLONEL CECIL EDWARD KEITH-FALCONER** (S) who was born at St Leonard's Forest, Horsham, Sussex 11th October 1860 and died in action near Belmont, South Africa 10th November 1899.

He represented the school XI in 1877-8, played in the FA Cup Final for Clapham Rovers 1879 with Prinsep and Growse, as well as turning out for The Swifts and the OCs. He was a centre-forward who was also a wing forward and described as a "good wing, is faster than he appears to be; always plays well and backs up without tiring". Later he was described as "a fair centre, but slow". Keith-Falconer played for the school cricket XI in 1878, and was reputed to have scored the first century for the team. He was the grandson of the 7th Earl of Kintore and son of an army major. He joined the army in 1881 with the Sussex Militia till 1883 and then the 5th Northumberland Fusiliers 1883-7. He was appointed ADC to the Governor and C in C of Victoria, Australia and then ADC to the Governor of the Cape of Good Hope 1889-92. A promotion to Captain in 1892 eventually led to him passing out in the Staff College with honours. Between 1895-8 he was with the 13th Sudanese Battalion, seeing action in Dongola and the Nile. He was mentioned in dispatches several times and promoted Lt-Colonel in November 1898. Eventually he was killed in Boer War action with the 5th Regiment of Fusiliers. Earlier in 1899 he got married. At the time of his death his home was 25 Granville Place, Portman Square.

EDWARD FREDERIC GROWSE (G) was the 1st XI captain at this time and he was born at Brentwood, Essex 8th July 1860. He died on board ship in the Red Sea on 10th November 1908.

Growse was in the Charterhouse 1st XI 1876-8, being captain in 1878. Balliol College, Oxford 1879 where he did not get a Blue but he did play in the FA Cup final that year for Clapham Rovers as well as playing for Essex and the London FA against Birmingham at the Aston Lower Ground (7th Feb 1880). The school played against a team from Brentwood in the early period and possibly this was the link. Growse was "a fast centre-forward, sometimes brilliant who worked hard and was sometimes too excitable. He must learn not to get offside when backing up." He was a good cricketer, in the 1st XI from 1875 until 1878 and captained

in 1877. He played for Essex for a period around 1880 when the county achieved first class status. He won Blues for sprinting in 1880 and 1881 finishing second in the Oxford 400 yards twice. He went abroad to serve the Empire and was lost to sport.

COTSFORD M BURDON (G), captain in 1878, went to New College, Oxford, became an Oxford Blue in 1879 when he also gathered an XI that visited the school. As a farmer, he later migrated to Canterbury, New Zealand.

In November 1878 a Greyfriars FC played at the school with Parry, AJ Wake and Page in the line up. The Greyfriars CC (1874) later became the Old Carthusian Club.

By 1879 the rules of the OC club and the club colours of brown, black and orange stripes were established. The club report for 1879/80 mentioned that: "The result of the last year's matches was most satisfactory from a social point of view, but if we are to keep up our football reputation, individuals must make greater efforts to play regularly." Such planning quickly led to the success in the FA Cup!

AWF Wilson captained the Oxford XI, playing as a half back, along with Page and Burdon another forward.

By 1880 the OC colour scheme was altered to pink, dark blue and cerise. In 1880 the customary match at the start of the term was "Seven against Eleven" and then "Eleven played Seventeen" and the XI lost the last game of the term only when they played the OC XI which two

School team 1881-2. Standing: FH Brown, KH Eddis, WN Cobbold, A Amos, LW King-Harman, AM Walters, W Rayner. Sitting: AI Vintcent, EB Sewell, AK Henley, TW Blenkiron. School archive

weeks later won the FA Cup.

The 1881 Cup Final was the last final between two amateur sides (see chapter 5) – the Old Carthusians and the Old Etonians. On the way to the final, the Headmaster would announce to the school the OC results by posting a telegram on the noticeboard – and every boy knew this significance, singing the success "till the roof rang".

Oxford University AFC records show the OCs played them in 1881-2, drawing 1-1. They played again in 1882-3, 1886-7, 1893-4, 1896-7, 1897-8 and 1899-1901.

CJ Weir in his book on the *History of Oxford University AFC* writes that the OCs kept up their twice-yearly fixture with the University

and EG Colvin played for a Cambridge team that beat Oxford 2-1 on 12th February 1881.

In the OQ 1881 a "Scratch Sixes" competition was held at the suggestion of the *Carthusian*. Teams were made up from pupils who had won their Caps. 1881-2 was a very successful season for the school, with all 16 out of 16 matches being won. 53 goals were scored for and 14 against.

Between 1881 and 1885 various OCs brought teams under the names of WH Norris (g), J Vintcent (W), whilst the Reverend CC Tancock from Brooke Hall also presented a team to play. HA Carter (RS) and WG Morrison (W) also arranged sides to play though neither had any pedigree in school teams or elsewhere.

the f.a. cup 1881 to 1892

With the growing strength of the Football Association, Charles Alcock introduced The Challenge Cup for the associated teams, an idea based on the inter-house competition (known as Cock House) at Harrow School. Alcock captained the Wanderers side that won the first FA Cup. In that final, four members of the Cup committee were involved: Alcock himself, Captain Francis Marindin of the Royal Engineers, the opposition, Betts the goal scorer and the referee Alfred Stair.

In 1871, fifteen teams entered the first Cup competition, but by the time withdrawals had occurred only twelve clubs and thirteen teams were involved. By the 21st century, thirteen rounds are played, originally regional and, after about nine months, the seven hundred or so entrants are reduced to two finalists playing before a world-wide audience at Wembley.

This first final, between the Wanderers and the Royal Engineers, on 16th March 1872, was played at the Kennington Oval. The pitch had no cross bar, only a tape, no nets, no line markings for the half-way line or centre circle and no free kicks or penalties were awarded – however such was the interest that 2000 spectators turned up wearing their favours. Both teams adopted a 1-2-7 formation. There was no recognisable goalkeeper and the teams ran around as though they were children in a playground. Despite the Royal Engineers going a man down after 10 minutes due to a broken collar bone, the game surprisingly only ended up 1-0! In the 1872-3 competition, the Wanderers, as holders,

were exempt from playing in any of the qualifying rounds and not only had byes through to the final but also were allowed to choose its venue.

From small beginnings the competition has become the massive commercial concern that spans the globe. The Old Carthusians did not enter the cup until 1879, the year of the club's formation and at that time they were likely to be drawn against a team from the inaugural group that first played in the competition. The club

FA Cup. Football Association

report at the end of 1879-80 season said, "The result of last year's matches was most satisfactory from a social point of view, but if we are to keep up our football reputation, individuals must make greater efforts to play regularly."

The school played teams such as Barnes, Civil Service, Clapham Rovers and the other entrants to the cup included Crystal Palace (not associated with the modern club), Hampstead Heathens, Harrow Chequers, Hitchin, Maidenhead, Marlow, Reigate Priory, Royal Engineers (Chatham), Upton Park, the Wanderers, Queen's Park from Glasgow and Donington School near Spalding, in south Lincolnshire. From this gathering some teams scratched; the Scots found the cost of travelling unviable and the schoolboys withdrew before their first game having been drawn against Queen's Park and, although their headmaster was keen for his boys to take part in this competition, he could not justify travelling to Glasgow to play!! A hundred years later, for "old time sake", the school did make the trip to Glasgow to play Queen's Park and they lost.

The first twelve years of the competition were dominated by the Wanderers, the Old Etonians, the Royal Engineers and Oxford University. The Wanderers poached players from other clubs and by the time the competition was getting serious, the club found its supply of players limited and the club eventually disbanded. It was an amateur game and, as already shown, the Old Carthusians played their part from 1879.

That year, 54 teams started and the OCs played against Acton away at Gunnersbury Lane, winning 4-0, and in round two they lost to the only goal scored – by Wace for the Wanderers. Clapham Rovers won the trophy.

In 1880-1, 63 teams entered and the Carthusians, with an exceptional team, swept all before them, defeating Saffron Walden Town 7-0 (23/10/1880) in the first round at the Oval. *The Times* remarked that the only thing that Saffron Walden won was the toss. The next round match was against Dreadnought, an East London team, with the OCs winning 5-1 (11/12/1880). In the third round there was a bye and due to bad weather the OCs had not played for two months, so they went to Chatham

under-prepared to play on the Great Lines ground against the Royal Engineers. The OCs beat them 2-0 (19/2/1881), very much against the odds. Wynyard and Parry scored. This was a particularly impressive result because the Engineers had previously put six goals past Glasgow Rangers. A report said: "We must not forget to speak of the hospitality of the Royal Engineers which was abounded and thoroughly appreciated." Clapham Rovers (the holders) fell next 3-1 (19/3/1881), after extra time (1-1), at the Oval.

❧ ❧

The weather was delightfully fine, a great number of spectators were present and great enthusiasm shown by the partisans of either side... and only six minutes after the commencement of hostilities, Lloyd-Jones, from a corner kick by Weston gained the first event of the day. Despite being 0-1 down, the Carthusians, who were decidedly quicker on their feet than their opponents, kept up a succession of attacks and but for Birkett, the Rover's flag would have been lowered half mast on many occasions... and eleven minutes only having passed away since the ends were reversed, when, from a neat throw in by Prinsep, Page made his shot and Birkett who tried all he knew to stop the ball, missed his opportunity and it went through equalising matters. And so the game carried on till time was called.....after brief consultation it was agreed according to the present law that they should continue for half an hour longer. Ogilvie again won the toss and as before took the western side of the ground. Page having kicked off, the Carthusians looked as fresh and as confident as when they commenced... only four minutes having elapsed Parry, charging down the left side, made his effort, and succeeded in spite of Birkett's strenuous attempts to prevent him... to add to the general satisfaction, after a splendid run by Hansell, Page was instrumental in gaining a third and thus ended one of the best matches of the season.

❧ ❧

In the semi-finals they beat Darwen from Lancashire 4-1 (26/3/1881) on the Oval. The original referee was to be Mr Pierce-Dix of Sheffield but he was unavailable, so the honour went to

Major Marindin, a southerner! The umpires CH Wollaston (Wanderers) and EC Bambridge (Swifts) were also from the south. The FA turned down Northerners' protests and "before the game the referee entered our (OCs) dressing room and reported that the Darwen team were shod with boots covered in spikes and projecting studs, which could not be allowed. However the Carthusians raised no objection, for new boots could not be procured in a moment, but our feet and shins showed afterwards that the referee's report was justified." Later Darwen, who had donned new jerseys in blue and white stripes, objected to the Carthusian unpunctuality and lined up shouting "time" for some minutes before the game started. At last the defaulter, JFM Prinsep, the youngest player, turned up biting a large sandwich. Darwen scored the only goal of the first half and their supporters sent up clouds of carrier pigeons. Supporters back home in Lancashire were crowded around the local newspaper office celebrating their lead.

After half-time the Carthusians drew level in controversial circumstances when Hansell shot through the goal and the Darwen team protested that the ball had in fact passed between the upright and the guy rope. They also protested that the second goal, scored by Tod, had come after the ball had been out of play. Referee Marindin overruled the protest and Darwen clearly lost their composure as the Carthusians went right away from them, obtaining two more goals by Wynyard and Vintcent. The crowd in Darwen slipped away never to see their team reach such heights again.

In the final the Old Etonians were beaten 3-0 on Saturday, 9th April 1881, at the Oval, in front of 4500 people. On the way to the final the Carthusians were given a bye in round three whilst the OEs had a bye in the semi-final.

The winning team was described as the finest combination seen up to that time to carry off the trophy. EG Colvin, JFM Prinsep, EH Parry, AH Tod, WR Page and the brilliant Captain Wynyard were not only players of the highest class, but they brought almost to perfection the system of combination. If one were asked to say which team deserved to rank as the first really scientific eleven that the football world knew, one must answer, the Old Carthusians.

(Association Football – The Men Who Made It.)

Reports of the game mention that the OCs chose the Gasometer end and Macaulay of Eton kicked off at 3.45pm. The OCs were a young side averaging only 20 years and 310 days. W. Pierce Dix of the Sheffield FA refereed this final, with umpires EH Bambridge (the Swifts) and CHR Wollaston (the Wanderers). EH Parry became the first overseas player to captain a winning team in the final and this was the only final to be contested by two Old Boys' teams. The Carthusians were reported to be in the "pink of condition" whilst the Etonians clearly struggled in the second half. Wynyard scored after 25 minutes (1-0 at half time) and Parry (75 minutes) and Tod (80 minutes) put the final nails in the coffin as the Etonians tired.

The Sportsman describing the game reported:

It was windy day. Play for a time was pretty even until the OCs got the leather well into

Drawing of 1881 FA Cup goal. School archive

the opponent's half and after ten minutes Wynyard kicked a goal. Whitfield effected some fine runs down the left side of the ground but was well stopped by Richards. The Charterhouse defence proved equal to anything that the Etonians could throw at them and eventually with a well-timed rush the ball went into touch about ten yards from the opponents' lines. Prinsep took a throw in which he did so cleverly that Wynyard was able to send the ball between the posts."

Football.

ASSOCIATION CHALLENGE CUP.

OLD ETONIANS *v.* OLD CARTHUSIANS.

On Saturday, April 9th, the final tie for the Challenge Cup was played at Kennington Oval, in the presence of about 4000 spectators. The Old Etonians were known to possess a strong team, but the extraordinary form shewn by their opponents of late caused them to be the more fancied of the two. Play began at twenty minutes to four o'clock, when Macaulay kicked off for the Etonians, who had lost the toss, against a slight wind. The Carthusians at once returned the ball, and carried it up to the Eton goal line, but after two throws in by Prinsep, which caused the ball to go in close proximity to the posts, Macaulay ran it along the centre of the ground. A corner-kick soon fell to the Etonians, but their rivals got the ball away. Some exceedingly fast play followed, and repeated runs were made by Page, Wynyard, and Parry, and the latter tried to kick a goal, but failed. The Etonians made a sharp burst into their adversaries' territory after the kick off, but the ball was sent to the wrong side of the posts. A corner then fell to the Carthusians, and Wynyard almost headed the ball through. After two more close but ineffectual attempts to score, Prinsep threw the ball well in, and Wynyard kicked it between the posts. Eton now became the assailants, and a splendid shot by Anderson was only just saved by Gillett. Once more the Carthusians assumed the aggressive, and Wynyard kicked the ball underneath the bar; but, as the offside rule had been broken, the goal was disallowed. With the exception of a corner-kick to the Carthusians, nothing further of note happened up to half-time, when the sides changed ends. Eton now had the wind at their backs, and a corner nearly caused the downfall of their opponents' goal. Charterhouse, however, quickly reasserted themselves, and a combined run on the part of Page and Parry ended in a goal being kicked by the latter. This was soon followed by a third disaster for the Etonians, as the ball glanced between the posts off Tod's chest. There was only a few minutes' time now left, and although Eton strove hard to score, their efforts were ineffectual, and the Old Carthusians were thus pronounced victors by three goals to none. Referee, Mr. W. Pierce Dix; Umpires, Mr. E. H. Bainbridge (Swifts), and Mr. C. H. Wollaston (Wanderers).

Carthusian report of 1881 final. School archive

Having changed ends, the wind was now at the Etonians' backs. At about 75 minutes gone in the game, shortly after a disallowed goal by Parry for offside, he scored a goal which was described by the *Carthusian* as "a combined run on the part of Page and Parry which ended in a goal being kicked by the latter". Five minutes later *The Field* said that "all hopes of Eton retrieving their losses seemed groundless and their misfortunes were compounded by a third disaster as Richards made a kick at goal, the ball glanced between the posts off Tod's breast." *The Sporting Life* reported this to be "off an Etonian's body". Whatever the outcome, it was Page's telling run that opened up the Etonian defence.

The teams lined up thus:

	Old Carthusians	Old Etonians
Goal	LF Gillett	JFP Rawlinson
Full backs	EG Colvin	CW Foley
	WH Norris	TH French
Half backs	J Vintcent	Hon AF Kinnaird (capt)
	JFM Prinsep	B Farrer
Right side	WE Hansell	WJ Anderson
	LM Richards	JBT Chevalier
Centres	WR Page	RH Macaulay
	EG Wynyard	HC Goodhart
Left side	EH Parry (capt)	H Whitfield
	A.H Tod	PC Novelli

The OCs (1881 and 1894) and Wimbledon Football Club (1963 and 1988) are recorded as the only two clubs to have won both the FA Cup and the FA Amateur Cups. The OCs achieved this double first! Wimbledon beat Sutton United at Wembley in 1963 to win the Amateur Cup and then Liverpool in 1988 in the FA Cup. Records suggest that the Royal Engineers did the same in 1875 and 1908 but history cannot confirm, once and for all, that these two "Engineers" feats were achieved by teams from the same parent body. The team that won the 1908 Amateur Cup final was called the "Depot Battalion Royal Engineers".

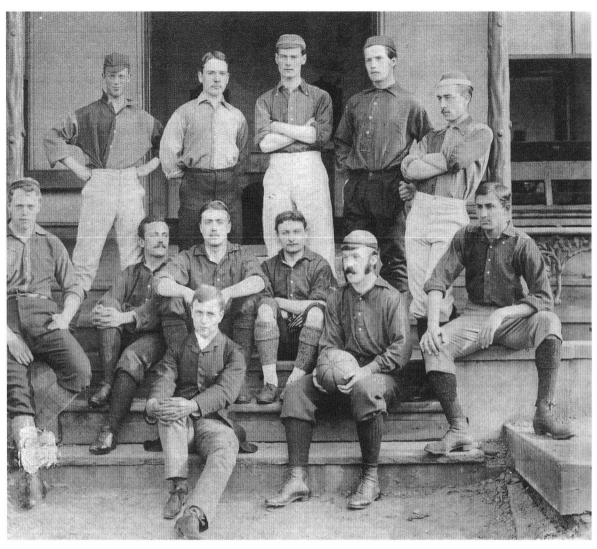

Members of the FA Cup winning team 1881. Back left: Richards, Norris, Colvin, Gillet, Hansell. Seated left: Wynyard, Tod, Prinsep, Page, Parry, Vintcent. Front: unknown. School archive

LEONARD FRANCIS GILLETT (D) Born in Derby 21st January 1861; died Austen's Close, Harbertonford near Totnes, Devon 23rd November 1915.

He was at Charterhouse 1874-9, went to Pembroke, Oxford in 1879 and got his BA in 1882. As well as being in the Cup side at 20 years old only, he won a Blue in 1882. He was a "most sure goalkeeper, very sharp". During his schooldays the school magazine said of him, "Has been of infinite service to the XI." He played for Notts County in 1882-3 losing in the semi-final of the Cup to the Old Etonians and he is recorded to be the first goalkeeper to play for Derby County, September

1884. By profession he became a civil and mining engineer and lived off his income in later years.

SIR ELLIOT GRAHAM COLVIN (PS) Born Almora (150 miles NE Delhi) India on 18th July 1861; died in Gang Bridge, St Mary Bourne, Andover, Hampshire on 2nd August 1940.

He was at Charterhouse between 1875-8, matriculating at King's College, Cambridge 1880. He played 1st XI football in 1878, got a Blue in 1881, when he also played in the Cup Final at the age of 19 and he then gained another Blue in 1882 and also played for the South

XI. He was "a good full back, difficult to pass, as he has plenty of pace and always sticks to his man. At different times he filled both posts of back and half-back, and always satisfactorily." He was also said to be a "first class back; fast, clever, and a powerful kick". He played in the school cricket XI (1876-8) played for Norfolk from 1878 and was a member of the MCC. He moved to India after his Cup Final appearance. He followed in his father's footsteps joining the Indian civil service in 1882, filling a number of posts for 36 years in local government. He retired in 1918. He was then appointed British delegate on the Inter-Allied Commission for war reparations in Sofia, Bulgaria and then on to other commissions which led to him being made a CSI in 1906 and his knighthood of that order in 1911.

Cup engraving. Christie's images

WALTER HARRY NORRIS (g) was born at Ashley House, Epsom on 8th April 1863 and died at Steane Park, Brackley, Northants 14th May 1931. Walter was at school from 1877 until 1880, playing in the XI in 1880. He was with the OCs in 1881 and represented the Surrey FA. He was a full back who reached the "top" very quickly. He was a "capital back, cool and with strong kick." He was a brewer by trade and was a director of the Brackley and Banbury Brewery.

SIR JOSEPH VINTCENT (W) Born in Mossel Bay, Cape Colony, South Africa on 12th November 1861 and died in Bulawayo, Southern Rhodesia on 14th August 1914. He attended the Diocesan College, Rondebosch then Charterhouse between 1877-80 playing in the XI in 1879. He went up to Trinity Hall, Cambridge, matriculating in 1880 with a BA, he gained his MA in 1884 and LL.B. He was a Cambridge Blue in 1883, playing also for Barnes, the Corinthians and the London FA. Vintcent was a half back, whose heading skills were noticed in this comment: "A very safe half

Winners medal. School archive

back, plays well to forwards, can place the ball almost where he likes, nearly as good with his head as his legs." He was described as "one of the best half backs in England, kicks well to forwards and rarely makes a mistake". He returned to South Africa in 1885, the year he played twice for the Corinthians. He played in the school cricket team in 1879 and was the brother of the South African test cricketer Charles Henry Vintcent. Joseph was a barrister who was called to the Bar on 26th January 1885. He returned to his home to be an advocate. Then he became a Crown Prosecutor in British Bechuanaland 1886-94, Judge of the High Court, Matebeleland 1894-8. He was Senior Judge of the High Court in Southern Rhodesia 1898-1914 and also in North-west Rhodesia in 1906. He was knighted in 1910.

Do not confuse him with James Edmund Vincent of Winchester and an Oxford Blue who opposed Joseph in the fifth round Cup tie between the OCs and Clapham Rovers in 1882-3.

Joseph's brother CH Vintcent (W) was the fourth son and was born 2.9.1866. He eventually worked back in the Transvaal, captaining the Transvaal football XI in 1890, the rugby team and winning the 100 yards championship all in the same year.

JAMES FM PRINSEP (RW) was born in India 27 July 1861 and died at Nairn, Scotland 22 November 1895. He was at school between 1874-8 and played in the school XI 1876-7. He then went to the Royal Military College, Sandhurst from 1878. He was a runner-up in the FA Cup with Clapham Rovers in 1879, being the youngest player to play in a Cup Final at 17 years and 245 days on 29th March 1879. Clapham lost to the Old Etonians 1-0. This record was eventually broken by Curtis Weston (17 years 119 days) of Millwall FC in 2004, an occasion that brought Prinsep's name into the national press. On their way to the final Clapham beat Forest School 10-1 on 7th December 1878. OCs, EF Growse and CE Keith-Falconer also played for Clapham. He was also the youngest to play for England (17 years 252 days) until Wayne Rooney broke the record in 2003. Prinsep played for the RMC Sandhurst, Clapham Rovers, Surrey FA, London FA, The South, The Rest v England and for England (see chapter 9).

He was an half back. "A fine half back, always cool, very strong in the legs and combining plenty of strength with great accuracy; kicks splendidly and with judgement; seldom makes a mistake; can kick the ball in any position and passes it admirably to his forward." W Unite Jones: "One of the prettiest half-backs that ever did duty for England, he was one of the most stylish players of his time." He played good club cricket, he was a member of the Free Foresters and the Grey Friars, a club for OCs. He played school cricket in 1877. He was a soldier with the Essex regiment 1882-5 and was at Khartoum in a vain attempt to save the besieged General Gordon. He joined the Egyptian Army in 1885-90, became a major and then came under British rule. He joined the Egyptian Coastguard service from 1890 until his death. He was living between Alexandria and 46, Thurloe Square in London at the time of his death. He was in Nairn, playing golf when he got pneumonia. This led to blood poisoning and kidney failure. He received two Royal Humane Society awards for rescuing men from the Nile. He saved two men, an English soldier and a Sudanese soldier, who had found themselves in difficulties a year apart on virtually the same date 1884 and 1885. E.G. Wynyard also won this award.

The marble 8-9th century well-head in Scholar Court at Godalming was given to the school by the family in OQ 1959.

WALTER EDWARD HANSELL (WV) was born in Norwich on 15th November 1860 and died at Heigham Hall, Norwich on 25th May 1938.

He was at school during 1873-8 appearing in the XI in his final year. He was an outside right and perhaps inconsistent as the pen picture reveals. "He was a fast wing, who shows some very good play but uncertain, and sometimes appears to get nervous in matches" although later he was "very fast and clever on the wing". He served on the FA Council between 1897-1900 for Norfolk County, helping to establish the county association. He was a good cricketer, playing for the county in 1889 and was a member of the MCC. He was a solicitor and Notary

Public in Norfolk from 1886, partner in Hansell and Hales of Norwich and later Under-sheriff of Norfolk. He joined the Norfolk Infantry Volunteer battalion 1879 reaching captain in the 3rd battalion in 1899. He died at his home in Pegg's Close, Sheringham.

LEWIS MATTHEW RICHARDS (UV) Born Swansea 14th September 1861; died 16, Sloane Gardens, London 30th November 1918. He was in the school XI in 1879 and 1880, Trinity College, Cambridge matriculation 1880, LL.B 1884. Played in the Cup winning team at the young age of 19. He gained a Cambridge Blue 1882. He played at inside right and was "a most useful forward, a splendid dribbler and sticks well to the ball". A useful cricketer he played at club level and was a member of the Free Foresters. He became a barrister, called to the bar at the Inner Temple on 17th November 1884. Practised as a Special Pleader on the South Wales circuit, he had a property in Swansea at Westcross House and was a Glamorgan JP. His wife was a judge.

WILLIAM ROBERT PAGE (VGg) Born at 11 Queen Street, Mayfair 12th December 1858 and died at 27 Westbourne Park, Paddington, on 30th June 1884. He was at Charterhouse between 1869-77, played 1st XI football in 1874-6 and was eventually captain. He matriculated at Queen's College, Oxford 1877, gained his Blue in 1878-9. Page also played for Berkshire, London FA, The South and for The Rest v England. He was a centre forward, renowned for dribbling, having "considerable pace and sticking to the ball in a wonderful manner". He "is small but has done great service by his dodgy dribbling". He was "one of the finest of his day, but should play more for his side and is rather accustomed to be played for". Page was regarded to be Cobbold's superior but he passed away before his time. He joined the Royal Irish Constabulary as a sub-inspector 1884 but tragically

died at 25 years old from meningitis and rheumatic fever. His father was a doctor.

MAJOR EDWARD GEORGE WYNYARD (Dg) Born in Saharanpur (Uttar Pradesh) India 1st April 1861; died at The Red House Knotty Green, Beaconsfield, Bucks, 30th October 1936 and was buried at Penn Church, Bucks.

His education began at Woodcote House, Windlesham. Then he joined Charterhouse 1874-7, playing for the School XI 1876 but moved to St Edward's School, Oxford 1877-9. He played for the London FA, Corinthians and St Edward's Rugby XV. He was a centre forward who scored in the FA Cup final. He was a "heavy forward, charging and dribbling well, always middles splendidly, with plenty of dash, making himself obnoxious to opposing backs". He kept playing into his thirties, playing twice for the Corinthians in 1893 and scoring five goals. He was president of the OC cricket and football club 1913-9. As a rugby player he was a "glorious three-quarter, and had he not gone into the army, he would have reached the top in rugby". As a cricketer he was a leader and he played in three test matches against Australia in 1896 and two against South Africa in 1905-6. He had to decline the invitation to tour Australia in 1897-8 due to army commitments and when he was invited to captain a tour to Australia in 1907-8, he could not accept because of family reasons. He did captain the MCC tour to New Zealand in 1906-7 and to the West Indies in 1904-5, when he topped the batting averages with 562 runs at 40.14. He also toured North America 1907, Egypt 1909, South Africa 1909-10, USA 1920 and Canada 1923 at the ripe old age of 62 when he topped the bowling averages with underarm lobs.

He played for Hampshire between 1878-1908 (not first class 1886-94) and was county captain 1896-9. His final first class match was against the MCC in 1912 and in all he scored 8318 first class runs at 33.00 with 13 centuries. His highest score of 268 was against Yorkshire. In 1896 he averaged 49.42 from 1038 runs coming second in the national averages. In 1915 he scored 1281 runs at 41.32 coming 15th. He was a member of the MCC, Free Foresters, MCC committee and represented the South African Cricket Association in England in 1908. He won the European Tobogganing championship at Davos in 1894, played county hockey for Hampshire, formed his own golf club called the "Jokers" made up from famous cricketing friends. He belonged to the Wimbledon GC (becoming an honorary life member in 1930) and the Oxford Graduates' Golf Society (hon. life member 1931). He joined the army in 1881 as a lieutenant in the Warwick Militia. He was with the King's Liverpool regiment in active service in Burma 1885-7 (Medal with clasp, DSO 1887, mentioned in dispatches twice). He became a captain in the Welsh Regiment 1890, adjutant Oxford University Volunteers 1899-1900, an instructor at the Royal Military College, Sandhurst 1900-3, when he retired. He was recalled for the Great War in September 1914 as a major with the King's Liverpool Rgt, then he was attached to the Army Ordnance Corps in May 1915. Middlesex Rgt November 1916, Commandant Thornhill Labour Camp 1916-9. He finally retired in April 1919 with an OBE. In 1895 he was awarded the Royal Humane Society medal for attempting to save a Swiss peasant from drowning in a lake in Davos, Switzerland. With a great sense of humour, Wynyard was annoyed that WG Grace withdrew from his XI to play against the RMC at Sandhurst in 1901. Wynyard dressed up as WG and batted for a few runs before being purposely hit on the head and retiring hurt. At lunch he appeared in half the disguise revealing himself not to be the great doctor.

EDWARD HAGARTY PARRY (G) Captained the OC XI in the 1881 FA Cup Final. Parry was a Gownboy, who was born in Toronto, Canada on 24th April 1855 and he died at 12 Dovedale Road, West Bridgford, Nottingham on 19 July 1931.

He was at Charterhouse between 1868-74

and in the 1st XI 1870-3 and captain in 1872-3. He then went to Exeter College, Oxford, matriculating 1874 with a BA in 1878 and an MA 1882. He played for Oxford University in the 1877 FA Cup Final, as captain, gaining Blues 1875-7. He also played for the Swifts, the Remnants, London FA, Bucks FA, The Rest v England, the South, Stoke Poges, Windsor and for Berks and Bucks. He played in full internationals v Wales 1879, 1882 and v Scotland 1882. He played inside left and was "a fast dribbler, and useful on the wing but is rather light and does not stand a charge". He scored goals consistently, "so that it did not seem to matter much". He played for the OCs that beat the South of England XI 3-1 in the FA Charity festival on 16th March 1889, scoring one of the goals. He scored five against Reading Minster in a first round cup match in 1883-4, four goals in beating Saffron Walden 7-0 in the cup first round in 1880-1 and three versus the Pilgrims in a 6-0 win in a first round match in 1882-3. Another hat-trick followed in that season's fourth round against the Royal Engineers(6-2) and his first hat-trick was in 1874-5 for Oxford University beating Brondesbury 6-0 in the FA Cup first round. Parry was a member of the FA Council in 1881. He was a decent cricketer playing in the school XI in 1872-4 and for the MCC. In 1874 he was joint winner of the Athletic Challenge Cup at school. In a soccer match, he once quietened a bumptious cadet from Sandhurst who had a disagreement with him on the field of play. The cadet soon realised who was talking to him when he asked Parry what he knew about the game and asked what club he had represented. He soon apologised when Parry told him of his success with the England team.

Parry became a schoolmaster at Felsted 1879-80 before settling at Stoke House School, Stoke Poges, near Slough 1881-1918, where he was headmaster from 1892. In 1907 he was chairman of the Private Schools' Association and sat on the council for many years. He helped run the Officers' Fund for sons of officers killed in the war. He suffered from ill health in his later years, suffering progressive blindness and physical weakness. He was buried at Plumtree

Church, West Bridgford, Nottingham. In 1881 the FA Cup went on display in the school and Parry wrote to Haig Brown's wife on 12th May saying, "I send to you the Association Challenge Cup which I hope you will allow us to put into your charge for the year, as Charterhouse is now its natural resting place."

ALEXANDER HAY TOD (G) Born at sea on 25th March 1857 and died in the Prince's Buildings, Clifton, Bristol on 22nd January 1942.

Tod entered Charterhouse as a Prize Scholar (Gownboys) in 1869 at the age of 12 and left in 1876. He was in the school XI in 1875-6. From Charterhouse he went to Oxford University, to Trinity College, matriculating in 1876 and gaining a BA in 1880 and an MA in 1883. He did not get a football Blue but was "an energetic forward, of great use in the proximity of the goal". Tod returned to the school in 1880 to teach and he captained the Cadet Corps from 1881 until 1905 and became the Housemaster of Verites in 1906. He was joint editor of the Register and author of *Charterhouse, a History* published by Bell's in a series on the Great Public Schools in 1900 and revised in 1919. In his history of the game, he wrote that "in Old Carthusian football to Wreford Brown, a Wreford Brown succeeds"; a comment on the famous Carthusian family and the influence that they had on the development of the game. Tod was regarded as the first organiser, secretary and historian of the club. He retired in 1920 and remained the treasurer of the War Memorial Fund from that time. (Do not confuse this Tod with Arthur Horatio who also played for Oxford and played in the 1877 final.)

Tod also refereed many of the school matches and started to give guidance after matches had been played. Coaching was given to the boys in Club games which were arranged by joining Houses together.

The *Carthusian* reported

> Most of the school came up to see the final, all Brooke Hall and Mrs Haig Brown in a

pink dress and beneath a pink parasol cheered all the players. It was a pleasant game won rather easily. In the evening both elevens were entertained by the Old Etonian club. Perhaps the main feature of the game was the formidable charging of Lord Kinnaird, yet all in fair play, with both elbows over the chest and kicking furiously. EH Parry was certainly the star.

In 1881-2, after three rounds, winning against Esher Leopards and Barnes, the Royal Engineers knocked out the OCs 0-2. It was not a good time for the OCs for they were then trounced on tour 0-8 by Queen's Park in Glasgow on 22nd December on a wet, windy and muddy Hampden Park. A dinner, commencing at 6pm, included eight courses and sixteen speeches. The next day they lost at Vale of Leven 2-1 and the tour continued at the Castle Ground, Nottingham, 1-5 and then went on to Bramall Lane, two days later, winning against Sheffield FC, 2-0.

But the following year, 1882-3, was exciting, taking on and beating the Pilgrims 6-0, then the Eton Ramblers 7-0, the Old Westminsters 3-2, the Royal Engineers 6-2 and then Clapham Rovers in the quarter-finals. Played at the Oval on the "lower side of the enclosure" the pitch was heavy and bare of grass. Rovers won the toss and defended the Crown Bath end of the ground. Going 3-0 up things were looking good for the OCs. Pawson got one goal back but Cobbold with a brilliant solo run restored the three goal lead. Lloyd-Jones and Ram then took advantage of unusual ill discipline in the OC camp, before they regained their composure and scored a late goal by Page: 5-3.

In the semi-finals, in March, on a neutral pitch at the Manchester football and cricket ground Whalley Range, against Blackburn Olympic, there was a 0-4 defeat and the Olympic went on to win the final. The OCs felt hard done by, having "a long and tedious journey" to this "neutral" pitch, which was in "strange condition" and only 16 miles from the Blackburn headquarters. Much was against them. Their opposition had prepared for the game at a nearby holiday resort, Blackpool! There was snow falling when the Blackburn team and supporters arrived by trains. Even the ball was not round and a thirty minute wait was forced while a round one was found. A crowd of 4000 saw a massive OC side tower over their opponents. Jack Hunter, the Olympic captain, marshalled his troops well and Dewhurst intercepted a misplaced pass to score first. By half time the pitch had cut up and it suited the lightweight northerners. With Cobbold out of form the game could not be retrieved. The section from the report in the *Carthusian*, opposite, tells the tale of woe!

The 1883-4 campaign was a modest affair, as the Old Foresters beat the OCs in round two, but the following season (1884-5) the OCs got to the semis again. Early round wins over Acton 7-1, played at Gunnersbury Lane and Marlow 5-3 with a bye to round four which was against Grimsby Town at home 3-0. The Grimsby game was played on Wandsworth Common on 25th January 1885. Grimsby travelled down with their 200 fans on a "football special" to enjoy their first game in the capital. They stayed at the Surrey Hotel on the edge of the common. Cobbold was in fine form and he scored the first. Taylor deflected a shot past his own goalkeeper and in the second half W Asling made three outstanding saves in the Grimsby goal to keep the score down. A journalist watching the game was very critical of the referee Morton P Betts, whom he claimed was coaching and favouring the home side. He was, however, generous about the Carthusian forwards, especially Cobbold whom he said provided "wonderful activity and correct shooting".

The OCs then met Chatham away in round 5, winning 3-0, and Church away 1-0. Church is a small district within Accrington. The Pickup Street ground had snow on it but was full to the brim with a crowd wishing to see such distinguished guests. Parry the captain scored the decider in an entertaining match. This took the team to meet Blackburn Rovers in the semis. This resulted in a 1-5 defeat despite Norris's excellence in the OC goal. Barmby scored the lone goal for a team that had Cobbold injured early on following a clash with Rovers' full back, Turner. Rovers won the cup beating Queen's Park from Glasgow.

THE FOOTBALL ASSOCIATION CHALLENGE CUP.

OLD CARTHUSIANS *v.* BLACKBURN OLYMPIC.

This match took place at Manchester on March 17th, and resulted in the defeat of the Carthusians by four goals to none. Parry kicked off at a quarter to four against a strong wind. The Football Association having taken the management out of the hands of the players, no one but the Committee are to blame for the non-appearance of the ball at the proper time, or for the match being played in a place much more convenient for one team than another, or for the captain of the Charterhouse team having only four days to get his men together; four of the team who would have played—one back, one centre forward, and two wings—were unable to. As soon as the ball was started, Last took it well into the enemies' quarters, but it was well returned by the opposing backs; but the backs on the other side were not so successful, their fault lay in kicking too high, and too hard against a strong wind, and this was a notable feature of the first half. The game began very fast, as in the first five minutes Blackburn threw the ball in twice; then the ball went behind the Old Carthusians' lines : then behind the Blackburn ; then Dewhurst made a fine run which resulted in a corner kick which hit the bar and bounded into play, but a catastrophe was well averted by Thompson, and the ball eventually went behind. On being kicked off, Hardman and Cobbold between them got the ball well down the ground, but were well stopped by Ward, who sent the ball well down the ground with the wind behind it; this was badly met by Norris, whose bad kick gave the Blackburn Olympic an opportunity, which they availed themselves of, and kicked the first goal five minutes from the start. Then followed a corner for Blackburn. A shot at goal saved by Thompson. Offside was given against a Blackburn forward shortly after. Another corner for Blackburn. W. E. Hansell had one good shot at their goal. Matthews then got cleverly away from them. Cobbold then had a shot, which was unsuccessful, after a run down chiefly by Last and Richards. The Old Carthusians then had a corner, but it was kicked behind. Blackburn off-side again. Off a throw in, the Charterhouse goal seemed doomed, but the goal was magnificently saved by

Beginning of report of Blackburn Olympic semi-final match 1883.
School archive

In 1885-6 the team lost a tense match 0-1 in the last sixteen, to West Bromwich Albion, who went on to the final. The match took place on 23rd January 1886 at Stoney Lane in front of a crowd of 8137. T Green scored the only goal of the match and the Albion team contained Bob Roberts (Albion's first ever international) in goal, Charlie Perry later capped three times for England, George Woodall (two caps) and Jem Bayliss up front, also an international. The wonderfully named Ezra Horton was the star of the era. 1885-6 was the first time the Albion had worn blue-and-white stripes having tried yellow-and-white quarters and chocolate-and-blue halves previously. All eleven players were born within a six mile radius of West Bromwich and seven of the team worked in the Salter's Spring factory which possibly explains the regular chant of "boing, boing" from the Albion terraces.

In 1886-7 it was Preston North End (the Invincibles) who knocked the Carthusians out of the cup in the last eight. This match was played at the Kennington Oval and the OCs just lost to Preston, all professionals, 1-2 . The *Preston Herald* of 5th May 1887 and other north-west papers gave full accounts of the match. The Preston team travelled by train, making their headquarters at the Covent Garden Hotel. The London & North Western Railway Company placed a bus at their disposal. Before the game the northerners visited the House of Commons. There was a reception of about six thousand spectators greeting the teams, mostly in favour of the Carthusians, giving them a most cordial welcome. The large attendance – for a midweek fixture – proved the hold that Association football had on the London crowd. Play was advertised to begin at 3.30pm, and Cobbold beat Ross in the toss and the game began at 3.35pm. The game was played on the Wednesday just before the weekend of the next round, the semi-final, for which West Bromwich Albion had already

Nottingham, on Saturday, March 7th, not more than 3000 spectators having mustered to witness this semi-final tie. Cobbold was injured early in the game, and was practically useless afterwards, which greatly militated against the Carthusians' chance of success, and the holders won by five goals to one. The Rovers, playing with a slight wind and the sun, were first to score, through the instrumentality of Brown. This reverse roused the Carthusians, who swarmed round the Rovers' goal, but all their shots were wild, and gradually the Lancastrians cleared their lines, and Norris had to save on two occasions. Again the "old boys," mainly owing to a fine run by Cobbold, made the Rovers act on the defensive, but Arthur was equal to the occasion. The Rovers now attacked, but could not break the defence of the brothers Walters, and at half-time the game stood one goal to nil, in favour of the Northerners. On the game being resumed, the Rovers took up the attack, and Norris running out to save a shot left the goal undefended, and Fecitt gained the second point by a good kick. This second reverse seemed to dishearten the Carthusians, who now played very wildly, and the Rovers, taking advantage of their confusion, added three more goals by Sowerbutts, Brown and Lofthouse. For the last ten minutes the Charterhouse boys played up well, and their efforts were rewarded by a goal from the foot of Barmby, directly after which, time was called, leaving the holders victorious by 5 goals to 1. Umpires, W. Beardshaw and W. Pierce-Dix; referee, C. W. Alcock. Sides :—

BLACKBURN ROVERS :—H. Arthur (goal), F. Suter and R. G. Turner (backs), H. McIntyre and J. Forrest (half-backs), J. Lofthouse and J. Douglas (left wing) J. Brown and J. Sowerbutts (centre), H. Fecitt and N. Walton (right wing).

OLD CARTHUSIANS :—W. H. Norris (goal), P. M. Walters and A. M. Walters (backs), G. F. A. England, A. Amos and F. J. Barmby (half-backs), W. N. Cobbold and L. Owen (left wing), L. M. Richards (centre), C. A. Smith and E. H. Parry (right wing.)

Carthusian report cup semi-final v Blackburn Rovers 1885.
School archive

qualified. Thomson kicked off for Preston from the Gasometer end into a slight breeze, playing on a superb, hard and fast surface. After a goalless first half, six minutes into the second half, Ainger and Smith made a good run on the right and passed the ball to Cobbold who dodging opponents planted the ball just out of Wharton's reach to the right of the goal, inspiring a scene of excitement rarely seen before at the Oval, with deafening shouts and sticks and hats flying into the air. It looked as though the great team from the north would be beaten at last. Cobbold was later "lamed" and out for the rest of the game. He was recorded to be prone to this for

OC XI v Preston North End at the Kennington Pavilion 1887. Top: TW Blenkiron, FJ Barmby, WH Ainger, CW Waddington, AM Walters, C Wreford Brown, Bottom: CA Smith, PM Walters, WN Cobbold, A Amos, L Owen. School archive

when he played against a northern side the previous year, word reached him that he would be "laid out in the first few minutes of the match" – and so he was! Aubrey Smith also was tripped from behind in the act of shooting and the game got very rough.

With only ten minutes left, Ross senior was brought down by PM Walters. The free kick was headed in by Graham. Preston had equalised minutes before time through a questionable free kick. In extra time, the North Enders secured victory when after seven minutes Gordon won the game with a shot that went in off AM Walters.

It is worth noting that the professionals claimed to have been "roughed up" by the Carthusians and "smashed up" also. The Prestonians being "knocked about unmercifully", naturally retaliated. A well dressed gentleman in the crowd was heard shouting to one of the Walters who was tackling Dewhurst "Play at him, jump on him, kill him, do anything with him!!" The *Herald* reported, "The game was what Lancashire people would call a rough one!".

Despite this the two teams were applauded as they left the field and Preston had to rush to catch their train at 8pm reaching home at 1.30am.

This struggle and travelling over 2000 miles in cup ties took so much energy out of the "Invincibles" that they lost their next game in the semi-final to West Bromwich Albion. At this point in their season they had played 39 club matches, winning 34 and scoring 212 goals and

C Aubrey Smith

One of the great characters in the team was **Sir C. AUBREY SMITH (UV)** who was born 21st July 1863 Brighton and died 1948.

From Charterhouse he went to St John's College Cambridge BA, where he played for the CUCC 1882-5 and later for Sussex CC 1882-92. He captained the first England cricket XI to South Africa in 1888-9. He was also a prolific Hollywood film star, an actor, who between 1911 and 1948 appeared in 76 films including the *Prisoner of Zenda, Six Glorious Years, Tarzan the Ape Man* and *The Lives of a Bengal Lancer*. Before making it as a movie star, he was the left winger in this OC side that played against Preston North End – proving to be the last challenge that the true amateurs made on the FA Cup. Aubrey Smith was a founder member of the English community cricket club in Hollywood, USA, a club that still exists. He married in 1896 Isabel, and he was awarded the CBE in 1938 and was knighted in 1944.

four cup ties scoring 14 goals. In 1889, having been unbeaten all season, Preston did the "double"; that is winning the English FA Cup and First Division of the league.

OCs:

C Wreford Brown (goal); AM and PM Walters (backs); A Amos, FJ Barmby, TW Blenkiron (half backs); CA Smith, WH Ainger (right wing); CW Waddington (centre); L Owen and WN Cobbold (left wing).

Preston North End:

Wharton (goal); Howarth and N Ross (backs); Robertson, Russell, Graham (half backs); Gordon and J Ross (right wing); Thomson (centre); Dewhurst and Drummond (left wing).

Umpires: Messrs MP Betts (Old Harrovians) and JC Clegg (president Sheffield Association).

Referee: Major Marindin (President Football Association).

The 1887-8 Cup campaign was famous for the 26-0 defeat of Hyde United by Preston NE but it also was noted for the success of the OCs who reached the quarter-finals, only to meet WBA again away at Stoney Lane, losing 2-4. Wreford Brown opted to play in goal and was quite magnificent whilst full back Locker broke his collar bone – 0-2 down and then, although Wilson pulled one back at half time, the game fell away in the second half going to 1-4, until Price made the final score a little more respectable.

Not needing to qualify through the preliminary rounds, a tough draw in the first round, in 1888-9, away to Wolverhampton Wanderers, was lost 3-4 in a superb game of football.

In 1889-90 a similar fate awaited the team as they lost to Wolves 0-2 away at the Molineux Pleasure Ground in round one with 12,000 watching.

In 1890-1 and 1891-2 having to qualify proved problematic and early exits heralded the end of the club's involvement in the FA Cup. By this time, 163 clubs had entered and WBA beat Aston Villa in the final, 3-0, before 25,000 at the Oval.

In 1892, the OCs left the competition to the professionals and the club won the first Amateur Cup in 1894. They had appeared in five quarter-finals, three semi-finals and of course won the final in 1881.

The Old Carthusians were invited guests as part of the Cup Final centenary celebrations at Wembley in 1972 organised by the FA. The club was presented with a centenary plate which is kept in the archives.

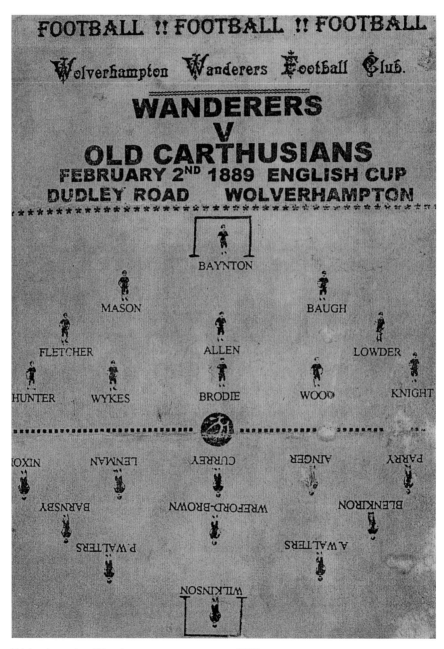

Wolverhampton Wanderers cup programme 1889. Wolverhampton Wanderers FC

FA CUP RESULTS OLD CARTHUSIANS 1879-1892 (OC scores first)

1879/80
Rd 1   v Acton 4-0 a
Rd 2   v Wanderers 0-1 a
54 teams entered

1880/81
Rd 1   v SaffronWalden Town 4-0
Rd 2   v Dreadnought 5-1
Rd 3   bye
Rd 4   v Royal Engineers 2-0
Rd 5   v Clapham Rovers 3-1 e
SF   v Darwen 4-1 n
F   v Old Etonians 3-0 n
P6 W6 F 24 A 3
63 clubs entered

1881/2
Rd 1   v Esher Leopold 5-0 a
Rd 2   v Barnes 7-1
Rd 3   v Royal Engineers 0-2
73

1882/3
Rd 1   v Pilgrims 6-0
Rd 2   v Etonian Ramblers 7-0
Rd 3   v Old Westminsters 3-2
Rd 4   v Royal Engineers 6-2
Rd 5   v Clapham Rovers 5-3
SF   v Blackburn Olympic 0-4 n
(Olympic went on to beat the Old Etonians in the final)
84

1883/4
Rd 1   v Reading Minster 10-1 a
Rd 2   v Old Foresters 2-7
100

1884/5
Rd 1   v Acton 7-1 a
Rd 2   v Marlow 5-3
Rd 3   bye
Rd 4   v Grimsby Town 3-0
Rd 5   v Chatham 3-0 a
Rd 6   v Church 1-0 a
SF   v Blackburn Rovers 1-5 n
(Blackburn R beat Queen's Park Glasgow in the final)
116

1885/6
Rd 1   v Chatham 2-0 a
Rd 2   v Upton Park 6-0
Rd 3   bye
Rd 4   bye
Rd   v West Bromich Albion 0-1 a
(WBA went on to lose to Blackburn Rovers after a replay in the final)
130

1886/7
Rd 1   v Reading 2-1
Rd 2   v Crusaders 4-2
Rd 3   v London Caledonians w/o
Rd 4   bye
Rd 5   v Leek 2-0 a
Rd 6   v Preston North End 1-2 e
126

1887/8
Rd 1   v Hanover Utd 5-0
Rd 2   v Watford Rovers 3-1 a
Rd 3   v Old Brightonians 5-0
Rd 4   bye
Rd 5   v Bootle 2-0
Rd 6   v West Bromich Albion 2-4 a
(WBA went on to beat Preston NE in final)
149

1888/9
exempt from qualifying rounds
Rd 1   v Wolverhampton Wanderers 3-4 a
(Wolves went on to lose to Preston in the final)
149

1889/90
exempt from qualifying rounds
Rd 1   v Wolverhampton Wanderers 0-2 a
132

1890/1
Pre Rd v Old Brightonians 4-3 a
Q2   v City Ramblers 8-0
Q3   v London Caledonians a 0-2
161

1891/2
Q2   v Old Etonians 4-6
163
44 appearances in total.

The arrival of the professionals led to many of the Old Boys sides withdrawing from the FA Cup and joining the FA Amateur Cup in 1894. The Old Carthusians won this Cup at the first time of asking.

a = away, n = neutral, e = extra time

a golden period 1882 to 1906

A POEM   March 1882

As I watched, in a struggle at football,
The earnest yet good-natured strife,
Me thought I discovered a moral
In the lessons it offered in life.

All are eager, yet all in their order,
Each side one harmonious whole,
And the backs keep the field, while the
    forwards
Press hard on the enemy's goal.

One is always in luck, on his fellow
Ill fortune seems ever to frown,
And one gets a spill, while another
Is making a splendid "run down".

But through the hot fight they engage in
True honour is always their guide,
And they seek not a shabby advantage
With "hands" or by playing "offside".

Whene'er, after honest endeavour,
One sees that his own time is gone,
He gives the good work to another,
Unselfishly "passing it on".

And if, by mishap in the melee,
One comes by a cross-shin or hack,
How bravely he bears it, nor seeks he
To pay it revengefully back.

But while we thus prose on the matter,
What's the score? For the playing is done;
Carthusian pluck and endurance
Have carried their three goals to one.

May we all, when life's struggle is ending
With conscience and character whole.
Ere yet "Time" is called by the Umpire,
Have made a "good shot at the goal".

In 1880 the Norfolk and Norwich Football Club was formed, the captain of which was WE Hansell (WV) who was in the OC Cup winning team. He helped establish the Norfolk Association in 1881 and played regularly for the county for 18 years. His team came to Charterhouse in LQ 1892 and was beaten 4-1.

Other missionaries included Charles Wreford Brown who helped foster the dribbling code in the Gloucestershire and Bristol area at the same time.

For the next ten years or so, Carthusians played a prominent role in the top flight of British football. Having won the FA Cup, OCs were regularly selected for international duty and for the many different representative sides forming all over the country. OCs also went on to help administer the game in various clubs and associations, as the game changed from being a leisurely amateur pastime into a professional business. Among those who made their names either playing for the school team, the OCs, universities, clubs or even their country were Carthusians who have left their mark on the history of the game.

A team called the Casuals existed as early as the 1870s and in 1882 the Corinthian Club was formed by NL 'Pa' Jackson, then the assistant secretary to the Football Association. The Corinthian's first match was on 26th October

1882 against St Thomas's Hospital at the Lambeth Palace grounds. The idea was to raise a team to beat the Scots, who were proving to be better than the English national side. Within four years the English team consisted of nine Corinthians and the team drew 1-1 with the "auld enemy". TW Blenkiron along with F. Bickley, an Old Etonian, helped found the club under Bickley's racing colours of chocolate and pink. These colours are still worn by the club today. Blenkiron was a man of the turf and at one time Chairman of the Directors of Kempton Park racecourse.

TW Blenkiron at school. School archive

THOMAS WALTER BLENKIRON (H) was a founder member of Casuals FC. He was born on 5th August 1864 and died on 19th September 1934 at Hove.

He was in the cricket XI 1880-3 (Capt '83), in the football 1880-2 (Capt '82) and he left school in CQ '83 to go to Trinity College, Cambridge LLB. where he played for the CUAFC, 1885-7, as a centre-half.

The Casuals Football Club was officially formed in 1883 and became the nursery for the Corinthian FC with the membership limited to Charterhouse, Eton and Westminster old boys. The Casuals lost to the OCs in the first Amateur Cup Final and then helped form the Isthmian League. In 1904, Manchester United's heaviest defeat, 3-11, was inflicted on them by the Corinthians with several Carthusians in the side including JCD Tetley – and Real Madrid adopted their club colours of all white. In 1907 when the Amateur Football Alliance split from the FA, the Casuals helped form the Southern Amateur League and became the first holders of the AFA Senior Cup, beating the OCs in the final. A tour of Brazil in 1910 inspired the founding of Corinthian Paulista FC, another corner of the world touched by the "English game". In 1921 the Casuals and the Corinthians met and it was C. Wreford Brown who proposed that the two clubs should eventually merge after an initial period of ground sharing at the Crystal Palace. Actually this did not happen until March 1939,

ready for the next season.

WILLIAM NEVILL COBBOLD (UV) was born on 4th February 1863 at Long Melford, Suffolk. He died on 8th April 1922 at 1, Richmond Gardens, Bournemouth. He was the third son of the Reverend Edward Augustus Cobbold of Tonbridge. William Cobbold's only son Geoffrey was a Lockite from summer term 1911 and his grandson Michael was a Verite from the summer term 1938. Michael's son Richard left Verites in OQ 1972 and his son Nicholas was also in Verites, leaving in OQ 1993. Nicholas was a prolific goal scorer in an U14B team as a Yearling.

Cobbold was a Junior scholar in LQ 1877 and was first placed into Uskites and then joined Verites. He played in the cricket XI 1881-2, football XI 1880-1 and left school in CQ 1882, to be the Rustat Scholar of Jesus College, Cambridge leaving with his MA. He played for Cambridge University 1883-6, was captain in the last

WN Cobbold at school. School archive

two years and never lost the Varsity match. He played twice for Cambridge v Oxford at tennis in doubles partnering HWW Wilberforce (later Sir Herbert Wilberforce) and never lost a set. At the CUAC sports he came second at the 100 yards timed at 10.2 seconds, a good reason for him avoiding getting caught offside. He won many prizes at Fives. "The Prince of Dribblers" was a powerful man with huge shoulders like an ox and he had a deadly intensity near to goal that few defences knew how to cope with. CB Fry nicknamed Cobbold "Nuts" because he was "of the very best Kentish cob quality, all kernel and extremely hard to crack". Described as the fastest dribbler the game has known he was the very antithesis of the chief dribblers in professional elevens at that time and his career was long and brilliant, like many of his runs. He was responsible for many tactical innovations including an attacking system adopted by the Corinthians involving the three inside-forwards passing at speed to one another. NS Creek in his *History of the Corinthian FC* (1933) wrote that Cobbold had a peculiar shuffling run and a wonderful knack of shooting at unexpected moments and angles. His shots were extremely accurate rather than hard. His weakness was that he never headed the ball. He played against

Scotland for England in 1883, 85, 86-7, v Wales 86-7, v Ireland 83 (24th Feb first cap scoring twice in his debut), 85, 87. His second goal against Ireland in 1883 was England's 50th goal in international football and he scored 6 in nine matches. He later joined the army and was a university tutor at West Wratting Park, Cambridgeshire 1886-1922 where he prepared pupils for various examinations at Oxford and Cambridge and for the army. He brought the local side to Charterhouse in 1895 and 1903. He was a founder of the Corinthian FC, played for Kent CC (not first class) in 1887 and married Hester Marian in 1891.

Even the professional half-backs regarded Cobbold as a very special player, compared favourably with the great Steve Bloomer of Derby County. His most memorable game was against Preston North End in the FA Cup sixth round. He was President OCFC and OCCC 1907-8.

His uncle, Thomas Clement Cobbold, was responsible for the foundation of Ipswich Town FC in 1878. Having been a Saunderite between 1848 and 1851, Thomas became Conservative MP for Ipswich in 1876. Founded by "public school boys" according to Brian Scovell's book on the Cobbold family *Football Gentry*, Ipswich Town was "an amateur club imbued with the principles of fair play. The players were dribblers and scrimmagers". The pupils of Ipswich School chose Thomas Clement to be their president and since he was pupil at the school and at Charterhouse it was said of him, "They were very fortunate to have Mr Cobbold because Charterhouse fostered the association game and Old Carthusians helped spread the game throughout the land." Mr Cobbold presented the ball for the first game at the original pitch at Broom Hill on Saturday 26th October. In 1936 a chance meeting between Captain John Murray Cobbold and Samuel Hill-Wood led to the development of the club. Cobbold gave a loan of £11,000 to enable it to turn professional.

In this period, the game developed and com-

PM Walters at school. School archive

bined back play was attributed to the Walters brothers, AM and PM, who later became conspicuous as English internationals. They had an uncanny understanding, as you would expect from brothers, and they won their first and last caps in the same matches.

PERCY MELMOTH WALTERS (H) PM was born on 30th September 1863 and died on 3rd October 1936 at Ashtead. He joined the school in OQ 1876, played in the cricket XI in 1879-80, but never got his colours in football. He formed a formidable pairing with his brother AM and left school in OQ 1880 to go to Oriel College, Oxford, where he got his MA, and played for the OUAFC in 1885. The brothers played for five years in succession against Scotland (see chapter 9) and appeared for the Old Carthusians and Corinthians in matches against Preston North End who were at the height of their fame. Percy's kicking was huge, he tackled fearlessly and observed the old-fashioned shoulder charge rule. He played for the OC XI in three Amateur Cup Finals and appeared in the LSC in 1895. Percy played 13 times for England and in club football he appeared for East Sheen and Epsom and Ewell FC. He was a Chancery Barrister LI by 1888 and fought in the Great War, after which he went to be a Bencher of Lin-

coln's Inn. OTC. He married Alice in 1896.

ARTHUR MELMOTH WALTERS (H) was born 26th January 1865 and died 2nd May 1941 at Holmwood.

He joined the school in CQ 1878, playing in the cricket XI in 1883, and the football team in 1881-2. After this he left school in CQ83 to go to Trinity College, Cambridge, where he gained his MA and played for the CUAFC between 1884-7 with his team conceding only one goal. In the OC XI, he played in the Amateur Cup Final in 1894 and also featured in the LSC 1895. He played nine times for his country (see chapter 9). He said of himself that he "will stop anyone, but should learn not to jump when charging". With his brother they remained "close" with pace and combination, playing for the Corinthians and East Sheen. He loved running, hurdles and held the school record (5' 9") for 40 years for the high jump. He became a solicitor in 1889 in London and then registrar of Charterhouse 1910-38. He was responsible for advising the Governors to sell off nearly all the landed property which had formed the main endowment since Sutton. This provided a substantial

AM Walters at school. School archive

fund for both parts of Sutton's Hospital. Secretary and treasurer of the Tercentenary Fund from 1911, he was also a jovial secretary of the Founder's Day Dinner and President of the OC Club 1927. A founder of the Corinthian FC, he married Amy in 1892.

These brothers were the best pair of England full-backs at the time and were a "household name". They played as a pair against Scotland in 1885 until 1890, excepting 1888 when AM could not play. In the book *Association Football and the men who made it* (Ed A Gibson and W Pickford) they were described as "fine specimens". PM weighed 13 stone and AM just over 12 stone; standing at nearly 6 feet tall.

With the England goalkeeper WR Moon they made a formidable triangle, working out a defensive scheme that enabled them to play for England during 1885 through to 1887 and against Scotland for three years running (1885-7). PM broke his leg at Oxford but this never dissuaded him from playing a hard game. The accidental death of their younger brother in a soccer match made the brothers give up playing temporarily in deference to their parents' wishes. AM was generally regarded as the better player and he would occasionally play at half-back and even fancied himself as a forward on his tours with the Corinthians. AM went to Cambridge and they played against each other in the Varsity match in 1884. They both played for the London FA.

In this era, centre-forward play was turned into a supreme art by GO Smith.

GILBERT OSWALD SMITH (H DAY) was born 25th November 1872 in Croydon, living in Godalming and died 6th December 1943 at Yaldhurst, Lymington. GO was at school from OQ 1886–CQ1892, representing the cricket XI 1889-92, captain 1890-2, football 1888-91; he received his colours after the Westminster match in March 1889 and first became captain in LQ 1890, leaving Charterhouse in CQ 92. His first big match for the Corinthian FC was against Queen's Park in 1893. A year later he was an

international. Smith was an OC XI Amateur Cup winner 1895 (goal) and 1897 (goal), he played in the London Senior Cup Finals 1895/6/7/9 and the London Charity Cup 1896/8, and in Dunn Finals 1903-5. He was at Keble College, Oxford for his MA. He represented the OUAFC 1893-96, Capt 96, OUCC 95-96, Surrey CCC 96, England International and captain (see chapter 9). He became an assistant master and later headmaster at Ludgrove Preparatory School, Wokingham until 1922. He ran the school with such footballing dignitaries at ATB Dunn (see chapter on Dunn Cup), WJ Oakley (Old Salopian) and WFH Stanbrough.

He captained the cricket XI three years running and against Westminster he scored 229 in 1892 out of 360. On the second day of the match the school was allowed out to watch him get his double century. He scored a century in the Freshman's match but had to wait until his third year for his Blue. He scored a 100 v Kent and 51 n.o. in the Varsity match. In 1896 he made 132 to win the game for Oxford who had to chase 330 in the second innings. Wisden described his movement in the field as graceful and quick.

He was the most famous Carthusian footballer and he went to Oxford with a considerable reputation. He played four times against Cambridge winning three times. In 1882 the Casuals included G.O.Smith in their team to play Shrewsbury School, whom they had not beaten in the first two encounters. Smith scored 8 as the Casuals recorded their first win 9-2 against the schoolboys. He recollected that, "the Corinthians of my day never trained and I can say that the need of it was never felt. We were all fit and I think could have played for more than one-and-a-half hours without being any the worse." He retired from the Corinthians as a player in 1902 but served on their committee for many years afterwards.

Known by his initials, his popularity ranked alongside the famous WG (Grace) as GO was just about the finest centre-forward of his decade. GO lived in a house called Hillcott (it may have been called Killcott) which stands on the main site of St Hilary's School in Godalming

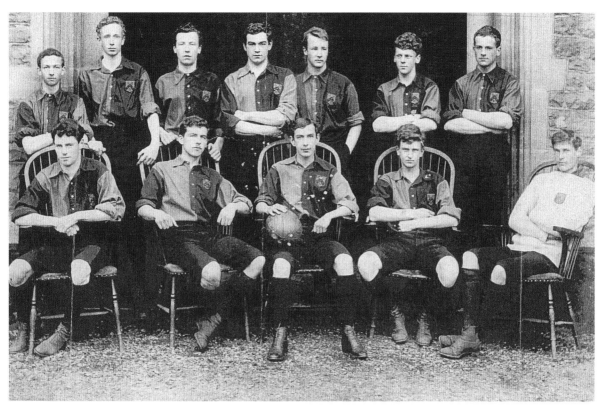

1890-1 school team. Standing: RJ Salt, AH Bailey, CD Hewitt, E Bramwell, IGP Alston, EH Bray, F Clark. Sitting: GS Wilson, EC Bliss, GO Smith (capt), WW Halsted, BKR Wilkinson. School archive

on Holloway Hill. The chimney bears the date 1870 and Robert Smith became owner in 1885. The finials on the roof, now removed, were in the shape of footballs. The field at the front of the house, now used as a games area for the young children, was 100 yards long and was made for the benefit of GO. The young boys still play football on this pitch. Smith had skills learned from the fast sandy pitches at Godalming and he would walk to school every day with the final mile being uphill. He and his two brothers played their first football at Branksome Preparatory School owned by Mr Sainsbury.

Playing in the 1890s he was slim and well balanced, with marvellous dribbling skills and body swerves, superior to anyone at his time – except for WE Gilliatt perhaps. GO rarely headed the ball but kept it on the ground where he had lightning speed. His positioning was superb and he made goals as well as scored them.

He scored 125 goals for the Corinthians in 131 matches and he scored 11 goals in 20 matches (1893-1901) for England, being captain at least 14 times. In the Sheriff of London Charity Shield, which pitched the best amateur against the best professional side, in 1898 GO captained the Corinthians to a draw against Sheffield United and in 1900 he scored in a memorable win 2-1 over Aston Villa. GO continued to play in the Dunn side, although he "retired" from soccer when he took over at Ludgrove and taught at Lancing College later in his career. He played in the first three finals, finally hanging up his boots in 1905. GO was part-author of the volume on *Football* in the Badminton Library.

In *Association Football and the men who made it*, published in 1906, Smith is described as the greatest centre-forward in the land. Never has there been in history any centre-forward equal to him. For ten years there was no rival. As a junior at school he played outside-right but the school report in 1888 said that he "improved towards the end of the season, dribbling and passing well, but is rather slow".

His great strength was passing and no defender could anticipate what he was going to do.

He had a deadly shot, he preferred subtlety to force and intellect to mere strength. He was slightly over "middle in height with a winsome face that bore traces of the pale cast of thought." He was modest and perhaps handicapped to a slight extent by diffidence and shyness. If he could not win by fair means he would not win by foul. He never whined nor grumbled nor did he shirk a tackle. Few could run as fast as he with a ball at his feet, he was king of athletes.

As the captain of the national side, all players, including the professionals, loved playing for him. Above all he had intellect, he always had something up his sleeve and the game had no better ornament. Ernest Needham, the Sheffield United international, said that "he was a good player when playing behind Smith but only a medium one when he played in front of him". It was said that "he'd eyes all round his shirt!"

Teaching at Ludgrove school under the headmastership of Smith was:

WALTER FARNELL HENNIKER STANBROUGH (G) who was born 20th April 1869

WFH Stanbrough at school. School archive

and died in Northampton 20th November 1950. He represented Charterhouse cricket in 1888, football 1886-7 and as captain. He left the school in CQ 1888 and went to Trinity College, Cambridge after which he became a schoolmaster. He played for an England XI in South Africa 1897, also played for the London FA. He was member of the OC XI that won the London Charity Cup 1898 and the Dunn Cup in 1903-5. His brother MH also played (see Amateur Cup chapter).

A man of true class was Charles Wreford Brown who served association football from the 1880s until the post Second World War period.

CHARLES WREFORD BROWN (G) was born 9th October 1866 at Clifton, Bristol and died on 26th November 1951 in Bayswater, London. He was a Gownboy from OQ 1880 playing in the school cricket XI, 1883-5, captain '85, football XI 1883-5, captain 1885. He left school OQ 85, going up to Oriel College, Oxford for his BA. He played for OUAFC XI in 1888-9, captain '89. He then played for England (see chapter 9) and for London FA. Wreford Brown was accredited with using the word "soccer" first c.1888, when he was asked at university what he was going to do, perhaps to play "some rugger" and he replied that "after brekker he would go and play soccer".

He was remembered as an outstanding centre-half despite being built on the small side. In his obituary in *The Carthusian* (March 1952) his position was described as being "either centre-half or centre-forward, being one of two centres"; in original line-ups there were at first six forwards, one of whom later became a centre-half.

He learned to play in goal one season when he was injured, assisting the OCs in that position when he left school. Indeed he was the keeper in the memorable FA Cup tie against Preston North End. He was a wonderful header of the ball, his ability to read the game and being so nimble enabled him to attack and defend equally well. He was extremely cool and never lost his head.

C Wreford Brown at school 1885. School archive

In 1887 he was down to play his usual position in goal for the OCs against Oxford, but there were two goalies and the team was short of a defender so he decided to play out-field. Having played so well he was invited to play at centre-half for Oxford against West Bromwich, retaining his place to play against Cambridge, and this enabled him to win his Blue and later to become captain.

He played four times at international level and for the Corinthians between 1889-1903, playing more than a hundred times. His first match was on the Christmas tour when he made his debut against Preston North End. He captained Corinthian tours to South Africa (1903), Sweden (1904) and the USA/Canada (1906). He played in the OC Amateur Cup Finals ('94, '97) and captained amateur international sides, including an FA XI in Germany 1899. Charles was responsible for the formation of the AFA in 1907 and became chairman. He managed a team to Canada in 1924. Even after the war he

played for the Corinthians against various schools. His last game was for the Old Gownboys at 61 years old against the House team in which his youngest son earned his colours. He was a member of the FA Council, vice-president 1944, on the international selection committee and member of team that toured Australia and New Zealand in 1937. He sat on the London FA and became Chairman of the FA. He managed the 1936 British Olympic soccer team in Munich, Germany and forbade them to give the "Nazi salute". The British team gave the "eyes right" at the opening ceremony instead. Charles is believed to be the only Carthusian to have shaken hands with Hitler. He also was officiating on behalf of the FA in the notorious match against Germany in 1938 when the team were "obliged" to give the Nazi salute before the match. There is more on this in the War Years chapter.

He won his OUCC Blue in 1887, given for promise rather than extreme ability. He was injured playing against Surrey so that he was not able to play against Cambridge in the Varsity match. He also played for Gloucestershire county cricket XI, being a good bat and slow bowler, and played for Clifton FC in the Western league. He acted as a legal adviser and football legislator between 1886-98, when he was a solicitor in London. He served in WW1, joining the 3rd Grenadier Guards. He played chess for Great Britain in the 1924 Olympic Games and British Championship at Hastings 1933. He was the second of five brothers, had three sons in Gownboys and became President of the OC Club in 1921-3. He married Helen in 1901, and then Agnes 1936. His brother-in-law was WJH Curwen.

On a South African tour in 1903 the referee adjudged one of the Corinthians to have committed a foul in the penalty area. As captain, Wreford Brown instructed the goalkeeper to stand aside to allow the opposition a free shot. Later on the tour when awarded a penalty, Wreford Brown deliberately shot wide. Charles was very much part of the setting up of the Arthur Dunn cup competition. He played in three victorious finals, with his brother O.E. in two of them.

A Amos at school. School archive

There was no official coaching in these early days but there was always advice, as the Captains' Register reveals. The boys learned by watching and playing against some of the best players in the country. The fixture list shows that famous Old Boys and their contemporaries from Oxford or Cambridge, for example, all enjoyed visiting the school to play against the XI. Eventually it was apparent that other teams were taking matters more seriously, so that they could beat Charterhouse at its own game.

ANDREW AMOS (R G) was born on 20th September 1863, the eldest child of Rev James Amos, Vicar of St Stephen, Southwark. He died on 2nd October 1931 in London.

Junior and Senior Scholar, Exhibitioner at Charterhouse, he played in the football XI in 1881. Amos left school in CQ82 to be Scholar of Clare College, Cambridge where he got his MA (senior optime in the Tripos 1885).

He played for the CUAFC 1884-6, as a left half-back, winning three Varsity matches and also for England (see chapter 9). He played for

the London FA, Hitchin Town and the Corinthians and was part of a formidable half-back line in that team. Creek said that he was probably the best left-back in the history of the Corinthian FC. He was a great theorist who laid down the principles of the wing-half game and took the line that perfect backs will always stop perfect forwards. He was ordained in 1888 after a curacy in Gateshead and then joined the Clare College Mission in 1889, ending up in Rotherhithe 1922. He served as a councillor on the Bermondsey Borough council. He had a strong personality with definite Catholic convictions, married Susan and finished his career in the Diocese of Southwark.

He preached the Founder's Day sermon in 1924 taking the very characteristic text, "A fine fight".

The Charterhouse football XI of 1881-2 included Amos, Cobbold and Walters. No wonder the school won all its matches. Matches were played against:

Brooke Hall, Vintcent's XI, Clapham Rovers, WH Norris's XI, RMC Sandhurst, an Oxford XI, Pilgrims, OCs (1881), WG Morrison's XI, Royal Engineers, a Cambridge XI, Westminster, an Oxford XI, RMC Sandhurst, Old Westminsters, OCs (1882)

The Charterhouse School team also included:
In goal: L King-Harman,
backs: A Amos, AD Murray, EB Sewell
halves: TW Blenkiron AM Walters
centres: AI Vintcent, KH Eddis,
oneside: inside WN Cobbold outside EH Brown,
otherside: inside AK Henley (capt), outside W Rayner.

Amos wrote to the *Carthusian* referring to this team and using the phrases that described "peculiarities of play". The three half-back game did not take on until 1885 when England played in a match against Scotland. He said that the team stuck to one side of the ground – the left in the first half and the right in the second.

Oxford University AFC 1883. Top: L. Owen. Bottom: E.T. Hardman and C.J. Cornish. OUAFC archive

In the last game of the term, unbeaten, the XI played the OCs and things were not looking good. In their blue jerseys with narrow red lines, knickerbockers tight at the knee, no bars nor studs on boots, no shin guards – the latter being regarded as "funk".

Prinsep had a pot shot towards the end of the game that hit Amos in the face, knocking him down – and he got much applause for saving a certain goal.

The following year, 1882, LF Gillett and LML Owen played for Oxford whilst EG Colvin and LM Richards played for Cambridge. Blackburn Rovers lost to the Old Etonians 1-0 in the FA Cup. Blackburn Olympic returned to the Oval in 1883 to beat the Etonians and this heralded the domination of the competition by professionals, once payment had been made legal in 1885. Arthur Dunn played for the Eton side and he later gave his name to the Arthurian League and the associated Arthur Dunn Cup competition.

In 1883 two-handed throw-ins were made law. Between 1882 and 1887 Cambridge dominated the Varsity match. The 1883 match included three Carthusians on the Oxford team (ET Hardman, CJ Cornish and LML Owen – all forwards) and three for Cambridge (J Vintcent, a half-back, EJ Wilson and WN Cobbold – both forwards).

The introduction of a combination of passing tactics to the discouragement of dribbling was noted as the difference between the two ages of Association play. The shape of 1-2-3-5 became the accepted system of play as the influence from the Scots and the northern team had its affect on Cambridge and the Corinthians. WN Cobbold playing for Cambridge in 1883 was associated with this growing style of play. The "back play" particularly was exceptionally performed by the Walters brothers, who played against each other in the 1885 Varsity match, and A Amos, a light blue from 1884-6.

In LQ 1884, FW Sewell's team playing against the school may well have been linked to the Wanderers, a team he played for. At the Kennington Oval in February, Amos, AM Walters and Cobbold played for Cambridge and Owen captained the dark blues.

That year the Governing Body acquired the land to the west of Princes Avenue which is now called Under Green. Big Ground used to have that name, being next to "Upper" Green. As the game became more popular so the grounds were extended.

The success of Carthusian football was spread far and wide. In China a "Carthusian XI" was made up from two Wesleyan missionaries who played "a very foul game". The list of countries touched by Carthusian football internationally goes as far afield as the Transvaal, Harvard in the USA and, of course, Brazil. But there was also a diffusion of ideas closer to home.

In 1887 two Carthusians, including Frederick G Leatham (RS), went to the Agricultural College at Downton, Hampshire, helping to establish the game and playing "soccer to perfection". Gordon B Winch (H) left Charterhouse in LQ 1894 to go to Trinity College, Cambridge, where he was the promoter and first secretary of the Cambridge Football League.

In the *History of West Bromwich Albion F.C.* it is recorded that in 1885-6 the club emerged as national cup fighters *par excellence*. In the third season of entry to the cup, WBA won through to the final "after defeating such formidable opponents as Wolverhampton Wanderers, the Old Carthusians and Small Heath (later to become Birmingham City)".

In 1885 the Charterhouse formation was following the national trend to have five forwards, three half-backs, two backs and one goalkeeper. The old goalposts were quite thin, about the thickness of the bar, but a tape and a little flag flew at the top of each post. These posts were fixed in their places by ropes and tent pegs. Fags carried them from the pavilion each day and there were no nets.

In this period, teams formed by old boys included AK Henley (RG), RL Escombe (BG),

Cambridge UAFC team 1886. Back left A Amos. Front 2nd from left to right: TW Strother, 4th is WN Cobbold, AM Walters, TW Blenkiron is 2nd right. CUAFC archives

GSK Ashby (D), E Escombe (G), HJ Carson (H), D Crossman (B) and AJ Webbe's team from Harrow or possibly Oxford also made up the fixture list. RL Escombe was an original member of the Corinthian committee.

ARTHUR C NIXON (H) was born 18th April 1867 and died 16th February 1900 at Ladysmith.

He joined Charterhouse in CQ 1880, played in the cricket XI in 1886 and the football XI in 1885-6. He left Charterhouse in CQ '86 and went up to Trinity College, Cambridge, gaining his BA. In February 1888 he represented Suffolk County against Northamptonshire. Woodbridge FC was his stated club. He was a CUAFC XI Blue in 1889 and played for the London FA. He became secretary of the Casuals FC and secretary of the OCs in 1890. He was commissioned in the 5th Lancers 1894, fighting in the Boer war in 1899.

WE Gilliat 1885 at school. School archive

In this season the first professional, James Forrest, played for England, wearing a different styled jersey to the others. He earned £1 a week from Blackburn Rovers but was not paid by the club in his international week because he had been paid by England. PM Walters made his first Varsity match whilst his brother AM, Amos, TW Blenkiron and Cobbold, the captain, played for the other side.

Nine pitches were laid out on Under Green in 1886, the pavilion was built and a groundsman was employed. NL Jackson, famed with the Corinthians, first suggested the idea of awarding caps for internationals. FJ Barmby, a cool half-back with a powerful shot, played in the Oxford side whilst TW Strother (in goal), Walters, Amos, Blenkiron and Cobbold, as captain again, filled the Cambridge team.

In LQ 1887 the OCs sent down to Charterhouse their FA Cup team (missing four players) to warm up against the school. Their next cup tie, the quarter-final, was to be against Preston North End – or "the Invincibles" as they were becoming known. In the Varsity match AM Walters, Blenkiron and WH Ainger played for Cambridge. This was the year that the centre circle was added to the pitch markings.

During the 1886-7 season **WALTER EVELYN GILLIAT (G)** played for the XI. Walter was born 22nd July 1869 in Stokes Poges and died 2nd January 1963 at Woking.

He was in the Charterhouse cricket XI 1888 and left school CQ 1888. He went to Magdalen College, Oxford MA. Played OU football 1892, Woking FC and England (see chapter 9). Rated alongside the great Cobbold and Page, he only got one Blue and one cap. He was an inside-forward; "very lightly built, he was extraordinarily foot clever and was better with his head than most Carthusians". A weak knee prevented him from playing more for the "Blues". He was ordained Reverend in 1895 and married Georgina in 1901. He became President the OC Club in 1948. His sons IWA and JHH were distinguished OCs in the 1920s and 1930s. His

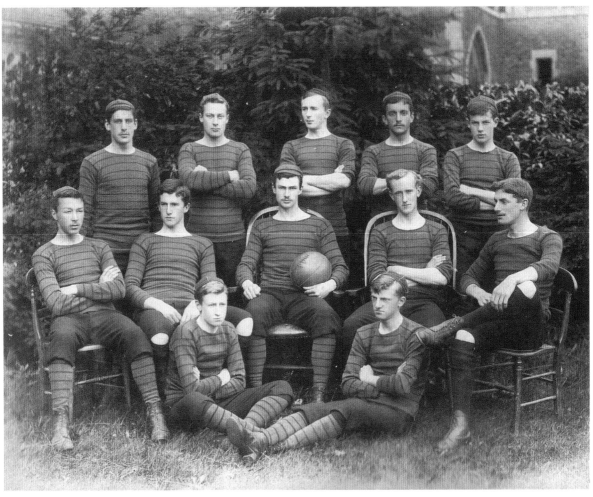

School team 1886. Standing: AC Nixon, WA Shaw, FG Leatham, HC Price, WFH Stanbrough.
Middle row: HS Steele, ES Currey, CH Tyler (capt), HJ Carson, RGT Baker Carr. Sitting: G Pim, GC Leman.

grandson RMC gained Oxford Blues in soccer and cricket, captaining Hampshire C.C. in the 1970s and becoming a Housemaster and Second Master and Admissions Registrar at the school in the 1990s, retiring from Charterhouse in 2004.

EDMUND SAMUEL CURREY (V) was born on 28th June 1868 and died 12th March 1920. He was the seventh son of Edmund Charles of Malling Deanery, Lewes. Leaving school in the summer 1886 to go to Magdalen College, Oxford, to get his BA, he played for OUAFC 1888-90 and was captain in his final year. He played for England (see chapter 9). As well as playing for the OCs, he also turned out for the

Corinthians and the Casuals (1885-6), the Sussex Dolphins (1889-91) and Sussex. He became a solicitor in 1895 and married Helene Sanson of Edinburgh in 1907.

The 1888 Varsity match saw the end of the Cambridge winning run. Oxford had five future internationals and these included C Wreford Brown at centre-half and ES Currey. To this talented group another Carthusian, C Waddington, helped defeat the light blues, for whom CH Tyler played.

On Founder's Day LQ 1889 against the Sussex Dolphins, three of the school team were singing at the Old Charterhouse and one was "away in search of a scholarship". To make

*Old Carthusians FC 1889. Left to right: S Furber, SC Dickinson, HC Price, AM Walters, TW Blenkiron,
EC Streatfeild, S Tewson, TO Jones, PG Rathbone, WE Gilliat, WH Bagshaw.* School archive

matters worse "we were photographed which had the effect of making our backs take up attitude". Sydney Tewson's (G) XI visited in OQ 1889 and were beaten 6-1. Tewson became a tea planter in Ceylon and was murdered by a native in December 1897. In this year's Varsity match HM Walters, from Haileybury, the brother of the famous twins, got his Blue. He had played rugby but was adapted to a "rushing" inside-right. Playing under instructions to take the man and let PR Farrant (Repton), his outside-right, take the ball, he most unfortunately in one of his rushes met his opponent's knee and died of his injuries at Oxford. The Varsity match was drawn and LR Wilkinson, Wreford Brown (capt) and ES Currey played for Oxford, while AC Nixon played for the opposition.

LEONARD RODWELL WILKINSON (BS) was born 15th October 1868 son of Col Josiah Wilkinson of Highgate (L 23). He entered Saunderites OQ 1882 as a Junior and later Senior scholar, played in the cricket XI 1885-7 as captain in his final year. He made the football XI as a goalkeeper 1886 and left the school for Christ Church, Oxford, 1887. He was the Holford Exhibitioner, gained an MA and represented Oxford athletics in the hurdles 1890-1 and the OUAFC 1889-91. He played football for Eng-

LR Wilkinson at school. School archive

Oxford University AFC 1894-5. Back: RJ Salt (second from right). Middle: CB Fry (left), CD Hewitt, EC Bliss, GO Smith (second from right). OUAFC archive

land (see chapter 9), and in the 1894 Amateur Cup Final winning team. He became a barrister, Oxford Circuit, Director of Continental Gas Association and British Gas Light Co., married Laura 1898 and died at Emery Down, New Forest, 9th February 1913.

In 13th February 1890 the snow was covering the ground. The eldest son of the HRH Prince Christian of Schleswig-Holstein and HRH Princess Helena of Great Britain and Ireland was Prince Christian Victor who went to Wellington. The princess was the daughter of Queen Victoria and their second son, John FCAG Albert (S) (Prince of Schleswig-Holstein) was at Charterhouse. All this led to a game of football against this "royal team" in LQ 1890, which the school won 5-0.

Nets were first used in 1890 reputedly in a match involving the Liverpool Ramblers (see chapter 15) but not in a Cup Final until 1892 . The following OCs played in the Varsity match;

Wilkinson and Currey (capt) for Oxford with MH Stanbrough, now an international on the other side. Currey was a big fast centre with a fine left foot. He could, however, have his off days. Sadly Wilkinson "slipped up" causing one of the three goals to be scored.

In 1891, a referee and two linesmen became established as controllers of the game and the penalty kick was introduced. The advent of the penalty kick, originally proposed by William McCrum of the Irish Football Association, caused a considerable stir amongst the amateur clubs, who saw the principle of the penalty kick as an affront to the ethics of their game. When free-kicks were introduced the gentleman players objected to the assumption that they might purposely break the laws. Extending the game to accommodate a penalty kick was included in law 7 after Stoke lost the opportunity to equalise at the end of a match when the Aston Villa goalkeeper booted the ball over the stand to waste time, bringing the game to a conclusion. Curiously the goalkeeper was allowed to handle the ball out of the penalty area as far as the half-way line until 1912. The famous playboy and Welsh goalkeeper, Leigh Richmond Roose, made the most of this freedom to colour his art by launching huge kicks from well outside the penalty area, playing as a sweeper for much of the game.

At Queen's Club the Varsity match contained Wilkinson, NF Shaw, for the dark blues and Stanbrough in light blue. The Cambridge side had toured prior to the big game and played against Aston Villa, Bootle, Preston and the Blackburn Rovers. Maybe this had been too strenuous for them as they lost the match 2-1.

The 1892 Varsity match included WE Gilliat who ranked alongside Cobbold and Page as a fine dribbler. Needless to say, in the match his knee "went" in the first ten minutes. The Oxford shooting was dire and after the game the four fit forwards took a ball to the shooting range only to sky to all corners of the ground. CB Fry played in this game and was prone to "let Cambridge in by his fancy kicking". Oxford had a bad game and Fry was to prove a better player against the pros than against the amateurs. EC Bliss and Shaw added to the Oxford team whilst Stanbrough captained Cambridge and EC Streatfeild played alongside him in a game that was abandoned due to fog – despite the trick of the goalkeepers having bells to ring periodically to give an idea of where the goals were. LH Gay of Brighton College is reported to have wandered off to the side of the pitch to ring his bell and distract the opposing forwards

Nets were used in the Cup Final for the first time, an invention of the chief engineer of the Mersey Tunnel, John Alexander Brodie.

In the 1892-3 season, Veale reports that he had not seen any better performance by a school XI than that against the OC XI which needed a practice match before a cup tie. EH Bray and AD Fordyce as backs were brilliant and steady. R Hunt, short but fast, scored the winning goal just before the end making it 2-1. Coming off

the field, C Wreford Brown's comment to Captain Wynyard was, "Well I'll be damned!"

Teams for this game were:-

OC XI: LR Wilkinson, EF Buzzard, EC Bliss, GS Wilson, C Wreford Brown, Hon RH Lindsay, CD Hewitt, RJ Salt, GO Smith, Capt EG Wynyard, MH Stanbrough.

School: GP Lea, EH Bray, AD Fordyce, WU Timmis (sub for AB Winch), G Wreford Brown, CB Ward, GC Vassall, JB Dyne, R Hunt, HPO Broadbent, H Crabtree. The formidable OC XI was beaten.

Richard Hunt (RH) scored 20 goals in the 1891-2 season including five against Westminster. He then scored 19 in OQ 1893 after which he left the school to go to Magdalen, Oxford. Clearly his shooting was good because he also was in the Ashburton winning eights in 1891 and 1892. In the Carthusian match 1893 his shooting was described as " hardly consistent"!!

During the 1893 Varsity match GO Smith made his mark. Originally placed at outside-right, his school position, he was asked to fill in at centre-forward for Oxford and he never looked back. F Street, the captain, said of Smith that "the most remarkable feature of his game was the way in which he fed his wings, drawing the defence in the direction of one wing and then placing the ball with extraordinary precision at the very feet of the other, unmarked winger." EC Bliss and EF Buzzard played at half-back, CD Hewitt, RJ Salt partnered Smith up front. Fry, who had complained about the "old crocks" he had to play with the previous year, collided with Buzzard who had to leave the ground and it was then that Cambridge scored. Oxford eventually won 3-2.

Wilmot and Streatfeild described the Eleven football ground in 1894 as one which

> cannot be styled sightly, being in fact a mere arid waste between the fives courts and the chapel; grass there is none, though a few weeds do show their heads in the 'close season', only to be ruthlessly trampled under foot when the 'twenty-two men' start work

OUAFC 1899 Team. Back: ER Turnbull (second left), CF Ryder (second right), EM Jameson (middle second left), GC Vassall (middle centre). OUAFC archive

again in September; but this is unavoidable, as the sandy soil cannot be expected to stand the wear and tear of almost incessant football from September to April.

Conditions like this can be understood even today when the school suffers a drought in the summer or too many games are played on Big Ground in succession; the grass turns brown and creeping vetch succeeds.

The Varsity match in 1894 involved Buzzard, Bliss, Smith and Hewitt for Oxford and GS Wilson for Cambridge.

1893-4 was the twelfth season of the Corinthian FC history and the England team playing against Wales at Wrexham was basically the Corinthian FC XI. Wales lost 5-1 and C Wreford Brown and GO Smith featured in the line-up. Another occasion in 1895 against Wales saw a similar full representation from the Corinthian FC, this time

including MH Stanbrough. In those days it would not be unusual to field two England teams on the same day against Wales and Ireland – an amateur team playing one match and a professional another.

FKW Girdlestone with WAE Austen formed the Unders' Football League, for 264 boys under sixteen, in 1894. This was a serious attempt to organise games with a league system especially involving the youngest boys in the school. Austen was in Robinites and Pageites and he captained the XI in 1893-4. The league consisted of twenty-four teams and they all played each other. Each new boy was assigned a team, boys of the same house being together. This was refined in 1899.

In the records there is an obsession with kick-off times, which were often late due to the uncertainty of the travelling arrangements. The 1894 match against Godalming, where Petrie was playing for the town side, was described as "a poor specimen of Scotch professionalism"; the visiting team seemed "to forget that they were not playing amongst themselves but against gentlemen (of Charterhouse)". Matches against Godalming drew much attention and when Godalming played Guildford a large crowd gathered at either venue. Carthusians were often commandeered into the local side and one London paper described a team picked from these teams as the "Hot Village Lot". Names such as HR, GO and DM Smith, GC and SH Vassall, Bertram Evans (son of the Rev HJ Evans of Gownboys), AR Haig Brown (son of the Headmaster), WLH Moss (son of the Lockite housemaster) and CB Fry, a master at Charterhouse, would thrill the supporters at the local derby.

In the OC match against Oxford University the Carthusians came up against GO Smith who scored 7 goals in a 10-0 victory for the dark blues.

GILBERT CLAUDE VASSALL (P, DAY) was born Hardington-Mandeville, Somerset on 5th April 1876 and died 19th September 1941 in Park Town, Oxford.

He played for the football XI between 1892-4 and left the school in CQ 1894. He became the Bible Clerk at Oriel College, Oxford, where he got his MA. He played for the OUAFC 1896-99, captained his team in 1899, was in the OC XI, played in the LCC '96, ADC 04-07, '09, '10. He also played for the London FA, Somerset CCC 1902-5 as a fast bowler. He was a Casual, he toured with the Corinthians at Easter 1904 in Hungary, summer 1906 to USA/Canada. He played in the Corinthian XI in 1904 in the Sheriff of London Shield match beating Bury the FA Cup holders 10-3 at Queen's Club. Turned down the opportunity to play for England against Ireland (see chapter 9). Gilbert played in six winning Dunn teams. He was a hard shooting outside-right. He also represented the OUAC in the long jump '96-99, became President in 1899 of OUAC v Harvard. He won the long jump three times v Cambridge University

(23ft 5in – a record at the time) and was runner up in the Amateur Championships in 1899. He became co-headmaster of the Dragon School, Oxford and was described by parents as having "the grand secret of teaching". He took an interest in Oxford House, Bethnal Green – a charity – and introduced the relay system and other athletics to university. He married Rosa first and then in 1929 Brenda.

In 1895 the Varsity match saw a change of tactics which involved using GO Smith as a withdrawn centre-forward, allowing his speedy inside-forwards to run onto through balls. Bliss was captain for Oxford, Salt, Smith and Hewitt played against EH Bray and HJ Broadbent. Smith played mainly for England and the Corinthians in the autumn of 1895 but in the Lent term he made the Oxford side more efficient. So for the 1896 Varsity match the Oxford team was "linked together". GO scored a goal that nobody else would have done: "GO was twenty yards out from goal towards the corner flag and practically on the touchline. He obviously had to centre but he saw the goalie off his line, so he placed the ball with a left foot slice over the keeper's head." Oxford won 1-0. GC Vassall appeared for Oxford and EH Bray was captain for Cambridge and supported by CB Ward. He was a formidable player with speed and weight.

CB FRY had played for the Casuals before he left Repton as a schoolboy and after teaching at Charterhouse (1896-8) he dabbled with journalism, subsidising his career as an amateur cricketer – his best sport. Fry also played for the Corinthians and full-back for Southampton in the Southern League, gaining an international cap in 1901 and playing in the 1902 Cup Final against Sheffield United.

The match against the OC Internationals was played at Queen's Club, 16th December 1896, but the fog was so thick it was impossible to see what was happening.

In 1897 the masters' pavilion committee bought the land to the east of Prince's Avenue known as Lessington with Lessington House built on the land. Lessington Brake still stands by studio where the pony and trap, used to pick up boys from the station, was stabled.

The Varsity match this year was rich with Carthusians. HM Turnbull was in goal, WU Timmis played at full-back, Wilson, Vassall and EM Jameson, SL Darvell and RH Laird made up the Oxford team. For Cambridge, JT McGaw was the Cambridge goalie, playing behind Bray and AJ Davidson.

On 15th October 1898 there was the first game on Lessington when a 3rd XI played against the Rev GB Raikes's (an Old Salopian, Oxford Blue and English international) 2nd XI. Standing by the headmaster's garden wall near the main entrance to the house an engraved stone tablet marks what was previously the boundary to Charterhouse's land.

CHARLES FREDERICK RYDER (G) was born on 24th February 1879, being the second son of George W Ryder of Keymer, Sussex. Leaving school in the summer 1897, he went to Magdalen College, Oxford (Demyship) where he won a Blue for tennis 1900 and 1901 and played for OUAFC 1899-01. Played one "unofficial" international at centre/inside-forward for England v Germany 1901 at White Hart Lane. He served in the Sudan political service, Lt-Col of the General Staff during WW1 earning an OBE and the Order of the Nile. He married Elizabeth Harman in 1925. Died 15th February 1960.

The Varsity match of 1898 involved the following: Timmis, Wilson, Jameson, Vassall and Laird for Oxford; AR Haig-Brown for Cambridge.

In 1899 the last game of the century was against the Old Internationals on Wednesday 20th December at Queen's Club and the weather was favourable (for London).

The House leagues were refined to accommodate an A division that held fourteen teams and a B division that had twelve. During the OQ they played every team in their own division and then in LQ the top seven in A joined with the top six from B to form a "Senior Cup Division". The remainder went into a "Junior Cup Division". Matches lasted an hour and points were awarded as in the Association League. Goals were recorded just in case there were equal points. This arrangement ensured that each boy had plenty of games to play.

The Varsity match in 1899 ended in thick fog and the Oxford team took themselves off afterwards to tour abroad in Austria and Bohemia – the first tour of its kind for a university. They played the Bohemians, beating them 3-0, and then the German Club, winning 9-0. Jameson had to spend some of his time explaining to the press that Oxford had not accepted bribes to beat the Czech team by fewer goals than the German club team. ER Turnbull, Vassall (capt), CF Ryder and Jameson, who organised the tour, played for Oxford. Haig Brown and LH Wace were in the Cambridge team. Vassall spent most of his time either delivering after-dinner speeches or trying to maintain discipline.

On 15th March 1900 there was a match against Eton – actually called J Wormald's XI because his team did not want to be known as "Eton". The Eton archives hold no record of this match.

On 17th March there was the 500th match at Godalming and this was against the OC Internationals. GO Smith was captaining England against Ireland so he was unable to play, but the team was still entirely made up from internationals. CH Wild played for Oxford University, with Jameson (captain) and Ryder. At Oxford, the University team moved location to Iffley Road where they found the pitch very wet compared to the Parks.

On 6th March 1901 Charterhouse played Oriel College, Oxford, who had just won the "College Cup". The school posted a 6-1 win, showing their superiority. In February that year Wild and Ryder got their Blues for the Oxford side.

Left: RA Bense Pembroke. Right: OT Norris. School archive

AH Tod described the playing of house matches before Christmas with "violent" enthusiasm whereas Junior matches in LQ were decided often by the nature of the annual epidemic!

In 1902 the Westminster match remained the highlight of the year. Matches were played against various Oxford and Cambridge colleges, usually managed by an OC. There were Old Boys' games against the Etonians, Wykehamists, Bradfield Waifs and Reptonians. Games against the military, for example RMC Sandhurst and RMA Woolwich, filled the growing fixture card – as well as matches with some of the emerging clubs such as Beckenham, Barnes and West Wratting.

Robert Graves wrote in *Goodbye to All That* that he had not been permitted to play football due to a weak heart. He describes the dominance of the "bloods" – members of the football and cricket teams – who were the ruling elite in the school. The eleventh man in the side, even though he might be a member of the under fourth form, had more prestige than the top scholar.

Oh we are the bloods of the place,
We shine with superior grace
At the goal or the wicket, at footer or
    cricket,
And nothing our pride can efface.

The worms of the sixth we despise…
We count them as dirt in our eyes.

*(Aristophanic parody quoted by
Noel Annan Roxburgh of Stowe)*

Full of beer after an away match against the Casuals, they returned to school and disrupted a school debate, forcing it to be closed. Even on a Sunday the Bloods swaggered down the aisle in chapel, having the right to walk arm in arm and wear distinctive clothes such as butterfly collars and jackets with slits up the back. The Blood steps still exist in front of Verites, although the understanding that only Bloods may use them has long disappeared.

This year saw only one Carthusian making the Oxford side, CH Wild, and there was nobody selected for Cambridge.

OSWALD THOMAS (TOM) NORRIS was born Chipstead, Surrey 1st July 1883. Charterhouse cricket XI 1900-2, capt 1902, football XI 1900-1, capt 1901. Left school CQ 1902 for Oriel College, Oxford. OUAFC 1902-5 capt 05. He was a good back and appeared in four Varsity matches, captain in 1905. He was in the

Corinthian XI 1905. Far left: GC Vassal, seventh from left OT Norris, next to TS Rowlandson with goalie top and cap. WU Timmis is third from right. David Roy and Replay Publishing

Corinthian side 1902 touring South Africa in 1903 and Sweden 1904, and went to Hungary with OUAFC in 1907, and he played in the Dunn winning sides of 1903 and 1905 and for OUCC in his second year but a thumb injury prevented him actually playing in the Varsity match. The following year he had a poor run of form and did not get selected for the game against Cambridge. So he was selected to play for Oxford as was C. Wreford Brown but never actually played in the major game. He once hit a ball down the "old Weekite steps" (behind Memorial Chapel) and ran eleven in a house match. He also scored 246 for the Friars in one innings. Four brothers were Carthusians and two grandsons were in Weekites. He made his money as a wine merchant and was asked to go forward as Lord Mayor but he declined. He always was benevolent towards Brooke Hall and the school – for example he gave money anonymously to build the "old Gym" and made munificent gifts to the Carthusian Trust. Tom fought in the Great War, RASC; and was a brilliant creative farmer, Young Farmers' Club President, CBE 1957 for services to the NFYFC, Governor 1951-73, President OC Club 1960,

married Evelyn 1911. He died at Tilgate, Sussex 22nd March 1973.

GV Goodliffe was in the dark blue team 1903.

Regular school games with Winchester began in 1904 and 2nd XI games became more regular, including the home and away game against Cranleigh. In December 1904 Veale refereed a school match and had to give the first penalty on Big Ground against the Old Reptonians. Mr Tod, the official referee, was taken ill during the match and Veale took over. He gave the penalty for hand ball against the opposition and "Woe was me!" he reported. There was no penalty mark and nobody seemed to know how to take it! AS Cockburn, one of the school half-backs, came to the rescue and showed everyone what should be done. Veale never refereed another game. Norris continued to play for Oxford whilst TS Rowlandson was in the Cambridge goal.

1905 saw Norris gain another Blue and he was joined by WJH Curwen and RA Bence-Pembroke.

Nial PKJO'N McCleland (S) probably the longest named Carthusian ever (apart from John FCAG Albert (S) (Prince of Schleswig-Holstein), left the school in the summer of 1906 to go up to Pembroke College, Cambridge, where he became a familiar figure on the tow-path and a Fellow and Bursar as well as Honorary Treasurer of the CUAFC.

JCD Tetley made the Oxford side this year along with Curwen, Norris (as captain), Bence-Pembroke and IE Snell. Queen's Club, the Varsity match venue, was like a swamp after heavy rain and the lighter Cambridge side won after Norris was carried from the ground injured. Snell was very big and strong and the only Oxford forward likely to get the ball to travel in the mud. Having scored, he was put at full-back and the initiative was lost.

Mordaunt HC Doll (V) left school to go to Trinity College, Cambridge. He played Amateur football for England AFA XI against Bohemia in 1911, as well as representing Middlesex CCC 1911-19.

In 1907, Bence-Pembroke captained Oxford, Snell played at full-back, again heading many crosses away, and he was partnered by Tetley. VG Thew played for Cambridge.

Repton beat the school in their first encounter 0-4 in 1907 and in 1908 the match was played as late as 22nd December. The Varsity game saw RLL Braddell in the Oxford team and Thew played again for Cambridge. This was a period when the university sides had to decide whether to join with the newly formed AFA or stay with the FA. As the "split" occurred it would mean that the university teams would not be allowed to play the professionals if they went with the AFA. Playing amateur teams was less financially

1902-3 School team. Top: C Lee, RD England, JCD Tetley, DF Seth Smith, Middle: GT Branston, IE Snell, RA Bence-Pembroke, GL Bickersteth, AA Drew. Front: RB Taylor, RH Allen. School archive

VG Thew. 1st XI captain 1904-06. School archive

their league, giving the students more suitable opposition.

The Oxford 2nd XI, the Centaurs, first had a match against Charterhouse in 1908-9 and the following year the school played OUAFC again. Braddell was picked for Oxford and he became university captain in 1910. JB Bickersteth and HJC Pears joined him in the Blues' side. Thew captained Cambridge for two consecutive years.

A.W Corrie (S) who played for the school XI in 1873-74 became President of the OCFC and OCCC from 1909-11. S Baker and RM Weeks were three Carthusians in the light blue side at this Varsity match. Bickersteth captained Oxford in 1911 and Weeks played against him. In 1912 CB Johnson and WIF MacDonald were in the Oxford XI against Weeks (the opposing captain) who had Baker in support. So the school was still sending decent players to the two major universities.

However, the match against the OC internationals due to be played at Queen's Club was last on the fixture card in LQ 1909 – and it was scratched. This may have signalled the end of the "Golden Period".

exciting but did lead to closer games. Even in the 1970s this issue arose when matches in the Blues' term were mostly against professional sides, fielding mixed teams usually too strong for the undergraduates. By the 21st century the Oxbridge teams had joined BUSF and played in

the f.a. amateur cup, london senior cup and others

Amateur Cup. School archive

On 16th March 1889, the OCs beat the South of England XI 3-1 in the FA Charity festival. The *Carthusian* describes the game "as made up between the OCs and the South of England". *Pastime* records that: "The selection of the two Southern teams for this match did not give general satisfaction, and when it was found that both would be playing below their full strength, the interest was further reduced." The *Carthusian* said: "The play needs little description – it was quite too uninteresting." It appears that Ford, the opposition goalie, let one soft shot through his legs from W.H. Ainger. Parry added the second finding himself on the left of the goal when he was actually a right-winger and, although distinctly offside, it was allowed. The unfortunate Ford caught a shot from C Wreford Brown and then promptly threw the ball at Cobbold who "returned the ball and scored a third goal".

Having left the FA Cup to the professionals, the OCs entered and triumphed in the newly-formed F.A. Amateur Cup, a unique double at the time and a record that the club shares with the now defunct Wimbledon Football Club who won the Amateur Cup in 1963 and the FA Cup in 1988 (see FA Cup chapter 5). On 8th February 1893 the rules for this new competition were drawn up and 81 teams joined in. Many Old Boys' teams entered but by 1904 few remained as once again competition from amateur league clubs pushed the "gentleman" to one side. In the 1893-4 campaign, the OCs played the Crusaders at home, winning 4-2 in the first round. The Crusaders were previously known as Brent-

Winners medal 1897. School archive

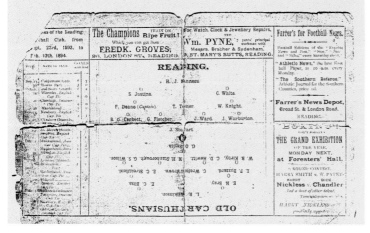

The oldest known Reading Football Club programme in existence, printed for the Amateur Cup game against Old Carthusians on February 17th, 1894.

Reading programme. Reading AFC archive

wood. The second round saw a match at Reading FC, with the OCs winning 4-1, watched by 1000 people. Having been contacted by the club's historian, David Downs, in May 2006, he told me that the programme from that game, held on 17th February 1894, was the earliest known Reading football programme. The Carthusian team for this match was published as: Wilkinson, Bray, Bliss, Buzzard, Wreford Brown, Streatfeild, Kirby, Hewitt, Smith, Stanbrough, Wilson, and the referee was Captain Pulteney of the Royal Engineers. Wreford Brown and Kirkby did not play but DC Leman and Timmis did.

This match was played at Caversham football ground and both teams and spectators had to get to the pitch by ferry across the river from Adams and Gyngell's boathouse at 1d a trip. The *Carthusian* and the *Reading Mercury* reporting the match both show "R Hunt" at centre-forward. Indeed an "R Hunter" also mysteriously appears on team sheets at this time, including an Amateur Cup tie against the Crusaders on 3rd February 1894. Actually Richard Hunt had just left the school and may well have been drafted in at centre-forward. He had scored regularly for the XI in his two seasons in the team. It is believed by some that this was actually GO Smith trying to remain anonymous. The description of R Hunt's significant contribution to the game suggests that it could have been GO and why he did not want to be named on the list is not known, although he may have wished his performance not to have been discovered by his university team selectors. Another "ringer", "AN Brown", was listed alongside GO for the OCs against the Old Westminsters that season too. In 2007 the school team played a Reading FC academy team on 7th February on Big Ground, losing 0-6.

THE FOOTBALL ASSOCIATION AMATEUR CUP.

FINAL TIE.

The Old Carthusians beat the Casuals at Richmond on Saturday, April 7th, by two goals to one, and became the first holders of the Amateur Cup. Both teams are to be congratulated on the excellence of the contest. The dribbling of Stanbrough and R. Topham, the great half-back game of Wreford Brown (who is certainly one of the very best halves that ever lived), some of A. M. Walters's art as a full back, and stout goal-keeping at each end, were points that gave to the match an invigorating freshness. There are still many who find in the dribbles, the long passes, and the rushes quite as much attraction as all the fine finish of the short passing game now generally practised among the great professional clubs. The match was splendid to watch, and the interest was sustained during every minute. There was not a great deal to choose between the sides, although the impression left by Wreford Brown, Walters, and Stanbrough lent heavy weight to the feeling that Charterhouse was really the better team. However, they won, and a victory was never more popular. The crowd evidently looked upon the Casuals as lacking the legitimate rights of a club; the cause of this idea was no doubt the large and varied membership. And in some of the unkind epithets that were hurled at the team a section of the crowd showed, to put it lightly, extremely bad manners. The attendance on this glorious afternoon at Richmond ran up to some 4000, a company that must be gratifying to the promoters of the competition, in the early stages of which there was a little lethargy in the attention bestowed by the public. The Duke and Duchess of Teck are familiar visitors to the Richmond Athletic Ground, and they and their daughter, the Duchess of York, received a hearty welcome on this occasion. They were spectators of the whole of the play. The captains of the teams—Wreford Brown and R. Topham—had the honour of being presented to the Royal visitors before the match began. It should be noted that the withdrawal of G. O. Smith, who was called away to play for England, rather disorganised the front rank of the Carthusians. For his place in the centre had to be filled by a half-back, E. F. Buzzard, who did not quite realize the way that it is necessary for a good centre to get the ball out to the wings. Hence Stanbrough had little to do until the halves took upon themselves the duty of feeding him. And when Stanbrough did get an opening or two he quickly put the Carthusians ahead. In order to curb this strong left wing, the Casuals transposed their full backs, Lodge, who was late in turning up, going over to the right. But these tactics did not work so well as those which preceded them. The Casuals did a lot of pressing to begin with, and Topham, closing in from the right, had the ball well passed to him by Perkins, and he scored in four minutes from the start. For some time after this the attention of the spectators was bent on the fine defence of the Carthusians, notably Walters at back and Wreford Brown at half. It was after a sharp attack by the Casuals that the players named got the ball out to Stanbrough, who dribbled brilliantly down the left wing, and by a skilful middle gave Buzzard an easy opening for a goal. So the scores were brought level at the end of thirty-five minutes. Buzzard and Topham each missed what seemed an inevitable point. Then just before the interval Wreford Brown again got the ball up to Stanbrough, who finished another great piece of dribbling with a second goal. The second half of the match was fast and exciting. Stanbrough executed a lot of fine work on the left wing, while Wreford Brown nearly scored with a long shot. Harrison was hard pressed more than once. Lodge kicked well, and the Casuals, after having the worst of the match, made a big attempt to equalise in the last ten minutes. Any openings they had were lost by lofty kicking, and the Carthusians won the match by 2 goals to 1. Mr. T. Gunning was the referee, and the sides were as follows :—

CASUALS :—A. E. Harrison (goal), L. V. Lodge, C. O. S. Hatton (backs), R. R. Barker, A. G, Topham, J. E. Grieveson (half-backs), H. A. Rhodes, T. B. Rhodes, T. N. Perkins, F. W. Carlton, R. Topham (captain) (forwards).

Everyone will, we are sure, join us in most hearty congratulations to the Old Carthusian Football Club on this splendid victory, and especially to the team in general, and its most energetic Captain, C. Wreford Brown, in particular. That this, and like successes, may attend the team next year, is the earnest wish of everyone connected with Charterhouse.

Carthusian report of first Amateur Cup final. School archive

Great Marlow came next in the quarter final at home on Godalming recreation ground, with a victory to the OCs 4-1.

Wreford Brown was again unavailable because his was "trying to score off the examiners at Oxford" and Wilson was also missing because "his college authorities failed to properly appreciate football".

Then the OCs beat Bishop Auckland in the semi-final at the neutral Nottingham Forest ground 5-1. This match was scheduled on the same day that Notts County, who had won through to the FA Cup Final, were playing a league game in town. The kick off was at the same time, affecting the semi-final gate which numbered only two hundred. Bishop Auckland would soon become one of the great teams in the history of the cup.

In the final tie on 7th April 1894, at the Athletic Ground, Richmond, the Carthusians overcame the Casuals 2-1 in front of a crowd of up to 4000. The game was watched by the Duke and Duchess of York with their daughter, Princess May (later to be Queen Mary), and before the game the captains, Wreford Brown and R Topham, were presented to the royal visitors. That day, GO Smith was called away to play for England against Scotland in front of 40,000 at Celtic Park and EF Buzzard, a left half, very much a fill in, had to get used to playing as a centre and spreading the play to the wings. The Casuals scored after a few minutes through R Topham and this was just as well since their left back, LV Lodge, had missed his train and turned up ten minutes late for the game. The Carthusians gradually settled and the new formation began to work with Stanbrough giving Buzzard an opening to score the equaliser. Stanbrough then finished a great piece of dribbling with a goal. The referee was Mr T Gunning and the team was: LR Wilkinson, AM Walters, EH Bray, EC Bliss, C Wreford Brown, EC Streatfeild, CD Hewitt, GA Richardson, EF Buzzard, GS Wilson (1 goal) MH Stanbrough (1 goal).

The Carthusian complimented Stanbrough and Topham on their dribbling and Wreford Brown on being "one of the best halves that ever lived". Clearly there were still elements of the Charterhouse game that survived. For example, the dribbles, the long passes and rushes were found by many just as attractive "as all the fine finish of the short passing game now generally practised among the great professional clubs".

MH Stanbrough at school. School archive

MAURICE HUGH STANBROUGH (G) Born 2nd September 1870, Cleobury North, Salop; died 17th December 1904, Broadstairs.

He was at Charterhouse first in OQ 1884. Brother WFH also played football. He played cricket for the XI in 1889, football in 1888 and left in CQ '89. He went up to Caius College, Cambridge, got his BA and played for CUAFC in 1890-2, he won his Blue at outside left. He played against Oxford three times with two victories and in his last year his team won 5-1. Played for the London FA, Eastbourne, OC XI in the Amateur Cup 1894 (1 goal), '95, '97 (1 goal), LSC '95, LCC '96, ADC 1903.

He represented England (see chapter 9). He had a reputation for clever forward play and he was a dashing runner. Slightly built he was one of the best left-wing players in the amateur game, being the despair of the full-back playing against him. *Pastime* magazine (28th February 1894) states, "He has plenty of pace, he passes accurately, middles beautifully and shoots at goal with deadly accuracy." Injury limited his performances but he turned out for the Corinthians and the OCs. He was a schoolmaster who taught at Elstree, Stanmore, Eastbourne and at St Peter's, Broadstairs.

In the 1894-5 Amateur Cup there was a walk over given by Swindon in round one and a victory over Tottenham Hotspur away at the Tottenham ground, Northumberland Park, 5-0, in round two (Saturday 13th March) with a crowd of 3000. Spurs were opponents again, five days later, in the London Charity Cup semi-final at Leyton, watched by 1200 people and the OCs won this time, 3-0. GO Smith scored twice. Between these two games GO Smith and the Walters played for England against Wales on Monday 15th March. On the Spurs side that time was Ernest Payne who had moved from Fulham previously. In *The Carthusian* he is reported to have had "the best sprint of the day" chasing a ball down the pitch. When he signed for his new club, he had no kit and Spurs obligingly found his kit and gave him ten shillings to buy boots. This contravened the amateur rules and Spurs became suspended by the London FA. Spurs at this point turned professional.

In round three, 30th March, Crewe Alexander was put aside 1-0. This was an unpleasant match "with the opponents bent on tripping and lofty kicking". Just before the finish of the game their outside left was dismissed for abusive language to the referee. "The language and play of the opposing team was so bad that some of the Carthusians wished to retire at half-time."

LONDON SENIOR CUP.

FINAL.

The following is reprinted from *The Sportsman* :—

OLD CARTHUSIANS *v.* CASUALS.—History has very nearly repeated itself this season in connection with the Charterhouse players. Last year, after reaching the final stage in the Amateur, London Senior and Charity Cup contests, they had to rest content with winning the first-named trophy. This season they once more arrived in the closing scenes for all three, but in the Charity Competition lost to London Caledonians, whilst the Middlesbrough team wrested the Amateur Cup from them. On April 30th, however, the Old Boys made some amends by carrying off the London Senior, but although they won easily, their display was far from being a high-class one. The weather was fine, but the turf at the Queen's Club was very long and caused the ball to travel somewhat slowly, whilst there were not more than about 800 or 900 people present. Neither side was up to full strength, but in this respect the Casuals suffered most, and the lot they had to rely upon distinguished themselves by an utter lack of combination. Toone kicked off from the top end of the ground at 4.35. The Casuals ran down, but Hewitt and Kirby at once returned, and were becoming exceedingly dangerous when Fry cleared. Kirby returned to the charge, and Smith headed into Lawrence's hands. The Carthusians kept up the pressure, and Buzzard came within an ace of scoring, whilst after a corner Tringham nearly got through, but nevertheless the play was not fast or particularly good. A quarter of an hour from the start a run by Tringham and Richardson ended in the former scoring, and this was the only point scored in the first half. After change of ends the game degenerated into a farce almost, C. P. Wilson and Compton were continually making mistakes, whilst Hilleary was seldom dangerous. The Carthusians penned their rivals, and after Smith had hit the bar with a swift shot and the Old Boys had forced a couple of corners, the O.C.s centre forward placed his side another point ahead. Then, from a pass by Smith, Richardson headed through, and directly after Kirby put on two goals in quick succession. Tringham then scored with a shot that hit Lawrence and knocked him clean over. The goal-keeper was considerably shaken, but he stopped a rare hot one from Richardson directly after, and when the whistle blew the score was: Old Carthusians, six goals ; Casuals, 0. Teams:

The Old Carthusian record is as follows :—

LONDON CHARITY CUP.

Clapton	...	...	4—0
Tottenham Hotspur	...	...	3—0
London Caledonians	...	...	1—3

LONDON SENIOR CUP.

Old Foresters	...	...	8—0
Clapton	...	...	4—1
Old Westminsters	...	...	5—0
Casuals	...	...	6—0

AMATEUR CUP.

Tottenham Hotspur	...	...	5—0
Crewe Alexandra	...	...	1—0
South Bank	...	...	1—1
,, (re-played tie)	...	...	3—2
Middlesbrough	...	...	1—2

TOTAL.

London Charity Cup	...	...	8—3
London Senior Cup	...	...	23—1
Amateur Cup	...	...	11—5
Total	...		42—9

An Old Carthusian has kindly forwarded us an extract from the *Pall Mall Gazette*, and as we think it may interest our readers, we venture to insert it :—

No club has more reason to complain of the frost than the Old Carthusians, who, having entered for three cup competitions and being greatly fancied to win the lot, found all their matches thrown together at the end of the season and all their hopes cruelly dashed to the ground. The best trained athlete finds football a most exhausting game, and it is not therefore surprising that with untrained amateurs an average of three matches a week should prove to be too much for them. It was unfortunate for the Carthusians that they were so successful in the earlier ties, for had they been knocked out of one competition they might have won in the other two. As it is, they were beaten by the London Caledonians for the Charity Cup, by Middlesbrough for the Amateur Cup (of which they were the holders), and they have to console themselves with their single success in the London Association Cup final. The Old Boys, besides being stale, were very unlucky in losing the services of Wreford Brown, who sprained his ankle early in the match with the London Caledonians. Only those who have played with or against this clever little half-back can appreciate the difference his presence makes to a team. It is safe to assert that Middlesbrough would not now possess the Amateur Cup if he had been playing against them, and it is probable that if the accident had not happened to him in the Charity tie the Caledonians would not be happy in the possession of the handsome trophy presented by Sir Reginald Hanson.

Carthusian article reporting London Senior Cup triumph and explanation for staleness of players at the end of a long season. School archive

OFFICIAL CARD.—Printed and Sold on the Ground ONLY.

ESSEX COUNTY CRICKET GROUND, LEYTON,

Thursday, April 16.

LONDON SENIOR CUP—FINAL.

OLD CARTHUSIANS v. CASUALS.

CASUALS.

[RIGHT.]   [LEFT.]

GOAL.
A. G. S. Lawrence

BACKS
A. G. P. Baines   W. G. Adams

HALF-BACKS
H. A. Fauthmell   R. R. Barker   C. O. S. Hatton

FORWARDS.
R. L. Hilleary   F. H. Bryant   G. F. Fernie   S. S. Taylor   C. F. Drake

FORWARDS.
W. R. Kirby   B. Murdoch   G. O. Smith   E. M. Tringham   C. D. Hewitt

HALF-BACKS.
G. S. Wilson   A. N. Other   S. R. Darvell

BACKS.
E. H. Bray   G. E. B. Pritchett   E. F. Buzzard

GOAL.

OLD CARTHUSIANS.

[RIGHT.]   [LEFT.]

REFEREE   ...

Programme for the London Senior Cup Final.
School archive

Old Carthusians 1895. Back: A Foster, RJ Salt, BKR Wilkinson, PM Walters. Middle: RF Buzzard, CD Hewitt, GO Smith, C Wreford Brown, EH Bray, AM Walters. Front: HJ Broadbent, WE Kirby. School archive

After this undesirable match the team beat South Bank in a replay (after a 1-1 draw at Headingly, Leeds on April 13th). Some 300 supporters followed the Carthusians. *The Carthusian* reported, "We believe South Bank is in North Yorkshire which accounts for some of the weird expressions used during the match." Seven days later the replay was won 3-2 at Derby with a very poor gate. The game went through two periods of extra time (two-and-a-half hours of football) by which time the game had deteriorated and the crowd showed little interest. The OCs lost the final to Middlesbrough at Headingly, Leeds 1-2 on 27th April 1895, in front of 4000 – mostly northerners. There was drizzle and a driving wind which affected the play and without Wreford Brown the Carthusians were "weak and stale". Smith scored the first goal in the second half and following "a long dropping free kick from half-back by Allport, Mullen in true northern forethought disposed of goalkeeper Wilkinson by

knocking him back into the net before the ball dropped. For some reason this was not noticed by the referee, seeing that he was decidedly offside." The final winning goal was scored by Mullen in the last minutes of the match.

Those who played that day were: BKR Wilkinson, Walters AM and PM, EF Buzzard, (Kite), EC Streatfeild, CD Hewitt, HJ Broadbent, GO Smith, GS Wilson and MH Stanbrough. (Smith scored the goal.) Referee: Mr RE Lythgoe.

Wreford Brown could not play in this game and he was, according to *The Carthusian*, "replaced by _____ who was in splendid form". There was also no name given in the team list published in the June 1895 edition, with a space left in the halves. Although R. Samuel in his *The Amateur Cup Results Book* does give the name of "Kite" whose name does not appear in school records. A bit of a mystery then, until one reads *The Times* for 29th April 1895 which names a curious fellow in the

MARCH, 1896.]   THE CAR

but there was no further scoring, and the teams will consequently have to meet again.   Teams :

OLD CARTHUSIANS :—J. T. McGaw (goal), E. H. Bray, E. C. Bliss (backs), A. Vassall, C. Wreford Brown, E. F. Buzzard (half-backs), M. H. Stanbrough, W. F. H. Stanbrough (left wing), G. O. Smith (centre), G. S. Wilson, G. C. Vassall (right wing) (forwards).

LONDON CALEDONIANS :—F. Burton (goal), W. Hay (capt.), H. W. Moffatt (backs), J. Russell, T. Harvey, L. H. Mackenzie (half-backs), R. H. Howie, A. Whitehead (right wing), J. W. Murison (centre), F. Whitehead, R. Kidd (left wing) (forwards).

REFEREE :—Lieut. Simpson (Hon. Sec. L.F.A.).

THE AMATEUR CUP.
SECOND ROUND.

v. DARLINGTON :—Great interest centered in this re-played tie at Darlington on Saturday, Feb. 22nd (the Skernesiders having played a draw a week previous in London), and over five thousand spectators passed the turnstiles. Matters looked bad when the visitors (who were but weakly represented) scored twice through the Stanbroughs, but in the last quarter of an hour Darlington equalised. Within five minutes of the re-start the home team registered another point, and ten minutes afterwards added another. The Carthusians played up pluckily, but though they had by far the best of the argument in the last twenty minutes, they only scored once, and at the finish of a hard-fought game had to retire beaten by four goals to three. Teams :

OLD CARTHUSIANS :—J. T. McGaw (goal), A. Massey, A. D. Fordyce (backs), E. Garnett, J. L. Lock, W. A. E. Austen (half-backs), B. Murdoch, A. J. Davidson, F. R. Barwell, W. F. H. Stanbrough, M. H. Stanbrough (forwards).

DARLINGTON :—Henderson (goal), Morris, Bird (backs), Cambell, T. Waites, Johnson (half-backs), Dyane, Almond, Lowes, Boyle, Bowes (forwards).

REFEREE :—Mr. E. Ramsbottom (Liverpool).

LINESMEN :—Messrs. Howcroft (Redcar) and Penton (Liverpool).

Carthusian article March 1896 showing strongest team above and the Amateur Cup team below which was much weakened. School archive

Carthusian eleven as A du C Kite . There is no record of this character in the school Register but, having looked carefully, one discovers that some member of Girdlestoneites' house (a Duck-ite) had been drafted in for the match!! There is no obvious reference in school or the house registers to explain who this was. In 1894, 1895 and again 1897, the OCs appeared in the finals of the FA Amateur Cup, the London Senior Cup and the London Charity Cup. On each occasion, too many matches in such a short time prevented them from doing the "treble".

In the 1895-6 competition there was a round one walkover again when Oxford City scratched. The next opponents were Darlington and after "the Skernesiders had played a draw 1-1 a week previous in London" in round two, the

away fixture at Feethams, ended as a 3-4 defeat. Sadly the OCs were depleted owing to the absence of many first choice players who could not travel north for that game. The two *Carthusian* reports show how changed the amateur cup side was. Darlington lost to Bishop Auckland in the semi-final.

The OCs won the cup again in 1896-7 beating Bristol South End 10-0 away in the first round. They then played Ealing, winning 2-1 at home, and then the Old Westminsters at home 3-1. Great Marlow were the opponents in the semi-final and this resulted in a 2-1 win at Maidenhead, after a 0-0 draw at Leyton. The Marlow Club at that time was successful enough

THE AMATEUR CUP.
REPLAYED FINAL TIE.
To the Editor of the Carthusian.

SIR,—Feeling that on such an important occasion as the replayed Final Amateur Cup Tie your paper should be represented, I appointed myself to a post on your staff and joined the Old Carthusian party that left London by the 5.45 Great Northern express on the 15th April last, for Darlington.

Jameson, burdened with a pack of patience cards, was the first player to put in an appearance. The other players continued to arrive at intervals, and I recognised Bliss by a treatise on International Law, and Timmis by the number of "stodgers" consumed in the refreshment room. Hewitt was the last, as usual, to arrive. Mr. Longworth and Mr. Becker, as representatives of Brooke Hall, completed the party, and took the places of Wreford Brown, who had gone north the day before in order to see an importunate client, and W. F. H. Stanbrough, who, in view of the near approach of the open Golf Championship, had gone to Sandwich to practise.

The most striking feature of the journey up was an attempt by one of the travellers to hit a red-bearded Yorkshire postman who was peering in at our dining saloon. The net result was a broken window.

On arriving at Darlington we were delighted to find it was raining, as this probably meant the tie would be played on a heavy ground. Owing to the large crowd which had come down to see the train arrive, it was some time before we were able to leave the station and drive off to the King's Head, where the team were to stay.

The chief items of interest on Good Friday morning were the rude awakening of G. O. Smith and Bray by two of the Clapham Rovers' team, who were on tour up north and staying at the same hotel, the rain, which we hoped would continue, the consumption of hot-cross buns, a grand vocal trio in a half-built villa by Smith, Bray and Buzzard—the last named appearing in the *rôle* of Plunket Greene—and a magnificent oratorio by Hewitt in the *grand salon* of the hotel. In the afternoon most of the party expended sevenpence and

The report on Stockton replay by the correspondent. School archive

saw a Northern League match between Crook and Darlington, on the ground on which our tie was to be played on the morrow. Those who saw it left the ground fully convinced that they had witnessed the foulest exhibition of football that could be reasonably expected for the money. The doings of the rest of the party, are they not chronicled in the *Sporting Life's* issue of the 17th April?

On the 17th we awoke to find that Wreford Brown had arrived in the small hours of the morning, and that the *Sporting Life* had kindly decided that if the morning broke fine we should take walking exercise. As the morning broke wet, the only walking exercise taken was round the billiard tables.

After lunch the team, which was completed by Stanbrough's arrival from York, was photographed, and then drove to the ground. The rain still continued to descend, and in consequence our hopes of success rose, as the team, despite their training on the School ground, invariably do better when the going is heavy than when the ground is dry and fast.

The start of the game was delayed for some little time owing to one of the linesmen not having arrived. Wreford Brown lost the toss, and our opponents taking advantage of the little wind there was, G. O. Smith kicked off about ten minutes after the advertised time. The first few minutes' play went in favour of Stockton, who got down to Wilkinson's end and caused that player to use his hands. Following the goal kick our left wing got possession of the ball from Smith's pass, and Hewitt made a brilliant run, ending up with a magnificent shot from the corner, which completely beat Hamilton the goal-keeper of the Stockton Football and Cricket Club Co., Limited, and passed through the goal close to the right-hand post. Encouraged by this success, gained as it was but seven minutes from the start, our team pressed hard for some time, but without success. The Stockton men at last cleared by means of a free-kick for "hands" and took the ball right down the field, their final shot going just outside the post. Our left wing again got away from the kick off, but the ball went over the line and our opponents again visited our end, Timmis at length relieving with a big kick. Stanbrough was next conspicuous with a run on our right, but he was finally pulled up by the opposing captain, and Wilkinson, when hard pressed, effected a clever save from a shot by their right wing. Our forwards again broke away, and Timmis next distinguished himself with a long shot, which Hamilton just managed to clear in time. Stockton then returned to the attack, and, securing a couple of fruitless corners, for some minutes kept our defence very busy, but our backs and halves proved equal to all emergencies, and tackled and marked their men with commendable persistency. Wilkinson at length got the ball away, and Smith sent in a capital shot, which was saved at the expense of a corner. Even play followed for some time, but shortly before the interval the Stockton right wing got away and the outside sent in a fast shot, which Wilkinson just managed to save with his foot. The whistle blew soon afterwards for

half-time, with the score still standing 1—0 in our favour. The supporters of the Old Carthusians had at this period every reason to be satisfied with their display, as besides the material advantage of a goal the exchanges had ruled distinctly in their favour.

As soon as our opponents had finished discussing the contents of their black bottle—a feature of modern football which for some reason or other has not yet been adopted by Old Carthusians—the game was resumed, as our players were anxious to catch the express back to town, and standing still in the rain was by no means pleasant.

On re-starting both goalkeepers were soon called on, Smith giving the Stockton keeper a stinging shot, which he kept out by conceding a corner-kick. The Stockton right wing then broke away, but Bray relieved, and Buzzard and Smith returned to the attack. Give-and-take play ensued for some time, and several shots were sent in by both sides, the Stockton outside right on one occasion having only Wilkinson to beat at close range, and driving the ball yards outside the post. After this we again visited their end for a short time, but our opponents rallied and attacked our goal so persistently for at least ten minutes, that it certainly looked as if our bad luck in final ties was going to stick to us and that we were doomed to defeat. At last their right half put in a long dropping shot, and one of their forwards pushing Bray over from behind and then charging Wilkinson when he was neither playing the ball nor obstructing an opponent, the ball bounced into the net, and the teams were again level.

Stimulated by this success and the contents of the black bottle before mentioned, our opponents returned to the bombardment of our goal, and it looked any odds on their scoring again. After several anxious minutes' play, however, Smith and our left wing suddenly broke away, and after passing and re-passing right down the ground, Buzzard placed the ball in the net from Smith's final pass when in an awkward position for taking aim. This second goal seemed to take all the show out of Stockton, and within three minutes of Buzzard's goal the score was standing 4—1 in our favour. Our third goal was got by Smith after some more excellent passing between himself and the left wing, and the fourth was obtained by Buzzard after a good single-handed rush down the centre of the field, his shot being taken when some distance out of goal. This four minutes' piece of play was the best piece of work in the match, and was of so brilliant a character that it was alone well worth the long journey to Darlington to see. Of course these goals placed the issue beyond doubt, as but ten minutes remained for play, and our opponents played like a beaten team, albeit they once or twice got close to our goal on sufferance. The only other noteworthy feature of the game was some capital work by Stanbrough and Jameson, the latter sending in a fast shot which just skimmed the bar. The whistle blew with the score unaltered, and so Old Carthusians were returned the Diamond Jubilee winners of the Amateur Cup.

Wreford Brown and a few of the team stayed to have

The report on Stockton replay by the correspondent (continued). School archive the Cup and medals presented to them; and Wreford Brown returned thanks on behalf of the O.Cs. The other players, finding it hopeless to get through the crowd, returned to the hotel as speedily as possible, in order to scrape off the mud with which they were coated from head to foot.

Without doubt the balance of the play during the game was distinctly in our favour, and it was generally admitted in Darlington after the match that the better team had won.

Turning to the individual players, Wilkinson, who was evidently very nervous on the way to the ground, made some splendid saves in goal, and owing to an unfair charge, had no chance with the goal that Stockton got. It is a pity that he is not a stronger kicker-off from goal. Timmis played a good hard game from start to finish, and seemed to fairly revel in the vigorous play. Bray was also very good, and as usual made some beautiful kicks from very difficult positions. Darvell—our only Welsh International—and Bliss, both played a persistently hard game, worrying their opponents and giving every opportunity to their own forwards. Wreford Brown was—Wreford Brown. Anyone who had only seen him play in the semi-final and final ties of this competition, would have believed that he was only just starting his football career with Old Carthusians instead of having played with them for the last ten years and more. There is no doubt that the team plays better as a whole when he is there to captain them, and it will indeed be a bad day for Old Carthusians when he decides that he is too much of a "stiff 'un" to turn out for them any more.

Coming to the forwards, Hewitt, Buzzard, and Smith combined splendidly, and the four minutes' play after Stockton got their goal evidently came as an eye-opener to the spectators who kindly obliged by whistling the "Dead March in Saul" when we obtained our third goal. Hewitt's goal—the first he has got for O.Cs. since the beginning of last year's cup tie season—was a brilliant effort, and he had the pace of the opposing backs from start to finish. Buzzard on this occasion played far better than he had previously done this season, and showed that when he gets his "tail up" he is a difficult man to stop. His first goal was the turning-point of the game, and as he got the winning goal for O.Cs. in the Amateur final of 1894, he can look back to his final ties in this competition with the utmost satisfaction. G. O. Smith, who was still a bit lame, was as usual the making of the forwards, and his value to the team is, to use an Irishism, most apparent when he is absent. Stanbrough and Jameson as a pair suffered by comparison with the left wing, but they both worked their hardest. The former, as he always does, got through an enormous amount of work, and hustled the opposing backs continually. He had his reward in the shape of a deliberate blow over the left eye from an opponents' fist, and a gold medal. Jameson was much better in the second than the first half. At present he seems clumsy and lacks control over the ball, but another season's play will doubtless remedy this. It is a gratifying feature to find the

School is still sending out players of a calibre good enough to represent O.Cs. in their most important engagements in the season following that in which they represented the School.

Of the Stockton team so far as football was concerned, the two backs and goalkeeper played best. They however keep a man who can hit straight from the shoulder and has apparently taken lessons from C. J. N. Fleming, the Scotch International threequarter, as to how a collar by the neck should be effected. As far as one could judge from seeing them play in London and Darlington, their success is due to the kick-and-rush style of play combined with a remarkable aptitude for playing a foul game without being seen by the referee.

After the match was over, the following curious document was on sale.

Carthusians 4   Stockton 1

> SACRED TO THE MEMORY OF THE
>
> ## UNFORTUNATE STOCKTONIANS,
>
> WHO MET THEIR DOOM AT FEETHAMS, DARLINGTON,
>
> ON SATURDAY, APRIL 17TH, 1897.
>
> Three weeks ago at Tufnell Park — But now to-day we've gone amiss
> We had a right to crow; — And lost our chance to sup:
> For splendid football there we played — For we felt sure to taking back
> Which ended in a draw. — The English Amateur Cup.
>
> WITH OLD CARTHUSIANS' KIND REGARDS.

Evidently Mr. Alfred Austin and the Surrey poet have a dangerous Northern rival.

All the party with the exception of Wilkinson and Hewitt returned to town by the 5.54 express; and so ended a most enjoyable and satisfactory trip. Rumour has it that Hewitt was seen in the dead of night in the neighbourhood of Northallerton carrying a bicycle over five-barred gates and hedges, but there is no doubt that he has since arrived back in Town, as he has been seen in the flesh by

YOUR DARLINGTON CORRESPONDENT.

OLD CARTHUSIANS:—B. K. R. Wilkinson (goal), E. H. Bray, W. U. Timmis (backs), H. Darvell, C. Wreford Brown, E. C. Bliss (half-backs), C. D. Hewitt, W. F. H. Stanbrough (left wing), G. O. Smith (centre), E. F. Buzzard, E. M. Jameson (right wing) (forwards).

STOCKTON:—T. Hamilton (goal), E. Brannan, C. Wilson (backs), R. Shaw, R. Murray, W. Monteith (half-backs), T. Robson, G. Lee (right wing), Halfpenny (centre), G. Sanderson, T. Lakey (left wing) (forwards).

REFEREE:—Mr. A. Kingscott, Derby.

————

The report on Stockton replay by the correspondent. School archive

to entertain Paris as an opposition at the beginning of the century, and this is the first time a French team played on English soil.

Finally, the Stockton team were formidable opponents in the final at Tufnell Park, Holloway, on 27th March. Wind, a dry pitch and hard ground in the first match made the game difficult "with much excessive violent and ragged play". The *Carthusian* describing the Stockton men, said that "the extraordinary emulation aroused by the importance of this game also manifested itself in the promiscuous kicking of their opponents and occasionally their comrades. Torn clothing and contusions were so palpably evident that the referee at half-time thought well to examine the boots of the players." Following a 1-1 draw the OCs eventually travelled to Darlington on 17th April and conquered in the north-east, at the Feethams ground 4-1 before 10,000 spectators.

The Editor of the *Carthusian* at the time joined the tour party, leaving London on the 5.45pm Great Northern express on 15th April. The account of his journey and experience makes entertaining reading (previous pages).

The team was: BKR Wilkinson, EH Bray, WU Timmis, S Darvell, C Wreford Brown, EC Bliss, GS Wilson, EF Buzzard, CD Hewitt, GO Smith (1), WH Stanbrough, EM Jameson.

In the second match Hewitt (1), Buzzard (2), Smith (1) scored the goals in what was the Diamond Jubilee.

In the winning team were those named above except for EM Jameson in place of Wilson.

The OCs never appeared in the Amateur Cup after that and the Old Malvernians became prominent in the competition for a few years, winning the 1901-2 final 5-1 against Bishop Auckland. The Westminsters and Etonians continued to play for a few more years also.

Tanner at Wembley. Pegasus v Bishop Auckland. School archive

Charterhouse's last contact with this cup was in 1951 when John Tanner played for the famous Pegasus side at Wembley in front of 100,000. He scored the winning goal over Bishop Auckland, helping the old boys of Oxbridge to an extraordinary 2-1 victory.

WALTER HENRY AINGER (R g)
born 7th February 1864, died 6th January 1948 at Newcastle.

At school LQ 1876-CQ '82. He did not play in school XI. Went to St John's College, Cambridge, MA. CUAFC 1887, forward. Played for the London FA on several occasions in 1888-9. Chaplain to 1st VB (5th Northumberland) Fusiliers, Vicar, Canon of Newcastle 1928-48. Honorary Canon after 1929. Married Edith 1898.

ARTHUR JOHN LAST (DG)
born 24th May 1862, died 21st May 1928 Hildenborough.

Left school CQ '80. He played for the London FA v Nottingham at the Oval 3rd November 1883, but never played in the XI at school. Solicitor.

ARTHUR C NIXON (H)
born 18th April 1867, died 16th February 1900 at Ladysmith.

Joined the school CQ 1880, cricket XI 1886, football XI 1885-6. Left CQ '86, Trinity College, Cambridge, BA. CUAFC XI Blue '89, played for the London FA. Secretary Casuals FC and secretary OCFC 1890-2 seasons. 5th Lancers 1894, Boer war 1899.

GEORGE AUSTIN GARDINER (Rg)
born 14th October 1872, died 9th October 1912.

Played in the XI 1891-92, Left CQ 92, New College, Oxford. OC XI, LCC '98, LSC '99.

JOHN THOBURN MCGAW (B)
born 13th August 1872, died 21st April 1952. Left CQ '90, Trinity College, Cambridge. CUAFC '97, LCC '96.

EDWARD FARQUHAR BUZZARD (g)
born 20th December 1871, died 17th December 1945

In the Football XI 1889-90, left CQ 1890. Magdalen College, Oxford, MA. OUAFC '93-4, OC XI, Three Amateur Cups '94, '95, '97 (2 goals). London Senior Cup '95-'97, London Charity Cup '96. Regius Professor of Medicine, Royal College Physicians 1907 and Physician to George VI as Sir E Farquhar Buzzard. CB Fry in *Life Worth Living* wrote that "he hoped he was as good a Regius Professor as he was a footballer". Married May in 1899.

EDWARD CHAMPION STREATFEILD (g)
born 16th June 1870, died 22nd August 1932

In the football XI 1887-8, left CQ '88, Pembroke College, Cambridge, BA.

CUCC '90-3, CUAFC '91-2, Amateur Cup '94, '95.

FRANK REINAGLE BARWELL (RG)
born 6th November 1875, died 20th March 1943.

School XI 1891-2, left CQ '92, Amateur Cup '97, LSC '97, '99,

Married Mabel 1908.

EDWARD HUGH BRAY (RS)
born 15th April 1874, died 27th November

1950 at Rye.

Joined school SQ '88, cricket XI 1891-3, football 1890-3, captain 1892-3.

Left CQ '93. Trinity College, Cambridge, BA. CUAFC 1895-7, captain '96. Played for the OC XI, Amateur Cup 1894 and '97. LSC 1895-7, '99. LCC '95, '98, London FA (1895-8) CUCC 1896-7 Middlesex County wicketkeeper and bat. 1895-99. East India Merchant Sheriff of Calcutta 1916 WW1 Brig-Gen of Indian contracts, Knighted 1917, CSI 1919. Married 1912 Constance.

SYDNEY DARVELL (D)

born 17th May 1874, died 22nd June 1944.

Left CQ '92, Keble College, Oxford, OUAFC '97.

OC XI, Amateur Cup '97, LSC '96-7, '99 LCC '98.

Played for Wales v Ireland and Scotland '97.

HERBERT JOHN BROADBENT (S)

born 27th August 1874, died 26th March 1951.

In the XI 1892, left OQ '92, Jesus College, Cambridge. CUAFC '95, OC XI, Amateur Cup '95.

WILLIAM UDAL TIMMIS (W)

born 1st November 1874 Orchard View, Bickley, Kent, died 24th January 1921.

Buried St Luke's, Bromley.

In the XI 1893-94, left CQ '94 Balliol College, Oxford, BA.

OUAFC '97-8 OC XI Amateur Cup '97 LSC '97, '99 LCC '98 AD '03-6, '08. "He had all the best qualities for that position." Still played in his late 30s.

Corinthians v Bury FC 5th March 1904 (10-3). Toured with them to South Africa 1903, Hungary and Scandinavia 1904, Germany and Holland and Canada and USA in 1906. Secretary of the club 1906-20. Amateur International

Cap 1907; played for Amateurs v Professionals. Oxford representative on FA Council. Barrister. Great War commission in Grenadier Guards (Special Reserve). Married Phyllis Bowater (d. of Sir J. and Lady Frederick)

COPLEY de Lisle HEWITT (B)

born 28th October 1871, died 30th September 1941, Aylesford.

In the football XI 1889-90, left CQ '91, Magdalen College, Oxford, MA. OUAFC XI 1893-95, OCs in 1890s. FA Amateur Cup Finals '94, '95, '97. LSC '94-7, '99, LCC '96, '98. Played for the London FA (1895-8). Barr Inner Temple 1897; W Circuit; Clerk to Commissioner of Taxes, City of London 1916-41. WW1 Sub-Lt RNVR. Helped organised London's weapons' week. JP, High Sheriff of Kent 1929. Governor Maidstone GS and Dover College. Friend of Baden-Powell; County Commissioner Kent Scouts. His baritone voice was outstanding. Married Alice 1905.

EDWARD CHURCH BLISS (g)

born 10th October 1872, died 6th December 1923.

In the football XI 1888-91, left CQ '91, Oriel College, Oxford, MA. OUAFC '92-95, OC XI, FA Amateur Cup '94, '97, LSC '97, '99. Barrister. Married Rosalind 1897.

BERNARD KEDINGTON RODWELL WILKINSON (S)

born 14th November 1872, died 24th January 1918. Brother LR Wilkinson also a goalkeeper who played for England.

School XI 1889-91, left CQ '91, New College, Oxford, MA. Amateur Cup '95, '97 (goal), LSC '95, '97. Married Margaret 1900.

GEORGE SHEPLEY WILSON (L)
born 8th Sepember 1873, died Tunbridge Wells 26th December 1928 Junior and Senior scholar OQ '87.

School XI 1889-91, left CQ '91, Scholarship Pembroke College, Cambridge.

CUAFC '94, OC XI, Amateur Cup '94 (goal) '95, LSC '96, LCC '96, Married Jane, daughter of Henry Melville Scott Malden of Frant (OQ '75) 1907.

GEORGE ARTHUR RICHARDSON (RG)
born 18th November 1872, died 31st January 1933.

Left CQ '91, Caius College, Cambridge, BA. Amateur Cup '94.

EDWARD MELLOR JAMESON (P)
born 27th November 1877, died 25th November 1958.

School XI 1893-6, Capt 1895-6, left CQ '96, Exhibitioner Oriel College, Oxford, MA.

OUAFC '97-00, Capt '00, OC XI, Amateur Cup '97. Curate of St Leonard's, Bridgnorth, 1903 and Assistant Master, Charterhouse, 1906.

Married Valeria only daughter of J.Davidson of Buenos Aires.1903.

DOWNTON CURTIS LEMAN (P)
born 14th October 1868, died 27th April 1942. CQ '87 Trinity College, Cambridge. Solicitor 1893.

Played various Amateur Cup ties. Described in April 94 *Carthusian* as "does not seem to have the knack of putting himself in a good position to take a pass, and so did not shine very much."

Married 1895 Patience Helen.

Between 1893-4 and 1905-6 the OCs entered

DC Leman at school. School archive

the London Football Association Senior Cup. The cup was first played for in 1882-3 and is still competed for. In their first final (1893-4) the OCs lost to the Old Foresters 1-2. In the 1894-5 final the Casuals were defeated 6-1, a year later the Casuals were beaten again 3-1. In 1896-7 against the 3rd Grenadier Guards we lost 2-5 and in 1897-8 we lost to Ilford 1-2 in the semi-final. The following year (1898-9) the OCs beat London Caledonians 2-1 in the final and their last appearance in the competition was in 1905-6 losing to the New Crusaders in the last 16. There is a gap in the record between 1899 and 1905.

C Wreford Brown served on the committee from its inauguration in 1894 until 1905 and a good number of OCs played in the representative team that played against Sheffield, Notts County under what was described as mixed rules, Sheffield rules, London rules and Association rules depending on where the games were played.

Those who played were: JFM Prinsep, WR Page, EH Parry, WKW Jenner, EF Growse, CD Learoyd, J Vintcent, EG Wynyard, AJ Last, GF England, A Amos, PM and AM Walters, AC Nixon, HW Ainger, C Wreford Brown, CD

Hewitt, EH Bray, MH Stanbrough, GO Smith, GC Vassall, WF Fox, A Wade, TW Downing, AG Bower. It is possible that others played but they may not have been entered on the team lists under another club.

In 1930 on 3rd December the London Football Association played Charterhouse school at Godalming and won 12-1. The results show more drubbings annually until 1936 and then from 1947 when JD Tanner played against his old school until 1954. The London FA was prestigious enough to play as a team in the Inter Cities Fairs Cup, a European Cup competition, and of course by this time the team was made up from professionals such as Jack Kelsey, the Arsenal and Wales goalkeeper, and Danny Blanchflower from N. Ireland and Spurs.

THE LONDON CHARITY CUP FINALS

1890-1 lost to the Casuals 2-5 after a 1-1 draw
1892-3 lost to the Crusaders 1-2
1894-5 lost to the London Caledonians 1-3
1895-6 beat Ilford 4-0
1896-7 lost to the Casuals 5-0
1897-8 beat Casuals 3-0
1898-9 lost to Clapton 2-1
1899-1900 lost to Clapton 3-0, after a 1-1 draw

The formation of a London League was regarded as a possibility with all the top named teams having a place in it. This did not emerge for sometime and by the time the league was founded, the OCs were unlikely to commit the club to a competition such as this. Eventually, the OCs joined the Old Boys' league for a while in the 1960s and then, of course, the Arthurian league was formed.

PLAYERS IN OTHER CUPS

WALTER REGINALD KIRBY (RS)

born 5th March 1873, died 19th July 1920.
School XI 1890, left school OQ '90,
LSC '95, '96.

EDGAR MONTGOMERY TRINGHAM (W)

born 2nd August 1873, died 9th February 1949, left school LQ '89,
OC XI, ADC '97, LSC '95-97, LCC '96.

REGINALD JOHN SALT (S)

born 2nd March 1874, died 19th October 1963.
School XI 1890-2, Left CQ '92, New College, Oxford.
OUAFC '93-5.

GERALD WREFORD BROWN (G)

born 19th August 1874, died 11th March 1956 at Eastbourne.
Charterhouse OQ 1888, Football XI 1892, left CQ 1893, Oriel College, Oxford, MA. Ordained 1899, Vicar from 1914-27. WW1 Chaplain to the forces.

CHARLES BLYTH WARD (RG)

born 27th December 1874, died 23rd April 1950.
School XI 1891-93, left CQ '93, Trinity College, Cambridge. CUAFC '96, OC XI, LCC '96, '98.
Married Mary 1899.

BERNARD MURDOCH (L)

born 29th September 1876, died 16th March 1933.
School XI 1894-5, left CQ '95, OC XI, LSC '96.
Married Amy 1904.

ALAN RODERICK HAIG BROWN (H) See War Years chapter.

An Amateur Cup Finalist was **ERNEST BARTON PROUD** (V) who did not play school football but who went back to his home region and played in goal for Bishop Auckland in the Northern league for ten years. Born 6th December 1880, he went to King James I GS and then Charterhouse. He gained three amateur caps v France 1907 and Belgium and Germany 1908 and an amateur cup winners medal in 1900 with two losers medals in 1902 and 1906. He played cricket for Bishop Auckland and Durham county (as did his son) and he became president of both. He was also president of Bishop Auckland FC, CC, the local league and Durham FA. He became a solicitor in 1903 with the family firm, he married Dorothy in 1909 and fought in the Great War with the S. Staffs Rgt. Died Bishop Auckland 15th June 1967.

the arthur Dunn cup and arthurian League 1903–2008

A photo of the Arthur Dunn Cup and FA Cup with 2005–6 team. Back: S Henkes, A Mezzetti, J Dauman, W Young, H Nash, J Golder, F Palley, J Kibbey, H Ellis-Hill. Front: M Bailey, P Leal, W Frost, C Ingham, T Savage, T Burke-Murphy, H Toulson. School archive

By the end of the 19th century it was clear that the OCs would no longer be a force in the major national competitions. Many amateur teams refused to acknowledge the penalty kick and this did not amuse the Football Association. There was an amateur split in this last decade, with teams in the Middlesex and Surrey counties refusing to accept the FA resolution on professional football which stated that all county FAs should admit professional clubs to membership. In 1906 rebellious clubs were branded as outlaws and the Amateur Football Defence Association (now Alliance) was founded in 1907, led by Lord Alverstone (Richard Everard Webster), an OC and Lord Chief Justice of England 1900-17. Alverstone, a fine athlete at school, was president of the AFA from 1907 until 1947. The Casuals stayed true to their amateur beliefs, becoming founder members of the Southern Amateur League, and they launched the AFA Senior Cup which the OCs played in against the Casuals losing 1-3 in the first final. This split lasted until 1914 when the AFA became affiliated to the FA. Needless to say some schools may have drifted towards rugby during this time. Even in the first season of the Arthur Dunn Cup, the FA claimed that the referees being used were not registered and that the Arthur Dunn clubs objected to the FA rule relating to penalty kicks being regarded as contrary to their code of conduct. The FA wanted all the Dunn clubs to be affiliated to them but of course the clubs involved were reluctant to be under such tight control. Thankfully the issue eventually was resolved thanks to the diplomatic skills of the committee.

On 12th October 1901, Arthur Dunn, an Old Etonian, Cambridge Blue in 1883-4 and English international, who played both at forward and full-back, read a newspaper article that suggested that amateur football was on the decline. It was headed "Amateur Clubs and the English Cup". The article read: "It has been said that amateur football is on the decline, that is not what it was, and that its ultimate significance is,

in fact, merely a matter of time." Dunn wrote to an old friend, Norman Malcolmson (OE), his wife's brother, suggesting the formation of an old boys' association. Malcolmson was secretary of the FA cup committee until February 1920, as well as the public school representative on the FA Council. Dunn had a vision of a cup for old boys' teams to enable them to maintain a good standard of competition and the initial tournament took place in 1902-3. Dunn had died prematurely at 41 and never saw his idea come to fruition; nevertheless the cup lives on and celebrated its hundredth year in 2002-3. His grand-daughter, Jane Sawyer, keeps the family link by presenting the cup at each final. At Dunn's memorial service, the OCs and both the school football team and cricket teams sent floral tributes and GO Smith was at his graveside. Dunn had founded Ludgrove School with the idea that he prepared boys to go on to Eton. Smith took over the running of Ludgrove School with WJ Oakley, another famous Salopian and Corinthian footballer. Owing to this commit-

OC XI Joint winners Dunn Cup 1903. OT Norris, Capt. W Simpson (Referee), CH Child, CF Ryder, AR Haig-Brown, TS Rowlandson. Front: OE Wreford Brown, WU Timmis, WFH Stanborough, GO Smith, CW Wreford Brown, MH Stanbrough. School archive

ment, Smith retired from international football.

Charles Wreford Brown, along with Malcolmson and many fine footballers of that time, had the whole competition finalised only 14 weeks after Dunn's death. In its first year the following old boys' teams were represented on the General Committee and played in the competition: Bradfield, Brighton, Charterhouse, Eton, Felsted, Forest, Harrow, Lancing, Malvern, Repton, Rossall, Shrewsbury, Westminster and Winchester

In the first round of the first competition (1902-3) the OCs met Lancing Old Boys and won 3-0. They then played the Felstedians and won 3-1 after a 0-0 draw. This left them with the Reptonians in the semi-final who were beaten 5-2 and then they went on to the first Dunn final.

The original final was played between the OCs and the Old Salopians in a game that resulted in two drawn matches. They therefore shared the cup. In the first match at the Crystal Palace on 28th March before a crowd of about 1000, Captain Simpson was the referee and WG Grace, who was in the stand, saw the Salopians dominate the early game, taking the lead after 10 minutes. Heavy rain and wind blowing down the ground disturbed the flow of play but the skill of players enabled a good fast match to be played. The Salopians went in front through HN Edwards cutting in from the left. An error by the Salopian goalie, who ran out of his goal and missed his kick, allowed the Carthusians to draw level through Haig Brown who, finding an open net, ran the ball into the goal. Before half-time H Morgan-Owen, a Welsh international, got another splendid goal for the Salopians but Ryder's goal, half an hour into the second half, enabled the OCs to equalise at 2-2. Only ten minutes each way of extra time was allowed since both teams had booked dinner at the Café Royal that evening.

The second match was played at Ealing FC "somewhere near Gunnersbury Lane" on the 1st April and ended 2-2 again.

GO Smith got a second of time that he needed and shot into the top right-hand corner of the goal. After the interval the Carthusians scored again very quickly through a swivelled shot by Smith. Craig for Shrewsbury had a significant

effect on the game and goals by Morgan-Owen and Alexander drew the score level in the second half.

The Carthusian team contained nine Blues, including three internationals and the other two players had played "unofficial" internationals against Germany and South Africa. In 1903 ten Carthusians played in the Varsity match; seven for Oxford.

It is a remarkable coincidence that in the 100th match, the same two schools played each other, this time at the Imperial College Sports Ground at Cobham in 2003.

From 1902-3 the OCs won the next three finals. The Salopians were also in the 50th year final losing to the Wykehamists at Tooting and Mitcham FC.

The final of 1903-4 was played at Queen's Club against the Old Rossallians. Smith's two goals brought about the 2-0 win in a game where there was only one foul given by the referee Captain Simpson. The OCs beat the Cholmeleians 4-1, the Salopians 2-0, the Reptonians 5-0 on their way to the final. The team was the same as the previous final.

In 1904-5 the OCs beat the Reptonians at Queen's Club, in a close game again 2-0. Smith and Vassall scored. En route the OCs beat the Bradfield Waifs 4-0, the Foresters 11-2, the Cholmeleians 5-0, and the Malvernians 4-2.

Team: TS Rowlandson, IG Witherington, WU Timmis, WJH Curwen, C Wreford Brown, OT Norris, GC Vassall, WFH Stanbrough, GO Smith, CF Ryder, WW Bruce.

In 1905-6 the OCs met the Old Reptonians again at Queen's Club and the match ended in the same score. Crowds were increasing and so was the number of teams starting in round one. Clearly the "interest in amateur football was not dying out", reported *The Times*.

Team: Rowlandson, Timmis, JCD Tetley, B Tuff, D Grahame, Curwen, RA Bence-Pembroke (1 goal), RH Allen, OL Trenchman (1 goal), IE Snell and Vassall.

The Malvernians (4-1), the Cranleighians (4-

1), the Westminsters (3-3, 3-0) and the Aldenhamians (1-0) fell by the wayside.

The Cup was presented to the winners at the dinner at the Trocadero in the evening after the game.

In 1906-7 the OCs lost their first game ever, in the third round to the Old Brightonians. The game went to 3-3 at full time and 5-4 in extra time. Even the Brighton goalkeeper scored.

Then there were two more victories in 1907-8 beating the Old Wykehamists 2-1 at Queen's Club. Grahame and Vassall scored and the OCs beat the Etonians 13-0, the Johnians 9-1, the Salopians 2-1 and the Malvernians 2-0.

Team: Rowlandson, Timmis, Tetley, B Tuff, Grahame, Curwen, CE Deacon, Trenchman, HK Waller, Snell and Vassall.

IVAN EDWARD SNELL (RL) was born 25th April, played in the football XI 1901-2 and the cricket XI 1903. He won the Public Schools boxing heavyweight title 1903 and he left for Christ Church, Oxford, BA, that summer. Played for OUAFC 1906 and 1907 as a formidable player of 6 feet tall and 15 stone. He played for the Corinthians until 1914, touring Canada and Brazil. AFA XI v France 1911-2 and Bohemia 1913. He also ran the hurdles and threw the hammer. He was called to the Bar 1909, SE Circuit; Great War Bt-Maj The Black Watch: Staff: 3M:W; MC was a magistrate 1925-48. Married Marjory and died Mengeham House, Hayling Island 29th August 1958.

In 1909-10 the final was played at Weybridge Rose FC (described as "pretty if rather inaccessible") located in Walton Road, before a small crowd of only 250 or so. The Rossallians were 0-1 up at half-time. In the second half the OCs came good to run out winners 2-1 with goals from Curwen and Vassall to take the cup for the fifth time in eight years.

They beat the Westminsters 4-1, the Aldenhamians 2-0, the Reptonians 5-2 on the way.

Team: Rowlandson, Tetley, RLL Bradell, Rev JG Birch, Grahame, JB Bickersteth, AA Tyler, Curwen, RM Weeks, Vassall and LR Burrows.

Both teams celebrated as usual at the Trocadero restaurant, the annual post final venue.

The 1910-1 final was contested by the OCs again at Ealing with Lord Alverstone watching. The Reptonians were deserving victors 1-0.

Play ceased as war began.

In this period the committee decided that only old boys of the school could play in the competition following the success of Claude Ashton who influenced the 1920 final on behalf of the Wykehamists.

Three more finals were won by the OCs between 1920-1 and 1922-3. In 1921 the Aldenhamians were defeated 2-0 at Queen's Club. Williams and Reiss scored.

Team: HCD Whinney, AG Bower, JSF Morrison, P Fraser, AGH Butcher, J Pollock, RT Thorne, JG Williams, PQ Reiss, HRH Williams, RH Whalley.

The Wellingburians (7-2), Cholmeleians (4-1), the Reptonians (3-1) were beaten on the way.

JOHN SF MORRISON (W) was born 17th April 1892 and died 28th January 1961 at Farnham.

1st XI cricket captain (wicket-keeper) and 1st XI football in his last year at school, leaving 1911. Trinity College, Cambridge BA, where he gained a triple Blue with CUCC 1912, 1914, scoring 233 n.o. v MCC in two and three-quarter hours, and after the war he captained the XI in 1919. Football 1913-14, also captain 1919. Teamed up with AG Bower as a formidable full-back line up. Played for Sunderland FC under the captaincy of Charles Buchan. Massive, fit and fearless, he was a law unto himself. Buchan told how he was allowed a quart of beer before the game and at half-time. As a Corinthian defender he played a major role in the defeat of Blackburn Rovers in the FA Cup on 12th January 1924.

He gained a golf Blue in 1919, was made a Major and was awarded the RFC, RNAS and RAF M, DFC with Bar as well as Italian Silver

JFS Morrison at school. School archive

Team: HM Ward-Clarke, AG Bower, JSF Morrison, GW Shilcock, BCA Patchitt, P Rucker, R Thorne Thorne, JG Williams, HRH Williams, BG Bearman, DLM Thompson.

In 1922-3 the Malvernians were beaten 5-1 at the Spotted Dog, Forest Gate (the home of Claton FC) with HRH Williams completing a hat trick. JG Williams and Bearman completed the tally.

The Reptonians (2-1), Wellingburians (3-2), Westminsters (6-0) were beaten on the way.

Team: HM Ward-Clarke, AG Bower, JSF Morrison, FE Powell, GW Shilcock, BCA Patchitt, IAW Gilliat, JG Williams, HRH Williams, BG Bearman, RH Whalley.

A quiet period occurred until the era of GT Hollebone, who was a close friend of the Dunn family. Encouraged by Mrs Helen Dunn to help organise OC football, he soon brought more success for the club with a win in 1935-6. This campaign began with a draw against the powerful Aldenhamians 2-2 and in the replay the OCs

and Bronze medals for valour. He played for Somerset cricket 1920 and for Northumberland, was an Amateur international footballer v Wales in 1920. Played golf for England in 1930 v Ireland and was the Amateur Golf Champion of Belgium 1929. Golf architect. Group Captain in the WW2 with the RAFVR.

Married Elizabeth first and then Gwendoline 1938.

The following year, 1922, the Old Aldenhamians were beaten 2-1 at the Army Sports Ground, Leyton. Williams opened the scoring but the opposition drew level and RJ Thorne Thorne scored the winner, running from the half-way line, beating three men. A crowd of a 1000 watched him secure the victory.

The Malvernians (6-2), Reptonians (6-1), Wellingburians (2-0) were also beaten.

Gerry Hollebone. School archive

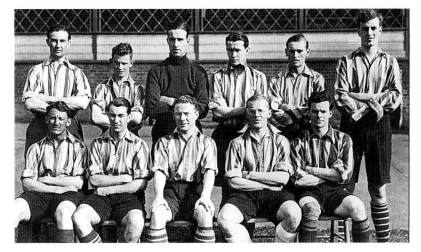

Cup winning team 1936. David Roy and Replay Publishing

OLD CARTHUSIANS
Winners 1936

(Back Row)
J C Moss, J L Field,
H M Mitton, J G Dunbar,
S C Gillchrest, R M Hollis.

(Front Row)
D A Pott, W F Moss,
G T Hollebone, K P S Caldwell,
A J Wreford Brown.

were 0-4 down at half-time. A change of tactics (putting the Moss brothers down the wings) left the opposition in their wake winning 5-4. After that the Wellingburians (3-0) and Cholmeleians (5-1) were beaten.

The OCs went on to win at the Crystal Palace over the Bradfieldians 2-0 with JG Dunbar scoring two goals, one in each half. *The Times* reported that Dunbar would "hurl himself cheerfully and to no little effect against anyone or anything between himself and the ball". The *Morning Post* began its report thus:

> Although the Old Carthusians were clearly fast enough to have run off with the Arthur Dunn Cup before the match without fear of being caught by the Old Bradfieldians, they preferred to put themselves to the trouble of taking the trophy by lawful means after all, it is as well; to have an alternative scheme in reserve, and it would have been a pity rashly to disturb the halcyon charm that a precocious March had bestowed upon the scene of such a stern if bloodless conflict, graced by the presence of Mrs Arthur Dunn.

ANTHONY J WREFORD BROWN (G) was born 26th October 1912, died 2nd September 1997.

At school OQ 1925 – SQ 1931. Head of House, Captain 1st XI football and cricket.

Won Amateur Championships Eton Fives (Kinnaird Cup) with T R Garnett (OQ '28).

Worcester College, Oxford, MA. First-class cricket for Oxford and Sussex cricket in 1934.

Assistant master Charterhouse SQ 1935–CQ 1976. WW2 Capt 60th rifles (Q's Westminster) and one of the first to cross the Rhine into Germany. Housemaster Weekites LQ 1954–LQ 1970, retired CQ 1976. He was a member of the

AJ Wreford Brown. School archive

OLD CARTHUSIANS
Winners 1939

(Back Row)
E H Ades, A J Wreford Brown,
J B Lyon, A R Woods,
P L Richards, S C Gillchrest,

(Front Row)
J L Field, K P S Caldwell,
G T Hollebone (Capt.),
W F Moss, R M Hollis.

Cup winning team 1939. David Roy and Replay Publishing

1936 Dunn side and he also scored in the 1939 win. After the War he joined Brooke Hall and as a master he played in victorious Dunn finals in 1947 (scoring a goal) and 1949. Founder member of Jim Swanton's Arabs CC in 1935. Coached football Charterhouse 1946-52 and the cricket team with PBH May in 1947-8. His football teams were particularly good at the end of the 40s and he wrote: "It is possible for boys to take games too seriously and also too lightly...football and cricket are sociable gaieties, yet good education as well like fiddling and dancing." OC Golf. Married Christine. He had two older brothers.

His father was the famous Charles (one of five brothers) who played his last game of football against Anthony's Gownboys at the age of 61.

His uncle was Oswald E.

Goals from Wreford Brown and Field led to the 1938-9 win at the Hurlingham Club beating the Cholmeleians 2-1 on a very windy day. Gerry Hollebone was once again the captain. En route the OCs beat the Foresters 3-0, the Wykehamists 2-1, Bradfieldians 1-0 after 2-2.

The draw for the 1939-40 cup was made but the war stopped further competition and the draw was not used until 1946-7. The com-

TOP: *ACTION IN THE GOALMOUTH DURING THE 1939 FINAL.*

Programme and photo of 1939 final. Replay Publishing

OLD CARTHUSIANS
Winners 1947

(Back Row)
D P Rowat, F A Peet,
H P Cunningham, A K Hughes,
J G Larking, G L Howard.

(Front Row)
J D P Tanner, K P S Caldwell,
R M Hollis (Capt.),
A J Wreford Brown, J C Daukes.

Cup winning team 1947. David Roy and Replay Publishing

mittee reformed in 1945 and was pleased to hear from the Old Boys that they were happy to continue the competition, which for so long has kept the spirit of the amateur alive in the public schools.

In the post-war period, the final was won in 1946-7 at Lloyds Bank, Beckenham beating the Reptonians 3-1, with two goals from the right-winger John Tanner and AJ Wreford Brown. Tanner was very flexible and a tactic was to switch him to centre-forward during the match. He was able to keep his shots low and he had an

1949 Team with cup. Hollis is holding the cup. David Roy and Replay Publishing

OLD CARTHUSIANS
Winners 1949

(Back Row)
D L Benke, P C G Larking,
P B H May, V R Goodridge,
A Hastings, K R Dolleymore.

(Front Row)
M J Rimell, A J Wreford Brown,
R M Hollis (Capt.), J G Larking,
P Bennett.

Cup winning team 1949. David Roy and Replay Publishing

unerring eye for goal. This helped beat the Aldenhamians 3-0, the Wykehamists 4-2 and the Salopians 5-0 in the first three rounds.

John Daukes later became Clerk to the Charterhouse Governing Body. He lived in a house called "Chaucers" on the Seale Road and later that house was bought and lived in by the Corney family, the son Chris becoming a Duckite and footballer, in 2004.

Playing at that time was:
FRANK ANTONY PEET (G) who was born 5th May 1922, died 27th August 2003

In school between S 36-S 41, WW2 Capt RE. Brasenose College, Oxford, BA, OUAFC Blue 1947, Fives 1946 and Pegasus. LSE, Colonial service, Gray's Inn 1952 Solicitor. 1964 married June.

In 1948-9 at Tooting and Mitcham FC, Sandy Lane, there was a win over the Salopians 2-0, even without Tanner. This was an unattractive final despite the pedigree of the two rivals. Too many individuals trying to impress with heavy tackling meant there were few cohesive moments. "But everyone enjoyed the hearty scrambles for the ball and it was all great fun." Despite Ken Shearwood, the great Oxford University and Pegasus FC centre-half, moving forward, the Salopians were not able to crack open the Carthusian defence.

On the way to the final the OCs beat the Lancing OBs (3-1), the Wykehamists gave a walk-over and then Brentwood 5-1. Larking and Goodridge scored the goals. *Team:* see above.

RALPH MALLORY HOLLIS (G) was born 11th October 1916 and died 3rd May 1981.

Joined Charterhouse OQ 1930 until CQ 35. He was a school monitor and played 1st XI cricket and football for two years each. He went on to be an Exhibitioner at Brasenose College, Oxford gaining his MA. He played in the 1939 Dunn final and his motto was "they shall not pass". He captained the team to three Dunn victories (1947, '49 and '51) after the Second World War having previously been up to Oxford winning a Blue in 1935-7. He resuscitated the OCFC after the war "virtually single-handed". He had a fearsome sliding tackle from full-back. In a memorable game against the Royal Marines the crowd mimicked our calls adding "right Cecil, yours Percival!!" It was not until the OCs were leading 9-0 that the frenetic cries turned to bored groans of "declare". He served during WW2 as a Lt in the RNVR. He became a Solicitor in 1947. Later he was a member Charterhouse Governing Body. Married 1952 Elsie Lorna.

PETER BH MAY (S) was born 31st December

John May. School archive

Peter May. School archive

On Big Ground v Repton 1950 semi-final. David Roy and Replay Publishing

1929 at Reading and died 27th December 1994 Dunsfold, near Godalming.

Joined school SQ 1947. Went up to Pembroke College, Cambridge BA. Played CUCC 1950-2 and football 1949-52 (captain 51-2). Played OC football including three consecutive Dunn finals winning in 1949 and 51. Surrey CCC 1950, Capt 1957-62 (county champions 52-8), England 1951-61, Captain 41 times v Australia, W Indies, S Africa, Pakistan, India and NZ. Lloyds 1953. Married Virginia 1959.

He played for the cricket 1st XI at the age of fourteen and he won Blues at Cambridge for both sports. Of course he played for Surrey and England, captaining his country to 21 wins in 41

tests post war. He later became a test selector 1965-8, then chairman of selectors 1982 and a second spell in 1985. CBE 1981. President MCC 1980-1.

Peter's brother John was a committed footballer too and John's son Charles was captain of the school XI and played some OC football in the 1980s.

John Tanner, who could turn on a sixpence and was a class apart, May and his brother John (JWH), Derek GW Goodliffe (who played for Millwall after the war) and Tim RH Savill, were

ABOVE: *1951, G R Scott (Captain, Old Wellingburians), Bill Chivers (referee) and P Bennett (Captain, Old Carthusians), waiting for the penny to drop.*

RIGHT: *Goalmouth action during the 1951 Final.*

1951 *Action from final.* David Roy and Replay Publishing

the very back-bone of the club in this era. John Larking was a veteran midfielder playing alongside the terrier-like Wreford Brown. Geoff Howard had become a fearsome full-back whilst Jim Prior contributed that element of reliability that would characterise his political life.

It was in this period that the famous Pegasus football team was formed with players such as Ken Shearwood of Lancing and John Tanner.

In the 1950s the OC Club had an arrangement with Hampstead Cricket Club to use their ground from September to March. This lasted for 20 years until the club moved to the school. The club eventually agreed to have a formal constitution and HCD Whinney was selected as the

first president. Jo J Ullman (W) and Simon JE Easton (G) were the driving forces behind the modernisation of the OC Club.

In 1950-1 at Tooting again, the Wellingburians were beaten 4-2, when the "wind and a light ball, of an unexpected orange tint, reduced the masters of the game to mediocrity". Savill (2), Tanner and Williams scored in a game that was exciting to the final minutes. Peter Bennett was a metaphoric brick wall in goal whilst John Larking was a dextrous winger, who later "retired" to become a goalkeeper.

The route to the final included the Brentwoods 5-0, the Salopians 6-3 and the Reptonians 4-1. Jim Prior, later to become a member of

Cup winning team 1951. David Roy and Replay Publishing

OLD CARTHUSIANS
Winners 1951

(Back Row)
J W H May, A G Williams,
M J Rimell, G Clarke,
J M L Prior, T R H Savill.

(Front Row)
P B H May, R M Hollis,
P Bennett (Capt.), J D P Tanner,
J G Larking.

Cup winning team 1951. David Roy and Replay Publishing

Parliament, scored all four at Repton and was paraded around Euston Station on a luggage trolly when the OCs arrived back in London

The next victory was in 1953-4 against the Salopians at Tooting and Mitcham, winning 2-0. Savill and Whinney scored and the cup was presented by Arthur Dunn's daughter Mrs Andrew Shirley. The Lancing OBs (0-0, 6-0), Westminsters (4-3), Reptonians (3-0) were overcome on the way. *Team*: See below.

As Tanner elegantly slipped past the age of 30, he was still playing but he found injury a problem and this was not surprising considering his ability to accelerate. Peter May was drawn to cricket inevitably but his young brother John carried on the family tradition supported by the robust Derek Goodliffe. Nick Fair was at full-back, with Graham Clarke and Howard there was a solidarity in front of the brave Larking in goal. Mike Whinney was to become Bishop of Southwark. Sadly David Miller missed this game, having been injured playing for Pegasus the previous week.

There was another gap in the successes until 1961-2 at Wealdstone, when there was a win over the Malvernians 2-1. Savill put the OCs into the lead, Malvern equalised late on to force extra time and Jakobson settled it as the Carthusians had more in the tank at the end of the game. The extra period brought the best football of the match and Lees shot only to see the goalie mishandle and Jakobson was on hand to bring the cup back to Charterhouse.

Having the best record in the competition, this was a good all round team led by DB Lees, who had played for the Army in his National Service. Lees and his brother JM formed a for-

Cup winning team 1954. David Roy and Replay Publishing

OLD CARTHUSIANS
Winners 1954

(Back Row)
A G Williams, M H D Whinney,
J N Fair, M G Varcoe,
G Clarke, J W H May.

(Front Row)
J D P Tanner, D H G Goodliffe,
T R H Savill (Capt.),
J G Larking, G L Howard.

Cup winning team 1962. David Roy and Replay Publishing

OLD CARTHUSIANS
Winners 1962

(Back Row)
J M Lees, D S Mace,
A T C Allom, R F Buckley,
J N Garrow, A P Blumer.

(Front Row)
D H Goodliffe, F E Kung,
D B Lees (Capt.), T R H Savill,
T R Jakobson.

midable partnership and the vociferous and gigantic Ants Allom in goal made for an impressive core to the team. Jeremy Tomlinson (Old Reptonians) wrote that "Allom kept goal but though back trouble curtailed his football career his ominous presence could be felt from the touchline instead." Big Ground had a wonderful playing surface and many a full-back trained in Third Division North methods would end up in the beech hedge near the touchline attempting to tackle a tricky and fast winger.

Team: See above.

D.B. LEES (L) was born 23rd November 1936.
Played in the school XI 1953-5, captained the OC XI team in 1962 and played for the Army during National Service.

During the 1962-3 season the Arthurian League was started but fixtures were not completed due to the dreadful winter conditions between December and March. Charterhouse eventually beat Westminster in the first round and succumbed to the Malvernians including George Chesterton in his only match for the OMs in the Dunn. He was co-opted at the last minute while he was eating house lunch with the boys. The game went to 3-3 at full-time 4-3 to the Carthusians but late goals brought a 5-4 defeat, much to George's relief.

Cup winning team 1977. David Roy and Replay Publishing

OLD CARTHUSIANS
Winners 1977

(Back Row)
M Herbert-Smith (sub),
J M Bennett,
S J E Easton, H M Martin,
J D Holder, K R Ellis.

(Front Row)
A D Marks, I A Stewart,
A Adomakoh, L K Walton (Capt.),
P C Godby, C Comninos.

Louis Adomakoh v the School. School archive

LOUIS ADOMAKOH (R) was born 25th April 1957 in Accra, Ghana. Louis was at Charterhouse 1970-OQ 1974. He played in the 1st XI LQ 1972-OQ 74 and for the Public Schools XI 1973-5. Went to Downing College, Cambridge 1975-78 BA law. CUAFC 1977, he was the first Ghanaian to be awarded a Blue. Louis was a stalwart of the OC XIs for the next 20 or so years, still playing and scoring at the age of 50 in 2007. Arthurian League representative XI. He was also a fine athlete and decent cricketer. There were four brothers and a sister, all of whom attended Charterhouse and all very good at a variety of sports. He worked for Unilever and in a small firm later becoming a director of his own training company.

There was a further period of quiet until 1976-7 where the Dunn final was played at Crystal Palace against the Brentwoods beating them 3-0 after the Brentwoods missed a penalty early on. Lee Walton, Bennett (pen) and James Holder scored the goals. On the way the OCs beat the Bradfieldians 6-1, Lancing OBs 6-1 and the Wykehamists 5-1; pretty convincing stuff with seventeen goals in the bag with only three conceded. AAY (Louis) Adomakoh (R) started his incredible and illustrious career as an OC footballer.

Simon Easton, Howard Martin, Holder, Keith Ellis, Peter Godby and Carlo Comninos all sent boys to the school and who all contributed to school football in a significant way.

In 1981-2 the OCs won the final at Dulwich Hamlet FC beating the Malvernians 3-0. Alan Stewart, a Leeds United trialist, and Peter Godby were part of a free scoring team and they had also only conceded three goals in the cup that year, thanks to Simon Easton's marshalling of the defence in front of the bearded goalkeeper Keith Ellis. Richard Oulton, Hugo Pratt and Godby scored in the final. They beat the Ardinians 7-0, Reptonians 7-1 (4-0 up after twenty minutes) and the Brentwoods 2-1. This was a double year, for the 1st XI also won the league title. *Team: See over.*

LEE K WALTON (H) was born 25th April 1952.

He captained the OC XI in 1977 and 1982 which was the Double Year (also won Argonaut

OLD CARTHUSIANS
Winners 1982

(Back Row)
I A Stewart, T C R Whalley,
K R Ellis, M W G Doggart,
G D T Pride, J D Holder (sub),
H E Pratt.

(Front Row)
M G Herbert-Smith, L K Walton,
R A C Oulton (Capt.),
P C Godby, S J E Easton.

Cup winning team 1982. David Roy and Replay Publishing

trophy). His father was Kent Walton, the ITV wrestling commentator. This was a year when the OCs also won the Cricketer Cup and the Halford Hewitt Golf competition for Old Boys. Only the Reptonians have equalled this feat.

The cup was won in 2000-1 at the Imperial College Sportsground, Cobham, beating the Bradfieldians, a first division side, 4-1. The veteran Jason Golder held the back line and even Louis Adomakoh, well into his 40s, had a spell on the pitch, enabling him to hold a record of playing in four decades of Dunn football. A Cambridge Blue, Public Schools representative and legend in Old Boys' football, Louis appeared in the 1977,

1984, 1991 and 2001 finals. He was still playing regularly in 2003-4, as was Golder in 2005-6.

Golder, Mitten, Nash and Webb scored.

On the way: Beat the Salopians 2-1, Witleians 4-2, Westminsters 4-2. *Team:* See below.

In 2001 Edward J Rees (L) who played for the Combined Universities, captained the winning Dunn team with Graham Brooke (S), an Oxford Blue and university captain. Duncan Austin (H) also won his Blue with Brooke.

Matthew Bailey (V) also captained an ISFA Cup Final team in 2000, this time at Filbert Street, Leicester City against Shrewsbury School, losing 0-1. He played his first Dunn final in his first year of leaving school and appeared again in 2003, 2006 and 2008.

The 2005-6 season proved to be a very suc-

OLD CARTHUSIANS
Winners 2001

(Back Row)
L J Webb, H Nash,
M J Mitten, W R Frost,
R Taylor, M T Bailey,
J A Jarvis.

(Front Row)
T E B Walker. A A Y Adomakoh,
J C Golder, E J Rees (Capt.),
N P Waters, G R C Brooke,
D C M Stern.

Cup winning team 2001. David Roy and Replay Publishing

Centenary Cup Final team, 2003. Back: H Nash, JE Green, WJS Clark, MT Bailey, R Tayler, PSS Leal, MJ Mitten, Front: DCM Stern, EJ Rees, JC Golder, TEB Walker, S Henkes, GRC Brooke, AJ Viall.
David Roy and Replay Publishing

cessful one for the OCs as Henry Nash (g) led his squad to the premiership title and to the Arthur Dunn Cup Final. In the league it was a hot contest all season with the Etonians, the league and cup holders, and the Harrovians. By 18th March there was a head to head with Harrow on a blustery pitch "W", the OC pitch, a week after the Carthusians had won their way into the Dunn final by beating the Haileyburians on Big Ground 4-3. The Harrovians went in front early on but a Beckham-like free kick by Alan Mezzetti and three further goals forced Harrow to give in. So with the league title under their belts the OCs met the Old Westminsters on the Imperial College ground at Udney Park, Teddington on Saturday 1st April at 3pm. This was a particularly auspicious occasion for David Roy, a long servant of the Arthurian League and Cup and a former star for the OWs. His son Edward was in the team enjoying a good game

personally and the league one side gave the Carthusians a number of concerns, especially in the first half with the wind at their backs. It was, however, the captain who opened the scoring for the OCs half way through the first half after an excellent interchange with Matt Bailey on the left. Nash pivoted onto his trusty right foot and shot, hitting the underside of the bar. Everyone played on as the goalie, veteran Jim Kershen, scrambled the ball clear, but the linesman Mr PG Holliman adjudged the ball to have crossed the line (1966 style) and so the deadlock was broken. James Kibbey (g) in goal made three crucial saves as the pinks pressed but another opportunist goal by Nash in the late second half took the drive out of Westminster and the Charterhouse old boys ran home confidently, to win their twentieth final in 26 attempts. The man of the match might have been Kibbey who had not played in goal above 1st tics level and a couple

Action from Centenary Cup Final. David Roy and Replay Publishing

*Members of Committee in Brooke Hall before Arsenal game.
J Merrick (committee), P Hill-Wood (guest), D Miller (President),
N Leale (Chairman).* School archive

To celebrate the 125th year since the Old Carthusians Football Club won the FA Cup, a match was played on a verdant Big Ground on 29th April 2006.

On a beautiful sunny afternoon, an Arsenal Youth XI coached by Steve Bould provided the opposition. The young Gunners contained six international representatives including Armand Traore from France and captain Mark Randall an England U17 cap, who recently both played for the Arsenal 1st XI.

The Old Carthusians withstood some early pressure on a superb pitch and, after 15 minutes, playing an excellent series of passes involving Pedro Leal and Matt Bailey, captain Henry Nash was put in to score a fine goal. More pressure from the Arsenal team did not dent a determined Carthusian defence and with goalkeeper Will Young in outstanding form and veteran Jason Golder, in his last game for the XI, never faltering, the Arsenal boys could not get on terms. In the second half, however, pressure eventually told and two scrappy goals allowed the visitors to sneak ahead. Even after this there were two goal-line clearances at the Arsenal end.

A crowd of over 500 enjoyed a game played in the best spirits, overseen by ex FIFA referee, Ray Lewis. Guests invited to witness this match included Peter Hill-Wood the Arsenal chairman, Barry Bright on behalf of the FA, Jane and Peter Phillips from Godalming Town FC and Ken Shearwood of Lancing College, a member of the amateur club Pegasus, famed for their cup exploits in the 1950s. Special guest was Arthur Milton, the last amateur to play for the full England XI. He was also a first class cricketer who played for his country.

David Miller OC, the famous sports writer, was largely responsible for arranging the event with club Chairman Nick Leale and his committee giving him support.

of senior house matches, but David Miller, the club president, picked out Seb Henkes as the rock on which the victory was founded. Jason Golder received a silver tankard to commemorate his 50th and last Dunn game as he promised his lovely family that he would retire from the 1st XI circuit.

Team: JM Kibbey, T Burke-Murphy, JC Golder, HA Toulson, JA Dauman, CGC Ingham, AWJ Mezzetti, MT Bailey, S Henkes, PSS Leal, H Nash with WR Frost, T Savage and RP Burke-Murphy as subs.

James Kibbey had never played school team football to any serious level but had appeared in the Duckite House team, even in a house final. There were seven 1st XI captains in the starting XI. This squad just about played for the whole of the season and this continuity no doubt contributed to their success. Ross Tayler played the odd game in goal and Humphrey Ellis-Hill also joined the squad.

Charles Ingham (W) captained the ISFA Six-a-side Cup winning team in 2003. He arrived with minutes to spare before the final, having been held up by traffic on the A3. Despite his lateness, typically, without any preparation, he was included in the starting eleven and gave an athletic performance on the right and left side of the Carthusian' five man midfield.

OLD CARTHUSIANS
Runners up 1991

(Back Row)
A Viall, J Kemball,
N Waters, J Aubrey,
M Kerevan, R Faulkner,
C May.

(Front Row)
M G Herbert-Smith,
A Adomakoh, J Golder (Capt.),
K R Ellis, R A C Oulton.

Runners up 1991. David Roy and Replay Publishing

In 2006 and 2008 the OC 1st XI was invited to play in the Greenland Cup, a pre-season tournament, invented to bring the winning teams from the various "genuine" amateur leagues in the south-east.

If the 2005-6 season was a successful one for the OCs, it was surpassed in 2007/08 following on from the school's success that season each of the OC teams competing the Arthurian League won its respective division; the OC 1st team led by Henry Nash won the Premier division; the OC 2nd XI, captained by Will Frost(W), won the 2nd Division and the OC 3rd team under James Kibbey(g) won Division 4. To add to this the OC 1st XI completed its second double in three years by carrying off the Arthur Dunn Cup and the Veterans' team, led by Nick Waters made it a clean sweep by picking up the Derrick Moore Trophy. The presentation dinner at the Imperial Hotel, Russell Square was a great night for the Carthusians and was made all the sweeter when the club, unexpectedly, picked up the Bill Chivers Sportsmanship Trophy into the bargain. The League victory had been a tense affair: although the Old Carthusians eventually won the league with a record number of points, they were pushed all the way by Old Brentwoods. Three matches from the end of the season the OCs suffered their only defeat at Brentwood and were left needing four points from their last two

matches to be assured of success. A nervy match on Lessington against Old Westminsters saw the team 0-1 down at half-time despite having had all the match. Second half goals from Charlie Ingham and Patrick Millington Buck (g) secured an important victory and left just one point to be gained against already relegated Bradfieldians a fortnight hence. In between was the small matter of the Arthur Dunn final, also against Old Brentwoods. As two years previously the final was held at the Imperial College sports ground in Teddington on April 19th. A healthy crowd witnessed a tight game where the vigorous tackling of the Old Brentwoods left little room for the Old Carthusians to play with any sort of freedom or flair. The OCs were gifted an early goal when the Old Brentwoods' goalkeeper allowed a fairly tame Matt Bailey free-kick to slip through his hands and into the net. The game then deteriorated into a war of attrition with the Carthusians resisting all Brentwoods' attempts to muscle themselves into the game. Mid-way through the second half Matt Bailey had the ball in the net again after Jamie Cameron (g) had twice hit the woodwork, but the effort was ruled offside. Then, on the stroke of full time Old Brentwoods were inches wide with a free header following a free kick and the Carthusians breathed a sigh of relief and were able to celebrate taking the Arthur Dunn Cup once again. Bouyed by this success, the Old Carthusians were never going to let the chance of the "double" disappear against already relegated Old Bradfieldians and, on the following Saturday, they clinched the Premier Lague title with a comfortable 4-0 victory.

The OCs have been losing finalists in six finals, the first one being in 1911 which was held at Ealing with Lord Alverstone (OC) looking on. Alverstone became the first president of the A.F.A. A loss to Repton 0-1 was the result.

Other defeats were in 1929 losing to the Wykehamists 0-3 at the Crystal Palace, 1950 to the Wykehamists 1-3 at Tooting with Peter May scoring the OC goal, in 1984 at Dulwich 0-2 to Lancing, 1991 to Repton after a drawn final 1-1 at Motspur Park with Mark Kerevan scoring the OC goal. Then there was a goalless first half but the OCs were totally outplayed 0-4 in the second. In 2003, the centenary final was lost 1-2 to the Salopians after Matthew Mitten put the OCs ahead.

The captain of this defeated team was Tom Walker (W) who in 1993 captained the ISFA Cup Final team, playing at Craven Cottage, Fulham, against Forest School, losing after extra time (2-2) on penalties.

Semi-finals were lost in 1909, 1928, 1953, 1955, 1957, 1966, 1967, 1971, 1974, 1981, 1986, 1989, 1994, 1996.

The record at the centenary in 2003 was: played 241, won 149, ranking second to the Malvernians in success. GO Smith scored 5 goals in finals with HRH Williams getting the hat trick in 1923. There have been 39 semi-final appearances.

THE ARTHURIAN LEAGUE

This league for Old Boys was founded in 1961 and in that time the Old Carthusians have won the following titles:

Premier League (once First Division)
1978-9 (also won Argonaut trophy), 1981-2 ("double" and won Argonaut Trophy), 1987-8, 2005-6 won by OC I (including the "double") and 2007-8 (including the 'double'.

The Vic Merrett Memorial Cup (played between the Arthurian and Old Boys' League winners) 2006 won by OC I for the first time.

Division Two
1986-7 won by the OC II and 2007-8

Division Three
1977-8, 1981-2, 1983-4 won by the OC II

Arthur Dunn Cup Winners 2008. Back row: J Cameron A Mezzetti C Ingham P Millington Buck W Young W Clark F Palley R Griston. Front row: T Walker S Henkes H Nash (capt) M Bailey J Dauman H Toulson

Division Four
1999-00 won by the OC III and 2007-8
Division Five
1978-9, 1985-6, 1998-9 won by the OC III.
The Junior League Cup (the equivalent of the Dunn for lower XIs)
1993-4, 1999-00 won by the OC II and 2003-4 won by the OC III.
Derrick Moore Veterans Trophy (Over 35s)
1992-3, 1994-5. 2002-3, 2003-4 winners and 2007-8
2004-5, 2005-6 Runners up
Bill Chivers Sportsmanship Trophy
1988-9, 1995-6, 2001-2, 2003-4 and 2007-8 won by the club.

The OCFC continues to play with three senior teams weekly based at the school for home games using the Peter May Pavilion and the Long Room bar as their club house. Training takes place in Battersea Park on a Wednesday evening. The Veterans XI play in the Derrick Moore Cup, an annual knock-out cup with a plate. An Under 23 team has been established to attract recent leavers to the club, playing friendlies against Arthurian teams. The OCs play five XIs against the school early in OQ and provide a team against a Leavers XI in March as the season and Long Quarter closes.

CHAPTER 9

the war years 1914-1945

By 1914, many Carthusians were recorded as having left the school before the end of their planned education, to join the war effort. School football fixtures were unreliable and more military teams came to play – such as the 60th Rifles.

Nearly one thousand Carthusians lost their lives in the tragedies of the Great War and the Second World War. They are remembered by the monument of the Memorial Chapel. Six of these young men, who were particularly good footballers, played for the Corinthian FC. Two of them, John Fosdick and John Tetley, were travelling in August 1914 with twelve other Corinthian tour footballers on a ship, the Aragon, to Brazil when, on landing at Pernambuco, the first main landfall on the continent, they heard of the European conflict. Along with two other tour members, Cockburn and Wilkinson, they immediately left the ship and returned home to fight. They soon perished in the trenches.

JH Fosdick. School archive

JOHN HYLAND FOSDICK (g) The only son of Frederick of Ipswich and Alice Fosdick of Cullenswood, Eastbourne. Born 2nd March 1895, he joined the school under Harold Crabtree's Girdlestoneites and he went up to Pembroke College, Cambridge where he gained a Blue as a freshman in September 1913. He played three times against the Corinthians and for the combined Oxbridge XI. He was a freshman cricketer in 1914. From his old corps, the CUOTC in which he held a commission (13th June 1914),

he served with the South Wales Borderers while waiting to join the 7th Battalion, Rifle Brigade in which he was promoted to lieutenant. Helping to defend the Hooge crater in Flanders created on 19th July – a tunnel had been dug previously and filled with explosives under the German lines. On 30th July the Germans tried to regain the position using flame throwers for the first time. Fierce fighting occurred but the British troops eventually regained the crater. Fosdick was killed by shrapnel wounds to the head, in action on 31st July 1915. He was 20 years old. He lies in the Lijssenthoek military cemetery (I.A.5), and is listed on memorials in All Saints Church, Eastbourne.

In 1917 **JOHN CD TETLEY**, a Daviesite, was also killed in action at Houlthurst Forest, Belgium, on 9th October 1917. This was during the

A variety of caps and badges won by Tetley for OCs, OUAFC, AFA, Corinthians. Tetley family archive

build up to the Third Battle of Ypres (Passchendale) when he was part of the advance on the ridge. His body was found and his personal effects included a cigarette case, damaged watch and Freemason's certificate. His memorial is at Tyne Cot. He was born on 11th April 1885, first son of Frank from Buenos Aires, and he joined the school in OQ 1899; left Summer 1903. He went up to Oriel College, Oxford, gained an MA, played football for the university between 1906-7, played Corinthians, for the AFA and then became a solicitor. Captain in the 3rd Grenadier Guards. He played right back against Manchester United in the famous 11-3 victory in November 1904. He married wife Sybil Edwards of Novington Manor, Sussex 1912. His great-grandson played in 1st XI goal 2005-6.

WILFRED JH CURWEN (g) was born 14th April 1883, son of John M and died on the 9th May 1915, being killed in action at Ypres, Belgium. His memorial is shown on Panel 6 and 8, Ypres, Menin Gate. He was an only son.

He was in the cricket XI 1901-2, football XI 1900-1, rackets pair 1901-2 and he left school CQ 1902 to get a BA at Magdalen College, Oxford. He played for the OUAFC 1901-2 and 05-6 and also for OUCC 1906, Surrey CCC 1909, was Captain of the AFA English XI v Bohemia 1908 and 09. Was in the 2nd VB Royal Fusiliers in 1900 and retired 1905. In the Great War, he chose to be a Capt in the 6th Battalion attached to the 3rd Royal Fusiliers.

He was another family member of the Wreford Brown's, a brother-in-law who played in the first five Dunn finals.

OSWALD ERIC WREFORD BROWN (G) was born the sixth son of

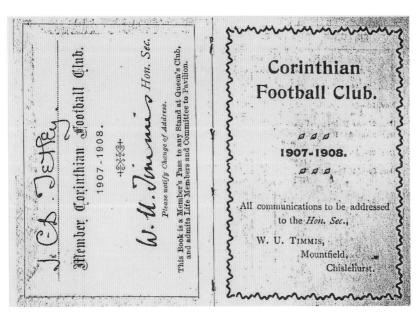

Tetley's Corinthian FC membership card 1907-8. Tetley family archive

WJH Curwen at school. School archive

William at Clifton, Bristol on 21st July 1877. Brother of Charles. In WW1 Capt 9th Northumberland Fusiliers, he died of wounds suffered on

July 4th 1916 three days later in action near Corbie, Albert on the Somme. Buried Plot 1, Row B, Grave 48, Corbie communal cemetery extension. He was described by his men as "a leader who would put his men first and pay attention to the comforts of his men before his own".

He played school cricket 1894-6 and was captain '96. He was also in the football XI '95 leaving school in CQ 96. He played for England v Germany 1899 and Gloucestershire CCC 1900. He appeared in the 1903 and '04 Dunn finals, won the London Senior Cup in 1899 and worked in the London Stock Exchange 1902-16. A partner in the firm with P de La Penha.

THOMAS SOWERBY ROWLANDSON (L)

was born 22nd February 1880 in Newton Morrell, Darlington, son of Samuel and Isabel. He died, killed in action 15th October 1916 and

OE Wreford Brown at school. School archive

TS Rowlandson. Cambridge University AFC archive

was buried at the Becordel-Becourt military cemetery on the Somme 18th September 1916.

He was in the football XI 1897, the rackets pair 1897and he left the school OQ 97, to go to Trinity Hall, Cambridge, where he played for CUAFC 1902-4 and also played billiards v Oxford 1904. He was the goalkeeper in the Sunderland league XI 1904-5, an England Amateur international v Ireland 1907 and v Holland 1907. He also led English XIs to South Africa, Budapest, Norway, Sweden and Canada. He played for the Corinthians and in the first six Dunn finals in goal. He became a magistrate in the North Riding 1912. During WW1 he was commissioned Lieutenant in the 2/4th Battalion Yorks Regt. 5th September 1914 and gave his family home over to the Red Cross as a hospital. Served in the Great War and was present at the second battle of Ypres, at Hooge and on Hill 60. Transferred to the 1/4th Battalion Yorkshire Regt (North Riding territorials) 15th January. Made Captain 8th October 1915, he was serving on the Somme when he was killed. His adjutant said of him: "I have always thought of him the finest type of Englishman....his death was just as fine as his life. He died where of all places I think he would have chosen to be – on the parapet of a German trench ahead of his men. A Bosche bomb hit him on the shoulder; death must have been instantaneous. No words of mine can tell you what he was to us...." (Newspaper cutting). Awarded the M, MC January 1916.

ALAN RODERICK HAIG BROWN (H) 5th son of Rev Canon William Haig Brown, the Headmaster and Master of Charterhouse, born 6th September 1877, he was killed in action 25th March 1918; along with 15,000 others during this chaotic campaign, at Bapaume on the Somme and buried at Achiet-Le-Grand communal cemetery extension. Lt Col with the 23rd Battalion Middlesex Regt. and was awarded the DSO.

He played for the school XI 1895-6, left CQ '96 to go to Pembroke College, Cambridge, where he got his BA. He played for CUAFC 1898-9 and ran for the college. Played some games for Brighton and Hove Albion. He was the author of books such as *Sporting Sonnets*, *My Game Book* and *The OTC and the Great War*. He became an assistant master at Lancing College in 1899, where he joined the 2nd VB R Sussex Regt. in 1906 and ran the Lancing College OTC from 1906-15. His cadets shot at Bisley.

He played for the OC XI, LCC '98, LSC '99, ADC 1903.

Married Violet Wrackleford, Dorset 1907.

During the OQ 1914, at school, Charterhouse "A" played Godalming on December 26th and there were more "A" XI games as the Charterhouse team was decidedly weakened by the loss of older players.

The entry in the Captain's Register ceased after 1915 for a few years and there is no explanation for this apart from the distraction of the conflict on the continent. However a valuable resource was kept in what is called the Captain's Book; *Rules and Advice*. Various snippets were written in as they were thought of by the captain at the time, including gems such as "A stretcher is always kept at the Lodge in Prince's Avenue in case of accident" and "No shootabout (sic) are to be held on the north end of Ground D; fellows with colours please enforce this."

There was advice about practice, studs (especially with the away games), how to arrange trials and Turning Up. The captain would give advice about the Winchester match, which involved a two-and-a-half-hour "taxi" journey, with lunch and tea taken at the college. Accounts of matches had to be sent to the editor of the *Carthusian* and to *The Field* magazine as well as *The Sportsman* at 139/140 Fleet Street and *The Morning Post*.

Colour Sunday is the second last of the OQ now, but in 1915 it was the second last of the LQ. This was when the captain posted the list of all colours from 1st XI to Clubs.

The advice from the captain to ensure that the

"brake" (pony and trap) from the Angel Hotel was ordered well in advance before visiting teams needed picking up from the station, was brought on because during the war the occupation of the Witley Camp by soldiers meant that the brake was called upon more often. There was also a stable at Lessington Brake, the bargate house near studio.

In 1916 a one-off match with Shrewsbury was planned but it never took place. However, by 1922 regular fixtures were played, originally at the Crystal Palace to save travelling and possibly to avoid the advantage of playing at home. The Charterhouse pitch was free draining on sandstone and the Shrewsbury pitch heavy with mud, so neither away side won a match during the time up to 1940.

It was recorded in LQ 1918 that the "whole system of football in the school was altered". 1st tics was the best team in each House bar the 1st XI players. The Etceteras was the next best team and there was also the Yearlings. Finally "Big House" ran a 2nd tics team which included all other footballers.

IAW Gilliat was the captain in 1919 and wrote about the value of a coach for the XI. This was the Rev EM Jameson whose XIs regularly played against the school, usually the first match of the OQ in that period. He came from Oriel College, Oxford and was the Housemaster of Bodeites from OQ 1921 until summer 1936, retiring from the school in 1938. He returned to teach during the war and died on 25th November 1958.

Players who were under 16 and a half were being encouraged to play more often so that they benefited from coaching and playing on Big Ground. It was recorded by VE Morgan that the Headmaster refused to allow these fellows to go to away matches and miss school, so junior games against Westminster had to stop. Games against local teams therefore were to be encouraged.

Max Beerbohm in the *Carthusian* December 1920 reflected that he could not bear the thought of leaving Charterhouse, for life after that was an anticlimax. "He could not forget the goal that Gownboys kicked against Hodgsonites…".

In 1920-1 over the Christmas holidays, the school hosted a football competition for elementary schools on Broom and Lees. Four schools attended including the Godalming Council School, the National School and Farncombe National School, playing for the Charterhouse Shield. Mr Fletcher organised this event.

In 1921, PWC Hollowell became the "Games Master". He was a boy at Charterhouse playing both 1st XI cricket and football, leaving in Summer 1916 to study at Magdalene College, Cambridge. He played for the CUAFC 1919-20, took a 1st in Maths and was awarded the MC with Bar in the Great War. He returned to teach at Charterhouse between 1921-58 and was Housemaster of Bodeites 1936-50, succeeding Jameson.

BASIL CA PATCHITT (W) born 12th August 1900, became captain of football and cricket left the school in the summer term 1919 to join Trinity College, Cambridge where he gained his BA and a Blue for the university team in 1921. Cap-

BCA Patchitt at school. School archive

tained The Amateurs v The Professionals at Stamford Bridge 1923. He then played for England in 1923 (see chapter 10). He played for the Corinthians and Castleford Town FC.

He was a mining engineer (coal) in Yorkshire (hence Castleford connection) and then taught at Rosehill School, Banstead. Captain in South African Engineer Corps (tunnelling company) in WW2, married Mary McArthur 1926. Then became a production engineer for Bedaux Company in 1935 and was sent to the gold mines of Johannesburg, retiring in 1963.

John TR Graves (G) left Charterhouse in the summer 1921 to go to St John's College Oxford. Having a distinguished career in education and becoming a partner at Sandroyd School in 1949, he also wrote *The Boys' Book of Association Football*.

GERARD TREVOR HOLLEBONE (g) was born 3rd September 1912 (father OC C 1894). He went up to Trinity College, Cambridge where he gained his BA and played for the CUAFC. He was a Captain in the RA intelligence Corps and then joined the Stock Exchange in 1946.

He captained the OC team in two Dunn finals just before the Second World War. He was close friend of the Dunn family who persuaded him to revitalise the Old Carthusians FC that had been through a bad patch. In 1934 he began to run the club and in that season the OC XI were pitted against the Aldenhamians, a formidable team at the time. After a drawn game and being 0-4 down at half-time he changed tactics and brought on the Moss brothers whose wing play caused havoc in the Aldenham defence, the OCs won 5-4. They went on to the final and beat the Old Bradfieldians. Three years later in 1939 they beat the Cholmeleians 2-1. He played OC cricket and he retired from soccer in 1945 and continued as a committee member as well as helping with organising the Dunn. Married Eileen 1942.

During the 1920s **ALFRED GEORGE BOWER** (R), who was born on 10th November 1895 at Bromley and died at Gorey, Jersey 30th June 1970, made his mark on English football. A boy at Charterhouse from the LQ 1910 until CQ 1914, he served in the Great War as a Private in the HAC and as a Captain in the 1st London Regiment. He then joined the Stock Exchange

GT Hollebone at school. School archive

AG Bower at school. School archive

from 1919-54.

He was the OC president, known as "Baishe" and the last amateur footballer to captain England, achieving this honour never having played for the Charterhouse 1st XI (see chapter 9). He played in the hat trick winning Dunn team from 1922 and for the OCs and Casuals in the Isthmian league and for the Corinthians. They were the top amateur side in the country that had several stirring FA Cup runs including an epic against Brighton and Hove Albion in 1923 that ended in a second replay and a defeat in front of 43,780 at a neutral Stamford Bridge. He helped beat Blackburn Rovers the following year, losing in the next round to West Bromwich Albion. With Morrison alongside him, Charterhouse was well represented in the top flight of football during this period. Whilst playing for the Corinthians against Suffolk County at Ipswich in the 1920s his team was awarded a penalty for hand ball. Bower informed the referee that they never attempted to profit from such kicks and promptly tapped the ball slowly towards the goalkeeper. He played for Chelsea for several seasons and was known as a player who had never committed an international foul and became a favourite of the crowds. He was a member of the FA Council 1928-33 and president of both the Dunn competition and the Old Carthusians from 1947 to 1963. Married Marjorie Irma.

HERBERT RH WILLIAMS (V) was born on 7th June 1900 and died 17th September 1974. Joined the RAF in 1918, played for the Essex CC XI 1919-20 and became a shipbroker in Brazil. Reputed to have played for the Corinthians FC in Brazil between 1922-4 and for a Brazil XI in 1927.

VERNON E MORGAN (V) captained 1st XI football and left school with many successes in athletics in LQ 1923. At Christ Church, Oxford he played for the Blues and won the 3 miles var-

sity event in 1925 as well as being part of the relays in 1924. He represented Great Britain in the Amsterdam Olympics 1928, the Empire games in Hamilton, Canada in 1930 and was the South African mile record holder in 1929. He went on to write on sport and became a member of the Football Writers' Association and in the Second World War he was a war correspondent. He gained an OBE and was awarded the Olympic Diploma of Merit – at the time, only the fourth person to be given such an honour.

GS Fletcher wrote in 1923-4 that Repton sides were always "heavy" and it was advisable to wear leg guards. He reported the new fixture against Shrewsbury which was to be played at Crystal Palace (the old ground) unfortunately after the end of the Quarter. The Headmaster eventually allowed it to be played at Shrewsbury. With the acquisition of Northbrook grounds the captain developed a system called "Fragments" which involved Houses being grouped together rather like Clubs and two teams from each being made up. A new system of Club matches was created in OQ 1924 and 1st XI players became more involved with the less able players, thereby spreading the "word" down the school.

Advice was given to ensure that the referee played the "penalty kick" in the Westminster game because they were always "apt to trip a player as he is scoring a goal". The usual punishment apparently was a free kick which meant trying to score through a crowded penalty area.

In 1924 after the Oxbridge term finished, Old Carthusians came back to play against their Houses. The captain at the time, AH Williams, acted as host to an OC team that came to Charterhouse to play against other clubs at the school. The OCs played on a South of France tour, beating Menton 2-1 and losing to Cannes 0-4, played in front of the Queen of Romania and Lord Balfour.

1923 – 1924.

There is very little that has been altered. Mr Hollowell still does the accounts, and we still have no 1st Tie turning up on Thursdays. This seems to work quite well. There were a few alterations with regard to the 1st XI. With apologies to the previous captain, I am quite certain we had too many matches during 1922-23 and by Long Quarter many of the side were stale. Accordingly I have tried to reduce the number of fixtures and I succeeded in dropping about 4 or 5. But we had one important new match. It was against Shrewsbury at the Crystal Palace on the first day of the Christmas holidays. It was a great success and we hoped to have it there every year. Unfortunately the two schools do not break up on the same day next season, so the match cannot be played there. The headmaster has, however, given leave for it to be played at Shrewsbury.

I have written in anything that seemed necessary, and I have put a few hints overleaf.

G.S. Fletcher.

Captain 1923-24

GS Fletcher's captain's log with advice about the Shrewsbury game. School archive

GEORGE D KEMP-WELCH (H) left in the summer of 1925 and whilst at Sydney Sussex, Cambridge, he won his Blue in 1928, captained the university in 1930 and played cricket for Cambridge as well as for Warwickshire between 1927-35. In 1931 he played for the Gentlemen v the Players and married Diana, the daughter of Stanley Baldwin (later the 1st Earl Baldwin of Bewdley). He was killed by enemy action in 1944.

By 1928 there was discontent over the standard of football in the school so a new system of trials was established. I am afraid that Mr PWC Hollowell was described as a "rotten coach" by the 1st XI captain, JLH Fletcher. He also warned the players not to accept the beer at the Lancing lunch because "it is fermented". Although he advised future captains not to stop at Horsham on the way back from Lancing without the Headmaster's permission, he did this with his team and got caught. His 1929 advice for the Lancing game was to "arrive at the ground two minutes before the kick off; having a shootabout before the game only tires you out. Do not have a tosh (bath) before the game – it weakens you."

Journey time to Repton was just 5 hours by train – not dissimilar to today's times – leaving Godalming at 12.23 and getting to Repton at 5.20pm. Tickets for 12 people totalled £14.17.

C Middleton was captain 1929-30.

AJ Wreford Brown captained in 1931 and the programme for the Shrewsbury game involved arriving at the school at 4.30pm, then having a six course meal in the "Shop" before going to a school concert. Thence to the Headmaster's house where there was more food and the advice was to slip away politely to get a good night's sleep. Wreford Brown also mentioned that training should not include "toe to toe walking if you have weak ankles or knees because this might wreck yourself". Also to prepare for the Repton match a player should "take two or three walks in the fortnight before the game over as much plough(field) as possible". The team should watch as much "pro-football" as possible to pick up useful tips and dodges.

1931 Winchester used a "T" ball which had a thinner cover and is blown up much harder than at Charterhouse. On their boggy ground this led to different playing conditions entirely. So intense was the rivalry that the captain took

himself and two colleagues to watch Winchester play a few days before the big game. In a dry year (and the game was played on the first Thursday in March) the ground would be as hard as Big Ground. Thus long studs would be useless. If you asked RV Lewis, the present U14 A-team coach, for his opinion of Winchester's pitch and match ball, not much has changed! Home advantage often keeps the two teams close together.

There was reference regarding hockey which is described as a "minor sport and must not be allowed to interfere with football. Don't let any member of the two top teams get too keen on the game". There was also excellent advice about tying the laces of the boot half-way up to just over the instep which "enables a fellow to get his toe down for shooting and seems to make passing more accurate".

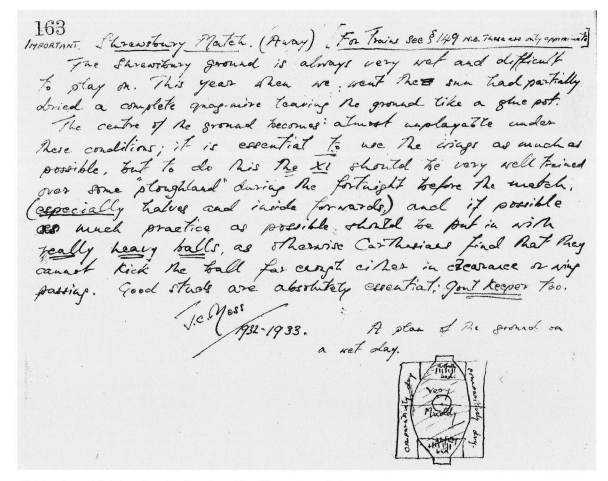

JS Moss's captain's log showing the plan of the Shrewsbury pitch. School archive

There was some sensible advice about the 2nd XI and the need to give the players more attention and raise the profile of the team.

JC Moss drew a plan of the Shrewsbury pitch to make the future captains aware of the state of the mud. "Ploughland and heavy balls for practice is recommended to teach the team how to cope with the glue pot."

He warned future captains that at Lancing the steep slope away from the Chapel makes things difficult – they always play uphill first if it is a dry day – then there will be wind.

At Westminster the ground as we know is very greasy but hard on top like ice. It makes it hard to stop and turn and therefore, in the first quarter of an hour players find it hard to get their legs. "Sling the ball about more because Westminster like to play a close passing game. They also have a professional coach and there is a marked degree of accurate passing."

At Bradfield it is essential for the goalie to take a cap with him since the sun shines directly into the eyes. "Bradfield tend to be rather big and tough and often kick the ball too hard."

On 6th May payment was made by the OC Club for four guineas to secure four complimentary tickets to the 1931 Cup Final, the 50th anniversary of the FA Cup victory, to be sent to members of the 1881 Cup winning side.

During the 1931-2 season the Old Carthusians are recorded as having played an AFA Cup match against Ipswich Town FC. On the 2nd January they played away and forced a 4-4 draw but lost the return a week later on the 9th, 4-2 at home.

By the 1932-3 season changes were made again to the Turning Up system; Yearlings was abolished and Colts (UXVI) was set up. 2nd tics was the less able UXVIs "young duds". Etceteras was over XVIs only and 1st tics was to include any UXVI who had house colours, making it a slightly better team. There seemed to be a wish to help the better junior players.

In 1933 the Corinthian Football School at Highbury was regarded as a good Summer holiday exercise and new ideas were brought back to school – such as heading tennis. The fee for the course was one guinea.

Advice for the away game at Repton, encouraged the school secretary to try to persuade the Repton captain, when you visit them, that "dress clothes" are not necessary. The Repton headmaster does not mind you going to dinner in "sportings" but odious fours and check garments are strongly discouraged. In the event of evening dress being worn, endeavour to keep boiled shirt un-creased. Their field is of colossal dimensions (136 x 68yards apparently); try not to be put off by Morgan-Owen (the famous footballer) who is extremely vociferous and not a little annoying as he runs the Repton game from the touch line.

For the Godalming match, tickets were 7 pence each and the money goes to the Mayor's "Pull Together Fund". After the match the dignitaries are invited to high tea at the "Angel" and be prepared to make a response to the President's speech and remember to tip the waitresses.

By 1933-4 BC Lee, eventually to be the Girdlestoneites housemaster, was the man to ask for advice and he would give it willingly but he never offered advice without being asked. At this time there was an extraordinary sportsman in the school who never fulfilled his potential.

This was:

JOHN MILLINGTON LOMAS (g), a true all rounder, was the younger brother of GW. Born on 12th December 1917, he joined the school in the OQ 1931. His brother was a school monitor and 2nd XI player in his time but JM had a much more colourful school career. In his first LQ in 1932 he played in U16 house racquets, winning the final against Bodeites. In SQ 32 he played in the house cricket team and also starred in the Yearlings House XI that won House Cup.

In OQ32 JM played in a house football XI that lost to Verites 0-12 in the final.

In the CQ 33 the house played 10 games of cricket, won half and he got his 1st XI colours. In LQ 34 JM was in house hockey team and he received 2nd XI colours and in SQ 34 he was captain of the house team that played 10 but lost 7 matches. He won his 1st XI cricket

JM Lomas at school. School archive

saders, Toc H, the HAC, Repton and the Casuals. In the house racquets the pair lost to B in the final. In LQ 37, he remained as head monitor, was still in the house hockey XI that won the cup v Pageites. He won the racquets singles cup for the third year in succession and received athletics colours. He left the school at the end of the LQ. At Oxford for two years before the war, he played for the university in 1937 and 1938, he was secretary of the OUAFC 1939 and played cricket 1938. He also played for the Corinthians in the cup and in the Dunn side in 1939. He was a quick, neat and beautifully balanced footballer rather in the mould of GO Smith. In the war he joined the RNVR and was invalided out in 1940. He was in the Admiralty 1940-1, then back to Oxford to get a 1st in law and became an official fellow at New College, Oxford. He died in London on 4th December 1945. Illness took its toll.

colours and averaged 52.5, winning the school batting cup. In OQ 34, JM and AG Leatham scratched to Bodeites in the final of house racquets but JM got 1st XI colours for football and was made Captain of Racquets. In the LQ 35 JM won the singles racquets and played for the school at Queen's. In the SQ 35, he was awarded his 1st XI colours and won the batting average cup again. In OQ 35, he captained the house football team. He was vice-captain of school football.

In LQ 36, JM was in the house hockey winning final v Bodeites and also in the 1st tics team. He was awarded a major scholarship to New College, Oxford (classics). In SQ 36, JM captained the house cricket losing to Verites in the final and he captained the school XI scoring 2000 runs in his career. He captained the public schools XI at Lords. By OQ 36 he was head monitor, on the Games Committee, and captain of the house football XI that won the house final beating Gownboys. He captained school football and racquets, playing at Queen's three years running. During that football season he scored four goals five times against the Army Cru-

JB Lyon thought that brightening up the trials could be achieved by inviting some members of Brooke Hall to play in them. During the 1938-9 season, Sir Stanley Rous and Charles Wreford Brown turned their attention to the country's schools on behalf of the Football Association supported by the public schools, and held summer coaching schemes at Oxford and Cambridge universities alternately.

JDP Tanner was captain in 1939-40 and he was later to become the chairman of the FA Coaching Committee. He wrote that a lot of the coaching guide was "bunkum" especially the advice about having baths! He does, however, recommend that "Mansfield" boots are the best on the market. AL Irvine in *Sixty Years at School* mentions having JDP Tanner (Denys) in his house. Tanner's father was sending him to Marlborough but was persuaded that soccer at Charterhouse would suit his son better. As a remarkable prep school player he then went on to captain Charterhouse in the first year of the war, moving then to lead Oxford University AFC after the war. He played war-time football for Huddersfield Town FC and then once for their

JDP Tanner's captain's log. School archive

league team after the war.

Irvine said he was "also a very good Head of House, living harmoniously with some intellectuals extremely unlike himself".

JOHN DP TANNER (P) was born 2nd July 1921, died 25th October 1987, joined the school in the Summer term 1940, went up to Brasenose College, Oxford MA. Played for the OUAFC 1948, CU Eton fives 1949, Ass. Sec OU appointments committee. In WW2 he was a Captain in the Indian Armoured Corps, 1951 textile industry in Yorkshire. He gained amateur caps 1947-8, an Amateur Cup winners medal (Pegasus FC) 1951. He was the last Carthusian to earn an amateur cap v Ireland February 1947, scoring three times and as an Oxford Blue he scored twice in his first varsity match and captained in 1948 a thrilling 5-4 win over Cambridge at White Hart Lane. He also played for

Huddersfield (his home club debut 25 August 1948 against Derby County at the Baseball Ground – he was on the losing side but scored from the right wing) and scored the decisive second goal for Pegasus in the famous 1951 Amateur Cup Final against Bishop Auckland at Wembley in front of a full house of 100,000. He scored in the semi-final against Harwich and Parkstone the following year in a 6-0 win but missed the final due to injury. Tanner had searing pace and an ability to make goal scoring look easy. He served on the FA Coaching Committee, played in three Dunn winning sides 1947 (two goals), 1951 and 1954 and in the 1950 defeat. Played for the London FA. He had the distinction of being only one of two amateurs to play in the old First Division and in First Class cricket. He played for Oxford UCC but did not get a Blue. Playing for the Oxfordshire Minor County XI he scored a century in his only match. He was also a good tennis player and member Carthusian Society committee. Small, tough, loyal with a Yorkshire sense of humour, he remained devoted to his old school and his Carthusian friends.

Geoffrey Green for *The Times* on the FA Amateur Cup Final in 1951 reported:

100,000 people watched the students of Cambridge and Oxford Universities beat the famous northern amateurs Bishop Auckland, 2-1 at Wembley. It was Tanner, who was more and more to have a decisive influence on affairs. With ten minutes left Pegasus settled matters with a second goal. Pawson, Johnny Dutchman (who taught at Chigwell) and Tanner split the defence with their ground passing and Tanner's shot went home low into the corner. It was Dennis Saunders (who later taught at Malvern) who held the cup in his hands.

Tanner, the May brothers, Dereck GW Goodliffe (who played for Millwall just after the war) and TRH Savill, who had a sweet left foot, were the backbone of the OC club at that time. Goodliffe went on to own Dulwich Hamlet FC and the school and OCs had connections with the club in the 1980s playing at their ground on occasions. The Dunn final was held there on a number of occasions too. The Goodliffe's Dulwich Hamlet team was victorious in the Amateur Cup Final of 1934. HF Benka played in that side and D Levy was in the Ilford team playing against Dulwich in that final. Benka's son, Peter, was also a formidable sportsman, particularly in the golfing world and who became a member of the Charterhouse governing body.

In 1941 there was a reduced fixture-list due to expenses. The school played Bradfield twice, and Wellingborough at home, and the other opponents generally were service teams from the local area. It was written in the *Carthusian* that "the lack of quality of matches is beginning to coming more acute as there are practically no pre-war amateur sides available". School matches were reduced to Bradfield home and away and Malvern came into the orbit. Various army

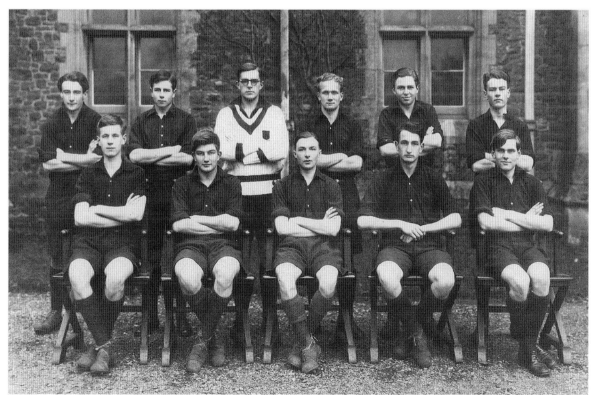

JDP Tanner's 1939-40 school team. Back row: R Finlayson, FA Peat, P Bennett, BMS Hoban, DAN Allen, MF Dean. Front row: AJM Milne, JG Larking, JD Tanner, HP Cunningham, HC Churchill Davidson. School archive

sides made up opposition but they were "very talkative".

January and February 1942 provided the worst winter since 1895 – snow and frosts curtailing much of the football and the results from that period were very thin.

OQ 1943 saw the result of the war on four years of preparatory school football and the standard at Charterhouse was poor as a result.

The captain advised never go to Sandhurst in a truck provided by the army because the journey will make you "sea-sick".

In OQ 1944 and LQ 1945 the captain wrote that the Malvern match away was lost, and it was a shocking game on a pitch ankle deep in mud off which the cows had to be driven by the combined efforts of the two teams before the kick off.

In LQ 1945 a match against Winchester was played at Redhill on 31st March, in the holidays. The initiative was that of Mr AH Leppard who wanted to show the "local talent that it is possible to play a really hard game without questioning the motives of the opposition if one was sent for six". After the game, a three-course meal was provided for the team by GJ Searle (OC) and the profits from the match (a large crowd) went to the Army Cadet Corps.

CHAPTER 10

international football

CW Alcock, a member of the famous Wanderers, was elected to the Football Association and his vision saw the formation of not only the FA Cup, but also the first official internationals. He wrote to a Glasgow newspaper inviting Scottish players to take part in a contest against England. There were five matches played at the Kennington Oval between 5th March 1870 and 24th February 1871. The Scottish team was made up from exiles living in England. With only Queen's Park operating as a club of any note, it took the persuasive powers of Archibald Rae, the club's secretary, to help Alcock raise the two sides that played at Glasgow's Partick ground on 30th November 1872, kicking off at 2.20pm with a crowd of 4000 in attendance. There was no Carthusian selected and the result was 0-0.

By 1879, when England ventured into internationals against Wales, EH Parry was chosen. Carthusians were then regularly selected to play for their country for the next twenty years.

THOMAS CHARLES HOOMAN performed in four pre-official internationals against Scotland in 1871 (both matches) and 1872 (both matches) and was chosen for the first full matches in 1872-3 but was unavailable.

CHARLES EDWARD BURROUGHS NEPEAN, having Scottish ancestry, played in pre-official internationals in 1871 and 1872 for Scotland against England. **EDWARD HAGARTY PARRY** became the first Carthusian to play in a full international v Wales on 18th January 1879 at the Kennington Oval. The team won 2-1 in front of 200 people. Parry then played against Scotland at First Hampden, Glasgow on 11th March 1882, when England lost 1-5. A crowd of 10,000 witnessed the humiliation! A 5000 crowd saw him score in a 3-5 defeat by Wales at the Racecourse Ground, Wrexham two days later.

JAMES FM PRINSEP, registered with the Clapham Rovers club, made one solitary appearance for England. He was also the youngest player to play for England at 17 years 252 days at that time and this record remained until Wayne Rooney of Manchester United broke the record in 2003. Prinsep played for The Rest v England initially and for England in his historic full international v Scotland on 5th April 1879. This was a 5-4 victory for England at the Kennington Oval with 4500 in attendance. That day Prinsep played against another Carthusian, CEB Nepean (also see chapter 3) and was later selected for the Scotland game in 1881-2, but was unavailable.

The Corinthian spirit dominated English football in the early period of international football and although the players were true amateurs, footballers were gradually being given hero status by the growing following of supporters throughout the country. Along with this inevitably money played its part.

James Corbett in his book *England Expects – A history of the England football team* quotes, "The pick of the heroes were the brothers Arthur and Percy Walters, two Charterhouse old boys who had formed a defensive pairing for the Corinthian FC, turned out for their respective universities and for their country." England may never find another pair as capable as these two. They played international football for five years until the untimely death of their younger brother, who died whilst playing football. This tragedy persuaded them to abide with their parents' wish that they retire from the sport. They were cut short in their prime.

ARTHUR MELMOTH WALTERS. His nine international appearances were always with his brother against Scotland in 1885,86,87,89 and 1890, v Wales 1887,89,90 and v Ireland 1885. In all he played 9 times and bowed out of the England team with his brother after playing at Hampden Park against Scotland in 1890.

These brothers were the best pair of full-backs for England at the time and were a "household name". They played as a pair against Scotland in 1885 until 1890 except in 1888 when AM could not play.

With the England goalkeeper WL Moon they made a formidable triangle, working out a defensive scheme that enabled them to play for England from 1885 through to 1887 and against Scotland for three years running.

PERCY MELMOTH WALTERS played 13 times for England *v Scotland* on:

AM and PM Walters formidable full backs for England. School archive

21st March 1885 at Kennington Oval, with Cobbold and Amos.

27th March 1886 at Second Hampden, 1-1 draw (11,000 crowd).

19th March 1887 Leamington Road, Blackburn, 2-3 defeat (12,000).

17th March 1888 as the only OC at Hampden Park in a 5-0 win (10,000).

13th April 1889 Kennington Oval (10,000), 1-2 defeat.

April 5th 1890 Hampden, 1-1 (26,379).

Matches *v Ireland*:

28th February 1885, Whalley Range, Manchester, 4-0 win (6000).

13th March 1886 at Ballynafeigh Park, Belfast (4500) 6-1 win and he was the only Carthusian in the team,

7th April 1888 – once again he was the only OC playing in England's 5-1 win in Belfast (7000).

Matches *v Wales*:

29th March 1886 at Wrexham.

26th February 1887 at Kennington Oval.

23rd February 1889 at Victoria Ground, Stoke, 4-1 win (6000) and 1890 at the Racecourse Ground with Currey and AM. He captained England on five occasions.

EDMUND SAMUEL CURREY played for England against Wales on 15th March 1890 as a centre-forward, coming in as a "student" aged 22 years 46 days, replacing George Cotterill (CUAFC, Old Brightonians and Corinthians) at the Racecourse Ground Wrexham. He scored twice on debut and missed a hat trick when he hit the post. 5000 were in the crowd. He also appeared against Scotland at inside-forward, on 5th April 1890 at Hampden with 26,379 watching, but was "fagged out against them" so the *Athletic News* reported.

A meeting in Manchester in December 1882 brought together the four home nations which formed an association to look after international rules. Out of this the Home Championship was inaugurated in 1883-4. Matches against teams outside the home nations were to come later.

Corbett also describes the forward WN Cobbold as "....the real star of the national team. In many ways he was the first modern footballer, a man who actually considered where he was running and who he was playing to, rather than putting his head down and simply charging blindly onwards." Cobbold played for Cambridge University and then for England.

WILLIAM NEVILL COBBOLD played against Ireland, winning his first cap and scoring twice on 24th February 1883 at Aigburth CC, Liverpool (2500). His second goal was England's 50th goal in international football.

He then played against Scotland and scored once at Bramall Lane, Sheffield on 10th March 1883 in front of 7000. His third cap was gained v Ireland on 28th February 1885. On 21st May 1885 he played at the Kennington Oval against Scotland with the Walters and Amos. The following year, 1886, he played at Second Hampden v Scotland. On 29th March he saw Amos, another OC, score against Wales. On 5th February 1887, Cobbold scored twice against Ireland at Bramall Lane beating the Irish 7-0 (6000 crowd). He then scored against Wales on 26th February at the Kennington Oval (4500) and finished his personal international career in a defeat on 19th March 1887 against Scotland 2-3 at Leamington Road, Blackburn (12,000). In the end he scored 6 times in nine matches.

After Cobbold's retirement, there was the instigation at NL 'Pa' Jackson's suggestion of the international cap being awarded to any player representing his side from 1886.

ANDREW AMOS played for England v Scotland in 1885 at the Oval and v Wales in 1886, scoring one goal and creating another from his corner. Amos was a player of immense ability

and it is surprising that he only played twice.

By 1888 the new Football League kicked off and the division between professionals and amateurs was even more significant. Despite the rift, GO Smith made his debut against the Irish in February 1893, having previously been a schoolboy at Charterhouse, a Blue at Oxford and by his debut he was playing regularly for the Corinthians. Gibson and Pickford in *Association Football and the men who made it* wrote that GO was "great in all the qualities which go to make up the man who is the keystone of the arch of a team, it was in the making and receiving of passes that he excelled."

Smith was a typical Carthusian who played football for fun and who remained a true amateur unaffected by the status that he achieved in his seven years at the top. Sir Frederick Wall, the secretary of the FA, wrote that Smith was a "man without petty pride" and Steve Bloomer had "immense admiration" for his striking partner. He was invariably courteous to his professional team-mates who would shake hands with any player.

GILBERT OSWALD SMITH was an England International twenty times.

v Scotland:

7th April 1894 Celtic Park, 2-2 (45,107). The day the OCs won the FA Amateur Cup with Buzzard taking GO's place.

4th April 1896 Celtic Park, 1-2 (57,000)

3rd April 1897 Crystal Palace, 1-2 (37,000) capt.

2nd April 1898 Celtic Park, 3-1 win (40,000)

8th April 1899 Villa Park, Birmingham, 2-1 win, one goal (22,000) capt.

7th April 1900 Celtic Park, 1-4 (64,000) capt.

30th March 1901 Crystal Palace, 2-2 (35,000) capt. His last appearance in an England shirt.

v Wales:

12th March 1894 Racecourse Ground, 5-1 win (5500), when he did not get on the score line.

He was not picked for the next match v Scotland but, after a late injury, got in so successfully that he linked well with the professional forwards Bassett (WBA) and Goodall (Derby County).

18th March 1895 Queen's Club, 1-1 (13,000)

16th March 1896 Arms Park, Cardiff, 9-1 win, he scored twice (10,000) capt.

29th March 1897 Bramall Lane, 4-0 (5000) capt.

28th March 1898 Racecourse Ground, one goal, 3-0 (4000) capt.

20th March 1899 Ashton Gate, Bristol, 4-0 (10,000) capt.

26th March 1900 Arms Park, 1-1 (20,000) capt

v Ireland

25th February 1893 Perry Barr, 6-1, one goal (10,000)

7th March 1896 Solitude, Belfast, 2-0 win, one goal (12,000) capt.

February 1897 Trent Bridge Nottingham, 6-0 (14,000) capt.

5th March 1898 Solitude, 3-2 win, one goal (12,000) capt.

GO Smith. Prolific England centre forward. School archive

18th February 1899 Roker Park, Sunderland 13-2 win, scored four, with hat-trick between the 59th and 63rd minutes (13,000) capt.

17th March 1900 Lansdowne Road 2-0 win (8000) capt.

v Germany

1901. In an unofficial international which was not recorded in the FA minutes at White Hart Lane, GO Smith presided over a 12-0 win in which Reginald Foster scored 6 goals. It was reported that "the English played in a nice leisurely game that spelled no exertion".

He scored 11 goals in 20 matches (1893-1901) for England, being captain 14 times (at least) with ten of these in consecutive matches.

As the captain of the national side, all players, including the professionals, loved playing for him. Above all he had intellect, he always had something up his sleeve and the game had no better ornament. Ernest Needham, the Sheffield United international, said that "he was a good player when playing behind Smith but only a medium one when he played in front of him". It

C Wreford Brown player and administrator for FA.
School archive

was said that "he'd eyes all round his shirt!"

In 1898 with GO winning his 13th cap, England beat Scotland 3-1 at Celtic Park in front of 40,000 people. Imagine the trains and cars, omnibuses and people flocking through the city to watch this spectacle. With Steve Bloomer, a real super-star from Derby County at inside right and GO up front, Charles Wreford Brown led a formidable team. Fred Wheldon on scoring the first goal within minutes of the start was greeted by a "jumping for joy" captain who took out a gold sovereign from his shorts pocket and placed it into the lucky goal scorer's hand. He did the same when Bloomer scored the first of his two goals and then when he secured the game with the third goal. After this game Wreford Brown invited all the English players to his rooms for champagne – such class!!

CHARLES WREFORD BROWN played for England v Ireland, 2nd March 1889 at Anfield Road in a 6-1 win (crowd 6000) as a 22-year-old centre half. He was next selected v Wales 1894 and was captain against them in 1895. He captained the England team with Steve Bloomer and GO Smith in his forward line against Scotland 2nd April 1898 when aged 31. Thus he won four caps in 9 years. He captained amateur international sides in South Africa 1903, Scandinavia 1904 and Canada and USA in 1906 and 1911. He managed a team to Canada in 1924.

He was a member of the FA Council and vice-president from 1944, was on the international selection committee and member of the team that toured Australia and New Zealand in 1937.

He managed the 1936 British Olympic soccer team in Munich, Germany and forbade them to give the "Nazi salute". The British team gave "the eyes right" at the opening ceremony instead but Charles is believed to be the only Carthusian to have shaken hands with Hitler. He also was officiating on behalf of the FA in the notorious match against Germany in 1938 when the team was "obliged" to give the Nazi salute before the match. There is more on this below.

Wreford Brown ran the line in two matches

during the 1920 Olympics and in an international match against France in 1925 in Paris.

LEONARD RODWELL WILKINSON was the goalkeeper for England v Wales 7th March 1891 at Newcastle Road, Sunderland in a 4-1 win, 15,000 in attendance.

WALTER EVELYN GILLIAT became an England international v Ireland, 25th February 1893, scoring 3 goals between 10 and 30 minutes into the game on his debut. (Four other "one cap" English internationals have done this.) England won 6-1 and he was never picked again!

1893-4 was the twelfth season of the Corinthian FC history and the England team playing against Wales at Wrexham was basically the Corinthian FC XI. Wales lost 5-1 and C

Wreford Brown and GO Smith featured in the line up. Another occasion in 1895 against Wales saw a similar full representation from the Corinthian FC, this time including MH Stanbrough. In those days it would not be unusual to field two England teams on the same day against Wales and Ireland, an amateur team playing one match and a professional another.

During this season, the final of the Amateur Cup was played on 7th April 1894. The Carthusians overcame the Casuals 2-1 in front of a crowd of up to 4000. That day, GO Smith was called away to play for England against Scotland in front of 45,107 at Celtic Park.

MAURICE HUGH STANBROUGH represented England against Wales 1895 with Charles Wreford Brown as his captain, and also played v Canada, 19th December 1891 – not regarded as an official international due to Canada's status.

Harpies XI at school 1890s. Darvell sitting left, WU Timmis, back right. School archive

WALTER FARNELL HENNIKER STANBROUGH played for an England XI in South Africa 1897.

On 6th March 1897 **SYDNEY DARVELL** was selected to play for Wales against Ireland at Solitude, Belfast and later on 20th March at home at the Racecourse Ground, Wrexham against Scotland. The Welsh went 1-3 up at half-time but caved in to lose 4-3 in the first match with 10,000 spectators. Half that attendance appeared for a second match which was drawn 2-2. Darvell played alongside stars such as Billy Meredith of Manchester City and Morgan Morgan-Owen of Oxford University and an Old Salopian.

GILBERT CLAUDE VASSALL was chosen to play for England v Ireland in 1899 (18th February) but it clashed with the Varsity soccer match and he chose to captain his university team.

OSWALD ERIC WREFORD BROWN captained England v Germany 1899 when the FA sent a touring party to Germany, the first steps towards making the game global. Two years later an amateur contest was played in which the Germans were routed 12-0 at White Hart Lane. Four days later the professionals had their turn and scored 10 past the hapless visitors. Canada sent a team to the Oval for a friendly and was soundly beaten 6-1.

By the beginning of the new century GO Smith had retired from the international scene. CB Fry of Repton, Oxford, the Corinthians and Southampton (and he himself an international full-back), said of Smith that "GO was a genius in football and like all geniuses he rose on stepping stones of his real self by taking infinite pains in terms of natural gifts." In Fry's view only Bloomer, a professional who completed a lucrative transfer to Middlesbrough in 1905, shot harder and straighter than GO.

On Saturday 17th March 1900 Charterhouse played the 500th match since the school moved to Godalming. The OC team was entirely made from Internationals. Those available for selection were: A Amos, WN Cobbold, ES Currey, S Darvell, WE Gilliatt, EH Parry, JFM Prinsep, GO Smith, MH Stanbrough. AM Walters, PM Walters, LR Wilkinson, CF Wreford Brown, OE Wreford Brown, GC Vassall. The result was 5-0 to the OCs.

CHARLES FREDERICK RYDER played in the unofficial international match for England v Germany 1901 at White Hart Lane with GO Smith.

At the turn of the century many of the foreign associations were formed and great international teams began to grow. The Milan football club was founded by an Englishman in 1899 and touring began as transport became more flexible, although the FA was not prepared to send full sides out into the wilds of the continent. The Home championship was still the centrepiece of international football and the XIs gradually became filled with professionals. Some vestiges of amateur influences in the game remained personified by players such as Vivian Woodward who played for Tottenham Hotspur and Chelsea, clung to his amateur status and was considered knowledgeable enough and able to set a good example to his men on the field to be a captain and leader. The professionals were not held in high esteem and it was vital that the FA had a reliable man to show their team the way.

GO Smith also noted the difference in play between the amateurs and the professionals. The amateur style was faster with pace, forward passes, being intent on out running the backs. The professionals reached the goal by degrees using the full backs or half backs or a deep lying forward. The "gung ho" approach to football was attractive but tactically naïve.

Sadly the FA was also inward looking when it

came to international football and the body seemed content to ignore the growth of the game beyond British shores. In May 1904 seven countries on the continent founded the Federation Internationale de Football Association (FIFA). The FA was surprised at such a swift development and eventually the home nations joined – by 1907. Despite this "entente cordial" no member country of FIFA was invited to England until Belgium visited in 1923. In 1907 the FA required all county associations to admit professional clubs and to protect and preserve amateur football the Amateur Football Defence Foundation was formed. This soon became known as the Amateur Football Allianace (AFA) and the two associations ran separately until 1913.

The formation of the England amateur team in 1906, when this split occurred, provided the Corinthians with an outlet for their dreams, whilst the professional game moved onwards like a juggernaut in the "full" side. The Great Britain team, with Woodward at the helm, won the Olympic gold medal in 1900 in Paris and again in London 1908. The English amateur team then won the 1912 Stockholm Olympics title comfortably. Thirteen AFA international matches were played during the "years of separation" and a number of Carthusians were involved.

WILLIAM UDAL TIMMIS Amateur International Cap v Ireland 7th December 1907 at White Hart Lane, winning 6-1, and Holland at Feethams 21st December when England won 12-2. There was another match at HVV Platz, De Diepput, Den Haag on 1st April 1907 which England won 8-1 (crowd 8000).

JSF Morrison with the ball and AG Bower on his left in the Corinthian side that beat Blackburn Rovers 1924. Replay

THOMAS SOWERBY ROWLANDSON was the goalkeeper for England amateur international v Ireland 1907 and v Holland 1907. He also led English XIs to South Africa, Budapest, Norway, Sweden and Canada.

ERNEST BARTON PROUD, who never played for the school (see Chapter 7), gained three amateur caps, including one v France at Parc de Princes (crowd 1500) on 1st November 1907. Against Belgium on 18th April 1908 at Leopold CB Platz, Brussels, England won 8-2 and in Mariendorf, Berlin, on 20th April 1908, Germany lost.

WJH CURWEN played for the AFA international side v Bohemia 1908 with **BERTRAM TUFF** who was born 18th March 1883. He played football for the school 1898-1900 and left LQ 1901. He was an outstanding forward who played in the XI for three years, being captain in his last year. He scored five goals against Westminster in 1900 and during that season he scored 44 goals in 20 games. He played for the OCs before he left school, playing with internationals and Blues. He joined the Corinthians but ill health limited his appearances for them. Member of Dunn winning sides 1906 and 1908. Served in the Great War Lt RNVR. He died 26, Kensington Gate, London on 6th November 1953.

JCD TETLEY was in the AFA side against France 1911.

IE SNELL represented the AFA England XI v France 1912 and Bohemia 1913 as did **VG**

THEW who represented the AFA against Northern France in Tourcoing, with Rowlandson in goal. The AFA won 13-0. **RLL BRADDELL,** then with Oxford University AFC, was also invited to play during this period.

MORDAUNT HC DOLL played in an international against Bohemia 1911 and for the AFA England XI against Bohemia in 1913.

The first official English foreign tour took place in 1908 to Austria, Hungary and Bohemia but then nothing happened abroad until a friendly against Belgium in 1921 in Brussels and then in 1923 a tour to Belgium, France and Sweden.

BASIL CA PATCHITT captained the Amateurs v the Professionals at Stamford Bridge in 1923 and made his debut at half-back or full-back and as captain of the full side against Sweden on 24th May in Stockholm, winning 4-2 (14,500). He was captain again in the next game that ended in a 3-1 win for his team.

He therefore gained two full international caps in Stockholm playing alongside the professionals as an amateur, a remarkable achievement at this stage of football's history.

ALFRED GEORGE "Baishe" **BOWER** gained five senior caps between 1924 and 1927, captaining on three occasions. He played against:

Northern Ireland 20th October 1923 at Windsor Park losing 1-2 (crowd 23,000)

Belgium 1st November 1923 in Antwerp 2-2 draw (40,000) and 8th December 1924 at The Hawthorns winning 4-0 (15,405) as captain.

Unfortunately Bower was not picked to play in the first international match to be held at the new Wembley Stadium, when England played out a 1-1 draw with the Scots on 12th April 1924.

Cartoon JFS Morrison portrayed in cartoon form as he helped vanquish the professional Blackburn Rovers. Football Association and Replay

He was the last amateur to captain England against Wales on 12th February 1927 at the Racecourse Ground, Wrexham. Dixie Dean scored two of England's goals in a 3-3 draw in front of a 16,000 crowd. That year Dean scored 12 goals in seven matches.

Wales 28th February 1925 at the Vetch Field, Swansea 2-1 win (8000) captain.

This was alongside 13 amateur caps he was awarded between 1922 and 1928. There were matches played outside of the "Home tournament", for example, against *France* on 5th May 1921 when 30,000 watched the French go down 2-1 at the Stade, General John Joseph Pershing,

Paris. Against *South Africa* on 11th October 1924, 10,000 spectators witnessed a 3-2 win at the Dell, Southampton and later on 26th November 1924 at White Hart Lane, 12,000 saw the English win by the same margin.

JOHN SF MORRISON was an amateur international footballer v Wales in 1920. This match was played at Penydarren Park, Merthyr Tydfil, 14th December. England won 9-0.

RJP THORNE THORNE played in an amateur international v *Wales* 1921.

HERBERT RH WILLIAMS reputedly played for a Brazil XI whilst living there in 1927.

Gradually the FA became more adventurous and by 1938 a European tour, led by FA officials Charles Wreford Brown, and the new FA secretary Stanley Rous, met the British Ambassador Sir Neville Henderson in Berlin. Hitler's Germany was in the process of marching into Austria, war was in the air and the England officials on May 14th were asked by Henderson to tell the team to present the Nazi salute at the pre-match presentation after the Germans had "stood for the British national anthem, in order to get the crowd in good temper". One version of the story tells that the team was informed to give the salute by one of the two officials (unnamed but almost certainly Wreford Brown) at the last minute, as they were about to leave the dressing room. Stanley Matthews and his colleagues were apprehensive and indeed the dressing room "erupted". The official went away and returned minutes later with an "order" from Henderson to comply, since the situation in Europe was so precarious. The players were eventually persuad-

ed that compliance would also probably affect the way in which the game was to be played. The team did as they were told and England thrashed their opponents 6-3.

Despite this victory Eddie Hapgood said that what happened at that presentation ceremony was the worst moment of his life. Hapgood's story claimed that he had been instructed earlier by Wreford Brown and Rous to inform his team, which he did. Hapgood had been told by Wreford Brown that both he and Rous felt sick about the whole affair but under the circumstances it was the correct thing to do. As it was, the team members were well entertained by the German people and felt no animosity towards their hosts at that time.

The Times reported that "the English team immediately made a good impression by raising their arms in the German salute while the band played the German National Anthem".

JOHN DP TANNER was the last Carthusian to earn an amateur cap. Tanner played against *Wales* 29th March 1947 at Somerton Park, Newport winning 4-1. Also played against *Ireland* on 8th February 1947 at Haig Avenue, Southport in a 3-1 victory. The following year he played at Solitude, Belfast against the Irish (7th February) 5-0 win.

After the Second World War, our next closest recognition for international honour was David Miller, a flying winger, who sadly was not picked for the full England amateur squad despite playing in a series of international trials for the Olympics during the 1956 season. International recognition for Carthusians now rests with the Independent Schools' FA representatives. Over the years many Carthusians have made it to the full squads of what was originally the Public Schools' FA and its modern equivalent, ISFA at U16 and U19 level; a great achievement.

CARTHUSIAN INTERNATIONALS

	v SCOTLAND	v WALES	v IRELAND	v OTHERS
TC HOOMAN	1871/2 (unofficial)			
CEB NEPEAN				Scotland v Eng 1871/2 (unofficial)
EH PARRY	1882	1879, 82		
JFM PRINSEP	1879			
WN COBBOLD	1883(1)/5/6/7	1886/7 (1)	1883(2)/5/7(2)	
A AMOS	1885	1886(1)		
AM WALTERS	1885/6/7/9/90	1887c/9/90	1885	
PM WALTERS	1885/6/7/8/9/90c	1886/7/9/90c	1885/6c/8	
C WREFORD BROWN	1898c	1894/5	1889	
ES CURREY	1890	1890(2)		
LR WILKINSON		1891		
MH STANBROUGH		1895		Eng v Canada 1891am.
WFH STANBROUGH				Eng v S Africa 1897am.
WE GILLIAT			1893(3)	
GO SMITH	1894/6c/7c/8/9c(1) 00c/1c	1894/5/6c(2)/7c/8(1)/9c 00c	1893(1)/6c(1)/7c/8c(1) 99c(4)/00c	
GC VASSALL			1899 am.	
OE WREFORD BROWN				Eng v Germany 1899 am.
SL DARVELL				Wales v Scotland and Ireland 1897
CF RYDER				Eng v Germany 1901 am.
WU TIMMIS			1901 am.	Eng v Holland 1907 am.
TS ROWLANDSON			1907 am.	Eng v Holland 1907 am.
EB PROUD				Eng v France 1907, v Belgium, Germany 1908 both am.
MHC DOLL				Eng XI v Bohemia 1911 am.
JSF MORRISON		1920 am.		
RJP THORNE THORNE		1921 am.		
BCA PATCHITT				Eng v Sweden 1923 x 2
AG BOWER		1925c 1920/2/3/4/6 am.	1923 1922/3/4/5, 27 am.	Eng v Belgium 1923/24c Eng v France 1920 am. Eng v S Africa 1924 am.
JDP TANNER		1947 am.	1947/8 am.	

(1) = goals scored   c = captain   CAPITALS = full England cap   *am.* = amateur cap

the post war years 1945-78

In OQ 1945, after the war, the school managed to revive the established fixtures with Repton and Shrewsbury and then BC Lee (Brutus, as he became) the Girdlestoneite housemaster handed over the care of the team to A (Tony) J Wreford Brown in 1946-7. Tim RH Savill in the Captain's Register wrote on the subject of referees by describing Sergeant Scott, the Gownboy butler, "as a tricky customer and you have to flatter him a bit as he thinks a lot of himself; however he will referee once flattered enough".

In OQ 1946 Charterhouse played Highgate for the first time and the venue was the Chelsea Football Ground. Charterhouse won 4-0. The record states, "Charterhouse played well against opponents who clearly knew the game and who were noticeably good at heading the ball." The following season, on 7th December 1947, Stamford Bridge was again the venue with a win for Charterhouse 3-0. There is no reference to how or why the pitch was chosen, save it being approximately half way between the two schools.

A Hastings 1947-8 recorded, "AJ Wreford Brown (Tony) became Master in Charge after he had returned from the war. Wreford Brown had a long pedigree and became a legend in the school." He was still a member of Brooke Hall when I joined the staff in 1974, and he proved his reputation as a determined and skilful sportsman.

Tony wrote the article overleaf to support a tour to Bermuda by the school team in 1984, organised by Paul Dinkenor, a young history beak and Cambridge Blue.

David Miller, whose contributions to this period of school football have been invaluable, described AJWB as

> a fanatical enthusiast, who led more by emotion than science. Gatherings before a first eleven match on the Friday evening, in his fourth form classroom, in the gaunt post-war years under a bare austerity light-bulb with-

TRH Saville. School archive

'Many Memories"

A.J. Wreford-Brown,
Old Gownboy, Ex-Housemaster Weekites,
Ex-M/C 1st XI Football and Cricket,
Oxford University Harlequin.

Good luck to the Charterhouse tour in Bermuda; you will be good ambassadors I am sure, will enjoy yourselves, give enjoyment, play good football, and enjoy meeting your opponents after the match.

My own experience of Association Football has been long and happy. My father was occasionally the England captain about the turn of the last century. He also was the F.A. member in charge of the England side at the Olympic Games in Munich before the last world war. One of his vague duties was to see that all the England team were safely installed on the various trains travelling to the varied destinations. My father (perhaps there is something in heredity) was occasionally forgetful. Certainly on one occasion during this tour all the English eleven were to be seen peering out of the train windows shouting —Faster, Wreford, faster", as the F.A. member in charge was to be seen galloping after the rear carriage in a desperate, but mercifully successful, effort to join his side.

After the last world war I had a wonderful time, putting my moderate talents to work helping to run the Charterhouse 1st XI soccer. As I was also helping with the 1st XI cricket and the fives, my time was filled, but I loved it all and if you have people like Peter May around you do not have to worry about results much. As far as I can remember the Charterhouse first fives pair beat the Charterhouse second pair in the Final of the Public Schools competition.

But in my soccer memories I recollect many Carthusians that I have admired particularly, either for their company or for their outstanding soccer skill or for their great contribution to Carthusian football.

I am over seventy years old now so my memory (nevery very good) has caused me to leave out many others I have admired, so please forgive the countless omissions. A. G. Bower (one of the last amateurs to play in a full England XI), C. Wreford-Brown, G.O. Smith (famous Corinthians), Gerard Hollebone (Cambridge captain), Bill Moss (Oxford captain), and his brother Jock, the Whinney family, father and son Michael, Tim Savill, John Tanner, David Miller (player and writer), Hugh Cunningham, Douglass Pott, Simon Easton, the Pratts, father and son, and Brian Young's godson, Alan Stuart.

I do have my non-Charterhouse soccer heroes also: Bobbie Charlton, Alex James, Stanley Rous, K. E. Hegan (Corinthians and Army), H. Thompson (Pegasus), G. Green (Salopian), and some non-soccer heroes: two Lords – Lord Ismay (Carthusian) and Lord Hailsham. Two educational heroes: George Turner and Frank Fletcher.

An old man is now "remembering with advantages" no doubt, but I am in fact being accurate, for I am not an ingenuous historian-Marxist such as Christopher Hill and A.J.P. Taylor and I can see that far from life being "the march forward" of history after thesis, anti-thesis, and synthesis, it is in fact *often* "a more backward" after thesis, anti-thesis, and synthesis. So, of course, it is with football. Nowadays it is a little nauseating to me to see the things you take for granted as good, because the professionals (those who play for money) do it – that is to say, rushing about like a lot of monkeys kissing each other after the scoring of a goal (such displays we used to think all right for the foreigners but not for the British); rolling over into the penalty area if fouled outside it in order to gain a penalty; one moment lying on the ground writhing in pain as if with a leg broken in two places, the next moment racing down the wing to score from the resulting free kick; abusing the referee; doing a lap of honour waving to their masters, the crowd, in thanks for not having been actually hit on the head by a spectator's glass bottle or not having been buried under a sea of toilet paper. These things, I say, are not necessarily a march forward in soccer. But in technique, in tactics that work out every inch of the soccer ground mathematically in training the footballers (only professionals can manage full-time training) so that their bodies and muscles emerge one hundred percent fit, there has been a great march forward. They are highly skilled, the modern footballers.

But as with everything in this great Mystery there are some things that are better, some things that are worse. Patrick R. Chalmers got it right in his poem "Roundabouts and Swings", about a gypsy trying to make his living at a travelling fair.

"'E thumped upon the footboard and 'e lumbered on again to meet a gold-dust sunset down the owl-light in the lane; An' the moon she climbed the 'azels, while a nightjar seemed to spin that Pharaoh's wisdom o'er again, 'is sooth of lose-and-win; For "up an' down an' round", said R, "goes all appointed things, An' losses on the roundabouts means profits on the swings!" "

Good luck and good fellowship to all soccer players everywhere, and in particular to Carthusians on this tour.

The Bermuda tour undertaken by the school team in 1984

out a shade, could be particularly nerve-chilling and inspirational, impressing upon us our duty as much as any ambition. Here was instilled the ethic of the game from the Corinthians, passed on to him by his father Charles, and thence on to us, attentive yet often uncertain schoolboys, at least until we had the security of having played half-a-dozen games or been given second eleven colours. His philosophy was essentially based in two areas: winning the ball, fearsomely and fearlessly, as he had done so conspicuously himself as a terrier-like wing-half, and then sweeping goalwards with arrow-like thrusts through the middle or down the wings. It was essentially a long passing style not necessarily in the air, but what was missed was greater emphasis on the short ball game which would have come from a closer association with the professional game. It always struck us that it was a contradiction for the cricket eleven to have the benefits of the wisdom of coaching from a former professional, George Geary or Doug Wright, but for young footballers, in a much more integrated team game, to be reliant on the experience of an amateur. On the other hand Wreford Brown instilled what few professionals would have done: a love of the challenge, the old fashioned honour of losing when having played so well, of representing the school and the game. He could not tolerate the half-hearted and the greatest virtue you could have as one of his players was trying your utmost when knowing that you were not playing well. He epitomised the maxim that sport is a microcosm of life itself.

Miller also recognised the prolonged encouragement and expert advice given to younger members of the school by George Ullyott who, with a chemistry degree from Brasenose, Oxford, became the housemaster of Hodgsonites and later Careers master. He understood the refinements of the game and taught that the game was essentially about simplicity and retaining possession of the ball through good technique.

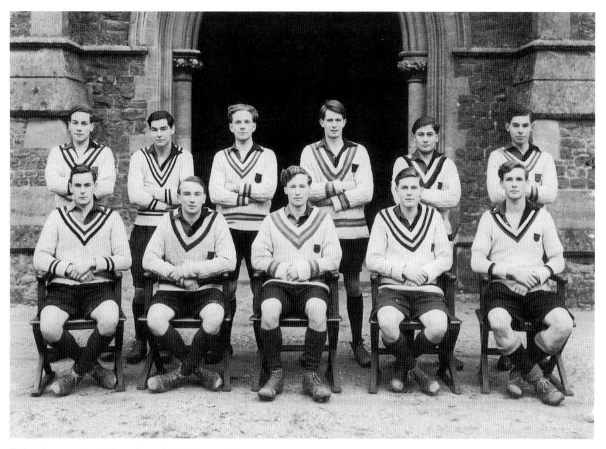

School team 1946. Standing: DGW Davis, DP Johnson, JR Anthony, BHD Mills, VJPD Marrot, BW Seaman Sitting: PBH May, DP Rowat, TRH Savill, A Hastings, BSCG Randall. School archive

It was noted by the captain, Hastings, that there was a strengthening of hockey in the LQ and this threatened to overthrow football after Christmas; but this did not materialise and a compromise between the two sports was eventually made.

Michael Whinney, the captain in 1948-9, was an exemplary captain and personality on the field – as he would be in later life in the church. This was not a particularly successful team but Whinney led them with vigour as a hard running and boisterous right-winger.

In 1949 M David C Jenks (B) was a "vocal, runabout, robust captain who could hoof the ball halfway to Guildford and sometimes with an opponent attached". IM Paton (W) was a quick tenacious full-back and JNB King (D) exhibited the same qualities at wing-half. John May (S) in the midfield provided articulate, accurate service to his forwards and in some ways he was a superior player to his more famous brother, having an influence on the increased thought in the game and emphasising the need for possession of the ball. It was a pity that he was not given a wider stage, such as Oxbridge, to display his talents. Up front, DF Spargo (G) was a neat, if lightweight leader alongside PD Smithson (G), the pair capable of winning any match given enough ball. This supply did come excitingly but erratically from MRP Young (V) and CK Edwards (D). Peter Bennett was a brick wall in goal, as he would be for many years with the OCs.

During the 1950s Richard (Dick) H Crawford, fresh from Cambridge and captain of both the Magdalene College football and cricket teams, ran the side and he paid attention to minute detail in his approach to coaching. He sat on the Games Committee, chairing it and for years ran Yearlings' football with a variety of assistants, all of whom spoke warmly of Dick's devotion to Charterhouse sport. In this period

1951 Team. Standing: D Miller, CTH Whinney, ML Bayman ,RF Tuck, DM Brundan, RJK Spurrell. Sitting: RP Carless, RC Pegler, AJ Barclay, TM Gladstone, R Blumer. School archive

Ken Armstrong (Chelsea) and Ron Reynolds (Spurs) were assigned as professionals by the F.A. to coach at the school on a fixed number of visits. The idea of course was to promote the national game. Billy Wright (Wolves and England captain) and Jimmy Hill (Fulham and media star) also visited. David Miller wrote of RHC that

> he was a considered, thoughtful coach, almost bookish in the same way as, say, Ron Greenwood at West Ham – more brain than passion. As a former inside-forward, he was creative and believed in the virtues of possession, or accurate passing, of players moving in support of each other off the ball; less gusto with more refinement. He would pose as many questions about a match, before and after, as he would give answers. He had a conception of the kind of collective play that was just beginning to take shape at Tottenham Hotspurs in the 1950s under Arthur Rowe, but what young boys needed and

lacked was visible demonstration of this, which was never available from friendly fixtures at that time against such senior opposition as the physical Army Crusaders or the rugby-style Old Etonians. Dick Crawford would be remembered as an avuncular friend.

In the fifties professionalism was an anathema. When it was proposed to the Headmaster, Brian Young, a new young incumbent from Eton, that in the interests of efficiency it might be a good idea to take to away matches, in addition to a twelfth man, our own specialist linesman, Michael Perrin (D), who was actually familiar with the laws of the game, we might as well have suggested installing a cocktail cabinet in the pavilion. This was an era when for some schoolmasters, sport was still exclusively a pastime rather than a subject for expertise. Maybe they were right.

The 1950 team was skippered excellently by John May, and it was an attacking side with

Anthony J Barclay (G) proving to be one of the most exciting wingers. Richard C Pegler (g) was a dominant and forceful central striker with Tim M Gladstone (L) a swift, sharp-footed partner. Rod Tuck (D), who competed in the biathalon for Britain in the Olympics, with Jeremy Lack and Whitney Sadler, produced a penetrating team. MRP Young, CAH Monk (G), GER Lloyd (D) provided the craft, while RP Carless (R) was an outstanding goalkeeper at only sixteen years old. JN Fair possessed an "unusual" technique at full-back. The following year, with four strong players returning, the side was very impressive in AJWB's last season in charge. They crashed at Repton in heavy conditions but R Blumer (W) and David M Brundan (G) were oaks in defence with RJK Spurrell (G) and Lack being inventive in midfield supplying Tuck, a ramrod in attack.

By 1952 the team was "middling", lacking pace in midfield where Graham Pratt (G) had the ideas, being an intelligent schemer, but had rare support. He saw his two sons captain the XI in the 1980s. Basil Gemmel, a wing-half, was one of the most natural games players to arrive in the school at that time, and so with Sadler

(G), Brundan and Brian R Good (D) they formed a solid back line, but erratic attacking play did not help. Richard O Knox (B) brought guile on the wing and CR White (V), a thoughtful inside-forward, endeavoured to give opportunities to the speedy winger David Miller (D). Carless was still outstanding in goal.

DAVID MILLER (D) born 1st March 1935, was in the school XI 1951-3, taking the captaincy in his final year. He represented the Corinthian Casuals Public Schools' XI 1952-3 and left Charterhouse in Cricket Quarter 1953 for Peterhouse, Cambridge, gaining Blues for football (1954 and 55) and athletics. He played for Sussex, the AFA, Eastbourne Town, Ilford, Cambridge City, the Corinthian Casuals FC and Portsmouth reserves. At his best he was selected for FA XIs and Pegasus in the "great days" (1953-7) and in 1956 he was in the training squad for the British Olympic soccer team. On 19th March at Loftus Road, Miller played for an England Amateur XI against Queen's Park Rangers and the UAU. Despite playing in a vic-

Graham Pratt 1952. School archive

Miller at school 1952. School archive

1956 Team. Standing: AAH White, JGS Matterson, ATC Allom, A MacLeay, MR Gardiner. Seated: GPF Steed, AP Hansell, DR Tomlinson, DC Burrows, DJ Sparshatt. School archive

torious team, beating QPR 3-2, he was the only player not selected for the following match at Wembley against Scotland, which awarded a full amateur cap. As the Olympic squad eventually was whittled down to 15, he was omitted and at that point he decided to concentrate his efforts on journalism. David became a sports' journalist with *The Times*, the *Sunday Telegraph*, then the *Daily Express* and the *Daily Telegraph*. He has become a leading sports' writer with many books to his name including a biography of Matt Busby, Stanley Matthews and Sebastian Coe as well as being considered a leading author on the Olympics. He is married with two children and lives in Norfolk. President OCFC.

In the 1960s, Keith Garland, an Oxford Blue, ran the side for several years but left the school

as Roy Woodcock arrived. Roy, another Oxford man, was better known for his cricketing prowess, having been a highly successful schoolboy bowler at the RGS Worcester and then at Oxford for the university. As inter-regnum, Dick Crawford and Tony Darbyshire took over the helm at a point when Charterhouse football was not at its best, as David Miller (D) and R Malory Hollis (G) observed. The 2nd XI had a game against the Huddersfield Amateurs, one of the great amateur clubs, and JDP Tanner brought a star-studded team to play the 1st XI in OQ 1961, mainly as a practice match.

Roy Woodcock (RGW) established a link with Dario Gradi, who has been the manager of Crewe FC, a gentleman and in 2008 one of the longest serving professional managers in the country. He was an FA coach and prior to that a schoolmaster. Len Walker also came along as the professional, being employed by Aldershot FC,

Roy Woodcock 1972. School archive

when the club was last in the football league. The system of 2-3-5 changed in that time along with development of football in the 1960s and inevitably the World Cup success in 1966 affected the way that football was played at Charterhouse. That year LG Thompson wrote to the *Carthusian* reporting that Jimmy Hill, "the bearded and enterprising Chairman of the Professional Footballers' Association, had been coaching at Eton College and that the school XI had been playing splendidly and had beaten Charterhouse." He asked, "Did Charterhouse not think that a professional might help them very greatly?"

RICHARD GILLIAT, born 20 May 1944 in Ware, Hertfordshire, was prominent in HM Martin's 1st XI in 1962 (Howard Martin was captain for two OQs) and Gilliat went on to

1962 Team. Standing: JMM Hooper, GR Biggs, JN Coleclough, RM Baker, N de Grunwald, NP Hill. Seated: PM Bailhache, RMC Gilliat, HM Martin, HGL Powell, AD Marks. School archive

The Centenary match 1963 v Westminster. Mike Hooper at the back post. School archive

play for Oxford University getting a Blue and captaining his side at football and cricket as well as winning a Blue at tennis. He scored four against Bradfield in OQ 1962 described by the *Telegraph* correspondent, Henry Blofeld, as "mesmerising the opposition". More famous for his exploits in running Hampshire's county championship side in 1973 (a side that included Richard V Lewis our present cricket professional and U14 soccer coach), Gilliat was a clever footballer who scored goals. Frequent match reports on games in the national press referred to him being the outstanding player on the pitch. He returned to Charterhouse in his retirement from cricket to become a housemaster of his old house Gownboys, and then second master.

In LQ 1963 no games were played due to the wintry conditions that affected the whole of the country.

OQ 1963 saw the hundredth year of the Westminster match, in which a talented JMM (Mike) Hooper made the pass for AE Weir to settle the game. The *Daily Telegraph* correspondent at the time described "the stately, turquoise air of Brooke Hall" as he enjoyed a celebratory dinner with the various dignitaries of both schools. On the day eighty-two benches ringing Big Ground were filled with spectators. AD Marks was the winning captain.

MIKE HOOPER took over the captaincy in the following year and continued his success as a goal provider and scorer. Howard Fabian described the scene of the Bradfield match at Charterhouse: "Brilliant sunshine, a billiard table pitch and the lovely autumn colours combined to make a picture of perfection. The football played by Charterhouse was by no means out of place in this setting." Mike Hooper was an "all-round genius" rather like many of his contemporaries at the time, starring at soccer, racquets, tennis and most importantly cricket. He also chipped in with hockey, cross country and anything he was asked to take part in. Mike's prowess as a batsman took him to play for Surrey and the MCC, adding weight to the Friars and he watches his son Harry perform with equal talent, now in OC XIs.

There were two excellent results including a 3-3 draw at Repton and the 3-1 beating of Shrewsbury. The number of games played against adult sides during the season gave the team little chance of developing its game and consequently the record was unbalanced.

In OQ 1966 the Shrewsbury match was lost 4-7, and we beat Westminster 8-0.

Duckites won the house cup beating H 2-0 and there were Yearlings fixtures being played as well as some U15, U16, 3rd and 2nd XI games (see chapter on the Fixture Card).

In LQ 1967 saw William M Gray (P) captain the side and in the U15s a young Lee Walton (H), son of Kent Walton the famous TV wrestling commentator, scored 26 goals out of his team's 39 in 13 games. Lee went on to do great things and became a respected member of OC football and local club cricket.

OQ 1967 had John M Bennett (g) as a prolific goal scorer and although the XI lost at Repton 1-8, they did beat Shrewsbury 4-1. Hodgsonites won the house cup over Verites but the match had to be played on Lessington due to snow on Big Ground.

LQ 1968 David Eccles (P) was making his name in the school goal and he continued to be a foremost member of the OCFC. The XI played 10 and won 5 beating Westminster 3-1 and Eton 7-0.

In OQ 1968 there is a reference to an opposition called Arsenal, though no report can be found and the XI lost 0-2. There were Yearlings matches being played and the XI's opponents included Hampton, Corinthian Casuals, Shrewsbury, Highgate, Winchester, Repton and Eton. A member of Brooke Hall, a linguist, Bernard Hanauer, a hero from the Second World War who had played soccer for Holland and Portsmouth and thrown the javelin in the Olympics, coached the 2nd XI.

LQ 1969 saw Chris Rose (g) take over the captaincy and Lee Walton in OQ 1969 scored 12 goals in a moderate season, but the school did gain its first victory away since 1947 at Repton (4-1) on an icy pitch. Champagne flowed afterwards. Alan Stewart (S) scored twice and James Holder and Walton added one each. Shrewsbury were also beaten 2-1 and there was a first fixture and a 3-0 win against King Edward's School, Witley, a local derby. There were other very good victories over all schools' opponents and a 1-1 draw at Ardingly. Clearly there was a talented cohort at senior level.

John Peters, a young Oxford graduate, was coaching a very successful U16 XI that won 9

James Holder, Alan Stewart and Peter Godby. School archive

and drew 2 out of 12 matches. He was soon to take over the 1st XI.

In OQ 1970 Nick Wisdom (R) was in the XI. He was diminutive, rather like his famous father, but tenacious and he scored a crucial goal against Shrewsbury away in the 3-3 draw. Nick did a very good impersonation of his father. He played alongside his captain Lee Walton (H) in a team that only won 4 out of 10 school games. The house match system was changed to a split league and Gownboys won the Cup under the new arrangements.

Roy Woodcock, master in charge of cricket, also ran the Geography department and eventually was made Verites' housemaster – something had to go. He handed over the running of football to John Peters (JP), a Welshman who had been up at Oxford where he had played college football as a goalkeeper. In this period Charter-

house was blessed with some very fine players who later became the backbone of the Old Carthusian side, so successful in the late 70s. Keith Ellis (R), Alan Stewart (S) and Louis Adomakoh (R) were foremost in the success gained by the XIs. Stewart was a shrewd and skilled forward with a knack for goals who had trialled for Leeds United.

In OQ 1971 Alan Stewart led the team and Repton were beaten away again 3-1 and Shrewsbury forced a draw 1-1 at home. Peter Godby (H) was a leading forward in that side, who played for the Southern Public Schools and he has also played Vets football for the OCs following an illustrious career with the OC 1st XI. James Holder (g) made the XI – they were both to go up to Cambridge and both their sons had success in the school XIs. Saunderites won the house cup. Louis Adomakoh was called up to

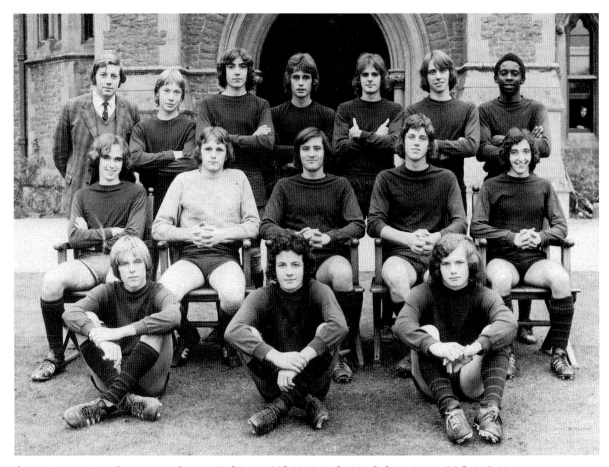

School team 1973. Back row: J Peters. IA Gibson, MG Herbert-Smith, C Comninos, JM Schofield, TD Middleton, AA Adomakoh. Middle row: MWG Doggart, KR Ellis, PLM Williams, RC Ecob, SJ Faull. Bottom row: SR North, AHR Napolitano, DWT Levy. School archive

the XI after an OQ with the Under 15s. Around the same time Simon "Billy" North was also elevated. Against an uncompromising Surrey University team, the boys were "kicked all over the place" and at 2-3 down looked doomed to defeat. A penalty late in the game, given by JP, allowed the XI to draw!

Mark Faldo (G) was captain of the LQ 1972 side and Alan Stuart scored 30 goals that term. The best result was over Millfield, a team described as "very professional", and they eventually reached the National Schools' semi-finals.

John Peters and Bernard Hanuaer took the XI to Luxembourg at Exeat in OQ 1972. The team played several matches including one against the national select schools XI. The tour was blamed for a lethargic performance against Shrewsbury on their return. In that side was Peter Oundjian (S), a fine footballer but an even better violinist, who is now world renowned, Mike Doggart (S), Martin Herbert-Smith (g) and the captain was Tony Forbes-Watson (V). Louis Adomakoh played for the Public Schools XI at the Skegness ESFA Festival, and matches were played against Brian Glanville's team, the Chelsea Casuals. Verites won the house cup.

In LQ 1973 Roger Ecob (P) was captain and Keith Ellis had played in every 1st XI game since OQ 1971.

Jamaica was the destination for the OQ 1973 XI that toured with the Headmaster, Brian Rees, JP and Richard Thorpe (DRT). This exciting tour was based at Kingston at the Calabar High

School and five matches were played including one against the National School XI. The results were favourable. Paul Williams (B) led the team, Carlo Comninos (g), Steven Faull (D), Simon de L North (R) and Jerry Scholfield (V) made the tour party. This XI was particularly strong and they beat the OCs, the Oxford Centaurs (5-0) in one of those games where "everything went right" including an exchange of passes between Adomakoh and North from the half-time kick-off that resulted in a goal. A win over Shrewsbury was secured with Ellis saving a crucial penalty. Chelsea FC, under David Sexton, brought their full team to the school to train and play an exhibition game against the school. This was a big affair and the local press and the whole school supported the event. Jimmy Hill, the TV pundit, and Geoffrey Green of *The Times* were present.

The following Quarter (LQ 1974) was a little quieter but very successful with 67 goals scored in 14 games, due mainly to the experience in Jamaica. Left winger, Guy Walker (L) slotted 13 goals, I suspect rather in the style of his very talented son, James (g), a deft player, who played in 2003/4.

Will, the younger son, also played in the 2007-8 side. Adomakoh scored 24 goals including three hat-tricks and made the Public Schools XI for a second year running.

In OQ 1974 Paul Williams continued to lead a very good team containing Adomakoh, Walker, Herbert-Smith, Comninos and Tim Middle-

1974 Team: RAC Oulton, D Glover, R Hughes, GH Walker. School archive

Collage of photos taken during centenary celebration. November 1976. OCs v D. Miller's XI.
Team: B Wakefield, C Joy, R Huvven, R Gillard, H Moxon, M Smith, P Vaughan, A Gregory, D Miller, S Szemereny,
T Williams, A Pawson

ton (B). Williams had been in the side since he was a Remove in LQ 1971 (the age gap would not be allowed by the FA today). Walker scored 31 goals in the calendar year. The best victory was over Shrewsbury away 4-0 especially since the fixture which began in 1922, favoured the home team. Indeed this was the first win since 1948. The team won 11 but lost to Bradfield and Repton.

Robinites won the house match over Bodeites with Adomakoh scoring the only goal.

It was my first Quarter at Charterhouse and my U15 team lost only their first game to a Charterhouse-in-Southwark XI, coached by Bert Nolan, a long standing and well respected member of the Southwark Boys' Club. In 13 matches they won 10 captained by George Andrews (G). Bill Higginson, the ex-Middlesex cricketer and our professional, helped me on Saturdays especially so I could continue playing in the then Athenian League.

1975 LQ saw an XI with a large numbers of untried players. Simon North led the team and Robin Phillips (g) scored the goals. Due to inclement weather only two 1st XI games were possible against Bedales and Westminster. By the time these were completed the 1st XI record for 1974-5 was P18 W14 Drawn 1, excellent under any circumstances.

The A XI functioned after January playing against the following opposition: Elmbridge School, Ottershaw, Gordon Boys, Brooke Hall, Corinthian Casuals, RMA Sandhurst, Douai, Steyning GS, St John's Leatherhead, Farnham College, Box Hill School, Christ's Hospital, JP's XI.

The B XI was coached by DR Thorpe.

Adomakoh made his hat-trick appearance for the Public Schools XI.

Ivor Gibson (G) inherited a new side in OQ 1975 as the Oxbridge pupils left, so rebuilding was the order of the day. He played for the South and Andrew Cussins (S) was in the XI, his

School team 1976. Back row: Tom Bury, Mark Lovill, Neil Ostrer, Adrian Shepherd, Tristan Whalley, Chris Mole, Robin Philips. Front row; Clive Swabey, George Andrews, Hugh Reynolds, Paul Cummins, Alex Kirkbride. Photo RPM Trollope

father, Manny, being a well-known director at Leeds United. Andrew's son, Sam, made his way through to the 1st XI in 2006. The team lost only once, to Shrewsbury, on Big Ground. Duckites beat Robinites in the house cup, the U16 XI won 12 and drew 2 out of 15 matches.

In LQ 1976 the Old Bradfieldians, another long standing fixture, drew with the 1st XI and Graham Roope the Surrey and England cricketer failed to save the home team's penalty that equalised the game. By the end of the term the school's complete record from 1975-6 was remarkable: Played 25 Won 11 Drawn 10.

On November 27th, OQ 1976 the OCs played the school in celebration of their centenary. Brian Rees, the Headmaster, referred to the day when Sir Harold Thompson and Sir Stanley Rous both visited to help the celebrations. On a sunny day, there was marvellous game of football between the OCs and a David Miller XI.

Harold Thompson presented the club with a silver salver to mark the occasion and then future coach of the Wales International squad, Mike Smith, played in the opposition. The Headmaster remarked: "It is a great pity that our predecessors did not take out a patent on the game. Had they done so our income might now be as those of the fortunate possessors of oil fields, our fees reduced to nil and Brooke Hall be clothed in ermine." *Team*: TEO Bury, MN Lovill, NM Ostrer, AW Shepherd, TCR Whalley, CC Mole, R Phillips, C Swabey, GA Andrews, HB Reynolds, PA Cummins, AP Kirkbride.

During this season the OCs had a fantastic run of victories, playing 32 games and winning 26 with a tally of 128 goals. Alan Stewart would be singled out as his top scored with 30 goals. Peter Godby, Lee Walton and Alan Bennett each scored over 20. They reached the Argonaut Trophy final and won the Dunn.

Richard Hughes handed over the school's 1st XI captaincy to Hugh Reynolds (B). He also led

1978. Tim Piper scores against Shrewsbury. School archive

his house team to win the house cup over H. He had a most distinguished Quarter and proved to be a brave and popular captain. It was Ken Shearwood's last year in charge of Lancing's football and he was a legend, having played for the mighty Pegasus and written a very informative book on the success of that side in the 1950s. The XI drew 1-1 away and had other victories over Ardingly and Bradfield as well as the Oxford Centaurs led by Richard Oulton (OC,W).

In LQ 1977 the hockey team celebrated 100 years of hockey at Charterhouse and the footballers continued to enjoy their LQ sport and it appears that there was no distinction between 1st XI and A XI during this term. Neil Ostrer's (W) XI played 15 matches and 10 were won. There were games against Pembroke College, Cambridge and Haileybury. Brian Pearce, a schoolmaster working at Lanesborough prep school, took over as the Training Officer for the Guildford referees association and he was asked to present sessions on refereeing to the boys at Charterhouse, as part of what was known as Tuesday Activity. This ran for nearly 30 years with Brian handing over to David Hutchison when he retired and moved to the west country. He also worked tirelessly for the Arthurian League referees. Brian refereed the Charterhouse v Eton match on Big Ground on 17th October 1981, with Myles Harfield, a boy at the school, assisting as a linesman. Brian Young's son, Tim, would have been the Eton master in charge.

Jeremy Kemball was the Charterhouse captain and Richard McCourt played – both old boys from Brian's school. After the match one of the Etonians was left behind by the coach and had to be driven to Guildford station by the referee!

The OQ 1977 saw a visit by Crystal Palace players including George Graham, Mel Blyth and Alan Harris. They ran a coaching session with Tristan Whalley's (R) team. Tristan played for the South XI, led his side in the house match final but was beaten by Duckites 1-0 in an enthralling game. Richard Lewis arrived to replace TWH (Bill Higginson). W.A. Shepherd (B) also played for the South and in goal was the very genial Clive Swabey (L) who could be described as one of life's characters – they say you have to be mad to be a goalkeeper! Sadly Clive died prematurely in 2006. Richard Doggart (G) proved to be a valuable member of the team although injury haunted him later and Alex Kirkbride (g) won his colours; he became a published underwater photographer!

In LQ 1978 bad weather caused the cancellation or abandonment of four matches and a new fixture was played against Wellington College, arch rivals in hockey and cricket.

Tristan Whalley continued to captain the team and in OQ 1978 under Paul Cummins (D) the team toured Jersey at Exeat being hosted by Victoria College, although we stayed in a hotel called the Cornucopia. JP's last 1st XI won nine games and gave him a rousing send off. David Miller's son Gavin played in the school team.

Saunderites won the house cup beating W 3-2, exactly 100 years after the first final, won by Saunderites.

CHAPTER 12

1979 to 1992

In LQ 1979, I, as a young member of Brooke Hall, took over running the school's soccer. I joined Brooke Hall in September 1974 and gained the Full Coaching Licence, the top FA award in 1979. The Liverpool Ramblers were on the fixture card, along with Alleyn's, Exeter College Oxford, the FA Colts (a local schools' representative side) and an away match against the Cambridge Falcons. Chris Mole (P) led the A XI and players such as Hugo Pratt (G), Geoff Pride (D), Warren Barbour (V) and Richard Haynes (S) were in the side and served the Old Carthusians in the next decade or so. Chris Mole's son is playing U16A football in 2008.

In OQ 1979 Oxbridge candidates in their seventh term added experience to the senior sides and three 1st XI away trips to Malvern, Shrewsbury and Repton had to be endured. Hugo Pratt (G) the captain was positive in his attitude and commitment to the team, and he was good enough to play for the Southern Public Schools XI. Alan Lathwood played for the South also and along with Nigel Pendrigh (P) became a "Blood". The OQ began with a tour to Jersey playing against teams such as Victoria College, which we lost 0-4. David Miller's XI, the Old Carthusians and Brooke Hall continued to be adult additions to the fixture card and to show the progress the team made during the term, Victoria College were beaten when they returned at Exeat on their tour. At this time we had the luxury of two qualified referees and linesmen in the school C Harfield (H) and C Ruddle (P) who took advantage of a Surrey referees' association course to qualify and help out

with adjudication. We also sent players to prep schools on Monday afternoons to help with coaching. The Leavers XI went to Dulwich Hamlet to play against the Old Carthusians (courtesy of the Goodliffe family) and to hold Repton to a 1-1 draw at the end of the season away was very satisfying. Bob Wright and Richard Lewis (the cricket professional) ran the 2nd XI. There were three 3rd XI games. The U16As played a match against a Southampton FC Youth XI. Saunderites won the house cup.

The number of teams playing football in the 1980s grew rapidly and along with hockey and cricket was a major sport catering for 8 or more teams each week. Fixtures cards regularly included B XIs and the biggest problem the school experienced was trying to find opposition to match us.

Charles May (W), John May's son and Peter May's nephew, captained the 1980 LQ XI and as the fixtures got tougher, the results were not so impressive. Millfield appeared in the fixture card and although previous results were not encouraging, the XI beat them 2-1. A combined squad of beaks and boys took on the Cambridge Falcons over a weekend visit to the university town at half term. Jeremy Kemball (R), who became Master in Charge of Football at Westminster, was in the side, as was Nick Blanchard (S) and Doug Fordham (H) who all went on to play with the Old Carthusians with great enthusiasm. The 2nd XI during this term lost one game and won eleven.

OQ 1980 saw the "retirement" of Dick Crawford (see p156) from running Yearlings

Team talk with Charles May on MJB's right at back. Jeremy Kemball with hands on hips. 1980.

soccer. He is still visiting Big Ground, giving advice, and he has been particularly helpful in supporting this historical record. Charlie May continued as the captain for this Quarter and he had some hard work to do to gel the side. He won a place in the Public Schools' B XI. Elizabeth College, Guernsey visited us at Exeat. There was a good draw with Shrewsbury, and Paul Dinkenor's 2nd XI lost only once in 13 matches. A Cambridge Blue and member of Brooke Hall, Paul was a talented and popular coach. Daviesites won the house cup beating Verites.

Charles May continued to captain the XI in LQ 1981, his second year of captaincy and the team did not fare well, winning only 4 games. The fixture list was tough but a defeat by Haileybury 0-9 away was hard to explain, even though the away pitch was described as a cow field! However, Haileybury had beaten Brentwood 6-0 previously, so they were a decent team. Chelsea trained at Charterhouse with their manager, the World Cup hero Geoff Hurst, and played a friendly against a mixed XI of beaks and boys afterwards. Bobby Gould, a journeyman footballer, showed his enthusiasm for the game by scoring a hat-trick. There was also a Sunday match against the "Match of the Day Commentators" XI containing some well known pundits from TV such as John Motson and Martin Tyler. The school team won 3-2. A team from HMS *Rothesay* also visited the school, the Corps' Naval Section's adopted ship.

In OQ 1981 a short tour to Tideswell in Derbyshire was led by the new captain, Jeremy Kemball, who later in the year played for the Public Schools' side against the FA Youth and in the English Schools' Festival at Skegness. He was an immensely talented Carthusian who played for the Scottish Universities and, after teaching at Charterhouse for a short period, went to Westminster to run the soccer with considerable success.

The OCFC celebrated the centenary of winning the FA Cup and five matches against the club were played on Gaudy day. The XI was sponsored for goal scoring during the term and this raised £250 for "Sport for the Disabled". Paul Newman (D) played for Southern Public Schools' U16 XI. The Under 15 XI scored over 100 goals in 14 games, losing once to a local school, Broadwater, 2-3. The U14A XI was unbeaten with Dick Crawford still offering advice to Bob Noble. Jimmy Allen (P) scored 28 goals and Ben Haghighi (H) 27 in a remarkable team. The U15A lost one game out of 14. Verites won the house cup.

In LQ 1982 Paul Dinkenor ran the A XI. During this period the XI had a torrid time but did return a victory 6-0 over Haileybury, making up for last year. Jason Gard (G) ran his heart out to lead his team from the front and a marvellous group of players including Rick Faulkner (H), Karl Frearson (W), James Reid (B) and Bruce Mellstrom (B) would have better seasons. Karl's son joined the school in OQ 2008.

In March an U16 XI and an U15 XI went on tour to Belgium. The tour party included Jason Golder (P), and Trevor Kidson (B) who became a Housemaster at Bradfield. There was also Harry Pratt (G), Graham's son and Hugo's brother, soon to be captain of football, and George Asprey (V), now a professional actor.

Bruce Mellstrom was the captain of the 1982 OQ team and became Chairman of the OCFC giving long and distinguished service. The 1st XI visited Tideswell and played against Bolton School and King Edward VII in Sheffield. All four senior teams won against Lancing and Winchester and the Under 16 XI followed on from last year, losing only once. Harry Pratt (G), Chris Coe (G), Ben Haghighi played for the Southern Public Schools XI. From that XI, Jon Aubrey (B) went on to make many appearances for the Old Carthusians, particularly developing the reputation of an uncompromising centre-back. A 0-0 draw against Repton and a 5-0 win over Westminster rounded off a moderate season's results. Hodgsonites and Verites met again in the house cup and drew, with no extra time they shared the trophy.

In LQ 1983 victory over the Corinthian Casuals was a great joy and a draw with Millfield a worthy effort too. James Reid captained the side, the Bs won 6 out of 10 games and the U16s toured the Manchester area playing Bolton and

Dick Crawford and Bob Noble with the Yearlings. 1980.

Manchester GS with a visit to Maine Road thrown in. James went on to teach and coach at Barfield prep.

In OQ 1983 the XI only lost once to schools (therefore not including the OC match 0-1) and this was to a good Malvern side 0-2. Highlights in this extraordinary term were scoring six against Shrewsbury at home and then seven away at Repton – rare results. Obe Ibru (H) netted consecutive hat-tricks in these two matches whilst James Davis (D) tallied 14 goals in the term. Karl Frearson (W) the captain was a talented player who became a beak at Eton and Jason Golder a stalwart in defence became a feared and respected centre-back in the Old Boys circuit. He was still playing in the OC 1st XI in 2005-6. Julian Waters (V) a useful winger now presents football on Sky Sports, whilst Don Pennant (V) whose dribbling skills unlocked the Salopian defence and Ross Tayler (D), goalkeeper in the 2002 Dunn win, also kept up their OC appearances. Rick Faulkner played for the South and also the Public Schools' B XI. In this term the 2nd XI drew once and won the rest of its games, the 3rd XI lost once in eleven, the U16s

lost once in eleven, the U15s lost only two and so did the Yearlings team. Verites completed a hat trick of wins in the house cup (see 1982).

I took a year long sabbatical to New Zealand from January 1984. The A XI seemed to have a confidence about it with good victories against an OC XI and the Oratory. A "Stanley Matthews XI" made up of beaks, Old Carthusians and boys turned out at RMA Sandhurst. Two Pratts, two Prides and three Adomakohs were in the squad with the famed England, Blackpool, Stoke City and winger on the touchline as coach. PSD, who arranged the visit of the legend, and Richard Lewis ran this game and the Charterhouse XI won 3-2. It was sad that I was away, unable to play under my boyhood hero. Another mixed side went to Cambridge and took on the Falcons, drawing 1-1. Jay Griffiths (g) scored 14 goals in 11 games.

The highlight at the end of the 1984 LQ was a tour to Bermuda organised by Paul Dinkenor. He selected his U16 players mainly, including Alex Viall (D), Nick Waters (V) and Nick Adomakoh (R) who were prominent members of the squad. From 27th March until the 10th April

1983 Team. Back row: R Faulkner, P Van Hengel, R Tayler, O Ibru, J Golder, J Waters, MJB,
Front row: D Pennant, H Pratt, H Meesman, K Frearson, J Davies, C Coe

Below: Sir Stanley Matthews with Jay Griffiths (tourist)

Jay Griffiths (G) with Stanley Matthews 1984

the tour party played six matches against local school sides mainly, but twice against the National youth XI, had a drinks reception with Governor of Bermuda and were well hosted by the Siddle family.

With only three players remaining in the XI, 1984 was going to be a tricky year and with me away, the onus was with Richard Lewis the cricket professional and qualified soccer coach to run the side. He had great support from Brooke Hall and especially Nigel Cooper who ran the Turning Up programme. Lew had a great term with wins over Bradfield and Repton (3-1 at home) as highlights. Harry Pratt followed his brother by captaining the team and Nick Ado-makoh (R) proving to be a chip off the old

block. Jason Golder (P) played for the South, Ed Baker (W) scored 11 goals and Alex Viall (D) with Mark Kerevan (H) proved to be strong characters in this team and they all continue their careers with the OC Club. The U16s had a good term losing once and the Yearlings were unbeaten. Daviesites won the house cup, beginning a run of four consecutive victories.

The LQ 1985 XI should have been captained by Harry Pratt (G) who struggled to keep fit and Jason Golder (P) took over and won a place in the South XI. He had seven OQ colours to back him up, so the team was pretty strong. This was Julian Alliott's (W) year and he played well at left back and continued his interest in the sport at Haileybury where he teaches and runs their football. The team lost once to Hampton and had a notable draw with the Corinthian Casuals and won all other school matches. The B XI was led by MC Jackson (R) (Cosmo) who was elevated to the As and has taught and run football at Hurtwood House for many years.

Alex Viall's OQ 1985 team toured the Hague district pre-season and won seven matches and drew two out of the fourteen played in the term. He sustained a serious injury that kept him out of the XI for several games and the team was never quite the same. For the Eton match our keeper Andrew Cooley (P) was injured, to be replaced on the players choice by Howard Croathall (g), a rugby-playing Kiwi. We lost. A 1-3 deficit at Winchester was turned round in a fine performance by Adam Spiegel (g), son of the famous film-maker, Sam, "producing" a 4-3 victory. The 2nd XI lost once. Daviesites continued the run of victories in the house match final with the school captain setting a fine example and Charlie Jenkins scoring a hat-trick. In September the school hosted a Prep Schools' six-a-sides for the first time and this attracted 16 local teams. This competition grew to 32 the following year. Nick Waters (V), Julian's brother, held the left-wing position and continued his career with the Old Carthusians. In the Public Schools' Sixes we reached the semi-final of the Plate.

The captain of the LQ 1986 XI was Jon Gough (V) and his goalkeeper was a rugby full-back and ex-4th XI keeper, Edward Brockman (g), a real surprise find. One of the beauties of LQ is the emergence of players like him from the shadows. Tom Beaumont (W), a centre-back, who could head the ball a "mile", earned himself a place in the Southern public schools' side. Against the Bs, Cosmo Jackson returned to play for Hurtwood House and the Army Crusaders had a General playing for them!

George Stonehouse, a Liverpudlian, retired this year and he has been responsible for catering in school for a decade. He got most animated when he saw on the fixture card that "Liverpool R" were playing the school. He thought this was the reserves rather than the Ramblers and was set to produce a special tea.

The captain of the OQ 1986 team, Bob Goodliffe (D) was not a colour and only one colour returned to support him. The team toured Holland again and the school entered the Surrey County Cup at U19 level (and also in the U15 age group). Charlie Jenkins (D) played for the South and ex-captain Jeremy Kemball joined Brooke Hall. Daviesites won the house final for the third year running, with Jenkins proving to be the match winner. Names from this year's football included Andrew Leale (V) who went to Tonbridge to teach and run football, Charlie Whinney (G) a long-serving OC footballer with a long family history and Dick Cowling (R) more likely to be found on the hockey or cricket pitch but nevertheless a decent 2nd XI player. Neil Stevens scored four against Westminster at Vincent Square. Seven wins and two draws, including the away game against Shrewsbury where Andrew Ivermee (H) equalised with a 25 yarder, was a respectable record for such an inexperienced side.

The Army Crusaders have been playing against the school for decades and they are made up from the officers. They travel from their various barracks to play football against the schools and they present to the school that gives

them the best game of football a Rose Bowl at the end of their season. Charterhouse won this in LQ 1987 and the Master in Charge was invited to their splendid annual military dinner! Bob Goodliffe (D) kept the family in the record books as the captain, Steve Mellstrom (B), made his mark and he played on with the Old Carthusians following in his brother, Bruce's footsteps. Jimmy Lunnon (S) made it into the B XI and I am pleased to say that his company was responsible for sponsoring Charterhouse kit in 2004.

Leonard Islef (R) captained the side from the goal in OQ 1987 and even the "hurricane" in mid October did not affect our fixtures at home against Eton that Saturday. We played on, regardless of the damage done around the school with boys marking out pitches and repairing goals whilst the groundstaff, under Ron Perrin, went about clearing fallen trees. This side drew seven matches including Eton, Shrewsbury and Repton and won eight. The senior squad toured Godalming's twin town of Mayen in Germany and we also played a warm up fixture against a Southampton FC XI. There was a ridiculously long match at Winchester when we seemed to play 100 minutes into the dark evening. A thick fog at Repton in which we employed four linesmen to help the "short sighted ref" did not ruin our visit and we drew 1–1. Mark Strecker scoring, not surprisingly, from 25 yards. Piers Gorman scored the school's 100th goal against Shrewsbury. Seb Henkes (G) sustained an injury early in the season and we missed him although he has paid his dues back to the OCFC over the past 20 odd years. Graham Brooke (S) and Duncan Austin (H), both later to play for Oxford University in 1992 and 1993, made their way into the side. Brooke played for the ISFA B XI and captained OUAFC and Gorman eventually won his place in the full Public Schools' side. Daviesites, led by Gorman, extended their run to four house match wins.

LQ 1988 was not a vintage year and the record in the Carthusian refers to prima donnas; only three games were won. Pity poor Leonard Islef (R) the goalie and captain who had to stand behind a side apparently "bereft of drive and determination". The Bs had a better time of things and Lunnon, Giles Drew (S) and James Scholefield (V) had an influence on that.

The following season, OQ 1988, we returned to Mayen for pre-season, but despite a potentially good side we won only six and drew five matches in the term. On November 3rd the Old Carthusians played a Wimbledon FC XI to commemorate both clubs being the only two clubs to win both the FA Cup and the Amateur Cup. The professionals won 5-1. Giles Schofield (S), a long-serving member of the OC Club organised the fixture. It was also the 125th year from the first officially recorded game against Westminster (actually the 117th game). This was played out on Vincent Square and we lost 1-4. Fate! Edward Grayson, the famous sports' lawyer and Corinthian historian, recorded his thoughts in the *Carthusian* (March 1989). In the XI was Duncan Austin (H) who was captain with Brooke in support. Jerry Scholefield (V) was an unorthodox centre-forward, Rowan Ewart-White (V) played at the back and Jim Merrick

(S) appeared on the left. All these continued to play OC football late into the 20th century and Merrick is still going strong in the 21st. The win over Malvern was our first away win against them since 1942, a draw versus Repton and a win over Shrewsbury, both at home, proved to be highlights. Verites won the house cup.

In LQ 1989, Graham Brooke and Piers Gorman were selected to play for the ISFA XI at the ESFA Annual Festival of Football at Skegness over the Easter period. The A XI was very successful, winning 8 and drawing 2 of their 11 fixtures. The Leavers played an ISFA Masters XI at the end of the term. One odd feature was the defeat of Collyers School, Horsham (my old school) 5-1 with three goals coming from near post corners, delivered by Brooke. Whilst Bas Clark (S) was tormenting defences with his pace, Seb Henkes (G) and Duncan Austin also had important roles to play. The captain Rowan Ewart-White waxed lyrical over the team, its supporters and even the groundsman Ron Per-

1987 Team. Back row: G Pascoe, A Leale, P Scott, P Gorman, D Austin, G Brooke
Front row: D Tinslay, M Gray, L Islef, M. Strecker, S Henkes, J Hare.

rin, who produced such a wonderful surface for his side to play on! Rowan is as eloquent now as he was then.

The driest summer since 1976 and the warmest year since records began made the OQ 1989 pitches hard and brown. The U14 intake was particularly strong and they toured Guernsey in December. We would benefit from this year group three years later when we reached the final of the first ISFA Cup. By now the school was fielding five senior sides, and seven junior teams. There were six colours in the Verite House team that won the house cup and thus there was a run of success for them over the next few years (and not just in soccer). The school hosted the southern ISFA trials in September, and the prep school sixes was thriving. Ed Ashby (V) captained a side to seven wins and three draws. Jim Merrick was his sturdy vice-captain and Chris Sale (H) played for the South against the North. Matt Mitten led the forwards and he was to play a part in OC football later on, as did Ed Rees (L), who eventually became captain of the 1st XI and the Old Carthusians. His family gave the Senior Sixes Trophy to us won by Lockites in the first year. Ed played for ISFA. Rob Ashby (V) Ed's younger brother played as a fifth and Giles Drew (S) proved to be a fully fledged OC footballer for many years. Bas Clark continued to bring his speed and ability to jump very high to both 1st XI and OC teams. His performance on Big Ground against Westminster brought an accolade from the *Daily Telegraph*. The team did not tour before the season but did play against Farncombe Athletic in a pre-season warm up. The season's results were not flattering but a win over Shrewsbury and a 4-0 defeat of Westminster helped the team finish the quarter in style. In the Surrey Cup we reached the semi-final to be beaten by Heath Clark College 1-6 and we played well!

LQ 1990 saw Edward Ashby (V) continue the captaincy and his younger brother Robert played for ISFA U16s. Snow interfered with some fixtures especially away at the Oratory, Reading where we were due to play on their new and much appreciated flat pitch. Unfortunately we were moved to their old pitches on the

chalky slopes of the Berskhire Downs.

The summer was hotter and drier than the last one but the OQ 1990 house sixes competition was played in a December blizzard. Ed Rees captained the XI and played against the FA Youth for the newly named Independent Schools XI in March 1991. Winning six games and drawing two was not a good record although Andy Gompertz (V) with a hat-trick against Ardingly and ten goals in the term proved to be a valuable striker. Dan Peters (R), son of John Peters, earned his colours in defence as an uncompromising tackler. There was a friendly against El Allson School from Cairo, Egypt, which we won 5-0, but a defeat by Winchester followed – Charterhouse having 90% territory, an inexplicable result. The development of the U15As was impressive as they won ten games and drew three in their season. This year we secured the help of Mike Godfrey, a freelance football coach who stayed with us for eleven years. He ran the Surrey Youth XI and gave a number of our boys experience of playing at this higher level. Lockites won the house cup.

Jeremy Kemball coached the A XI this term (LQ 1991), just as he decided to move on to Westminster School to teach. The A XI was a young side with Brian Souter's son, Martin, keeping goal, Dan Peters in defence and Matt Mitten as captain. Their youthfulness did suggest that there were better years to come.

In OQ 1991, Richard Thorpe and John Peters renewed their partnership by taking on the Under 14 Cs. This team fulfils two major roles; one of providing players for higher teams and secondly in the role of representing Charterhouse football against prep school 1st XIs. By now outside referees such as Roger Matthews, Barry Morse, David Woolcott, Keith and Steven Birch and Manuel Bello particularly have helped us for a decade or more. Hodgsonites had another win in the house cup. Andy Gompertz played for ISFA B and Ben Wakeham (H) played for the ISFA U16s and Martin Souter (S) for the South XI.

The school XI, captained by Mike Daly, won ten games and drew two. He was ably supported by Robert Ashby (V) whose 12 goals in the term crowned his three years in the XI. Brett Akker (D) in goal and Rupert Green (L) were to feature in the success of the 1992-3 team. Anton McCourtie (B) scored a hat-trick against Ardingly, slipping their offside trap with his pace.

One odd fact involved Phil Shearer (L), an average footballer playing 2nd XI at best, who when he left Charterhouse helped run a diving school in the Turks and Caicos Islands. He was selected to play for his "country" in the World Cup qualifiers! There were not many eligible males on the island, he told me.

Nick Leale (V) was the 2nd XI captain and he has been a major force in the Old Carthusians FC, most recently taking over from Bruce Mellstrom as chairman. The U16 XI continued their very good form winning all their matches with Leigh Webb (B) scoring 27 goals and Ben Wakeham (H), son of OC Lord John Wakeham, finding the net 18 times. Ed Reid (g), now a Brooke Hall beak and a superb schoolmaster, was playing in the U16B goal.

The LQ 1992 XI contained young players

Brett Akker and Anton McCourtie at English Schools' Festival

that would make their mark in the next year or so. Mike Daly was captain, Matt Pegler (L) was clever midfield player and Rupert Green (L) and Leigh Webb were beginning to show how effective they would be in the coming OQ. Nick Kidd (R), a diminutive but extremely able winger, scored 5 goals as did Rob Cunningham-Brown (g) but Webb got the golden boot with his tally of 9. The Bs only lost once in their last game of the term to Christ's Hospital away. Sean Brazier (H), Michael Pate (B) and Barney Weigand (B) emerged as useful players.

OQ 1992 saw the XI start with four old colours and an experience of playing in the Gothia Cup in Sweden during the previous summer. Brett Akker (D) was a brilliant goalkeeper and a popular captain. Under his eye were some very talented and resilient players. In the Surrey Cup the XI played three games including two very good wins against St Joseph's from Tooting and Richmond College using squad players to ease the burden of the number of matches being played. With our entry into the newly formed Boodle's Independent School's Cup (see Chapter 14) our "friendly fixtures" seemed less important in a way, but we beat Forest 3-0, Ardingly 3-0, Bradfield 2-0, Winchester 6-1, Shrewsbury 2-0 away and Westminster 3-2 away. There were defeats also but Webb and McCourtie proved to be prolific goalscorers, with the former showing great awareness and the latter electric pace and strength. Add to that Wakeham's endeavour in midfield alongside Green's silky skills and Tom Walker's timing at the back, this was a well balanced side that did not know when it was beaten. Hodgsonites made it two wins on the trot. Hodgsonites played Verites and after extra time it was 1-1 and, with the light fading fast, it went to penalties. After the first round of five it was 4-4, after the second round of sudden death it was 9-9. Verites missed and Sean Brazier kept his nerve to slot the 20th penalty kick home.

In the ISFA Sixes at Forest in December, Lord Wakeham's son, Ben, was pitted against John Major's son in our game against Kimbolton. Peer against Prime Minister!

CHAPTER 13

1993 to 2007

In LQ 1993, as a result of getting to the final of the Surrey Schools' Cup, the team qualified for the National Schools' Cup (sponsored by Snickers) and our first round game was played in January against Taunton's from Southampton who were old campaigners in this competition and who reached the final that year. We lost 0-2. The Surrey Senior Schools' Cup Final was played at Carshalton FC's ground against Wilson's from Wallington, another well organised team and, despite our best efforts and a lively crowd bathed in floodlights, we lost 0-1. Wilson's also reached the last eight of the nationals. So there were no victory celebrations but the school XI had many wonderful football experiences, not to be forgotten.

Occasionally exceptional teams come around and the one that emerged from the OQ 1992 was mainly a first year sixth form team. It was remarkable that this side was to play a big part in the newly formed Boodle and Dunthorne Independent Schools' Cup. Mark Dickson, the Master in Charge at Shrewsbury, master minded the new competition, a break away from the traditional friendlies. In this first year, Charterhouse made its way to the final at Fulham FC, Craven Cottage in March 1993 (see ISFA Cup Finals chapter 14).

During OQ 1993, with eight colours returning, things should have been even better, but results did not favour us. We lost to an emerging Ardingly side 0-3 in the ISFA Cup and bowed out of the Surrey Cup in the quarter-finals. During the term the XI had some outstanding moments, scoring hatfuls of goals, but when it

came to the crunch, in the cup, in the 'friendlies' at Shrewsbury and Repton, the team did not cut the mustard. The playing record was from 18 games, 11 were won and 1 drawn with an average of 3 goals a game for and 2 against. It was clear where the problems were! Tom Walker (W) captained the side and played for the South; Leigh Webb would have played for the ISFA side but was on tour with the cricket XI. In his two seasons at 1st XI level he scored 37 goals, including five against Forest in one game. Jamie Jarvis (W), a very influential member of the team, missed much of the season through illness and we had to do our best without his service from the right wing.

In the house final Hodgsonites played a Yearling, Dan Ray, in goal and nerves got the better of him, whilst outfield the star players, Tassell, Younie and Wakeham, made an exciting game of it even when V were 4-1 up. Hodgsonites pulled back to 4-4 only to see the inspirational Dan Stearn (V) complete his hat-trick to finish the game at 5-4.

Other school teams had excellent terms with the 2nd XI being unbeaten and the U14A also winning ten out of ten.

One major feature of the LQ 1994 was the win against St Bede's, Hailsham, in which captain Leigh Webb scored 7 out of 9. He proceeded to score 16 times more including 3 hat-tricks. In his full Charterhouse career he scored 170 goals and 76 at the 1st and A XI level. Leigh and Guy Tassell (H) played for ISFA at Morecambe, Tassell being a last minute replacement, a reward that pleased his supportive OC grandfather.

Ben Wakeham gave great power to the midfield and James Dauman (V), a Yank at Charterhouse, filled our right-back spot and they both also continue to play OC football. Will Frost (W) was described as someone who was the "find of the season" and he is still a reliable member of the OC club, not a great technical player by his own admission but utterly enthusiastic and effective in his play. Ed Reid (g) made his debut in goal for the A XI and of course he is now a much appreciated member of Brooke Hall. The team made up for last year's embarrassing defeat by Douai (see chapter 14) scoring 10 against them, then 10 more against Cranleigh. Needless to say this side was always exciting to watch.

The final game of the season was against the Old Carthusians and the A XI won 1-0 thanks to the OC keeper Chris Bayman (g) being distracted by chatting to a Duckite fourth who happened to be walking behind his goal. The team won seven and drew four matches. Four of Webb's 23 goals came in the 5-5 draw with an ISFA Schoolmasters XI.

OQ 1994 presented us with a major problem in that there were no colours returning. After a tour to Maastricht, the XI was eventually made up from four 2nd XI colours, six under 16s, four players who came from the "shadows" and, for the first time, two New Zealand schoolboys who were at Charterhouse on "exchange" for the OQ. Both of these boys came as football scholars and they were very good, but conscience did not allow us to play them both in the XI at the same time. There were an unhelpful number of injuries to add to our woes. In the end Toby Dolman (V) led his side to seven wins in twenty matches and two draws. Toby Smith who eventually captained the Old Carthusians, was in this side as were Sean Brazier (H) and Tim Raven (G) who both also played regularly for the old boys. Weekites won the house match final beating Lockites. Duckites were knocked out in the semi-final on penalties by Lockites but this was the beginning of a remarkable run of success for the house in the senior house cup.

The school XI team was captained by a goalkeeper, Jon Shenkman (g), in LQ 1995 and,

despite his best efforts, this team did not do well; ten games were played, we lost 7 and drew 3 with no victories. Safe to say this was not a very good Quarter!

In OQ 1995 the XI won 7 and drew 2 games. Ian Hayes (B) led the side with great dignity and as Head of School he was also leading Charterhouse at a difficult time in its history. It was on tour in Holland that we heard of the demise of Peter Hobson, the Headmaster. Hayes' XI was not the most gifted and successful team but in Nick Frendo (B) there was a natural goal scorer, whose hat-trick against Ardingly was very special. Andrew Hollingsworth (L) was a quick and precise winger, who with a number of youngsters learning the game suggested that the future would be more successful. This was the year when our great rivals Westminster were strong. They beat us in the cup and we managed a draw in a bad tempered game in the "friendly" on Big Ground. The Shrewsbury match was marked as a memorial to Piers Rimmell (P) who tragically died in a car accident. Piers had left Charterhouse and was at school at Varndean College in Brighton. Many of the players wanted to attend his memorial service so we went ahead and put together a side of youngsters who did valiantly but lost against the powerful northerners. We also staged a memorial game between Piers' two schools, Charterhouse and Varndean School. In this term the U14Bs won every match and Duckites beat Pageites in the house cup.

In LQ 1996 David Carmichael (D) who joined the school as a sixth former took over the captaincy of the side in his final LQ. Of the 12 matches played 5 were won and 3 drawn with successes over the Liverpool Ramblers, the Army Crusaders, the Hamilton Accies, St Bedes and the Old Carthusians. A leavers match at the Guildford Spectrum was a highlight at the end of the season arranged by Peter Britten (g) and his family.

Phil Westcott's (g) team of OQ 1996 played 19 games winning 12 and drawing 1, an excellent return for a talented side. Lancing beat us 0-3 twice (once in the Cup) and they went on to win the ISFA Cup. Repton beat us too and we lost in the semi-final of the Surrey Cup. But victories over Eton, Bradfield and Malvern made up for these reverses. This team had won all its matches as U14s and there was plenty of talent on show. Andrew Hollingsworth actually went on to play a high standard of cricket and Toby Savage (W) preferred hockey, as did Anthony Smith (V). Henry Nash (g), Henry Toulson (g) and James ter Haar (G) are in OC sides now and Mike Gillespie (R) who did not play enough to win his colours was a gifted all rounder who has returned to Brooke Hall. Ed Breeze (P), an imposing goalkeeper, played for the South.

This was the year when the pitches on Northbrook were restructured to accommodate the Sir Greville Spratt (an old Duckite) track and the Yearlings' pitch sits nicely in the centre of it. Sadly the contractors appeared to have had a loss of memory when the drainage was being added, as this pitch is the only one in the school still to be waterlogged after heavy rain. Duckites won the house final against Verites and they also won Colts and Yearlings.

Phil Westcott (g) lead a successful LQ 1997 team that won 4 and drew 5 of its matches. The house match final delayed from OQ had to be played on a Sunday at the beginning of Quarter and I, at the ripe old age of 46 years, played for the Hamilton Accies negotiating a 4-4 draw against the school. The school beat Chigwell 6-1 and Will Adie (G), a talented but sometimes unpredictable striker, scored a hat-trick against the Corinthian Casuals in a 3-4 defeat. Ross Noades, the son of the well-known Crystal Palace FC chairman (at the time) and businessman, was in the squad.

A tour to Holland with three teams (1st, U16 and U15) gave the players for OQ 1997 an ideal warm up and, despite some very dry pitches at school early on, injuries were relatively rare. The XI was one of the best I had coached, winning 12 out of 18 games with 4 draws and 64 goals scored. Nick Gay (V) scored 25 and Andrew Hollingsworth 16. Henry Toulson (g) was a focussed and effective captain and is still bringing his enthusiasm to OC football. Gay is reputed to have scored 100 goals in school soccer, 100 goals in hockey and taken a 100 wickets at cricket! Strong players such as Savage, Nash,

Pedro Leal (V), a Portuguese import, and Tim Burke-Murphy (G) made up the heart of a very good squad and are also the heart of the present OC XI. Toulson, Leal and Dieter Schneider (V) played for the South. A pleasant note to add to this period concerns Dan Ray (H), who as a Yearling played in a house match final a few years before. Dan then had a bad injury and missed the next two years sport. In the end he recovered and tended the goal for this XI with few problems. In the ISFA Cup, we did not get past the highly rated St Bede's, Manchester, losing on penalties after a brave 3-3 draw and we also held Ardingly at their peak, 3-3. But we scored 7 past Bradfield which was most embarrassing for them, 5 past Forest, 4 past Lancing and Eton and we beat Shrewsbury. Being 3-1 up at Repton we should have sealed another fantastic win but the wheels dropped off and they beat us 3-6 mainly because they had a very fast right-winger! Stamina played a part and the captain reminded me that 24 goals out of the 68 were scored in the final ten minutes of the games. Meanwhile the U16s were winning 10 matches and so did the U15s and the U14s, suggesting some good years ahead for Charterhouse football. Duckites lost to Verites in the house final.

Henry Nash (g), presently the OC 1st XI captain, was the captain of the LQ 1998 side and his team won 7 and drew 3 out of 13 matches scoring 40 goals and conceding only 19. Peter Deakin and Richard Lewis (the master in charge of school cricket and the cricket professional) ran the XI. Victories over the Liverpool Ramblers 5-2, Douai School 7-1, Glyn 5-0 stood out.

In OQ 1998 Pedro Leal captained the side supported by Schneider, Burke-Murphy, Iain Ure (R) and Phil White (g). Nick Gay was not as sharp as he had been the year before but boosted by a talented first year sixth, the team had a solid balance. Matthew Bailey (V), the son of the Master in Charge, made it into the team and the next year was to prove very exciting for everyone associated with Charterhouse football. An early and unfortunate exit in the cup to Latymer Upper 2-3, on a super September afternoon, was sad, but wins over Forest, Lancing, Malvern (6-0), Aldenham, Westminster and a marvellous

1997 team. Back: JCT Ho, IS Ure, TE Burke-Murphy, DJ Ray, DCW Schneider, PSS Leal, NSE Gay, MJB. Front: EJW Rees, H Nash, HA Toulson (captain), TNG Savage, AP Hollingsworth, MR Gillespie.

defeat of Repton thanks to Jon Goodrich's late strike, helped ease the pain. In the house cup Duckites were runners up, losing to Gownboys 2-3.

LQ 1999 was a term when the team won 7 games beating the likes of Bournemouth AFC U16s, the Army Crusaders, Sutton GS and the Reading Oratory. A confidence ran through the team and having had exciting draws with the Liverpool Ramblers, 4-4 and Collyer's Horsham, only losses to the Corinthian Casuals and Chigwell prevented an unbeaten term.

OQ 1999-LQ 2000 was a vintage season and as memorable as 1992-3. The school 1st XI won its way to the Boodle and Dunthorne ISFA Cup Final for a second time, at Leicester City's Filbert Street. 1800 pupils, friends and relatives supported the match against Shrewsbury which was to go the Salopians way, 0-1. Two finals and two defeats, but once again the experience gained by the team and its followers can never

be replaced (see ISFA Cup chapter 14). In the quarter this team won 11 out of 12 schools' friendlies including Eton 4-1, Lancing 3-0, Ardingly 6-0 and Shrewsbury 2-0. Matt Bailey headed the goal scorers with 13.

In the ISFA Sixes the squad lost to Manchester GS in the Plate Final on a very cold day in Bolton. In the house cup Duckites were winners over Verites. Jon Byrne (g) and Bailey played for ISFA on their Italian tour to Rimini and San Marino.

The team of OQ 2000 had a hard act to follow but Alan Mezzetti's (B) team did not let him down. Brentwood, having lost to us in the cup semi-final last year, got their own back in the ISFA Cup 3rd round, although we fought back to 4-3 in the dying stages on Big Ground. Will Clark led the line, scoring 18 goals and he played for ISFA. In the newly formed Southern Independent Schools' League organised by the statistician, Bob Noble, Charterhouse came top with the best percentage. The team also beat all our rivals including Ardingly and Repton and drew away at Shrewsbury on a heavy pitch. In the end the record was won 13, drew 2, lost 1. The captain, Clark and Chris Shelton have the unusual honour of never having lost a 1st XI game on Big Ground over two full seasons. The U16As also won their "league" and the U16Bs won 7 out of 7 matches.

In the house cup the winners were Gownboys who beat Duckites.

It was an extremely wet autumn and the excellent drainage on Charterhouse sandstone attracted Wimbledon FC to play some of their academy matches on Northbrook when their home pitches were unplayable. The link with Wimbledon is of interest to archivists who know that the Old Carthusians and this league club are the only two clubs to win both the FA Cup and the FA Amateur Cup.

The captain, Mezzetti, was ill during the LQ 2001 and could not lead his team in the fixtures set for that term. The team had mixed results but held the Corinthian Casuals Schools XI 2-2 – a fixture that dates back to 1883. There was also a match against the Royal Military Academy (2-5) and this dates back to 1878. In March 2001 I celebrated my 50th birthday by holding a veterans football match on Big Ground between Brooke Hall and the Old Carthusians and then a more youthful Charterhouse XI made up from pupils, staff and Old Carthusians entertained the Spurs Veterans All Stars.

In OQ 2001 the 1st XI selectors plucked Charlie Watson (G) from the 3rd XI and he solved a goal scoring problem, as he bagged 10 goals including a hat-trick against Eton in our 7-1 win in the centenary fixture. It was another satisfying term although the results were not quite as good as in previous years. We have been spoiled. Brentwood took our ISFA dreams away again with their Thai U17 international making the difference. However, nine wins out of ten games, following that set-back, meant that the

Will Clark v Winchester. Behind are Jon Jackson (right), James Toller (left)

Watson hat trick v Eton. Sol Sogbetun in background.

"informal" Southern Independent Schools' League was ours again. Richard Griston (g) was captain, a modest but brilliant, compact player, who could play anywhere on the pitch. We had a thriller against Shrewsbury, 3-2, scored another 7 against Aldenham, 4 against Westminster and 4 against St Bedes. After Watson's exploits, Nick Bunstead (P) and Paul Brennan (G), son of Simon Brennan, managed 5 goals each and eight other players contributed to the final tally of 37 goals. Brennan was to make 75 appearances for the A XI from the Removes and then the 1st XI. We conceded 13 in 15 matches losing only twice. This team had many fine individuals including James Green (V) who played for the South, J-J Williams (V) a silky passer of the ball and the agile Will Young (R) in goal. It was mentioned that the Leavers had lost only one game on Big Ground over their two years (see last year). The 3rd XI was unbeaten.

Having disposed of the star-studded Duckites in the semis, Lockites, a powerful team with few colours, beat Weekites in the house final.

LQ 2002 saw the team win 9 and draw 1 out of 12 matches. The As and Bs combined won 16 out of 21 matches, losing just three times. James Green (V) had been a reliable and tenacious defender who deserved to lead the side during this term. The Corinthians were dispatched 4-1, and only the powerful Millfield caused an upset

in the record. Richard Lewis's B XI matched this record with 7 wins and 1 draw out of 9. Freddie Mellor (L), the son of politician David, kept goal.

The team of OQ 2002 reached the ISFA Cup semi-final and met the northern favourites on Big Ground. Bolton School have a reputation for being good and they were. Despite our best efforts, trying to gel a team together in what was the hockey term, the opposition was too strong. Previously, the 1st round win over St Bede's Manchester 5-4 away from home was something of a miracle against the odds and Nick Bunstead's canny hat-trick won us the game with a battling performance. Fred Palley (g), the captain, scored a late equaliser against St Bede's, Hailsham away in the next round, leading the team to penalties and a decisive victory. During the term the XI won 9 and drew 4, losing only to Shrewsbury and Forest away. There was another victory over Repton whom we seem to have got closer to over the years. Palley was a tower of strength in the team and he had the knack of scoring goals from deep in defence when they were needed. In the LQ he scored 12 to make his point. Tom Marsden (G) played for the South and ISFA B XI taking his skilful passing game to Lilleshall for the Christmas trials against Shropshire Schools. The Man of the Season was Peter Handley (W) who came back after

*U16 Gothia Cup squad. Back row: PH Summers, AH Procter, AA Jurenko, WGR Holder, CP Lucas,
W-N Paes, BW Ryder-Smith. Middle row: RV Lewis, J.A Cameron, TF Bowry, A.N.H. Lam, JR Jenkins,
PB Millington Buck, M.J. Bailey. Front row: BM Tabone, CT de Laiglesia, HGC Schofield, HAJ Ross,
ED Walford, T Yabe.*

g v R house final. Penalty.

a bad eye injury sustained at the beginning of
last year's fixtures. In the first year sixth was
Harry Hooper (G) son of OC, Mike, who was to
have a major influence on school sport in his
final two years.

During the year Simon Allen, a member of

1st XI 2001. Back row: CM Bunstead, NEC Armstrong, PS Brennan, WH Young, TCC Marsden, FD Palley, NJ Bunstead, MJB. Front Row: S Sogbetun, JE Green, J-J Williams, RC Griston, (capt) MAA Cook, CEL Watson

Brooke Hall and once head boy and 1st XI goalkeeper at Lancing College, succeeded in qualifying at the FA Level 2 Coaching Certificate. By 2005 he had reached Level 3, a seriously well-earned award. In the summer of 2002 a squad of U16 players attended the Gothia Cup Youth tournament in Gothenburg putting these young players on a highly competitive stage. Their response was excellent and they will have learned much about playing the game at a different level. At the younger age group a very good side was forming at U14A with eleven victories out of 12 and the B XI won 10 games.

In house football Duckites won the Senior final over Robinites, taking the cup for the fourth time in seven years.

Simon Allen ran the A XI during LQ 2003 and his team had the strength of Fred Palley (g) at the helm and some mature players supporting him, such as Nick Bunstead, Ned Millington-Buck (g), Paul Brennan and Mike Stimpson (g). 46 goals were scored in 12 games with two losses to Millfield and away at the Oratory. 9 were put past the Army Crusaders, 6 past Cranleigh and 4 past Chigwell. This was side full of confidence and camaraderie.

For the first time, the school won the ISFA Crusader Six-a-side Cup at Brentwood in September, OQ 2003. I must admit over the years the school has not really taken this competition seriously and although there have been occasional flutters of success, usually in the Plate (one final appearance, losing to Manchester GS), the win this year was most gratifying.

ISFA Sixes Winners 2003. EC Jenner, RP Noble, OD Bardot, FN Barrow, Michael Askham (ISFA), CGC Ingham, TP Tennant, PB Millington Buck, JB Hunter, HP Hooper, T. Yabe, Clive Allen (ex England, Spurs), MJ Bailey.

the ISFA side playing out of position at right back.

In these past seven years, the school had played 110 games and won 77. Bob Noble reminds me that this record stands after he joined me as the Peter Taylor part of a Clough and Taylor duo! This year's team won 8 and drew 3 and had there been a natural goal-scorer I am sure the record would have been better. We only scored 26 goals all season. The defence did its bit by conceding only 11 goals. Tom Tennant kept five consecutive clean sheets

Charlie Ingham's (W) team had a magnificent tournament beating Oswestry, St Edmund's Canterbury and drawing with Ardingly, the team qualified for the main knock-out. Chigwell were disposed of in the last 16, Millfield outplayed us but we managed to force a draw (our goal coming from Patrick Millington-Buck (g)) and then won on penalties, with keeper Tom Tennant (R) literally saving the day. In the semis we played a strong Bradfield six and drew 1-1 again with a goal from Jon Hunter (V). In the shoot out it went to 4-4, then the keepers both scored and in sudden death we scored all five and Bradfield cracked. So on to the final to play St Edmund's again. What happened to all the northern teams? We won the final 3-0 and held the cup for the first time ever. Oli Bardot (W) and Harry Hooper (G) played in every game. Fred Barrow (R), who was dragged from his bed at 7.30am to replace an injured player, scored in the final and Take Yabe (P), only a fifth former, showed his individual class in every game he played.

It was another superb season with wins over all our rivals except Bradfield and Shrewsbury. The Bradfield game had to be played on their second XI pitch because the hot autumn had rendered their main pitch rutted and dangerous.

Ingham was a top-class athlete who had amazing power and speed. He won a place with

in the first half of the term and then four after Exeat. One rare occasion was against Aldenham when with injuries we decided not to disturb the 2nd XI or U16s for a sub but asked an occasional 5th XI player to sit on the bench just in case. At 1-0 up and the game going nowhere Dan Ezekiel (g) took the stage and within minutes met a cross with his head and scored. Fairy tale stuff! The U15A continued their good progress with 11 wins. During the term we had a visit from some footballers from Millwall FC who came and coached for an afternoon. This was engineered by Nick Carter's (g) father who acquired the coaching session at a charity "auction". Duckites won the house final over Daviesites.

In LQ 2004 Simon Allen was again in charge and 5 games were won and 5 lost. Our hold over the Corinthians continued, with Alec Stewart the famous England and Surrey cricketer playing on Big Ground, shortly after his retirement, but failing to help his side to a win. Millfield beat us again and it was good to see Gordon's School emerging as a decent footballing school having altered their status from an independent military school to a "fee paying" state boarding school. Consequently a number of useful sportsmen from the local area joined their ranks.

The Bs won 8 out of 12 with 2 draws. Richard Lewis and I master-minded their strate-

Charlie Ingham

gy and Justin Johnston-Taki (H), a very genial young man, scored his only goal in school football, in his final game. Bruce Forsyth's son JJ (g) also played.

In OQ 2004 seven Duckites made up the school's six-a-side squad when the ISFA competition was played at Repton. Eight Duckites played in the 1st XI which beat the Old Carthusians for the first time for many years. The XI, captained by Patrick Millington-Buck (g), won the unofficial Southern Independent schools' league, winning 11 and drawing 3 of their 17 matches. This might have been the smallest team ever, particularly in defence. Will Holder (g) son of James (OC-g) scored 12 goals. Luke Evans (W) played for the full ISFA U16 squad. James Walker (g) son of Guy (OC-L) and Jamie Cameron (g) both played for the South B. Charlie Nash (W), a fifth, scored a hat-trick at Westminster. George Ellis (V), a Remove and son of Keith Ellis (OC goalie-R) played in our cup game when regular Jon Jenkins was injured. We pitched an XI against our sister school from The Hill, Potstown, Pennsylvania and there was a Fathers v Brooke Hall charity match for Chase on Big Ground in March.

Duckites won the house final beating Weekites 2-1.

During the LQ 2005 the team lost a handful of matches and won a few under Simon's control, whilst the B and C XIs enjoyed the festivities of LQ football and weather.

In May, Sam Bird, a Weekite, who left Charterhouse after the fifth form to continue his education at Millfield and pursue his blossoming career in motor racing, played football in the Michael Schumacher's XI v Prince Albert's XI for charity as an advertisement for the Monaco grand prix. He also played in the ISFA Cup final with his new school.

During the summer of 2005 Nick Carter (g) had to leave the school's annual tour to the Gothia Cup early to join a Sky television programme called "Football Icon" based at Chelsea FC training grounds. Previously thousands of youngsters tried a series of football tests at various road shows around the country. Nick was chosen for the final 40 from these hopeful teenagers and he was invited to spend time at Chelsea's training ground to take part in games to select a final 12 boys. Nick did not succeed but he did appear on nationwide TV and he had made it to the final round!

During OQ 2005 we had high hopes for this XI; they certainly did not let us down. Despite being disappointed about the defeat by Lancing in the last 16 of the Boodles ISFA Cup where we were mugged by long throws, we only lost that game and had splendid victories over all our rivals. We played Highgate in a block fixture for the first time since 1991. A two week half term promised to upset our momentum but 34 of the top players, including some U16s, and two Spanish-speaking members of Brooke Hall, Simon Allen and Richard Noble, along with the master in charge, went to Valencia for four nights in November, a welcome break at a purpose-built resort. There was a new fixture against St Mary's Crosby in the cup (10-1 win) on the wind-swept coast of Lancashire. Once again we could not play the Hampton fixture due to a clash with cup matches and we could not agree on a date to play Shrewsbury – a great loss since this was to be Mark Dickson's last year as Master in Charge of the Shropshire school.

Duckites were clear favourites to win the house cup with all 14 squad players being 1st, 2nd or 3rd XI players. Lockites made a game of it by coming back from 2-0 down to draw level, with Ben Ryder-Smith prominent in his side's recovery, but Richard Rudden's strike following a corner settled the tie and made it four finals on the trot. Duckites also won the 1st tics and Yearlings Cups, as well as being finalists in the Colts. Ed Walford (g) played for the ISFA B XI and eventually the A XI, whilst Anthony Beddows (G) was a permanent fixture in the full IFSA U16 XI. Jamie Cameron played for the South A XI and Take Yabe the South B XI.

LQ 2006 saw the A XI win 8 matches. Take Yabe finished his career of four LQs of football and three OQs, with a goal in his final match.

OC Peter de Savary, entrepreneur, became chairman of the ailing Millwall FC.

The school returned on August 29th OQ 2006 and the grounds were still suffering from a long-term drought.

Against Forest in September 2006 the XI notched up a 7-0 win away and this was the 100th win for the pairing of Bob Noble and myself over nine years and a few weeks. Malvern were beaten the previous Wednesday 5-0 and this would prove to be the last OQ game between

Patrick Millington Buck

the two schools as Malvern changed codes to rugby in their autumn term. By half term the team had won 10 matches out of ten against schools and topped the South league (south sec-

Will Holder (in white)

Jack Tetley catches the ball v. OCXI. Charlie Nash, Harry Schofield, Charlie Clinton, Wayne Paes, Anthony Beddows, in maroon. Matt Bailey, Fred Palley, Seb Henkes facing in stripes.

tion). Brooke Hall completed their fixtures against the boys by playing a Chinese XI!! Probably the best supported game of the term.

The period after Exeat is always tougher and we suffered our first defeat at the hands of St Bede's, Hailsham who with this victory and not losing another game prevented us from getting into the first league cup final. St Bede's played instead and beat the winners of the northern section, Westminster, at the Corinthian Casuals ground in January. But there was consolation in an unusual November double defeating Repton and then Shrewsbury and two more ISFA cup wins at home to Latymer Upper and Manchester GS. We finished the Quarter with 16 wins and three draws scoring 55 goals and conceding 17. I think the 16 OQ wins was a modern day record. There was the prospect of an ISFA Cup semi-final in January also. Duckites won the house cup beating Lockites 2-1 in a dour game. Duckites also won the Junior and Yearlings cups, and both sixes competitions; an unprecedented feat.

Hugo Rubinstein in a tackle, Alex Mason watching.
Bob Noble and MJB in background.

1st XI 2006. Back row: JAF Hall, AED Mason, SJ Cussins, GHT Ellis, JR Satterthwaite, NA Carter, ASD Parsons, MJB Front row: L Evans, AN Beddows, HWH Rubinstein, CD Clinton (capt), CJ Nash, DK Bowman, OR Black.

The Cup run continued into the LQ and by beating Bury GS away in the semi-final, at the end of the January, the XI prepared with special fitness sessions to meet Hampton in Walkers Stadium, Leicester City FC on 5th March. This match was postponed due to waterlogging and had to be rearranged.

A phone call from Ray Lewis on behalf of ESFA on 27th February asking us if Charterhouse could host the under 18 schoolboys' international between England and Belgium was quickly confirmed and by the end of a frantic morning Lessington was roped off and looking in very good condition. Big Ground was too wet but the England schoolboys enjoyed Lessington, winning 5-2, a privilege for both parties.

So to the ISFA Cup final which brought another defeat for a gallant Charterhouse team pitted against the excellent Hampton. Neutrals thought we should have won, having dominated the first quarter of the game, but it was not to be as penalties were our downfall again (see ISFA Cup chapter 14).

During the 2007 OQ the school's six-a-side team won through to the ISFA Sixes final at St Bede's College Manchester with Sir Alex Ferguson as guest of honour. Qualifying in our group by scoring one goal and conceding none, the team thought themselves a little lucky to remain in the competition. Having beaten Victoria College, Jersey 3-0 and then Aldenham 1-0, the team went on to get rid of Brentwood at the semi-final stage and then met the hosts in the final. This could have gone either way but typically we did not spoil their party as we lost 1-2.

The squad of A Beddows (G) capt, G Ellis (V), H Peat (G), C Jamieson (W), J Rogers (V), S Parsons (V), W Walker (g), J Hall (L) were magnificent in their effort. Beddows dragged the team through the matches with his power and Ellis was eager as always to keep a clean sheet. George and Anthony played for the South and they both played ISFA B.

The OQ results were even more of a surprise as the team beat all records, conceding only 5 goals in their 19 school fixtures. There were

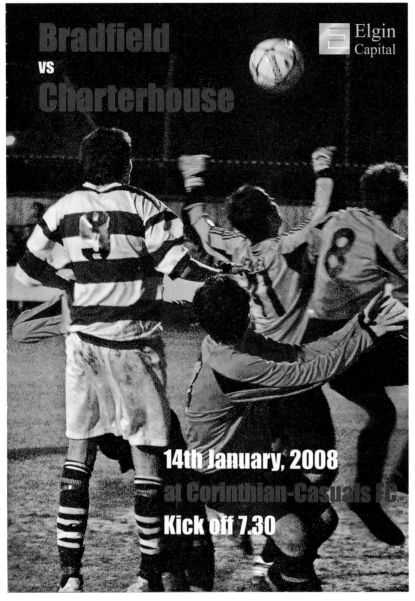

Programme Southern Independent School's League Cup Final

bled in after rebounds. In the second half we never looked back and the second goal came from our left back when George Adolphus (R), aiming for the far post, shanked it and caught the poor Bradfield goalie off his line. We have not had a lot of luck this season in front of goal but this fluke secured the game. The third goal came from a tidy move involving the captain again who found Jamie Hall in front of goal and he scored from short range. We also reached a second consecutive Boodle's ISFA Cup final against Millfield, originally planned to be played at the Walker's Stadium on 10th March at 7pm. With about three weeks to go we heard that Leicester's pitch would not be playable and after some negotiating Woking FC's ground, Kingfield, was made available (see chapter 14).

In the late 20th century, the very popular 1st 'tics (peripatetics) competition still exists, designed for all senior house players not in the 1st or 2nd XI squads. This always provided a social event to look forward to. The Senior and Junior house leagues were split into 5 and 6 teams each in 1970 to give more games, whilst 1st 'tics and 2nd 'tics involved each house playing others weekly. Colts had split leagues and the Yearlings' weekly league matches against every other house. As sport was reformed in the late 1990s, the Senior and Junior house match competitions were returned to knock out cups, with a plate for the first round losers. The others, 1st 'tics,

seven games played consecutively without conceding a goal and a total of 15 wins and 4 draws including our quarter-final Boodles ISFA win over Shrewsbury away. This record helped the team reach the Southern Independent Schools' League Cup final against Bradfield at the Corinthian Casuals Ground on 24th January 2008 at 7.30pm. Six coach loads of Carthusians supported this game which we won 3-0. After absorbing some lively pressure in the opening twenty minutes, a classic "slider" free kick, tried many times but rarely successfully, allowed the captain to cross a low ball that Rogers scram-

Southern Independent School League Cup Winners 2007-8

Colts and Yearlings remained as leagues, but 2nd 'tics was abandoned. In the late 1990s there was a big difference in the quality of house teams and the Yearlings had to be ranked into two groups of "Super Six" and "Friendly Five" to save too many heavy defeats. Junior teams involved Removes and Fourths, where previously Unders also included the Fifths. There is also a six-a-side tournament for Juniors and Seniors.

Edward Grayson in *Corinthians and Cricketers* reports the demise of Charterhouse football by writing, "The picture of Charterhouse football in the days of GO Smith and his great contemporaries makes all the sadder reading when one considers the present decline of football at the school." Nothing could be further from the truth! Perhaps we are not the foot-balling academy we used to be at the turn of the 19th century and rarely does a Carthusian footballer go to Oxbridge to win a Blue, but with eighteen or more school teams playing regularly and a 1st XI revered in ISFA, Charterhouse is still the team to beat. As ISFA Cup holders, southern league champions and having just had a record breaking season the school's football is in very good shape. Our Old Boys, remaining a 'closed' club, have maintained their amateur status and carry on their good work with dignity, presently Arthurian League champions and winning the final of the Arthur Dunn Cup. The OC 2nd XI won their league, the 3rd XI won theirs, the Vets were also victorious in their Cup and more importantly the club was awarded the Sportsmanship Trophy!

CHAPTER 14

the Boodles' isfa cup finals

T he Independent Schools' FA put in place a knock out cup for 1st XIs from HMC schools and Charterhouse was fortunate enough to make their way to the first final. This competition was the brain child of Mark Dickson, then the Shrewsbury master in charge of football who encouraged the famous jewellers, Boodle and Dunthorne, to sponsor the cup.

1992-3

On the way to the final the team played in some memorable matches but none so meaningful as the semi-final victory over our old rivals Shrewsbury on their pitch. When it was needed the Carthusians dug in and none more that game than Ben Wakeham, son of Lord Wakeham. Of course it would have been fitting for Mark Dickson's team to get to the final, since he founded the competition, but the Carthusians put on a superb display to run out 4-2 winners in extra time to spoil the party. Mark was to get his own back in the 2000 final! Twenty-eight teams entered this cup in 1992 and after four rounds the final was played at Craven Cottage on Tuesday March 16th at 7.45pm. David Elleray, a housemaster at Harrow School, refereed supported by Martin Bodenham and Rob Harris – both FIFA referees.

In the first round we played John Lyon School at Harrow and won comfortably 5-1 after two goals from Anton McCourtie. In the next round our oldest rivals, Westminster, came to Big

Ground and we also ran out 5-1 victors with a Leigh Webb hat-trick and so our quarter-final opponents were Bradfield on their own ground. This was a tense affair which we just edged 2-1 with a dramatic last minute winner from Ben Wakeham after Jamie Jarvis had equalised. After this, our epic trip to Shropshire in the Long Quarter was a great advert for schools' soccer and the sponsors would have been proud of their product.

The 1993 final was remarkable in that Quinton Fortune (who went on to play for Athletico Madrid, Manchester United and Bolton Wanderers) was in the Forest line up. Our super star goal-scorer, Leigh Webb, was left behind at school with measles which developed on the day of the game and he could not even watch the match. I remember his matron phoning me up to ask me what she should do! We had a good side but Forest was full of very accomplished players. A crowd of over 1600 watched Charterhouse cope admirably with their opposition at the Fulham FC ground. We had set a plan which included man marking their dangerous player, Fortune. Guy Tassell had that unenviable task which almost worked.

After an even first half, there was a break away goal and we were 1-0 up through Anton McCourtie with 20 minutes left. Forest pulled one back from a set piece to force a draw at full time. They went ahead through their star player in extra time but Charterhouse fought back and drew level after McCourtie and Alasdair Younie combined down the right to enable Jamie Jarvis to equalise at the death. Both teams tired and

1993 Finalists. Back row: Jamie Jarvis, Rob Cunningham-Brown, Doug Sadler, Martin Souter, Guy Tassell, Leigh Webb, Ben Wakeham, MJB. Seated: Alasdair Younie, Anton McCourtie, Brett Akker, Rupert Green, Mike Pate, Tom Walker. Absent: Barnie Weigand.

then penalties had to be taken which Charter-house, exhausted, just could not handle, missing the first three kicks! So there was a defeat, but what a game, what an occasion and what a marvellous season.

The whole event was brilliantly organised, bringing a huge crowd from Godalming, backed up by many friends and OCs from the London area. Forest of course had a large support too. Changing in the Cottage, a floodlit pitch and first-class officials made for a great occasion. There was a formal reception afterwards and much celebration despite the result.

The next school match, by the way, was against Douai School, away, on the following Wednesday, which we lost 2-3!

1999-2000

A victory over Winchester 2-0, with goals from Jon Byrne and Will Clark in the first round, set us up for an away match at QEGS, Blackburn. After a delightful stop-over at the "Chimneys" guest house, we trained on a wet and blustery morning but found their pitch in excellent condition. We rode our luck when Tim Blake headed a certain goal off our line from a corner towards the end of the game. Ian MacAuslan and the captain, Matt Bailey, scored our goals by the 60th minute. With the game balanced at 2-2, after extra time, it came down to penalties and Dominic Heaton-Watson played the psychological game with their shooters to secure a 5-4 result. In the Blackburn side was a young Chris Porter who later played at Bury, Oldham and Motherwell.

The quarter final eventually was played late in the term, away at Bury GS 2-1 on a slushy, mud heap of a pitch in December. The game should

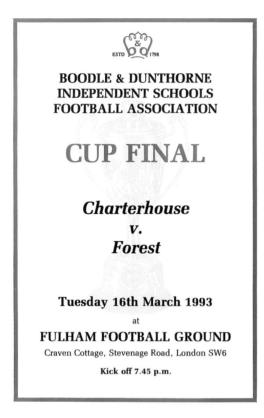

**BOODLE & DUNTHORNE
INDEPENDENT SCHOOLS
FOOTBALL ASSOCIATION**

CUP FINAL

*Charterhouse
v.
Forest*

Tuesday 16th March 1993

at

FULHAM FOOTBALL GROUND

Craven Cottage, Stevenage Road, London SW6

Kick off 7.45 p.m.

1993 Match programme

not really have been played but we needed to get the game over before the end of term and they agreed. Their master in charge was Mark Aston, son of John, who starred in the Manchester United European Cup win at Wembley. Despite being put under the cosh by an aggressive home team, Matt Bailey and Jon Jackson scored within four minutes of each other midway through the second half. Bury got one back and Matt Smith cleared off the line in the final minutes following their desperate last minute surge. As we travelled back to Manchester on the metro we looked back at the playing fields and saw a brown mass which looked like a First World War battlefield.

LQ 2000 therefore included preparations for the ISFA Cup semi-final. We had to keep our feet on the ground and play as much football as possible – a problem with half the team in the hockey squad. Godalming Town helped us out by letting us train and play under their floodlights, and we managed friendlies to bring the team

together, but it turned out this was never going to be enough. Brentwood have been one of the more successful teams in the cup and once again we were playing away in January. Trying to blend the team together with some playing hockey would be a problem and indeed we lost our striker, Will Clark, who had stepped on a hockey ball in practice. Any route to a final is going to be challenging and this sequence of away matches and quality of opposition would test the best of any school XI in the country. Beating Brentwood on the way in the semi-final was a real bonus although our goal had a charmed life. However a 2-0 victory away from home seemed comfortable. We hit Brentwood hard in the first half scoring twice through Jackson and Chris Shelton. By the second half we were under pressure and managed to dig in and survive. Jon Goodrich almost snatched a third on the break and our defence performed heroics for much of the second half. Two coach loads of Carthusians came to watch and it made a difference having the support of friends on a distant field.

In school matches through the season, only one match was lost against Repton, and this was away on a bad day for the team. For the rest, the team won every game, eleven of them, with 37 goals coming freely and a mean defence conceding only 6 including 3 against Repton! Matthew Bailey (V) led his team from the front and even in the last game at Filbert Street, his swashbuckling style was maintained to the bitter end. He scored 13 goals and with Will Clark (g) and Jon Jackson (g) there was a potent strike force. Chris Shelton (D), Ian MacAuslan (R), Jon Goodrich (L) and James Toller (D) provided attacking support whilst the defence was as solid as the record shows. Matt Smith (D), Jon Byrne (g), Sam Spinks (D), Alan Mezzetti (B) and Tim Blake (D) formed a formidable unit with Dominic Heaton-Watson (B), the son of another member of Brooke Hall, Richard Heaton-Watson, the final line of defence.

The preparation for the final involved a night at a hotel in Quorn paid for by one of the parents and we had a morning training session at a local pitch and a nervous wait for the evening

Anton McCourtie scores to put Charterhouse 1-0 in front

The Captains and Officials before the Kick Off

ISFA CUP FINAL 1993

Jarvis equalises in extra time

CHARTERHOUSE v FOREST

McCourtie on the ball

Photographs by B R Souter and R W Smeeton

Rupert Green receives his medal from Jimmy Hill

A near miss

Collage of photos from 1993 final

Collage of photos from 2000 final

kick off. Our specially embroidered kit had not been unwrapped until the evening of the match, when we found that some of the heat pressing had stuck the two sides of the shirt together! This situation was rescued only after some worrying moments. Shrewsbury and Charterhouse are the best of friends and fiercest rivals so it was no wonder that the ISFA Cup Final attendance record of over 1700 was broken that evening at Filbert Street.

The game was heart-breaking because we had all the early pressure and could not score. Shrewsbury as expected were no push over and in the second half scored a goal from a long

2000 final. Back row: Ben Deschampsneufs, Will Clark, Chris Shelton, Jon Byrne, Sam Spinks, Alan Mezzetti, Richard Burke-Murphy, Richard Griston. Front row: James Toller, John Goodrich, Dominic Heaton-Watson, Matthew Smith, Matthew Bailey, John Jackson, Ian MacAuslan, Tim Blake.

shot. 0-1 down meant all hands to the pumps and despite the determined attempts of all the team, with cramps setting in, we could not reach

---

BOODLE & DUNTHORNE INDEPENDENT SCHOOLS FOOTBALL ASSOCIATION

CUP FINAL

Charterhouse
v.
Shrewsbury

Monday, 20th March 2000
at
LEICESTER CITY FOOTBALL CLUB
Filbert Street, Leicester

Kick-off 7.00 p.m.

2000 Match programme

---

parity. Two finals, seven years apart, two close defeats.

Having a top school team succeeding in such a prestigious competition gives the school a lift and although the hockey team was disrupted occasionally by the march to the final it would be fair to say that the LQ hockey team had a good run of results, their best season ever, on the back of this confidence. PR was good too and as *The Times* reported of the game, "Emile Heskey was surely never exhorted to greater efforts to the strains of Jerusalem or the Star Wars theme as rendered by the Charterhouse orchestra!"

2006-7

Having gone away to St Mary's School, Crosby last year in the Cup we were drawn against them this year in the 2nd round. We won 10-1 last time but it was not such a cake-walk in 2006, as we conceded a sparkling own goal by Sam Cussins from wide left-back just before half-time. St Mary's put up fierce resistance and despite all our best efforts the equaliser was not coming. We only secured a win in the 81st and 82nd minutes when Hugo Rubinstein scored a characteristic headed goal and Sam Parsons shot

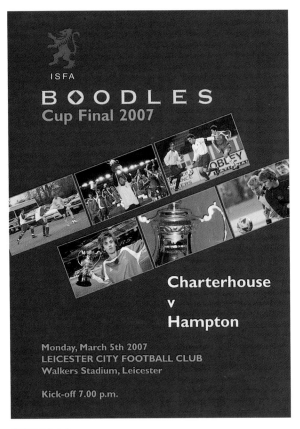

2007 Match programme

from the edge of the penalty area to help us have a cheerful journey home!

Latymer Upper 3-1 gave us a slight scare but some solid team play and a third goal by Charlie Clinton sealed a good victory in front of a lively crowd. Manchester GS came to us and a win by 2-1 was a well deserved victory in front of the school. Beddows and Nash scored. We were then drawn away for a semi-final fixture at Bury GS, bringing reminiscences of the 1999-2000 campaign. Actually the day was fair and several degrees warmer than last time. The pitch had good grass on it and we played strong and well-organised football, winning comfortably 2-0. Rubinstein and Carter scored.

The other semi-final was where the top ranks were and Hampton reached their third final beating Millfield 2-1 away. The final was destined originally for 19th March when our term had finished. Pre-empting that we might qualify, the organisers brought the final forward to 5th March which sadly went pear-shaped as depression after depression crossed the country bring-

ing rain that made the pitch waterlogged on the day and unplayable. We arrived at Walker's Stadium, Leicester to hear the news and we were allowed to see the pitch which quite honestly looked in perfect condition. Nobody from ISFA was there to help assess the situation, apart from me, but the schools do not have a leg to stand on and phone calls had to be made at the last minute to stop the 16 coaches and dozens of OCs, parents, guests and friends from travelling. Having been taken to the plateau of performance the bubble had burst and we had to wait for a new date for the final. After some considerable negotiation, Mark Dickson plumped for Friday 27th April at 7pm at Walker's Stadium, Leicester City FC. The whole procedure had to start again but we had four weeks holiday. Hampton finished term on 31st March but went back after us on 25th April. During the Easter break training at Battersea with the OCs was one opportunity to bring the players together but never more than half a dozen were able to take advantage. Running on the beach, skiing and occasionally getting a game with a local side was the best that the players could achieve. So by 17th April as the Carthusians returned, a very warm and dry spell of weather suited cricket more than football and with limited time to prepare the players snatched every opportunity

Hugo Rubinstein could not get the final touch to score a winner v Hampton. Sam Parsons is number 12

Back left: MJB, M Manches, C Jamieson, J Carnegie-Brown, A Mason, D Bowman, J Satterthwaite, S Cussins, S Parsons, J Rogers, RPN. Front left: C Harper, L Evans, A Beddows, H Rubinstein, C Clinton, C Nash, G Ellis, O Black.

Charlie Clinton

Hugo Rubinstein

Anthony Beddows

Charlie Nash scores

Collage of photos from 2007 final

to practice. A friendly against Godalming Town FC on the Tuesday before the final was our only full match.

Arriving at the Walker's Stadium it was a great feeling to be inside a proper ground and our crowd arrived in their coach-loads. Inside the dressing rooms there were all the trappings of a pro club and it was a privilege to experience it. The *Carthusian* reports:

As in their two previous visits to the ISFA Cup final, Charterhouse came away disappointed. They had proved the equal of a much vaunted Hampton team in everything but penalty kicks. Sadly, equal was not good enough. But what an occasion it was! And what a fight the team put up! Sixteen coaches transported almost the entire school to the Walkers Stadium, home of Leicester City FC, for the final. An enormous logistical operation in itself, it was made doubly difficult by the fact that the ground was deemed unfit on March 5th the original date for the final and the new date involved travelling on a Friday afternoon in the CQ. Nevertheless, all arrived safely and on time and the Charterhouse spectators, bedecked for the most part in pink tee-shirts and pink beanies and wearing commemorative scarves, gave the team rousing support from start to finish. The game began at a frenetic pace and Charterhouse were soon in the lead with a spectacular goal (opposite) from Charlie Nash after only two minutes. His shot into the bottom corner of the net subsequently won him the Chris Saunders award for the Golden Moment of the game. Charterhouse continued to press and after 18 minutes were awarded a penalty when the irrepressible Nash was upended in the box. Had they scored, the game would surely have been theirs for the taking, but sadly, with the goalkeeper diving the wrong way, the ball went the wrong way too and shaved the outside of the post. Hampton drew heart from this and, while they were unable to make any impression up to half-time, neither were Charterhouse able to extend their advantage. It still appeared that Charterhouse would prevail, however - not least because they were clearly the fitter side - but with fifteen minutes left on the clock, a carelessly conceded free kick led to the Hampton equaliser and gave the opposition a

great lift. As fatigue and cramp set in, the game dwindled into a draw and twenty minutes of extra time still could not separate the sides. And so it came to penalties. Hampton dispatched theirs with the aplomb and efficiency of a crack German unit, while Charterhouse showed rather more English fallibility and the Cup slipped from their grasp.

2007-8

During the OQ, to get to another final was furthest from our dreams but by 23rd January, Anthony Beddows had led his team to another celebration by winning four matches, each one away and each one to the furthest parts of the country. After a first round bye, a 2nd round match at Blackburn against QEGS was fairly daunting for this new team, but on a superb pitch against a young opposition Beddows showed the way with two goals in a 4-0 win. Jack Rogers, and Charlie Watson completed the rout. So confident were we so that we gave Rob Procter the sub-goalkeeper a run out up front. This was a strong performance and since this XI did not concede many goals (5 in 20 games through the season) there was always a chance of victory. The boys decided that a curry was a very good way of gelling the team together, a

Anthony Beddows – the inspirational captain

decision made only when our hotel on the Preston Road had a power cut and could not produce food.

When the balls came out of the hat for the last 16, we were heading to Newcastle for the first time, playing the Royal Grammar School. Their beak, Peter Shelley, had arranged to play the tie at Whitley Bay FC, a real treat for us on a sunny but blustery day. We re-enacted the great 19th century Old Carthusian FC visits to the northeast, during the Amateur Cup's halcyon days, by dressing up in period sports' wear and Bob Noble was the bag man with wing collar and waistcoat. Every trip needed a theme and this worked as a distraction in the morning before the game. The home pitch was spacious and had a good surface so we had no excuses. The first half went well as we played brilliant football down wind but we were only 1-0 up at half-time following Beddows's header from a corner. We then proceeded almost to throw the game, finding it difficult to get out of our half. In the end it was a decent win after a tense second half. The train journey home was fun.

Surely a home game next but needless to say the draw was destined to give us Shrewsbury away in the last eight. They should have come to us for the traditional game, so we swapped venues and played on a much improved Shrewsbury pitch against a team who fancied their chances.

We knew how good they were but maintained our confident approach to the game, as we had done in the previous ties. Shrewsbury away needed no special themes although the traditional pre-match rituals of curry and an Italian meal for the coaches were repeated. In front of their lively crowd, a number of our parents and many interested neutrals, it was a very even game that ended 2-2, after extra time. Charlie Watson at the back post and then Tom Kimmins scored our goals in normal time. Then there were penalties which brought back ghosts from last year's final. We need not have worried because after drawing 4-4 in the first round, our extra penalty takers did us proud and a poor Salopian rattled the bar to give us victory. There were tense moments as George Ellis, Sam Parsons and then George Adolphus were thrown into the limelight. As their penalties went in their fathers jumped gleefully together like over-excited schoolboys. Some celebration then occurred, walking proudly off the Salopian turf, their crowd drifting away. A large meal on the way home was the boys' reward, paid for by the grateful parents. The two goals we conceded meant that our goal had been breached five times only in the term – surely the secret of our success.

The last hurdle was to be jumped in the Long Quarter, so the winter break and Christmas holiday interrupted our momentum. We were

George Ellis makes the vital save

Oli Black wins the game

drawn to travel to Chester and meet King's School who had won the Cup twice before and had a good pedigree. We did not get a chance to watch them because their games prior to the semi-final had been called off due to water-logged pitches. Their pitch was in very good condition on a blustery, dry day and on a lush turf we dominated the game but only managed one goal via Beddows's cross and Hall's clever header. King's were spirited and young and no doubt will do well next year. But it was our triumph and another final beckoned in March.

We heard a week later that it was to be Millfield who had comfortably beaten Haileybury, surprise members of the final four. Coincidently, their old boys had made their way into the Arthur Dunn semi-finals also, a great step for a Lent term soccer school. Another final at Leicester City was set for 10th March but a phone call two weeks before the day from the hard working Mark Dickson told me that the pitch would not be playable because it had been in a state all season and the club could not accommodate us. The ISFA diplomatic machine went into action and guest of honour for the final, Martin Tyler, helped us acquire Kingfield at Woking instead. The boys were not over excited by this but a final is a final wherever it is played.

As we prepared for this fourth final, a game against the OCs on a mid February Sunday afternoon and then another game against Didcot Town FC away the following Sunday, gave the squad a chance to play together. Injuries acquired in 1st XI hockey matches and A XI games meant that we did not actually play the full side together between the semi-final and final. It did allow Tom Bray (W) the opportunity to step up to the squad and as a fifth former he had achieved something that he would not have dreamed of during the OQ when he was playing for the Under 16 A XI. The hockey team was also having a good term and the last school match before the final ended with an 8-1 demolition of Epsom College, leaving Jamie Hall, the school's striker, full of confidence after helping himself to a hat-trick. The A XI footballers played St Bede's, Hailsham two days before the final and careful substitutions protected the

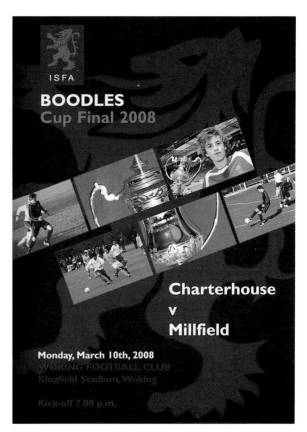

2008 Match programme

players but probably engineered a 0-1 defeat to a lively side that the full 1st XI had struggled to beat in September.

As the final drew near so did a deep depression over the Atlantic with tornadoes on the eastern seaboard of the USA, bringing the threat of storm force winds and heavy rain to the Woking pitch. We waited with baited breath. Disaster struck as torrential rain fell with gusts of 60 mile an hour winds during the early hours of Monday March 10th forcing a postponement at 8.30 am. This was another disappointment and the emotional stress of reorganising another venue was beginning to takes its toll. Mark Dickson, knowing that both sides wanted to get the game played before the end of term, tossed a coin at 5pm on the Monday evening and Charterhouse won the choice of venue for the first Boodles' ISFA Cup final to be played at a school the following Wednesday. With only two days to spare, we had to think about the organisation at Charterhouse amongst the usual day-to-day events such as hashes at 2.15 until 3.40pm, annual commitments such as the Godalming Music Festival and the fact that we also had Reading FC arriving with a young academy side to play Charterhouse at 4.15pm.

It was as fate had contrived to bring the school success after three previous failed attempts in a tense and momentous game in front of the school on the historic Big Ground. Millfield arrived with their talented squad included the ESFA goalkeeper and several members of the ISFA squad. Conditioned to a peak of fitness they began the afternoon as favourites and so on a beautifully sunny but very blustery day the game kicked off in front of Martin Tyler the guest of honour and hundreds of pupils, school staff, OCs, parents and friends.

Nick Pelling, Charterhouse's 2nd XI coach, wrote this account of the game.

Nick Pelling's account of the 2008 ISFA Cup Final

The Boodles ISFA Cup Final 2008: The Whale has Landed.

The Victorian headmaster Haig Brown looked unruffled in the turbulent breeze, seemingly immune to the emotions inherent in the occasion. As the young players jogged onto the pitch they drifted past the little stone plaque that silently offered up the information that only a mere 127 years before, the Old Carthusians had lifted the original FA Cup. In a way, just possibly, football was returning to at least one of its historic homes. Even those that thought little about these things could feel the tug of History in the wind. Haig Brown, however, simply concentrated on balancing the school in his right hand. But then again, manly self control is easy for statues.

For many years Charterhouse has not had an entirely happy relationship with the finals of this relatively new competition. Three times finalists and three times losers, there was an unspoken hoodoo hanging over the game. To say that the coaching duo of Bailey and Noble had developed the equivalent of Captain Ahab's obsession with the big football whale would be silly, but there was something odd in the way the pair scanned the horizon. Earlier omens had not been

good. For a while it was a fixture without a home, thanks to problems at Leicester City, and then it became the fixture that the hard Woking rain would not allow, and then, worryingly, it seemed it was the fixture that had run out of school diary time. But, in the end a flipped coin brought the game spinning back to Big Ground.

On the actual day almost the entire school frothed and tumbled around the edge of the pitch as the powerful figure of premiership referee Howard Webb got the game under way. In the late winter sunshine Charterhouse began brightly. Hall and Rogers looked lively up front and for a while the supposedly superior Millfield team could find no rhythm. But gradually they began to play football and Charterhouse started to look a little ragged. Jamieson was booked on twenty-six minutes and then just before half-time the wind dropped, and time itself stood still, as a ball looped up over goalkeeper George Ellis and the crowd sensed it might just drop under the bar. Instead, it bounced off the bar and breathing was resumed among the faithful. Just before half-time Rogers bravely headed from beneath the Millfield keeper's flailing arms but the ball flashed over. By half-time it was honours about even.

In the second half, Millfield began to press and cunningly substituted the wind for a different wind that opened new angles against the House defence. The crowd grew a little subdued. Several Mexican waves broke flimsily on the rocks of worried faces. And yet Charterhouse occasionally flared into action: a marvellous shot on the turn by Hall underlined the fact that this was a game balanced on a waning knife-edge. As the match moved towards its climax, Millfield made a substitution but the maroon back four stood firm, Adolphus almost making light of his chores. Watson fought for everything, but it was the sight of a cramp-struck Beddows, however, which did most to suggest that the Charterhouse ship was about to go down. And yet the captain stayed at his station, though this proved to be a location falling further and further back.

In extra time the lofty school flag was pulled almost off its moorings by the wind, but still flapped and fluttered away. The defence seemed similarly yanked about but amazingly resilient. At the heart of it

Jamieson yelled and cajoled while Black quietly set about extinguishing small fires around the box. As extra time came towards its end, it slowly dawned that the game that could not find a way to start had become the game that could not find a way to end. Without a goal it was not perhaps a great game but it was in a way a quite exceptional display of old fashioned grit by Charterhouse.

During the penalties, never have so many Carthusians been so silent. Even for Millfield's penalties, each individual's confrontation with the agony of choice seemed to cast a soundless spell. There were particular moments when the suspense reached an awful crescendo. On the fifth penalty, when defeat was just a kick away, it was Kimmins, not Haig Brown, who held the whole of the school in his hand – or at least on the end of his foot. He despatched it with no fuss, to the overwhelming relief of most. Harry Peat and Sam Parsons faced similar moments of destiny and held their nerves, though there was a hint of a slice in Harry's audacious top right selection. Then, suddenly it was the hands of goalkeeper George Ellis who grabbed an opportunity. The chance to lift the ISFA jinx fell to the redoubtable Oli Black. He did it with aplomb and the entire crowd of educated and civilised young Carthusians dissolved into mayhem.

It wasn't quite a miracle, and manly self control was maintained amongst the beaks, and the statues, but for many, and two coaches in particular, the hoodoo was finally blown away.

2008 Cup Winners. Back row: George Adolphus, Sam Parsons, Oli Black, Anthony Beddows, George Ellis Jack Rogers, Harry Peat, Tom Bray, Rob Procter. Front row: Peter Doggart, Tom Kimmins, Charlie Jamieson, Charlie Clinton, Jamie Hall, Will Walker, Dan Linden

ENDNOTE

This has been a rather biased account and it should be admitted that Millfield were a little unlucky, exceptionally able and magnanimous in defeat. For those that worry about these things, the final score was 8-7. NSP

The boys enjoyed a large party in the Squirrel afterwards with their parents and friends. The film company that videoed the match joined them showing the game again on the pub's TV screen; who knows what the local clientele felt about that. Beddows and Ellis slept with the two cups their team had won during the season.

As the strains of "Jerusalem" echo around Chapel during the final service of the LQ, this marvellous season is now behind us; three finals, unbeaten in school games, a watertight defence and great camaraderie and undying spirit that those Carthusians from the Golden period of soccer would have admired. The whole school was lifted at the end of another intensely busy LQ and the pupils can say that they were there to witness another cup final and another victory. I can finish off the narrative of this book now a happy man.

the fixture card

Referring to the list of fixtures played since 1862 there are many different types of "foreign" opposition to have pitted their skills against the pupils of Charterhouse. Early fixtures were mainly home games against elevens brought together by members of the teaching staff (Mr Page), Old Carthusians (NJ Abdy) or an enthusiastic friend of the school and the game such as Lord Kinnaird. Brooke Hall turned out a team and only during the 1990s did they cease to play the 1st XI, finding the gap between the two teams too great. Brooke Hall still plays house teams and some of the lesser school teams including the Chinese XI. Some clubs such as St Bartholomew's Club, the Civil Service and the Crusaders were regulars in this early period.

February 1864 saw the fist match against an Old Carthusians team and this fixture has varied over the years from a match against an all star International XI in the late 19th century, to the five fixtures now regularly played on the first Saturday of OQ. Inevitably OCs from Oxford and Cambridge, London University and the London Hospitals appeared with sides.

For example, G Cardale was a local day boy who went to Oriel College, Oxford and brought an XI to play in 1862. HC Malkin (G) was a scholar at Trinity College, Cambridge and he was an assistant master in 1862-3 when he raised a visiting team. He later became the first president of the Greyfriar Cricket Club (1874-9) which eventually founded the OC Club. HH Gilbert (W) and KA Muir MacKenzie (SG), who was captain of the school team in 1862-3, both brought teams. The Honourable FG Pelham was an Old Etonian who played cricket for Cambridge and Sussex. His team played the school in 1865. James Butter (G) went to Balliol, Oxford and his "Oxford" side played the school in 1866-7 when he was the Gownboy Master.

The first recorded schools' fixture was against Westminster in 1863. This we regard as the longest played schools' fixture in history. Westminster had played Harrow

Football.

FOOTBALL MATCHES FOR 1880—81.

October	2nd, v. Brooke Hall	At Charterhouse.
„	16th, v. Clapham Rovers	„
„	23rd, v. Sandhurst	„
November	6th, v. Old Etonians	„
„	13th, v. Remnants	„
„	20th, v. Old Carthusians	„
„	27th, v. Old Harrovians	„
December	4th, v. Pilgrims	„
„	11th, v. Wanderers	„
January	29th, v. H. A. Carter's Eleven	„
February	5th, v. Remnants	„
„	12th, v. Brooke Hall	„
„	26th, v. Westminster	„
March	11th, v. Sandhurst	„
„	19th, v. Clapham Rovers	„
„	26th, v. Old Carthusians	„

Fixture list 1880-1

and Eton prior to this and indeed the match in 1863 was 'the first match for many years'. By 1865 the school team was considered to be worthy opponents for the legendary "Wanderers", a team that dominated football into the 1880s. The Wanderers were originally known as Forest, emanating from Epping in Essex. Another group of assorted public school boys made up the Remnants who tried to follow the standard set by the Wanderers.

After the watershed of 1863, when the Association was formed, more teams emerged and fewer "internal games" at school were necessary. The Harrow Chequers, Old Etonians and West Kent begin to appear frequently on the fixture card around the late 1860s. The Royal Engineers, also a dominant force at the time, played from 1868 although of course there is no confirmation of which XI they would have turned out, but the names in the Captain's Book do suggest that the leading players of their time did come to Godalming. It was regarded as a privilege to play the school.

As the FA Cup was inaugurated, Charterhouse was hosting matches against Clapham Rovers, Walthamstow, Barnes, a club formed as early as 1838, and Crystal Palace. Some of these clubs were in the hat in 1871-2 when the first cup draw was made. Of course this coincided with the school's move from London to the spacious Godalming site. The fixture against the Civil Service that year was reported to have been the first foreign match played at Godalming.

Winchester played us in 1873 but there was then a gap in fixtures until 1902; however by then the Old Wykehamists had been playing us since 1887. AL Irvine wrote to the *Carthusian* in December 1958 to explain that the Register was wrong in dating the first match against Winchester as 1904. He said that he had a record of the two schools playing on February 26th 1902. He had met the Winchester captain of that time who was a junior contemporary of his at school and college. He had left his t'other'un (prep school) at the same time as the prospective Charterhouse captain of 1901-2 and had invited the Charterhouse XI to visit Winchester at the end of the season for an unofficial match. By

that time the captain had left unexpectedly and the replacement was OT Norris (later in 1958 a member of the school's Governing Body). The match appeared in the fixture list as CJ de B Sheringham's XI but the actual match is given in the March *Carthusian* 1902 as a win for the school 2-0.

The Weyside Club formed in 1870 played in red and white harlequin shirts and Reigate Priory, the Swifts and a curiously named team, Gitanos who played in Battersea Park, made frequent visits to the school.

During 1875 is recorded the first "Army" fixture and these increased in number around the war years and of course brought a foreign flavour to the school, as we played Canadian teams, for example, who would have been stationed at Witley or nearby in one of the many Surrey heathland barracks. Aldershot may have been a town side but could have been another military team. The Royal Military College at Sandhurst became regular opponents from 1878 as did the RMA at Woolwich. We have played matches against the college from Sandhurst in recent years.

In 1876 the Bradfieldian Waifs and then, one year later, the Old Harrovians sent teams here as did the Old Reptonians in 1880. Repton is in Derbyshire, so one presumes these were London based old boys, who, like today, represent their school in the Arthurian League.

WW Drew's XI in 1877 probably came from King's, Cambridge, his destination after he had been in Gownboys as Head of School, captain of cricket and in the football XI between 1871-3.

As football prospered in the school, amongst the old boys and nationally, so more prestigious teams came to play; Oxford XIs, the famous Corinthians and the Casuals, then two separate clubs and well known internationals such as Cobbold and Smith provided teams made up from their footballing friends. WTB Hayter (LH) led his team to play the XI in 1878 and in 1927 he was made the Master of the Charterhouse. In the Cup winning year, 1881, WH Norris who had been school captain and who later played in the Cup Final provided opposition. WG Morrison (W) led his team to a 7-0 defeat in LQ 1882 and with TW Blenkiron (H) founded the Casuals AFC. The Rev CC Tancock organised a team in 1882-3 and during 1886-96 he was the headmaster of Rossall School and later headmaster at Tonbridge 1899-1907. AJ Webbe was an Old Harrovian who played for Middlesex CCC and his team played in 1885 as did AK Henley's (Rg) who captained the school team in 1881.

The Corinthians were founded in 1872 and the Casuals a year later in 1873. The Corinthians club began when Blenkiron, with F Buckley, set the wheels in motion and used Buckley's racing colours of pink and chocolate on the shirts. The Casuals club was a "nursery" to the great Corinthians and this probably explains why the school played the Casuals more frequently than their more prestigious partners. In 1921 the two clubs agreed to work more closely and it was C Wreford Brown who said that "this meeting is of the opinion that efforts should be made to obtain a suitable ground in the London area which might be used by both clubs". This ground was to be at the old Crystal Palace.

The Corinthians were in decline during 1907-14 during the period when the amateurs and professionals split. The club could no longer play competitively against the professionals and some of the best players moved to bigger clubs. The Great War took its toll also and the club suffered but gradually re-established itself in the 1920s, especially in the FA Cup. At this time Carthusians AG Bower and JFS Morrison were ever present.

In 1887, the school first played Godalming FC, but once again it is not easy to decipher what this team represented. Today the school still plays the local Godalming and Guildford FC, albeit their youth team, and sometimes we are lucky enough to play on their ground, under floodlights. Other local teams have played including Dennis Athletic whom I suspect are associated with the lorry manufacturer, Dennis of Guildford, whose original factory was sited south-west of the town.

As football developed and leagues formed, the school began to lose some of the club fixtures and more Old Boys sides (Old Rossalians, Old Brightonians) filled the gaps. 1894 saw the first match against the Liverpool Ramblers who still tour in the south bringing three teams to us. The Ramblers club is made up from old boys in the north-west region and local players, lucky enough to have their own grounds in Crosby, Merseyside. One may regard the Ramblers as the northern equivalent of the Corinthian Casuals, a club determined to promote football in the schools and to give every school leaver a chance to play.

The Lessington ground was first played on in 1898 and this suggests that there was now room for more games on impressive pitches. By the

Football.

Football Fixtures, Season 1908–9 :—

Date.		Opponents.	Where Played.
Saturday,	Oct. 3, 1908	1st XI. v. A. H. Tod, Esq.'s XI. ..	Charterhouse
Saturday,	,, 10. ..	1st XI. v. R.M.A. Woolwich	,,
Saturday,	,, 17. ..	1st XI. v. Weybridge	,,
Saturday,	,, 24. ..	1st XI. v. Casuals	,,
Saturday,	,, 31. ..	1st XI. v. R.M.C. Sandhurst ..	,,
Wednesday,	Nov. 4. ..	1st XI. v. P.C. Smythe, Esq.'s XI. ..	,,
Saturday,	,, 7. ..	1st XI. v. Kenley	,,
Saturday,	,, 14. ..	1st XI. v. Beckenham	,,
Wednesday,	,, 18. ..	1st XI. v. Outcasts..	,,
Saturday,	,, 21. ..	1st XI. v. Liverpool Ramblers ..	,,
Saturday,	,, 28. ..	1st XI. v. Addiscombe Park ..	,,
Wednesday,	Dec. 2. ..	1st XI. v. Oxford University " A"	,,
Saturday,	,, 5. ..	1st XI. v. B. H. Willett, Esq.'s XI. ..	,,
Saturday,	**,, 12. ..**	**1st XI. v. OLD CARTHUSIANS ..**	**Charterhouse**
Tuesday,	**,, 22. ..**	**1st XI. v. REPTON .. .. ..**	
Wednesday,	**,, 23. ..**	**1st XI. v. OLD INTERNATIONALS**	**Queen's Club**
Saturday,	Jan. 30, 1909	1st XI. v. Emeriti	Charterhouse
Wednesday,	Feb. 3. ..	1st XI. v. C. D. White, Esq.'s XI. ..	,,
Saturday,	,, 6. ..	1st XI. v. Clapham Rovers	,,
Wednesday,	,, 10. ..	1st XI. v. Casuals	,,
Wednesday,	,, 17. ..	1st XI. v. Reigate Priory	,,
Saturday,	,, 20. ..	1st XI. v. Oriel College, Oxford ..	,,
Saturday,	,, 27. ..	1st XI. v. Oxford University " A"	,,
Wednesday,	Mar. 3. ..	1st XI. v. Old Wykehamists ..	,,
Saturday,	**,, 6. ..**	**1st XI. v. WESTMINSTER ..**	**Charterhouse**
Tuesday,	**,, 9. ..**	**1st XI. v. WINCHESTER ..**	**Winchester**
Saturday,	,, 13. ..	1st XI. v. Norsemen	Charterhouse
Saturday,	,, 20. ..	1st XI. v. Lancing Old Boys ..	,,
Wednesday,	Oct. 21. 1908	2nd XI. v. Cranleigh	Charterhouse
Saturday,	,, 31. ..	2nd XI. v. Reigate St. Marys ..	,,
Wednesday,	Nov. 11. ..	2nd XI. v. Cranleigh	Cranleigh
Saturday,	Dec. 19. ..	2nd XI. v. C. K. Denny, Esq.'s XI.	Charterhouse
Saturday,	Feb. 18. 1909	2nd XI. v. R.M.C. Sandhurst 2nd XI.	,,
Wednesday,	,, 24. ..	2nd XI. v. R. C. Peache, Esq.'s XI. ..	,,
Wednesday,	Mar. 10. ..	2nd XI. v. Brooke Hall	,,
Monday,	Oct. 12, 1908	House Matches, 1st Round.. ..	Charterhouse
Monday,	Nov. 2. ..	House Matches, 2nd Round	,,
Monday,	,, 23. ..	House Matches, Semi-Final	,,
Tuesday,	Dec. 8. ..	House Matches, Final	,,

Fixture card 1908-9

Football.

Fixtures for Oration Quarter, 1921 :—

Date.	Opponents.	Where Played.
Sat., Sept. 24.	1st XI *v.* Rev. E. M. Jameson's XI	Charterhouse
Sat., Oct. 1.	1st XI *v.* Toc H.	,,
Sat., ,, 8.	1st XI *v.* Old Foresters	,,
Wed., ,, 12.	1st XI *v.* University Coll., London	,,
Sat., ,, 15.	1st XI *v.* Old Malvernians ...	,,
Sat., ,, 22.	1st XI *v.* Magdalen Coll., Oxford	,,
Wed., ,, 26.	1st XI *v.* Stage F.C.	,,
Sat., ,, 29.	1st XI *v.* Old Bradfield Boys ...	,,
Wed., Nov. 2.	1st XI *v.* BRADFIELD	**Bradfield**
Sat., ,, 5.	1st XI *v.* LANCING	**Charterhouse**
Wed., ,, 9.	1st XI *v.* Jesus Coll., Cambridge ...	,,
Sat., ,, 12.	1st XI *v.* R.M.A., Woolwich ...	,,
Thur., ,, 17.	1st XI *v.* REPTON	**Repton**
Wed., ,, 23.	1st XI *v.* Trinity Coll., Oxford ...	Charterhouse
Sat., ,, 26.	1st XI *v.* University Coll., Reading	,,
Sat., Dec. 3.	1st XI *v.* Old Carthusians ...	,,
Sat., ,, 10.	1st XI *v.* Corinthians	,,
Wed., ,, 14.	1st XI *v.* Oxford University Centaurs	,,
Sat., Oct. 15.	2nd XI *v.* Old Carthusian "A" ...	,,
Wed., ,, 19.	2nd XI *v.* No. 3 Coy. R.M.C. ...	,,
Wed., Nov. 20.	"A" team *v.* Bedales	,,

Fixture card 1921

First World War there were a number of military opposition available – for example the Artists Rifles and the Hampshires. There was also developing an established fixture card against schools.

There were two matches against Eton in 1900-1 and 1901-2, neither of which were "sanctioned" by Eton and not acknowledged by their "games committee". The next time we played Eton was in 1943.

Curiously, it was Repton again who became the third regular school to play us, in 1907. Interesting stories emerge about the journeys made to each school and the entertainment. These days we play Repton midweek and tend to make the journey in a day by minibus. In 2007 we helped Repton celebrate their 450th year with a match on Saturday 10th November. We won 3-1. Harrow played us from 1915, until they changed codes in 1928. Harrow picked up soccer again in the Lent Term 1980s and have since proved successful in the round ball game.

We have never managed to play them in LQ as we are not able to offer a "block". Bradfield also joined our fixture list in 1915. Drummond Athletic appeared for a couple of years and this was another local engineering firm set on the Aldershot Road. Lancing played us from 1917 and there was one lone match against Aldenham from near Watford in 1920 after which the fixture was not played again until 1977.

In 1922 Shrewsbury became part of the season's fixture card and they remain our most favourite fixture. The Salopians always play a good standard and they are meticulously well behaved. Under Robin Trimby in the 1980s and then Mark Dickson, Shrewsbury have been a major force in the north. Trimby was one of the great schoolmaster footballers, an Oxford Blue, amateur international and member of the famous Pegasus team. He also was the headmaster of the experimental FA School at Lilleshall in its first few years. Charterhouse and Shrewsbury produced a sponsors' dream in the ISFA Cup Final of 2000. Two traditional boarding schools competing for the prestigious Boodle and Dunthorne Trophy as it was known, was an ideal crowd puller. As you will have read in chapter 14, Charterhouse lost! It was a special moment for the Shrewsbury master in charge, Mark Dickson, who has organised the ISFA Cup since its inception in 1992.

Being very much part of the "association", Charterhouse has been able to attract some colourful opposition and the London FA would be one. Their teams, adult in the 1930s and later "Minors", proved strong opponents; a good lesson would be learned in these games but maybe they were not good for morale. Eight goals seemed to be a common score against and a defeat of 0-17 is recorded. There was a fixture against the Surrey Senior League, against Charterhouse in Southwark our "linked" charity and Camberley Town, then in the Isthmian League, visited one Saturday when both teams had a spare date. I was playing for the club at that time.

Fixture card 1962-3

In 1935 the first all schools' fixture list is recorded. By 1938 we played Malvern and during the war years matches against some teams occurred twice. One school, Wellingborough from Northamptonshire, played us twice in 1941 only. It is also worth marking the first two fixtures against Highgate School that took place in 1946 and 1947 at Stamford Bridge. Matches between the two schools continue rather intermittently in the 1970s and 80s. The fixture has recently been revived.

By the 1950s there were as many as 17 1st XI matches played in the OQ and about seven in the LQ, depending on the weather. There was a 2nd XI and sometimes a 3rd, with U16 and U15 teams turned out. In 1964 the first Yearlings matches were played.

In the 1970s gradually the school played fewer club sides and more schools. This helped change the results record since the Carthusians were no longer playing against fit mature men from Old Boys' sides, probably fresh from National Service. There was a 70% loss rate against these adult teams which must have weighed hard on morale.

In an attempt to get more experience playing against schoolboys, Hampton Grammar School and Middlesex GS were included and later the school played teams such as Camberley and Frimley GS, Woking GS, Godalming College and Farnham College. These proved to be testing games and when the college system was

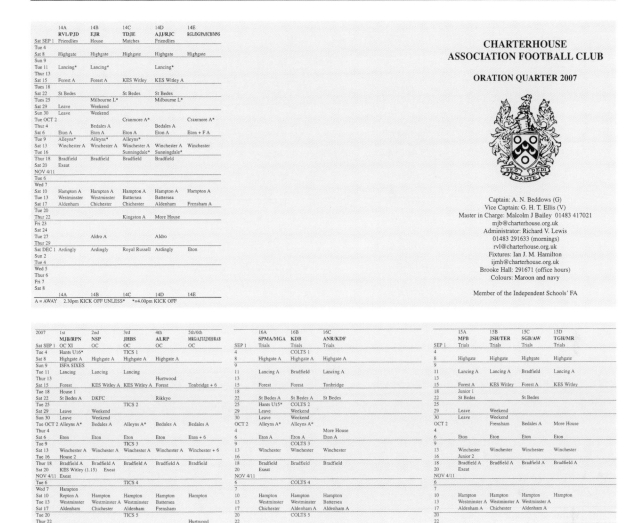

Fixture card 2007

introduced we found that we were playing against players who were well over 18 and possibly even on the rebound from being apprentices at league clubs. Consequently the games were a little one-sided although it is fair to say that the Carthusians always did their best. In the Surrey Schools Cup the competition was eventually divided into a schools section and a colleges section.

We also host a number of tour sides from the USA including our twin school, The Hill from Pottstown, Pennsylvania, as well as teams from Australia and New Zealand.

Adult matches continued to take their share of the list with the Chelsea Casuals. (Brian Glanville's XI – he is an OC and a well known sports' writer), David Miller's XI (an OC and another major sports' writer) and Surrey University. Gradually more "public schools" opponents were added, such as King Edward's, Witley, Bedales and Ottershaw. These smaller schools were relatively easy opposition whereas Millfield was a different matter. The Channel Islands supplied teams such as Victoria College and Elizabeth College, who toured in the south and some of the rugby playing schools began Lent Term football. Christ's Hospital and Oratory are two who were very decent opposition and the Lent Term list expanded as many of these schools wanted to play us to test their strength.

The LQ fixture card was regarded as purely an A XI list by 1980 as hockey became the major sport for the whole of the term.

With terms dates changing frequently, trying to set a firm fixture list was a problem but by the 1980s there was a distinct pattern. The aim was to start with some friendly fixtures to try players out and then to build up the quality of the opposition towards Exeat. After half-term there was a need to start again and then to build towards the tough fixtures such as Repton and Shrewsbury. Leave weekends did not help with continuity as a Saturday was lost at the end of September and November. Losing three Saturdays over Exeat added to the total!

In 1992 the ISFA Cup began and this would mean travelling to one off fixtures further afield such as QEGS Blackburn, Kimbolton School and Bury GS. We also joined the Surrey Schools' Cup and despite getting to the final in 1993, we decided to withdraw from the competition due to fixture congestion. Having lost the final we still qualified for the ESFA national individual schools' cup and lost in the first round 0-2, against Taunton's College from Southampton, who were the Hampshire champions. Ardingly, Sussex champions, went on to win this cup later in the decade.

There have been matches against an Arsenal XI, Southampton Youth, Reading FC and a Chelsea XI. There was also a celebratory game against a Tottenham Hotspurs Vets XI to celebrate the master in charge's 50th birthday in March 2001. In 2004 a block fixture against Brentwood School was arranged for the first time although the school did play Brentwood in the early years, this was not recorded at the school. More recently the Premiership club Reading FC sent an academy team to play the A XI. During the OQ 2007 the school enjoyed several "firsts" including an away trip to the Royal Grammar School, Newcastle in the ISFA Cup, King's School, Chester also and the Under 15 XI played Truro School in their age group's national cup and St Edmund's School, Canterbury. All of these were successful.

appendices

I References

A Study in Charterhouse Life, Archibald K Ingram (Allen & Co)

The Amateur Cup Results Book, Samuel (Soccer books Limited) 2003

Association Football and the men who made it, Gibson and Pickard, 1906

Association Football ed AH Fabian and Geoffrey Green – Caxton series

BTW photos

Cambridge University Laws of Association Football

Captain's Books

The Carthusian

The Centenary History of the Arthur Dunn Cup, Roy, Bevan, Hibberd and Gilbert (Replay Publishing), 2003

Charterhouse Old and New 1895, EP Eardley Wilmot and EC Streatfeild

Charterhouse Registers, R Arrowsmith

Charterhouse, A History of the School, A Quick

Charterhouse, A History, Tod (Bell)

Charterhouse, EM Jamieson (Blackie)

Christie's Images

Comedy of Errors, King Lear, William Shakespeare

Corinthians and Cricketers, Edward Grayson (Yore Publications)1996

The Early FA Cup finals and the Southern Amateurs (1872, 1883), Warsop (Soccer Data), 2004

Edwardians at Play Sport 1890, 1914, Brian Dobbs (Pelham Books)

England Expects, James Corbett (Aurum), 2006

England Football Fact Book, Freddi (Guiness), 1991

The FA Cup, complete results, Brown (Soccer Data), 1999

The Field magazine

The Footballer's Fireside Book, Delaney (The Sportsmans' Book Club), 1961

Football and All That, Giller (Hodder), 2004

From a New Angle, Veale

Goodbye to all that, Robert Graves

The Greyfriar

The History of CUAFC, Weir (Yore Publications), 2004

The History of Football, Heatley (Past Times), 2003

The History of OUAFC, Weir (Yore Publications), 1998

The History of the Football Association (Naldrett), 1953

History of London, William Fitzstephen

History of the Corinthians, FNS Creek (Longmans), 1933

History of West Bromwich Albion FC, Peter Morris

ISFA Cup Final programmes, Mark Dickson

Kicking and Screaming, Taylor and Ward (Robson), 1995

The Lost Trophy, the complete history of the FA Cup 1871, 1895, Tony Onslow, 2006

The Men who made the Town (B Scovell)

The Official Illustrated History of the FA Cup, Butler (Headline), 1996

Orientations, Richard Storrs

Pegasus, Ken Shearwood (OUP), 1975

The People's Game, James Walvin, 1975

Roger Smeeton

The Rules of Association Football 1863, Melvyn Bragg (Bodelian, from 12 Books that changed The World), 2006

Samuel Pepys Diaries

Shrewsbury School Football, an Illustrated History, Mark Dickson, Robin Trimby et al, 1995

The Sporting Life

The Sportsman

Start of Play, Rice (Prion), 1998

The Times

To the Palace for the Cup, an affectionate history of the Crystal Palace, Bevan, Hibberd and Gilbert (Replay Publishing), 1999

II Charterhouse Association Football
1st XI colours

1861-62
GJ Cookson capt
BF Hartshorne
J Lant
KA Muir-MacKenzie
JT Hodgson
FWH Somerset
CJ Hawkins
Hon FS O'Grady
M Muir MacKenzie
ER Eardley Wilmot
CE Boyle

1862-63
GJ Cookson capt
BF Hartshorne
J Lant
KA Muir-MacKenzie
JT Hodgson
Hon FS O'Grady
M Muir MacKenzie
CE Boyle
L Ogden
CA Sumner
EL Pearson

1863-64
KA Muir-MacKenzie capt
JT Hodgson
Hon FS O'Grady
M Muir MacKenzie
L Ogden
EL Pearson
HH Cameron
GE Smythe
LH Stevenson
GS Davies
AC Seymour

1864-65
Hon FS O'Grady capt
M Muir-MacKenzie
L Ogden
HH Cameron
GE Smythe
AC Seymour
ECS Gibson
CP Scott
OS Walford
WW Cooper

1865-66
M Muir-MacKenzie capt
ECS Gibson
CP Scott
OS Walford
WW Cooper
RW Macan
JP Abraham
JP Middleton
CEB Nepean
WL Boreham
JA Foote

1866-67
ECS Gibson capt
OS Walford
CEB Nepean
WL Boreham
JA Foote
CH Wade
W Wallace
E Venables
AS Mammatt
HH Murray-MacKenzie
EA Hammick

1867-68
CEB Nepean capt
W Wallace
E Venables
EA Hammick
FG Paulson
R Dunn
FF Brown
AF Russell
TC Hooman
HJ Almond
CC Boyle

1868-69
FF Brown capt
AF Russell
CA Bushnell
JF Inglis
HL Matthews
HVB Smith
AL Phillips
GC Carter
EF Brown
FR Byng
EV Ravenshaw

1869-70
HS King capt
D Barry
JF Inglis
GC Carter
EF Brown
TP Gandell
EV Ravenshaw
CG Inglis
CG Paget
GW Hervey

1870-71
D Barry capt
JF Inglis
GC Carter
EF Brown
TP Gandell
EV Ravenshaw
CG Inglis
CG Paget
GW Hervey
EH Parry
W Dorling

1877-72
GC Carter capt
EF Brown
TP Gandell
EV Ravenshaw
CG Paget
EH Parry
WC Williams
WW Drew
GE Staveley
AH Gipps
WH Thompson

1872-73
TP Gandell capt
EH Parry capt LQ1873
WC Williams
WW Drew
AH Gipps
HW Davies
HG Jeaffreson
FH Firth
NJ Abdy
E Williams
JC Hanson
FJ Synge

1873-74
EH Parry capt
WW Drew
HG Jeaffreson
NJ Abdy
E Williams
FJ Synge
LC Park
A Orford
HD Verelst
A Wynne-Corrie
EM Short

1874-75
NJ Abdy capt
HG Jeaffreson
A Orford
EM Short
WR Page
AH Tod
HB Southwell
A Wilson
RLW Curzon
H MacGeorge
RL Hulton

1875-76
EM Short capt
WR Page
AH Tod
AW Wilson
CA Reeve
CP Cornish
AJ Wake
WT Hayter
RSS Baden-Powell
GD Keightley
LH Burrows

1876-77
WR Page capt
WT Hayter
GD Keightley
EF Growse
JE Eddis
AJ Parry
HW Devenish
JF Prinsep
SF Smith
EG Wynyard
A Keightley

1877-78
EF Growse capt
JF Prinsep
CM Burdon capt LQ1878
WEC Frith
EG Colvin
WE Hansell
SL Medlicott
CE Keith-Falconer
EJ Wilson
OG Evan Thomas
HM Hull

1878-79
CM Burdon capt
LD Jackson capt LQ1879
EJ Wilson
HM Hull
LM Richards
LF Gillett
JNG Pollock
HC Rutter
HM Holman
GS Guiness
WL Vyvyan
EE James
ET Hardman

1879-80
EM Pollock capt
LM Richards
WL Vyvyan
J Vintcent
A Rayner
CK Hamilton
WG Morrison
WA Hamiton
AK Henley
AI Vintcent
BHT Frere

1880-81
GK Harrison capt
A Rayner
WG Morrison
WA Hamilton
AK Henley
AI Vintcent
TW Blenkiron
WN Cobbold
LML Owen
CW Wright
WH Norris

1881-82
AK Henley capt
AI Vintcent
TW Blenkiron
WN Cobbold
EH Brown
AM Walters
A Amos
W Rayner
KH Eddis
EB Sewell
LW Keith-Falconer
FE Messent

1882-83
TW Blenkiron capt
AM Walters
CH Vintcent
LA Vintcent
HA Steward
HL Brookes
D MacNeil
RVI Forbes
ES Fardell
WM Cleaver
HS Ponsonby
OH Latter

1883-84
HA Steward capt
RVI Forbes capt LQ1884
CH Vintcent
HS Ponsonby
CH Evan Thomas
GA Coulby
JM Walker
C Wreford Brown
AL Hansell
FJ Richardson
HS Spark
CW Waddington
W Barnett

1884-85
CH Evan Thomas capt
C Wreford Brown
WM Crowdy
CW Wright
BH Drake
CH Tyler
HL Lewis
CD Morrison
G Laird
AJ Mosty
FJ Cooper
ES Currey
HJ Carson

1885-86
C Wreford Brown capt
CH Tyler capt LQ1886
ES Currey
HJ Carson
HS Steele
RGT Baker-Carr
HC Price
RF Daglish
CW Parry
WA Shaw
AC Nixon
GC Leman
FG Leatham
WE Stanbrough
G Pim

1886-87	1887-88	1888-89	1889-90	1890-91
HC Price capt	WFH Stanbrough capt	RM Cowie capt	FP Armstrong capt	GO Smith capt
WA Shaw capt LQ1887	S Furber	NF Shaw capt LQ1889	GO Smith capt LQ1890	EC Bliss
FG Leatham	FA Earle	DF Macfie	EC Bliss	WW Halsted
WFH Stanbrough	WE Gilliatt	CM Rayner	G Head	BKR Wilkinson
G Pim	NF Shaw	MH Stanbrough	RE Rising	GS Wilson
HC Lowther	SC Dickinson	WH Wakefield	WW Halstead	CD Hewitt
DC Leman	DF Macfie	JG Woodhouse	BKR Wilkinson	E Bramwell
FF Harrison	EC Streatfeild	GC Barker	EF Buzzard	EH Bray
LR Wilkinson	RM Cowie	FL Vogel	GS Wilson	WR Kirby
EC Rutter	A Foster	GO Smith	CD Hewitt	ID Ogilvy
S Furber	GA Roper	EC Bliss	RW Wade	GW Dawson
FA Earle	CM Rayner	G Head	E Bramwell	IGP Alston
WE Gilliat		FP Armstrong	GH Woodbridge	RJ Salt
EW Timmis				AH Bailey
CG Lewis				F Clark

1891-92	1892-93	1893-94	1894-95	1895-96
GO Smith capt	EH Bray capt	RD Fordyce capt	WAE Austen capt	EM Jameson capt
EH Bray	CB Ward	GC Vassall	CH Wilson	GW Ryder
RJ Salt	AD Fordyce	R Hunt	EM Jameson	GS Smith
H Foster	RD Fordyce	GP Lea	HRB Hancock	CB Hulton
RH Frith	G Wreford Brown	WU Timmis	EN Broome	AR Haig Brown
CB Ward	H Crabtree	CH Wilson	AH Laird	W Renshaw
GA Gardiner	GC Vassall	WAE Austin	GW Ryder	FW Tomlinson
AD Fordyce	R Hunt	EM Jameson	JP Benson	CF Ryder
WH Wild	HJ Broadbent	E Garnett	HLP Walsh	SH Vassall
FR Barwell	AB Winch	HRB Hancock	SG Wallace	AHP Horne
RD Fordyce	GP Leach	FF Salden	B Murdoch	OE Wreford Brown
	HPO Broadbent	AJ Davidson		HC Hollebone

1896-97	1897-98	1898-99	1899-1900	1900-01
GS Smith capt	H Musker capt	CH Wild capt	AH Liddle capt	B Tuff capt
CF Ryder	WLH Moss	RB Timmis	RAB Trower	WHM Finch
W Renshaw	CW Gordon	BH Leatham	B Tuff	JWS Malden
SH Vassall	CH Wild	KWE Evans	JS Gardner	C de M Kellock
WLH Moss	TS Rowlandson	RAB Trower	RCAS Hobart	WJH Curwen
AL Scott	HC Hollebone	AH Tompson	ES Chance	OT Norris
GS Churchill	RB Timmis	BGB Leechman	GB Good	GV Goodliffe
AH Morris	BH Leatham	B Tuff	WHM Finch	AB Pratt
CW Gordon	GH Fox	JS Gardner	JWS Malden	FA Bowring
RR Forbes	KWE Evans	AH Liddle	HK Waller	RA Bence-Pembroke
CD Mucklow	G Crosdale	RC Greenwood	S Johnston	K Fisher
MFR Wingfield	GN Clarke	WD Sturrock	AP Strange	HG Bagnall
H Musker	RAB Trower			
CH Wild				

1901-02	1902-03	1903-04	1904-05	1905-06
OT Norris capt	RA Bence-Pembroke capt	JS Strange capt	VG Thew capt	VG Thew capt
WJH Curwen	IE Snell	RH Allen	EL Firth	CT Gooch
GV Goodliffe	GL Bickersteth	RB Taylor	JC Mackwood	LM Peet
FA Bowring	JS Trange	F Johnston	JH Rucker	JSPS Greig
IE Snell	GT Branston	VG Thew	TRG Lyell	JB Bickersteth
GL Bickersteth	AA Drew	EL Firth	GM Reid	RLL Bradell
RA Bence-Pembroke	CB Lee	RE Grice-Hutchinson	AS Cockburn	JH Dixon
BT Verry	DF Seth Smith	ES Cripps	GG Newman	JT Parry
AR Cheale	RD England	JC Mackwood	HA Gilbert	RH Deneke
AL Preston	RH Allen	KD Barbour	CT Gooch	WK Tillie
JS Strange	JCD Tetley	JH Rucker	HJC Pears	EH Preston
	RB Taylor	R Walker	LM Peet	AW Waterhouse

1906-07	1907-08	1908-09	1909-10	1910-11
CT Gooch capt	FHL Rushton capt	CB Johnson capt	HA Wellesley capt	L Gjers capt
RLL Braddell	CB Johnson	S Baker	CO Fricker	R Boosey
JT Parry	S Baker	WG Gabain	RE Norris	EI Gibbons
EH Preston	AGH Livesey	RM Weeks	L Gjers	JSF Morrison
AW Waterhouse	CK Rhodes	WIF Macdonald	R Boosey	LH Davidson
FHL Rushton	SA Pike	HA Wellesley	EI Gibbons	FN Sidebotham
CP Mead	WG Gabain	CO Fricker	GCW Dowling	K King
J Gjers	A Stuart	RE Norris	W Steer	KO Smithers
A Marshall	RB Murray	EB Trower	NE Burdon	NE Burdon
RS Evans	RW Russell	RCH Kingdon	GW Polson	R Faulkner
J Pegram	RM Weeks	JRT Benn	HN Dixon	H Welsey-Smith
WC Wardle	AP Wilson	ERC Booth	RM Bruce	
GD Jameson		AF Wharton		
		HB Emley		

1911-12	1912-13	1913-14	1914-15	1915-16
PS Lampard capt	AS Chambers capt	GV Hinds capt	AB Chadwick capt	AHG Butcher capt
NE Burdon	JH Fosdick	AB Chadwick	E Cawston capt LQ1915	RLG Garth
RG Morrison	ED Fox	PS Handley	JC Ritchie	D Dunlop
D St GK Boswell	CES Rucker	JG Young	AG Vlasto	PWC Hollowell
JH Fosdick	EA McNair	FS Burnett	KJN Hansell	RL Hall
EOC Goodall	JAL Hopkinson	AM Walters	FG Emley	V Reiss
HD Vernon	AJT Bland	GML Smith	JES Anderson	DHM Leggatt
FS Letten	GV Hinds	KW Gray	FW Winterbotham	G Tinley
AL Ford	G Steel	E Cawston	RLG Garth	FH Martin
AS Chambers	AB Chadwick	GNP Humphries	BB Edge	CN Brownhill
AB Johns	DG Liddle	JC Ritchie	AHG Butcher	JM Wells
ED Cox		PQ Reiss	D Dunlop	JB Beck
CES Rucker		AG Vlasto	PWC Hollowell	

1916-17	1917-18	1918-19	1919-20	1920-21
AHG Butcher capt	JM Wells capt	BCA Patchitt capt	IAW Gilliat capt	IAW Gilliat capt
DHM Leggatt capt 1917	HRH Williams	FE Powell	RE Balnd	FH Barnard
JB Beck	EL Lavenstein	EV Daldy	CB Mordaunt-Smith	HEM Benn
JM Wells	BCA Patchitt	RC Gregory	HM Ward Clarke	AJP Parker
HC Halliley	RH Whalley	JA Hardicker	AFP Wheeler	EC Austin
BG Bearman	RJP Thorne-Thorne	PA Fraser	LG Cox	PM Anderson
JM South	E Wesley-Smith	HS Tegner	GR Wade	VE Morgan
HN Vintcent	PW Rucker	EA Mahaler	ID McIlwraith	EG Waldy
HRH Williams	THP Beeching	IAW Gilliat	FH Barnard	HM McGusty
WG Camidge	Hon DFC Erskine		GB Garnett	CFP Lowe
DW Bennett	FE Powell		HEM Benn	PK Bamber
EL Lavenstein	DJT Peacock		KG Rigden	
TH Penlington	AM Stearn		HG Chevis	
BCA Patchitt			GE Sclater	
RH Whalley				
CW Stokes				

1921-22	1922-23	1923-24	1924-25	1925-26
VE Morgan capt	VE Morgan capt	GS Fletcher capt	AH Williams capt	TC Johnson capt
AW Kiggell	EC Doresa	LHA Clarke	TC Johnson	JHG Gilliat
RPW Shackleton	GT Kenyon	BP Massey	AL Stock	RJ Seligman
FL Barker	JHA Clarke	KM Goodbody	GD Kemo Welch	DI Deakin
HC Gill	GS Fletcher	JG St G Shute	JD Pritchard	JEF Vogel
CG Varcoe	BP Massey	KDC Nation-Dixon	JHG Gilliat	AH Head
JG Bearman	RC Hoyle	FHD Pritchard	CJ D'Arcy Hildyard	AT Pritchard
MP Griffiths-Jones	KM Goodbody	MS Murdoch	RW Hall	RB Beare
EC Doresa	CJ Quiney	JN Carter	R Dobson	JC Connell
AR Harvie	BE Malek	AH Williams	RJ Seligman	MW Delaforce
GT Kenyon		GE Blundell	DI Deakin	BCM Palmer
		CIP Rishworth		

1926-27	1927-28	1928-29	1929-30	1930-31
AH Head capt	EMC Heath capt	JLH Fletcher capt	C Middleton capt	AJ Wreford Brown capt
AT Pritchard	RS Davies	GOS Striven	KL Stock	GT Hollebone
RB Beare	JLH Fletcher	C Middleton	FRS Jeavons	WF Moss
RS Davies	PG Wreford Brown	GL Stumbles	IT McGaw	NS Pope
MX Pickstone	WH Lydall	RW Craddock	AJ Wreford Brown	DA Pott
E St A Glynn	VLC Johnson	JWR Hunt	EB Hacking	AH Edmundson
JH Fletcher	JPR Hale	KL Stock	GT Hollebone	JR Lowe
EMC Heath	JD Morton	FRS Jeavons	ASC Hulton	JS Greening
GR Chetwynd Stapylton	GOS Stiven	IT McGaw	WF Moss	JH King
HE Weatherall	C Middleton	LS Cohen	NS Pope	GL Paver
PG Wreford Brown	GL Stumbles	AJ Wreford Brown	GH Baines	JFH Carson
	HA Clarke	CR Spencer		FCL Matthews
	DR Godfrey	BE Godfrey		TE Watson
	RW Craddock			RF Merz

1931-32	1932-33	1933-34	1934-35	1935-36
WF Moss capt	JC Moss capt	JL Field capt	DFM Roberts capt	PR Crompton capt
DA Pott	KPS Caldwell	SC Gillchrest	RM Hollis	ADC Dowding
RF Merz	RAP Woodbridge	PL Richards	J de D Yule	JM Lomas
JA Brown	HEK Field	DFM Roberts	ADC Dowding	GG Dunbar
TCH Pearson	RH Blackwell	BSM Carson	JC Daukes	PRC Hobart
AC Rabagliati	JL Field	JB Frith	PR Crompton	EH Ades
JC Moss	SC Gillchrest	WL Paynter	GE Hodgson	AR Woods
DG Drakeford	PL Richards	RM Hollis	JM Lomas	P Rhodes
JG Dunbar	DFM Roberts	JA Trapman	JHE Guest	AH Beane
KPS Caldwell	RD Bowen	J de D Yule	MA Melford	PE Nesbitt
DW Tyler	BSM Carson	RPR Powell	GG Dunbar	RG Greene
EF Farrington		ADC Dowding	PRC Hobart	RW Hayes
		JC Daukes		CA Vanbergen
				BH Groves
				AK Hughes

1936-37	1937-38	1938-39	1939-40	1940-41
JM Lomas capt	JB Lyon capt	JAE Sharp capt	JDP Tanner capt	AJM Milne capt
RW Hayes	RD Geppert	JDP Tanner	JG Larking	FA Peet
BH Groves	RC MacCunn	JS Mc E Sceales	HP Cunningham	LCW Figg
AK Hughes	GW Rothery	JG Larking	AJM Milne	ADH Hawley
PF Beane	JAE Sharp	JB Swinbank	HC Churchill Davidson	PH Blanchard
JB Lyon	AH Miskin	NCA Hawley	P Bennett	JDF Watson
RD Geppert	L Stone	HP Cunningham	BMS Hoban	JPL Sharp
RA Orton	JDP Tanner	UE Larsen	FA Peet	J McK N Roberts
WD Bramwell	JS Mc E Sceales	AJM Milne	MF Dear	P Spencer
DL Benke	DG Anthony	BD Holme-Summer	R Finlayson	AS Lovett
RC MacCunn	JG Larking	J Bennett	DAN Allen	RS Evans
RW Rothery	JB Swinbank	B Travers		MW Nesbitt
JAE Sharp				NH Benke

1941-42	1942-43	1943-44	1944-45	1945-46
PH Blanchard capt	RW Sword capt	JL Godden capt	MJ Rimell capt	BH Price capt
AS Lovett	RW Holder	MJ Rimell	GD Spratt	AJ Rimell
RS Evans	GT Metcalfe	GD Spratt	EA Bishop	TJ Aitchison
NH Benke	RDF Watson	PB Cross	PSI Godden	AG Williams
RM Lahaye	GE Seager	A Crole-Rees	JAN Pollock	PM Lind
PCG Larking	EC Dalgety	IG Lovesy	BH Price	TRH Savill
RC Towers	JL Godden	EA Bishop	TRF Fenwick	DP Rowat
MEH Le Gallais	DJC Stevenson	PSI Godden	AJ Rimell	EP Wilson
RW Sword	MJ Rimell	EC Whitley	PA Vlasto	A Hastings
RW Holder	GD Spratt	EL Williams	AM Cranstoun	PBH May
EW Lomas	JG Elliott	JAN Pollock	H Le Bas	GL Howard
JD Bendit	GN Whitfield	BH Price	JM Waddell	BSCG Randall
GT Metcalfe	RA Saager	AC Robertson	WNB Parker	
RDF Watson				
GE Seager				

1946-47	1947-48	1948-49	1949-50	1950-51
TRH Savill capt	A Hastings capt	MHD Whinney capt	MDC Jenks capt	JHW May capt
DP Rowat	DP Johnson	MS Schofield	DF Spargo	JN Fair
A Hastings	NRL Saunders	MDC Jenks	IM Paton	MRP Young
PBH May	DP Johnson	DHG Goodliffe	JHW May	AJ Barclay
BSCG Randall	DG Millar	MJ Perkins	JN Fair	MC Varcoe
DGW Davis	NR Burt	DF Spargo	MC Donne	RC Pegler
DP Johnson	SC Norman	PJ Pelly	JNB King	CAH Monk
VJPD Marrot	MHD Whinney	RD Richardson	DAN Vansittart	TM Gladstone
BHS Mills	JK Divett	IM Paton	CK Edwards	JC Astwood
JR Anthony	PG Nathan	HOJ Gibbon	PD Smithson	RP Carless
G Clarke	MJ Archibald	JHW May	GJ Agate	R Blumer
RL Whitby	SEA Kimmins	JC Kay	TC Frankland	WJS Clutterbuck
BW Seaman	IF Murray-Brown	RIM Scott	MRP Young	GER Lloyd
		JNM Pickersgill		

1951-52	1952-53	1953-54	1954-55	1955-56
AJ Barclay capt	D Miller capt	GE Pratt capt	GB Gauntlett capt	DS Mace capt
RC Pegler	RP Carless	P Rubin	DS Mace	MNS Ruddock
TM Gladstone	DM Brundan	DR Curtis	DB Lees	RE Stephens
RP Carless	BR Good	HC Cairns	RF Buckley	FSK Tunnock
R Blumer	WN Sadler	IM O'Brien	MNS Ruddock	TR Jakobson
CTH Whinney	AJ McIntosh	GB Gauntlett	R Gardiner	CJ Forsyth
D Miller	CR White	CC Davis	RE Stephens	AP Hansell
RJK Spurrell	GE Pratt	DS Mace	PD Capper	AF Ramsey
DM Brundan	RO Knox	DB Lees	FSK Tunnock	DR Tomlinson
RF Tuck	P Rubin	BNS Gemmell	TR Jakobson	DC Burrows
ML Bayman	DR Curtis	RF Buckley		GPF Steed
JPN Parker	RIG Hardcastle			RIM Standring
J Lack				

1956-57	1957-58	1958-59	1959-60	1960-61
DR Tomlinson capt	AAH White capt	JPN Hallam capt	MR Willcocks capt	GS Parke capt
AP Hansell	MR Gardiner	EP Visser	JM Topham	JN Garrow
DC Burrows	MGV Harrison	SRV Tham	AP Blumer	JGS Pilch
GPF Steed	RS Evans	PC Gibb	HJH Taylor	PM Draper
DJ Sparshatt	PL Levy	P Strathern	WJ Mallinson	HM Martin
ATC Allom	IS Gordon	TH Reed	GS Parke	CNH Cain
JGS Matterson	JPN Hallam	MR Willcocks	NA Marks	H Arnold
A MacLeay	SRV Tham	JE Gabriel	NJK Mark	CC King
AAH White	PHS James	GM Faulkner	HC Sharp	RMC Gilliatt
MR Gardiner	EP Visser	MLFC Konig	SFD Knight	HGL Powell
MGV Harrison	PC Gibb	JM Topham	EJ Craig	PJ Sweet
	JM Agace	AP Blumer	JGS Pilch	ARD Lorenz
	P Strathern	HJH Taylor	JN Garrow	WD Vorley
	TH Reed	PMS Tham		

1961-62
HM Martin capt
PM Draper
CNH Cain
H Arnold
RMC Gilliatt
HGL Powell
PJ Sweet
PM Bailache
AD Marks
N de Grunwald
AP Hopkins

1962-63
HM Martin capt
RMC Gilliatt
HGL Powell
PM Bailache
AD Marks
N de Grunwald
JN Colecough
GR Biggs
RM Baker
JMM Hooper
NP Hill
AP Hopkins

1963-64
AD Marks capt
PM Bailache
RM Baker
JMM Hooper
NP Hill
DM Drayson
JPG Randel
BME MacFarlane
AW Weir
RM Sutton
MS Dark
MT Coleclough
PM Ashton
MJ Samuelson
FT Hobbs

1964-65
JMM Hooper capt
AW Weir
RM Sutton
BME MacFarlane
MT Coleclough
FT Hobbs
MJ Samuelson
JC Ravenscroft
JR Gimson
SJE Easton
RD Gough
MA Godfrey
RW Bidwell
CK Price

1965-66
MT Coleclough capt
JR Gimson
SJE Easton
MA Godfrey
PW Makin
WM Gray
AG Simmons
JM Bennett
RP Kennedy
MH Cohn
MR Deans
NJT Aston
MT Ward

1966-67
WM Gray capt
JM Bennett
RP Kennedy
MH Cohn
MR Deans
NJT Aston
MT Ward
DA Eccles
IRB Perkins
NC Provis
PF Howard

1967-68
MH Cohn capt
MR Deans
JM Bennett
DA Eccles
IRB Perkins
NC Provis
NG Woodwark
EJW Gieve
GAH Johnson
RFW Wild
ACM Rintoul

1968-69
DA Eccles capt
M Ritchie
CJ Rose
JP Hannyngton
PHC Foster
DB Lowe
LK Walton
WRS Critchley
JM Horner
NT Carter
PCC Grizzelle

1969-70
CJ Rose capt
LK Walton
PCC Grizzelle
MP Gandell
JR Wallis
JM Horne
AG Lysley
VM Gibson
MRP Power
PMC Talbot

1970-71
LK Walton capt
PWA Hughes
JR Wallis
FG Lyle
IA Stewart
VM Gibson
N Wisdom
SJ Gale
JG Hooper
PC Godby
MH Faldo
JD Holder
RH Gibson

1971-72
IA Stewart capt
PC Godby
MH Faldo
JD Holder
CSN Williams
PL Williams
AD Forbes-Watson
AJ Norman
CHO Jay
SJ Faull
KR Ellis
PAJ Bennett

1972-73
AD Forbes-Watson capt
KR Ellis
CHO Jay
JJ Cama
RC Ecob
MWG Doggart
PH Oundjian
PL Williams
SJ Faull
TJC Parker
AAY Adomakoh
JP Victor

1973-74
PL Williams capt
KR Ellis
RC Ecob
MWG Doggart
SJ Faull
AAY Adomakoh
DWT Levy
C Comninos
MG Herbert-Smith
IA Gibson
SR de L North
TD Middleton

1974-75
PL Williams capt
DWT Levy
AAY Adomakoh
C Comninos
MG Herbert-Smith
IA Gibson
SR de L North
TD Middleton
RAC Oulton
GH Walker
RJM Hughes
CC Belchamber

1975-76
IA Gibson capt
DWT Levy
RJM Hughes
CC Belchamber
AJ Cussins
MA Blanchard
HB Reynolds
RC Phillips
JC Cunningham
JS Hayllar
NM Ostrer
SC Parker
PC Goodliffe
NC Frankland

1976-77
HB Reynolds capt
CC Belchamber
NM Ostrer
TEO Bury
TCR Whalley
PA Cummins
C Swabey
MN Lovill
CC Mole
GA Andrews
WA Shepherd
AP Kirkbride

1977-78
TCR Whalley capt
PA Cummins
C Swabey
MN Lovill
AP Kirkbride
CC Mole
WA Shepherd
ML Faull
GDT Pride
C St R Mole
RC Doggart
AOY Adomakoh

1978-79
PA Cummins capt
CC Mole
GDT Pride
TJ Piper
MJ Bishop
SC Speak
HE Pratt
DC Allison
AH Beck
W Barbour
WGR Haynes
WH Webbe
RC Doggart
JW Barrett
G Miller

1979-80
HE Pratt capt
MJ Bishop
DC Allison
WGR Haynes
AJ Lathwood
CWH May
ARR Best
NJJ Pendrigh
DA Fordham
SP Raymonde
SJ Gard
HS Kirkbride

1980-81
CWH May capt
DA Fordham
JJ Kemball
JS Lloyd
JW Gard
RJ Nelson
NJ Blanchard
DE Bonham-Carter
SC Toombs
GDA Spooner
PAF Cuff

1981-82
JJ Kemball capt
DA Fordham
DE Bonham-Carter
JW Gard
R McCourt
JDE Myers
DJ Morley
TDJ Marshall
CAN von Weiler
JD Reid
PR Durnford
JC Davies

1982-83
BR Mellstrom capt
JD Reid
JC Davies
KJ Blake
K Frearson
PD Newman
AG Proctor
JD Aubrey
CJL Bayman
RN Faulkner
O Ibru
PD van Hengel

1983-84
K Frearson capt
JC Davies
RN Faulkner
PD van Hengel
GH Meesman
O Ibru
R Tayler
JS Waters
DNH Pennant
CA Coe
JC Golder
GH Pratt

1984-85
GH Pratt capt
CA Coe
NKP Adomakoh
JC Golder
SW Wattar
AJ Viall
W Wooldridge
EJM Baker
AP Spiegel
JH Gough
CC de Wolff
MJ Kerevan

1985-86
AJ Viall capt
EJM Baker
AP Spiegel
JH Gough
MJ Kerevan
TL Beaumont
DRS Neill
ARR Cooley
RW Faulkner
NP Waters
CD Jenkins
JF Alliott

1986-87
RB Goodliffe capt
CD Jenkins
AJ Zervos
HC Bedford
NRK Payne
AE Ivermee
SC Mellstrom
MC Gray
LF Islef
M Strecker

1987-88
LF Islef capt
M Strecker
MC Gray
JCD Hare
AJ Leale
P Gorman
DA Tinsley
DJ Austin
GRC Brooke
PW Scott
S Henkes
GRD Pascoe

1988-89
DJ Austin capt
P Gorman
GRC Brooke
S Henkes
RB Ewart-White
SJ Wheatley
NH Benham
RMF Harris
JP Scholefield
EM Ashby
JL Merrick
CJA Sale

1989-90
EM Ashby capt
JL Merrick
CJA Sale
EJ Rees
GD Butler
AMD Spray
MS Dawson
JD Wallace
WHG Fraser
MJ Mitten
ITI Clark
G Drew

1990-91
EJ Rees capt
JD Wallace
MJ Mitten
RJ Ashby
JGR Bower
JJ Hodson
DGP Lazell
ANW Gompertz
MWR Grindley
MT Daly
DJ Peters
NRC Kidd

1991-92
MT Daly capt
RJ Ashby
ANW Gompertz
DJ Peters
NRC Kidd
MK Pegler
RGS Sadler
AJ Proctor
AS McCourtie
BJ Akker
RMH Green
ME Dolman
ET Bennett

1992-93
BJ Akker capt
RMH Green
AS McCourtie
ET Bennett
AM Pate
DWM Sadler
LJ Webb
TEB Walker
JA Jarvis
BF Wakeham
GH Tassell
BE Weigand
AR Younie
R Cunningham-Brown

1993-94
TEB Walker capt
BF Wakeham
DWM Sadler
LJ Webb
GH Tassell
JA Jarvis
BE Weigand
AR Younie
R Cunningham-Brown
MA Souter
TCN Guy
DCM Stern
JA Dauman

1994-95
TC Dolman capt
TA Smith
JP Shenkman
GA Waller
SD Brazier
ID Hayes
DM Roberts
DW Carmichael
BJ Robertson
NP Frendo
JR Dyson
POH Rimmell

1995-96
ID Hayes capt
DW Carmichael
NP Frendo
JR Dyson
TCH Raven
WM Lidstone
PA Westcott
CI Hogan
EAJ Breeze
JDM ter Haar
ADW Smith

1996-97
PA Westcott capt
CI Hogan
EAJ Breeze
JDM ter Haar
ADW Smith
PA Britten
MA Saunders
WP Adie
HA Toulson
TNG Savage
AP Hollingsworth
EJW Rees

1997-98
HA Toulson capt
TNG Savage
AP Hollingsworth
EJW Rees
H Nash
DJ Ray
JCT Ho
MR Gillespie
NSE Gay
TE Burke-Murphy
PSS Leal
DCW Schneider
IS Ure

1998-99
PSS Leal capt
NSE Gay
TE Burke-Murphy
DCW Schneider
IS Ure
JAM Wallis
CWSJ Beaumont
ASB Poulsen
PGH White
MT Bailey
MWE Smith
JC Jackson
D Heaton-Watson

1999-2000
MT Bailey capt
MWE Smith
JC Jackson
D Heaton-Watson
IT MacAuslan
JWL Toller
JP Byrne
SJ Spinks
TS Blake
JA Goodrich
WJS Clark
AWJ Mezzetti
CT Shelton

2000-01
AWJ Mezzetti capt
WJS Clark
CT Shelton
SM Hunter
BCB Deschampsneufs
ERWKT Hancock
EC Mulligan
RP Burke-Murphy
RC Griston
J-J Williams
JE Green
MAA Cook
S Sogbetun

2001-02
RC Griston capt
J-J Williams
JE Green
MAA Cook
S Sogbetun
WH Young
NEC Armstrong
CEL Watson
CM Bunstead
FD Palley
PS Brennan
TCC Marsden
NJ Bunstead

2002-03
FD Palley capt
PS Brennan
TCC Marsden
NJ Bunstead
NJ Hatton
PMC Handley
BPM Barnett
ES Millington Buck
DE Simmonds
DJ Katte
JJM Ball
CGC Ingham
JHP Hooper
JB Hunter
MStH Stimpson

2003-04
CGC Ingham capt
JHP Hooper
JB Hunter
MStH Stimpson
OD Bardot
MKL Armstrong
TP Tennant
FN Barrow
EC Jenner
DW Bourne
PB Millington Buck
JH Walker
T Yabe

2004-05
PB Millington Buck capt
T Yabe
JH Walker
JR Jenkins
PH Summers
HGC Schofield
WGR Holder
JA Cameron
ED Walford
WW-N Paes
AWBV Saunt
CD Clinton

2005-06
HGC Schofield capt
ED Walford
WGR Holder
JA Cameron
W-NW Paes
CD Clinton
T Yabe
BW Ryder-Smith
CT De Laiglesia
JEC Tetley
JN Fyler
HWN Rubinstein
CJ Nash
AN Beddows

2006-07
CD Clinton capt
HWH Rubinstein
CJ Nash
AN Beddows
L Evans
SJ Cussins
JR Satterthwaite
DK Bowman
NA Carter
GHT Ellis
OR Black
ASD Parsons
AED Mason

2007-8
AN Beddows capt
GHT Ellis
OR Black
ASD Parsons
JFW Rogers
HRO Peat
G Adolphus
JAF Hall
CW Jamieson
CP Watson
TCA Kimmins
PCG Doggart
RA Procter
WG Walker

III Masters in charge from 1919 and Captains

Masters in charge

1919	Rev Edward M Jameson	1953	Richard H Crawford	1970	John Peters
1921	Patrick WC Hollowell	1962	Keith Garland	1980	Malcolm J Bailey
1933	Brutus Lee	1967	Antony Darbyshire		
1945	Anthony J Wreford Brown	1970	Roy G Woodcock		

Captains

Year	Name		Year	Name		Year	Name	
1862	GJ Cookson	S	11	L Gjers	R	60	GS Parke	V
63	GJ Cookson, BF Hartshorne V	S	12	PS Lampard	g	61	HM Martin	V
64	KA Muir Mackenzie	SG	13	AS Chambers	S	62	HM Martin	V
65	HFS O'Grady	G	14	GV Hinds	S	63	PM Bailache	H
66	MJ Muir Mackenzie	S	15	AB Chadwick S, E Cawston	B	64	JMM Hooper	G
67	ECS Gibson	G	16	AHG Butcher V, DHM Leggatt	G	65	MT Coleclough	V
68	CEB Nepean	G	17	JM Wells	D	66	WM Gray	P
69	FF Brown	VG	18	BCA Patchitt	W	67	MH Cohn	B
70	HS King	G	19	IAW Gilliat	G	68	DA Eccles	P
71	D Barry	S	20	IAW Gilliat	G	69	CJ Rose	g
72	TP Gandell G, CC Carter	SG	21	VE Morgan	V	70	LK Walton	H
73	EH Parry	G	22	VE Morgan	V	71	I A Stewart	S
74	EH Parry	G	23	GS Fletcher	L	72	AD Forbes Watson	V
75	NJ Abdy	S	24	AH Williams	G	73	PL Williams	B
76	EM de Short	Gg	25	TC Johnson	D	74	PL Williams	B
77	WR Page	VGg	26	AH Head	G	75	IA Gibson	G
78	EF Growse	G	27	EMC Heath	V	76	HB Reynolds	B
79	CM Burdon G, LD Jackson	G	28	JLH Fletcher	L	77	TCR Whalley	R
80	EM Pollock	H	29	C Middleton	B	78	PA Cummins	D
81	CK Harrison	S	30	AJ Wreford Brown	G	79	HE Pratt	G
82	AK Henley	Rg	31	WF Moss	W	80	CWH May	W
83	TW Blenkiron	H	32	JC Moss	W	81	JJ Kemball	R
84	HAH Steward BG, RAV Forbes	D	33	JC Field	V	82	BR Mellstrom	B
85	CH Evan-Thomas	G	34	DFM Roberts	P	83	K Frearson	W
86	C Wreford Brown G, CH Tyler	BG	35	PF Crompton	V	84	GH Pratt	G
87	HC Price RP, RPWA Shaw	V	36	JM Lomas	g	85	AJ Viall	D
88	WFH Stanborough	G	37	JB Lyon	S	86	RB Goodliffe	D
89	RM Cowie H, NF Shaw	V	38	JAE Sharp	G	87	LF Islef	R
90	FP Armstrong V, GO Smith	H	39	JDP Tanner	P	88	DJ Austen	H
91	GO Smith	H	40	AJM Milne	g	89	EM Ashby	V
92	GO Smith	H	41	PH Blanchard	S	90	EJ Rees	L
93	EH Bray	RS	42	RW Sword	S	91	MT Daly	H
94	RD Forsdyce	H	43	JL Godden	W	92	BJ Akker	D
95	WAE Austen	RP	44	MJ Rimell	W	93	TEB Walker	W
96	EM Jameson	P	45	BH Price	R	94	TC Dolman	V
97	GS Smith	P	46	TRH Savill	W	95	ID Hayes	B
98	H Musker	W	47	A Hastings	g	96	PA Westcott	g
99	CH Wild	G	48	MHD Whinney	G	97	HA Toulson	g
1900	AH Liddle	RG	49	MDC Jenks	B	98	PSS Leal	V
01	B Tuff	H	50	JWH May	S	99	MT Bailey	V
02	OT Norris	W	51	AJ Barclay	G	2000	AWJ Mezzetti	B
03	RA Bence-Pembroke	S	52	D Miller	D	01	RC Griston	g
04	JS Strange	g	53	GE Pratt	G	02	FD Palley	g
05	VG Thew	W	54	GB Gauntlett	L	03	CGC Ingham	W
06	VG Thew	W	55	DS Mace	L	04	PB Millington Buck	g
07	CT Gooch	W	56	DR Tomlinson	W	05	HGC Schofield	g
08	FHL Rushton	g	57	AAH White	S	06	CD Clinton	D
09	CB Johnson	D	1958	JPN Hallam	V	07	AN Beddows	G
1910	HA Wellesley	V	59	MR Willcocks	L			

IV Old Carthusian Football Blues

OXFORD in *italics*, CAMBRIDGE in BOLD

DATES	NAME	LEFT	House	DATES	NAME	LEFT	House
1873	*CEB NEPEAN*	o69	G	*1906/7*	*IE SNELL*	s03	L
1875/6/7*	*EH PARRY*	s74	G	**1907/8/9*/10***	**VG THEW**	L01	W
1878	**NJ ABDY**	s 76	S	*1908/9/10**	*RLL BRADDELL*	s07	H
1878/9*	*AWF WILSON*	s79	S	*1909/10/1**	*JB BICKERSTETH*	L06	S
1878/9	*WR PAGE*	L77	VGg	*1909*	*HJC PEARS*	L05	RP
1879	*CM BURDON*	o78	G	**1910**	**EH CUTHBERTSON**	s02	V
1881/2	**EG COLVIN**	s78	PS	**1910/1/2***	**RM WEEKS**	s09	V
1881	*ET LLOYD*	s74	H	**1910/1/2**	**S BAKER**	s04	V
1882	*LF GILLETT*	o78	D	*1912*	*CB JOHNSON*	s10	D
1882/3*/4*	*LML OWEN*	s81	D	*1912/3*	*WIF MACDONALD*	o04	S
1882	**LM RICHARDS**	s80	UV	*1913/4+ 20**	*JSF MORRISON*	s11	W
1883	**EJ WILSON**	s79	UL	*1913*	*L GJERS*	s11	R
1883	*J VINTCENT*	L80	W	*1913/4*	*HD VERNON*	s09	S
1883	*ET HARDMAN*	o79	G	**1914**	**D-St GK BOSWELL**	s12	H
1883	*CJ CORNISH*	s76	G	**1914**	**JH FOSDICK**	s13	g
1883/4/5*/6*	*WN COBBOLD*	s82	UV	**1920/1**	**PWC HOLLOWELL**	s16	W
1884/5/6	*A AMOS*	s82	Rg	*1920/1*/2**	*AHG BUTCHER*	o16	V
1884/5/6/7	**AM WALTERS**	s83	H	*1921*	*HCD WHINNEY*	o17	G
1885	*PM WALTERS*	s80	H	*1922/3*	*HM WARD CLARKE*	o19	V
1885/6/7	**TW BLENKIRON**	s83	H	*1922*	*PA FRASER*	o18	R
1886	*FJ BARMBY*	s82	US	**1922**	**RJP THORNE THORNE**	s18	S
1886	*TW STROTHER*	o82	H	*1922/3/4**	*FH BARNARD*	s21	W
1887	*WH AINGER*	s82	Rg	**1922**	**BCA PATCHITT**	o19	w
1888/9*	*C WREFORD BROWN*	s85	G	*1923*	*VE MORGAN*	L23	V
1888/9/90*	*ES CURREY*	s86	V	**1924**	**FE POWELL**	L19	H
1888	*CW WADDINGTON*	s84	BG	*1925/6/7*	*ECG HARLOW*	s21	g
1888	**CH TYLER**	s86	BG	*1925*	*IAW GILLIAT*	s21	G
1889	**AC NIXON**	s86	H	*27/8**	*GS FLETCHER*	s24	L
1889/90/1	*LR WILKINSON*	s87	BS	**1928/9**	**JOHNSON TC**	s26	D
1890/1/2*	*ME STANBROUGH*	s89	G	**1929/30/1***	**GD KEMP-WELCH**	s25	H
1891/2	*NF SHAW*	s89	V	**1930**	**BEARE RB**	o22	g
1891/2	*EC STREATFEILD*	s88	g	**?**	**KHE BOWEN**	s32	W
1892/3/4/5*	*EC BLISS*	s91	g	*1933*	*C MIDDLETON*	s30	B
1892	*WE GILLIAT*	s88	G	*1933/4/5**	*WF MOSS*	s26	W
1893/4	*EF BUZZARD*	s90	g	**1934/5***	**GT HOLLEBONE**	o26	g
1893/4/5	*CDeL HEWITT*	s91	B	*1935*	*JEB HILL*	o27	R
1894	*GS WILSON*	s91	L	*1935*	*JL FIELD*	o29	V
1895	*HJ BROADBENT*	s92	S	*1935/6/7*	*SC GILLCHREST*	L34	G
1895/6*/7	*EH BRAY*	s93	RS	*1936*	*KPS CALDWELL*	s33	g
1893 + 95	*RJ SALT*	s92	S	*1936/7/8*	*RM HOLLIS*	s35	G
1893/4/5/6*	*GO SMITH*	s92	H	*1938/9*	*JM LOMAS*	s37	g
1896/7/8/9*	*GC VASSALL*	s94	P	*1939*	*PR CROMPTON*	s36	V
1896	**CB WARD**	s93	Rg	*1940*	*CA VANBERGEN*	s36	P
1897	**JT McGAW**	s90	B	*1941 + 42*	*LCW FIGG*	s41	W
1897	**AJ DAVIDSON**	s94	G	**1942**	**HC CHURCHILL DAVIDSON**	s36	V
1897	*HM TURNBULL*	s94	P	*1943+44+45*	*CMG ELLIOTT*	o39	H
1897	*SL DARVELL*	s92	D	*1947 + 49**	*JDP TANNER*	s40	P
1897/8	*WU TIMMIS*	s94	W	*1948*	*FA PEET*	s41	G
1897/8	*CH WILSON*	s95	G	**1950/1/2***	**PBH MAY**	s47	S
1897/8/9/00*	*EM JAMESON*	s96	P	**1955/6**	**D MILLER**	s53	D
1897/8	*RH LAIRD*	s95	W	*1964/5/6**	*RMC GILLIAT*	s63	G
1898/9	**AR HAIG-BROWN**	s96	H	**1978**	**L ADOMAKOH**	o74	R
1899	*LH WACE*	o94	H	*1992/3*	*DJ AUSTEN*	s89	H
1899	*ER TURNBULL*	s95	P	*1992/3**	*G BROOKE*	s89	S
1899/00/1	*CF RYDER*	s97	g				
1900/1/2/3	*CH WILD*	s99	G	Date of Leaving	o = Oration		
1903	*GV GOODLIFFE*	s02	Rg		s = Summer		
1903/4	**TS ROWLANDSON**	o97	L		L = Long		
1903/4/5/6*	*OT NORRIS*	s02	W		* = captain		
1905/6	*WJH CURWEN*	s02	g		recorded at Charterhouse		
1905/6/7*	*RA BENCE-PEMBROKE*	s03	S		McCleland NPKJO	s06	S
1906/7	*JCD TETLEY*	s03	D		not on CUAFC boards		

Houses (in order of foundation)

S = Saunderites	L = Lockites	B = Bodeites
V = Verites	W = Weekites	P = Pageites
G = Gownboys	H = Hodgsonites	R = Robinites
g = Girdlestoneites	D = Daviesites	U = Uskites

V Old Carthusian International Footballers
(see also p 138)

	v SCOTLAND	v WALES	v IRELAND	v OTHERS
TC HOOMAN	1871/2 (unofficial)			
CEB NEPEAN				Scotland v Eng 1871/2
EH PARRY	1882	1879/82		
JFM PRINSEP	1879			
WN COBBOLD	1883(1)/5/6/7	1886/7 (1)	1883(2)/5/7(2)	
A AMOS	1885	1886(1)		
AM WALTERS	1885/6/7/9/90	1887c/9/90	1885	
PM WALTERS	1885/6/7/8/9/90c	1886/7/9/90c	1885/6c/8	
C WREFORD BROWN	1898c	1894/5	1889	
ES CURREY	1890	1890(2)		
LR WILKINSON		1891		
ME STANBROUGH		1895		*Eng v Canada 1891*
WFH STANBROUGH				*Eng v SAfrica 1897*
WE GILLIAT			1893(3)	
GO SMITH	1894/6c/7c/8/9c(1)	1894/5/6c(2)/7c/8(1)/9c	1893(1)/6c(1)/7c/8c(1)	
	00c/1c	00c	99c(4)/00c	*v Germany 1901*
GC VASSALL			1899	
OE WREFORD BROWN				*Eng v Germany 1899*
SL DARVELL				Wales v Scotland and Ireland 1897
CF RYDER				*Eng v Germany 1901*
WU TIMMIS			1907	*Eng v Holland 1907*
EB PROUD				*Eng v France 1907*
				v Belgium, Germany 1908
TS ROWLANDSON			1907	*v Holland 1907*
MHC DOLL				*Eng XI v Bohemia 1911*
JSF MORRISON		*1920*		
RJP THORNE THORNE		*1921*		
BCA PATCHITT				Eng v Sweden 1923 x 2
AG BOWER		1924c/27c	1923	Eng vBelgium 1923/24c
		1920/2/3/4/6		*Eng v France 1920*
			1922/3/4/5, 27	*Eng v S Africa 1924*
HD MOLSON				*Canada 1924-27*
JDP TANNER		*1947*	*1947/8*	

(1) = goals scored   c = captain   capitals=full side   *italics = amateur ints.*

VI House Cup Final Winners

Year	Winner		Year	Winner		Year	Winner
1878	Saunderites		1934	Verites		1990	Lockites
1879	Verites		1935	Weekites		1991	Hodgsonites
1880	Girdlestoneites		1936	Girdlestoneites		1992	Hodgsonites
1881	Lockites		1937	Girdlestoneites		1993	Verites
1882	Final not contested		1938	Daviesites		1994	Weekites
1883	Gownboys		1939	Pageites		1995	Girdlestoneites
1884	Gownboys		1940	Girdlestoneites		1996	Girdlestoneites
1885	Gownboys		1941	Girdlestoneites		1997	Verites
1886	Saunderites		1942	Girdlestoneites		1998	Gownboys
1887	Gownboys		1943	Hodgsonites		1999	Girdlestoneites
1888	Hodgsonites		1944	Girdlestoneites		2000	Gownboys
1889	Verites		1945	Weekites		2001	Lockites
1890	Hodgsonites		1946	Gownboys		2002	Girdlestoneites
1891	Saunderites		1947	Gownboys		2003	Girdlestoneites
1892	Hodgsonites		1948	Saunderites		2004	Girdlestoneites
1893	Pageites		1949	Gownboys		2005	Girdlestoneites
1894	Girdlestoneites		1950	Saunderites		2006	Girdlestoneites
1895	Pageites		1951	Bodeites		2007	Verites
1896	Lockites		1952	Daviesites			
1897	Weekites		1953	Saunderites			
1898	Verites		1954	Lockites			
1899	Verites		1955	Saunderites			
1900	Saunderites		1956	Saunderites			
1901	Lockites		1957	Hodgsonites			WINS
1902	Gownboys		1958	Saunderites		G	27
1903	Weekites		1959	Hodgsonites		g	21
1904	Gownboys		1960	Verites		V	19 and 2 shared
1905	Gownboys		1961	Gownboys		S	17
1906	Gownboys		1962	Gownboys		H	10 and 2 shared
1907	Girdlestoneites		1963	Hodgsonites		W	10
1908	Gownboys		1964	Verites		D	8
1909	Girdlestoneites		1965	Verites		L	6
1910	Weekites		1966	Girdlestoneites		P	3
1911	Saunderites		1967	Hodgsonites/Verites		R	3
1912	Saunderites		1968	Verites		B	1
1913	Weekites		1969	Gownboys			
1914	Saunderites		1970	Gownboys			
1915	Weekites		1971	Saunderites			
1916	Verites		1972	Verites			
1917	Verites		1973	Robinites			
1918	Verites		1974	Robinites			
1919	Robinites		1975	Girdlestoneites			
1920	Gownboys		1976	Hodgsonites			
1921	Gownboys		1977	Girdlestoneites			
1922	Gownboys		1978	Saunderites			
1923	Gownboys		1979	Saunderites			
1924	Daviesites		1980	Daviesites			
1925	Saunderites		1981	Verites			
1926	Gownboys		1982	Hodgsonites/Verites			
1927	Gownboys		1983	Verites			
1928	Gownboys		1984	Daviesites			
1929	Gownboys		1985	Daviesites			
1930	Weekites		1986	Daviesites			
1931	Weekites		1987	Daviesites			
1932	Verites		1988	Verites			
1933	Gownboys		1989	Verites			

VII 1st XI Football Results
OQ to present and LQ up to 1979
compiled by Bob Noble
(Oration Quarter-Long Quarter is a season)
Home games in bold, aet = after extra time
Team names and goal descriptions as written in Captain's Book or Carthusian account

School fixtures

Aldenham

Date	Year	Opponent	Result	Score
Nov 10th	1920	Charterhouse	won	3-0 (Barnard 2, Gilliat)
Nov 15th	1977	Charterhouse	won	1-0 (Mole)
Nov 14th	1978	**Aldenham**	won	1-0 (Pride)
Nov 13th	1979	Charterhouse	won	4-0 (Haynes 2, Raymonde, Lathwood)
Nov 11th	1980	**Aldenham**	won	2-1 (Cuff 2)
Nov 10th	1981	Charterhouse	lost	1-2 (McCourt)
Nov 9th	1982	**Aldenham**	lost	1-3 (Proctor)
Nov 15th	1983	Charterhouse	won	4-1 (Davis 2, Ibru, Pennant)
Nov 13th	1984	**Aldenham**	drew	0-0
Nov 12th	1985	Charterhouse	lost	1-4 (Faulkner)
Nov 11th	1986	**Aldenham**	won	2-1 (Jenkins, o.g.)
Nov 10th	1987	Charterhouse	won	3-0 (Leale 2, Henkes)
Nov 8th	1988	**Aldenham**	won	3-0 (Scholefield 2, Ashby)
Nov 7th	1989	Charterhouse	drew	1-1 (E Ashby)
Nov 6th	1990	**Aldenham**	won	2-1 (Mitten, Kidd)
Nov 5th	1991	Charterhouse	won	3-0 (Pegler, Ashby, Gompertz)
Nov 14th	1992	**Aldenham**	lost	2-3 (McCourtie 2)
Nov 13th	1993	Charterhouse	won	4-2 (Younie 2, Webb, o.g.)
Nov 12th	1994	**Aldenham**	drew	2-2 (Brazier, Raven)
Nov 11th	1995	Charterhouse	won	1-0 (Raven)
Nov 16th	1996	**Aldenham**	won	4-3 (Adie 2, Savage 2)
Nov 15th	1997	Charterhouse	won	1-0 (Savage)
Nov 14th	1998	**Aldenham**	won	3-0 (Bailey, Burke-Murphy, Beaumont)
Nov 13th	1999	Charterhouse	won	4-0 (Bailey 2, Byrne, Shelton)
Nov 11th	2000	**Aldenham**	won	5-0 (Burke-Murphy, Holmes, o.g., Mulligan, Clark)
Nov 10th	2001	Charterhouse	won	7-0 (C Bunstead, Watson 2, Brennan 2, Williams, Palley)
Nov 30th	2002	**Aldenham**	won	5-2 (Bunstead, Marsden, Palley, Millington Buck, o.g.)
Nov 29th	2003	Charterhouse	won	2-0 (Millington Buck, Ezekiel)
Nov 27th	2004	**Aldenham**	won	3-1 (Lucas, Walker, Millington Buck)
Nov 19th	2005	Charterhouse	won	1-0 (Cameron)
Nov 18th	2006	**Aldenham**	drew	1-1 (o.g.)
Nov 17th	2007	Charterhouse	won	3-1 (Jamieson 2, Beddows)

Alleyn's Dulwich

Date	Year	Opponent	Result	Score
Sept 27th	2000	**Alleyn's**	won	2-0 (Clark 2)[ISFA 2]
Oct 2nd	2007	**Alleyn's**	won	1-0 (Beddows)

Ardingly College

Date	Year	Opponent	Result	Score
Oct 15th	1969	**Ardingly**	drew	1-1 (Walton)
Oct 14th	1970	Charterhouse	drew	1-1 (Godby)
Oct 13th	1971	**Ardingly**	won	5-2 (Godby 3, Stewart, Holder)
Oct 11th	1972	Charterhouse	won	1-0 (Doggart)
Oct 10th	1973	**Ardingly**	won	4-1 (Scholfield 2, Adomakoh, Middleton)
Oct 9th	1974	Charterhouse	won	5-0 (Adomakoh, Walker 2, Middleton 2)
Oct 8th	1975	**Ardingly**	lost	0-1
Oct 6th	1976	Charterhouse	won	3-1 (Reynolds, Cummins, Shepherd)
Oct 5th	1977	**Ardingly**	drew	2-2 (Adomakoh, Shepherd)
Oct 4th	1978	Charterhouse	won	3-1 (Piper, Cummins, Haynes)
Oct 3rd	1979	**Ardingly**	lost	1-2 (Haynes)
Oct 1st	1980	Charterhouse	won	5-0 (Gard 2, Cuff 2, Myers)
Sept 29th	1981	**Ardingly**	lost	1-3 (Challen)
Sept 28th	1982	Charterhouse	won	2-1 (Waters 2)
Sept 27th	1983	**Ardingly**	won	3-0 (Davis 2, Ibru)
Oct 2nd	1984	Charterhouse	won	6-0 (Baker 3)
Oct 1st	1985	**Ardingly**	won	2-1 (Kerevan, Abdali)
Sept 30th	1986	Charterhouse	won	1-0 (Jenkins)
Sept 29th	1987	**Ardingly**	drew	1-1 (Hare)
Sept 27th	1988	Charterhouse	drew	2-2 (Henkes, Scholefield)
Sept 26th	1989	**Ardingly**	drew	0-0
Sept 25th	1990	Charterhouse	won	7-2 (Gompertz 3, Daly, Wallace, Mitten, o.g.)
Sept 24th	1991	**Ardingly**	won	5-2 (McCourtie 3, Kidd 2)
Sept 29th	1992	Charterhouse	won	3-0 (McCourtie 3)
Sept 28th	1993	**Ardingly**	lost	1-5 (Drayson)
Nov 16th	1993	Charterhouse	lost	0-3 [ISFA 3]
Sept 27th	1994	Charterhouse	lost	1-5 (Robertson)

Date	Year	Opponent	Result	Score
Nov 7th	1995	**Ardingly**	lost	3-4 (Frendo 3)
Nov 12th	1996	Charterhouse	lost	0-2
Oct 14th	1997	**Ardingly**	drew	3-3 (Hollingsworth, Gay 2)
Nov 28th	1998	Charterhouse	lost	0-1
Nov 27th	1999	**Ardingly**	won	6-0 (Bailey 2, Clark 2, Jackson, Toller)
Nov 25th	2000	Charterhouse	won	2-0 (Clark, Mulligan)
Nov 24th	2001	**Ardingly**	won	1-0 (Williams)
Nov 23rd	2002	**Ardingly**	won	3-2 (Bunstead, Millington Buck, Barnett)
Dec 4th	2004	Charterhouse	won	4-0 (Clinton 2, Millington Buck, Yabe)
Dec 3rd	2005	**Ardingly**	won	2-1 (Cameron, Delaiglesia)
Dec 3rd	2006	Charterhouse	won	3-0 (Rubinstein 2, Satterthwaite)
Dec 1st	2007	**Ardingly**	won	6-0 (Beddows 2, Walker, Hall, Peat, Parsons)

Bedales

Date	Year	Opponent	Result	Score
Jan 31st	1973	Charterhouse	won	3-0
Oct 27th	1973	**Bedales**	won	5-0 (Williams, Middleton, Faull, Adomakoh, Napolitano)
Jan 26th	1974	Charterhouse	won	3-0 (Adomakoh, North, Scholfield)
Jan 25th	1975	Charterhouse	won	2-1 (North, Phillips)
Jan 24th	1976	Charterhouse	won	1-0 (Cunningham)
Nov 24th	1976	**Bedales**	won	

Bolton GS

Date	Year	Opponent	Result	Score
Sept 7th	1982	**Bolton GS**	lost	1-4 (o.g.)
Sept 7th	1983	**Bolton GS**	lost	3-6 (Griffiths, Meesman, Haghighi)
Feb 3rd	2003	Charterhouse	lost	0-5 [ISFA Cup(semi-final)]

Bradfield

Date	Year	Opponent	Result	Score
Mar 10th	1915	**Bradfield**	won	5-2 (Hansell 3, Dunlop, Spafford)
Nov 10th	1915	Charterhouse	won	8-0 (Reiss 7, Tinley)
Oct 28th	1916	**Bradfield**	won	3-2 (Tinley 2, Bearman)
Oct 20th	1917	Charterhouse	won	6-0
Nov 12th	1919	**Bradfield**	won	5-3 (Gilliat 3)
Nov 24th	1920	Charterhouse	won	3-0 (MacGusty, Kiggell 2)
Nov 2nd	1921	**Bradfield**	lost	1-2 (Morgan)
Nov 22nd	1922	Charterhouse	won	1-0 (Fletcher)
Nov 3rd	1923	**Bradfield**	won	3-0 (Massey, Shute, Fletcher)
Nov 19th	1924	Charterhouse	won	4-0 ((Kemp Welch 2, Sharp 2)
Nov 25th	1925	**Bradfield**	lost	0-2
Dec 1st	1926	Charterhouse	won	2-1 (Weatherall, Fletcher)
Nov 30th	1927	**Bradfield**	won	3-1 (Middleton, Fletcher, Davies)
Nov 14th	1928	Charterhouse	won	5-0 (Cohen, Craddock, Jeavons 3)
Nov 27th	1929	**Bradfield**	drew	0-0
Nov 12th	1930	Charterhouse	won	3-1 (Paver, Moss 2)
Nov 21st	1931	**Bradfield**	drew	1-1 (Dunbar)
Nov 4th	1933	**Bradfield**	drew	2-2 (Trapman, Frith)
Nov 3rd	1934	Charterhouse	won	3-1 (Hodgson, Lomas, Daukes)
Nov 2nd	1935	**Bradfield**	lost	2-3 (Ades, Dowding)
Oct 31st	1936	Charterhouse	won	4-1 (Stone, Lomas)
Oct 30th	1937	**Bradfield**	drew	1-1 (Geppert)
Oct 29th	1938	Charterhouse	won	3-0 (Tanner 3)
Oct 28th	1939	**Bradfield**	drew	2-2 (Tanner, Finlayson)
Oct 26th	1940	Charterhouse	won	4-0 (Spencer 3, Evans)
Nov 16th	1940	**Bradfield**	won	5-2 (Figg 4, Hawley)
Oct 25th	1941	**Bradfield**	won	2-1 (Evans, Lahaye)
Nov 15th	1941	Charterhouse	won	4-0 (Evans 3, Lahaye)
Oct 24th	1942	Charterhouse	drew	1-1 (Crole-Rees)
Nov 24th	1942	**Bradfield**	drew	0-0
Nov 27th	1943	**Bradfield**	drew	0-0
Nov 18th	1943	Charterhouse	won	1-0 (Crole-Rees)
Oct 28th	1944	Charterhouse	won	4-0 (Godden 2, Wilson, M Rimell)
Nov 18th	1944	**Bradfield**	won	3-2 (Spratt 2, Godden)
Oct 27th	1945	**Bradfield**	won	4-0 (Howard 2, May, Wilson)
Oct 26th	1946	Charterhouse	won	6-0 (Savill 2, May 2, Mills, Gemmel)
Oct 25th	1947	**Bradfield**	won	3-1 (Burt, Whinney, Janes)
Oct 23rd	1948	Charterhouse	lost	0-1
Oct 22nd	1949	**Bradfield**	lost	3-4 (Jenks, Gladstone, o.g.)
Oct 28th	1950	Charterhouse	won	3-1 (Pegler 2, Yanneghas)
Oct 27th	1951	**Bradfield**	won	5-2 (Miller 3, Tuck, Pegler)
Oct 25th	1952	Charterhouse	drew	1-1 (Miller)
Oct 24th	1953	**Bradfield**	lost	0-1
Oct 23rd	1954	Charterhouse	drew	1-1 (Ruddock)
Oct 22nd	1955	**Bradfield**	drew	3-3 (Burrows, Tunnock, Sparshatt)

Oct 27th	1956	Charterhouse	drew	2-2 (White, Sparshatt)	
Oct 26th	1957	Bradfield	lost	0-3	
Oct 25th	1958	Charterhouse	drew	0-0	
Oct 24th	1959	Bradfield	drew	1-1 (o.g.)	
Oct 22nd	1960	Charterhouse	lost	0-2	
Oct 28th	1961	Bradfield	drew	2-2 (Gilliat 2)	
Oct 27th	1962	Charterhouse	won	6-1 (Gilliat 4, Hooper, Martin)	
Oct 26th	1963	Bradfield	lost	1-4 (Hooper)	
Oct 24th	1964	Charterhouse	won	3-0 (Hooper, Weir 2)	
Oct 23rd	1965	Bradfield	lost	0-2	
Oct 22nd	1966	Charterhouse	won	2-1 (Bennett)	
Oct 28th	1967	Bradfield	lost	1-2 (Gieve)	
Oct 26th	1968	Charterhouse	lost	0-1	
Oct 25th	1969	Bradfield	won	2-0 (Walton, Grizelle)	
Oct 24th	1970	Charterhouse	won	2-1 (Godby, Hughes)	
Oct 23rd	1971	Bradfield	lost	0-4	
Oct 21st	1972	Charterhouse	won	3-0 (Doggart, Stone, Parker)	
Oct 20th	1973	Bradfield	lost	1-2 (	
Oct 19th	1974	Charterhouse	lost	1-3 (Adomakoh)	
Oct 18th	1975	Bradfield	drew	1-1 (	
Oct 16th	1976	Charterhouse	won	2-1 (Belchamber, Ostrer)	
Oct 15th	1977	Bradfield	drew	0-0	
Oct 14th	1978	Charterhouse	won	1-0 (Farrow)	
Oct 13th	1979	Bradfield	won	2-1 (Raymonde 2)	
Oct 11th	1980	Charterhouse	lost	1-2 (McCourt)	
Oct 10th	1981	Bradfield	lost	0-4	
Oct 9th	1982	Charterhouse	won	3-0 (Proctor 2, Newman)	
Oct 8th	1983	Bradfield	won	3-1 (Faulkner, Davis, Pennant)	
Oct 13th	1984	Charterhouse	won	2-1 (Gough)	
Oct 12th	1985	Bradfield	won	1-0 (Baker)	
Oct 11th	1986	Charterhouse	lost	0-1	
Oct 10th	1987	Bradfield	drew	1-1 (Gray)	
Oct 8th	1988	Charterhouse	drew	1-1 (Brooke)	
Oct 7th	1989	Bradfield	lost	0-1	
Oct 6th	1990	Charterhouse	drew	1-1 (Gompertz)	
Oct 5th	1991	Bradfield	lost	0-2	
Oct 10th	1992	Charterhouse	won	2-0 (Webb 2)	
Nov 19th	1992	Bradfield	won	2-1 (Jarvis, Wakeham) [ISFA Cup 3]	
Oct 9th	1993	Bradfield	lost	1-2 (o.g.)	
Oct 8th	1994	Bradfield	lost	0-1	
Oct 7th	1995	Bradfield	won	3-2 (Frendo, A Smith, Lidstone)	
Oct 5th	1996	Charterhouse	won	2-1 (Saunders, Hollingsworth)	
Oct 4th	1997	Bradfield	won	7-0 (Gay 3, Hollingsworth 2, Nash, Beaumont)	
Oct 3rd	1998	Charterhouse	drew	1-1 (Burke-Murphy)	
Oct 19th	2000	Charterhouse	won	3-0 (Deschampsneufs, Clark, Williams)	
Oct 18th	2001	Bradfield	won	2-0 (Watson, Brennan)	
Oct 17th	2002	Charterhouse	drew	2-2 (Bunstead, Millington Buck)	
Oct 16th	2003	Bradfield	lost	0-3	
Nov 2nd	2004	Charterhouse	drew	3-3 (Clinton, Holder, Yabe)	
Oct 20th	2005	Bradfield	won	2-0 (Holder, Delaiglesia)	
Oct 19th	2006	Charterhouse	won	3-0 (Rubinstein, Parsons, Carter)	
Oct 18th	2007	Bradfield	drew	0-0	
Jan 28th	2008	Corinthian Casuals	won	3-0 (Rogers, Adolphus, Hall) [SIS League Final]	

Brentwood

Jan 25th	1999	Brentwood	won	2-0 (Jackson, Shelton) [ISFA Cup Semi-final]	
Oct 17th	2000	Charterhouse	lost	3-4 (Clark 2, Mulligan) [ISFA Cup 3]	
Sept 27th	2001	Charterhouse	lost	0-4 [ISFA Cup(1)]	
Sept 28th	2004	Charterhouse	lost	1-2 (Paes) [ISFA Cup (1)]	
Nov 13th	2004	Brentwood	drew	1-1 (Cameron)	

Bury GS

Dec 4th	1999	Bury	won	2-1 (Bailey, Jackson) [ISFA Cup 4]	
Jan 29th	2007	Bury GS	won	2-0 (Carter, Rubinstein)[ISFA Cup Semi-final]	

Camberley & Frimley CGS

Oct 1st	1969	Charterhouse	lost	0-2	
Sept 29th	1970	Charterhouse	lost	0-1	

Chichester HS

Nov 9th	1996	Charterhouse	won	7-1 (Adie 3, Savage 2, Hollingsworth, o.g.)	

Collingwood

Sept 28th	1971	Charterhouse	lost	1-2	
Dec 4th	1973	Charterhouse			

Collyer's, Horsham

Nov 21st	1973	Collyer's			
Oct 2nd	1974	Charterhouse	won	3-2 (Walker)	
Oct 1st	1975	Collyer's			
Sept 29th	1976	Charterhouse			
Nov 23rd	1977	Collyer's	won	3-1 (Shepherd, Kirkbride, Doggart)	
Dec 13th	1979	Charterhouse	drew	2-2 (Raymonde, Haynes)	

Coulsdon College

Nov 29th	1993	Charterhouse	lost	2-3 (Webb, Aldridge) [Surrey Cup]	

Croydon College

Nov 19th	1990	Charterhouse	lost	1-2 (Bower) [Surrey Cup Quarter Final]	

De La Salle Jersey tour

Sept 8th	1979	De la Salle, Jersey	won	2-0 (Haynes 2)	

Elizabeth College Guernsey tour

Oct 25th	1977	Charterhouse	lost	2-4 (Mole, Doggart)	
Sept 9th	1980	Elizabeth College	drew	2-2 (Cuff, o.g.)	
Oct 22nd	1980	Charterhouse	lost	1-3 (Spooner)	
Oct 22nd	1987	Charterhouse	won	4-2 (Gray 3, Leale)	
Oct 18th	1990	Charterhouse	won	3-2 (Gompertz 2, Rees)	

Epsom & Ewell

Oct 17th	1996	Charterhouse	won	4-2 (Savage, Adie, Westcott, Saunders) [Surrey Cup]	

Esher College

Oct 16th	1991	Charterhouse	won	5-0 (Ashby 3, McCourtie, Pegler)[Surrey Cup]	

Eton

15th Mar	1900	Charterhouse	won	4-1 (Tuff 3, Good)	
14th Mar	1901	Eton	won	5-0 (Tuff, Goodliffe, Bense Pembroke 3)	
Feb 18th	1943	Eton	won	4-3 (Spratt, Edwards, Dalgety 2)	
Feb 10th	1944	Charterhouse	won	3-1 (Rimell, Spratt, Crole-Rees)	
Feb 10th	1945	Eton	drew	1-1 (Pollock)	
Feb 14th	1946	Charterhouse	won	10-1 (Wilson 4, May 3, Savill 2, Price)	
Feb 9th	1948	Charterhouse	won	3-0 (Divett 2, Whinney)	
Feb 10th	1949	Eton	won	2-0 (Goodliffe, Kay)	
Feb 9th	1950	Charterhouse	drew	2-2 (Vansittart, Young)	
Feb 8th	1951	Eton	won	8-2 (Pegler 5, Barclay, Yannaghas, Monk)	
Feb 7th	1952	Charterhouse	won	3-2 (Parker, Pegler, Miller)	
Feb 5th	1953	Eton	won	3-2 (Hardcastle 2, White)	
Feb 4th	1954	Charterhouse	lost	0-4	
Feb 3rd	1955	Eton	drew	2-2 (Buckley, o.g.)	
Feb 9th	1956	Charterhouse	won	6-2 (Steed 2, Forsyth, Jakobson, Tunnock, o.g.)	
Feb 7th	1957	Eton	won	2-1 (o.g., Visser)	
Feb 6th	1958	Charterhouse	drew	1-1 (Agace)	
Feb 5th	1959	Eton	won	5-1 (Gibb, Faulkner, Topham, Taylor 2)	
Feb 4th	1960	Charterhouse	drew	1-1 (Taylor)	
Feb 9th	1961	Eton	lost	2-3 (Powell, Gilliat)	
Feb 8th	1962	Charterhouse	won	3-0 (Gilliat 3)	
Feb	1963	No match - snow			
Feb 6th	1964	Charterhouse	won	3-0 (Weir 2, Hooper)	
Feb 4th	1965	Eton	won	4-1 (Easton, Weir, Hooper 2)	
Feb 10th	1966	Charterhouse	won	2-0 (Bennett, Gimson)	
Feb 9th	1967	Charterhouse	won	3-0 (Deans 2, Provis)	
Feb 10th	1968	Charterhouse	won	7-0 (o.g., Carter 2, Bennett 2, Deans, Rintoul)	
Feb 6th	1969	Eton	won	2-0 (Foster 2)	
Feb 5th	1970	Charterhouse	drew	1-1	
Feb 4th	1971	Eton	won	5-0 (Godby, Holder, Gibson, Stewart 2)	
Oct 16th	1971	Charterhouse	won	2-1 (Godby 2)	
Oct 14th	1972	Eton	lost	1-3	
Oct 13th	1973	Charterhouse	drew	1-1	
Oct 12th	1974	Eton	lost	0-2	
Oct 11th	1975	Charterhouse	won	1-0 (Hayllar)	
Oct 9th	1976	Eton	lost	1-4	
Oct 8th	1977	Charterhouse	drew	0-0	
Oct 21st	1978	Eton	lost	0-2	
Oct 20th	1979	Charterhouse	won	2-0 (Haynes, Bishop)	
Oct 18th	1980	Eton	drew	0-0	
Oct 17th	1981	Charterhouse	drew	0-0	
Oct 16th	1982	Eton	lost	0-1	
Oct 15th	1983	Charterhouse	drew	0-0	
Oct 20th	1984	Eton	drew	2-2	
Oct 19th	1985	Charterhouse	lost	2-3 (Jenkins, Neill)	
Oct 18th	1986	Eton	drew	1-1 (Jenkins)	
Oct 17th	1987	Charterhouse	drew	0-0	
Oct 15th	1988	Charterhouse	drew	0-0	
Oct 14th	1989	Charterhouse	lost	0-2	
Oct 13th	1990	Eton	lost	0-2	
Oct 12th	1991	Charterhouse	drew	1-1 (Ashby)	
Oct 17th	1992	Eton	drew	1-1 (Webb)	
Oct 16th	1993	Charterhouse	won	1-0 (Webb)	
Oct 15th	1994	Eton	won	2-0 (Frendo, Dolman)	
Oct 14th	1995	Charterhouse	lost	0-1	
Oct 12th	1996	Eton	won	3-0 (Hollingsworth 2, Westcott)	
Oct 11th	1997	Charterhouse	won	4-2 (Toulson, o.g., Savage, Gay)	
Oct 10th	1998	Eton	lost	0-3	
Oct 9th	1999	Charterhouse	won	4-1 (Clark, Byrne, Bailey, Toller)	

Oct 7th	2000	Eton	won	2-0 (Williams 2)
Oct 6th	2001	Charterhouse	won	7-1 (Bunstead 2, Watson 3, Palley, Cook)
Oct 5th	2002	Eton	drew	1-1 (Brennan)
Oct 4th	2003	Charterhouse	drew	0-0
Nov 4th	2003	Eton	lost	1-2 (Bourne) [ISFA Cup 3]
Oct 9th	2004	Eton	lost	2-3 (Clinton, Holder)
Oct 8th	2005	Charterhouse	won	1-0 (Cameron)
Oct 7th	2006	Eton	won	4-1 (Satterthwaite, Black, Cussins, Carter)
Oct 6th	2007	Charterhouse	drew	0-0

Fairfields

Nov 11th	1997	Charterhouse	lost	1-2 (Burke-Murphy) [Surrey Cup Quarter final]

Farnham College

Nov 1st	1993	Farnham College	won	5-4 (Webb 3, Wakeham, Stern) [Surrey Cup]

Forest

Sept 29th	1979	Charterhouse	drew	1-1 (Gard)
Sept 27th	1980	Charterhouse	lost	0-1
Sept 26th	1981	Charterhouse	won	3-1 (McCourt, Fordham, Gard)
Sept 25th	1982	Charterhouse	drew	4-4 (Proctor, Waters, Frearson, Aubrey)
Sept 24th	1983	Charterhouse	won	3-2 (Frearson 2, Davis)
Sept 29th	1984	Charterhouse	won	2-0
Sept 28th	1985	Charterhouse	drew	2-2 (Spiegel, Abdali)
Sept 27th	1986	Charterhouse	won	3-2 (Zervos, Dow, Jenkins)
Sept 26th	1987	Charterhouse	won	3-1 (Leale 2, Gray)
Sept 24th	1988	Charterhouse	drew	1-1 (Sale)
Sept 23rd	1989	Charterhouse	drew	1-1 (Sale)
Sept 22nd	1990	Charterhouse	drew	0-0
Sept 21st	1991	Charterhouse	lost	0-4
Sept 26th	1992	Charterhouse	won	3-0 (Webb 2, o.g.)
Mar 16th	1993	Craven Cottage	drew	2-2(McCourtie, Jarvis)[ISFA Cup Final] aet lost 0-3 on pens
Sept 25th	1993	Charterhouse	won	5-0 (Webb 5)
Sept 24th	1994	Charterhouse	lost	1-3 (Frendo)
Sept 23rd	1995	Forest	drew	0-0
Sept 21st	1996	Charterhouse	drew	1-1 (Smith)
Sept 20th	1997	Forest	won	5-3 (Hollingsworth 3, Gay, Leal)
Sept 19th	1998	Charterhouse	won	4-2 (Jackson, Leal 2, Wallis)
Sept 18th	1999	Forest	won	2-1 (Clark 2)
Sept 16th	2000	Charterhouse	won	2-1 (Mezzetti, Williams)
Sept 15th	2001	Charterhouse	won	2-1 (Watson, Williams)
Sept 14th	2002	Forest	lost	1-2 (Ingham)
Sept 13th	2003	Charterhouse	won	4-2 (Ingham, Yabe, Hunter, Bourne)
Sept 18th	2004	Forest	won	3-1 (Yabe, Delaiglesia, Lucas)
Sept 17th	2005	Charterhouse	won	6-0 (Delaiglesia, Cameron, Fyler 3, Holder)
Sept 16th	2006	Forest	won	7-0 (Beddows, Rubinstein, Clinton 2, Nash, Evans, Cussins)
Sept 15th	2007	Charterhouse	won	4-0 (Kimmins, Beddows, Hall 2)

Fulbrook College

Oct 18th	1995	Charterhouse	drew	1-1 (Savage) [Surrey Cup] *won on penalties aet*
Oct 1st	1997	Fulbrook College	won	9-1 (Nash 3, Gay, Hollingsworth, Leal, Savage, Burke-Murphy o.g.) Surrey Cup]

Godalming College

Sept 17th	1980	Charterhouse	drew	2-2 (Cuff 2)
Sept 16th	1981	Charterhouse	won	4-2 (Gard 2, Davis 2)
Sept 15th	1982	Godalming College	lost	1-2 (Newman)
Sept 21st	1983	Godalming College	won	1-0 (Pennant)
Sept 26th	1984	Godalming College	won	6-1 (Wattar 3, Baker 2)
Sept 25th	1985	Godalming College	won	4-0 (Spiegel, Baker 2, Kerevan)
Sept 24th	1986	Godalming College	won	2-1 (Zervos 2)
Sept 23rd	1987	Godalming College	won	4-3 (Leale 2, Gray, Strecker)
Sept 20th	1988	Godalming College	won	3-1 (Brooke 2, Gorman)
Sept 20th	1989	Godalming College	won	2-0 (Sale, Clark)
Sept 19th	1990	Godalming College	lost	0-3
Sept 11th	1991	Charterhouse	lost	2-4 (Daly, Ashby)
Nov 11th	1991	Charterhouse	lost	0-2 [Surrey Cup Quarter final]

Guildford Technical College

Jan 20th	1971	Charterhouse	won	4-0 (Godby 2, Stewart, Gibson)

Haileybury

Jan 22nd	1977	Charterhouse	won	3-0 (Foley-Brickley, Whalley, Ostrer)

Hampton School

Feb 12th	1958	Charterhouse	won	2-1 (Gibb, Visser)
Nov 16th	1960	Hampton	lost	2-3 (Powell, Garrow)
Nov 11th	1961	Charterhouse	won	6-2 (Gilliat 4, Arnold, Bailhache)
Nov 10th	1962	Charterhouse	won	2-0 (Gilliat 2)
Nov 9th	1963	Charterhouse	lost	0-1
Nov 7th	1964	Hampton	drew	1-1 (Davis)

Nov 12th	1966	Hampton	lost	1-2 (Cohn)
Nov 11th	1967	Hampton	lost	1-2 (Rintoul)
Nov 9th	1968	Hampton	lost	1-4 (Foster)
Nov 8th	1969	Charterhouse	won	1-0 (Walton)
Nov 7th	1970	Hampton	won	3-1 (Stewart, Walton, Wallis)
Nov 6th	1971	Charterhouse	won	6-0 (Godby 2, Stewart 2, Holder, Williams)
Oct 16th	1974	Charterhouse	won	2-1 (Adomakoh 2)
Oct 15th	1975	Hampton		
Nov 27th	1991	Charterhouse	won	3-2 (Ashby, Gompertz, Pegler)
Oct 13th	1993	Charterhouse	won	6-1(Wakeham 2 Cunningham-Brown 2 Webb 2) [Surrey Cup]
Nov 23rd	1994	Charterhouse	won	
Nov 13th	2002	Charterhouse	won	4-0 (Marsden 2, Brennan, Katté)
Nov 12th	2003	Charterhouse	won	2-0 (Hunter, Millington Buck)
Nov 8th	2006	Charterhouse	drew	1-1 (o.g.)
Apr 27th	2007	Walkers Stadium	drew*	1-1 (Nash) [ISFA Cup Final] *lost 2-4 on penalties aet*
Nov 14th	2007	Charterhouse	won	2-0 (Rogers, Kimmins)

Harrow

Mar 20th	1915	Harrow	won	5-2 (Dunlop 2, Hansell 3)
Mar 11th	1916	Charterhouse	won	4-2 (Tinley, Leggatt, Reiss 2)
Mar 10th	1917	Harrow	won	4-3 (Bennett 2, Williams, Whalley)
Mar 13th	1918	Charterhouse	won	5-0 (Patchitt)
Mar 27th	1919	Harrow	lost	3-4 (Mordaunt-Smith 3)
Feb 24th	1920	Charterhouse	won	4-0 (Gilliat 3, Barnard)
Mar 3rd	1921	Harrow	drew	2-2 (Gilliat 2)
Feb 25th	1922	Charterhouse	won	1-0 (Doresa)
Feb 17th	1923	Harrow	won	5-2 (Shute, Kenyon, Morgan, Fletcher, Johnson)
Mar 1st	1924	Charterhouse	won	7-1 (Fletcher 2, Carter 4, Pritchard)
Mar 3rd	1925	Harrow	drew	1-1 (Deakin)
Feb 13th	1926	Charterhouse	won	3-1 (Glynn, Connell, Deakin)
Feb 12th	1927	Harrow	lost	0-4

Hautlieu GS Jersey tour

Oct 27th	1978	Hautlieu GS	won	3-0 (Mole 2, Piper)

Heath Park

Nov 23rd	1989	Charterhouse	lost	1-6 (E Ashby) [Surrey Cup Semi-final]

Highgate

Dec 18th	1946	Stamford Bridge	won	4-0 (Savill 2, May 2)
Dec 17th	1947	Stamford Bridge	won	3-0 (Whinney 2, Hastings)
Nov 22nd	1961	Charterhouse	lost	2-4 (Gilliat 2)
Nov 21st	1962	Highgate	lost	1-3 (de Grunwald)
Nov 20th	1963	Charterhouse	lost	2-8 (Randel, Bailhache)
Nov 18th	1964	Highgate	drew	1-1 (Weir)
Nov 17th	1965	Charterhouse	won	1-0 (Bennett)
Dec 3rd	1966	Charterhouse	lost	0-1
Nov 22nd	1967	Highgate	won	2-1 (Bennett, Provis)
Nov 20th	1968	Charterhouse	won	6-0 (Foster 3, Carter, Walton, Ritchie)
Nov 19th	1969	Charterhouse	won	1-0 (Walton)
Nov 18th	1970	Highgate	lost	0-3
Nov 17th	1971	Charterhouse	won	3-0 (Godby, Holder, Faull)
Nov 15th	1972	Highgate	won	1-0 (Parker)
Nov 14th	1973	Charterhouse	won	3-1 (Faull, o.g., Adomakoh)
Nov 12th	1975	Charterhouse	drew	0-0
Nov 10th	1976	Highgate	lost	2-8
Nov 9th	1977	Charterhouse	won	3-0 (Mole, Shepherd 2)
Nov 8th	1978	Highgate	drew	1-1 (Mole)
Nov 7th	1979	Charterhouse	won	1-0 (Haynes)
Nov 5th	1980	Highgate	drew	1-1 (Gard)
Oct 24th	1981	Charterhouse	drew	0-0
Oct 23rd	1982	Charterhouse	won	1-0 (Ibru)
Oct 22nd	1983	Highgate	won	2-0 (Davis 2)
Nov 17th	1984	Highgate	lost	1-3
Nov 16th	1985	Highgate	won	3-1 (Kerevan 2, Jenkins)
Nov 15th	1986	Charterhouse	drew	0-0
Nov 14th	1987	Highgate	drew	0-0
Nov 12th	1988	Charterhouse	won	2-0 (Benham, Austin)
Nov 11th	1989	Highgate	won	3-0 (Sale, R Ashby, Mitten)
Nov 10th	1990	Charterhouse	lost	2-3 (Wallace, Gompertz)
Nov 9th	1991	Highgate	won	3-0 (Ashby, Gompertz, Pegler)
Sept 10th	2005	Charterhouse	won	3-1 (Delaiglesia, Clinton. Nash)
Sept 9th	2006	Highgate	won	2-0 (Nash, Parsons)
Sept 8th	2007	Highgate	won	2-0 (Hall, Jamieson)

John Lyon

Oct 1st	1992	John Lyon	won	5-1 (McCourtie2 Webb Wakeham Cunningham-Brown) [ISFA Cup 1]

Kimbolton

Sept 23rd	1993	Kimbolton	won	4-1 (Younie, Wakeham, Guy 2) [ISFA Cup 1]
Sept 19th	2000	Kimbolton	won	1-0 (Mezzetti) [ISFA Cup1]

King Edward VII Sheffield-tour

Sept 9th	1982	King Edward VII	won	3-2 (Ibru, Proctor, Frearson)
Sept 8th	1983	King Edward VII	lost	0-2

KES Witley

Oct 22nd	1969	KES Witley	won	3-0 (Walton, o.g. 2)
Oct 21st	1970	Charterhouse	drew	0-0
Oct 20th	1971	KES Witley	drew	2-2
Oct 18th	1972	Charterhouse	won	4-2 (Doggart, Faull, Gibson, o.g.)
Oct 17th	1973	KES Witley		
Nov 27th	1974	Charterhouse	won	6-0 (Walker 4, Adonakoh, Middleton)
Sept 16th	1992	Charterhouse	won	3-0 (Webb, o.g.2)
Sept 15th	1993	KES Witley	drew	2-2 (Wakeham, Sadler)
Sept 14th	1994	Charterhouse	won	5-0 (Frendo 2, Smith 3)
Sept 13th	1995	KES Witley	won	1-0 (Frendo)
Sept 18th	1996	Charterhouse	won	4-2 (Hollingsworth, Savage, Westcott, Smith)
Sept 17th	1997	KES Witley	won	5-1 (Gay 3, Hollingsworth, Burke-Murphy)
Nov 11th	1998	Charterhouse	won	1-0 (Leal)
Nov 10th	1999	KES Witley	won	4-0 (Clark, Blake, Goodrich, Jackson)
Nov 7th	2000	Charterhouse	drew	1-1 (Clark)
Oct 21st	2006	KES Witley	won	5-1 (Clinton 2, Carter, Parsons, Mason)
Oct 20th	2007	Charterhouse	won	1-0 (Rogers)

King's School Chester

Jan 23rd	2008	Chester	won	1-0 (Hall) [ISFA Cup Semi-final]

Lancing

Mar 31st	1915	Lancing	won	7-1 (Reiss, Dunlop 2, Cawston 4)
Nov 10th	1917	Charterhouse	won	2-0
Oct 19th	1918	Lancing	won	4-0 (King)
Nov 15th	1919	Charterhouse	won	6-2 (Austin 2, Gilliat 4)
Nov 6th	1920	Lancing	won	3-1 (Gilliat 2, Anderson)
Nov 5th	1921	Charterhouse	drew	1-1 (Doresa)
Nov 4th	1922	Lancing	drew	1-1 (Fletcher)
Oct 31st	1923	Charterhouse	won	5-1 (Fletcher 2, Shute 3)
Nov 1st	1924	Lancing	lost	2-6 (Beare, Kemp Welch)
Oct 31st	1925	Charterhouse	won	6-0 (Deakin 4, Seligman, Connell)
Oct 30th	1926	Lancing	lost	1-2 (Glynn)
Oct 29th	1927	Charterhouse	won	4-3 (Robertson, Davies, Bruce Jones, Hale)
Oct 27th	1928	Lancing	won	9-0 (Spencer 2, Cohen, Craddock 3, Jeavons, Fletcher 2)
Oct 26th	1929	Charterhouse	won	4-0 (Jeavons 2, Wreford Brown, Hulton)
Nov 1st	1930	Lancing	drew	0-0
Oct 24th	1931	Charterhouse	drew	1-1 (Cardew)
Oct 21st	1933	Charterhouse	won	6-1 (o.g., Gillchrest 2, Frith 3)
Oct 20th	1934	Lancing	lost	1-2 (Daukes)
Oct 19th	1935	Charterhouse	won	5-1 (Ades, Greene 2, Dunbar, o.g.)
Oct 17th	1936	Lancing	won	3-2 (Hughes 2, Lomas)
Oct 16th	1937	Charterhouse	lost	1-3 (Swinbank)
Oct 15th	1938	Lancing	won	6-0 (Larking, Beattie, Tanner 3, Swinbank)
Oct 14th	1939	Charterhouse	lost	0-1
Dec 16th	1944	Charterhouse	won	8-0 (Spratt 5, Godden 2, Bishop)
Oct 20th	1945	Lancing	won	2-1 (Wilson 2)
Nov 23rd	1946	Charterhouse	won	8-2 (May 4, Savill 3, Seaman)
Oct 18th	1947	Lancing	drew	1-1 (Hastings)
Oct 16th	1948	Charterhouse	won	3-1 (Atkinson, Whinney, o.g.)
Oct 15th	1949	Lancing	won	1-0 (Smithson)
Oct 14th	1950	Charterhouse	won	6-0 (Monk 3, Pegler 2, Bayman)
Oct 13th	1951	Lancing	won	3-0 (Spurrell, Miller 2)
Oct 11th	1952	Charterhouse	won	7-1 (Miller 3, Pratt 3, White)
Oct 10th	1953	Lancing	drew	2-2 (Wilkinson, Mace)
Oct 9th	1954	Charterhouse	lost	1-2 (Ruddock)
Oct 8th	1955	Lancing	won	3-1 (Jakobson, Forsyth 2)
Oct 13th	1956	Charterhouse	won	2-1 (Sparshatt, White)
Nov 30th	1957	Lancing	won	4-1 (Harrison, Agace, White, Gardiner)
Oct 11th	1958	Charterhouse	won	4-3 (Gibb 2, Topham 2)
Oct 10th	1959	Lancing	lost	1-5 (Topham)
Oct 15th	1960	Charterhouse	lost	1-5 (Powell)
Oct 14th	1961	Lancing	won	2-1 (Powell, Arnold)
Oct 13th	1962	Charterhouse	won	2-0 (Gilliat, Hopkins)
Oct 12th	1963	Lancing	lost	1-2 (Weir)
Oct 10th	1964	Charterhouse	drew	1-1 (Weir)
Oct 9th	1965	Lancing	lost	0-3
Oct 8th	1966	Charterhouse	lost	0-2
Oct 7th	1967	Lancing	lost	1-2 (Bennett)
Oct 5th	1968	Lancing	lost	0-3
Oct 4th	1969	Charterhouse	won	3-1 (Stewart, Walton 2)
Oct 3rd	1970	Lancing	won	2-1 (Wallis, Godby)
Oct 2nd	1971	Charterhouse	lost	1-4
Oct 7th	1972	Lancing	won	1-0 (Doggart)
OQ	1973	cancelled due to illness		
Oct 5th	1974	Lancing	won	5-2 (Middleton 3, Walker, Gibson)
Oct 4th	1975	Charterhouse	drew	0-0

Oct 2nd	1976	Lancing	drew	1-1 (Cummins)
Oct 22nd	1977	Charterhouse	lost	1-3 (Shepherd)
Oct 7th	1978	Lancing	won	3-0 (Piper 2, Farrow)
Oct 6th	1979	Charterhouse	lost	0-1
Oct 4th	1980	Lancing	won	2-1 (May 2)
Oct 3rd	1981	Charterhouse	won	1-0 (Gard)
Oct 2nd	1982	Lancing	won	3-1 (o.g., Newman, Frearson)
Oct 1st	1983	Lancing	won	3-1 (Davis 2, Faulkner)
Oct 6th	1984	Lancing	lost	1-2
Oct 5th	1985	Charterhouse	drew	0-0
Oct 4th	1986	Lancing	lost	1-2 (Gray)
Oct 3rd	1987	Charterhouse	won	1-0 (Gray)
Oct 1st	1988	Lancing	lost	0-2
Sept 30th	1989	Charterhouse	lost	0-2
Sept 29th	1990	Lancing	drew	0-0
Sept 28th	1991	Charterhouse	drew	0-0
Oct 3rd	1992	Lancing	lost	0-2
Oct 2nd	1993	Charterhouse	won	4-3 (Guy 2, Wakeham, Cunningham-Brown)
Oct 1st	1994	Lancing	lost	1-2 (Waller)
Sept 30th	1995	Charterhouse	lost	1-3 (Streatfeild)
Sept 28th	1996	Lancing	lost	0-3
Oct 15th	1996	Lancing	lost	0-3 [ISFA (2)]
Sept 27th	1997	Charterhouse	won	4-1 (Gay, Leal 2, Hollingsworth)
Sept 29th	1998	Lancing	won	2-0 (Leal, Wallis)
Sept 25th	1999	Charterhouse	won	3-0 (Bailey, Clark 2)
Sept 23rd	2000	Lancing	won	1-0 (Burke-Murphy)
Sept 22nd	2001	Charterhouse	lost	1-2 (Griston)
Sept 21st	2002	Lancing	won	2-0 (Barnett, Marsden)
Sept 20th	2003	Charterhouse	won	4-0 (Jenner, Yabe, Walker, Bardot)
Sept 25th	2004	Lancing	won	4-2 (Clinton, Millington Back, Holder, Cameron)
Sept 24th	2005	Charterhouse	won	1-0 (Beddows)
Nov 10th	2005	Lancing	lost	1-2 (Holder) [ISFA Cup 3]
Sept 23rd	2006	Lancing	won	3-0 (Beddows, Mason, Satterthwaite)
Sept 11th	2007	Charterhouse	won	1-0 (Rogers)

Latymer Upper

Sept 23rd	1998	Charterhouse	lost	2-3 (Bailey, Jackson) [ISFA Cup 1]
Nov 10th	2004	Charterhouse	won	2-1 (Holder 2)
Nov 15th	2006	Charterhouse	won	3-1 (Carter, Parsons, Clinton) [ISFA Cup 3]

Malvern

Nov 18th	1939	Charterhouse	won	3-2 (Figg, Larking, Tanner)
Nov 28th	1942	Harrow School	won	5-0 (Godden, Spratt 2, Dalgety, o.g)
Dec 1st	1943	Charterhouse	lost	0-3
Nov 29th	1944	Malvern	lost	0-4
Nov 21st	1945	Charterhouse	won	3-1 (May 2, Howard)
Oct 28th	1972	Charterhouse	drew	0-0
Sept 27th	1973	Malvern	drew	1-1 (Doggart)
Oct 26th	1974	Charterhouse	won	4-0 (Walker 2, Middleton, Adomakoh)
Oct 25th	1975	Malvern	drew	0-0
Oct 23rd	1976	Charterhouse	lost	1-3
Oct 11th	1977	Charterhouse		
Oct 10th	1978	Charterhouse	drew	0-0
Oct 9th	1979	Malvern	drew	1-1 (Bowers)
Oct 7th	1980	Charterhouse	won	3-1 (Gard, McCourt, Bonham-Carter)
Oct 6th	1981	Charterhouse	drew	0-0
Oct 5th	1982	Malvern	lost	0-1
Oct 4th	1983	Charterhouse	lost	0-2
Oct 9th	1984	Malvern	lost	0-2
Oct 8th	1985	Charterhouse	lost	0-1
Oct 7th	1986	Malvern	lost	1-5 (Jenkins)
Oct 6th	1987	Charterhouse	won	2-1 (Leale, Scott)
Oct 11th	1988	Malvern	won	1-0 (Henkes)
Oct 10th	1989	Charterhouse	won	4-2 (Rees, Hodson, o.g., Sale)
Oct 9th	1990	Malvern	won	2-1 (Mitten 2)
Oct 8th	1991	Charterhouse	won	2-0 (Gompertz, Ashby)
Oct 7th	1992	Malvern	lost	0-2
Oct 6th	1993	Charterhouse	won	3-2 (Wakeham, Webb, Cunningham-Brown)
Oct 4th	1994	Malvern	drew	1-1 (Frendo)
Oct 4th	1995	Charterhouse	won	2-0 (Frendo 2)
Sept 25th	1996	Charterhouse	won	2-1 (Adie 2) [ISFA Cup 1]
Oct 7th	1997	Malvern	won	2-0 (Gay, o.g.)
Oct 7th	1998	Charterhouse	won	6-0 (Jackson 2, Gay 2, Bailey, Beaumont)
Oct 5th	1999	Malvern	won	3-1 (Clark 2, Jackson)
Oct 4th	2000	Charterhouse	won	5-1 (Clark, Burke-Murphy, Mezzetti 2, Shelton)
Oct 2nd	2001	Malvern	won	3-1 (Sogbetun, Palley, Watson)
Oct 2nd	2002	Charterhouse	drew	2-2 (Brennan, Katté)
Sept 30th	2003	Malvern	won	2-0 (o.g., Walker)
Oct 10th	2004	Charterhouse	won	4-0 (Holder 2, Delaiglesia, Walker)
Oct 4th	2005	Malvern	won	3-0 (Holder, Delaiglesia 2)
Sept 13th	2006	Charterhouse	won	5-0 (Beddows 2, Clinton 3)

Malvern change to Lent Term football

Manchester GS

Oct 7th	2003	Charterhouse	won	1-0 (Jenner) [ISFA Cup 2]
Nov 28th	2006	Charterhouse	won	2-1 (Beddows, Nash) [ISFA Cup 4]

Merton

Oct 11th	1990	Charterhouse	won	4-2 (Mitten 2, Gompertz 2) [Surrey Cup]

Millfield

Jan 29th	1972	Charterhouse	won	3-2 (Doggart, Cragg, Adomakoh)
Jan 27th	1973	Millfield	lost	0-6
Mar 12th	2008	Charterhouse	won	0-0 aet 8-7 penalties (ISFA Cup Final)

Oratory Reading

Jan 30th	1974	Charterhouse	won	4-0 (Adomakoh 3, Walker)
Jan 28th	1976	Oratory		
Jan 26th	1977	Charterhouse	won	4-0 (Whalley 2, Kirkbride, Shepherd)
Jan 23rd	1980	Charterhouse	drew	0-0

Oxted

Nov 2nd	1994	Charterhouse	won	2-0 (Robertson, Dyson) [Surrey Cup]

Purley College

Oct 8th	1992	Charterhouse	won	3-2 (Webb 3) [Surrey Cup]

QEGS Blackburn

Oct 21st	1999	Blackburn	drew	2-2 (MacAuslan, Bailey) [ISFA Cup 3] *won on penalties* aet
Oct 10th	2007	QEGS Blackburn	won	4-0 (Rogers, Beddows 2, Watson) [ISFA Cup 2]

Reigate GS

Sept 29th	1977	Charterhouse	won	5-0 (Adomakoh, Mole 2, Shepherd, Whalley)
Sept 28th	1978	Charterhouse	won	3-0 (Cummins, Farrow, Miller)
Sept 19th	1979	Charterhouse	won	4-1 (Haynes 2, Kirkbride, Doggart)

Repton

Dec 19th	1907	Repton	lost	0-4
Dec 22nd	1908	Charterhouse	won	2-1 (Macdonald, Johnson)
Dec 21st	1909	Charterhouse	won	2-0 (Boosey 2)
Dec 21st	1910	Repton	drew	2-2 (Wesley Smith, Boosey)
Dec 20th	1911	Leyton	lost	0-2
Nov 20th	1912	Charterhouse	lost	0-2
Nov 20th	1913	Repton	lost	0-2
Nov 18th	1914	Charterhouse	won	3-2 (Cawston, Hansell, Paull)
Nov 18th	1915	Repton	lost	5-6 (Hall 3, Tinley, Reiss)
Oct 31st	1917	Repton	lost	1-3 (Lavenstein)
Dec 4th	1918	Charterhouse	drew	1-1 (Kiggell)
Nov 20th	1919	Repton	won	3-1 (Gilliat, Austin, Mordaunt Smith)
Nov 18th	1920	Charterhouse	won	2-0 (MacGusty 2)
Nov 17th	1921	Repton	lost	0-3
Nov 16th	1922	Charterhouse	lost	0-2
Nov 13th	1923	Repton	lost	3-4 (Shute 2, Fletcher)
Nov 11th	1924	Charterhouse	lost	0-2
Nov 12th	1925	Repton	drew	2-2 (Seligman, Deakin)
Nov 11th	1926	Charterhouse	won	1-0 (Beare)
Nov 10th	1927	Repton	lost	1-4 (Middleton)
Nov 8th	1928	Charterhouse	lost	1-2 (Craddock)
Nov 7th	1929	Repton	lost	2-4 (Greening, Jeavons)
Nov 6th	1930	Repton	lost	3-4 (Samuelson, Paver, Pope)
Nov	1931	Repton	lost	0-6
Nov 9th	1933	Repton	lost	0-2
Nov 8th	1934	Charterhouse	won	2-1 (Guest, Dowding)
Nov 7th	1935	Repton	lost	1-2 (Hayes)
Nov 5th	1936	Charterhouse	won	7-2 (Lomas 4, MacCunn, Hughes, Orton)
Nov 5th	1937	Repton	drew	1-1 (Stone)
Nov 3rd	1938	Charterhouse	lost	0-3
Nov 1st	1945	Repton	lost	0-2
Nov 12th	1946	Charterhouse	won	2-1 (May 2)
Nov 11th	1947	Repton	won	1-0 (Whinney)
Nov 20th	1948	Charterhouse	won	3-1 (Kay, Goodliffe, Spargo)
Nov 19th	1949	Repton	lost	0-1
Nov 25th	1950	Charterhouse	won	3-0 (Monk, Gladstone 2)
Nov 24th	1951	Repton	lost	1-6 (Gladstone)
Nov 22nd	1952	Charterhouse	lost	1-2 (Knox)
Nov 21st	1953	Repton	lost	2-3 (Ruddock 2)
Nov 20th	1954	Charterhouse	lost	1-4 (Percival)
Nov 19th	1955	Repton	drew	1-1 (Forsyth)
Nov 24th	1956	Charterhouse	lost	1-3 (Steed)
Nov 23rd	1957	Repton	lost	2-6 (Harrison, o.g.)
Nov 22nd	1958	Charterhouse	lost	1-3 (Strathern)
Nov 21st	1959	Repton	lost	0-4
Nov 19th	1960	Charterhouse	lost	0-2
Nov 25th	1961	Repton	lost	0-1
Nov 24th	1962	Charterhouse	won	5-1 (Gilliat 3, Martin, Powell)
Nov 23rd	1963	Repton	lost	2-7 (Randel, Bailhache)

Nov 21st	1964	Charterhouse	lost	3-4 (Hooper 2, Weir)
Nov 20th	1965	Repton	drew	3-3 (Gray, Deans, Eatson)
Dec 7th	1966	Repton	drew	0-0
Dec 2nd	1967	Repton	lost	1-8 (Cohn)
Nov 30th	1968	Charterhouse	lost	2-5 (Carter, Hannyngton)
Nov 29th	1969	Repton	won	4-1 (Stewart 2, Holder, Walton)
Nov 28th	1970	Charterhouse	lost	1-2 (Walton)
Nov 27th	1971	Repton	won	3-1 (Godby, Stewart 2)
Nov 25th	1972	Charterhouse	lost	2-3 (Williams, Doggart)
Nov 24th	1973	Repton	won	3-1 (Adomakoh 3)
Nov 23rd	1974	Charterhouse	lost	0-2
Dec 3rd	1977	Repton	lost	1-2
Dec 2nd	1978	Charterhouse		
Dec 1st	1979	Repton	drew	1-1 (Bishop)
Nov 29th	1980	Charterhouse	lost	0-3
Nov 28th	1981	Repton	drew	2-2 (Myers, Bonham-Carter)
Nov 27th	1982	Charterhouse	drew	0-0
Dec 3rd	1983	Repton	won	7-0 (Ibru 3, Davis, Pratt, Pennant, Griffiths)
Dec 1st	1984	Charterhouse	won	3-1 (Golder, Baker 2)
Dec 1st	1985	Repton	lost	2-3 (Kerevan, Spiegel)
Nov 29th	1986	Charterhouse	lost	0-2
Nov 28th	1987	Repton	drew	1-1 (Strecker)
Nov 26th	1988	Charterhouse	drew	2-2 (Sale, Merrick)
Nov 25th	1989	Repton	lost	1-3 (Sale)
Nov 24th	1990	Charterhouse	lost	0-2
Nov 23rd	1991	Repton	lost	0-1
Nov 28th	1992	Charterhouse	drew	0-0
Oct 23rd	1993	Repton	won	2-1 (Webb 2) [ISFA Cup 2]
Nov 27th	1993	Repton	lost	1-2 (Wakeham)
Nov 26th	1994	Charterhouse	lost	0-6
Nov 25th	1995	Repton	lost	1-3 (Westcott)
Dec 3rd	1996	Charterhouse	lost	2-6 (Britten, Smith)
Nov 29th	1997	Repton	lost	3-6 (Hollingsworth, Gay, Nash)
Nov 17th	1998	Charterhouse	won	1-0 (Goodrich)
Nov 16th	1999	Repton	lost	0-3
Nov 14th	2000	Charterhouse	won	3-2 (Clark 2, Deschampsneufs)
Nov 13th	2001	Repton	lost	0-1
Nov 26th	2002	Charterhouse	won	3-1 (Millington Buck, Palley, Katté)
Nov 25th	2003	Repton	won	3-0 (Bourne 2, Millington Buck)
Nov 23rd	2004	Charterhouse	won	2-1 (Nash, Lucas)
Nov 22nd	2005	Repton	won	3-1 (Cameron 2, Holder)
Nov 21st	2006	Charterhouse	won	4-2 (Carter 3, Clinton)
Nov 10th	2007	Repton	won	3-1 (Hall 2, Jamieson)

Reynalds

Nov 1st	1989	Charterhouse	won	3-0 (Sale 2, Wallace) [Surrey Cup]

Richard Challoner's

Oct 2nd	1991	Richard Challoner's	won	3-2 (Bennett, McCourtie, Ashby) [Surrey Cup]
Nov 27th	1996	Richard Challenor's	lost	0-1 [Surrey Cup Semi Final] aet

Richmond College

Oct 14th	1987	Charterhouse	won	1-0 [Surrey Schools]
Oct 19th	1988	Richmond College	lost	1-2 (Gorman) [Surrey Cup]
Dec 2nd	1992	Charterhouse	won	6-4 (McCourtie 4, Jarvis, Aldridge) [Surrey Cup]

RGS Newcastle

Nov 7th	2007	Whitley Bay FC	won	1-0 (Beddows) [ISFA Cup 3]

Royal Russell

Nov 29th	1975	Charterhouse	won	7-0 (Belchamber 2, Phillips 2, Parker 2, Ostrer)
Dec 6th	1978	Charterhouse	won	

Salesian College

Oct 20th	1976	Charterhouse		
Nov 9th	1989	Charterhouse	won	4-2 (R Ashby, Fraser, Mitten 2) [Surrey Cup]

Shrewsbury

Dec 19th	1922	Charterhouse	drew	0-0
Dec 18th	1923	Crystal Palace	won	4-0 (Fletcher, Carter, Shute 2)
Dec 20th	1924	Shrewsbury	lost	0-1
Jan 29th	1926	Charterhouse	drew	1-1 (Palmer)
Dec 18th	1926	Shrewsbury	lost	1-5 (Glynn)
Dec 18th	1928	Crystal Palace	abnd	0-2
Dec 18th	1929	Crystal Palace	lost	1-2 (Hulton)
Dec	1930	Shrewsbury	lost	3-6 (Samuelson, Pope, Greening)
Dec 17th	1931	Charterhouse	drew	4-4 (WF Moss, JC Moss 3)
Dec 16th	1933	Charterhouse	won	3-1 (Trapman, Frith, Gillchrest)
Dec 1st	1934	Shrewsbury	drew	2-2 (Daukes, Hodgson)
Nov 23rd	1935	Charterhouse	won	7-1 (Lomas 2, Greene 2, Dowding, Hayes, Crompton)
Nov 21st	1936	Shrewsbury	lost	1-2 (Hughes)
Nov 20th	1937	Charterhouse	won	2-1 (Stone, Larking)
Nov 19th	1938	Shrewsbury	lost	1-10
Nov 7th	1945	Charterhouse	drew	2-2 (Howard, Wilson)
Nov 6th	1946	Shrewsbury	lost	1-4 (Mills)
Dec 15th	1947	Charterhouse	drew	2-2 (Nathan, o.g.)

Nov 10th	1948	Shrewsbury	won	2-1 (Goodliffe, Kay)
Nov 9th	1949	Charterhouse	drew	1-1 (May)
Nov 15th	1950	Shrewsbury	drew	0-0
Nov 14th	1951	Charterhouse	won	7-0 (Barclay 2, Miller 2, Pegler, Spurrell, o.g.)
Nov 12th	1952	Shrewsbury	lost	1-5 (Miller)
Nov 11th	1953	Charterhouse	lost	0-1
Nov 10th	1954	Shrewsbury	drew	1-1 (Buckley)
Nov 9th	1955	Charterhouse	won	2-0 (Steed, Tunnock)
Nov 14th	1956	Shrewsbury	drew	1-1 (Burrows)
Nov 13th	1957	Charterhouse	drew	0-0
Nov 12th	1958	Shrewsbury	lost	0-2
Nov 11th	1959	Charterhouse	won	2-1 (Blumer, Willcocks)
Nov 9th	1960	Shrewsbury	drew	0-0
Nov 15th	1961	Charterhouse	won	2-0 (Arnold, de Grunwald)
Nov 14th	1962	Shrewsbury	lost	1-2 (Marks)
Nov 13th	1963	Charterhouse	won	3-1 (Hill, Hooper, Weir)
Nov 11th	1964	Shrewsbury	lost	2-3 (Weir 2)
Nov 10th	1965	Charterhouse	won	3-1 (Cohn, Bennett, Easton)
Nov 16th	1966	Shrewsbury	lost	4-7 (Kennedy 2, Provis, Deans)
Nov 15th	1967	Charterhouse	won	4-1 (Bennett 3, Cohn)
Nov 13th	1968	Shrewsbury	lost	0-5
Nov 12th	1969	Charterhouse	won	2-1 (Stewart, Walton)
Nov 11th	1970	Shrewsbury	drew	3-3 (Walton 2, Wisdom)
Nov 10th	1971	Charterhouse	drew	1-1 (Godby)
Nov 11th	1972	Shrewsbury	lost	0-2
Nov 10th	1973	Charterhouse	won	2-1 (Ecob, Adomakoh)
Nov 9th	1974	Shrewsbury	won	4-0 (Oulton, Middleton 2, Williams)
Nov 8th	1975	Charterhouse	lost	0-3
Oct 13th	1976	Shrewsbury	lost	0-2
Nov 26th	1977	Charterhouse	lost	0-1
Nov 25th	1978	Charterhouse	drew	1-1 (Piper)
Nov 24th	1979	Shrewsbury	lost	0-1
Nov 22nd	1980	Shrewsbury	lost	1-2 (May)
Nov 21st	1981	Charterhouse	drew	1-1 (Bonham-Carter)
Nov 20th	1982	Shrewsbury	lost	1-2 (Frearson)
Nov 26th	1983	Charterhouse	won	6-3 (Ibru 3, Davis, Pennant, Faulkner)
Nov 24th	1984	Shrewsbury	lost	0-1
Nov 23rd	1985	Charterhouse	lost	0-1
Nov 22nd	1986	Shrewsbury	drew	1-1 (Ivermee)
Nov 21st	1987	Charterhouse	drew	1-1 (Gorman)
Nov 19th	1988	Shrewsbury	won	1-0 (Brooke)
Nov 18th	1989	Charterhouse	won	1-0 (Wallace)
Nov 17th	1990	Shrewsbury	lost	1-2 (Rees)
Nov 16th	1991	Charterhouse	lost	1-2 (Gompertz)
Nov 21st	1992	Shrewsbury	won	2-0 (McCourtie 2)
Feb 1st	1993	Shrewsbury	won	4-2 aet (Green, Webb, McCourtie, Jarvis) [ISFA Semi-final]
Nov 20th	1993	Charterhouse	lost	0-3
Nov 19th	1994	Shrewsbury	lost	0-1
Nov 18th	1995	Charterhouse	lost	1-5 (Hollingsworth)
Nov 23rd	1996	Shrewsbury	lost	1-2 (Smith)
Nov 21st	1997	Charterhouse	won	1-0 (Gay)
Nov 20th	1998	Shrewsbury	lost	0-3
Nov 19th	1999	Charterhouse	won	2-0 (Clark, Byrne)
Mar 20th	1999	Filbert Street	lost	0-1 [ISFA Cup Final]
Nov 17th	2000	Shrewsbury	drew	1-1 (Cook)
Nov 16th	2001	Charterhouse	won	3-2 (Brennan, Armstrong 2)
Oct 19th	2002	Shrewsbury	lost	1-2 (Palley)
Oct 18th	2003	Charterhouse	lost	1-2 (Bourne)
Nov 19th	2004	Shrewsbury	lost	0-3
Nov 24th	2006	Shrewsbury	won	1-0 (Rubinstein)
Dec 4th	2007	Shrewsbury	drew	2-2 (Watson, Kimmins) [ISFA Cup 4] *won on penalties* 8-7 aet

Spelthorne

Oct 31st	1990	Charterhouse	won	2-1 (Gompertz, Ashby) [Surrey Cup]

Steyning GS

Sept 14th	1983	Charterhouse	won	6-0 (Davis 2, Pennant, Ibru, Frearson, Haghighi)
Sept 19th	1984	Charterhouse	won	7-2 (Wattar 3, Kerevan 2)
Sept 18th	1985	Charterhouse	won	3-2 (Jenkins 3)
Sept 17th	1986	Charterhouse	won	4-3 (Leale 3, Jenkins)
Sept 15th	1987	Charterhouse	lost	1-2 (Gray)
Sept 14th	1988	Charterhouse	won	2-1 (Austin, Benham)
Sept 13th	1989	Charterhouse	won	4-0 (Clark 2, Sale 2)
Sept 12th	1990	Charterhouse	won	1-0 (Mitten)
Sept 18th	1991	Charterhouse	won	2-1 (McCourtie, Peters)
Sept 23rd	1992	Charterhouse	drew	3-3 (McCourtie 2, Wakeham)
Sept 21st	1994	Charterhouse	won	1-0 (Frendo)
Sept 20th	1995	Charterhouse	won	3-0 (Frendo, A Smith, Raven)
Oct 2nd	1996	Charterhouse	won	3-1 (Adie 2, Hollingsworth)
Nov 19th	1997	Charterhouse	drew	0-0

St Andrew's Leatherhead

Oct 2nd	1995	Charterhouse	won	4-3 aet (Lidstone, Hayes 2, Hamblin) [Surrey Cup]

St Bede's Hailsham

Nov 8th	1997	Charterhouse	won	6-1 (Leal 2, Hollingsworth 2, Beaumont, Savage)
Nov 7th	1998	Charterhouse	won	2-1 (Beaumont, Wallis)
Nov 6th	1999	Charterhouse	won	3-0 (Toller, Bailey 2)
Nov 4th	2000	Charterhouse	won	4-1 (Clark 3, Burke-Murphy)
Nov 3rd	2001	Charterhouse	won	4-0 (Marsden, Armstrong, N Bunstead 2)
Nov 9th	2002	St Bede's	drew	3-3 (Bunstead, Barnett, Palley) [ISFA 3] *won on penalites* aet
Nov 8th	2003	Charterhouse	drew	2-2 (Hunter, Millington Buck)
Nov 6th	2004	Charterhouse	won	1-0 (Millington Buck)
Oct 11th	2005	Charterhouse	won	3-0 (Delaiglesia, Cameron, Clinton) [ISFA Cup 1]
Nov 12th	2005	St Bede's	drew	2-2 (Delaiglesia 2)
Nov 11th	2006	Charterhouse	lost	0-1
Sept 22nd	2007	St Bede's	won	2-1 (Hall, Black)

St Bede's Manchester

Sept 29th	1994	St Bede's, Manchester	lost	0-4 [ISFA (1)]
Sept 24th	1997	St Bede's, Manchester	drew	3-3 (Hollingsworth 2, Nash) [ISFA 2] *lost on pens* aet
Oct 9th	2002	St Bede's, Manchester	drew	5-5 (Bunstead 3, Ball, Millington Buck) [ISFA 2 *won on penalites* aet

St Joseph's College

Nov 4th	1987	Charterhouse	lost	1-3 (Gray) [aet] [Surrey Cup]
Nov 11th	1992	Charterhouse	won	3-1 (McCourtie 2, Webb) [Surrey Cup]

St Mary's Crosby

Sept 28th	2005	St Mary's Crosby	won	10-1 (Nash, Holder 2, Clinton 2, Walford, Delaiglesia 3, Beddows) [ISFA Cup 1]
Oct 11th	2006	St Mary's, Crosby	won	2-1 (Rubinstein, Parsons) [ISFA Cup 2]

Taunton College Southampton

Jan 18th	1993	Taunton College	lost	1-2 (McCourtie) [ESFA Cup 1]

Victoria College Jersey tour

Nov 10th	1951	Charterhouse	drew	1-1 (Whinney)
Oct 22nd	1974	Charterhouse	won	5-0 (Walker 2, Middleton, Adomakoh, Belchamber)
OQ	1975	Charterhouse	won	3-1 (Phillips, Ostrer, Cunningham)
Oct 25th	1976	Charterhouse	won	4-1 (Ostrer 2, Shepherd, Phillips)
Oct 20th	1977	Charterhouse	drew	1-1
Oct 26th	1978	Victoria College	won	2-1 (Mole, Bishop)
Nov 30th	1978	Charterhouse	won	2-0 (Piper 2)
Sept 10th	1979	Victoria College	lost	0-4
Oct 23rd	1979	Charterhouse	won	3-0 (Bishop 2, Raymonde)
Oct 22nd	1981	Charterhouse	won	1-0 (Myers)
Nov 29th	1996	Charterhouse	won	1-0 (Saunders)
Nov 5th	1997	Charterhouse	drew	4-4 (Gay 4)

Wellingborough

Nov 6th	1940	Charterhouse	won	6-2 (Evans 2, Spencer 2, Lovett, Figg)
Nov 26th	1941	Charterhouse	won	7-2 (Lahaye 4, Evans, Larking, Lovett)

Westminster

OQ	1863	Vincent Square	lost	0-2
Nov 23rd	1864	Vincent Square	lost	1-2 (McKenzie)
Nov 22nd	1865	Charterhouse	drew	0-0
Nov 21st	1866	Vincent Square	won	1-0 (Walford)
Mar 1st	1875	Charterhouse	won	2-0 (Curzon 2)
Feb 19th	1876	Vincent Square	lost	0-1
Feb 17th	1877	Charterhouse	won	2-0 (Parry, Eddis)
Feb 16th	1878	Charterhouse	won	1-0 (Growse)
Feb 22nd	1879	Charterhouse	won	4-2 (Jackson, Hull, one out of scrimmage)
Feb 21st	1880	Vincent Square	won	4-3 (Pollock 2, Vyvyan, Rayner)
Feb 26th	1881	Godalming	won	3-2 (Cobbold 2, Owen)
Feb 25th	1882	Vincent Square	won	3-2 (Cobbold 2, Vintcent)
Feb 24th	1883	Charterhouse	won	5-1 (Steward 2, Brookes 2, CH Vintcent)
Feb 23rd	1884	Vincent Square	lost	1-2 (Vintcent)
Feb 28th	1885	Charterhouse	won	3-0 (Galsworthy 2, Cooper)
Feb 27th	1886	Westminster	lost	2-4 (Sheppard, Currey)
Mar 12th	1887	Charterhouse	won	1-0 (Pim)
Mar 10th	1888	Vincent Square	drew	3-3 (Gilliat, Dickinson, Stanbrough)
Mar 2nd	1889	Charterhouse	won	8-0 (Stanbrough 2, Armstrong 4, Barker, Smith)
Mar 8th	1890	Vincent Square	won	8-0 (Buzzard 4, GO Smith 3, Wilson)
Feb 28th	1891	Charterhouse	drew	2-2 (Clark 2)
Feb 27th	1892	Vincent Square	won	5-0 (Smith 2, Salt)
Feb 25th	1893	Charterhouse	won	5-0 (Hunt 5)
Mar 3rd	1894	Vincent Square	won	6-0 (Vassall, Hancock 2, Jameson, Fordyce 2)
Mar 9th	1895	Charterhouse	won	6-0 (Austen, Walsh, GW Ryder, CF Ryder, Wallace, Hancock)

Date	Year	Venue	Result	Score
Mar 14th	1896	Vincent Square	won	2-0 (Vassall, Ryder)
Feb 27th	1897	Charterhouse	won	3-1 (Gordon 2, Ryder)
Mar 5th	1898	Vincent Square	lost	1-4 (Moss)
Feb 25th	1899	Charterhouse	lost	1-2 (Tuff)
24th Feb	1900	Vincent Square	won	7-2 (Tuff 5, Trower 2)
23rd Feb	1901	Charterhouse	won	6-0 (Goodliffe, Tuff 3, Bense Pembroke 2)
22nd Feb	1902	Vincent Square	won	2-0 (Farquharson, Bowring)
Feb 21st	1903	Charterhouse	won	2-1 (Bense Pembroke 2)
Feb 20th	1904	Vincent Square	won	1-0 (Taylor)
Mar 4th	1905	Charterhouse	won	4-0 (Pears 3, Lyell)
Mar 3rd	1906	Vincent Square	won	3-0 (Parry 3)
Mar 2nd	1907	Charterhouse	won	3-0 (Parry, Pegram 2)
Feb 29th	1908	Vincent Square	won	4-0 (Pike 3, Livesey)
Mar 6th	1909	Charterhouse	won	2-1 (Norris, Macdonald)
Feb 26th	1910	Vincent Square	drew	1-1 (Dixon)
Feb 25th	1911	Charterhouse	won	4-1 (Faulkner, Boosey, Sanderson 2)
Feb 24th	1912	Vincent Square	drew	1-1 (Fosdick)
Feb 22nd	1913	Charterhouse	won	2-0 (Steel, Chambers)
Feb 7th	1914	Vincent Square	won	4-1 (Reiss 2, Smith, Ritchie)
Nov 28th	1914	Vincent Square	drew	3-3 (o.g., Hansell, Paull) [not recorded as school match]
Feb 20th	1915	Charterhouse	won	4-1 (Cawston 2, Ritchie, Reiss)
Mar 29th	1916	Vincent Square	drew	0-0
Nov 11th	1916	Vincent Square	won	6-2 (Bearman 3, Lavenstein, Williams 2)
Feb 28th	1917	Charterhouse	won	3-1 (Williams, Whalley, Lavenstein)
Nov 17th	1917	Charterhouse	won	9-0 (Lavenstein, Williams)
Mar 9th	1918	Vincent Square	won	3-0 (Williams 3)
Nov 30th	1918	Charterhouse	won	2-0
Nov 29th	1919	Charterhouse	won	8-0 (Austin 2, Gilliat 4, Mordaunt Smith, McIlwraith)
Feb 28th	1920	Vincent Square	won	6-0 (Gilliat 4, Barnard 2)
Feb 26th	1921	Vincent Square	won	3-1 (Barnard 2, Gilliat)
Feb 18th	1922	Charterhouse	won	3-0 (Bearman, Doresa, Kenyon)
Feb 24th	1923	Vincent Square	won	1-0 (Shute)
Feb 16th	1924	Charterhouse	won	5-1 (Rishworth, Carter, Fletcher 2, Massey)
Feb 18th	1925	Vincent Square	drew	1-1 (Seligman)
Nov 21st	1925	Charterhouse	won	3-0 (Palmer, Deakin 2)
Nov 20th	1926	Vincent Square	won	5-0 (Wreford Brown 2, Weatherall 2, Fletcher)
Nov 19th	1927	Charterhouse	lost	1-4 (Davies)
Nov 17th	1928	Vincent Square	lost	2-4 (Craddock, Cohen)
Nov 16th	1929	Charterhouse	won	4-0 (Jeavons 2, Moss, Greening)
Nov 15th	1930	Vincent Square	won	4-2 (Moss, Greening 2, Pope)
Nov 28th	1931	Charterhouse	won	4-1 (Dunbar 2, WF Moss 2)
Nov 18th	1933	Charterhouse	won	3-0 (Tuckwell 2, Frith)
Nov 17th	1934	Vincent Square	won	1-0 (Dunbar)
Nov 16th	1935	Charterhouse	drew	0-0
Nov 14th	1936	Vincent Square	won	2-0 (Hughes 2)
Nov 27th	1937	Charterhouse	drew	1-1 (MacCunn)
Nov 26th	1938	Vincent Square	won	3-1 (Larking, Tanner, Cunningham)
Jan 2nd	1943	Vincent Square	won	7-1 (Godden 4, Dalgety, Stevenson, Spratt)
Jan 8th	1944	Bank of England	won	4-0 (Godden 3, Spratt) *at Roehampton*
Jan 6th	1945	Bank of England	won	1-0 (Price) *played at Roehampton*
Dec 1st	1945	Charterhouse	won	7-0 (May 3, Howard 2, Savill 2)
Dec 7th	1946	Grove Park	won	10-1 (Savill 4, Marrot 2, Mills 2, May 2)
Dec 6th	1947	Charterhouse	won	5-1 (Burt 2, Whinney, Divett, o.g.)
Dec 4th	1948	Vincent Square	won	3-1 (Whinney, Atkinson, Gibbon)
Dec 3rd	1949	Charterhouse	won	3-1 (Vansittart, May, Agate)
Dec 2nd	1950	Vincent Square	drew	2-2 (May, Barclay)
Dec 1st	1951	Charterhouse	won	7-1 (Gladstone 3, Pegler 2, Tuck 2)
Nov 29th	1952	Vincent Square	drew	3-3 (Miller, Knox, White)
Nov 28th	1953	Charterhouse	won	3-0 (Buckley 2, Cairns)
Nov 27th	1954	Vincent Square	won	2-0 (Ruddock)
Nov 26th	1955	Charterhouse	lost	1-3 (o.g.)
Dec 1st	1956	Vincent Square	won	1-0 (Burrows)
Nov 27th	1957	Charterhouse	won	2-1 (Harrison, Topham)
Nov 29th	1958	Vincent Square	won	2-0 (o.g., Gibb)
Nov 28th	1959	Charterhouse	lost	0-1
Nov 26th	1960	Vincent Square	lost	1-4 (Arnold)
Dec 2nd	1961	Charterhouse	won	3-0 (Martin, o.g., Gilliat)
Dec 1st	1962	Vincent Square	won	2-0 (Gilliat, de Grunwald)
Nov 30th	1963	Charterhouse	won	1-0 (Weir)
Nov 28th	1964	Vincent Square	won	4-0 (Rolls, Hooper 3)
Feb 19th	1966	Vincent Square	won	5-0 (Howard 2, Deans 2, Simmons)
Feb 18th	1967	Charterhouse	won	8-1 (Deans 3, Bennett 4, Provis)
Feb 1st	1968	Vincent Square	won	3-1 (Deans, Foster 2)
Feb 1st	1969	Charterhouse	won	1-0 (Walton)
Jan 31st	1970	Vincent Square	drew	2-2 (Stewart, Holder)
Jan 30th	1971	Charterhouse	won	4-0 (Godby, Stewart 2, Holder)
Feb 5th	1972	Vincent Square	won	6-2 (Stewart 2, Williams 2, Faull, Adomakoh)
Feb 3rd	1973	Charterhouse	won	3-2
Feb 2nd	1974	Vincent Square	drew	1-1 (Adomakoh)
Feb 1st	1975	Charterhouse	won	5-0 (Gibson, Oulton 3, Phillips)
Jan 31st	1976	Vincent Square	drew	0-0
Jan 29th	1977	Charterhouse	drew	1-1 (Wilson)

Date	Year	Venue	Result	Score
Jan 28th	1978	Charterhouse	won	5-1 (Mole 2, Mole, Whalley, Adomakoh)
Jan 27th	1979	Vincent Square	cancelled-weather	
Jan 26th	1980	Charterhouse	drew	1-1 (Bowers)
Nov 25th	1980	Vincent Square	won	3-2 (Myers 2, Mellstrom)
Mar 9th	1982	Charterhouse	lost	0-2
Dec 7th	1982	Vincent Square	won	5-0 (Newman 3, Frearson, Ibru)
Dec 6th	1983	Vincent Square	drew	2-2 (Griffiths, Pennant)
Dec 4th	1984	Vincent Square	won	5-1 (Baker 2, Golder)
Dec 4th	1985	Charterhouse	won	3-1 (Kerevan 2, Neill)
Dec 2nd	1986	Vincent Square	won	5-1 (Leale, Stevens 4)
Dec 1st	1987	Charterhouse	won	3-1 (Leale 2, Henkes)
Nov 29th	1988	Vincent Square	lost	1-4 (Brooke)
Nov 28th	1989	Charterhouse	won	4-0 (Clark 2, Sale, Mitten)
Dec 4th	1990	Vincent Square	won	3-2 (Ashby, Mitten, Rees)
Dec 3rd	1991	Charterhouse	won	4-3 (Ashby 2, Gompertz, Pegler)
Oct 13th	1992	Charterhouse	won	5-1 (Webb 3, Younie, Wakeham)[ISFA 2]
Dec 1st	1992	Vincent Square	won	3-2 (McCourtie, Aldridge 2)
Nov 30th	1993	Charterhouse	won	6-2 (Younie 4, Webb, Tassell)
Nov 29th	1994	Vincent Square	lost	0-3
Sept 28th	1995	Charterhouse	lost	0-1 [ISFA Cup 1]
Nov 28th	1995	Charterhouse	drew	1-1 (Westcott)
Nov 26th	1996	Vincent Square	won	1-0 (Hollingsworth)
Nov 25th	1997	Charterhouse	won	1-0 (o.g.)
Nov 24th	1998	Vincent Square	won	5-1 (Jackson, Wallis, Leal 2, Gay)
Nov 23rd	1999	Charterhouse	won	4-0 (Toller, Byrne, Shelton, Bailey)
Nov 21st	2000	Vincent Square	won	3-0 (Clark 2, Sogbetun)
Nov 20th	2001	Charterhouse	won	4-0 (o.g., N Bunstead, Brennan, Watson)
Nov 19th	2002	Vincent Square	won	3-1 (Barnett 2, Palley)
Nov 18th	2003	Charterhouse	drew	0-0
Nov 17th	2004	Vincent Square	won	5-1 (Nash 3, Yabe, O'Brien)
Nov 15th	2005	Charterhouse	won	2-0 (Walford, Cameron)
Nov 30th	2006	Vincent Square	drew	1-1 (Bowman)
Nov 27th	2007	Charterhouse	won	1-0 (Jamieson)

Wilson's, Wallington

Date	Year	Venue	Result	Score
Mar 4th	1993	Carshalton FC	lost	0-1 [Surrey Cup Final]
Nov 16th	1994	Charterhouse	lost	0-4 [Surrey Cup]

Wimbledon College

Date	Year	Venue	Result	Score
Nov 23rd	1995	Charterhouse	lost	0-2 [Surrey Cup Quarter Final]
Nov 20th	1996	Charterhouse	won	5-3 aet (Adie, Westcott, Savage, Smith, Browne)[Surrey Cup]

Winchester

Date	Year	Venue	Result	Score
26th Feb	1902	Winchester	won	2-0 (Verry, Goodliffe)
Mar 3rd	1904	Charterhouse	drew	1-1 (Walker)
Mar 1st	1905	Winchester	lost	3-4 (Gilbert, Reid, Lyell)
Mar 8th	1906	Charterhouse	lost	0-2
Mar 12th	1907	Winchester	won	1-0 (Parry)
Mar 10th	1908	Charterhouse	won	5-0 (Pike 2, Stuart, Rushton, Livesey)
Mar 9th	1909	Winchester	won	6-3 (Weeks 3, Johnson 2, Wharton)
Mar 8th	1910	Charterhouse	won	2-1 (Boosey, Dunlop)
Mar 9th	1911	Winchester	lost	2-4 (Rücker, Boosey)
Mar 12th	1912	Charterhouse	won	9-0 (Boswell)
Mar 11th	1913	Winchester	won	2-0 (Steel, Chambers)
Mar 12th	1914	Charterhouse	won	8-2 (Reiss 2, Hinds 2, Smith 2, Ritchie 2)
Mar 25th	1915	Winchester	won	4-1 (Ritchie, Butcher, Hansell 2)
Mar 23rd	1916	Charterhouse	lost	1-4 (Tinley)
Mar 6th	1918	Winchester	drew	1-1
Apr 2nd	1919	Charterhouse	drew	1-1
Mar 4th	1920	Winchester	lost	2-4 (Mordaunt Smith, Cox)
Mar 10th	1921	Charterhouse	drew	0-0
Mar 9th	1922	Winchester	won	1-0 (Doresa)
Mar 7th	1923	Charterhouse	won	2-1 (Kenyon 2)
Mar 6th	1924	Winchester	won	4-2 (Fletcher, Carter 2, Rishworth)
Mar 5th	1925	Charterhouse	lost	0-1
Mar 4th	1926	Winchester	lost	0-1
Mar 2nd	1927	Charterhouse	lost	2-3 (Weatherall, Fletcher)
Mar 6th	1928	Winchester	lost	1-3 (Morton)
Mar 7th	1929	Charterhouse	lost	0-2
Mar 6th	1930	Winchester	won	3-1 (Moss, Middleton 2)
Feb	1931	Charterhouse	lost	0-2
Mar 2nd	1932	Winchester	won	2-0 (Dunbar, WF Moss)
Mar 1st	1934	Winchester	won	3-1 (Richards, Gillchrest, Dowding)
Feb 28th	1935	Charterhouse	won	2-1 (Hodgson, Dunbar)
Mar 4th	1937	Charterhouse	lost	1-2 (Benké)
Mar 3rd	1938	Winchester	lost	1-4 (Holme-Sumner)
Feb 23rd	1939	Charterhouse	drew	2-2 (*rushed 2*)
Feb 22nd	1940	Winchester	lost	0-1
Feb 27th	1941	Charterhouse	won	2-1 (Lovett, Larking)
Feb 25th	1943	Charterhouse	won	2-1 (Dalgety, Godden)
Feb 24th	1944	Winchester	won	3-0 (Spratt, Crole-Rees 2)
Feb 22nd	1945	Charterhouse	won	2-0 (Spratt, Price)
Mar 31st	1945	Redhill	won	2-1 (Godden, Spratt)
Feb 21st	1946	Winchester	lost	1-2 (Wilson)
Feb 19th	1948	Winchester	drew	1-1 (Archibald)
Feb 25th	1949	Charterhouse	won	3-2 (Kay, Ritchie, Spargo)

Date	Year	Opponent	Result	Score
Feb 23rd	1950	Winchester	lost	2-3 (Frankland, Jenks)
Feb 22nd	1951	Charterhouse	lost	0-1
Feb 21st	1952	Winchester	lost	1-2 (Pegler)
Feb 19th	1953	Charterhouse	won	2-1 (White, Pratt)
Feb 18th	1954	Winchester	won	5-4 (Lees 2, Ruddock 3)
Feb 17th	1955	Charterhouse	lost	1-2 (Forsyth)
Feb 23rd	1956	Winchester	won	3-2 (Jakobson, Burrows, o.g.)
Feb 21st	1957	Charterhouse	won	1-0 (Gibb)
Feb 20th	1958	Winchester	won	2-1 (Harrison, Agace)
Feb 19th	1959	Charterrhouse	lost	2-5 (Taylor, Visser)
Feb 18th	1960	Winchester	lost	2-4 (Pilch, Topham)
Feb 23rd	1961	Charterhouse	lost	0-1
Feb 22nd	1962	Winchester	won	1-0 (de Grunwald)
Feb	1963	No match - snow		
Feb 20th	1964	Winchester	won	2-1 (Weir, Hill)
Feb 18th	1965	Charterhouse	won	5-3 (Hooper 3, Weir 2)
Nov 27th	1965	Winchester	lost	1-4 (Deans)
Nov 23rd	1966	Winchester	won	1-0 (Cohn)
Nov 25th	1967	Charterhouse	lost	1-3 (Deans)
Nov 23rd	1968	Winchester	won	1-0 (Foster)
Nov 22nd	1969	Winchester	won	4-0 (Holder, Stewart, Lyle, Walton)
Nov 21st	1970	Charterhouse	won	3-0 (Godby, Stewart, Walton)
Nov 20th	1971	Winchester	drew	3-3 (Williams, Stewart, Faull)
Nov 18th	1972	Charterhouse	lost	0-2
Nov 17th	1973	Winchester	won	2-1 (Adomakoh)
Nov 16th	1974	Charterhouse	won	2-0 (Walker, Adomakoh)
Nov 15th	1975	Winchester	drew	1-1 (Peet)
Nov 13th	1976	Charterhouse	won	4-0 (Mole 3)
Nov 12th	1977	Winchester	won	1-0 (Shepherd)
Nov 4th	1978	Charterhouse	drew	0-0
Nov 10th	1979	Winchester	won	3-0 (Pratt, Haynes 2)
Sept 8th	1980	Guernsey tour	won	7-1 (Myers 5, Maddison, McCourt)
Nov 8th	1980	Charterhouse	lost	0-1
Nov 7th	1981	Winchester	lost	0-3
Nov 6th	1982	Charterhouse	won	3-1 (Newman, Ibru 2)
Nov 5th	1983	Winchester	drew	1-1 (Pennant)
Nov 10th	1984	Charterhouse	won	4-2 (Golder, Wattar)
Nov 9th	1985	Winchester	won	4-3 (Jenkins 2, Kerevan, Faulkner)
Nov 8th	1986	Charterhouse	won	4-0 (Jenkins, Gray, Payne, Bedford)
Nov 7th	1987	Winchester	drew	2-2 (Gray, Stone)
Nov 5th	1988	Charterhouse	lost	1-3 (Benham)
Nov 4th	1989	Winchester	won	3-0 (Merrick, Butler, Mitten)
Nov 3rd	1990	Charterhouse	lost	0-1
Nov 2nd	1991	Winchester	won	3-0 (Gompertz 2, Pegler)
Nov 7th	1992	Charterhouse	won	6-1 (Webb2 Wakeham Wiegand McCourtie CunninghamBrown)
Nov 6th	1993	Winchester	won	8-0 (Webb 3, Younie 2, Cunningham-Brown 2, Guy)
Nov 5th	1994	Charterhouse	won	2-0 (Waller, Brazier)
Nov 4th	1995	Winchester	won	3-2 (Frendo 2, A Smith)
Oct 19th	1996	Charterhouse	won	3-1 (Westcott 2, Smith)
Oct 18th	1997	Winchester	won	5-1 (Toulson, Burke-Murphy, Gay 2, o.g.)
Oct 17th	1998	Charterhouse	drew	0-0
Sept 30th	1999	Charterhouse	won	2-0 (Byrne, Clark) [ISFA Cup 2]
Oct 16th	1999	Winchester	won	2-0 (Bailey 2)
Oct 14th	2000	Charterhouse	won	5-1(Burke-Murphy, Clark, Shelton, Deschampsneufs, Mezzetti)
Oct 13th	2001	Winchester	won	2-0 (Sogbetun, Watson)
Oct 12th	2002	Charterhouse	drew	2-2 (Millington Buck 2)
Dec 3rd	2002	Charterhouse	won	2-1 (Barnett, Millington Buck) [ISFA Cup 4]
Oct 11th	2003	Winchester	won	4-0 (Bourne, Hooper, Millington Buck, Walker)
Oct 16th	2004	Charterhouse	won	3-1 (Walker, Holder, Paes)
Oct 15th	2005	Winchester	drew	1-1 (Cameron)
Oct 14th	2006	Charterhouse	won	2-1 (Satterthwaite, Carter)
Oct 13th	2007	Winchester	drew	0-0

Woking CGS

Date	Year	Opponent	Result	Score
Jan 27th	1965	Charterhouse	lost	0-1
Feb 2nd	1966	Charterhouse	won	7-2 (Howard 2, Cohn 2, Deans 3)
Feb 1st	1967	Woking	lost	3-4 (Bennett 3)
Jan 24th	1968	Charterhouse	won	2-1 (Bennett, Foster)
Jan 22nd	1969	Charterhouse	lost	0-2

OLD CARTHUSIAN TEAMS

Old Carthusians

Date	Year	Opponent	Result	Score
Feb 24th	1864	Charterhouse	won	5-0 (O'Grady) *moved to cloisters after 2-0*
Nov 30th	1864	Charterhouse	drew	2-2 (Mackenzie, *team effort*)
Feb 24th	1865	Charterhouse	won	3-2 (O'Grady, *squash*, Smythe)
Nov 29th	1865	Charterhouse	lost	1-3 *first half on Under green (1-0) 2nd half in cloisters*
Nov 30th	1866	Charterhouse	won	1-0 (*rush*) 13 a side
Feb 13th	1867	Charterhouse	won	5-0 (Macan, Boreham, Mammatt, Nepean 2)
Nov 1st	1867	Charterhouse	drew	1-1 (Foote) *second half in cloisters 14 a side*
Feb 24th	1868	Charterhouse	lost	0-2 *played in cloisters*
Nov 11th	1869	Charterhouse	won	3-0 (Barry, King) *2nd half in cloisters*
Feb 24th	1870	Charterhouse	drew	1-1 *2nd half in cloisters*
Feb 23rd	1871	Charterhouse	lost	0-1 *2nd half in cloisters*
Nov 30th	1871	Charterhouse	drew	1-1 (*rush*) 13 a side *2nd half in cloisters*
Nov 14th	1872	Charterhouse	drew	2-2 (Gandell, Gipps) (14 a side)
Mar 13th	1873	Charterhouse	won	4-3 (Jeaffreson 2, Abdy)
Nov 13th	1873	Charterhouse	won	6-2 (Drew 4, Parish, Jeaffreson)
Mar 13th	1874	Charterhouse	won	10-2 (Parry 2, Reeve, Corrie 4, Drew 2, Tod)
Nov 12th	1874	Charterhouse	won	5-2 (Reeve, Merriman, Page, Tod 2)
Feb 25th	1875	Charterhouse	lost	1-2 (Short)
Nov	1875	Charterhouse	won	6-5 (Brown,Short,Cornish,Burrows 2,Keightley)
Mar 11th	1876	Charterhouse	won	5-1 (*squash*, Wilson 2,Williams, Page)
Nov 25th	1876	Charterhouse	drew	1-1 (Page)
Mar 22nd	1877	Charterhouse	won	5-1 (Evan-Thomas, Page 3, Hayter)
Nov 24th	1877	Charterhouse	lost	3-5 (Evan-Thomas, Hansell, Wilson)
Mar 16th	1878	Charterhouse	won	8-1 (Growse, Evan-Thomas 2, Wilson 3, Princep, Hansell)
Nov 23rd	1878	Charterhouse	won	2-1 (Burdon, Jenner)
Mar 22nd	1879	Charterhouse	lost	1-6 (Wilson)
Nov 29th	1879	Charterhouse	drew	4-4 (Rayner 3, Pollock)
Mar 27th	1880	Charterhouse	lost	3-5 (Morrison, Richards 2)
Nov 27th	1880	Charterhouse	won	7-1 (Morrison 3, Owen, Vintcent 3)
Mar 16th	1881	Charterhouse	lost	1-6 (Walters)

(Old Carthusians won the FA Cup on April 9th with 7 of the same team)

Date	Year	Opponent	Result	Score
Nov 26th	1881	Charterhouse	won	5-2 (Rayner, o.g, Vintcent 2, Henley)
Mar 25th	1882	Charterhouse	won	3-1 (Eddis, Rayner, Cobbold)
Nov 25th	1882	Charterhouse	lost	1-3 (C Vintcent)
Mar 20th	1883	Charterhouse	won	5-3 (L Vintcent 2, Fardell, C Vintcent 2)
Dec 1st	1883	Charterhouse	lost	1-2 (Steward)
Mar 15th	1884	Charterhouse	lost	0-2
Dec 13th	1884	Charterhouse	lost	0-3
Mar 21st	1885	Charterhouse	won	2-1 (Martyn, Cooper)
Dec 5th	1885	Charterhouse	won	8-0 (Price 3, Currey 3, Wreford-Brown, Tewson)
Dec 12th	1885	Charterhouse	lost	0-5 OC Cup Team
Mar 20th	1886	Charterhouse	won	6-0 (Currey 5, Nixon)
Dec 11th	1886	Charterhouse	lost	0-3
Feb 19th	1887	Charterhouse	lost	2-5 (Pim 2)
Dec 10th	1887	Charterhouse	won	3-1 (Gilliat, Dickinson, Earle)
Mar 3rd	1888	Charterhouse	won	4-0 (Gilliat 2, Rayner, Cowie)
Dec 8th	1888	Charterhouse	lost	1-5 (Pierce)
Mar 30th	1889	Charterhouse	lost	4-6
Mar 15th	1890	Charterhouse	drew	1-1 (Buzzard)
Dec 6th	1890	Charterhouse	drew	2-2 (Wilson, Hewitt)
Mar 14th	1891	Charterhouse	won	4-1 (Clark 2, Wilson 2)
Mar 12th	1892	Charterhouse	drew	0-0
Dec 10th	1892	Charterhouse	lost	2-3 (Broadbent 2)
Mar 18th	1893	Charterhouse	won	4-2 (Vassall 2, Hunt, Fordyce)
Mar 29th	1893	Charterhouse	won	2-1 (Dyne, Hunt) OC Cup Team
Dec 9th	1893	Charterhouse	won	4-2 (Vassall, Jameson 2, Wilson)
Dec 7th	1895	Charterhouse	lost	2-5 (Vassall 2)
Dec 12th	1896	Charterhouse	won	6-4 (Ryder, Vassall 2, Gordon 2, Renshaw)
Dec 16th	1896	Old Internationals	lost	0-5 At Queen's Club
Dec 11th	1897	Charterhouse	lost	0-9
Dec 10th	1898	Charterhouse	lost	0-1
Dec 22nd	1898	Old Internationals	lost	2-4 (Trower, Gibson) At Queen's Club
Dec 9th	1899	Charterhouse	lost	1-2 (Tuff)
Dec 20th	1899	Old Internationals	drew	2-2 (Melchers-Ahrens 2) At Queen's Club

Recorded as 500th school match

Date	Year	Opponent	Result	Score
Mar 17th	1900	Charterhouse	lost	0-5
Dec 15th	1900	Charterhouse	won	2-0 (Ferguson, Tuff)
Dec 19th	1900	OC Internationals	lost	1-5 (Tuff) At Queen's Club
Dec 14th	1901	Charterhouse	won	3-0 (Goodliffe, Sharp, Verry)
Dec 13th	1902	Charterhouse	lost	0-4
Dec 17th	1902	Old Internationals	lost	0-4 At Queen's Club
Dec 12th	1903	Charterhouse	lost	0-3
Dec 23rd	1903	Old Internationals	lost	2-4 (Barbour, Taylor) At Queen's Club
Dec 17th	1904	Charterhouse	drew	1-1 (Gilbert)
Dec 9th	1905	Charterhouse	drew	1-1 (Gooch)
Dec 20th	1905	Old Internationals	won	3-2 (Parry, o.g., Greig) At Queen's Club
Dec 15th	1906	Charterhouse	lost	0-1
Dec 14th	1907	Charterhouse	lost	0-1
Dec 12th	1908	Charterhouse	lost	2-3 (Johnson, Weeks)
Dec 11th	1909	Charterhouse	lost	0-3
Dec 9th	1911	Charterhouse	lost	0-2
Dec 14th	1912	Charterhouse	lost	0-2
Nov 29th	1913	Charterhouse	lost	1-2 (Hinds)
Dec 13th	1919	Charterhouse	lost	3-6 (Gilliat 2, Austin)

Date	Year	Team	Result	Score (scorers)
Dec 4th	1920	Charterhouse	lost	1-2 (Gilliat)
Dec 3rd	1921	Charterhouse	lost	1-4 (Percival)
Dec 9th	1922	Charterhouse	drew	0-0
Dec 15th	1923	Charterhouse	lost	3-4 (Shute 3)
Dec 17th	1924	Charterhouse	lost	2-3 (Sharp, Stock)
Dec 4th	1926	Charterhouse	lost	3-5 (Nicholson, Glynn, Pearce)
Dec 3rd	1927	Charterhouse	won	4-3 (Davies 3, Morton)
Dec 1st	1928	Charterhouse	lost	1-4 (Jeavons)
Nov 30th	1929	Charterhouse	lost	2-4 (Greening, Moss)
Mar 5th	1932	Charterhouse	won	2-0 (JC Moss, Dunbar)
Feb 10th	1934	Charterhouse	lost	1-2 (Dowding)
Feb 9th	1935	Charterhouse	lost	1-4 (Ades)
Dec	1935	Charterhouse	won	6-0
Feb 27th	1937	Charterhouse	lost	1-4 (Benké)
Feb 19th	1938	Charterhouse	lost	1-6 (Stone)
Feb 18th	1939	Charterhouse	lost	1-2 (Larking)
Feb 14th	1948	Charterhouse	lost	1-2 (Archibald)
Feb 12th	1949	Charterhouse	lost	0-6
Feb 11th	1950	Charterhouse	lost	0-3
Feb 10th	1951	Charterhouse	lost	0-7
Feb 9th	1952	Charterhouse	drew	2-2 (Tuck, Pegler)
Jan 31st	1953	Charterhouse	won	2-0 (Pratt, Knox)
Feb 5th	1955	Charterhouse	lost	1-3 (Buckley)
Feb 2nd	1957	Charterhouse	lost	0-2
Feb 1st	1958	Charterhouse	won	7-2 (Agace 2, Gibb 2, White, Visser, Harrison)
Oct 18th	1958	Charterhouse	lost	1-9 (Gibb)
Oct 17th	1959	Charterhouse	lost	0-11
Feb 13th	1960	Charterhouse	lost	2-3 (Taylor, Knight)
Oct 8th	1960	Charterhouse	won	3-2 (Garrow 2, Pilch)
Sept 30th	1961	Charterhouse	won	3-2 (Gilliat, de Grunwald 2)
Sept 29th	1962	Charterhouse	lost	1-5 (o.g.)
Sept 28th	1963	Charterhouse	lost	0-3
Sept 26th	1964	Charterhouse	lost	0-4
Oct 2nd	1965	Charterhouse	lost	0-5
Oct 1st	1966	Charterhouse	lost	1-7 (Bennett)
Sept 30th	1967	Charterhouse	lost	2-4 (Bennett, Deans)
Sept 28th	1968	Charterhouse	drew	1-1 (Foster)
Sept 20th	1969	Charterhouse	drew	1-1 (Walton)
Sept 19th	1970	Charterhouse	lost	1-3 (Walton)
Sept 18th	1971	Charterhouse	won	2-0 (Williams, o.g.)
Sept 23rd	1972	Charterhouse	lost	2-3 (Oundjian 2)
Sept 22nd	1973	Charterhouse	won	2-0 (Adomakoh, Scholfield)
Sept 21st	1974	Charterhouse	drew	1-1 (North)
Sept 20th	1975	Charterhouse		
Sept 11th	1976	Charterhouse		
Nov 27th	1976	Charterhouse		
Oct 1st	1977	Charterhouse		
Sept 23rd	1978	Charterhouse	lost	0-2
Sept 22nd	1979	Charterhouse	lost	2-4 (Doggart, Kirkbride)
Sept 20th	1980	Charterhouse	lost	1-4 (Cuff)
Sept 19th	1981	Charterhouse	drew	1-1 (Fordham)
Sept 18th	1982	Charterhouse	lost	2-4 (Waters, Ibru)
Sept 17th	1983	Charterhouse	lost	0-1
Sept 22nd	1984	Charterhouse	lost	1-3
Sept 21st	1985	Charterhouse	lost	2-7 (Jenkins, Viall)
Sept 20th	1986	Charterhouse	lost	0-3
Sept 19th	1987	Charterhouse	lost	0-4
Sept 17th	1988	Charterhouse	lost	0-2
Sept 16th	1989	Charterhouse	lost	2-4 (E Ashby, Sale)
Sept 15th	1990	Charterhouse	lost	1-8 (Wallace)
Sept 14th	1991	Charterhouse	lost	0-5
Sept 19th	1992	Charterhouse	lost	1-5 (Wakeham)
Sept 18th	1993	Charterhouse	lost	1-5 (Younie)
Sept 17th	1994	Charterhouse	lost	1-5 (Conn)
Sept 16th	1995	Charterhouse	lost	2-3 (Frendo, Raven)
Sept 14th	1996	Charterhouse	lost	1-4 (Smith)
Sept 13th	1997	Charterhouse	lost	2-8 (Nash, Hollingsworth)
Sept 12th	1998	Charterhouse	lost	0-5
Sept 11th	1999	Charterhouse	lost	0-3
Sept 9th	2000	Charterhouse	lost	0-3
Sept 8th	2001	Charterhouse	lost	0-4
Sept 7th	2002	Charterhouse	lost	0-1
Sept 6th	2003	Charterhouse	lost	0-3
Sept 11th	2004	Charterhouse	won	2-0 (Delaiglesia 2)
Sept 3rd	2005	Charterhouse	lost	1-2 (Delaiglesia)
Sept 2nd	2006	Charterhouse	drew	1-1 (Satterthwaite)
Sept 1st	2007	Charterhouse	lost	0-1

Brooke Hall

Date	Year	Team	Result	Score (scorers)
Oct	1875	Charterhouse	won	3-0
Oct 4th	1876	Charterhouse	won	6-1 (Eddis, Williams, Burrows, Keightley 2, Page)
Feb 10th	1877	Charterhouse	won	5-0 (Evan-Thomas, Parry 3, Page)
Oct 13th	1877	Charterhouse	won	2-0 (*squash*, Master)
Feb 9th	1878	Charterhouse	won	7-0 (Frith 3, Wilson, Growse 2, Hansell)
Feb 5th	1879	Charterhouse	won	6-1 (Wilson 3, Richards 2, Guinness)
Oct 4th	1879	Charterhouse	won	5-0 (Richards 2, Vyvyan, Tucker, Pollock)
Feb 14th	1880	Charterhouse	won	7-3 (Rayner 4, Richards 2, Walters)
Oct 20th	1880	Charterhouse	won	7-1 (Currey Morrison 3, Escombe 2, Henley)
Feb 9th	1881	Charterhouse	won	5-0 (Vintcent, Henley, Harrison, Cobbold, Morrison)
Oct 1st	1881	Charterhouse	won	5-0 (Eddis 2, Henley, Blenkiron, Brown)
Feb 17th	1951	Charterhouse	drew	2-2 (Young 2)
Feb 16th	1952	Charterhouse	won	4-1 (Pegler, Miller 2, Tuck)
Feb 14th	1953	Charterhouse	lost	2-3 (White, Knox)
Feb 13th	1954	Charterhouse	drew	2-2 (Buckley, Ruddock)
Feb 12th	1955	Charterhouse	won	4-0 (Forsyth, Lees, Percival, Buckley)
Dec 7th	1955	Charterhouse	lost	2-3 (Burrows, Tunnock)
Dec 15th	1956	Charterhouse	won	1-0 (Burrows)
Dec 17th	1958	Charterhouse	drew	1-1 (Gwyn Rees)
Dec 9th	1959	Charterhouse	won	1-0 (Taylor)
Dec 7th	1960	Charterhouse	drew	2-2 (Arnold, Garrow)
Oct 3rd	1973	Charterhouse	won	6-0 (Adomakoh 2, Scholfield, Middleton, Grizzelle, North)
Sept 25th	1974	Charterhouse	won	3-0 (North, Middleton 2)
Nov 20th	1976	Charterhouse	won	4-1 (Ostrer 2, Belchamber, Shepherd)
Nov 19th	1977	Charterhouse	won	8-0 (Shepherd 3, Cummins 2, Kirkbride, Doggart, Mole)
Nov 18th	1978	Charterhouse	won	5-0 (o.g., Pride 2, Piper 2)
Dec 14th	1979	Charterhouse	won	4-2 (Raymonde, Haynes, Doggart, Bishop)
Dec 13th	1980	Charterhouse	lost	2-3 (Gard, Spooner)

Middlebriars

Date	Year	Team	Result	Score
Nov 27th	1879	Charterhouse	won	4-1

OTHER OPPONENTS

Achaeans

Date	Year	Team	Result	Score (scorers)
Oct 30th	1909	Charterhouse	won	2-0 (Bruce, Dixon)
Mar 11th	1911	Charterhouse	lost	2-5 (Boosey, Rücker)
Feb 21st	1912	Charterhouse	won	2-1 (Chambers, Ford)
Mar 1st	1913	Charterhouse	won	3-1 (Steel, Chambers, Liddle)

Addiscombe Park

Date	Year	Team	Result	Score (scorers)
Nov 28th	1908	Charterhouse	won	4-0 (Weeks 3, Johnson)

ADO, Holland tour

Date	Year	Team	Result	Score (scorers)
Sept 3rd	1986	ADO	lost	3-4 (Mellstrom 2, Leale)

Aldershot

Date	Year	Team	Result	Score (scorers)
Dec 2nd	1874	Charterhouse	drew	1-1 (Short)

Alzheim, Germany tour

Date	Year	Team	Result	Score (scorers)
Aug 26th	1988	Alzheim	won	2-1 (Clarke)

Amateur Athletic Club

Date	Year	Team	Result	Score (scorers)
Nov 30th	1867	Charterhouse	won	3-1 (Nepean 2, Foote)

Arsenal

Date	Year	Team	Result	Score
Oct 23rd	1968	Charterhouse	lost	0-2

Ashburnham Rovers

Date	Year	Team	Result	Score (scorers)
Sept 27th	1884	Charterhouse	won	4-2 (Crowdy, Wreford Brown, Burrell, Adams)
Sept 26th	1885	Charterhouse	won	2-1 (Parry, Wreford Brown)

Avengers

Date	Year	Team	Result	Score (scorers)
Oct 16th	1867	Charterhouse	won	6-0 (Nepean 4, Foote 2)
Nov 20th	1867	Charterhouse	won	3-1 (Wallace, Hammick, Nepean)

Bank of England

Date	Year	Team	Result	Score (scorers)
Sept 25th	1954	Charterhouse	lost	3-4 (Ruddock, Hornett, o.g.)
Feb 16th	1957	Charterhouse	lost	1-3 (Visser)
Feb 15th	1958	Charterhouse	won	3-2 (White 2, Gibb)

Bankstown City FC, Sydney tour

Date	Year	Team	Result	Score (scorers)
Oct 3rd	2006	Charterhouse	lost	1-2 (Mason)

Barnes

Date	Year	Team	Result	Score (scorers)
Dec 7th	1870	Charterhouse	drew	0-0
Feb 4th	1871	Barnes	lost	0-3
Oct 21st	1871	Charterhouse	won	1-0 (Davies)
Nov 14th	1885	Charterhouse	won	5-0 (Daglish, Parry, Currey, Leatham, o.g.)
Nov 20th	1886	Charterhouse	won	2-0 (Leman 2)
Feb 1st	1896	Charterhouse	won	7-2 (Jameson 2, Horne 2, Haig Brown 2, Ryder)
Dec 5th	1896	Charterhouse	won	3-1 (Ryder, Mucklow, Gordon)
Nov 27th	1897	Charterhouse	drew	1-1
Oct 29th	1898	Charterhouse	won	5-0 (Timmis, Trower, Evans 2, Leechman)
7th Feb	1900	Charterhouse	won	8-0 (Tuff 4, Trower 2, Malden 2)
14th Nov	1900	Charterhouse	lost	3-5 (o.g., Malden, Fisher)
27th Nov	1901	Charterhouse	won	6-0 (Bense Pembroke 5, Goodliffe)

Beaufrays, Holland tour

Sept 3rd	1998	Beaufays	won	4-1 (Schneider, Gay2, Wallis)

Beckenham

Oct 5th	1901	Charterhouse	won	2-1 (Goodliffe 2)
Oct 3rd	1902	Charterhouse	lost	0-4
Oct 3rd	1903	Charterhouse	drew	1-1 (Taylor)
Nov 19th	1904	Charterhouse	won	3-0 (Reid, Tillie, Cockburn)
Nov 18th	1905	Charterhouse	lost	1-2 (Greig)
Nov 17th	1906	Charterhouse	lost	0-1
Nov 16th	1907	Charterhouse	drew	1-1 (Wilson)
Nov 14th	1908	Charterhouse	won	4-1 (Norris 2, Macdonald 2)
Nov 20th	1909	Charterhouse	lost	2-5 (Dunlop, Bruce)
Dec 17th	1910	Charterhouse	won	2-0 (Boosey, Sanderson)
Feb 1st	1913	Charterhouse	won	2-1 (Hinds, Liddle)
Jan 31st	1914	Charterhouse	lost	0-1

Brentwood (Crusaders from 1887)

Mar 19th	1884	Charterhouse	lost	0-3
Nov 1st	1884	Charterhouse	won	1-0 (Price)
Mar 18th	1885	Charterhouse	lost	0-4
Oct 10th	1885	Charterhouse	lost	0-1
Mar 24th	1886	Charterhouse	drew	0-0
Mar 23rd	1887	Charterhouse	lost	1-3 (Stanbrough)
Dec 3rd	1887	Charterhouse	drew	1-1 (Stanbrough)
Oct 12th	1889	Charterhouse	won	2-0 (Halsted, Armstrong)
Feb 8th	1890	Charterhouse	lost	1-2 (Wilson)
Oct 11th	1890	Charterhouse	drew	2-2 (Wilson 2)
Feb 7th	1891	Charterhouse	lost	0-4
Oct 17th	1891	Charterhouse	lost	1-3 (Wild)
Feb 13th	1892	Charterhouse	drew	2-2 (Vassall, Smith)
Oct 22nd	1892	Charterhouse	drew	1-1 (Broadbent)
Feb 11th	1893	Charterhouse	won	2-0 (Vassall, Broadbent)
Nov 18th	1893	Charterhouse	won	1-0 (Hancock)
Feb 24th	1894	Charterhouse	lost	2-5 (Jameson, Davidson)
Nov 17th	1894	Charterhouse	won	2-1 (CF Ryder, GW Ryder)
Nov 9th	1895	Charterhouse	lost	1-3 (Moss)

Brentwood Rovers

Feb 2nd	1907	Charterhouse	won	3-0 (Pegram, Shrager, Jameson)

Calabar HS, Jamaica tour

Jan	1974	Calabar HS	won	1-0 (Faull)

Castricum AFC, Holland tour

Aug 29th	1995	Casticum AFC	won	5-0 (Adie 2, Frendo, Hamblin, Carmichael)

Casuals

Oct 24th	1883	Charterhouse	drew	1-1 (Brown)
Feb 20th	1884	Charterhouse	lost	2-3 (Brown 2)
Oct 8th	1884	Charterhouse	lost	0-1
Feb 25th	1885	Charterhouse	won	2-1 (Currey 2)
Mar 25th	1885	Charterhouse	drew	3-3 (Crowdy, Galsworthy, Martyn)
Oct 7th	1885	Charterhouse	lost	0-1
Feb 24th	1886	Charterhouse	won	2-1 (Parry, Price)
Mar 27th	1886	Charterhouse	won	1-0 (Nixon)
Oct 6th	1886	Charterhouse	drew	1-1 (Price)
Feb 23rd	1887	Charterhouse	won	3-2 (Taylor 2, Earle)
Oct 5th	1887	Charterhouse	won	2-0 (Furber 2)
Nov 5th	1887	Charterhouse	won	4-1 (Gilliat 3, Dickinson)
Mar 24th	1888	Charterhouse	drew	2-2 (Rayner, Earle)
Oct 3rd	1888	Beaufrays	won	3-1 (Stanbrough 2, Woodhouse)
Nov 28th	1888	Charterhouse	won	2-0 (Stanbrough, Price)
Oct 2nd	1889	Charterhouse	drew	3-3 (Halsted, o.g., Armstrong)
Mar 22nd	1890	Charterhouse	drew	2-2 (Wade 2)
Oct 1st	1890	Charterhouse	won	2-1 (Merriman, Hewitt)
Mar 25th	1891	Charterhouse	lost	1-3 (Wilson)
Oct 14th	1891	Charterhouse	won	6-5 (Smith 2, Crabtree, Salt, Wild 2)
Oct 5th	1892	Charterhouse	lost	2-4 (Broadbent, Ward)
Feb 15th	1893	Charterhouse	won	3-2 (Hunt 2, Fordyce)
Oct 4th	1893	Charterhouse	lost	2-5 (Peers, Fordyce)
Feb 14th	1894	Charterhouse	won	3-1 (Davidson 2, Jameson)
Oct 3rd	1894	Charterhouse	drew	2-2 (GW Ryder, Wallace)
Oct 23rd	1895	Charterhouse	lost	3-7 (Horne 2, Haig Brown)
Feb 5th	1896	Charterhouse	won	4-3 (Green, Vassall 2, Jameson)
Nov 7th	1896	Charterhouse	won	2-0 (Moss 2)
Feb 10th	1897	Charterhouse	drew	1-1 (Forbes)
Nov 20th	1897	Charterhouse	lost	1-2 (Gordon)
Feb 12th	1898	Charterhouse	won	7-1 (Moss 4, Crosdale 2, Trower)
Nov 19th	1898	Charterhouse	won	3-2 (Tuff 2, Evans)
Feb 11th	1899	Charterhouse	won	3-0 (Evans, Tuff 2)
Nov 15th	1899	Charterhouse	won	3-2 (Waller, Sharp, Tuff)
Feb 13th	1901	Charterhouse	lost	0-2
Nov 23rd	1901	Charterhouse	won	2-1 (Verry, Bense Pembroke)
Feb 19th	1902	Charterhouse	won	1-0 (Goodliffe)
Nov 19th	1902	Charterhouse	lost	0-1
Mar 4th	1903	Charterhouse	won	4-1 (Bense Pembroke 2, Allen, Taylor)
Nov 4th	1903	Charterhouse	lost	1-3 (Allen)
Mar 2nd	1904	Charterhouse	won	1-0 (Walker)

Oct 29th	1904	Charterhouse	lost	1-3 (Lyell)
Mar 8th	1905	Charterhouse	lost	0-3
Oct 28th	1905	Charterhouse	won	2-1 (Gooch, Preston)
Feb 17th	1906	Charterhouse	won	3-2 (Preston, Greig, Parry)
Sept 29th	1906	Charterhouse	lost	0-1
Oct 24th	1906	Charterhouse	won	5-1 (Preston 2, Parry 3)
Feb 16th	1907	Charterhouse	lost	1-6 (Preston)
Oct 26th	1907	Charterhouse	won	4-1 (Wilson 3, Livesey)
Feb 15th	1908	Charterhouse	lost	0-1
Oct 24th	1908	Charterhouse	lost	1-3 (Macdonald)
Feb 10th	1909	Charterhouse	won	2-1 (Johnson, Norris)
Oct 23rd	1909	Charterhouse	won	2-1 (Boosey 2)
Feb 9th	1910	Charterhouse	lost	0-4
Oct 22nd	1910	Charterhouse	lost	0-3
Feb 8th	1911	Charterhouse	won	2-0 (Gjers, Wesley Smith)
Oct 21st	1911	Charterhouse	won	2-1 (Ford 2)
Oct 19th	1912	Charterhouse	lost	1-4 (Hinds)
Feb 5th	1913	Charterhouse	lost	2-4 (Hinds, Liddle)
Oct 18th	1913	Charterhouse	lost	2-3 (Cawston, Hinds)
Feb 4th	1914	Charterhouse	lost	4-6 (Hinds 4)
Feb 7th	1923	Charterhouse	won	5-3 (Kenyon, Bett 2, Johnson, Doresa)
Feb 6th	1924	Charterhouse	drew	1-1 (Fletcher)
Feb 4th	1925	Charterhouse	lost	2-5 (Sharp, Deakin)
Feb 3rd	1926	Charterhouse	lost	1-4 (Seligman)
Feb 1st	1928	Charterhouse	lost	1-2 (Fletcher)
Jan 31st	1929	Charterhouse	lost	1-3 (Jeavons)
Jan 29th	1930	Charterhouse	won	6-4 (Pope, Jeavons 5)
Jan 28th	1931	Charterhouse	lost	2-5 (Matthews, Greening)
Jan 27th	1932	Charterhouse	lost	2-6 (Dunbar, JC Moss)
Jan 31st	1934	Charterhouse	lost	3-4 (Gillchrest, Dunbar, Powell)
Jan 30th	1935	Charterhouse	drew	2-2 (Dunbar, Hodgson)
Feb 6th	1937	Charterhouse	won	5-2 (Lomas 4, MacCunn)

Charterhouse-in-Southwark

Dec 12th	1936	Charterhouse	lost	2-3 (Benké)
Dec 9th	1939	Charterhouse	won	6-3

Civil Service

Nov 11th	1863	Charterhouse	won	2-0 (Hartshorne)
Feb 3rd	1864	Charterhouse	won	3-2 (*rush*)
Mar 19th	1864	Charterhouse	won	4-0 (Hodgson 2, Mackenzie, *rush*)
Oct 19th	1864	Charterhouse	lost	0-1
Nov 16th	1864	Charterhouse	won	4-0
Feb 1st	1865	Charterhouse	won	1-0 (Walford)
Mar 11th	1865	Charterhouse	won	1-0 (Cameron)
Oct 18th	1865	Charterhouse	drew	2-2 *first use of 'goal' rather than 'game'*
Nov 15th	1865	Charterhouse	won	2-1 (Walford 2)
Mar 7th	1866	Charterhouse	won	4-0 (Scott, Walford, Middleton, Nepean)
Nov 14th	1866	Charterhouse	won	3-0 (Mammatt/Nepean 2, Boreham)
Jan 30th	1867	Charterhouse	won	3-0 (Foote/Wallace/Mammatt, Venables, Wallace)
Mar 13th	1867	Charterhouse	won	1-0 (Walford)
Nov 13th	1867	Charterhouse	won	5-0 (Nepean 3, Boyle, o.g.)
OQ	1868	Charterhouse	won	3-0
Oct 13th	1869	Charterhouse	drew	1-1 (Barry)
Oct 19th	1870	Charterhouse	won	3-0 (*squash* 2, Neish) *1st half in cloisters*
Feb 8th	1871	Charterhouse	lost	0-1
Oct 11th	1871	Charterhouse	won	2-1 (Empson, Parry)
Feb 8th	1872	Charterhouse	won	6-0 (Parry 2, Ravenshaw, Gandell, Paget, Stavely)
Oct 16th	1872	Charterhouse (Godalming)	won	4-0 (Firth 2, Davies, Gipps)
Nov 15th	1882	Charterhouse	won	8-0 (Spring Rice, C Vintcent, Brookes 2, Eddis 3, Steward)

Clapham Rovers

Oct 20th	1869	Charterhouse	won	5-1 (Inglis 3, Barry, Matthews)
Jan 26th	1870	Charterhouse	lost	0-2
Nov 23rd	1870	Charterhouse	won	2-1 (Inglis, o.g.)
Feb 15th	1871	Charterhouse	lost	0-1
Mar 3rd	1877	Charterhouse	won	2-0 (Page 2)
Oct 20th	1877	Charterhouse	won	4-1 (Frith, Prinsep, Growse, Evan-Thomas)
Oct 19th	1878	Charterhouse	won	3-1 (Hansell, Richards, Jackson)
Oct 18th	1879	Charterhouse	won	4-1 (Pollock 2, Morrison, Richards)
Mar 20th	1880	Charterhouse	lost	1-6 (Richards)
Oct 16th	1880	Charterhouse	won	3-0 (Owen, Escombe, Cholmeley)
Oct 15th	1881	Charterhouse	won	5-3 (Rayner 2, Cobbold 3)
Oct 14th	1882	Charterhouse	drew	1-1 (Steward)
Oct 13th	1883	Charterhouse	won	2-0 (Galsworthy, Steward)
Oct 18th	1884	Charterhouse	won	1-0 (Martyn)
Feb 14th	1885	Charterhouse	won	2-0 (Holroyd, Crowdy)
Oct 14th	1885	Charterhouse	won	2-0 (Price, Daglish)
Oct 9th	1886	Charterhouse	won	1-0 (Price)
Feb 22nd	1888	Charterhouse	won	1-0 (Dickinson)
Oct 18th	1890	Charterhouse	won	6-0 (Bramwell, Smith, Wilson 2, Merriman 2)

Oct 24th	1891	Charterhouse	won	7-0 (Smith 4, Salt, Crabtree, Wild)
Feb 6th	1909	Charterhouse	won	5-1 (Weeks 5)
Feb 5th	1910	Charterhouse	won	3-1 (Dixon, Polson 2)
Feb 4th	1911	Charterhouse	won	3-1 (Boosey, Wesley Smith 2)

Corinthians

Mar 14th	1883	Charterhouse	won	3-0 (Fardell 2, L Vintcent)
Mar 5th	1884	Charterhouse	lost	1-2 (Vintcent)
Oct 8th	1919	Charterhouse	lost	2-6 (Mordaunt Smith, Gilliat)
Feb 16th	1927	Charterhouse	lost	2-3 (Fletcher, Weatherall)
Feb 19th	1930	Charterhouse	lost	1-3 (Pope)
Feb 17th	1932	Charterhouse	won	3-2 (WF Moss 2, Samuelson)
Feb 21st	1934	Charterhouse	lost	1-2
Feb 2nd	1935	Charterhouse	drew	3-3 (Daukes, Dowding)
Feb 20th	1937	Charterhouse	lost	0-7
Jan	1938	Charterhouse	lost	2-4 (Larking, McMillan)

Corinthian Casuals

Feb 15th	1941	Charterhouse	lost	2-4 (Davidson, Hawley)
Oct 18th	1941	Charterhouse	won	1-0 (Larking)
Oct 17th	1942	Charterhouse	lost	2-3 (Dalgety, Seager)
Oct 16th	1943	Charterhouse	lost	1-4 (Crole-Rees)
Oct 14th	1944	Charterhouse	lost	4-5 (Godden)
Feb 17th	1945	Charterhouse	lost	1-3 (Wilson)
Oct 13th	1945	Charterhouse	lost	3-4 (Savill, o.g., Wilson)
Oct 12th	1946	Charterhouse	drew	2-2 (Savill, Gemmel)
Nov 29th	1947	Charterhouse	drew	2-2 (Burt 2)
Jan 31st	1948	Charterhouse	lost	0-3
Nov 27th	1948	Charterhouse	lost	2-6 (Gibbon, Ritchie)
Jan 29th	1949	Charterhouse	lost	2-4 (Atkinson, Goodliffe)
Oct 8th	1949	Charterhouse	drew	1-1 (Edwards)
Jan 28th	1950	Charterhouse	lost	2-3 (May, Carver)
Oct 7th	1950	Charterhouse	lost	2-4 (Bayman 2)
Jan 27th	1951	Charterhouse	lost	1-3 (Barclay)
Oct 6th	1951	Charterhouse	lost	1-3 (o.g.)
Jan 26th	1952	Charterhouse	lost	0-4
Oct 4th	1952	Charterhouse	lost	1-2 (Cupitt)
Jan 24th	1953	Charterhouse	lost	3-4 (Pratt, White, Hardcastle)
Oct 3rd	1953	Charterhouse	lost	0-5
Jan 23rd	1954	Charterhouse	lost	0-5
Oct 2nd	1954	Charterhouse	drew	4-4 (Ruddock 2, Lees, Percival)
Jan 22nd	1955	Charterhouse	lost	1-6 (Jakobson)
Oct 1st	1955	Charterhouse	won	7-5 (Forsyth 4, Burrows 2, Jakobson)
Feb 11th	1956	Charterhouse	lost	1-3 (Hornett)
Sept 29th	1956	Charterhouse	won	5-0 (Burrows, Agace 2, Steed, Sparshatt)
Feb 9th	1957	Charterhouse	lost	1-2 (Visser)
Sept 28th	1957	Charterhouse	lost	0-2
Feb 8th	1958	Charterhouse	lost	2-6 (Harrison, o.g.)
Sept 27th	1958	Charterhouse	lost	2-6 (Topham, Gibb)
Feb 7th	1959	Charterhouse	lost	2-3 (Faulkner, Visser)
Oct 3rd	1959	Charterhouse	lost	0-5
Jan 30th	1960	Charterhouse	lost	2-4 (Taylor, Lorenz)
Oct 5th	1960	Charterhouse	lost	2-6 (Powell 2)
Feb 4th	1961	Charterhouse	lost	1-6 (Lorenz)
Oct 7th	1961	Charterhouse	lost	0-2
Feb 3rd	1962	Charterhouse	won	4-1 (Powell 2, Gilliat, o.g.)
Oct 6th	1962	Charterhouse	lost	0-3
Oct 5th	1963	Charterhouse	lost	1-3 (Bailhache)
Feb 1st	1964	Charterhouse	lost	1-4 (Hooper)
Oct 3rd	1964	Charterhouse	lost	0-6
Jan 30th	1965	Charterhouse	drew	1-1 (Bidwell)
Feb 4th	1967	Charterhouse	lost	0-6
Jan 27th	1968	Charterhouse	lost	1-5 (Foster)
Jan 25th	1969	Charterhouse	lost	0-1
Jan 24th	1970	Charterhouse	lost	0-4
Jan 23rd	1971	Charterhouse	lost	1-9 (Stewart)

A XI fixtures only from 1972. No 1st XI results

Corinthians 'A'

| Dec 10th | 1921 | Charterhouse | lost | 2-8 (Doresa 2) |
| Feb 25th | 1928 | Charterhouse | lost | 1-12 (Davies) |

Cornwall College, Jamaica tour

| Jan | 1974 | Cornwall College | lost | 1-2 (Adomakoh) |

Crusaders

Jan 28th	1863	Charterhouse	lost	0-1
Nov 18th	1863	Charterhouse	won	2-0 (O'Grady 2)
Feb 17th	1864	Charterhouse	drew	0-0
Mar 5th	1864	Charterhouse	drew	0-0
Dec 6th	1864	Charterhouse	won	2-0
Feb 8th	1865	Charterhouse	drew	1-1 *(team effort)*
Dec 6th	1865	Charterhouse	drew	0-0
Feb 10th	1866	Charterhouse	drew	1-1
Mar 9th	1867	Charterhouse	drew	0-0 *first use of 'draw' rather than 'tie'*
Nov 6th	1867	Charterhouse	won	4-1 (Venables, Paulson, Foote, Nepean)

Crystal Palace

Nov 15th	1871	Charterhouse	won	3-1 (Parry, Gandell, Paget)
Jan 27th	1872	Charterhouse	won	1-0 (Gandell)
Dec 3rd	1873	Charterhouse	won	2-0 (Parry, Drew)

Diekirch, Luxembourg tour

| Nov 3rd | 1972 | Diekirch | lost | 1-2 (Oundjian) |

Dingley Dell

Nov 6th	1861	Charterhouse	lost	0-1
Nov 16th	1861	Charterhouse	drew	1-1 (Mackenzie)
Oct 29th	1862	Charterhouse	lost	0-2
Nov 12th	1862	Charterhouse	lost	1-2 (Hodgson)
Feb 4th	1863	Charterhouse	won	1-0 (O'Grady)
Feb 25th	1863	Charterhouse	drew	0-0
Nov 4th	1863	Charterhouse	won	2-0 (*rush*, Hartshorne)
Nov 25th	1863	Charterhouse	lost	0-3
Jan 27th	1864	Charterhouse	won	1-0

Ealing

| Mar 19th | 1910 | Charterhouse | drew | 2-2 (Boosey, Dixon) |

East Surrey Wanderers

| Mar 31st | 1888 | Charterhouse | lost | 4-5 (Stanbrough 3, o.g.) |
| Mar 20th | 1889 | Charterhouse | lost | 1-5 (Irvine) |

Emeriti

Nov 12th	1898	Charterhouse	won	5-0 (Evans, Greenwood 2, Sturrock, Gibson)
25th Oct	1899	Charterhouse	won	3-0 (Waller, Trower, Tuff)
27th Oct	1900	Charterhouse	won	10-0 (Tuff 8, Malden, Goodliffe)
Jan 30th	1909	Charterhouse	lost	0-1

Ewell

| Nov 28th | 1896 | Charterhouse | won | 6-0 (Gordon 2, Ryder, Vassall 3) |
| 28th Oct | 1899 | Charterhouse | won | 6-1 (Tuff 4, Waller, Trower) |

FC Quick, Holland tour

Sept 5th	1985	FC Quick 'C'	won	6-0 (Faulkner, Bedford)
Sept 6th	1985	FC Quick 'B'	won	3-1
Sept 2nd	1986	FC Quick	drew	1-1 (Cowling)

Garleen Zuig, Holland tour

| Sept 5th | 1998 | Garleen Zuig | won | 9-0 (Gay 4, Jackson 2, Leal, Schneider, Poulsen) |

Gitanos

Mar 16th	1870	Charterhouse	won	3-0 (Smith 2, Inglis)
Oct 22nd	1870	Charterhouse	won	3-0 (Brown, Ravenshaw, King)
Mar 5th	1873	Charterhouse	won	3-0
Mar 22nd	1873	Charterhouse	lost	1-3 (E Williams)
Nov 8th	1873	Charterhouse	lost	0-3
Mar 21st	1874	Charterhouse	won	5-2 (Parry, Tod, Page, Verelst, Synge)
Oct 31st	1874	Charterhouse	won	2-0 (Abdy 2)
Nov 6th	1875	Charterhouse	lost	1-3 (Short)
Mar 14th	1877	Charterhouse	won	5-0 (A Keightley 3, Page, Eddis)

Godalming FC

April 2nd	1877	Godalming	won	2-0 (Gilliat, Stanbrough)
Oct 29th	1887	Godalming	won	6-0
Nov 17th	1888	Godalming	won	3-0 (Barker 2, Smith)
Oct 19th	1889	Godalming	won	4-1 (Smith 2, Armstrong 2)
Nov 25th	1891	Charterhouse	lost	1-3 (Salt)
Sept 28th	1892	Charterhouse	won	4-1 (Fordyce 2, Vassall, Broadbent)
Oct 11th	1893	Charterhouse	won	5-3 (Fordyce, Vassall 2, Hunt 2)
Oct 10th	1894	Charterhouse	lost	3-4 (Anderson, Laird, GW Ryder)
Oct 12th	1895	Charterhouse	lost	2-3 (Moss 2)
Dec 2nd	1933	Godalming	won	3-2 (Frith, Field 2)
Nov 24th	1934	Charterhouse	lost	0-2
Nov 30th	1935	Charterhouse		
Nov 28th	1936	Charterhouse	lost	3-7 (Tanner)
Nov 11th	1939	Godalming	won	4-1
Nov 8th	1952	Charterhouse	won	8-0 (White 3, Miller 2, Pratt, o.g. 2)

Grand Amalgamated Mediocrities

| Nov 5th | 1862 | Charterhouse | lost | 2-3 (Yorke, Hodgson/Eardley-Wilmot) *in cloisters* |
| Nov 19th | 1862 | Charterhouse | drew | 0-0 |

Guildford FC

Oct 17th	1896	Charterhouse	won	2-0 (Moss, Vassall)
Oct 23rd	1897	Charterhouse	won	1-0 (Gordon)
Oct 22nd	1898	Charterhouse	lost	1-2 (Evans)
31st Jan	1900	Charterhouse	won	1-0 (Trower)
10th Oct	1900	Charterhouse	won	6-0 (Curwen, Malden, Tuff 4)
Nov 1st	1902	Charterhouse	drew	0-0
Oct 31st	1914	Charterhouse	lost	0-2
Feb 13th	1915	Charterhouse	drew	1-1 (Hansell)

Hampstead

| Oct 10th | 1914 | Charterhouse | won | 4-1 (Hansell 2, Harvie, Anderson) |

Feb 6th	1915	Charterhouse	won	6-4 (Hansell 4, Hall, Ritchie)
Oct 16th	1915	Charterhouse	won	10-0 (Hall 5, Tinley 3, o.g. 2)

Hants Schools' U16

Sept 12th	2000	Charterhouse	drew	4-4 (Burke-Murphy 2, Cook, Clark)
Sept 11th	2001	Charterhouse	drew	1-1 (Sogbetun)
Sept 10th	2002	Charterhouse	won	3-0 (Hooper, Hunter, Barnett)
Sept 9th	2003	Charterhouse	lost	1-2 (Bourne)
Sept 14th	2004	Charterhouse	drew	1-1 (Holder)
Sept 13th	2005	Charterhouse	won	2-1 (Walford, Fyler)
Sept 5th	2006	Charterhouse	won	4-2 (Mason, Beddows, Nash 2)
Sept 4th	2007	Charterhouse	drew	3-3 (Rogers, Watson, Hall)

Inns of Court

Feb 16th	1916	Charterhouse	lost	1-3
Nov 18th	1916	Charterhouse	lost	1-4 (Lewns)

Kenley

Feb 13th	1904	Charterhouse	lost	0-1
Feb 11th	1905	Charterhouse	won	4-0 (Reid 2, Rücker, Pears)
Nov 10th	1906	Charterhouse	won	5-0 (Jameson 2, Preston 2, Parry)
Nov 9th	1907	Charterhouse	won	2-0 (Livesey, Wilson)
Nov 7th	1908	Charterhouse	won	4-3 (o.g., Weeks 3)
Nov 6th	1909	Charterhouse	won	3-1 (Bruce, Norris, Dixon)
Nov 5th	1910	Charterhouse	won	2-0 (Sanderson, Boosey)
Nov 9th	1912	Charterhouse	lost	3-5 (Payne, Chambers 2)

Kilburn

Feb 13th	1864	Charterhouse	drew	0-0
Mar 12th	1864	Charterhouse	lost	0-1
Feb 22nd	1868	Middlesex County ground	drew	0-0

Kingston College, Jamaica tour

Jan	1974	Kingston College	lost	0-2

Laleham (Brooke Hall bachelors' house)

Nov 25th	1944	Charterhouse	won	10-0 (Godden 4, Spratt 3, Price, Vlasto, Fenwick)

Liverpool Ramblers

Dec 8th	1893	Charterhouse	won	2-1 (o.g., Hunt)
Nov 1st	1894	Charterhouse	won	2-0 (Turnbull, Laird)
Nov 28th	1895	Charterhouse	lost	3-5 (Haig Brown 2, Moss)
17th Nov	1900	Charterhouse	lost	1-3 (Malden)
30th Nov	1901	Charterhouse	drew	1-1 (Verry)
Nov 29th	1902	Charterhouse	won	1-0 (Tetley)
Nov 26th	1903	Charterhouse	lost	1-3 (Reid)
Feb 25th	1905	Charterhouse	won	4-0 (Reid 2, Gilbert, Lyell)
Feb 10th	1906	Charterhouse	won	2-1 (Tillie, Gooch)
Nov 23rd	1907	Charterhouse	won	5-0 (Wilson, Rhodes, Pike 2, Livesey)
Nov 21st	1908	Charterhouse	won	6-0 (Weeks 3, Norris 2, Macdonald)
Mar 12th	1910	Charterhouse	won	3-0 (Dunlop 2, Boosey)
Dec 3rd	1910	Charterhouse	won	1-0 (Sanderson)
Dec 2nd	1911	Charterhouse	won	7-0 (Ford 4, de Bernière Smith, Vernon, Rücker)
Mar 7th	1914	Charterhouse	lost	3-6 (Cawston, Smith 2)
Mar 6th	1920	Charterhouse	won	4-3 (Gilliat 4)
Mar 5th	1921	Charterhouse	lost	1-2 (Gilliat)
Mar 4th	1922	Charterhouse	lost	0-1
Mar 3rd	1923	Charterhouse	lost	1-2 (Doresa)
Mar 8th	1924	Charterhouse	lost	3-4 (Rishworth , Carter)
Feb 3rd	1951	Charterhouse	lost	0-7
Feb 7th	1953	Charterhouse	lost	1-2 (White)
Jan 28th	1956	Charterhouse	won	6-0 (Jakobson 2, Burrows, Tunnock, Hornett, Forsyth)
Jan 25th	1958	Charterhouse	lost	1-2 (Visser)
Jan 23rd	1960	Charterhouse	lost	2-12 (Craig, Taylor)
Jan 27th	1962	Charterhouse	lost	0-1
Jan 25th	1964	Charterhouse	lost	1-2 (Weir)
Jan 29th	1966	Charterhouse	lost	1-9 (Howard)
Jan 20th	1968	Charterhouse	won	2-1 (Bennett, Foster)
Jan 18th	1969	Charterhouse	lost	3-4 (Grizelle 2, Foster)
Jan 17th	1970	Charterhouse	lost	0-1
Jan 16th	1971	Charterhouse	lost	0-1
Jan 22nd	1972	Charterhouse	lost	1-2 (Stewart)
Jan 20th	1973	Charterhouse	won	2-0
Jan 19th	1974	Charterhouse	won	2-1 (Adomakoh 2)
Jan 17th	1976	Charterhouse	won	3-2 (Cummins, Shepherd, Cunningham)
Jan 15th	1977	Charterhouse		
Jan 20th	1979	Charterhouse	drew	1-1 (Frankland)
Jan 19th	1980	Charterhouse	lost	1-3 (Gard)

A XI fixtures only from 1981. No 1st XI results

London FA

Nov	1931	Charterhouse	lost	1-8 (JC Moss)

Oct 18th	1933	Charterhouse	lost	0-8
Oct	1934	Charterhouse	lost	1-7 (Hodgson)
Oct	1935	Charterhouse	lost	0-14
Oct 14th	1936	Charterhouse	lost	1-7 (Orton)
Oct 8th	1947	Charterhouse	lost	0-11
Oct 6th	1948	Charterhouse	lost	0-17
Oct 5th	1949	Charterhouse	lost	0-4
Oct 4th	1950	Charterhouse	lost	1-6 (Gladstone)
Oct 3rd	1951	Charterhouse	lost	1-7 (Miller)
Oct 1st	1952	Charterhouse	lost	0-5
Sept 30th	1953	Charterhouse	lost	1-6 (Wilkinson)
Sept 29th	1954	Charterhouse	lost	0-11
Oct 5th	1955	Charterhouse	lost	0-3

London FA Minors

Oct 3rd	1956	Charterhouse	lost	0-7
Oct 2nd	1957	Charterhouse	lost	0-4
Oct 1st	1958	Charterhouse	lost	0-11
Nov 18th	1959	Charterhouse	lost	1-9 (Taylor)

London Medical College

Oct 6th	1945	Charterhouse	won	4-1 (Savill, Price, Meyer 2)

Luxembourg Schools XI tour

Nov 7th	1972	Luxembourg Schools XI	drew	0-0

Maarheeves, Holland tour

Sept 4th	1998	Maarheeves	won	8-0 (Beaumont, Schneider, o.g., Leal, Richardson 3, Wallis)

Mayen FC, Germany tour

Sept 1st	1987	Mayen FC	lost	1-3
Aug 25th	1988	FC Mayen	lost	1-3

Mayen Gymnasium, Germany tour

Sept 3rd	1987	Mayen Gymnasium	won	1-0

Medical Students' Union

Feb 14th	1942	Charterhouse	won	6-0 (Larking 2, Seager 2, Lovett, Evans)

Merton Park

Nov 7th	1914	Charterhouse	lost	2-3 (Hansell, Dunlop)

Middlesex Grammar Schools U18

Feb 10th	1960	Charterhouse	lost	1-9 (Craig)

Norsemen

Mar 13th	1909	Charterhouse	drew	0-0
Nov 17th	1951	Charterhouse	won	3-2 (Miller 2, Pegler)
Oct 28th	1953	Charterhouse	lost	1-5 (Gemmel)
Oct 27th	1954	Charterhouse	drew	3-3 (Ruddock, Lees, Buckley)
Oct 26th	1955	Charterhouse	won	3-1 (Hornett 2, Sparshatt)

Occasionals

Sept 30th	1939	Charterhouse	won	7-0
Feb 10th	1940	Charterhouse	drew	1-1

Oranienstein-Stuhm tour

Mar 11th	1937	Charterhouse	won	1-0

Outcasts (C Wreford Brown's Old Internationals)

Dec 17th	1907	Charterhouse	lost	1-2 (Pike)
Feb 19th	1908	Charterhouse	won	3-2 (Weeks 2, Macdonald)
Nov 18th	1908	Charterhouse	won	2-0 (Booth, Macdonald)
Mar 16th	1909	Charterhouse	lost	1-2 (Weeks)
Nov 10th	1909	Charterhouse	lost	1-3 (Norris)
Mar 2nd	1910	Charterhouse	lost	0-3
Nov 9th	1910	Charterhouse	lost	2-3 (Boosey 2)
Nov 8th	1911	Charterhouse	lost	1-3
Mar 9th	1912	Charterhouse	drew	2-2 (Boswell, Ford)
Nov 13th	1912	Charterhouse	lost	1-3 (Gregson Ellis)
Mar 12th	1913	Charterhouse	lost	1-4 (Rücker)
Nov 5th	1913	Charterhouse	lost	2-5 (Gray, Ritchie)
Mar 18th	1914	Charterhouse	lost	2-4 (Ritchie, Smith)

Owls

LQ	1869	Charterhouse	won	7-0 *played in cloisters*

Pilgrims

Dec 4th	1880	Charterhouse	won	3-0 (Henley, Currey, Escombe)
Nov 19th	1881	Charterhouse	won	1-0 (Eddis)
Dec 16th	1882	Charterhouse	lost	0-2
Mar 17th	1883	Charterhouse	won	12-2 (Brookes 3,Fardell 3,L Vintcent 2, Walters, C Vintcent 3)
Nov 24th	1883	Charterhouse	won	4-1 (Barnett 2, Walker 2)
Nov 29th	1884	Charterhouse	drew	1-1 (Currey)

Reading Amateurs

Dec 18th	1909	Charterhouse	drew	2-2 (Bruce, Boosey)
Feb 17th	1912	Charterhouse	won	5-4 (Boswell 2, Ford 3)

Feb 15th	1913	Charterhouse	lost	3-6 (Chambers 3)
Mar	1917	Charterhouse	won	14-1

Reigate Priory

Nov 29th	1873	Charterhouse	won	3-0 (Parry, Drew, Synge)
Nov 21st	1874	Charterhouse	won	5-1 (Tod, Lovegrove, Page, Curzon, Short)
Nov 10th	1877	Charterhouse	won	10-0 (Medlicott 2, Growse 4, Smith, *rush*, Evan-Thomas, Frith)
Oct 16th	1886	Charterhouse	won	2-1 (Price, Timmis)
Oct 15th	1887	Charterhouse	drew	1-1 (Colvin)
Oct 13th	1888	Charterhouse	won	2-1 (Barker, Phelps)
Nov 16th	1889	Charterhouse	won	4-0 (Armstrong 2, Wilson, Hewitt)
Oct 10th	1891	Charterhouse	won	4-3 (Smith, Salt 2, Winch)
Mar 1st	1893	Charterhouse	won	4-0 (Dyne, Broadbent, Hunt, Neill)
Mar 7th	1894	Charterhouse	won	1-0 (Hancock)
Oct 13th	1894	Charterhouse	won	2-1 (Laird, GW Ryder)
Oct 26th	1895	Charterhouse	won	4-0 (GW Ryder, Horne 2, Haig Brown)
Feb 20th	1897	Charterhouse	won	2-1 (Moss, Fox)
Oct 16th	1897	Charterhouse	won	4-3 (Moss 3, Gordon)
Oct 8th	1898	Charterhouse	won	3-0 (Evans, Gibson, Greenwood)
Oct 19th	1899	Charterhouse	lost	0-1
Mar 9th	1901	Charterhouse	won	7-2 (Bense Pembroke, Tuff 6)
Feb 1st	1902	Charterhouse	drew	0-0
Feb 7th	1903	Charterhouse	lost	0-1
Feb 6th	1904	Charterhouse	lost	1-2 (Blagrove)
Feb 4th	1905	Charterhouse	won	1-0 (Lyell)
Feb 1st	1908	Charterhouse	won	2-1 (Johnson, Livesey)
Feb 17th	1909	Charterhouse	won	9-4 (Weeks 5, Norris 2, Kingdom, Macdonald)
Feb 16th	1910	Charterhouse	won	4-2 (Dixon, Boosey 3)
Feb 14th	1912	Charterhouse	won	2-1 (Boswell, Ford)
Nov 16th	1912	Charterhouse	lost	1-2 (Payne)
Nov 22nd	1913	Charterhouse	won	1-0 (Gray)

Remnants

Dec 11th	1880	Charterhouse	won	5-0 (Escombe, Morrison, Vintcent, Henley 2)
Feb 12th	1881	Charterhouse	won	4-1 (Vintcent 2, Owen, Cobbold)

Rheinlander FC, Germany tour

Aug 28th	1988	Rheinlander FC	lost	0-4

Richmond AFC

Nov 23rd	1898	Charterhouse	won	3-2 (Tuff 2, Trower)

Sherwood Foresters

Oct 8th	1941	Charterhouse	drew	1-1 (Evans)

St Bartholomew's Hospital

Oct 28th	1863	Charterhouse	won	2-0 (Mackenzie, Hodgson)
Feb 20th	1864	Charterhouse	aban	1-0 (Mackenzie) (*snow*)
Oct 19th	1946	Charterhouse	lost	2-4 (Anthony, Sher)

St Mary's College

Feb 20th	1943	Charterhouse	drew	1-1 (Spratt)
Jan 29th	1944	Charterhouse	drew	2-2 (Crole-Rees, Price)
Dec 2nd	1944	Charterhouse	lost	1-2 (Spratt)

St Thomas's Hospital

Oct 15th	1941	Charterhouse	won	3-0 (Evans 2, Lahaye)
Feb 19th	1944	Charterhouse	won	3-0 (Cranstoun 2,Price)
Feb 3rd	1945	Charterhouse	drew	6-6 (Spratt 3, Wilson 2, Pollock)
Nov 17th	1945	Charterhouse	lost	0-2
Feb 2nd	1946	Charterhouse	lost	2-3 (Marrot, Wilson)
Oct 5th	1946	Charterhouse	won	6-2 (May 2, Marrot 2, Mills, Gemmel)
Oct 4th	1947	Charterhouse	won	5-0 (Hastings 2, Divett 2, Millar)
Oct 2nd	1948	Charterhouse	won	1-0 (Smithson)
Oct 1st	1949	Charterhouse	won	3-1 (Smithson 2, Vansittart)
Sept 30th	1950	Charterhouse	won	5-2 (Gladstone 2, Young 2, Barclay)
Sept 29th	1951	Charterhouse	won	3-2 (Pegler, Duits, Barclay)
Sept 26th	1953	Charterhouse	won	9-2 (Mace 4, Wilkinson 3, Pratt, Buckley)

Strangers

Feb 27th	1867	Charterhouse	drew	0-0

Surbiton Hill

Nov 4th	1905	Charterhouse	won	3-1 (Preston 2, Crier)
Nov 27th	1909	Charterhouse	won	4-2 (Bruce 2, Dunlop, Steer)
Nov 26th	1910	Charterhouse	drew	
Nov 18th	1911	Charterhouse	won	4-3 (Ford, Rücker, de Bernière Smith, o.g.)
Dec 7th	1912	Charterhouse	won	2-1 (Liddle, Steel)

Surbiton Wanderers

Oct 11th	1884	Charterhouse	won	4-0 (Currey 2, Martyn, Wreford Brown)
Oct 24th	1885	Charterhouse	won	2-0 (Price 2)

Surrey Senior League

Mar 2nd	1935	Charterhouse	lost	1-3

Surrey Schools' U16

Sept 27th	1998	Charterhouse	won	3-2 (Burke-Murphy, Schneider, Gay)

Sussex Dolphins

Dec 15th	1888	Charterhouse	lost	0-5
Oct 9th	1889	Charterhouse	won	3-2 (Buzzard 2, Armstrong)
Oct 3rd	1891	Charterhouse	won	9-0 (Smith 5, Wild 4)
Dec 16th	1893	Charterhouse	won	6-1 (Hunt 3, Wilson, Vassall, Hancock)

Swifts

Mar 13th	1875	Charterhouse	won	3-2 (Tod 3)
Mar 28th	1877	Charterhouse	won	3-0 (Page 3)
Oct 10th	1877	Charterhouse	lost	1-3 (Medlicott)
Oct 12th	1878	Charterhouse	won	5-2 (Pollock, Wilson 2, Jenner 2)
Oct 29th	1884	Charterhouse	won	4-0 (Price 2, Wreford Brown, Currey)
Mar 4th	1885	Charterhouse	won	4-1 (Cooper, Crowdy 2, Galsworthy)
Nov 14th	1888	Charterhouse	won	3-2 (Rayner, Smith, Stanbrough)

The Stage FC

Oct 18th	1922	Charterhouse	won	10-0 (Carter 4, Doresa 3, Kenyon 2, Fletcher

Toc H

Oct 1st	1921	Charterhouse	won	4-1 (Doresa 2, Engelbach, Kiggell)
Nov 25th	1922	Charterhouse	won	3-1 (Doresa, Kenyon, Fletcher)
Nov 10th	1923	Charterhouse	lost	0-4
Oct 25th	1924	Charterhouse	lost	1-4 (Evans)
Oct 24th	1925	Charterhouse	won	4-2 (Branston 2, Deakin, Connell)
Oct 23rd	1926	Charterhouse	won	1-0 (Glynn)
Oct 22nd	1927	Charterhouse	won	4-3 (Hale 2, Davies, Robertson)
Oct 20th	1928	Charterhouse	lost	1-3 (Cohen)
Oct 19th	1929	Charterhouse	won	4-1 (Stock 2, Hulton, Greening)
Oct 18th	1930	Charterhouse	drew	3-3 (Greening, Pope, Samuelson)
Oct	1931	Charterhouse	won	3-1 (WF Moss 2, Field)
Sept 30th	1933	Charterhouse	won	3-2 (Trapman, Frith, Field)
Sept	1934	Charterhouse	won	6-1
Oct 5th	1935	Charterhouse	won	5-2 (Merz 2, Dunbar 2, Greene)
Oct 3rd	1936	Charterhouse	won	4-0 (Lomas 4)

Tunbridge Wells

Oct 17th	1863	Charterhouse	won	5-0 (Malkin 2, Boyle, Hodgson, *rush*)

University College Hospital

Dec 12th	1894	Charterhouse	won	4-0 (Hancock, Franks, Jameson 2)

University College London

Oct 12th	1921	Charterhouse	won	2-1 (Doresa, Morgan)
Feb 11th	1943	Charterhouse	won	2-0 (Spratt, Godden)

University College Reading

Nov 5th	1919	Charterhouse	lost	1-3 (Gilliat)
Oct 27th	1920	Charterhouse	won	4-2 (Gilliat, Barnard 2, Anderson)
Nov 26th	1921	Charterhouse	won	3-2 (Doresa 2, Kiggell)
Nov 8th	1922	Charterhouse	lost	2-3 (Doresa, Fletcher)
Nov 21st	1923	Charterhouse	lost	2-6 (Carter, Fletcher)

Vagrants

LQ	1869	Charterhouse	won	7-0 *played in cloisters*

Vere Technical College, Jamaica tour

Dec	1973	Vere Technical College	won	3-1 (Adomakoh, Williams, Doggart)

Walthamstow

Nov 5th	1870	Charterhouse	won	1-0 (Dorling)
Mar 11th	1871	Charterhouse	won	10-0 (Inglis 6)
Feb 10th	1872	Charterhouse	won	3-0 (Davies, Brown, Thompson)

Wanderers

Nov 8th	1865	Charterhouse	lost	0-1
Mar 3rd	1866	Charterhouse	lost	0-1
Nov 10th	1866	Charterhouse	won	1-0
Feb 23rd	1867	Charterhouse	drew	0-0
Oct 26th	1867	Charterhouse	lost	0-1
Nov 3rd	1869	Charterhouse	drew	2-2 (Barry, Inglis)
Mar 19th	1870	Charterhouse	drew	1-1 (Barry)
Nov 2nd	1870	Charterhouse	won	3 (Brown, King, Inglis)
Mar 1st	1871	Charterhouse	drew	2-2
Nov 8th	1871	Charterhouse	drew	1-1 (Paget)
Nov 26th	1873	Charterhouse	won	4-1 (Parry, Jeaffreson, Drew, Synge)

Watersgraafmere AFC, Holland tour

Aug 31st	1995	Watersgraafmere AFC	drew	2-2 (Adie 2)

Wednesday Strollers
Dec 3rd	1884	Charterhouse	lost	0-1

West Kent
Dec 4th	1867	Charterhouse	won	2-1 (Paulson, Nepean)

West Wratting Park
Dec 5th	1894	Charterhouse	won	4-0 (Laird, o.g., GW Ryder, Jameson)
Dec 4th	1895	Charterhouse	lost	0-2
Dec 5th	1903	Charterhouse	drew	0-0 (only 40 minutes in thick fog)

Westminster Technical College
Dec 12th	1942	Charterhouse	won	3-2

Weybridge
Oct 19th	1892	Charterhouse	won	6-1 (Hunt 2, Broadbent 2, Fordyce, Crabtree)
Oct 14th	1893	Charterhouse	won	4-1 (Neill, Hunt 2, Hancock)
Oct 20th	1894	Charterhouse	won	2-0 (Anderson, GW Ryder)
Nov 23rd	1895	Charterhouse	won	12-0 (Ryder 4, Haig Brown 2, Horne, Vassall 3 Jameson 2)
7th Oct	1899	Charterhouse	lost	0-6
12th Oct	1901	Charterhouse	won	4-0 (Curwen, Goodliffe, Dowson, Bense Pembroke)
17th Oct	1900	Charterhouse	won	6-0 (Malden 2, Tuff 2, Goodliffe 2)
Oct 11th	1902	Charterhouse	won	1-0 (Eckersley)
Oct 11th	1903	Charterhouse	won	3-0 (Reid 2, Allen)
Oct 15th	1904	Charterhouse	won	4-0 (Reid 2, Lyell 2)
Oct 19th	1907	Charterhouse	won	2-1 (Livesey, Rushton)
Oct 17th	1908	Charterhouse	won	6-0 (Norris 2, Macdonald, Weeks 3)
Oct 16th	1909	Charterhouse	lost	0-1
Oct 15th	1910	Charterhouse	won	5-1 (Dunlop, Sanderson 2, Boosey 2)
Oct 14th	1911	Charterhouse	won	3-1 (Fosdick, Ford)
Oct 12th	1912	Charterhouse	won	2-1 (Payne 2)
Oct 11th	1913	Charterhouse	drew	2-2 (Gray, Burnett)

Weyside Club
Mar 15th	1873	Charterhouse	lost	1-2
Oct 25th	1873	Charterhouse	won	6-0 (Parish 2, Parry 2, Abdy, Corrie)
Feb 7th	1874	Charterhouse	won	2-0 (Tod, Synge)
Oct 24th	1874	Weyside	won	4-0 (Abdy, Page 2, Tod)
Feb 27th	1875	Charterhouse	won	9-0 (Macgeorge 4, Page 3, Tod, Blackett)

Wiltz, Luxembourg tour
Nov 5th	1972	Wiltz	won	3-1 (Parker, Stone)

Woolmers HS, Jamaica tour
Jan	1974	Woolmers HS	drew	0-0

OXBRIDGE XIs

Cambridge XI
Feb	1868	Middlesex County ground	lost	1-2 (Venables)
Dec 14th	1875	Charterhouse	won	1-0 (Tod)
Dec 10th	1876	Charterhouse	won	4-1 (Boscawen, Page 2)
Nov 22nd	1879	Charterhouse	won	4-0 (Pollock, Richards, Rayner 2)
Feb 16th	1881	Charterhouse	won	7-1 (Morrison 2, Vintcent, Henley 3, Cobbold)
Feb 15th	1882	Charterhouse	won	1-0 (Eddis)

Cambridge 'A'
Nov 4th	1925	Charterhouse	lost	1-2 (Connell)
Nov 3rd	1926	Charterhouse	drew	1-1 (Beare)
Nov 2nd	1927	Charterhouse	lost	2-5 (Chetwynd Stapylton, Fletcher)

Cambridge Czechs
Dec 7th	1940	Charterhouse	drew	5-5 (Hawley, Figg 2, Lovett, Davidson)
Dec 3rd	1941	Charterhouse	won	3-2

Cambridge Falcons
Oct 31st	1928	Charterhouse	drew	2-2 (Jeavons, Spencer)
Oct 31st	1951	Charterhouse	lost	0-7
Oct 28th	1952	Charterhouse	lost	2-8 (White, Cupitt)
Jan 26th	1955	Charterhouse	lost	1-6 (Percival)
Jan 25th	1956	Charterhouse	lost	1-5 (Tunnock)
Jan 30th	1957	Charterhouse	drew	0-0
Jan 29th	1958	Charterhouse	lost	1-4 (White)
Jan 28th	1959	Charterhouse	lost	3-6 (Visser, Strathern, Faulkner)
Jan 27th	1960	Charterhouse	lost	3-12 (Pilch, Craig, Taylor)
Feb 15th	1961	Charterhouse	lost	2-8 (Powell 2)
Feb 14th	1962	Charterhouse	lost	1-3 (de Grunwald)
Feb 12th	1964	Charterhouse	won	2-0 (Hooper 2)
Feb 10th	1965	Charterhouse	lost	0-4

Cambridge OCs
Feb 26th	1890	Charterhouse	drew	1-1 (Hewitt)
Mar 4th	1893	Charterhouse	won	4-1 (Crabtree, Fordyce, *rushed*, Dyne)
Nov 22nd	1893	Charterhouse	lost	1-2 (Sladen)
Feb 9th	1921	Charterhouse	won	2-1 (Gilliat, MacGusty)
Feb 1st	1922	Charterhouse	lost	0-3
Jan 31st	1923	Charterhouse	won	6-1 (Fletcher 2, Doresa 3, Kenyon)
Jan 30th	1924	Charterhouse	won	6-0 (Rishworth 3, Carter 2, Fletcher)
Jan 31st	1925	Charterhouse	lost	0-1
Jan 30th	1926	Charterhouse	lost	0-2
Jan 29th	1927	Charterhouse	lost	0-2
Jan 28th	1928	Charterhouse	won	3-1 (Davies, Craddock, o.g.)
Feb 6th	1929	Charterhouse	won	6-2 (Fletcher 3, Cohen 2, Jeavons)
Feb 5th	1930	Charterhouse	lost	0-5
Feb 11th	1931	Charterhouse	lost	1-3 (Moss)
Jan 23rd	1932	Charterhouse	lost	2-4 (WF Moss 2)
Nov 22nd	1933	Charterhouse	won	5-1 (Hartland-Mahon, Gillchrest, Dunbar 2, Field)

Caius College Cambridge
Oct 30th	1897	Charterhouse	won	1-0

Clare College Cambridge
Nov 5th	1902	Charterhouse	drew	0-0
Nov 16th	1904	Charterhouse	won	6-0 (Reid 4, Pears 2)
Nov 3rd	1906	Charterhouse	won	3-0 (Pegram 3)

Eton Club Cambridge
Jan 25th	1971	Charterhouse	lost	1-2

Jesus College Cambridge
Nov 9th	1921	Charterhouse	won	1-0 (Bearman)
Nov 1st	1922	Charterhouse	drew	1-1 (Kenyon)

Pembroke College Cambridge
Nov 22nd	1924	Charterhouse	lost	0-3

Trinity College Cambridge (Trinity Rest)
Oct 6th	1888	Trinity Rest	drew	2-2 (Stanbrough)
7th Mar	1900	Trinity Rest	won	1-0 (Trower)
27th Feb	1901	Trinity Rest	drew	2-2 (Tuff 2)
Jan 28th	1905	Trinity Rest	won	3-1 (Lyell 3)
Feb 7th	1906	Trinity Rest	won	7-1 (Preston 2, Greig 3, Tillie, Parry)

Oxford 'A'
Dec 1st	1906	Charterhouse	lost	0-3
Dec 4th	1907	Charterhouse	lost	1-4 (Livesey)
Feb 27th	1909	Charterhouse	lost	1-3 (Weeks)
Nov 17th	1909	Charterhouse	won	1-0 (Boosey)
Dec 7th	1910	Charterhouse	lost	2-4 (Sanderson 2)
Dec 6th	1911	Charterhouse	drew	2-2 (Rücker, de Bernière Smith)
Feb 12th	1913	Charterhouse	drew	1-1 (Liddle)
Nov 11th	1913	Charterhouse	lost	1-4 (Smith)

Oxford XI
Dec 6th	1873	Charterhouse	won	3-2 (Tod, Jeaffreson, Drew)
Dec 15th	1874	Charterhouse	lost	1-3 (Tod)
Nov 27th	1875	Charterhouse	lost	1-3 (Wake?)
Nov 16th	1881	Charterhouse	won	1-0 (Vintcent)
Dec 6th	1882	Charterhouse	lost	2-6 (Eddis, Brookes)
Nov 19th	1884	Charterhouse	drew	1-1 (Cooper)
Nov 22nd	1941	Charterhouse	drew	1-1 (Lahaye)

Oxford University Authentics
Feb 10th	1937	Charterhouse	lost	2-4 (Hughes, Lomas)

Oxford University Centaurs
Jan 24th	1920	Charterhouse	drew	3-3 (Gilliat 3)
Feb 2nd	1921	Charterhouse	lost	1-4 (Anderson)
Dec 14th	1921	Charterhouse	lost	0-7
Dec 16th	1922	Charterhouse	lost	2-5 (Fletcher, Carter)
Feb 23rd	1924	Charterhouse	lost	1-4 (Carter)
Nov 26th	1924	Charterhouse	lost	0-2
Nov 18th	1925	Charterhouse	lost	1-3 (Deakin)
Nov 17th	1926	Charterhouse	drew	3-3 (Wreford Brown, Weatherall, Fletcher)
Feb 29th	1928	Charterhouse	won	4-2 (Fletcher, Hale 2, Davies)
Feb 20th	1932	Charterhouse	lost	1-2 (WF Moss)
Feb 14th	1934	Charterhouse	won	3-1 (Powell 2, Tuckwell)
Feb 13th	1935	Charterhouse	won	6-2 (Daukes 2, Ades 3, Hodgson)
Feb	1938	Charterhouse	lost	1-2
Feb 7th	1940	Charterhouse	lost	2-3 (Tanner 2)
Nov 16th	1946	Charterhouse	won	2-1 (Mills 2)
Oct 22nd	1947	Charterhouse	lost	0-1
Oct 20th	1948	Charterhouse	lost	0-3
Nov 12th	1949	Charterhouse	lost	1-6 (Edwards)
Oct 18th	1950	Charterhouse	lost	0-2
Nov 7th	1951	Charterhouse	won	4-2 (Pegler, Miller, Gladstone, Barclay)

Nov 5th	1952	Charterhouse	lost	2-5 (Miller, Surman)
Nov 4th	1953	Charterhouse	lost	1-3 (O'Brien)
Nov 3rd	1954	Charterhouse	lost	3-7 (Lees 3)
Nov 2nd	1955	Charterhouse	lost	0-6
Nov 7th	1956	Charterhouse	lost	0-3
Nov 6th	1957	Charterhouse	lost	0-5
Nov 5th	1958	Charterhouse	lost	2-5 (Gibb 2)
Nov 4th	1959	Charterhouse	lost	1-5 (Taylor)
Nov 2nd	1960	Charterhouse	lost	0-2
Nov 8th	1961	Charterhouse	lost	1-5 (Gilliat)
Nov 7th	1962	Charterhouse	lost	1-5 (Hooper)
Nov 6th	1963	Charterhouse	won	4-2 (Randel 2, Hill, Weir)
Nov 4th	1964	Charterhouse	lost	1-6 (Hooper)
Nov 3rd	1965	Charterhouse	lost	1-4 (Easton)
Nov 9th	1966	Charterhouse	lost	0-9
Nov 6th	1968	Charterhouse	lost	2-3 (Foster, Grizelle)
Nov 5th	1969	Charterhouse	lost	0-1
Nov 4th	1970	Charterhouse	lost	2-4 (Stewart, Walton)
Nov 3rd	1971	Charterhouse	won	1-0 (Godby)
Oct 31st	1973	Charterhouse	won	5-0
Oct 30th	1974	Charterhouse	drew	2-2 (Walker, Adomakoh)
Nov 17th	1976	Charterhouse	won	1-0 (Cummins)
Nov 16th	1978	Charterhouse		

Oxford Goblins

Dec 3rd	1890	Charterhouse	drew	1-1 (Wilson)

Oxford OCs

Oct 25th	1890	Charterhouse	won	5-0 (Wilson 2, Smith 2, Hewitt)
Nov 7th	1891	Charterhouse	won	2-0 (Salt, Smith)
Dec 11th	1895	Charterhouse	lost	1-6 (Horne)
Dec 9th	1896	Charterhouse	lost	1-7 (Mucklow)
Feb 20th	1924	Charterhouse	won	4-2 (Rishworth 3, Fletcher)
Feb 11th	1925	Charterhouse	lost	0-3
Feb 9th	1927	Charterhouse	drew	2-2 (Fletcher 2)
Feb 15th	1928	Charterhouse	lost	1-2 (Fletcher)
Feb 7th	1934	Charterhouse	won	5-3 (Dowding 3, Tuckwell 2)

Balliol College Oxford

Oct 31st	1894	Charterhouse	won	2-1 (GW Ryder, Austen)
Nov 27th	1895	Charterhouse	won	2-1 (Haig Brown 2)

Brasenose College Oxford

Feb 11th	1920	Charterhouse	won	3-1 (Gilliat 3)
Feb 19th	1921	Charterhouse	won	3-0 (Gilliat 2, Bamber)
Feb 11th	1922	Charterhouse	won	1-0 (Bearman)
Feb 14th	1923	Charterhouse	lost	1-7 (Shute)
Oct 23rd	1946	Charterhouse	won	3-1 (Savill 3)
Nov 5th	1947	Charterhouse	won	3-0 (Whinney 2, Burt)
Nov 3rd	1948	Charterhouse	lost	2-3 (Whinney 2)
Nov 2nd	1949	Charterhouse	won	2-1 (Vansittart 2)
Nov 1st	1950	Charterhouse	drew	2-2 (Young, Pegler)

Christ Church Oxford

Nov 10th	1886	Charterhouse	won	2-0 (Gilliat, Price)
Feb 11th	1888	Charterhouse	lost	0-2
Feb 20th	1889	Charterhouse	won	4-0 (Woodhouse 2, Phelps, Smith)
Oct 21st	1905	Charterhouse	won	6-1 (Preston, Greig, Gooch 2, Parry 2)

Exeter College Oxford

Feb 24th	1892	Charterhouse	won	9-0 (Smith 3, Salt 5, Barwell)
Jan 27th	1906	Charterhouse	won	4-2 (Parry 3, Preston)
Feb 4th	1920	Charterhouse	won	6-5 (Gilliat 4, Cox, Wade)

Hertford College Oxford

Feb 25th	1920	Charterhouse	won	7-0 (Gilliat 4, Barnard 3)

Keble College Oxford

Nov 9th	1892	Charterhouse	won	4-0 (Fordyce, Vassall, Broadbent, Bray)

Magdalen College Oxford

Nov 7th	1883	Charterhouse	lost	0-1
Nov 5th	1884	Charterhouse	drew	0-0
Nov 18th	1885	Charterhouse	lost	1-2 (Leatham)
Nov 17th	1886	Charterhouse	lost	0-1
Nov 16th	1887	Charterhouse	drew	0-0
Oct 31st	1888	Charterhouse	won	1-0 (Pierce)
Oct 30th	1889	Charterhouse	drew	3-3 (Buzzard, Hewitt, Smith)
Feb 25th	1891	Charterhouse	won	10-0
Nov 28th	1891	Charterhouse	won	1-0 (Smith)
Nov 23rd	1892	Charterhouse	won	2-1 (Broadbent, Hunt)
Feb 22nd	1893	Charterhouse	won	3-1 (Hunt, Vassall, Broadbent)
Nov 10th	1894	Charterhouse	drew	0-0
Nov 20th	1895	Charterhouse	won	2-1 (GW Ryder 2)
Oct 21st	1896	Charterhouse	won	2-1 (Gordon, Moss)
Nov 13th	1897	Charterhouse	lost	1-4 (Crosdale)
Nov 16th	1898	Charterhouse	won	2-0 (Greenwood, Trower)
10th Feb	1900	Charterhouse	lost	1-5 (Trower)
9th Feb	1901	Charterhouse	won	8-0 (o.g., Tuff 4, Bense Pembroke 3)

12th Feb	1902	Charterhouse	lost	1-3 (Verry)
Mar 7th	1903	Charterhouse	lost	0-1
Mar 9th	1904	Charterhouse	won	2-1 (Taylor 2)
Feb 23rd	1907	Charterhouse	won	4-1 (Parry 2, Pegram, Evans)
Feb 21st	1914	Charterhouse	lost	3-5 (Ritchie, Smith 2)
Jan 31st	1920	Charterhouse	lost	1-7 (Mordaunt Smith)
Jan 29th	1921	Charterhouse	lost	1-3 (Gilliat)
Oct 22nd	1921	Charterhouse	lost	1-2 (Engelbach)
Oct 25th	1922	Charterhouse	drew	2-2 (Carter, Doresa)
Nov 7th	1923	Charterhouse	won	5-1 (Kemp Welch, Shute 4)
Nov 5th	1924	Charterhouse	won	2-0 (Kemp Welch, Sharp)
Feb 19th	1927	Charterhouse	won	1-0 (Wreford Brown)

New College Oxford

Nov 15th	1893	Charterhouse	won	4-1 (Neill 2, Hancock, Hunt)
Nov 7th	1894	Charterhouse	won	4-2 (Laird, Franks, Haig Brown, Wallace)
Nov 21st	1903	Charterhouse	drew	0-0

Oriel College Oxford

Feb 26th	1896	Charterhouse	won	4-2 (Vassall, Ryder 2, Buzzard)
Feb 17th	1897	Charterhouse	drew	4-4 (Gordon 2, Mucklow, Ryder)
Feb 5th	1898	Charterhouse	lost	2-6 (Moss 2)
Feb 4th	1899	Charterhouse	drew	2-2 (Tuff, Good)
Feb 28th	1900	Charterhouse	won	6-2 (Tuff 3, Gimson 2, Waller)
Mar 6th	1901	Charterhouse	won	6-1 (Tuff 4, Bense Pembroke, Goodliffe)
Feb 18th	1903	Charterhouse	won	1-0 (Bense Pembroke)
Feb 22nd	1905	Charterhouse	drew	2-2 (Cockburn, Reid)
Feb 21st	1906	Charterhouse	won	1-0 (Peet)
Feb 9th	1907	Charterhouse	won	5-0 (Pegram 3, Jameson, Gooch)
Feb 12th	1908	Charterhouse	won	1-0 (Pike)
Feb 24th	1909	Charterhouse	won	3-0 (Macdonald, Weeks, Johnson)
Mar 1st	1911	Charterhouse	won	3-1 (Wesley Smith, Boosey 2)
Nov 15th	1911	Charterhouse	won	9-0
Nov 26th	1919	Charterhouse	won	3-0 (o.g., Mordaunt Smith, Gilliat)
Jan 28th	1922	Charterhouse	lost	0-3
Feb 21st	1923	Charterhouse	lost	0-3
Feb 13th	1924	Charterhouse	won	4-2 (Murdoch 2, Fletcher 2)
Feb 25th	1925	Charterhouse	lost	2-4 (Kemp Welch 2)
Feb 23rd	1927	Charterhouse	lost	1-3 (Weatherall)

Trinity College Oxford

Dec 2nd	1891	Charterhouse	lost	0-2
Mar 6th	1895	Charterhouse	drew	2-2 (Jameson 2)
Mar 1st	1899	Charterhouse	won	6-0 (Trower, Evans 2, Greenwood, Liddle, Tuff)
Feb 18th	1905	Charterhouse	won	5-2 (Burton 2, Greig 2, Reid)
Feb 23rd	1921	Charterhouse	lost	2-3 (Barnard 2)
Nov 23rd	1921	Charterhouse	lost	0-2
Nov 24th	1948	Charterhouse	drew	3-3 (Gibbon, Kay, Whinney)
Nov 23rd	1949	Charterhouse	drew	1-1 (Agate)
Nov 8th	1950	Charterhouse	drew	2-2 (Pegler 2)
Dec 5th	1951	Charterhouse	won	3-1 (Tuck 2, Miller)
Dec 3rd	1952	Charterhouse	lost	2-3 (White, Miller)
Dec 2nd	1953	Charterhouse	won	3-1 (O'Brien, Lees, Pratt)
Dec 1st	1954	Charterhouse	lost	2-5 (Percival)
Nov 30th	1955	Charterhouse	lost	2-3 (Burrows, o.g.)
Feb 1st	1961	Charterhouse	won	1-0 (Lorenz)
Jan 29th	1964	Charterhouse	won	6-0 (Hooper 2, Weir 2, Bailhache, o.g.)

University College Oxford

Nov 16th	1892	Charterhouse	won	4-1 (Hunt, Vassall 3)

Worcester College Oxford

Feb 5th	1921	Charterhouse	won	9-1 (Gilliat 5, Barnard 2, Anderson, MacGusty)

MILITARY XIs

Aldershot Division

Mar 4th	1876	Charterhouse	won	1-0 (Tod)
Mar 25th	1876	Charterhouse	won	2-1 (Tod, Williams)

Argyll & S Highlanders

Oct 2nd	1915	Charterhouse	lost	0-6
Oct 30th	1915	Charterhouse	won	13-0 (Reiss 4, Tinley 4, Hall 4, Brownhill)

Army Crusaders

Mar 1st	1922	Charterhouse	won	2-1 (Doresa, Crump)
Feb 28th	1923	Charterhouse	won	3-2 (Fletcher, Shute 2)
Oct 10th	1923	Charterhouse	won	3-2 (Murdoch, Fletcher 2)
Oct 4th	1924	Charterhouse	lost	0-2
Oct 3rd	1925	Charterhouse	lost	0-2
Oct 2nd	1926	Charterhouse	lost	0-2
Oct 1st	1927	Charterhouse	lost	0-3
Oct 3rd	1928	Charterhouse	lost	0-3
Oct	1929	Charterhouse	lost	3-5 (Abrams, Stock, Matthews)
Oct 1st	1930	Charterhouse	won	4-2 (*rushed* 2, Samuelson, Paver)

Oct	1931	Charterhouse	lost	2-4 (Samuelson, Hunt)	
Sept 27th	1933	Charterhouse	lost	0-5	
Sept	1934	Charterhouse	won	4-2 (Yule, Daukes 2, Dunbar)	
Sept 28th	1935	Charterhouse	won	4-0 (Ades, Lomas, Hayes 2)	
Sept 26th	1936	Charterhouse	won	4-3 (Lomas 4)	
Dec 9th	1950	Charterhouse	drew	2-2 (Pegler, Gladstone)	
Dec 8th	1951	Charterhouse	lost	1-2 (Miller)	
Dec 5th	1953	Charterhouse	lost	1-2 (Lees)	
Dec 4th	1954	Charterhouse	drew	2-2 (Ruddock)	
Dec 3rd	1955	Charterhouse	lost	1-3 (Steed)	
Oct 24th	1956	Charterhouse	lost	1-2 (Sparshatt)	
Oct 23rd	1957	Charterhouse	lost	1-5 (Agace)	
Oct 22nd	1958	Charterhouse	lost	4-6 (Gibb 2, Visser, Craig)	
Jan 31st	1959	Charterhouse	drew	4-4 (Gibb 2, Topham 2)	
Oct 21st	1959	Charterhouse	lost	1-3 (Lamaison)	
Oct 19th	1960	Charterhouse	lost	1-3 (Arnold)	
Oct 25th	1961	Charterhouse	won	3-2 (Arnold, o.g.2)	
Oct 24th	1962	Charterhouse	won	3-1 (Gilliat 2, Proud)	
Oct 23rd	1963	Charterhouse	won	3-2 (Drayson, Hooper, Weir)	
Oct 21st	1964	Charterhouse	won	6-2 (Weir 3, Easton, Hooper, Samuelson)	
Oct 20th	1965	Charterhouse	drew	1-1 (Easton)	
Oct 19th	1966	Charterhouse	won	2-0 (Bennett, Provis)	
Oct 18th	1967	Charterhouse	won	6-1 (Bennett 3, Deans, Provis, Cohn)	
Oct 16th	1968	Charterhouse	drew	3-3	

Army PT School
Nov 25th	1939	Charterhouse	won	4-1 (Larking, Finlayson, Tanner, Figg)

Artists' Rifles
Dec 5th	1914	Charterhouse	won	3-1 (Ritchie, Hansell, Paull)
Oct 18th	1916	Charterhouse	won	6-3 (Williams 6)

Canadian Field Artillery
Sept 25th	1918	Charterhouse	won	1-0 (Gilliat)

Canadian Field Engineers
Oct 2nd	1918	Charterhouse	lost	1-4 (Williams)

Canadian Brigade Artillery
Oct 9th	1918	Charterhouse	lost	0-3

125th Canadian Bttn
Feb 13th	1918	Charterhouse	won	4-0 (Williams, Whalley, Thorne 2)

Coldstream Guards
Oct 11th	1941	Charterhouse	lost	0-6
Dec 17th	1941	Charterhouse	drew	3-3
Nov 7th	1942	Charterhouse	won	5-3 (Godden 2, Spratt, Dalgety, Sword)
Dec 19th	1942	Charterhouse	lost	0-1

Dennis Athletic (Munitions)
April 1st	1916	Charterhouse	lost	1-2
Sept 30th	1916	Charterhouse	won	5-1 (Lewns, Gauntlett 2, Tinley 2)
Sept 29th	1917	Charterhouse	won	10-0 (Williams)

2nd Devonshire Regt
Nov 25th	1933	Charterhouse	lost	2-6

Drummond Athletic
Oct 9th	1915	Charterhouse	won	8-0 (Reiss, Dunlop 2, Tinley 3, Hall 2)

Duke of Cornwall's Light Infantry
Dec 9th	1908	Charterhouse	lost	0-1
Mar 5th	1910	Charterhouse	won	4-0 (Polson 2, Norris, Boosey)
Nov 23rd	1910	Charterhouse	won	3-0 (Boosey 2, Gjers)
Nov 22nd	1911	Charterhouse	drew	1-1

Gibraltar Barracks
Sept 13th	1981	Charterhouse	lost	3-4 (Gard, Davis, Challen)
Sept 12th	1982	Gibraltar Barracks	drew	2-2 (Proctor, Ibru)

Hants Regt
Mar 18th	1916	Charterhouse	won	5-2

London Yeomanry
Jan 25th	1941	Charterhouse	won	3-1 (Lahaye, Figg, Lovett)

5th Middlesex Regt
Jan 30th	1918	Charterhouse	lost	1-2

Mons OCTS
Feb 9th	1955	Charterhouse	lost	2-5 (Forsyth, Tunnock)
Sept 30th	1959	Charterhouse	lost	0-2
Oct 1st	1960	Charterhouse	won	4-0 (Powell 4)

OCB Bushey
Nov 16th	1918	Charterhouse	lost	1-2

OCD Eastbourne
Oct 12th	1918	Charterhouse	won	6-2

Queen's Bttn.
Nov 2nd	1940	Charterhouse	won	3-2 (Spencer 2, Hawley)

Queen's Royal Regt
Feb 8th	1941	Charterhouse	drew	2-2 (Lovett 2)
Feb 6th	1943	Charterhouse	won	3-1 (Crole-Rees 2, Wells)
Jan 31st	1942	Charterhouse	won	4-2

The Queen's Regt
Feb 11th	1914	Charterhouse	won	3-2 (Smith 2, Reiss)
Nov 3rd	1915	Charterhouse	won	5-2 (Hall, Reiss 2)

RA Subalterns
2nd Nov	1901	Charterhouse	won	1-0 (Kelly)

RAC Blackdown
Oct 2nd	1943	Charterhouse	drew	2-2 (Godden 2)
Jan 22nd	1944	Charterhouse	won	4-2 (Crole-Rees 2, Godden mi, Spratt)

RASC
Nov 20th	1940	RASC Training Btn	won	3-2 (Spencer, Figg, Evans)
Nov 23rd	1940	RASC Dorking	won	2-1 (Milne, Figg)
Feb 1st	1941	RASC Training Btn	won	9-3 (Evans 5, Figg, Hawley, Nesbitt, Lahaye)
Feb 22nd	1941	RASC Aldershot	lost	3-6 (Lahaye 2, Lovett)
Oct 4th	1941	RASC	won	2-1 (Lovett, Larking)
Oct 10th	1942	RASC Aldershot	lost	1-7 (Dalgety)
Nov 21st	1942	RASC Aldershot	drew	3-3 (Stevenson 2, Sword)
Nov 6th	1943	RASC Aldershot	lost	3-8 (Spratt 2, Pollock)
Oct 21st	1944	RASC	lost	2-6 (Vlasto, Wilson)
Jan 20th	1945	RASC	lost	0-1
Oct 15th	1952	RASC	lost	2-5 (Miller, White)
Jan 28th	1953	1st Trg Btn RASC	won	5-0 (Miller 3, Pratt, Knox)
Sept 24th	1955	1st Trg Btn RASC	lost	1-6 (Steed)

RFA
Nov 14th	1914	Charterhouse	won	8-1 (Hansell 4, Paull 3, Dunlop)

RGA Aldershot
Oct 6th	1917	Charterhouse	won	3-0
Oct 27th	1917	Charterhouse	lost	3-7

RMC Sandhurst
Mar 9th	1878	Charterhouse	lost	1-3 (Stubbs)
Nov 9th	1878	Charterhouse	won	4-2 (Richards, Jenner, Wilson, Burdon)
Mar 1st	1879	Charterhouse	won	5-2 (Vincent, Pollock, Guinness, Wilson 2)
Nov 8th	1879	Charterhouse	lost	1-2 (Rayner)
Mar 13th	1880	Charterhouse	won	3-2 (Vyvyan 2, *squash*)
Nov 6th	1880	Charterhouse	won	5-0 (Henley, *squash*, Escombe, Vintcent, Morrison)
Mar 12th	1881	Charterhouse	won	1-0 (*squash*)
Nov 5th	1881	Charterhouse	won	5-0 (King Harman 2, Henley, Cobbold, Vintcent)
Mar 11th	1882	Charterhouse	won	6-2 (Eddis 2, Cobbold 3, Vintcent)
Nov 11th	1882	Charterhouse	won	5-0 (Eddis 2, Steward, McNeill, C Vintcent)
Nov 17th	1883	Charterhouse	lost	2-3 (Steward 2)
Mar 1st	1884	Charterhouse	won	3-0 (Waddington 2, Brown)
Nov 15th	1884	Charterhouse	won	1-0 (Price)
Feb 13th	1886	Charterhouse	won	5-0 (Stanbrough 2, Nixon, Currey 2)
Mar 26th	1887	Charterhouse	won	2-0 (Earle, Stanbrough)
Nov 26th	1887	Charterhouse	won	2-0 (Furber, Gilliat)
Nov 24th	1888	Charterhouse	drew	1-1 (Barker)
Nov 23rd	1889	Charterhouse	drew	2-2 (Armstrong, Hewitt)
Nov 8th	1890	Charterhouse	won	4-3 (Wilson 3, Hewitt)
Nov 21st	1891	Charterhouse	drew	1-1 (Salt)
Nov 19th	1892	Charterhouse	won	4-1 (Vassall 2, Broadbent, Hunt)
Nov 25th	1893	Charterhouse	won	7-2 (Hunt 5, Hancock, Jameson)
Oct 27th	1894	Charterhouse	lost	0-2
Oct 19th	1895	Charterhouse	lost	2-4 (Jameson, Horne)
Oct 24th	1896	Charterhouse	won	7-1 (Moss 2, Ryder, Renshaw, Vassall 2)
Dec 4th	1897	Charterhouse	won	7-3
Nov 26th	1898	Charterhouse	won	13-1 (Tuff 4 Gibson 3 Evans 3 Trower, Leechman, Gardner)
25th Nov	1899	Charterhouse	won	6-1 (Waller 3, Gardner, Tuff, Trower)
20th Oct	1900	Charterhouse	won	2-1 (Tuff 2)
26th Oct	1901	Charterhouse	won	3-0 (Goodliffe, Bense Pembroke, Bowring)
Oct 25th	1902	Charterhouse	won	3-0 (Dowson 2, Snell)
Oct 25th	1903	Charterhouse	drew	1-1 (Allen)
Dec 3rd	1904	Charterhouse	drew	1-1 (Pears)
Dec 2nd	1905	Charterhouse	drew	1-1 (Preston)
Nov 24th	1906	Charterhouse	won	2-1 (Preston, Gooch)

Date	Year	Venue	Result	Score
Nov 2nd	1907	Charterhouse	won	5-1 (Pike 4, Wilson)
Oct 31st	1908	Charterhouse	won	4-1 (Weeks 3, Macdonald)
Oct 9th	1909	Charterhouse	drew	2-2 (Boosey, Norris)
Oct 8th	1910	Charterhouse	won	1-0 (Dunlop)
Mar 4th	1911	Charterhouse	lost	0-1
Oct 28th	1911	Charterhouse	won	2-1 (de Bernière Smith 2)
Feb 28th	1912	Charterhouse	won	4-1 (Letten, Ford 3)
Oct 9th	1912	Charterhouse	lost	3-4 (Payne, Rücker, Hinds)
Mar 5th	1913	Charterhouse	lost	1-2 (Rücker)
Oct 8th	1913	Charterhouse	lost	1-3 (Burnett)
Dec 19th	1914	Charterhouse	won	6-0 (Spafford, Hansell 3, Hall, Ritchie)
Mar 6th	1915	Charterhouse	won	6-3 (Butcher, Edge, Dunlop 3, Hansell)
Mar 17th	1915	Charterhouse	won	6-0 (Hansell 4, Dunlop, Reiss)
Oct 13th	1915	Charterhouse	lost	4-7 (Brownhill 2, Reiss, Tinley)
Dec 1st	1915	Charterhouse	lost	4-5 (Reiss 2, Tinley, Bell)
Oct 14th	1916	Charterhouse	won	4-3 (Williams 2, Bearman, Tinley)
Oct 21st	1916	Charterhouse	won	10-1 (Tinley 5, Williams 3, Bearman 2)
Feb 6th	1918	Charterhouse	won	3-1 (Williams 3)
Oct 15th	1919	Charterhouse	lost	1-5 (Gilliat)
Feb 7th	1920	Charterhouse	won	4-3 (Gilliat 4)
Oct 20th	1920	Charterhouse	lost	2-3 (Barnard, MacGusty)
Feb 16th	1921	Charterhouse	won	3-0 (Gilliat 2, Bamber)
Feb 15th	1922	Charterhouse	won	2-0 (o.g., Harvie)
Oct 28th	1922	Charterhouse	lost	2-4 (Fletcher, Doresa)
Oct 24th	1923	Charterhouse	drew	1-1 (Fletcher)
Oct 22nd	1924	Charterhouse	lost	0-4
Oct 21st	1925	Charterhouse	lost	0-10
Oct 20th	1926	Charterhouse	lost	1-4 (Fletcher)
Oct 19th	1927	Charterhouse	lost	2-7 (Bruce Jones, Robertson)
Oct 10th	1928	Charterhouse	won	3-1 (Craddock, Spencer, Jeavons)
Oct	1929	Charterhouse	drew	2-2 (Middleton, o.g.)
Oct 4th	1930	Charterhouse	drew	0-0
Oct	1931	Charterhouse	lost	1-6 (JC Moss)
Oct 4th	1933	Charterhouse	won	6-4 (Trapman, Tuckwell 4, Frith)
Oct	1934	Charterhouse	won	4-2 (Dowding, Dunbar 2, Daukes)
Oct 2nd	1935	Charterhouse	lost	1-3 (Lomas)
Oct 7th	1936	Charterhouse	lost	1-2 (Lomas)
Oct 7th	1939	Charterhouse	lost	1-2
Feb 12th	1944	Charterhouse	lost	1-5 (Crole-Rees)
Oct 1st	1947	Charterhouse	lost	0-2
Sept 28th	1949	Charterhouse	drew	1-1 (Frankland)
Sept 27th	1950	Charterhouse	won	3-0 (Gladsotne 2, Yannaghas)
Sept 26th	1951	Charterhouse	lost	0-3
Sept 24th	1952	Charterhouse	drew	2-2 (White, Miller)
Sept 27th	1952	Charterhouse	won	3-2 (Knox, Arnsby-Wilson 2)
Oct 14th	1953	Charterhouse	lost	1-2 (Buckley)
Oct 13th	1954	Charterhouse	drew	1-1 (Ruddock)
Oct 12th	1955	Charterhouse	lost	0-4
Oct 10th	1956	Charterhouse	won	2-1 (Burrows, Sparshatt)
Oct 9th	1957	Charterhouse	lost	0-5
Oct 8th	1958	Charterhouse	lost	1-4 (Topham)
Oct 7th	1959	Charterhouse	lost	0-3
Oct 12th	1960	Charterhouse	lost	2-3 (Powell 2)
Oct 11th	1961	Charterhouse	drew	2-2 (Hopkins, de Grunwald)
Oct 10th	1962	Charterhouse	won	4-2 (Proud 3, Gilliat)
Oct 9th	1963	Charterhouse	lost	1-5 (Drayson)
Oct 7th	1964	Charterhouse	won	1-0 (Weir)
Oct 6th	1965	Charterhouse	lost	0-2
Oct 5th	1966	Charterhouse	won	1-0 (Bennett)
Oct 4th	1967	Charterhouse	drew	2-2 (Bennett, Deans)
Sept 25th	1968	Charterhouse	lost	1-2
Sept 24th	1969	Charterhouse	lost	0-3
Sept 23rd	1970	Charterhouse	lost	1-4 (Walton)

Sandhurst 'A'

Date	Year	Venue	Result	Score
Sept 29th	1948	Charterhouse	lost	0-3

Sandhurst OCTU

Date	Year	Venue	Result	Score
Dec 4th	1940	Charterhouse	won	4-0 (Spencer 2, Evans 2)
Nov 8th	1941	OCTU Sandhurst	lost	1-5 (Hogg)
Feb 11th	1942	Charterhouse	drew	0-0
Oct 31st	1942	Charterhouse	lost	0-4
Oct 9th	1943	Charterhouse	lost	0-6
Dec 9th	1944	Charterhouse	won	7-6 (Spratt 3, Godden 2, Price 2)
Jan 26th	1946	Charterhouse	lost	0-4

RMA Woolwich

Date	Year	Venue	Result	Score
Nov 30th	1895	Charterhouse	won	2-0 (Moss, Scott)
Nov 2nd	1898	Charterhouse	won	4-2 (Wild, Gibson 2, Trower)
1st Nov	1899	Charterhouse	won	4-1 (Waller, Tuff, Gardner, Trower)
24th Nov	1900	Charterhouse	lost	1-2 (Tuff)
19th Oct	1901	Charterhouse	drew	1-1 (Bense Pembroke)
Oct 19th	1902	Charterhouse	won	2-0 (Bense Pembroke, Tetley)
Oct 17th	1903	Charterhouse	won	2-1 (Taylor, Allen)
Oct 22nd	1904	Charterhouse	lost	0-1
Oct 7th	1905	Charterhouse	won	5-2 (Greig 2, Parry, Preston, Tillie)
Oct 6th	1906	Charterhouse	won	7-0 (Parry 2, Pegram, Wardle, Preston 2, Gooch)
Oct 6th	1907	Charterhouse	won	5-0 (Pike 3, Livesey, Wilson)

Date	Year	Venue	Result	Score
Oct 10th	1908	Charterhouse	drew	1-1 (Weeks)
Oct 27th	1909	Charterhouse	won	11-0 (Boosey 5, Bruce 2, Dixon 3, Norris)
Oct 26th	1910	Charterhouse	won	4-2 (Dunlop, Booosey, Faulkner, Sidebotham)
Oct 25th	1911	Charterhouse	won	2-0 (Liddle, Wright)
Oct 30th	1912	Charterhouse	lost	2-3 (Payne, Chambers)
Oct 29th	1913	Charterhouse	lost	0-3
Oct 25th	1916	Charterhouse	won	5-2 (Bearman 2, Butcher, Tinley 2)
Oct 25th	1919	Charterhouse	drew	2-2 (Gilliat 2)
Feb 14th	1920	Charterhouse	won	4-0 (Barnard, Austin, Gilliat 2)
Nov 13th	1920	Charterhouse	won	3-1 (Anderson 2, Gilliat)
Nov 12th	1921	Charterhouse	lost	1-5 (Doresa)
Nov 29th	1922	Charterhouse	lost	0-2
Dec 3rd	1924	Charterhouse	lost	0-1

RMC 'C' Company

Date	Year	Venue	Result	Score
Oct 5th	1929	Charterhouse	drew	3-3 (Greening 3)

Royal Artillery

Date	Year	Venue	Result	Score
Nov 22nd	1902	Charterhouse	drew	2-2 (Snell 2)

Royal Engineers

Date	Year	Venue	Result	Score
OQ	1868	Middlesex County ground	drew	1-1 (Povah)
Nov 17th	1869	Charterhouse	lost	2-3 (Smith, Inglis)
Mar 5th	1870	Charterhouse	drew	0-0
Nov 30th	1870	The Oval	lost	0-5
Feb 1st	1882	Charterhouse	won	2-0 (Vintcent, Rayner)
Feb 14th	1883	Charterhouse	won	6-2 (C Vintcent 2, L Vintcent, Brookes 3)
Feb 13th	1884	Charterhouse	won	3-0 (Kerr, Brown, Walker)
Feb 11th	1885	Charterhouse	won	1-0 (Currey)
Mar 13th	1886	Charterhouse	won	5-0 (Currey 2, Nixon, Sheppard, Price)
Feb 26th	1887	Charterhouse	won	1-0 (Furber)
Mar 7th	1888	Charterhouse	drew	4-4 (Stanbrough, Dickinson 2, Dashwood)
Mar 13th	1889	Charterhouse	won	7-1 (Stanbrough 3, Woodhouse 2, Smith, Halsted)
Feb 19th	1890	Charterhouse	won	8-0 (Hewitt 3, Smith, Buzzard 2, Wade 2)
Feb 14th	1903	Charterhouse	won	6-0 (Barbour, Bense Pembroke, Snell 3, Branston)
Oct 11th	1939	Charterhouse	drew	3-3
Oct 21st	1939	Charterhouse	won	3-0
Oct 5th	1940	Charterhouse	won	9-0 (Hawley 3, Spencer 6)
Nov 30th	1940	Charterhouse	won	3-1 (Hawley 2, Spencer)
Feb 21st	1942	Charterhouse	lost	0-2
Dec 5th	1942	Charterhouse	won	3-1
Nov 27th	1943	Charterhouse	lost	0-3

RAF Gatwick

Date	Year	Venue	Result	Score
Feb 12th	1941	Charterhouse	lost	1-4 (Lovett)

RAF Horley

Date	Year	Venue	Result	Score
Nov 1st	1941	Charterhouse	won	3-2 (Lomas, Evans 2)

Royal Horse Artillery

Date	Year	Venue	Result	Score
Feb 18th	1942	Charterhouse	lost	0-3

Scots Cyclists

Date	Year	Venue	Result	Score
Feb 27th	1915	Charterhouse	won	5-0 (Hansell 2, Reiss 2, Pollock)

Sherwood Foresters

Date	Year	Venue	Result	Score
Nov 27th	1915	Charterhouse	won	2-0 (Reiss, Tinley)

The HAC

Date	Year	Venue	Result	Score
Nov 4th	1916	Charterhouse	lost	2-3 (Gauntlett 2)
Oct 17th	1925	Charterhouse	drew	4-4 (Palmer, Soole, Connell 2)
Oct 16th	1926	Charterhouse	lost	1-2 (Nicholson)
Oct 15th	1927	Charterhouse	lost	3-5 (Robertson, Fletcher, o.g.)
Oct 13th	1928	Charterhouse	won	7-2 (Craddock 3, Fletcher 3, Jeavons)
Oct 12th	1929	Charterhouse	drew	2-2 (o.g., Hulton)
Oct 11th	1930	Charterhouse	won	8-2 (Samuelson 4, Pope 2, Moss, Paver)
Oct	1931	Charterhouse	won	2-1 (JC Moss, WF Moss)
Oct 14th	1933	Charterhouse	won	3-1 (Trapman, Field 2)
Oct	1934	Charterhouse	won	5-1
Oct	1935	Charterhouse	won	8-0 (Hayes, Dunbar 4, Greene, Dowding 2)
Oct 10th	1936	Charterhouse	won	6-2 (Lomas 4, MacCunn 2)

4th Reserve Battalion Witley

Date	Year	Venue	Result	Score
Oct 23rd	1918	Charterhouse	lost	2-3

8th Rifles

Date	Year	Venue	Result	Score
Feb 16th	1946	Charterhouse	lost	3-7 (Howard, Wilson, Savill)

8th "The Buffs"

Date	Year	Venue	Result	Score
Nov 21st	1914	Charterhouse	won	5-0 (Harvie 3, Hansell 2)

Tenth Regiment

OQ	1875	Charterhouse	won	7-1 (Short 2, Burrows, Tod 3, o.g)

60th Rifles

Mar 27th	1915	Charterhouse	drew	3-3 (Ritchie, Dunlop 2)

105th Regiment

Feb	1876	Charterhouse	won	4-0 (Short, Keightley, Tod, Reeve)

Chelsea Sea Cadets

Nov 13th	1943	Charterhouse	lost	0-2
Oct 7th	1944	Charterhouse	drew	0-0
Nov 10th	1944	Charterhouse	drew	2-2 (Spratt, Whettem)

Navy XI

Dec 6th	1941	Charterhouse	lost	1-7 (Evans)

SELECT XIs made up from OCs, members of Brooke Hall and Friends of the school

Nov 26th	1862	GH Shaw's XI	won	1-0 (Somerset)
Dec 3rd	1862	GH Shaw's XI	drew	0-0
Feb 8th	1863	HH Gilbert's XI	won	4-1 (Lant, Hodgson, Hartshorne, O'Grady)*in cloisters*
Mar 18th	1863	HC Malkin's XI	drew	0-0
Feb 27th	1864	H Malkin's XI	won	2-0 (Makenzie, Hodgson)
Mar 2nd	1864	F Giles' XI	drew	0-0
Oct 12th	1864	M Mackenzie's IX	won	4-0 *9-a-side*
Nov 2nd	1864	HC Malkin's XI	won	3-1 (Ogden, O'Grady, Mackenzie)
Jan 25th	1865	K Mackenzie's XI	drew	2-2 (Mackenzie 2)
Mar 4th	1865	FG Pelham's XI	won	1-0 (Ogden)
Oct 25th	1865	HC Malkin's XI	won	1-0 (Middleton)
Nov 1st	1865	J Wearne's XI	won	1-0 (Walford)
Jan 28th	1866	AF Kinnaird's XI	lost	1-2
Feb 7th	1866	F Pownall's XI	won	1-0 (Mackenzie)
Oct 10th	1866	J Wearne's XII	drew	1-1 (Nepean)
Oct 24th	1866	CW Allcock's XI	won	2-0 (Nepean, Walford)
Oct 31st	1866	J Butter's XI	won	3-0 (Nepean 2, Venables)
Jan 26th	1867	AF Kinnaird's XI	drew	0-0
Feb 6th	1867	J Butter's XI	won	4-0 (Mammatt, Venables, Nepean 2)
Feb 6th	1868	CW Allcock's XI	won	2-0 (Hammick, Venables) *played in cloisters*
Oct 3rd	1869	CW Allcock's XI	won	3-0 (Nepean 2, Cameron)
Mar 23rd	1870	CF Reid's XI	won	2-1 (Bushnell, Smith)
Oct 5th	1870	CW Allcock's XI	lost	1-3 (Inglis)
Oct 4th	1871	CW Alcock's XI	won	3-2 (Staveley, Williams, Paget) *12 a side*
Oct 4th	1873	JC Merryman's XI	won	2-0 (Parry, Williams)
OQ	1874	EH Parry's XI	won	3-2 (Southwell 2, Short)
Oct 14th	1876	C Haig Brown's XI	won	8-2 (Page, Hayter 2, Keightley, Eddis 2, Williams, Boscawen)
Oct 21st	1876	EM Short's XI	won	5-1 (Page 3, Eddis, Keightley)
Nov 7th	1877	WR Page's XI	drew	1-1 (Evan-Thomas)
Nov 26th	1877	EH Parry's XI	lost	0-2
Dec 12th	1877	NJ Abdy's XI	won	5-2 (Keith Falconer, Burdon 2, Frith, Medlicott)
Dec 15th	1877	WW Drew's XI	won	2-1 (Burdon, Hansell)
Sept 28th	1878	WW Drew's XI	won	4-0 (Wilson, Richards, Jenner, Hansell)
Nov 13th	1878	WTB Hayter's XI	drew	2-2 (Hansell, Jenner)
Nov 30th	1878	JFM Prinsep's XI	won	4-3 (Burdon 2, Hansell, Wilson)
Feb 12th	1879	CM Burdon's XI	won	6-2 (Jackson, Richards 2, Guinness, Pollock, Vyvyan)
Feb 18th	1880	CM Burdon's XI	drew	1-1 (Vyvyan)
Jan 29th	1881	HA Carter's XI	drew	1-1 (Morrison)
Oct 8th	1881	J Vintcent's XI	won	4-3 (Vintcent, Eddis 2, Brown)
Oct 22nd	1881	WH Norris' XI	won	2-0 (Eddis [*charged through* by Rayner], Henley)
Jan 28th	1882	WG Morrison's XI	won	7-0 (Vintcent, Spurway, Cautley 2, Rayner 2, Henley)
Mar 8th	1882	ET Hardman's XI	won	2-1 (Henley, Cobbold)
Oct 7th	1882	Rev CC Tancock's XI	won	7-2 (Eddis 2, Messent 2, C Vintcent 2, L Vincent)
Sept 29th	1883	Rev CC Tancock's XI	won	5-2 (Ponsonby 3, Pearce, C Vintcent)
Oct 6th	1883	WN Cobbold's XI	drew	1-1 (Brown)
Dec 15th	1883	TW Blenkiron's XI	drew	1-1 (Walker)
Feb 2nd	1884	FW Sewell's XI	won	5-0 (Walker, Brown, Vintcent 2, Waddington)
Mar 26th	1884	WN Cobbold's XI	won	2-0 (Vintcent 2)
Oct 4th	1884	Rev CC Tancock's XI	won	2-1 (Wreford Brown, Price)
Oct 15th	1884	J Vintcent's XI	won	2-0 ((Price, Martyn)
Mar 11th	1885	AJ Webbe's XI	lost	0-1
Oct 3rd	1885	Rev CC Tancock's XI	won	5-1 (Wreford Brown 3, Currey, Price)
Dec 2nd	1885	AK Henley's XI	won	1-0 (Currey)
Feb 17th	1886	R Escombe's XI	won	3-0 (Pim 2, Stanbrough)
Sept 25th	1886	G Ashby's XI	won	6-0 (Earle 2, Price 2, Leman, Gilliat)
Oct 2nd	1886	AH Tod's XI	won	2-0 (Price 2)
Nov 6th	1886	CH Tyler's XI	won	2-1 (Pim, Price)
Jan 29th	1887	AC Nixon's XI	lost	1-3 (Gilliat)
Mar 9th	1887	E Escombe's XI	won	5-0 (Furber 3, Leman, Dickinson)
Oct 1st	1887	AH Tod's XI	won	2-0 (Gilliat, Furber)
Nov 19th	1887	HJ Carson's XI	won	4-2 (Furber 2, Gilliat, Stanbrough)
Dec 14th	1887	WN Cobbold's XI	lost	2-4 (Gilliat, Furber)
Sept 26th	1888	AH Tod'sXII	lost	1-6 (Woodhouse)
Dec 12th	1888	WN Cobbold's XI	won	9-1 (Rayner 4, Stanbrough 2, Pierce, Woodhouse, Bliss)
Sept 28th	1889	AH Tod's XI	won	2-1 (Halsted, Armstrong)
Oct 26th	1889	FS Tewson's XI	won	6-1 (Halsted, Buzzard, Armstrong 2, Head, Hewitt)
Feb 18th	1890	Prince Christian Victor's XI	won	5-1 (Buzzard 3, Wade, Hewitt)
Mar 12th	1890	D Crossman's XI	won	5-2 (Buzzard 2, Smith 2, Wilson)
Oct 4th	1890	AH Tod's XI	won	9-0 (Wade 4, Kirby, Merriman 2, Hewitt 2)
Oct 29th	1890	MH Stanbrough's XI	won	2-0 (Hewitt 2)
Oct 7th	1891	AH Tod's XI	lost	2-3 (Smith, Salt)
Dec 5th	1891	WN Cobbold's XI	won	3-2 (Salt, Foster, Winch)
Feb 10th	1892	WE Hansell's XI	won	2-1 (Salt, Smith)
Sept 24th	1892	AH Tod's XI	lost	1-5 (Ward)
Dec 15th	1892	EC Bliss's XI	lost	0-1
Oct 7th	1893	AD Fordyce's XI	won	1-0 (Fordyce)
Dec 2nd	1893	WN Cobbold's XI	won	1-0 (Fordyce)
Dec 6th	1893	EC Bliss's XI	lost	2-4 (Vassall, Jameson)
Sept 29th	1894	AH Tod's XI	won	2-0 (GW Ryder 2)
Sept 28th	1895	AH Tod's XI	lost	1-11 (Vassall)
Mar 7th	1896	AD Forsyth's XI	lost	1-3 (Vassall)
Sept 26th	1896	AH Tod's XI	won	3-2 (Moss, Vassall, Mucklow)
Nov 24th	1896	WAE Austen's XI	won	4-3 (Vassall, Gimson, Gordon Mucklow)
Dec 2nd	1896	WN Cobbold's XI	lost	1-3 (Mucklow)
Feb 24th	1897	NL Jackson's XI	won	4-1 (Mucklow, Ryder, Gordon, Moss)
Oct 9th	1897	AH Tod's XI	lost	1-9 (Moss)
Dec 15th	1897	GC Vassall'sXI	lost	2-3
Feb 19th	1898	LB Coulson's XI	won	8-1 (Trower 2, Moss, Evans, Crosdale 3, Routh)
Sept 24th	1898	AH Tod's XI	lost	2-5 (Sturrock, Trower)
Dec 14th	1898	GC Vassall's XI	lost	0-6
Dec 19th	1898	GO Smith's XI	lost	1-3 (Greenwood)
Feb 15th	1899	CF Ryder's XI	won	5-2 (Flower 2, Tuff 3)
Feb 22nd	1899	RF Evans's XI	drew	4-4 (Sturrock 2, Trower, Evans)
Sept 30th	1899	AH Tod's XI	drew	0-0
Dec 6th	1899	WN Cobbold's XI	lost	1-4 (Waller)
Dec 17th	1899	H Crabtree's XI	lost	0-2
Mar 10th	1900	MFR Wingfield's XI	won	4-2 (Trower, Malden, Gimson 2)
Sept 29th	1900	AH Tod's XI	lost	1-6 (Tuff)
Oct 6th	1900	RAB Trower's XI	won	4-1 (Tuff 4)
Nov 28th	1900	JM Hulton's XI	won	5-0 (Ferguson, o.g., Curwen 2, Bowring)
Mar 16th	1901	CH Wilson's XI	lost	1-5 (Bowring)
Sept 28th	1901	AH Tod's XI	lost	0-7
Sept 27th	1902	AH Tod's XI	drew	1-1 (Dowson)
Feb 4th	1903	WJH Curwen's XI	won	4-1 (Bense Pembroke 2, Tetley, Seth Smith)
Sept 26th	!903	AH Tod's XI	lost	1-2 (Taylor)
Jan 30th	1904	RA Bense Pembroke's XI	drew	1-1 (Taylor)
Mar 5th	1904	OT Norris's XI	won	3-2 (Walker 2, Johnston)
Oct 1st	1904	AH Tod's XI	lost	2-5 (Pears, Lyell)
Dec 10th	1904	BH Willett's XI	won	2-0 (Rücker, Mackwood)
Sept 30th	1905	AH Tod's XI	lost	1-7 (Greig)
Dec 16th	1905	AA Drew's XI	drew	1-1 (Tillie)
Oct 10th	1906	AH Tod's XI	lost	0-9
Dec 8th	1906	AA Drew's XI	won	2-0 (Braddell, o.g.)
Dec 19th	1906	C Wreford Brown's XI	lost	0-5 *played at Queen's Club*
Sept 28th	1907	AH Tod's XI	lost	0-7 *played as the opening of Broom & Lees*
Oct 12th	1907	RD England's XI	won	4-1 (Wilson, Pike 2, Livesey)
Dec 7th	1907	BH Willett's XI	lost	1-2 (Livesey)
Dec 10th	1907	JHD Sheppard's XI	won	2-0 (Livesey, Wilson)
Feb 8th	1908	CT Gooch's XI	drew	2-2 (Rushton, Pike)
Mar 4th	1908	CD White's XI	won	4-1 (Weeks, Pike, Livesey 2)
Oct 3rd	1908	AH Tod's XI	lost	3-5 (Norris, Weeks)
Nov 4th	1908	PC Smythe's XI	won	6-2 (Weeks 3, Macdonald 3)
Dec 5th	1908	BH Willett's XI	won	1-0 (Johnson)
Oct 2nd	1909	AH Tod's XI	lost	1-8 (Bruce)
Nov 13th	1909	CB Johnson's XI	lost	0-1
Dec 4th	1909	BH Willett's XI	lost	0-2
Feb 12th	1910	S Baker's XI	won	3-0 (Polson 2, Dixon)
Oct 1st	1910	AH Tod's XI	drew	2-2 (Boosey, Dunlop)
Nov 19th	1910	BH Willett's XI	drew	3-3 (Boosey, Sanderson, Dunlop)
Oct 7th	1911	AH Tod's XI	lost	0-2
Nov 11th	1911	L Gjers' XI	won	3-0 (Vernon, o.g., Ford)
Sept 28th	1912	AH Tod's XI	lost	1-4 (Liddle)
Oct 5th	1912	R Boosey's XI	lost	1-3 (Liddle)
Nov 23rd	1912	NE Burdon's XI	drew	2-2 (Gregson Ellis, Hinds)
Feb 8th	1913	BH Willett's XI	lost	0-1
Sept 27th	1913	AH Tod's XI	lost	2-4 (Gray, Griffith)
Nov 15th	1913	BH Willett's XI	drew	4-4 (Gray, Smith 3)
Dec 6th	1913	HD Vernon's XI	won	4-2 (Ritchie, Cawston, Hinds 2)

Oct 3rd	1914	BH Willett's XI	won	4-1 (Dunlop 2, Harvie 2)
Feb 12th	1916	GV Hind's XI	won	7-0 (Reiss 4, Garth, Tinley, South)
Mar 4th	1916	JCD Tetley's XI	lost	1-2 (Brownhill)
Mar	1917	C Wreford Brown's	won	6-1
Oct 18th	1919	E Cawston's XI	won	8-2 (Gilliat 3, Mordaunt Smith, Wade)
Dec 6th	1919	JM Wells' XI	lost	2-9 (Austin 2)
Sept 25th	1920	Rev EM Jameson's	won	7-1 (Gilliat 6, Barnard)
Oct 2nd	1920	AH Tod's XI	drew	2-2 (Gilliat, Anderson)
Sept 24th	1921	Rev EM Jameson's	won	3-1 (Bearman, Kiggell, Doresa)
Sept 30th	1922	Rev EM Jameson's	lost	2-4 (Morgan, Fletcher)
Oct 14th	1922	JG Williams's XI	drew	2-2 (Fletcher 2)
Sept 29th	1923	Rev EM Jameson's	drew	2-2 (Fletcher, Clarke)
Sept 27th	1924	Rev EM Jameson's	lost	2-5 (Kemp Welch 2)
Sept 26th	1925	Rev EM Jameson's	lost	0-3
Sept 25th	1926	Rev EM Jameson's	lost	0-3
Sept 28th	1927	Rev EM Jameson's	lost	0-3
Sept 29th	1928	Rev EM Jameson's	lost	3-4 (Fletcher 2, Craddock)
Sept 28th	1929	Rev EM Jameson's	lost	0-5
Sept 27th	1930	Rev EM Jameson's	lost	0-1
Sept	1931	Rev EM Jameson's	lost	1-2 (Samuelson)
Feb 24th	1932	C Middleton's XI	lost	2-6 (Dunbar, JC Moss)
Oct 3rd	1942	Headmaster's XI	won	1-0
Feb 9th	1946	AJ Wreford Brown's	won	2-0 (May, Savill)
Sept 27th	1947	AJ Wreford Brown's	lost	2-9 (Janes, Burt)
Jan 28th	1948	AJ Wreford Brown's	lost	3-8 (Janes, Burt, Whinney)
Sept 25th	1948	AJ Wreford Brown's	lost	1-2 (Smithson)
Feb 19th	1949	AJ Wreford Brown's	won	3-1 (Goodliffe, May, Pickersgill)
Sept 24th	1949	AJ Wreford Brown's	lost	0-2
Jan 21st	1950	AJ Wreford Brown's	lost	3-4 (Young 2, Carver)
Jan 17th	1979	Select XI	won	4-3 (Frankland 2, Pratt, Farrow)
Sept 25th	1979	David Miller's XI	lost	0-2
Sept 23rd	1980	David Miller's XI	lost	0-1
Sept 22nd	1981	David Miller's XI	lost	1-4
Sept 21st	1982	David Miller's XI	lost	2-5 (Newman 2)

OLD BOYS' TEAMS

Bradfield Waifs

Dec 16th	1876	Charterhouse	won	5-1 (Page 3, Hayter 2)
Dec 8th	1894	Charterhouse	won	2-1 (Anderson, Franks)
Dec 17th	1898	Charterhouse	won	3-0 (Evans, Trower 2)
Jan 25th	1902	Charterhouse	won	2-1 (Farquharson, Goodliffe)
Nov 14th	1903	Charterhouse	won	3-0 (Allen 2, Taylor)

Bradfield Old Boys

Oct 29th	1910	Charterhouse	won	1-0 (Dunlop)
Nov 25th	1911	Charterhouse	won	2-0 (de Bernière Smith, Ford)
Oct 26th	1912	Charterhouse	lost	2-5 (Rücker, Payne)
Oct 11th	1919	Charterhouse	won	7-0 (Gilliat 3)
Oct 23rd	1920	Charterhouse	won	3-1 (Barnard 2, MacGusty)
Oct 29th	1921	Charterhouse	won	2-0 (Doresa 2)
Nov 11th	1922	Charterhouse	won	4-1 (Doresa, Kenyon 2, Carter)
Nov 24th	1923	Charterhouse	drew	1-1 (Carter)
Nov 8th	1924	Charterhouse	lost	0-1
Nov 7th	1925	Charterhouse	lost	1-2 (Deakin)
Nov 6th	1926	Charterhouse	won	2-0 (Wreford Brown, Glynn)
Nov 5th	1927	Charterhouse	lost	1-3 (Davies)
Nov 3rd	1928	Charterhouse	lost	1-5 (Craddock)
Nov	1929	Charterhouse	lost	1-2 (Hulton)
Nov 8th	1930	Charterhouse	lost	2-4 (Hunt, Watson)
Oct 31st	1931	Charterhouse	lost	0-5
Oct 7th	1933	Charterhouse	won	2-1 (Gillchrest, Tuckwell)
Nov 10th	1934	Charterhouse	lost	0-9
Nov 2nd	1946	Charterhouse	lost	1-3 (May)
Nov 1st	1947	Charterhouse	drew	1-1 (Burt)
Oct 30th	1948	Charterhouse	won	2-1 (Gibbon 2)
Oct 29th	1949	Charterhouse	lost	0-4
Oct 21st	1950	Charterhouse	drew	2-2 (Young)
Oct 20th	1951	Charterhouse	lost	2-4 (Tuck 2)
Oct 18th	1952	Charterhouse	lost	0-3
Oct 17th	1953	Charterhouse	won	4-0 (Gemmel, Mace, Percival, Buckley)
Oct 16th	1954	Charterhouse	drew	2-2 (Ruddock 2)
Oct 15th	1955	Charterhouse	drew	1-1 (Jakobson)
Oct 20th	1956	Charterhouse	won	3-1 (Sparshatt 2, White)
Oct 19th	1957	Charterhouse	lost	2-3 (Slater, Visser)
Feb 18th	1961	Charterhouse	won	3-0 (Lorenz, Powell 2)
Feb 17th	1962	Charterhouse	won	3-0 (Powell 2, Bailhache)
Feb 15th	1964	Charterhouse	won	3-2 (Hooper 2, Weir)
Feb 13th	1965	Charterhouse	lost	0-1
Feb 16th	1966	Charterhouse	lost	3-5 (Bennett, Howard 2)
Feb 15th	1967	Charterhouse	won	3-2 (Bennett 2, Provis)
Feb 7th	1968	Charterhouse	drew	3-3 (Carter 2, Bennett)
Jan 29th	1969	Charterhouse	lost	1-3 (Foster)
Jan 28th	1970	Charterhouse	drew	1-1 (Hughes)
Jan 27th	1971	Charterhouse	won	2-0 (Godby, Gibson)
Jan 26th	1972	Charterhouse	drew	2-2 (Stewart 2)
Jan 24th	1973	Charterhouse	won	6-3
Jan 23rd	1974	Charterhouse	won	4-0 (Adomakoh, Walker 2, North)
Jan 21st	1976	Charterhouse	drew	1-1 (Phillips)

Jan 19th	1977	Charterhouse	drew	1-1 (Shepherd)
Jan 18th	1978	Charterhouse	won	2-0 (Whalley, Doggart)

Old Brightonians

Oct 18th	1893	Charterhouse	won	3-2 (Fordyce, Hunt 2)
Oct 24th	1894	Charterhouse	drew	1-1 (Anderson)
Oct 5th	1895	Charterhouse	lost	2-4 (GW Ryder, Horne)
Oct 10th	1896	Charterhouse	won	5-1 (Vassall 2, Renshaw, Ryder, Moss)

Old Cholmeleians

Feb 7th	1948	Charterhouse	lost	2-4 (Burt 2)
Feb 5th	1949	Charterhouse	won	4-2 (May, Jenks, Goodliffe, Jordan)
Feb 13th	1952	Charterhouse	won	4-3 (Pegler 2, Miller 2)
Feb 11th	1953	Charterhouse	drew	0-0
Feb 10th	1954	Charterhouse	won	2-0 (Pratt, Ruddock)
Jan 29th	1955	Charterhouse	won	1-0 (Hornett)
Jan 26th	1957	Charterhouse	won	3-2 (Visser, Gordon, White)
Jan 24th	1959	Charterhouse	lost	1-2 (Taylor)
Jan 28th	1961	Charterhouse	lost	0-4
Jan 23rd	1965	Charterhouse	lost	2-3 (Hooper, Weir)
Jan 28th	1967	Charterhouse	lost	0-3

Old Etonians

Feb 21st	1866	Charterhouse	won	3-1 (Mackenzie, Walford, Nepean)
Nov 6th	1880	Charterhouse	won	4-1 (Owen 2, Henley, Cobbold)
Feb 28th	1883	Charterhouse	won	2-1 (Steward 2)
Feb 6th	1886	Charterhouse	won	3-1 (Currey 3)
Oct 28th	1893	Charterhouse	drew	2-2 (Hunt 2)
Dec 8th	1897	Charterhouse	won	5-4
Dec 7th	1898	Charterhouse	won	4-2 (Tuff 2, Trower, Greenwood)
18th Nov	1899	Charterhouse	won	5-2 (Tuff 4, o.g.)
8th Feb	1902	Charterhouse	won	4-0 (Goodliffe 4)
Oct 17th	1951	Charterhouse	drew	2-2 (Gladstone, Pegler)

Old Foresters

Oct 20th	1906	Charterhouse	drew	2-2 (Preston, Pegram)
Oct 8th	1921	Charterhouse	won	4-0 (Griffith Jones, Doresa, Bearman, Kiggell)
Oct 27th	1923	Charterhouse	won	1-0 (Fletcher)
Oct 18th	1924	Charterhouse	lost	1-2 (Beare)

Harrow Chequers

Jan 31st	1866	Charterhouse	lost	0-2
Dec 8th	1866	Charterhouse	won	2-0 (Wallace, Boreham)

Old Harrovians

OQ	1868	Middlesex County ground	drew	0-0
Nov 17th	1877	Charterhouse	won	2-0 (Growse, Medlicott)
Nov 16th	1878	Charterhouse	won	4-1 (Jenner 2, Burdon, Jackson)
Feb 17th	1883	Charterhouse	won	5-1 (Steward 2, Brookes, C Vintcent, McNeill)
Mar 8th	1884	Charterhouse	won	5-2 (Vintcent 2, Walker, Brown, Coulby)
Feb 7th	1885	Charterhouse	drew	2-2 (Currey, Crowdy)
Nov 28th	1885	Charterhouse	won	5-0 (Price 4, Parry)
Nov 13th	1886	Charterhouse	won	2-1 (Leman, Gilliat)
Mar 19th	1887	Charterhouse	lost	0-2
Nov 12th	1887	Charterhouse	won	4-1 (Dickinson, Stanbrough 2, Gilliat)
Mar 17th	1888	Charterhouse	drew	1-1 (Earle)
Oct 20th	1888	Charterhouse	lost	0-5
Feb 9th	1889	Charterhouse	won	3-2 (Woodhouse 3)
Nov 9th	1889	Charterhouse	won	2-1 (Buzzard 2)
Feb 15th	1890	Charterhouse	drew	3-3 (Kirby, Wilson, Smith)
Nov 15th	1890	Charterhouse	lost	1-2 (Kirby)
Feb 14th	1891	Charterhouse	won	3-0 (Clark, Wilson 2)
Nov 14th	1891	Charterhouse	won	8-3 (Salt 5, Barwell 2, Broadbent)
Feb 6th	1892	Charterhouse	won	5-0 (Salt 4, Smith)
Oct 15th	1892	Charterhouse	won	3-0 (Crabtree, Broadbent, Vassall)
Feb 10th	1894	Charterhouse	won	7-1 (Dyne, Fordyce, Jameson, Hancock, Vassall 3)
Dec 14th	1895	Charterhouse	won	7-2 (Horne 3, Green 3, Haig Brown)
Dec 2nd	1922	Charterhouse	won	4-3 (Fletcher 3, o.g.)

Lancing Old Boys

Feb 3rd	1906	Charterhouse	won	5-0 (Greig 2, Crier, Preston, Tillie)
Jan 25th	1908	Charterhouse	won	4-1 (Livesey 3, Johnson)
Mar 20th	1909	Charterhouse	won	7-0 (Macdonald 4, Weeks 3)
Jan 29th	1910	Charterhouse	lost	1-3 (Gibbons)
Feb 18th	1911	Charterhouse	lost	2-3 (Wesley Smith, Sanderson)
Nov 30th	1912	Charterhouse	drew	3-3 (Liddle 2, Wesley Smith)

Old Malvernians

Mar 13th	1920	Charterhouse	lost	4-7 (Gilliat 3, Cox)
Oct 30th	1920	Charterhouse	won	3-1 (Anderson, Gilliat, Barnard)
Oct 15th	1921	Charterhouse	lost	0-1
Oct 21st	1922	Charterhouse	drew	3-3 (Doresa 2, Carter)
Oct 20th	1923	Charterhouse	lost	2-5 (Shute, Fletcher)

Oct 11th	1924	Charterhouse	drew	0-0
Oct 10th	1925	Charterhouse	lost	0-1
Oct 9th	1926	Charterhouse	lost	1-3
Oct 8th	1927	Charterhouse	won	6-3 (o.g., Davies 2, Hale 2, Fletcher)
Feb 15th	1930	Charterhouse	drew	2-2 (o.g., Greening)
Feb 18th	1931	Charterhouse	lost	4-10 (Moss 2, Nicholl-Carne, Greening)
Feb 6th	1932	Charterhouse	lost	3-6 (WF Moss, JC Moss, Dunbar)
Feb 3rd	1934	Charterhouse	lost	2-3 (o.g., Gillchrest)
Feb 16th	1935	Charterhouse	drew	4-4 (Dunbar 2, Daukes 2)
Feb 13th	1937	Charterhouse	won	2-1 (Benké, Hughes)
Sept 25th	1965	Charterhouse	drew	2-2 (Rolls, Bennett)
Sept 23rd	1967	Charterhouse	lost	0-2
Sept 21st	1968	Charterhouse	won	5-3
Sept 26th	1970	Charterhouse	lost	2-4 (Gibson, Walton)
Sept 25th	1971	Charterhouse	won	2-0 (Doggart, Stewart)
Jan 27th	1934	Charterhouse	lost	1-3 (Gillchrest)
Jan 26th	1935	Charterhouse	won	6-2 (Daukes 2, Dunbar 2, Hodgson, Ades)
Jan 30th	1937	Charterhouse	lost	1-5 (Page)
Jan	1938	Charterhouse	won	6-2
Nov 30th	1946	Charterhouse	won	3-0 (Savill 2, Seaman)
Oct 11th	1947	Charterhouse	lost	1-3 (Whinney)
Oct 9th	1948	Charterhouse	lost	2-5 (Jordan, Atkinson)
Nov 26th	1949	Charterhouse	won	4-2 (Agate 2, May, Edwards)
Nov 18th	1950	Charterhouse	won	4-0 (Pegler 3, Gladstone)
Nov 7th	1953	Charterhouse	won	3-0 (Lees 2, O'Brien)
Nov 6th	1954	Charterhouse	won	7-3 (Lees 4, Jakobson, Buckley, Seth-Smith)
Nov 5th	1955	Charterhouse	won	2-0 (Hornett, Jakobson)
Nov 10th	1956	Charterhouse	won	4-2 (Steed, Hughesdon, Sparshatt, Foster-Brown)
Nov 9th	1957	Charterhouse	lost	1-2 (Tham)
Nov 8th	1958	Charterhouse	lost	1-3 (Faulkner)

Old Reptonians

Nov 20th	1880	Charterhouse	won	9-0 (Morrison 4, Vintcent 2, Henley, Owen, Currey)
Mar 8th	1893	Charterhouse	lost	2-3 (Broadbent, Hunt)
Mar 4th	1896	Charterhouse	drew	0-0
Oct 3rd	1896	Charterhouse	drew	2-2 (Vassall, Laird)
Oct 2nd	1897	Charterhouse	lost	2-3 (Moss 2)
Oct 1st	1898	Charterhouse	won	7-1 (Greenwood 3, Trower, Evans 2. Gibson)
Nov 5th	1904	Charterhouse	won	4-2 (Lyell 2, Cockburn, Steer)
Nov 11th	1905	Charterhouse	lost	1-4 (Jameson)
Oct 25th	1930	Charterhouse	drew	3-3 (Pope 2, Samuelson)
Nov	1931	Charterhouse	lost	0-9
Feb 24th	1934	Charterhouse	drew	0-0
Feb 23rd	1935	Charterhouse	won	5-0 (Hodgson 4, Rhodes)

Old Rossallians

Mar 4th	1891	Charterhouse	won	4-0 (Smith 2, Salt, Wilson)
Nov 11th	1891	Charterhouse	lost	2-4 (Salt)
Nov 12th	1892	Charterhouse	won	4-0 (Hunt 3, Broadbent)
Oct 21st	1893	Charterhouse	won	6-1 (Vassall 2, Fordyce, Jameson 2, Hunt)
Nov 16th	1895	Charterhouse	won	3-0 (Hulton, Vassall, Haig Brown)

Old Westminsters

Feb 5th	1881	Charterhouse	won	3-0 (Hamilton, Henley, Morrison)
Mar 22nd	1882	Charterhouse	won	1-0 (Cobbold)
Feb 12th	1887	Charterhouse	won	3-1 (Pim, Furber 2)
Mar 16th	1895	Charterhouse	won	4-1 (CF Ryder 3, Murdoch)
Oct 27th	1906	Charterhouse	won	2-0 (Pegram 2)
Feb 1st	1911	Charterhouse	won	4-1 (Sanderson 3, Gibbons)
Jan 27th	1912	Charterhouse	won	3-1 (Ford 2, Boswell)
Jan 25th	1913	Charterhouse	lost	1-5 (Wesley Smith)
Nov 1st	1919	Charterhouse	won	8-1 (Mordaunt Smith 3, Austin 2, Gilliat 3)
Oct 16th	1920	Charterhouse	won	2-1 (Austin, Gilliat)
Feb 4th	1922	Charterhouse	lost	1-2 (Morgan)
Feb 10th	1923	Charterhouse	won	2-1 (Clarke, o.g.)
Feb 9th	1924	Charterhouse	won	3-0 (Fletcher, Rishworth, Murdoch)
Feb 7th	1925	Charterhouse	drew	3-3 (Deakin, Stock, Seligman)
Feb 6th	1926	Charterhouse	lost	1-3 (Deakin)
Feb 5th	1927	Charterhouse	won	7-0 (Fletcher 2, Weatherall 2, o.g., Wreford Brown, Beare)
Feb 4th	1928	Charterhouse	lost	1-6 (Hale)
Feb 2nd	1929	Charterhouse	won	5-1 (Fletcher 2, Jeavons 2, Spencer)
Feb 1st	1930	Charterhouse	won	5-1 (Hulton 3, Middleton, o.g.)
Jan 31st	1931	Charterhouse	lost	1-3 (Greening)
Jan 30th	1932	Charterhouse	won	5-1 (Dunbar 3, WF Moss 2)

Old Wykehamists

Feb 5th	1887	Charterhouse	won	5-0 (Stanbrough 2, Leatham, Furber, Leman)
Feb 16th	1889	Charterhouse	won	4-0 (Stanbrough, Smith, Woodhouse, Armstrong)
Nov 30th	1889	Charterhouse	drew	1-1 (Halsted)
Feb 21st	1891	Charterhouse	won	4-3 (Salt 2, Wilson 2)
Jan 30th	1892	Charterhouse	drew	0-0
Jan 28th	1893	Charterhouse	won	3-1 (Fordyce 2, Vassall)
Feb 7th	1894	Charterhouse	drew	2-2 (Jameson, Dyne)
Feb 19th	1896	Charterhouse	drew	1-1 (Horne)
Feb 26th	1898	Charterhouse	won	4-2
Dec 3rd	1898	Charterhouse	won	3-1 (Greenwood, Tuff, Trower)
Feb 26th	1908	Charterhouse	won	3-1 (Weeks, Pike 2)
Oct 28th	1933	Charterhouse	won	2-0 (Swinbank, Dowding)
Oct	1934	Charterhouse	drew	2-2
Oct 24th	1936	Charterhouse	lost	0-2
Oct 19th	1940	Charterhouse	won	4-2 (Spencer 3, Vlasto)
Nov 15th	1952	Charterhouse	lost	2-4 (Miller, Bright)
Nov 14th	1953	Charterhouse	lost	2-5 (Pratt 2)
Nov 13th	1954	Charterhouse	won	6-1 (Jakobson 3, Lees, Percival, Seth-Smith)
Nov 12th	1955	Charterhouse	won	4-3 (Steed 3, Tomlinson)
Nov 17th	1956	Charterhouse	lost	0-7
Nov 16th	1957	Charterhouse	lost	2-5 (White, Harrison)
Nov 7th	1959	Charterhouse	lost	1-3 (Topham)
Nov 5th	1960	Charterhouse	lost	1-6 (Powell)
Oct 21st	1961	Charterhouse	won	5-3 (de Grunwald, Arnold, Marks, Powell, Hopkins)
Oct 20th	1962	Charterhouse	won	4-2 (Proud 2, Gilliat 2)
Oct 19th	1963	Charterhouse	won	6-4 (Drayson 2, Hooper 2, Hill, Bailhache)
Oct 17th	1964	Charterhouse	won	5-2 (Samuelson 2, Weir 2, Hooper)
Oct 16th	1965	Charterhouse	lost	0-2
Oct 15th	1966	Charterhouse	lost	2-5 (Bennett 2)
Oct 14th	1967	Charterhouse	lost	1-3 (Deans)
Oct 12th	1968	Charterhouse	lost	4-8
Oct 11th	1969	Charterhouse	won	3-2 (Walton 2, Stewart)
Oct 10th	1970	Charterhouse	won	1-0 (Holder)
Sept 30th	1972	Charterhouse	drew	2-2 (Williams)
Sept 29th	1973	Charterhouse	won	1-0 (Adomakoh)
Sept 28th	1974	Charterhouse	won	5-4 (Walker 3, Williams, Adomakoh)
Sept 27th	1975	Charterhouse		
Sept 25th	1976	Charterhouse	won	3-1 (Cummins 2, Phillips)
Sept 24th	1977	Charterhouse		
Sept 30th	1978	Charterhouse		

VIII 1st XI Results by dates

Date	Opponent	Result	Score
Nov 6th 1861	Dingley Dell	lost	0-1
Nov 16th 1861	Dingley Dell	drew	1-1 (Mackenzie)
Oct 29th 1862	Dingley Dell	lost	0-2
Nov 5th 1862	GAM (Grand Amalgamated Mediocrities)	lost	2-3 (Yorke, Hodgson/Eardley Wilmot) *in cloisters*
Nov 12th 1862	Dingley Dell	lost	1-2 (Hartshorne/Hodgson)
Nov 19th 1862	G Cardale's XI (GAM)	drew	0-0
Nov 26th 1862	GH Shaw's XI	won	1-0 (Somerset)
Dec 3rd 1862	GH Shaw's XI	drew	0-0
Jan 28th 1863	Crusaders	lost	0-1
Feb 4th 1863	Dingley Dell	won	1-0 (O'Grady)
Feb 8th 1863	HH Gilbert's XI	won	4-1 (Lant, Hodgson, Hartshorne, O'Grady) *in cloisters*
Feb 25th 1863	Dingley Dell	drew	0-0
Mar 18th 1863	HC Malkin's XI	drew	0-0
Oct 17th 1863	Tunbridge Wells	won	5-0 (Malkin 2, Boyle, Hodgson, *rush= undecided scorer*)
Oct 28th 1863	St Bartholomew's	won	2-0 (Mackenzie, Hodgson)
Nov 4th 1863	Dingley Dell	won	2-0 (*rush*, Hartshorne)
Nov 11th 1863	Civil Service	won	2-0 (Hartshorne)
Nov 18th 1863	Crusaders	won	2-0 (O'Grady 2)
Nov 25th 1863	Dingley Dell	lost	0-3
Dec 3rd 1863	Westminster	lost	0-2
Jan 27th 1864	Dingley Dell	won	1-0
Feb 3rd 1864	Civil Service	won	3-2 (*rush*)
Feb 13th 1864	Kilburn	drew	0-0
Feb 17th 1864	Crusaders	drew	0-0
Feb 20th 1864	St Bartholomew's	aban	1-0 (Mackenzie) (*snow*)
Feb 24th 1864	Old Carthusians	won	5-0 (O'Grady) *moved to cloisters after 2-0*
Feb 27th 1864	H Malkin's XI	won	2-0 (Makenzie, Hodgson)
Mar 2nd 1864	F Giles' XI	drew	0-0
Mar 5th 1864	Crusaders	drew	0-0
Mar 12th 1864	Kilburn	lost	0-1
Mar 19th 1864	Civil Service	won	4-0 (Hodgson 2, Mackenzie, *rush*)
Oct 12th 1864	M Mackenzie's IX	won	4-0 *9-a-side*
Oct 19th 1864	Civil Service	lost	0-1
Nov 2nd 1864	HC Malkin's XI	won	3-1 (Ogden, O'Grady, Mackenzie)
Nov 16th 1864	Civil Service	won	4-0
Nov 23rd 1864	Westminster	lost	1-2 (Mackenzie)
Nov 30th 1864	Old Carthusians	drew	2-2 (Mackenzie, *team effort*)
Dec 6th 1864	Crusaders	won	2-0
Jan 25th 1865	K Mackenzie's XI	drew	2-2 (Mackenzie 2)
Feb 1st 1865	Civil Service	won	1-0 (Walford)
Feb 8th 1865	Crusaders	drew	1-1 (*team effort*)
Feb 24th 1865	Old Carthusians	won	3-2 (O'Grady, *squash*, Smythe)
Mar 4th 1865	FG Pelham's XI	won	1-0 (Ogden)
Mar 11th 1865	Civil Service	won	1-0 (Cameron)
Oct 18th 1865	Civil Service	drew	2-2 *first use of 'goal' rather than 'game'*
Oct 25th 1865	HC Malkin's XI	won	1-0 (Middleton)
Nov 1st 1865	J Wearne's XI	won	1-0 (Walford)
Nov 8th 1865	Wanderers	lost	0-1
Nov 15th 1865	Civil Service	won	2-1 (Walford 2)
Nov 22nd 1865	Westminster	drew	0-0
Nov 29th 1865	Old Carthusians	lost	1-3 *first half on Under green (1-0) 2nd half in cloisters*
Dec 6th 1865	Crusaders	drew	0-0
Dec 14th 1865	Charterhouse past & present vs Westminster past & present at Vincent Square		1-0 (Walford)
Jan 28th 1866	AF Kinnaird's XI	lost	1-2
Jan 31st 1866	Harrow Checquers	lost	0-2
Feb 7th 1866	F Pownall's XI	won	1-0 (Mackenzie)
Feb 10th 1866	Crusaders	drew	0-0
Feb 21st 1866	Old Etonians	won	3-1 (Mackenzie, Walford, Nepean)
Mar 3rd 1866	Wanderers	lost	0-1
Mar 7th 1866	Civil Service	won	4-0 (Scott, Walford, Middleton, Nepean)
Oct 10th 1866	J Wearne's XII	drew	1-1 (Nepean)
Oct 24th 1866	CW Allcock's XI	won	2-0 (Nepean, Walford)
Oct 31st 1866	J Butter's XI	won	3-0 (Nepean 2, Venables)
Nov 10th 1866	Wanderers	won	1-0
Nov 14th 1866	Civil Service	won	3-0 (Mammatt/Nepean 2, Boreham)
Nov 21st 1866	Westminster	won	1-0 (Walford)
Nov 30th 1866	Old Carthusians	won	1-0 (*rush*) *13 a side*
Dec 8th 1866	Harrow Checquers	won	2-0 (Wallace, Boreham)
Jan 26th 1867	AF Kinnaird's XI	drew	0-0
Jan 30th 1867	Civil Service	won	(Foote/Wallace/Mammatt, Venables, Wallace)
Feb 6th 1867	J Butter's XI	won	4-0 (Mammatt, Venables, Nepean 2)
Feb 13th 1867	Old Carthusians	won	5-0 (Macan, Boreham, Mammatt, Nepean 2)
Feb 23rd 1867	Wanderers	drew	0-0
Feb 27th 1867	Strangers	drew	0-0
Mar 9th 1867	Crusaders	drew	0-0 *first use of 'draw' rather than 'tie'*
Mar 13th 1867	Civil Service	won	1-0 (Walford)
Oct 16th 1867	Avengers	won	6-0 (Nepean 4, Foote 2)
Oct 26th 1867	Wanderers	lost	0-1
Nov 1st 1867	Old Carthusians	drew	1-1 (Foote) *second half in cloisters, 14 a side*
Nov 6th 1867	Crusaders	won	4-1 (Venables, Paulson, Foote, Nepean)
Nov 13th 1867	Civil Service	won	5-0 (Nepean 3, Boyle, o.g.)
Nov 20th 1867	Avengers	won	3-1 (Wallace, Hammick, Nepean)
Nov 30th 1867	Amateur Athletic Club	won	3-1 (Nepean 2, Foote)
Dec 4th 1867	West Kent	won	2-1 (Paulson, Nepean)
Feb 6th 1868	CW Allcock's XI	won	2-0 (Hammick, Venables) *played in cloisters*
Feb 13th 1868	Cambridge XI	lost	1-2 (Venables) *played at Middlesex Ground, Islington*
Feb 22nd 1868	N.Ns (Kilburn)	drew	0-0 *played at Middlesex Ground, Islington*
Feb 24th 1868	Old Carthusians	lost	0-2 *played in cloisters*
OQ 1868	Royal Engineers	drew	1-1 (Povah) *at Islington*
OQ 1868	Old Harrovians	drew	0-0 *at Islington*
OQ 1868	Civil Service	won	3-0 *at Battersea Park*
OQ 1868	Clapham Rovers	won	4-0
OQ 1868	Kilburn Club	drew	0-0 *at Islington*
LQ 1869	Vagrants	won	7-0 *played in cloisters*
LQ 1869	Owls	won	7-0 *played in cloisters*
LQ 1869	Old Carthusians	drew	2-2
LQ 1869	Wanderers	won	2-1
Oct 3rd 1869	CW Allcock's XI	won	3-0 (Nepean 2, Cameron)
Oct 13th 1869	Civil Service	drew	1-1 (Barry)
Oct 20th 1869	Clapham Rovers	won	5-1 (Inglis 3, Barry, Matthews)
Nov 3rd 1869	Wanderers	drew	2-2 (Barry, Inglis)
Nov 11th 1869	Old Carthusians	won	3-0 (Barry, King) *2nd half in cloisters*
Nov 17th 1869	Royal Engineers	lost	2-3 (Smith, Inglis)
Jan 26th 1870	Clapham Rovers	lost	0-2
Feb 24th 1870	Old Carthusians	drew	1-1 *2nd half in cloisters*
Mar 5th 1870	Royal Engineers	drew	0-0
Mar 16th 1870	Gitanos	won	3-0 (Smith 2, Inglis)
Mar 19th 1870	Wanderers	drew	1-1 (Barry)
Mar 23rd 1870	CF Reid's XI	won	2-1 (Bushnell, Smith)
Oct 5th 1870	CW Allcock's XI	lost	1-3 (Inglis)
Oct 19th 1870	Civil Service	won	3-0 (*squash* 2, Neish) *1st half in cloisters*
Oct 22nd 1870	Gitanos	won	3-0 (Brown, Ravenshaw, King)
Nov 2nd 1870	Wanderers	won	3-1 (Brown, King, Inglis)
Nov 5th 1870	Walthamstow	won	1-0 (Dorling)
Nov 23rd 1870	Clapham Rovers	won	2-1 (Inglis, o.g.)
Nov 30th 1870	Royal Engineers	lost	0-5 *at the Oval*
Dec 7th 1870	Barnes	drew	0-0
Jan 25th 1971	Eton Club, Cambridge	lost	1-2
Feb 4th 1871	Barnes	lost	0-3
Feb 8th 1871	Civil Service	lost	0-1
Feb 15th 1871	Clapham Rovers	lost	0-1
Feb 23rd 1871	Old Carthusians	lost	0-1 *2nd half in cloisters*
Mar 1st 1871	Wanderers	drew	2-2
Mar 11th 1871	Walthamstow	won	10-0 (Inglis 6)
Oct 4th 1871	CW Alcock's XI	won	3-2 (Staveley, Williams, Paget) *12 a side*
Oct 11th 1871	Civil Service	won	2-1 (Empson, Parry)
Oct 21st 1871	Barnes	won	1-0 (Davies)
Nov 8th 1871	Wanderers	drew	1-1 (Paget)
Nov 15th 1871	Crystal Palace	won	3-1 (Parry, Gandell, Paget)
Nov 30th 1871	Old Carthusians	drew	1-1 (*rush*) *13 a side 2nd half in cloisters*
Jan 27th 1872	Crystal Palace	won	1-0 (Gandell)
Feb 8th 1872	Civil Service	won	6-0 (Parry 2, Ravenshaw, Gandell, Paget, Stavely)
Feb 10th 1872	Walthamstow	won	3-0 (Davies, Brown, Thompson)
Feb 17th 1872	Barnes	drew	0-0
Mar 7th 1872	Old Carthusians	won	2-1 (Ravenshaw, *squash*) *2nd half in cloisters*
Mar 13th 1872	Clapham Rovers	lost	1-4 (Gandell)

Date	Opponent	Result	Score (scorers)
Mar 20th 1872	Wanderers	drew	1-1 (Paget)
Oct 16th 1872	Civil Service at Charterhouse Godalming	won	4-0 (Firth 2, Davies, Gipps)
Nov 14th 1872	Old Carthusians	drew	2-2 (Gandell, Gipps) (*14 a side*)
Dec 7th 1872	Barnes	won	3-0 (Parry, Firth, Verelst)
Dec 11th 1872	Wanderers	drew	0-0
Dec 14th 1872	Weyside	won	3-0
Mar 5th 1873	Gitanos	won	3-0
Mar 13th 1873	Old Carthusians	won	4-3 (Jeaffreson 2, Abdy)
Mar 15th 1873	Weyside	lost	1-2
Mar 22nd 1873	Gitanos	lost	1-3 (E Williams)
LQ 1873	Winchester	drew	1-1
Oct 4th 1873	JC Merryman's XI	won	2-0 (Parry, Williams)
Oct 25th 1873	Weyside	won	6-0 (Parish 2, Parry 2, Abdy, Corrie)
Nov 8th 1873	Gitanos	lost	0-3
Nov 13th 1873	Old Carthusians	won	6-2 (Drew 4, Parish, Jeaffreson)
Nov 26th 1873	Wanderers	won	4-1 (Parry, Jeaffreson, Drew, Synge)
Nov 29th 1873	Reigate Priory	won	3-0 (Parry, Drew, Synge)
Dec 3rd 1873	Crystal Palace	won	2-0 (Parry, Drew)
Dec 6th 1873	Oxford XI	won	3-2 (Tod, Jeaffreson, Drew)
Feb 7th 1874	Weyside	won	2-0 (Tod, Synge)
Mar 13th 1874	Old Carthusians	won	10-2 (Parry 2, Reeve, Corrie 4, Drew 2, Tod)
Mar 21st 1874	Gitanos	won	5-2 (Parry, Tod, Page, Verelst, Synge)
Oct 3rd 1874	EH Parry's XI	won	3-2 (Southwell 2, Short)
Oct 24th 1874	Weyside	won	4-0 (Abdy, Page 2, Tod)
Oct 31st 1874	Gitanos	won	2-0 (Abdy 2)
Nov 12th 1874	Old Carthusians	won	5-2 (Reeve, Merriman, Page, Tod 2)
Nov 21st 1874	Reigate Priory	won	5-1 (Tod, Lovegrove, Page, Curzon, Short)
Dec 2nd 1874	Aldershot	drew	1-1 (Short)
Dec 15th 1874	Oxford XI	lost	1-3 (Tod)
Feb 25th 1875	Old Carthusians	lost	1-2 (Short)
Feb 27th 1875	Weyside	won	9-0 (Macgeorge 4, Page 3, Tod, Blackett)
Mar 1st 1875	Westminster	won	2-0 (Curzon 2)
Mar 13th 1875	Swifts	won	3-2 (Tod 3)
Oct 7th 1875	Brooke Hall	won	3-0 (Parish 2, Reeve)
Nov 6th 1875	Gitanos	lost	1-3 (Short)
Nov 11th 1875	Old Carthusians	won	6-5 (Brown,Short,Cornish,Burrows 2,Keightley)
Nov 17th 1875	Tenth Regiment	won	7-1 (Short 2, Burrows, Tod 3, o.g)
Nov 27th 1875	Oxford XI	lost	1-3 (Wake)
Dec 14th 1875	Cambridge XI	won	1-0 (Tod)
Feb 12th 1876	105th Regiment	won	4-0 (Short, Keightley, Tod, Reeve)
Feb 19th 1876	Westminster	lost	0-1
Mar 4th 1876	Aldershot Division	won	1-0 (Tod)
Mar 11th 1876	Old Carthusians	won	5-1 (*squash*, Wilson 2,Williams, Page)
Mar 25th 1876	Aldershot Division	won	2-1 (Tod, Williams)
Oct 4th 1876	Brooke Hall	won	6-1 (Eddis,Williams,Burrows, Keightley 2,Page)
Oct 14th 1876	C Haig Brown's XI	won	8-2 (Page 3, Keightley, Eddis 2, Williams, Boscawen)
Oct 21st 1876	EM Short's XI	won	5-1 (Page 3, Eddis, Keightley)
Nov 25th 1876	Old Carthusians	drew	1-1 (Page)
Dec 10th 1876	Cambridge XI	won	4-1 (Boscawen, Page 2)
Dec 16th 1876	Bradfield Waifs	won	5-1 (Page 3, Hayter 2)
Feb 10th 1877	Brooke Hall	won	5-0 (Evan-Thomas, Parry 3, Page)
Feb 17th 1877	Westminster	won	2-0 (Eddis, Parry)
Mar 3rd 1877	Clapham Rovers	won	2-0 (Page 2)
Mar 14th 1877	Gitanos	won	5-0 (A Keightley 3, Page, Eddis)
Mar 22nd 1877	Old Carthusians	won	5-1 (Evan-Thomas, Page 3, Hayter)
Mar 28th 1877	Swifts	won	3-0 (Page 3)
Oct 10th 1877	Swifts	lost	1-3 (Medlicott)
Oct 13th 1877	Brooke Hall	won	2-0 (*squash*, Master)
Oct 20th 1877	Clapham Rovers	won	4-1 (Frith, o.g., Prinsep, Evan-Thomas)
Nov 7th 1877	WR Page's XI	drew	1-1 (Evan-Thomas)
Nov 10th 1877	Reigate Priory	won	10-0 (Medlicott 2, Growse 4, Smith, *rush*, Evan-Thomas, Frith)
Nov 17th 1877	Old Harrovians	won	2-0 (Growse, Medlicott)
Nov 24th 1877	Old Carthusians	lost	3-5 (Evan-Thomas, Hansell, Wilson)
Nov 26th 1877	EH Parry's XI	lost	0-2
Dec 12th 1877	NJ Abdy's XI	won	5-2 (Keith Falconer, Burdon 2, Frith, Medlicott)
Dec 15th 1877	WW Drew's XI	won	2-1 (Burdon, Hansell)
Feb 9th 1878	Brooke Hall	won	7-0 (Frith 3, Wilson, Growse 2, Hansell)
Feb 16th 1878	Westminster	won	1-0 (Growse)
Mar 9th 1878	RMC Sandhurst	lost	1-3 (Stubbs)
Mar 16th 1878	Old Carthusians	won	8-1 (Growse, Evan-Thomas 2, Wilson 3, Princep, Hansell)
Sept 28th 1878	WW Drew's XI	won	4-0 (Wilson, Richards, Jenner, Hansell)
Oct 12th 1878	Swifts	won	5-2 (Pollock, Wilson 2, Jenner 2)
Oct 19th 1878	Clapham Rovers	won	3-1 (Hansell, Richards, Jackson)
Nov 9th 1878	RMC Sandhurst	won	4-2 (Richards, Jenner, Wilson, Burdon)
Nov 13th 1878	WTB Hayter's XI	drew	2-2 (Hansell,Jenner)
Nov 16th 1878	Old Harrovians	won	4-1 (Jenner 2, Burdon, Jackson)
Nov 23rd 1878	Old Carthusians	won	2-1 (Burdon, Jenner)
Nov 30th 1878	JFM Prinsep's XI	won	4-3 (Burdon 2, Hansell, Wilson)
Feb 5th 1879	Brooke Hall	won	6-1 (Wilson 3, Richards 2, Guinness)
Feb 12th 1879	CM Burdon's XI	won	6-2 (Jackson, Richards 2, Guinness, Pollock, Vyvyan)
Feb 22nd 1879	Westminster	won	4-2 (Wilson 2, Richards, *scrimmage*)
Mar 1st 1879	RMC Sandhurst	won	5-2 (Vintcent, Pollock, Guinness, Wilson 2)
Mar 22nd 1879	Old Carthusians	lost	1-6 (Wilson)
Oct 4th 1879	Brooke Hall	won	5-0 (Richards 2, Vyvyan, Pollock 2)
Oct 18th 1879	Clapham Rovers	won	4-1 (Pollock 2, Morrison, Richards)
Nov 8th 1879	RMC Sandhurst	lost	1-2 (Rayner)
Nov 22nd 1879	Cambridge XI	won	4-0 (Pollock, Richards, Rayner 2)
Nov27th 1879	Middlebriars	won	4-1
Nov 29th 1879	Old Carthusians	drew	4-4 (Rayner 3, Pollock)
Feb 14th 1880	Brooke Hall	won	7-3 (Rayner 4, Richards 2, Walters)
Feb 18th 1880	CM Burdon's XI	drew	1-1 (Vyvyan)
Feb 21st 1880	Westminster	won	4-3 (Rayner, Pollock 2, Vyvyan)
Mar 13th 1880	RMC Sandhurst	won	3-2 (Vyvyan 2, *squash*)
Mar 20th 1880	Clapham Rovers	lost	1-6 (Richards)
Mar 27th 1880	Old Carthusians	lost	3-5 (Morrison, Richards 2)
Oct 2nd 1880	Brooke Hall	won	7-1 (Currey, Morrison 3, Escombe 2, Henley)
Oct 16th 1880	Clapham Rovers	won	3-0 (Owen, Escombe, Cholmeley)
Oct 23rd 1880	RMC Sandhurst	won	5-0 (Henley, *squash*, Escombe, Vintcent, Morrison)
Nov 6th 1880	Old Etonians	won	4-1 (Owen 2, Henley, Cobbold)
Nov 20th 1880	Old Reptonians	won	9-0 (Morrison 4, Vintcent 2, Henley, Owen, Currey)
Nov 27th 1880	Old Carthusians	won	7-1 (Morrison 3, Owen, Vintcent 3)
Dec 4th 1880	Pilgrims	won	3-0 (Henley, Currey, Escombe)
Dec 11th 1880	Remnants	won	5-0 (Escombe, Morrison, Vintcent, Henley 2)
Jan 29th 1881	HA Carter's XI	drew	1-1 (Morrison) *after extra time*
Feb 5th 1881	Old Westminsters	won	3-0 (Hamilton, Henley, Morrison)
Feb 9th 1881	Brooke Hall	won	5-0 (Vintcent, Henley, Harrison, Cobbold, Morrison)
Feb 12th 1881	Remnants	won	4-1 (Vintcent 2, Owen, Cobbold)
Feb 16th 1881	Cambridge XI	won	7-1 (Morrison 2, Vintcent, Henley 3, Cobbold)
Feb 26th 1881	Westminster	won	3-2 (Cobbold 2, Owen)
Mar 12th 1881	RMC Sandhurst	won	1-0 (*squash*)
Mar 16th 1881	Old Carthusians	lost	1-6 (Walters)

(Old Carthusians won the FA Cup on April 9th 1881 with 7 of the same team)

Date	Opponent	Result	Score (scorers)
Oct 1st 1881	Brooke Hall	won	5-0 (Eddis 2, Henley, Blenkiron, Brown)
Oct 8th 1881	J Vintcent's XI	won	4-3 (Vintcent, Eddis 2, Brown)
Oct 15th 1881	Clapham Rovers	won	5-3 (Rayner 2, Cobbold 3)
Oct 22nd 1881	WH Norris' XI	won	2-0 (Eddis [*charged through* by Rayner], Henley)
Nov 5th 1881	RMC Sandhurst	won	5-0 (King Harman 2, Henley, Cobbold, Vintcent)
Nov 16th 1881	Oxford XI	won	1-0 (Vintcent)
Nov 19th 1881	Pilgrims	won	1-0 (Eddis)
Nov 26th 1881	Old Carthusians	won	5-2 (Rayner, o.g., Vintcent 2, Henley)
Jan 28th 1882	WG Morrison's XI	won	7-0 (Vintcent, Spurway, Cautley 2, Rayner 2, Henley)
Feb 1st 1882	Royal Engineers	won	2-0 (Vintcent, Rayner)
Feb 15th 1882	Cambridge XI	won	1-0 (Eddis)
Feb 25th 1882	Westminster	won	3-2 (Cobbold 2, Vintcent)
Mar 8th 1882	ET Hardman's XI	won	2-1 (Henley, Cobbold)
Mar 11th 1882	RMC Sandhurst	won	6-2 (Eddis 2, Cobbold 3, Vintcent)
Mar 22nd 1882	Old Westminsters	won	1-0 (Cobbold)
Mar 25th 1882	Old Carthusians	won	3-1 (Eddis, Rayner, Cobbold)
Oct 7th 1882	Rev CC Tancock's XI	won	7-2 (Eddis 2, Messent 2, C Vintcent 2, L Vincent)
Oct 14th 1882	Clapham Rovers	drew	1-1 (Steward)
Nov 11th 1882	RMC Sandhurst	won	5-0 (Eddis 2, Steward, McNeill, C Vintcent)
Nov 15th 1882	Civil Service	won	8-0 (Spring Rice, C Vintcent, Brookes 2, Eddis 3, Steward)
Nov 25th 1882	Old Carthusians	lost	1-3 (C Vintcent)
Dec 6th 1882	Oxford XI	lost	2-6 (Eddis, Brookes)
Dec 16th 1882	Pilgrims	lost	0-2
Feb 14th 1883	Royal Engineers	won	6-2 (C Vintcent 2, L Vintcent, Brookes 3)

Date	Opponent	Result	Score (Scorers)
Feb 17th 1883	Old Harrovians	won	5-1 (Steward 2, Brookes, C Vintcent, McNeill)
Feb 24th 1883	Westminster	won	5-1 (Steward 2, L Vintcent, Brookes 2)
Feb 28th 1883	Old Etonians	won	2-1 (Steward 2)
Mar 14th 1883	Corinthians	won	3-0 (Fardell 2, L Vintcent)
Mar 17th 1883	Pilgrims	won	12-2 (Brookes 3, Fardell 3, L Vintcent 2, Walters, C Vintcent 3)
Mar 20th 1883	Old Carthusians	won	5-3 (L Vintcent 2, Fardell, C Vintcent 2)
Sept 29th 1883	Rev CC Tancock's XI	won	5-2 (Ponsonby 3, Pearce, C Vintcent)
Oct 6th 1883	WN Cobbold's XI	drew	1-1 (Brown)
Oct 13th 1883	Clapham Rovers	won	2-0 (Galsworthy, Steward)
Oct 24th 1883	Casuals	drew	1-1 (Brown)
Nov 7th 1883	Magdalen College	lost	0-1
Nov 17th 1883	RMC Sandhurst	lost	2-3 (Steward 2)
Nov 24th 1883	Pilgrims	won	4-1 (Barnett 2, Walker 2)
Dec 1st 1883	Old Carthusians	lost	1-2 (Steward)
Dec 15th 1883	TW Blenkiron's XI	drew	1-1 (Walker)
Feb 2nd 1884	FW Sewell's XI	won	5-0 (Walker, Brown, Vintcent 2, Waddington)
Feb 13th 1884	Royal Engineers	won	3-0 (Kerr, Brown, Walker)
Feb 20th 1884	Casuals	lost	2-3 (Brown 2)
Feb 23rd 1884	Westminster	lost	1-2 (Vintcent)
Mar 1st 1884	RMC Sandhurst	won	3-0 (Waddington 2, Brown)
Mar 5th 1884	Corinthians	lost	1-2 (Vintcent)
Mar 8th 1884	Old Harrovians	won	5-2 (Vintcent 2, Walker, Brown, Coulby)
Mar 15th 1884	Old Carthusians	lost	0-2
Mar 19th 1884	Brentwood	lost	0-3
Mar 26th 1884	WN Cobbold's XI	won	2-0 (Vintcent 2)
Sept 27th 1884	Ashburnham Rovers	won	4-2 (Crowdy, Wreford Brown, Burrell, Adams)
Oct 4th 1884	Rev CC Tancock's XI	won	2-1 (Wreford Brown, Price)
Oct 8th 1884	Casuals	lost	0-1
Oct 11th 1884	Surbiton Wanderers	won	4-0 (Currey 2, Martyn, Wreford Brown)
Oct 15th 1884	J Vintcent's XI	won	2-0 ((Price, Martyn)
Oct 18th 1884	Clapham Rovers	won	1-0 (Martyn)
Oct 29th 1884	Swifts	won	4-0 (Price 2, Wreford Brown, Currey)
Nov 1st 1884	Brentwood	won	1-0 (Price)
Nov 5th 1884	Magdalen College	drew	0-0
Nov 15th 1884	RMC Sandhurst	won	1-0 (Price)
Nov 19th 1884	Oxford XI	drew	1-1 (Cooper)
Nov 29th 1884	Pilgrims	drew	1-1 (Currey)
Dec 3rd 1884	Wednesday Strollers	lost	0-1
Dec 13th 1884	Old Carthusians	lost	0-3
Feb 7th 1885	Old Harrovians	drew	2-2 (Currey, Crowdy)
Feb 11th 1885	Royal Engineers	won	1-0 (Currey)
Feb 14th 1885	Clapham Rovers	won	2-0 (Holroyd, Crowdy)
Feb 25th 1885	Casuals	won	2-1 (Currey 2)
Feb 28th 1885	Westminster	won	3-0 (Galsworthy 2, Currey)
Mar 4th 1885	Swifts	won	4-1 (Cooper, Crowdy 2, Galsworthy)
Mar 11th 1885	AJ Webbe's XI	lost	0-1
Mar 18th 1885	Brentwood	lost	0-4
Mar 21st 1885	Old Carthusians	won	2-1 (Martyn, Cooper)
Mar 25th 1885	Casuals	drew	3-3 (Crowdy, Galsworthy, Martyn)
Sept 26th 1885	Ashburnham Rovers	won	2-1 (Parry, Wreford Brown)
Oct 3rd 1885	Rev CC Tancock's XI	won	5-1 (Wreford Brown 3, Currey, Price)
Oct 7th 1885	Casuals	lost	0-1
Oct 10th 1885	Brentwood	lost	0-1
Oct 14th 1885	Clapham Rovers	won	2-0 (Price, Daglish)
Oct 24th 1885	Surbiton Wanderers	won	2-0 (Price 2)
Nov 14th 1885	Barnes	won	5-0 (Daglish, Parry, Currey, Leatham, o.g.)
Nov 18th 1885	Magdalen College	lost	1-2 (Leatham)
Nov 25th 1885	Old Harrovians	won	5-0 (Price 4, Parry)
Dec 2nd 1885	AK Henley's XI	won	1-0 (Currey)
Dec 5th 1885	Old Carthusians	won	8-0 (Price 3, Currey 3, Wreford Brown, Tewson)
Dec 12th 1885	OC Cup team	lost	0-5
Feb 6th 1886	Old Etonians	won	3-1 (Currey 3)
Feb 13th 1886	RMC Sandhurst	won	5-0 (Stanbrough 2, Nixon, Currey 2)
Feb 17th 1886	R Escombe's XI	won	3-0 (Pim 2, Stanbrough)
Feb 24th 1886	Casuals	won	2-1 (Parry, Price)
Feb 27th 1886	Westminster	lost	2-4 (Sheppard, Currey)
Mar 13th 1886	Royal Engineers	won	5-0 (Currey 2, Nixon, Sheppard, Price)
Mar 20th 1886	Old Carthusians	won	6-0 (Currey 5, Nixon)
Mar 24th 1886	Brentwood	drew	0-0
Mar 27th 1886	Casuals	won	1-0 (Nixon)
Sept 25th 1886	G Ashby's XI (West Kent)	won	6-0 (Earle 2, Price 2, Leman, Gilliat)
Oct 2nd 1886	AH Tod's XI	won	2-0 (Price 2)
Oct 6th 1886	Casuals	drew	1-1 (Price)
Oct 9th 1886	Clapham Rovers	won	1-0 (Price)
Oct 16th 1886	Reigate Priory	won	2-1 (Price, Timmis)
Nov 6th 1886	CH Tyler's XI	won	2-1 (Pim, Price)
Nov 10th 1886	Christ Church	won	2-0 (Gilliat, Price)
Nov 13th 1886	Old Harrovians	won	2-1 (Leman)
Nov 17th 1886	Magdalen College	lost	0-1
Nov 20th 1886	Barnes	won	2-0 (Leman 2)
Dec 4th 1886	RMC Sandhurst	won	2-0 (Leman, Gilliat)
Dec 11th 1886	Old Carthusians	lost	0-3
Jan 29th 1887	AC Nixon's XI	lost	1-3 (Gilliat)
Feb 5th 1887	Old Wykehamists	won	5-0 (Stanbrough 2, Leatham, Furber, Leman)
Feb 12th 1887	Old Westminsters	won	3-1 (Pim, Furber 2)
Feb 19th 1887	Old Carthusians	lost	2-5 (Pim 2)
Feb 23rd 1887	Casuals	won	3-2 (Taylor 2, Earle)
Feb 26th 1887	Royal Engineers	won	1-0 (Furber)
Mar 9th 1887	E Escombe's XI	won	5-0 (Furber 3, Leman, Dickinson)
Mar 12th 1887	Westminster	won	1-0 (Pim)
Mar 19th 1887	Old Harrovians	lost	0-2
Mar 23rd 1887	Crusaders	lost	1-3 (Stanbrough)
Mar 26th 1887	RMC Sandhurst	won	2-0 (Earle, Stanbrough)
April 9th 1887	Godalming Cup Team	won	2-0 (Gilliat, Stanbrough)
Oct 1st 1887	AH Tod's XI	won	2-0 (Gilliat, Furber)
Oct 5th 1887	Casuals	won	2-0 (Furber 2)
Oct 15th 1887	Reigate Priory	drew	1-1 (Colvin)
Oct 29th 1887	Godalming	won	6-0
Nov 5th 1887	Casuals	won	4-1 (Gilliat 3, Dickinson)
Nov 12th 1887	Old Harrovians	won	4-1 (Dickinson, Stanbrough 2, Gilliat)
Nov 16th 1887	Magdalen College	drew	0-0
Nov 19th 1887	HJ Carson's XI	won	4-2 (Furber 2, Gilliat, Stanbrough)
Nov 26th 1887	RMC Sandhurst	won	2-0 (Furber, Gilliat)
Dec 3rd 1887	Crusaders	drew	1-1 (Stanbrough)
Dec 10th 1887	Old Carthusians	won	3-1 (Gilliat, Dickinson, Earle)
Dec 14th 1887	WN Cobbold's XI	lost	2-4 (Gilliat, Furber)
Feb 11th 1888	Christ Church	lost	0-2
Feb 22nd 1888	Clapham Rovers	won	1-0 (Dickinson)
Mar 3rd 1888	Old Carthusians	won	4-0 (Gilliat 2, Rayner, Cowie)
Mar 7th 1888	Royal Engineers	drew	4-4 (Stanbrough, Dickinson 2, Dashwood)
Mar 10th 1888	Westminster	drew	3-3 (Gilliat, Dickinson, Stanbrough)
Mar 17th 1888	Old Harrovians	drew	1-1 (Earle)
Mar 24th 1888	Casuals	drew	2-2 (Rayner, Earle)
Mar 31st 1888	East Surrey Wanderers	lost	4-5 (Stanbrough 3, o.g.)
Sept 26th 1888	AH Tod's XII	lost	1-6 (Woodhouse)
Oct 3rd 1888	Casuals	won	3-1 (Stanbrough 2, Woodhouse)
Oct 6th 1888	Trinity Rest	drew	2-2 (Stanbrough)
Oct 13th 1888	Reigate Priory	won	2-1 (Barker, Phelps)
Oct 20th 1888	Old Harrovians	lost	0-5
Oct 31st 1888	Magdalen College	won	1-0 (Pierce)
Nov 14th 1888	Swifts	won	3-2 (Rayner, Smith, Stanbrough)
Nov 17th 1888	Godalming	won	3-0 (Barker 2, Smith)
Nov 24th 1888	RMC Sandhurst	drew	1-1 (Barker)
Nov 28th 1888	Casuals	won	2-0 (Stanbrough, Price)
Dec 8th 1888	Old Carthusians	lost	1-5 (Pierce)
Dec 12th 1888	WN Cobbold's XI	won	9-1 (Rayner 4, Stanbrough 2, Pierce, Woodhouse, Bliss)
Dec 15th 1888	Sussex Dolphins	lost	0-5
Feb 9th 1889	Old Harrovians	won	3-2 (Woodhouse 3)
Feb 16th 1889	Old Wykehamists	won	4-0 (Stanbrough, Smith, Woodhouse, Armstrong)
Feb 20th 1889	Christ Church	won	4-0 (Woodhouse 2, Phelps, Smith)
Mar 2nd 1889	Westminster	won	8-0 (Armstrong 4, Smith, Barker, Stanbrough 2)
Mar 13th 1889	Royal Engineers	won	7-1 (Stanbrough 3, Woodhouse 2, Smith, Halsted)
Mar 20th 1889	East Surrey Wanderers	lost	1-5 (Irvine)
Mar 30th 1889	Old Carthusians	lost	4-6
Sept 28th 1889	AH Tod's XI	won	2-1 (Halsted, Armstrong)
Oct 2nd 1889	Casuals	drew	3-3 (Halsted, o.g., Armstrong)
Oct 9th 1889	Sussex Dolphins	won	3-2 (Buzzard 2, Armstrong)
Oct 12th 1889	Crusaders	won	2-0 (Halsted, Armstrong)
Oct 19th 1889	Godalming	won	4-1 (Smith 2, Armstrong 2)
Oct 26th 1889	FS Tewson's XI	won	6-1 (Halsted, Buzzard, Armstrong 2, Head, Hewitt)
Oct 30th 1889	Magdalen College	drew	3-3 (Buzzard, Hewitt, Smith)
Nov 9th 1889	Old Harrovians	won	2-1 (Buzzard 2)
Nov 16th 1889	Reigate Priory	won	4-0 (Armstrong 2, Wilson, Hewitt)
Nov 23rd 1889	RMC Sandhurst	drew	2-2 (Armstrong, Hewitt)
Nov 30th 1889	Old Wykehamists	drew	1-1 (Halsted)
Feb 8th 1890	Crusaders	lost	1-2 (Wilson)
Feb 15th 1890	Old Harrovians	drew	3-3 (Kirby, Wilson, Smith)
Feb 18th 1890	Prince Christian Victor's XI	won	5-1 (Buzzard 3, Wade, Hewitt)
Feb 19th1890	Royal Engineers	won	8-0 (Hewitt 3, Smith, Buzzard 2, Wade 2)
Feb 26th 1890	Cambridge OCs	drew	1-1 (Hewitt)
Mar 8th 1890	Westminster	won	8-0 (Smith 3, Buzzard 4, Wilson)

Date	Opponent	Result	Score (scorers)
Mar 12th 1890	D Crossman's XI	won	5-2 (Buzzard 2, Smith 2, Wilson)
Mar 15th 1890	Old Carthusians	drew	1-1 (Buzzard)
Mar 22nd 1890	Casuals	drew	2-2 (Wade 2)
Oct 1st 1890	Casuals	won	2-1 (Merriman, Hewitt)
Oct 4th 1890	AH Tod's XI	won	9-0 (Wilson 4, Kirby, Merriman 2, Hewitt 2)
Oct 11th 1890	Crusaders	drew	2-2 (Wilson 2)
Oct 18th 1890	Clapham Rovers	won	6-0 (Bramwell, Smith, Wilson 2, Merriman 2)
Oct 25th 1890	Oxford OCs	won	5-0 (Wilson 2, Smith 2, Hewitt)
Oct 29th 1890	MH Stanbrough's XI	won	2-0 (Hewitt)
Nov 8th 1890	Sandhurst	won	4-3 (Wilson 3, Hewitt)
Nov 15th 1890	Old Harrovians	lost	1-2 (Kirby)
Dec 3rd 1890	Oxford Goblins	drew	1-1 (Wilson)
Dec 6th 1890	Old Carthusians	drew	2-2 (Wilson, Hewitt)
Feb 7th 1891	Crusaders	lost	0-4
Feb 14th 1891	Old Harrovians	won	3-0 (Clark, Wilson 2)
Feb 21st 1891	Old Wykehamists	won	4-3 (Salt 2, Wilson 2)
Feb 25th 1891	Magdalen College	won	10-0
Feb 28th 1891	Westminster	drew	2-2 (Clark 2)
Mar 4th 1891	Old Rossallians	won	4-0 (Smith 2, Salt, Wilson)
Mar 14th 1891	Old Carthusians	won	4-1 (Clark, Wilson 2, Salt)
Mar 25th 1891	Casuals	lost	1-3 (Wilson)
Oct 3rd 1891	Sussex Dolphins	won	9-0 (Smith 5, Wild 4)
Oct 7th 1891	AH Tod's XI	lost	2-3 (Smith, Salt)
Oct 10th 1891	Reigate Priory	won	4-3 (Smith, Salt 2, Winch)
Oct 14th 1891	Casuals	won	6-5 (Smith 2, Crabtree, Salt, Wild 2)
Oct 17th 1891	Crusaders	lost	1-3 (Wild)
Oct 24th 1891	Clapham Rovers	won	7-0 (Smith 4, Salt, Crabtree, Wild)
Nov 7th 1891	Oxford OCs	won	2-0 (Salt, Smith)
Nov 11th 1891	Old Rossallians	lost	2-4 (Salt)
Nov 14th 1891	Old Harrovians	won	8-3 (Salt 5, Barwell 2, Broadbent)
Nov 21st 1891	RMC Sandhurst	drew	1-1 (Salt)
Nov 25th 1891	Godalming	lost	1-3 (Salt)
Nov 28th 1891	Magdalen College	won	1-0 (Smith)
Dec 2nd 1891	Trinity College, Oxford	lost	0-2
Dec 5th 1891	WN Cobbold's XI	won	3-2 (Salt, Foster, Winch)
Dec 12th 1891	Old Carthusians	lost	4-5
Jan 30th 1892	Old Wykehamists	drew	0-0
Feb 6th 1892	Old Harrovians	won	5-0 (Salt 4, Smith)
Feb 10th 1892	WE Hansell's XI	won	2-1 (Salt, Smith)
Feb 13th 1892	Crusaders	drew	2-2 (Vassall, Smith)
Feb 24th 1892	Exeter College	won	9-0 (Smith 3, Salt 5, Barwell)
Feb 27th 1892	Westminster	won	5-0 (Smith 2, Salt 2, *mêlée*)
Mar 12th 1892	Old Carthusians	drew	0-0
Sept 24th 1892	AH Tod's XI	lost	1-5 (Ward)
Sept 28th 1892	Godalming	won	4-1 (Fordyce 2, Vassall, Broadbent)
Oct 5th 1892	Casuals	lost	2-4 (Broadbent, Ward)
Oct 15th 1892	Old Harrovians	won	3-0 (Crabtree, Broadbent, Vassall)
Oct 19th 1892	Weybridge	won	6-1 (Hunt 2, Broadbent 2, Fordyce, Crabtree)
Oct 22nd 1892	Crusaders	drew	1-1 (Broadbent)
Nov 9th 1892	Keble College	won	4-0 (Fordyce, Vassall, Broadbent, Bray)
Nov 12th 1892	Old Rossallians	won	4-0 (Hunt 3, Broadbent)
Nov 16th 1892	University College	won	4-1 (Hunt, Vassall 3)
Nov 19th 1892	RMC Sandhurst	won	4-1 (Vassall 2, Broadbent, Hunt)
Nov 23rd 1892	Magdalen College	won	4-2 (Broadbent, Hunt)
Nov 26th 1892	Sussex Dolphins	won	5-1
Nov 30th 1892	New College	lost	1-2
Dec 3rd 1892	WN Cobbold's XI	lost	0-5
Dec 10th 1892	Old Carthusians	lost	2-3 (Broadbent 2)
Dec 15th 1892	EC Bliss's XI	lost	0-1
Jan 28th 1893	Old Wykehamists	won	3-1 (Fordyce 2, Vassall)
Feb 11th 1893	Crusaders	won	2-0 (Vassall, Broadbent)
Feb 15th 1893	Casuals	won	3-2 (Hunt 2, Fordyce)
Feb 22nd 1893	Magdalen College	won	3-1 (Hunt, Vassall, Broadbent)
Feb 25th 1893	Westminster	won	5-0 (Hunt 5)
Mar 1st 1893	Reigate Priory	won	4-0 (Dyne, Broadbent, Hunt, Neill)
Mar 4th 1893	Cambridge OCs	won	4-1 (Crabtree, Fordyce, *rushed*, Dyne)
Mar 8th 1893	Old Reptonians	lost	2-3 (Broadbent, Hunt)
Mar 18th 1893	Old Carthusians	won	4-2 (Vassall 2, Hunt, Fordyce)
Mar 29th 1893	OC Cup team	won	2-1 (Dyne, Hunt)
Oct 4th 1893	Casuals	lost	2-5 (Peers, Fordyce)
Oct 7th 1893	AD Fordyce's XI	won	1-0 (Fordyce)
Oct 11th 1893	Godalming	won	5-3 (Fordyce, Vassall 2, Hunt 2)
Oct 14th 1893	Weybridge	won	4-1 (Neill, Hunt 2, Hancock)
Oct 18th 1893	Old Brightonians	won	3-2 (Fordyce, Hunt 2)
Oct 21st 1893	Old Rossallians	won	6-1 (Vassall 2, Fordyce, Jameson 2, Hunt)
Oct 28th 1893	Old Etonians	drew	2-2 (Hunt 2)
Nov 15th 1893	New College	won	4-1 (Neill 2, Hancock, Hunt)
Nov 18th 1893	Crusaders	won	1-0 (Hancock)
Nov 22nd 1893	Cambridge OCs	lost	1-2 (Sladen)
Nov 25th 1893	RMC Sandhurst	won	7-2 (Hunt 5, Hancock, Jameson)
Dec 2nd 1893	WN Cobbold's XI	won	1-0 (Fordyce)
Dec 6th 1893	EC Bliss's XI	lost	2-4 (Vassall, Jameson)
Dec 8th 1893	Liverpool Ramblers	won	2-1 (o.g., Hunt)
Dec 9th 1893	Old Carthusians	won	4-2 (Vassall, Jameson 2, Wilson)
Dec 16th 1893	Sussex Dolphins	won	6-1 (Hunt 3, Wilson, Vassall, Hancock)
Feb 7th 1894	Old Wykehamists	drew	2-2 (Jameson, Dyne)
Feb 10th 1894	Old Harrovians	won	7-1 (Dyne, Fordyce, Jameson, Hancock, Vassall 3)
Feb 14th 1894	Casuals	won	3-1 (Davidson 2, Jameson)
Feb 24th 1894	Crusaders	lost	2-5 (Jameson, Davidson)
Mar 3rd 1894	Westminster	won	6-0 (Vassall, Hancock 2, Jameson, Fordyce 2)
Mar 7th 1894	Reigate Priory	won	1-0 (Hancock)
Mar 17th 1894	Old Carthusians	won	1-0
Sept 29th 1894	AH Tod's XI	won	2-0 (GW Ryder 2)
Oct 3rd 1894	Casuals	drew	2-2 (GW Ryder, Wallace)
Oct 10th 1894	Godalming	lost	3-4 (Anderson, Laird, GW Ryder)
Oct 13th 1894	Reigate Priory	won	2-1 (Laird, GW Ryder)
Oct 20th 1894	Weybridge	won	2-0 (Anderson, GW Ryder)
Oct 24th 1894	Old Brightonians	drew	1-1 (Anderson)
Oct 27th 1894	RMC Sandhurst	lost	0-2
Oct 31st 1894	Balliol College	won	2-1 (GW Ryder, Austen)
Nov 1st 1894	Liverpool Ramblers	won	3-0 (Turnbull, Laird, Haig Brown)
Nov 7th 1894	New College	won	4-2 (Laird, Franks, Haig Brown, Wallace)
Nov 10th 1894	Magdalen College	drew	0-0 *abandoned because of rain*
Nov 17th 1894	Crusaders	won	2-1 (CF Ryder, GW Ryder)
Nov 21st 1894	Trinity Rest	lost	1-2 (Franks)
Dec 1st 1894	Old Carthusians	drew	2-2 (Jameson, Laird)
Dec 5th 1894	West Wratting Park	won	4-0 (Laird, o.g., GW Ryder, Jameson)
Dec 8th 1894	Bradfield Waifs	won	3-1 (GW Ryder, Anderson, Franks)
Dec 12th 1894	University College Hosp	won	4-0 (Hancock, Franks, Jameson 2)
Mar 6th 1895	Trinity College	drew	2-2 (Jameson 2)
Mar 9th 1895	Westminster	won	6-0 (Austen, Walsh, GW Ryder, CF Ryder, Wallace, Hancock)
Mar 16th 1895	Old Westminsters	won	4-1 (CF Ryder 3, Murdoch)
Sept 28th 1895	AH Tod's XI	lost	1-11 (Vassall)
Oct 5th 1895	Old Brightonians	lost	2-4 (GW Ryder, Horne)
Oct 12th 1895	Godalming	lost	2-3 (Moss 2)
Oct 19th 1895	RMC Sandhurst	lost	2-4 (Jameson, Horne)
Oct 23rd 1895	Casuals	lost	3-7 (Horne 2, Haig Brown)
Oct 26th 1895	Reigate Priory	won	4-0 (GW Ryder, Horne 2, Haig Brown)
Nov 9th 1895	Crusaders	lost	1-3 (Moss)
Nov 16th 1895	Old Rossallians	won	3-0 (Hulton, Vassall, Haig Brown)
Nov 20th 1895	Magdalen College	won	2-1 (GW Ryder 2)
Nov 23rd 1895	Weybridge	won	12-0 (Ryder 4, Haig Brown 2, Horne, Vassall 3, Jameson 2)
Nov 27th 1895	Balliol College	won	2-1 (Haig Brown 2)
Nov 28th 1895	Liverpool Ramblers	lost	3-5 (Haig Brown 2, Moss)
Nov 30th 1895	RMA Woolwich	won	2-0 (Moss, Scott)
Dec 4th 1895	West Wratting Park	lost	0-2
Dec 7th 1895	Old Carthusians	lost	2-5 (Vassall 2)
Dec 11th 1895	Oxford OCs	lost	1-6 (Horne)
Dec 14th 1895	Old Harrovians	won	7-2 (Horne 3, Green 3, Haig Brown)
Feb 1st 1896	Barnes	won	7-2 (Jameson 2, Horne 2, Haig Brown 2, Ryder)
Feb 5th 1896	Casuals	won	4-3 (Green, Vassall 2, Jameson)
Feb 19th 1896	Old Wykehamists	drew	1-1 (Horne)
Feb 26th 1896	Oriel College	won	4-2 (Vassall, Ryder 2, Buzzard)
Mar 4th 1896	Old Reptonians	drew	0-0
Mar 7th 1896	AD Fordyce's XI	lost	1-3 (Vassall)
Mar 14th 1896	Westminster	won	2-0 (Vassall, Ryder)
Sept 26th 1896	AH Tod's XI	won	3-2 (Moss, Vassall, Mucklow)
Oct 3rd 1896	Old Reptonians	drew	2-2 (Vassall, Laird)
Oct 10th 1896	Old Brightonians	won	5-1 (Vassall 2, Renshaw, Ryder, Moss)
Oct 17th 1896	Guildford	won	2-0 (Moss, Vassall)
Oct 21st 1896	Magdalen College	won	2-1 (Gordon, Moss)
Oct 24th 1896	RMC Sandhurst	won	7-1 (Moss 2, Ryder, Renshaw, Vassall 2)
Nov 7th 1896	Casuals	won	2-0 (Moss 2)
Nov 24th 1896	WAE Austen's XI	won	4-3 (Vassall, Gimson, Gordon, Mucklow)
Nov 28th 1896	Ewell	won	6-0 (Gordon 2, Ryder, Vassall 3)
Dec 2nd 1896	WN Cobbold's XI	lost	1-3 (Mucklow)
Dec 5th 1896	Barnes	won	3-1 (Ryder, Mucklow, Gordon)
Dec 9th 1896	Oxford OCs	lost	1-7 (Mucklow)
Dec 12th 1896	Old Carthusians	won	6-4 (Ryder, Vassall 2, Gordon 2, Renshaw)
Dec 16th 1896	Old Internationals	lost	0-5 *played at Queen's Club*
Feb 10th 1897	Casuals	drew	1-1 (Forbes)
Feb 13th 1897	Oriel College	drew	4-4 (Gordon 2, Mucklow, Ryder)
Feb 20th 1897	Reigate Priory	won	2-1 (Moss, Fox)
Feb 24th 1897	NL Jackson's XI	won	4-1 (Mucklow, Ryder, Gordon, Moss)
Feb 27th 1897	Westminster	won	3-1 (Gordon 2, Ryder)

Date	Opponent	Result	Score
Oct 2nd 1897	Old Reptonians	lost	2-3 (Moss 2)
Oct 9th 1897	AH Tod's XI	lost	1-9 (Moss)
Oct 16th 1897	Reigate Priory	won	4-3 (Moss 3, Gordon)
Oct 23rd 1897	Guildford	won	1-0 (Gordon)
Oct 30th 1897	Caius College	won	1-0
Nov 13th 1897	Magdalen College	lost	1-4 (Crosdale)
Nov 20th 1897	Casuals	lost	1-2 (Gordon)
Nov 27th 1897	Barnes	drew	1-1 (Moss)
Dec 4th 1897	RMC Sandhurst	won	7-3 (Moss 3, Gordon 3, Trower)
Dec 8th 1897	Old Etonians	won	5-4 (Gordon 3, Crosdale 2)
Dec 11th 1897	Old Carthusians	lost	0-9
Dec 15th 1897	GC Vassall'sXI	lost	2-3 (Gordon, Crosdale)
Feb 5th 1898	Oriel College	lost	2-6 (Moss 2)
Feb 12th 1898	Casuals	won	7-1 (Moss 4, Crosdale 2, Trower)
Feb 19th 1898	LB Coulson's XI	won	8-1 (Trower 2, Moss, Evans, Crosdale 3, Routh)
Feb 26th 1898	Old Wykehamists	won	4-2 (Trower 2, Moss, Crosdale)
Mar 5th 1898	Westminster	lost	1-4 (Moss)
Sept 24th 1898	AH Tod's XI	lost	2-5 (Sturrock, Trower)
Oct 1st 1898	Old Reptonians	won	7-1 (Greenwood 3, Trower, Evans 2. Gibson)
Oct 8th 1898	Reigate Priory	won	3-0 (Evans, Gibson, Greenwood)
Oct 22nd 1898	Guildford	lost	1-2 (Evans)
Oct 29th 1898	Barnes	won	5-0 (Timmis, Trower, Evans 2, Leechman)
Nov 2nd 1898	RMA Woolwich	won	4-2 (Wild, Gibson 2, Trower)
Nov 12th 1898	Emeriti	won	5-0 (Evans, Greenwood 2, Sturrock, Gibson)
Nov 16th 1898	Magdalen College	won	2-0 (Greenwood, Trower)
Nov 19th 1898	Casuals	won	3-2 (Tuff 2, Evans)
Nov 23rd 1898	Richmond AFC	won	3-2 (Tuff 2, Trower)
Nov 26th 1898	RMC Sandhurst	won	13-1 (Tuff 4 Gibson 3 Evans 3 Trower, Leechman, Gardner)
Dec 3rd 1898	Old Wykehamists	won	3-1 (Greenwood, Tuff, Trower)
Dec 7th 1898	Old Etonians	won	4-2 (Tuff 2, Trower, Greenwood)
Dec 10th 1898	Old Carthusians	lost	0-1
Dec 14th 1898	GC Vassall's XI	lost	0-6
Dec 17th 1898	Bradfield Waifs	won	3-0 (Evans, Trower 2)
Dec 19th 1898	GO Smith's XI	lost	1-3 (Greenwood)
Dec 22nd 1898	Old Internationals	lost	2-4 (Trower, Gibson) *played at Queen's Club*
Feb 4th 1899	Oriel College	drew	2-2 (Tuff, Good)
Feb 11th 1899	Casuals	won	3-0 (Evans, Tuff 2)
Feb 15th 1899	CF Ryder's XI	won	5-2 (Flower 2, Tuff 3)
Feb 22nd 1899	RF Evans's XI	drew	4-4 (Sturrock 2, Trower, Evans)
Feb 25th 1899	Westminster	lost	1-2 (Tuff)
Mar 1st 1899	Trinity College	won	6-0 (Trower, Evans 2, Greenwood, Liddle, Tuff)
Sept 30th 1899	AH Tod's XI	drew	0-0
Oct 7th 1899	Weybridge	lost	0-6
Oct 19th 1899	Reigate Priory	lost	0-1
Oct 25th 1899	Emeriti	won	3-0 (Waller, Trower, Tuff)
Oct 28th 1899	Ewell	won	6-1 (Tuff 4, Waller, Trower)
Nov 1st 1899	RMA Woolwich	won	4-1 (Waller, Tuff, Gardner, Trower)
Nov 15th 1899	Casuals	won	3-2 (Waller, Sharp, Tuff)
Nov 18th 1899	Old Etonians	won	5-2 (Tuff 4, o.g.)
Nov 25th 1899	RMC Sandhurst	won	6-1 (Waller 3, Gardner, Tuff, Trower)
Dec 6th 1899	WN Cobbold's XI	lost	1-6 (Waller)
Dec 9th 1899	Old Carthusians	lost	1-2 (Tuff)
Dec 20th 1899	Old Internationals	drew	2-2 (Melchers-Ahrens 2) *at Queen's Club*
Jan 31st 1900	Guildford	won	1-0 (Trower)
Feb 7th 1900	Barnes	won	8-0 (Tuff 4, Trower 2, Malden 2)
Feb 10th 1900	Magdalen College	lost	1-3 (Trower)
Feb 17th 1899	H Crabtree's XI	lost	0-2
Feb24th 1900	Westminster	won	7-2 (Tuff 5, Trower 2)
Feb 28th 1900	Oriel College	won	6-2 (Tuff 3, Gimson 2, Waller)
Mar 7th 1900	Trinity College	won	1-0 (Trower)
Mar 10th 1900	MFR Wingfield's XI	won	4-2 (Trower, Malden, Gimson 2)
Mar 15th 1900	Eton (J Wormald's XI)	won	4-1 (Tuff 3, Good)
500th Match			
Mar 17th 1900	Old Carthusians	lost	0-5
Sept 29th 1900	AH Tod's XI	lost	1-6 (Tuff)
Oct 6th 1900	RAB Trower's XI	won	4-1 (Tuff 4)
Oct 13th 1900	Guildford	won	6-0 (Curwen, Malden, Tuff 4)
Oct 17th 1900	Weybridge	won	6-0 (Malden 2, Tuff 2, Goodliffe 2)
Oct 20th 1900	RMC Sandhurst	won	2-1 (Tuff 2)
Oct 27th 1900	Emeriti	won	10-0 (Tuff 8, Malden, Goodliffe)
Nov 14th 1900	Barnes	lost	3-5 (o.g., Malden, Fisher)
Nov 17th 1900	Liverpool Ramblers	lost	1-3 (Malden)
Nov 24th 1900	RMA Woolwich	lost	1-2 (Tuff)
Nov 28th 1900	JM Hulton's XI	won	5-0 (Ferguson, o.g., Curwen 2, Bowring)
Dec 15th 1900	Old Carthusians	won	2-0 (Ferguson, Tuff)
Dec 19th 1900	OC Internationals	lost	1-5 (Tuff)
Feb 9th 1901	Magdalen College	won	8-0 (o.g., Tuff 4, Bense Pembroke 3)
Feb 13th 1901	Casuals	lost	0-2
Feb 23rd 1901	Westminster	won	6-0 (Goodliffe, Tuff 3, Bense Pembroke 2)
Feb 27th 1901	Trinity Rest	drew	2-2 (Tuff 2)
Mar 6th 1901	Oriel College	won	6-1 (Tuff 4, Bense Pembroke, Goodliffe)
Mar 9th 1901	Reigate Priory	won	7-2 (Bense Pembroke, Tuff 6)
Mar 14th 1901	Eton	won	5-0 (Tuff, Goodliffe, Bense Pembroke 3)
Mar 16th 1901	CH Wilson's XI	lost	1-5 (Bowring)
Sept 28th 1901	AH Tod's XI	lost	0-7
Oct 5th 1901	Beckenham	won	2-1 (Goodliffe 2)
Oct 12th 1901	Weybridge	won	4-0 (Curwen, Goodliffe, Dowson, Bense Pembroke)
Oct 19th 1901	RMA Woolwich	drew	1-1 (Bense Pembroke)
Oct 26th 1901	RMC Sandhurst	won	3-0 (Goodliffe, Bense Pembroke, Bowring)
Nov 2nd 1901	RA Subalterns	won	1-0 (Kelly)
Nov 23rd 1901	Casuals	won	2-1 (Verry, Bense Pembroke)
Nov 27th 1901	Barnes	won	6-0 (Bense Pembroke 5, Goodliffe)
Nov 30th 1901	Liverpool Ramblers	drew	1-1 (Verry)
Dec 14th 1901	Old Carthusians	won	3-0 (Goodliffe, Sharp, Verry)
Jan 25th 1902	Bradfield Waifs	won	2-1 (Farquharson, Goodliffe)
Feb 1st 1902	Reigate Priory	drew	0-0
Feb 8th 1902	Old Etonians	won	4-0 (Goodliffe 4)
Feb 12th 1902	Magdalen College	lost	1-3 (Verry)
Feb 19th 1902	Casuals	won	1-0 (Goodliffe)
Feb 22nd 1902	Westminster	won	2-0 (Farquharson, Bowring)
Feb 26th 1902	Winchester	won	2-0 (Verry, Goodliffe)
Sept 27th 1902	AH Tod's XI	drew	1-1 (Dowson)
Oct 3rd 1902	Beckenham	lost	0-4
Oct 11th 1902	Weybridge	won	1-0 (Eckersley)
Oct 19th 1902	RMA Woolwich	won	2-0 (Bense Pembroke, Tetley)
Oct 25th 1902	RMC Sandhurst	won	3-0 (Dowson 2, Snell)
Nov 1st 1902	Guildford	drew	0-0
Nov 5th 1902	Clare Coll. Cambridge	drew	0-0
Nov 19th 1902	Casuals	lost	0-1
Nov 22nd 1902	Royal Artillery	drew	2-2 (Snell 2)
Nov 29th 1902	Liverpool Ramblers	won	1-0 (Tetley)
Dec 13th 1902	Old Carthusians	lost	0-4
Dec 17th 1902	Old Internationals	lost	1-4 (Bense Pembroke) *played at Queen's Club*
Feb 4th 1903	WJH Curwen's XI	won	4-1 (Bense Pembroke 2, Tetley, Seth Smith)
Feb 7th 1903	Reigate Priory	lost	0-1
Feb 14th 1903	Royal Engineers	won	6-0 (Barbour, Bense Pembroke, Snell 3, Branston)
Feb 18th 1903	Oriel College	won	1-0 (Bense Pembroke)
Feb 21st 1903	Westminster	won	2-1 (Bense Pembroke 2)
Feb 28th 1903	HK Waller's XI	drew	2-2
Mar 4th 1903	Casuals	won	4-1 (Bense Pembroke 2, Allen, Taylor)
Mar 7th 1903	Magdalen College	lost	0-1
Sept 26th 1903	AH Tod's XI	lost	1-2 (Taylor)
Oct 3rd 1903	Beckenham	drew	1-1 (Taylor)
Oct 11th 1903	Weybridge	won	3-0 (Reid 2, Allen)
Oct 17th 1903	RMA Woolwich	won	2-1 (Taylor, Allen)
Oct 25th 1903	RMC Sandhurst	drew	1-1 (Allen)
Nov 4th 1903	Casuals	lost	1-3 (Allen)
Nov 14th 1903	Bradfield Waifs	won	3-0 (Allen 2, Taylor)
Nov 21st 1903	New College	drew	0-0
Nov 28th 1903	Liverpool Ramblers	lost	1-3 (Reid)
Dec 5th 1903	West Wratting Park	drew	0-0 (played only 40 minutes in thick fog)
Dec 12th 1903	Old Carthusians	lost	0-3
Dec 23rd 1903	*Old Internationals*	lost	2-4 (Barbour, Taylor) *played at Queen's Club*
Jan 30th 1904	RA Bense Pembroke's XI	drew	1-1 (Taylor)
Feb 6th 1904	Reigate Priory	lost	1-2 (Blagrove)
Feb 13th 1904	Kenley	lost	0-1
Feb 20th 1904	Westminster	won	1-0 (Taylor)
Mar 2nd 1904	Casuals	won	1-0 (Walker)
Mar 3rd 1904	Winchester	drew	1-1 (Walker)
Mar 5th 1904	OT Norris's XI	won	3-2 (Walker 2, Johnston)
Mar 9th 1904	Magdalen College	won	2-1 (Taylor 2)
Oct 1st 1904	AH Tod's XI	lost	2-5 (Pears, Lyell)
Oct 15th 1904	Weybridge	won	4-0 (Reid 2, Lyell)
Oct 22nd 1904	RMA Woolwich	lost	0-1
Oct 29th 1904	Casuals	lost	1-3 (Lyell)
Nov 5th 1904	Old Reptonians	won	4-2 (Lyell 2, Cockburn, Steer)
Nov 16th 1904	Clare College	won	6-0 (Reid 4, Pears 2)
Nov 19th 1904	Beckenham	won	3-0 (Reid, Tillie, Cockburn)
Dec 3rd 1904	RMC Sandhurst	drew	1-1 (Pears)
Dec 10th 1904	BH Willett's XI	won	2-0 (Rücker, Mackwood)
Dec 17th 1904	Old Carthusians	drew	1-1 (Gilbert)
Jan 28th 1905	Trinity Rest	won	3-1 (Lyell 3)
Feb 4th 1905	Reigate Priory	won	1-0 (Lyell)
Feb 11th 1905	Kenley	won	4-2 (Reid 2, Rücker, Pears)
Feb 18th 1905	Trinity, Oxford	won	5-2 (Burton 2, Greig 2, Reid)
Feb 22nd 1905	Oriel College	drew	2-2 (Cockburn, Reid)
Feb 25th 1905	Liverpool Ramblers	won	4-0 (Reid 2, Gilbert, Lyell)

Date	Opponent		Score (scorers)
Mar 1st 1905	Winchester	lost	3-4 (Gilbert, Reid, Lyell)
Mar 4th 1905	Westminster	won	4-0 (Pears 3, Lyell)
Mar 8th 1905	Casuals	lost	0-3
Sept 30th 1905	AH Tod's XI	lost	1-7 (Greig)
Oct 7th 1905	RMA Woolwich	won	5-2 (Greig 2, Parry, Preston, Tillie)
Oct 21st 1905	Christ Church, Oxford	won	6-1 (Preston, Greig, Gooch 2, Parry 2)
Oct 28th 1905	Casuals	won	2-1 (Gooch, Preston)
Nov 4th 1905	Surbiton Hill	won	3-1 (Preston 2, Crier)
Nov 11th 1905	Old Reptonians	lost	1-4 (Jameson)
Nov 18th 1905	Beckenham	lost	1-2 (Greig)
Dec 2nd 1905	RMC Sandhurst	drew	1-1 (Preston)
Dec 9th 1905	Old Carthusians	drew	1-1 (Gooch)
Dec 16th 1905	AA Drew's XI	drew	1-1 (Tillie)
Dec 20th 1905	Old Internationals	won	3-2 (Parry, o.g., Greig) *played at Queen's Club*
Jan 27th 1906	Exeter College	won	4-2 (Parry 3, Preston)
Feb 3rd 1906	Lancing OB	won	5-0 (Greig 2, Crier, Preston, Tillie)
Feb 7th 1906	Trinity Rest	won	7-1 (Preston 2, Greig 3, Tillie, Parry)
Feb 10th 1906	Liverpool Ramblers	won	2-1 (Tillie, Gooch)
Feb 17th 1906	Casuals	won	3-2 (Preston, Greig, Parry)
Feb 21st 1906	Oriel College	won	1-0 (Peet)
Mar 3rd 1906	Westminster	won	3-0 (Parry 3)
Mar 8th 1906	Winchester	lost	0-2
Sept 29th 1906	Casuals	lost	0-1
Oct 6th 1906	RMA Woolwich	won	7-0 (Parry 2, Pegram, Wardle, Preston 2, Gooch)
Oct 10th 1906	AH Tod's XI	lost	0-9
Oct 20th 1906	Old Foresters	drew	2-2 (Preston, Pegram)
Oct 24th 1906	Casuals	won	5-1 (Preston 2, Parry 3)
Oct 27th 1906	Old Westminsters	won	2-0 (Pegram 2)
Nov 3rd 1906	Clare College	won	3-0 (Pegram 3)
Nov 10th 1906	Kenley	won	5-0 (Jameson 2, Preston 2, Parry)
Nov 17th 1906	Beckenham	lost	0-1
Nov 24th 1906	RMC Sandhurst	won	2-1 (Preston, Gooch)
Dec 1st 1906	Oxford 'A'	lost	0-3
Dec 8th 1906	AA Drew's XI	won	2-0 (Braddell, o.g.)
Dec 15th 1906	Old Carthusians	lost	0-1
Dec 19th 1906	C Wreford Brown's XI	lost	0-5 *played at Queen's Club*
Feb 2nd 1907	Brentwood Rovers	won	3-0 (Pegram, Shrager, Jameson)
Feb 9th 1907	Oriel College	won	5-0 (Pegram 3, Jameson, Gooch)
Feb 16th 1907	Casuals	lost	1-6 (Preston)
Feb 23rd 1907	Magdalen, Oxford	won	4-1 (Parry 2, Pegram, Evans)
Mar 2nd 1907	Westminster	won	3-0 (Parry, Pegram 2)
Mar 12th 1907	Winchester	won	1-0 (Parry)
Sept 28th 1907	AH Tod's XI	lost	0-7 *played as the opening of Broom & Lees*
Oct 6th 1907	RMA Woolwich	won	5-0 (Pike 3, Livesey, Wilson)
Oct 12th 1907	RD England's XI	won	4-1 (Wilson, Pike 2, Livesey)
Oct 19th 1907	Weybridge	won	2-1 (Livesey, Rushton)
Oct 26th 1907	Casuals	won	4-1 (Wilson 3, Livesey)
Nov 2nd 1907	RMC Sandhurst	won	5-1 (Pike 4, Wilson)
Nov 9th 1907	Kenley	won	2-0 (Livesey, Wilson)
Nov 16th 1907	Beckenham	drew	1-1 (Wilson)
Nov 23rd 1907	Liverpool Ramblers	won	5-0 (Wilson, Rhodes, Pike 2, Livesey)
Dec 4th 1907	Oxford 'A'	lost	1-4 (Livesey)
Dec 7th 1907	BH Willett's XI	lost	1-2 (Livesey)
Dec 10th 1907	JHD Sheppard's XI	won	2-0 (Livesey, Wilson)
Dec 14th 1907	Old Carthusians	lost	0-3
Dec 17th 1907	Outcasts	lost	1-2 (Pike)
Dec 19th 1907	Repton	lost	0-4
Jan 25th 1908	Lancing OB	won	4-1 (Livesey 3, Johnson)
Feb 1st 1908	Reigate Priory	won	2-1 (Johnson, Livesey)
Feb 8th 1908	CT Gooch's XI	drew	2-2 (Rushton, Pike)
Feb 12th 1908	Oriel College	won	1-0 (Pike)
Feb 15th 1908	Casuals	lost	0-1
Feb 19th 1908	Outcasts	won	3-2 (Weeks 2, Macdonald)
Feb 26th 1908	Old Wykehamists	won	3-1 (Weeks, Pike 2)
Feb 29th 1908	Westminster	won	4-0 (Pike 3, Weeks)
Mar 4th 1908	CD White's XI	won	4-1 (Weeks, Pike, Livesey 2)
Mar 10th 1908	Winchester	won	5-0 (Pike 2, Stuart, Rushton, Livesey)
Oct 3rd 1908	AH Tod's XI	lost	3-5 (Norris 2, Weeks)
Oct 10th 1908	RMA Woolwich	drew	1-1 (Weeks)
Oct 17th 1908	Weybridge	won	6-0 (Norris 2, Macdonald, Weeks 3)
Oct 24th 1908	Casuals	lost	1-3 (Macdonald)
Oct 31st 1908	RMC Sandhurst	won	4-1 (Weeks 3, Macdonald)
Nov 4th 1908	PC Smythe's XI	won	6-2 (Weeks 3, Macdonald 3)
Nov 7th 1908	Kenley	won	4-3 (o.g., Weeks 3)
Nov 14th 1908	Beckenham	won	4-1 (Norris 2, Macdonald 2)
Nov 18th 1908	Outcasts	won	2-0 (Booth, Macdonald)
Nov 21st 1908	Liverpool Ramblers	won	6-0 (Weeks 3, Norris 2, Macdonald)
Nov 28th 1908	Addiscombe Park	won	4-0 (Weeks 3, Johnson)
Dec 5th 1908	BH Willett's XI	won	1-0 (Johnson)
Dec 9th 1908	Duke of Cornwall's L I	lost	0-1
Dec 12th 1908	Old Carthusians	lost	2-3 (Johnson, Weeks)
Dec 22nd 1908	Repton	won	2-1 (Macdonald, Johnson)
Jan 30th 1909	Emeriti	lost	0-1
Feb 6th 1909	Clapham Rovers	won	5-1 (Weeks 5)
Feb 10th 1909	Casuals	won	2-1 (Johnson, Norris)
Feb 17th 1909	Reigate Priory	won	9-4 (Weeks 5, Norris 2, Kingdom, Macdonald)
Feb 24th 1909	Oriel College	won	3-0 (Macdonald, Weeks, Johnson)
Feb 27th 1909	Oxford University 'A'	lost	1-3 (Weeks)
Mar 6th 1909	Westminster	won	2-1 (Norris, Macdonald)
Mar 9th 1909	Winchester	won	6-3 (Weeks 3, Johnson 2, Wharton)
Mar 13th 1909	Norsemen	drew	0-0
Mar 16th 1909	Outcasts	lost	1-2 (Weeks)
Mar 20th 1909	Lancing OB	won	7-0 (Macdonald 4, Weeks 3)
Oct 2nd 1909	AH Tod's XI	lost	1-8 (Bruce)
Oct 9th 1909	RMC Sandhurst	drew	2-2 (Boosey, Norris)
Oct 16th 1909	Weybridge	lost	0-1
Oct 23rd 1909	Casuals	won	2-1 (Boosey 2)
Oct 27th 1909	RMA Woolwich	won	11-0 (Boosey 5, Bruce 2, Dixon 3, Norris)
Oct 30th 1909	Achaeans	lost	2-3 (Bruce, Dixon)
Nov 6th 1909	Kenley	won	3-1 (Bruce, Norris, Dixon)
Nov 10th 1909	Outcasts	lost	1-3 (Norris)
Nov 13th 1909	CB Johnson's XI	lost	0-1
Nov 17th 1909	Oxford University 'A'	lost	1-0 (Boosey)
Nov 20th 1909	Beckenham	lost	2-5 (Dunlop, Bruce)
Nov 27th 1909	Surbiton Hill	won	4-2 (Bruce 2, Dunlop, Steer)
Dec 4th 1909	BH Willett's XI	lost	0-2
Dec 11th 1909	Old Carthusians	lost	0-3
Dec 18th 1909	Reading Amateurs	drew	2-2 (Bruce, Boosey)
Dec 21st 1909	Repton	won	2-0 (Boosey 2)
Jan 29th 1910	Lancing OB	won	1-0 (Gibbons)
Feb 5th 1910	Clapham Rovers	won	3-1 (Dixon, Polson 2)
Feb 9th 1910	Casuals	lost	0-4
Feb 12th 1910	S Baker's XI	won	3-0 (Polson 2, Dixon)
Feb 16th 1910	Reigate Priory	won	4-2 (Dixon, Boosey 3)
Feb 26th 1910	Westminster	drew	1-1 (Dixon)
Mar 2nd 1910	Outcasts	lost	0-3
Mar 5th 1910	Duke of Cornwall's Lt I	won	4-0 (Polson 2, Norris, Boosey)
Mar 8th 1910	Winchester	won	2-1 (Boosey, Dunlop)
Mar 12th 1910	Liverpool Ramblers	won	3-0 (Dunlop 2, Boosey)
Mar 19th 1910	Ealing	drew	2-2 (Boosey, Dixon)
Oct 1st 1910	AH Tod's XI	drew	2-2 (Boosey, Dunlop)
Oct 8th 1910	RMA Woolwich	won	1-0 (Dunlop)
Oct 15th 1910	Weybridge	won	5-1 (Dunlop, Sanderson 2, Boosey 2)
Oct 22nd 1910	Casuals	lost	0-3
Oct 26th 1910	RMA Woolwich	won	4-2 (Dunlop, Booosey, Faulkner, Sidebotham)
Oct 29th 1910	Bradfield OB	won	1-0 (Dunlop)
Nov 5th 1910	Kenley	won	2-0 (Sanderson, Boosey)
Nov 9th 1910	Outcasts	lost	2-3 (Boosey 2)
Nov 19th 1910	BH Willett's XI	drew	3-3 (Boosey, Sanderson, Dunlop)
Nov 23rd 1910	Duke Of Cornwall's Lt I	won	3-0 (Boosey 2, Gjers)
Nov 26th 1910	Surbiton Hill	drew	0-0
Dec 3rd 1910	Liverpool Ramblers	won	1-0 (Sanderson)
Dec 7th 1910	Oxford University 'A'	lost	2-4 (Sanderson 2)
Dec 17th 1910	Beckenham	won	2-0 (Boosey, Sanderson)
Dec 21st 1910	Repton	drew	2-2 (Wesley Smith, Boosey)
Feb 1st 1911	Old Westminsters	won	4-1 (Sanderson 3, Gibbons)
Feb 4th 1911	Clapham Rovers	won	3-1 (Boosey, Wesley Smith 2)
Feb 8th 1911	Casuals	won	2-0 (Gjers, Wesley Smith)
Feb 18th 1911	Lancing OB	lost	2-3 (Wesley Smith, Sanderson)
Feb 25th 1911	Westminster	won	4-1 (Faulkner, Boosey, Sanderson 2)
Mar 1st 1911	Oriel College	won	3-1 (Wesley Smith, Boosey 2)
Mar 4th 1911	RMA Sandhurst	lost	0-1
Mar 9th 1911	Winchester	lost	2-4 (Rücker, Boosey)
Mar 11th 1911	Achaeans	lost	2-5 (Boosey, Rücker)
Oct 7th 1911	AH Tod's XI	lost	0-2
Oct 14th 1911	Weybridge	won	3-1 (Fosdick, Ford)
Oct 21st 1911	Casuals	won	2-1 (Ford 2)
Oct 25th 1911	RMA Woolwich	won	2-0 (Liddle, Wright)
Oct 28th 1911	RMC Sandhurst	won	2-1 (de Brenière Smith 2)
Nov 8th 1911	Outcasts	lost	1-3
Nov 11th 1911	L Gjers' XI	won	3-0 (Vernon, o.g., Ford)
Nov 15th 1911	Oriel College	won	9-0
Nov 18th 1911	Surbiton Hill	won	4-3 (Ford, Rücker, de Brenière Smith, o.g.)
Nov 22nd 1911	Duke of Cornwall's Lt I	drew	1-1
Nov 25th 1911	Bradfield OB	won	2-0 (de Brenière Smith, Ford)
Dec 2nd 1911	Liverpool Ramblers	won	6-0
Dec 6th 1911	Oxford University 'A'	drew	2-2 (Rücker, de Brenière Smith)
Dec 9th 1911	Old Carthusians	lost	0-2
Dec 13th 1911	Norsemen	won	7-0 (Ford 4, de Brenière Smith, Vernon, Rücker)
Dec 16th 1911	Beckenham	drew	0-0
Dec 20th 1911	Repton	lost	0-2 *played at Leyton*
Jan 27th 1912	Old Westminsters	won	3-1 (Ford 2, Boswell)

Feb 14th 1912	Reigate Priory	won	2-1 (Boswell, Ford)
Feb 17th 1912	Reading Amateurs	won	5-4 (Boswell 2, Ford 3)
Feb 21st 1912	Achaeans	won	2-1 (Chambers, Ford)
Feb 24th 1912	Westminster	drew	1-1 (Fosdick)
Feb 28th 1912	RMC Sandhurst	won	4-1 (Letten Ford 3)
Mar 4th 1912	Outcasts	drew	2-2 (Boswell, Ford)
Mar 9th 1912	Lancing OB	won	7-0
Mar 12th 1912	Winchester	won	9-0 (Boswell)
Sept 28th 1912	AH Tod's XI	lost	1-4 (Rücker)
Oct 5th 1912	R Boosey's XI	lost	1-3 (Liddle)
Oct 9th 1912	RMC Sandhurst	lost	3-4 (Payne, Rücker, Hinds)
Oct 12th 1912	Weybridge	won	2-1 (Payne 2)
Oct 19th 1912	Casuals	lost	1-4 (Hinds)
Oct 26th 1912	Bradfield OB	lost	2-5 (Rücker, Payne)
Oct 30th 1912	RMA Woolwich	lost	2-3 (Payne, Chambers)
Nov 9th 1912	Kenley	lost	3-5 (Payne, Chambers 2)
Nov 13th 1912	Outcasts	lost	1-3 (Gregson Ellis)
Nov 16th 1912	Reigate Priory	lost	1-2 (Payne)
Nov 20th 1912	Repton	lost	0-2
Nov 23rd 1912	NE Burdon's XI	drew	2-2 (Gregson Ellis, Hinds)
Nov 30th 1912	Lancing OB	drew	3-3 (Liddle 2, Wesley Smith)
Dec 7th 1912	Surbiton Hill	won	2-1 (Liddle, Steel)
Dec 14th 1912	Old Carthusians	lost	0-2
Jan 25th 1913	Old Westminsters	lost	1-5 (Wesley Smith)
Feb 1st 1913	Beckenham	won	2-1 (Hinds, Liddle)
Feb 5th 1913	Casuals	lost	2-4 (Hinds, Liddle)
Feb 8th 1913	BH Willett's XI	lost	0-1
Feb 12th 1913	Oxford University 'A'	drew	1-1 (Liddle)
Feb 15th 1913	Reading Amateurs	lost	3-6 (Chambers 3)
Feb 22nd 1913	Westminster	won	2-0 (Steel, Chambers)
Mar 1st 1913	Achaeans	won	3-1 (Steel, Chambers, Liddle)
Mar 5th 1913	RMC Sandhurst	lost	1-2 (Rücker)
Mar 11th 1913	Winchester	won	2-0 (Steel, Chambers)
Mar 12th 1913	Outcasts	lost	1-4 (Rücker)
Sept 27th 1913	AH Tod's XI	lost	2-4 (Gray, Griffith)
Oct 8th 1913	RMC Sandhurst	lost	1-3 (Burnett)
Oct 11th 1913	Weybridge	drew	2-2 (Gray, Burnett)
Oct 18th 1913	Casuals	lost	2-3 (Cawston, Hinds)
Oct 29th 1913	RMA Woolwich	lost	0-3
Nov 5th 1913	Outcasts	lost	2-5 (Gray, Ritchie)
Nov 11th 1913	Oxford University 'A'	lost	1-4 (Smith)
Nov 15th 1913	BH Willett's XI	drew	4-4 (Gray, Smith 3)
Nov 20th 1913	Repton	lost	0-2
Nov 22nd 1913	Reigate Priory	won	1-0 (Gray)
Nov 29th 1913	Old Carthusians	lost	1-2 (Hinds)
Dec 6th 1913	HD Vernon's XI	won	4-2 (Ritchie, Cawston, Hinds 2)
Jan 31st 1914	Beckenham	lost	0-1
Feb 4th 1914	Casuals	lost	4-6 (Hinds 4)
Feb 7th 1914	Westminster	won	4-1 (Reiss 2, Smith, Ritchie)
Feb 11th 1914	Queen's Regt	won	3-2 (Smith 2, Reiss)
Feb 21st 1914	Magdalen College	lost	3-5 (Ritchie, Smith 2)
Mar 7th 1914	Liverpool Ramblers	lost	3-6 (Cawston, Smith 2)
Mar 12th 1914	Winchester	won	8-2 (Reiss 2, Hinds 2, Smith 2, Ritchie 2)
Mar 18th 1914	Outcasts	lost	2-4 (Ritchie, Smith)
Oct 3rd 1914	BH Willett's XI	won	4-1 (Dunlop 2, Harvie 2)
Oct 10th 1914	Hampstead	won	4-1 (Hansell 2, Harvie, Anderson)
Oct 31st 1914	Guildford	lost	0-2
Nov 7th 1914	Merton Park	lost	2-3 (Hansell, Dunlop)
Nov 14th 1914	RFA	won	8-1 (Hansell 4, Paull 3, Dunlop)
Nov 18th 1914	Repton	won	3-2 (Cawston, Hansell, Paull)
Nov 21st 1914	8th "The Buffs"	won	5-0 (Harvie 3, Hansell 2)
Nov 28th 1914	Westminster	drew	3-3 (o.g., Hansell, Paull) [not recorded as school match]
Dec 5th 1914	Artists' Rifles	won	3-1 (Ritchie, Hansell, Paull)
Dec 19th 1914	RMC Sandhurst	won	6-0 (Spafford, Hansell 3, Hall, Ritchie)
Feb 6th 1915	Hampstead	won	6-4 (Hansell 4, Hall, Ritchie)
Feb 13th 1915	Guildford	drew	1-1 (Hansell)
Feb 20th 1915	Westminster	won	4-1 (Cawston 2, Ritchie, Reiss)
Feb 27th 1915	Scots Cyclists	won	5-0 (Hansell 2, Reiss 2, Pollock)
Mar 6th 1915	RMC Sandhurst	won	6-3 (Butcher, Edge, Dunlop 3, Hansell)
Mar 10th 1915	Bradfield	won	5-2 (Hansell 3, Dunlop, Spafford)
Mar 17th 1915	RMC Sandhurst	won	6-0 (Hansell 4, Dunlop, Reiss)
Mar 20th 1915	Harrow	won	5-2 (Dunlop 2, Hansell 3)
Mar 25th 1915	Winchester	won	4-1 (Ritchie, Butcher, Hansell 2)
Mar 27th 1915	60th Rifles	drew	3-3 (Ritchie, Dunlop 2)
Mar 31st 1915	Lancing	won	7-1 (Reiss, Dunlop 2, Cawston 4)] ["An XI" played]
Oct 2nd 1915	Argyll & S Highlanders	lost	0-6
Oct 9th 1915	Drummond Athletic	won	8-0 (Reiss, Dunlop 2, Tinley 3, Hall 2)
Oct 13th 1915	RMC Sandhurst	lost	4-7 (Brownhill 2, Reiss, Tinley)
Oct 16th 1915	Hampstead	won	10-0 (Hall 5, Tinley 3, o.g.)
Oct 30th 1915	Argyll & S Highlanders	won	13-0 (Reiss 4, Tinley 4, Hall 4, Brownhill)
Nov 3rd 1915	The Queen's Regt	won	5-2 (Hall, Reiss 2)

Nov 10th 1915	Bradfield	won	8-0 (Reiss 7, Tinley)
Nov 18th 1915	Repton	lost	5-6 (Hall 3, Tinley, Reiss)
Nov 27th 1915	Sherwood Foresters	won	2-0 (Reiss, Tinley)
Dec 1st 1915	RMC Sandhurst	lost	4-5 (Reiss 2, Tinley, Bell)
Feb 12th 1916	GV Hind's XI	won	7-0 (Reiss 4, Garth, Tinley, South)
Feb 16th 1916	Inns of Court	lost	1-3
Mar 4th 1916	JCD Tetley's XI	lost	1-2 (Brownhill)
Mar 11th 1916	Harrow	won	4-2 (Tinley, Leggatt, Reiss 2)
Mar 18th 1916	Hants Regt	won	5-2
Mar 23rd 1916	Winchester	lost	1-4 (Tinley)
Mar 29th 1916	Westminster	drew	0-0
April 1st 1916	Dennis Athletic	lost	1-2
Sept 30th 1916	Dennis Athletic	won	5-1 (Lewns, Gauntlett 2, Tinley 2)
Oct 14th 1916	RMC Sandhurst	won	4-3 (Williams 2, Bearman, Tinley)
Oct 18th 1916	Artist Rifles	won	6-3 (Williams 6)
Oct 21st 1916	RMC/RMA 'A'	won	10-1 (Tinley 5, Williams 3, Bearman 2)
Oct 25th 1916	RMA Woolwich	won	5-2 (Bearman 2, Butcher, Tinley 2)
Oct 28th 1916	Bradfield	won	3-2 (Tinley 2, Bearman)
Nov 4th 1916	HAC, Richmond	lost	2-3 (Gauntlett 2)
Nov 11th 1916	Westminster	won	6-2 (Bearman 3, Lavenstein, Williams 2)
Nov 18th 1916	Inns of Court	lost	1-4 (Lewns)
Feb 28th 1917	Westminster	won	3-1 (Williams, Whalley, Lavenstein)
Mar 10th 1917	Harrow	won	4-3 (Bennett 2, Williams, Whalley)
Mar 1917	C Wreford Brown's XI	won	6-1
Mar 1917	Reading Amateurs	won	14-1
Sept 29th 1917	Dennis Athletic	won	10-0 (Williams)
Oct 6th 1917	RGA Aldershot	won	3-0
Oct 20th 1917	Bradfield	won	6-0
Oct 27th 1917	RGA Aldershot	lost	3-7
Oct 31st 1917	Repton	lost	1-3 (Lavenstein)
Nov 10th 1917	Lancing	won	2-0
Nov 17th 1917	Westminster	won	9-0 (Lavenstein, Williams)
Jan 30th 1918	5th Middlesex Regt	lost	1-2
Feb 6th 1918	RMC Sandhurst	won	3-1 (Williams 3)
Feb 13th 1918	125th Canadian Bttn	won	4-0 (Williams, Whalley, Thorne 2)
Mar 6th 1918	Winchester	drew	1-1
Mar 9th 1918	Westminster	won	3-0 (Williams 3)
Mar 13th 1918	Harrow	won	5-0 (Patchitt)
Sept 25th 1918	Cdn Fld Artillery	won	1-0 (Gilliat)
Oct 2nd 1918	Cdn Fld Engineers	lost	1-4 (Williams)
Oct 9th 1918	Cdn Brigade Artillery	lost	0-3
Oct 12th 1918	OCD Eastbourne	won	6-2
Oct 19th 1918	Lancing	won	4-0 (King)
Oct 23rd 1918	4th Res Bttn Witley	lost	2-3
Nov 16th 1918	OCB Bushey	lost	1-2
Nov 30th 1918	Westminster	won	2-0
Dec 4th 1918	Repton	drew	1-1 (Kiggell)
Mar 27th 1919	Harrow	lost	3-4 (Mordaunt Smith 3)
Apr 2nd 1919	Winchester	drew	1-1
Oct 8th 1919	Corinthians	lost	2-6 (Mordaunt Smith, Gilliat)
Oct 11th 1919	Bradfield OB	won	7-0 (Gilliat 3)
Oct 15th 1919	RMC Sandhurst	lost	1-5 (Gilliat)
Oct 18th 1919	E Cawston's XI	won	8-2 (Gilliat 3, Mordaunt Smith, Wade)
Oct 25th 1919	RMA Woolwich	drew	2-2 (Gilliat 2)
Nov 1st 1919	Old Westminsters	won	8-1 (Mordaunt Smith 3, Austin 2, Gilliat 3)
Nov 5th 1919	Univ Coll, Reading	lost	1-3 (Gilliat)
Nov 12th 1919	Bradfield	won	5-3 (Gilliat 3, Austin, Mordaunt Smith)
Nov 15th 1919	Lancing	won	6-2 (Austin 2, Gilliat 4)
Nov 20th 1919	Repton	won	3-1 (Gilliat, Austin, Mordaunt Smith)
Nov 26th 1919	Oriel College	won	3-0 (o.g., Mordaunt Smith, Gilliat)
Nov 29th 1919	Westminster	won	8-0 (Austin 2, Gilliat 4, Mordaunt Smith, McIlwraith)
Dec 6th 1919	JM Wells' XI	lost	2-9 (Austin 2)
Dec 13th 1919	Old Carthusians	lost	3-6 (Gilliat 2, Austin)
Jan 24th 1920	OU Centaurs	drew	3-3 (Gilliat 3)
Jan 31st 1920	Magdalen College	lost	1-7 (Mordaunt Smith)
Feb 4th 1920	Exeter College	won	6-5 (Gilliat 4, Cox, Wade)
Feb 7th 1920	RMC Sandhurst	won	4-3 (Gilliat 4)
Feb 11th 1920	Brasenose College	won	3-1 (Gilliat 3)
Feb 14th 1920	RMA Woolwich	won	4-0 (Barnard, Austin, Gilliat 2)
Feb 24th 1920	Harrow	won	4-0 (Gilliat 3, Barnard)
Feb 25th 1920	Hertford College	won	7-0 (Gilliat 4, Barnard 3)
Feb 28th 1920	Westminster	won	6-0 (Gilliat 4, Barnard 2)
Mar 4th 1920	Winchester	lost	2-4 (Mordaunt Smith, Cox)
Mar 6th 1920	Liverpool Ramblers	won	4-3 (Gilliat 4)
Mar 13th 1920	Old Malvernians	lost	4-7 (Gilliat 3, Cox)
LQ 1920	University College	drew	3-3
Sept 25th 1920	Rev EM Jameson's XI	won	7-1 (Gilliat 6, Barnard)
Oct 2nd 1920	AH Tod's XI	drew	2-2 (Gilliat, Anderson)
Oct 16th 1920	Old Westminsters	won	2-1 (Austin, Gilliat)
Oct 20th 1920	RMC Sandhurst	lost	2-3 (Barnard, MacGusty)

Date	Opponent	Result	Score (scorers)
Oct 23rd 1920	Bradfield OB	won	3-1 (Barnard 2, MacGusty)
Oct 27th 1920	Univ College, Reading	won	4-2 (Gilliat, Barnard 2, Anderson)
Oct 30th 1920	Old Malvernians	won	3-0 (Anderson, Gilliat, Barnard)
Nov 6th 1920	Lancing	won	3-1 (Gilliat 2, Anderson)
Nov 10th 1920	Aldenham	won	3-0 (Barnard 2, Gilliat)
Nov 13th 1920	RMA Woolwich	won	3-1 (Anderson 2, Gilliat)
Nov 18th 1920	Repton	won	2-0 (MacGusty 2)
Nov 24th 1920	Bradfield	won	3-0 (MacGusty, Kiggell 2)
Dec 4th 1920	Old Carthusians	lost	1-2 (Gilliat)
Jan 29th 1921	Magdalen College	lost	1-3 (Gilliat)
Feb 2nd 1921	OU Centaurs	lost	1-4 (Anderson)
Feb 5th 1921	Worcester College	won	9-1 (Gilliat 5, Barnard 2, Anderson, MacGusty)
Feb 9th 1921	Cambridge OCs	won	2-1 (Gilliat, MacGusty)
Feb 16th 1921	RMC Sandhurst	won	3-0 (Gilliat 2, Bamber)
Feb 19th 1921	Brasenose College	won	3-0 (Gilliat 2, Bamber)
Feb 23rd 1921	Trinity Oxford	lost	2-3 (Barnard 2)
Feb 26th 1921	Westminster	won	3-1 (Barnard, Gilliat)
Mar 3rd 1921	Harrow	drew	2-2 (Gilliat 2)
Mar 5th 1921	Liverpool Ramblers	lost	1-2 (Gilliat)
Mar 10th 1921	Winchester	drew	0-0
Sept 24th 1921	Rev EM Jameson's XI	won	3-1 (Bearman, Kiggell, Doresa)
Oct 1st 1921	Toc H	won	4-1 (Doresa 2, Engelbach, Kiggell)
Oct 8th 1921	Old Foresters	won	4-0 (Griffith Jones, Doresa, Bearman, Kiggell)
Oct 12th 1921	Univ College London	won	2-1 (Doresa, Morgan)
Oct 15th 1921	Old Malvernians	lost	0-1
Oct 22nd 1921	Magdalen College	lost	1-2 (Engelbach)
Oct 29th 1921	Bradfield OB	won	2-0 (Doresa 2)
Nov 2nd 1921	Bradfield	lost	1-2 (Morgan)
Nov 5th 1921	Lancing	drew	1-1 (Doresa)
Nov 9th 1921	Jesus, Cambridge	won	1-0 (Bearman)
Nov 12th 1921	RMA Woolwich	lost	1-5 (Doresa)
Nov 17th 1921	Repton	lost	0-3
Nov 23rd 1921	Trinity, Oxford	lost	0-2
Nov 26th 1921	Univ Coll, Reading	won	3-2 (Doresa 2, Kiggell) *abandoned due to fog*
Dec 3rd 1921	Old Carthusians	lost	1-4 (Percival)
Dec 10th 1921	Corinthians 'A'	lost	2-8 (Doresa 2)
Dec 14th 1921	OU Centaurs	lost	0-7
Jan 28th 1922	Oriel College	lost	0-3
Feb 1st 1922	Cambridge OCs	lost	0-3
Feb 4th 1922	Old Westminsters	lost	1-2 (Morgan)
Feb 11th 1922	Brasenose College	won	1-0 (Bearman)
Feb 15th 1922	RMC Sandhurst	won	2-0 (o.g., Harvie)
Feb 18th 1922	Westminster	won	3-0 (Bearman, Doresa, Kenyon)
Feb 25th 1922	Harrow	won	1-0 (Doresa)
Mar 1st 1922	Army Crusaders	won	2-1 (Doresa, Crump)
Mar 4th 1922	Liverpool Ramblers	lost	0-1
Mar 9th 1922	Winchester	won	1-0 (Doresa)
Sept 30th 1922	Rev EM Jameson's XI	lost	2-4 (Morgan, Fletcher)
Oct 14th 1922	JG Williams's XI	drew	2-2 (Fletcher 2)
Oct 18th 1922	The Stage FC	won	10-0 (Carter 4, Doresa 3, Kenyon 2, Fletcher)
Oct 21st 1922	Old Malvernians	drew	3-3 (Doresa 2, Carter)
Oct 25th 1922	Magdalen College	drew	2-2 (Carter, Doresa)
Oct 28th 1922	RMC Sandhurst	lost	2-4 (Fletcher, Doresa)
Nov 1st 1922	Jesus, Cambridge	drew	1-1 (Kenyon)
Nov 4th 1922	Lancing	drew	1-1 (Fletcher)
Nov 8th 1922	Univ Coll, Reading	lost	2-3 (Doresa, Fletcher)
Nov 11th 1922	Bradfield OB	won	4-1 (Doresa, Kenyon 2, Carter)
Nov 16th 1922	Repton	lost	0-2
Nov 22nd 1922	Bradfield	won	1-0 (Fletcher)
Nov 25th 1922	Toc H	won	3-1 (Doresa, Kenyon, Fletcher)
Nov 29th 1922	RMA Woolwich	lost	0-2
Dec 2nd 1922	Old Harrovians	won	4-3 (Fletcher 3, o.g.)
Dec 9th 1922	Old Carthusians	drew	0-0
Dec 16th 1922	OU Centaurs	lost	2-5 (Fletcher, Carter)
Dec 19th 1922	Shrewsbury	drew	0-0
Jan 31st 1923	Cambridge OCs	won	6-1 (Fletcher 2, Doresa 3, Kenyon)
Feb 7th 1923	Casuals	won	5-3 (Kenyon, Bett 2, Johnson, Doresa)
Feb 10th 1923	Old Westminsters	won	2-1 (Clarke, o.g.)
Feb 14th 1923	Brasenose College	lost	1-7 (Shute)
Feb 17th 1923	Harrow	won	5-2 (Shute, Kenyon, Morgan, Fletcher, Johnson)
Feb 21st 1923	Oriel College	lost	0-3
Feb 24th 1923	Westminster	won	1-0 (Shute)
Feb 28th 1923	Army Crusaders	won	3-2 (Fletcher, Shute 2)
Mar 3rd 1923	Liverpool Ramblers	lost	1-2 (Doresa)
Mar 7th 1923	Winchester	won	2-1 (Kenyon 2)
Sept 29th 1923	Rev EM Jameson's XI	drew	2-2 (Fletcher, Clarke)
Oct 10th 1923	Army Crusaders	won	3-2 (Murdoch, Fletcher 2)
Oct 20th 1923	Old Malvernians	lost	2-5 (Shute, Fletcher)
Oct 24th 1923	RMC Sandhurst	drew	1-1 (Fletcher)
Oct 27th 1923	Old Foresters	won	1-0 (Fletcher)
Oct 31st 1923	Lancing	won	5-1 (Fletcher 2, Shute 3)
Nov 3rd 1923	Bradfield	won	3-0 (Massey, Shute, Fletcher)
Nov 7th 1923	Magdalen College	won	5-1 (Kemp Welch, Shute 4)
Nov 10th 1923	Toc H	lost	0-4
Nov 13th 1923	Repton	lost	3-4 (Shute 2, Fletcher)
Nov 21st 1923	Univ Coll, Reading	lost	2-5 (Carter, Fletcher)
Nov 24th 1923	Bradfield OB	drew	1-1 (Carter)
Dec 15th 1923	Old Carthusians	lost	3-4 (Shute 3)
Dec 18th 1923	Shrewsbury	won	4-0 (Fletcher, Carter, Shute 2) *at Crystal Palace*
Jan 30th 1924	Cambridge OCs	won	6-0 (Rishworth 3, Carter 2, Fletcher)
Feb 6th 1924	Casuals	drew	1-1 (Fletcher)
Feb 9th 1924	Old Westminsters	won	3-0 (Fletcher, Rishworth, Murdoch)
Feb 13th 1924	Oriel College	won	4-2 (Murdoch 2, Fletcher 2)
Feb 16th 1924	Westminster	won	5-1 (Rishworth, Carter, Fletcher 2, Massey)
Feb 20th 1924	Oxford OCs	won	4-2 (Rishworth 3, Fletcher)
Feb 23rd 1924	OU Centaurs	lost	1-4 (Carter)
Mar 1st 1924	Harrow	won	7-1 (Fletcher 2, Carter 4, Pritchard)
Mar 6th 1924	Winchester	won	4-2 (Fletcher, Carter 2, Rishworth)
Mar 8th 1924	Liverpool Ramblers	lost	3-4 (Rishworth , Carter)
Sept 27th 1924	Rev EM Jameson's XI	lost	2-7 (Kemp Welch 2)
Oct 4th 1924	Army Crusaders	lost	0-2
Oct 11th 1924	Old Malvernians	drew	0-0
Oct 18th 1924	Old Foresters	lost	1-2 (Beare)
Oct 22nd 1924	RMC Sandhurst	lost	0-4
Oct 25th 1924	Toc H	lost	1-4 (Evans)
Nov 1st 1924	Lancing	lost	2-6 (Beare, Kemp Welch)
Nov 5th 1924	Magdalen College	won	2-0 (Kemp Welch, Sharp)
Nov 8th 1924	Bradfield OB	lost	0-1
Nov 11th 1924	Repton	lost	0-2
Nov 19th 1924	Bradfield	won	4-0 (Kemp Welch 2, Sharp 2)
Nov 22nd 1924	Pembroke Cambridge	lost	0-3
Nov 26th 1924	OU Centaurs	lost	0-2
Dec 3rd 1924	RMA Woolwich	lost	0-1
Dec 17th 1924	Old Carthusians	lost	2-3 (Sharp, Stock)
Dec 20th 1924	Shrewsbury	lost	0-1
Jan 31st 1925	Cambridge OCs	lost	0-1
Feb 4th 1925	Casuals	lost	2-5 (Sharp, Deakin)
Feb 7th 1925	Old Westminsters	drew	3-3 (Deakin, Stock, Seligman)
Feb 11th 1925	Oxford OCs	lost	0-3
Feb 18th 1925	Westminster	drew	1-1 (Seligman)
Feb 25th 1925	Oriel College	lost	2-4 (Kemp Welch)
Mar 3rd 1925	Harrow	drew	1-1 (Deakin)
Mar 5th 1925	Winchester	lost	0-1
Sept 26th 1925	Rev EM Jameson's XI	lost	1-3 (Deakin)
Oct 3rd 1925	Army Crusaders	lost	0-2
Oct 10th 1925	Old Malvernians	lost	0-1
Oct 17th 1925	The HAC	drew	4-4 (Palmer, Soole, Connell 2)
Oct 21st 1925	RMC Sandhurst	lost	0-10
Oct 24th 1925	Toc H	won	4-2 (Branston 2, Deakin, Connell)
Oct 31st 1925	Lancing	won	6-0 (Deakin 4, Seligman, Connell)
Nov 4th 1925	Cambridge 'A'	lost	1-2 (Connell)
Nov 7th 1925	Bradfield OB	lost	1-2 (Deakin)
Nov 12th 1925	Repton	drew	2-2 (Seligman, Deakin)
Nov 18th 1925	OU Centaurs	lost	1-3 (Deakin)
Nov 21st 1925	Westminster	won	3-0 (Palmer, Deakin 2)
Nov 25th 1925	Bradfield	lost	0-2
Jan 29th 1926	Shrewsbury	drew	1-1 (Palmer)
Jan 30th 1926	Cambridge OCs	lost	0-2
Feb 3rd 1926	Casuals	lost	1-4 (Seligman)
Feb 6th 1926	Old Westminsters	lost	1-3 (Deakin)
Feb 10th 1926	Oxford OCs	lost	0-5
Feb 13th 1926	Harrow	won	3-1 (Glynn, Connell, Deakin)
Feb 20th 1926	Magdalen College	won	3-1 (Glynn, Connell, Copeman)
Feb 24th 1926	Oriel College	lost	1-4 (Deakin)
Mar 4th 1926	Winchester	lost	0-1
Sept 25th 1926	Rev EM Jameson's XI	lost	0-3
Oct 2nd 1926	Army Crusaders	lost	0-2
Oct 9th 1926	Old Malvernians	lost	1-3 (Morton)
Oct 16th 1926	The HAC	lost	1-2 (Nicholson)
Oct 20th 1926	RMC Sandhurst	lost	1-4 (Fletcher)
Oct 23rd 1926	Toc H	won	1-0 (Glynn)
Oct 30th 1926	Lancing	lost	1-2 (Glynn)
Nov 3rd 1926	Cambridge 'A'	drew	1-1 (Beare)
Nov 6th 1926	Bradfield OB	won	2-0 (Wreford Brown, Glynn)
Nov 11th 1926	Repton	won	1-0 (Beare)
Nov 17th 1926	OU Centaurs	drew	3-3 (Wreford Brown, Weatherall, Fletcher)
Nov 20th 1926	Westminster	won	5-0 (Wreford Brown 2, Weatherall 2, Fletcher)
Dec 1st 1926	Bradfield	won	2-1 (Weatherall, Fletcher)
Dec 4th 1926	Old Carthusians	lost	3-5 (Nicholson, Glynn, Pearce)
Dec 18th 1926	Shrewsbury	lost	1-5 (Glynn)
Jan 29th 1927	Cambridge OCs	lost	0-2
Feb 5th 1927	Old Westminsters	won	7-0 (Fletcher 2, Weatherall 2, o.g., Wreford Brown, Beare)
Feb 9th 1927	Oxford OCs	drew	2-2 (Fletcher 2)
Feb 12th 1927	Harrow	lost	0-4
Feb 16th 1927	Corinthians	lost	2-3 (Fletcher, Weatherall)
Feb 19th 1927	Magdalen College	won	1-0 (Wreford Brown)

Date	Opponent	Result	Score (scorers)
Feb 23rd 1927	Oriel College	lost	1-3 (Weatherall)
Mar 2nd 1927	Winchester	lost	2-3 (Weatherall, Fletcher)
Sept 28th 1927	Rev EM Jameson's XI	lost	0-3
Oct 1st 1927	Army Crusaders	lost	0-3
Oct 8th 1927	Old Malvernians	won	6-3 (o.g., Davies 2, Hale 2, Fletcher)
Oct 15th 1927	HAC	lost	3-5 (Robertson, Fletcher, o.g.)
Oct 19th 1927	RMC Sandhurst	lost	2-7 (Bruce Jones, Robertson)
Oct 22nd 1927	Toc H	won	4-3 (Hale 2, Davies, Robertson)
Oct 29th 1927	Lancing	won	4-3 (Robertson, Davies, Bruce Jones, Hale)
Nov 2nd 1927	Cambridge 'A'	lost	2-5 (Chetwynd Stapylton, Fletcher)
Nov 5th 1927	Old Bradfieldians	lost	1-3 (Davies)
Nov 10th 1927	Repton	lost	1-4 (Middleton)
Nov 19th 1927	Westminster	lost	1-4 (Davies)
Nov 30th 1927	Bradfield	won	3-1 (Middleton, Fletcher, Davies)
Dec 3rd 1927	Old Carthusians	won	4-3 (Davies 3, Morton)
Jan 28th 1928	Cambridge OCs	won	3-1 (Davies, Craddock, o.g.)
Feb 1st 1928	Casuals	lost	1-2 (Fletcher)
Feb 4th 1928	Old Westminsters	lost	1-6 (Hale)
Feb 15th 1928	Oxford OCs	lost	1-2 (Fletcher)
Feb 25th 1928	Corinthians 'A'	lost	1-12 (Davies)
Feb 29th 1928	OU Centaurs	won	4-2 (Fletcher, Hale 2, Davies)
Mar 6th 1928	Winchester	lost	1-3 (Morton)
Sept 29th 1928	Rev EM Jameson's XI	lost	3-4 (Fletcher 2, Craddock)
Oct 3rd 1928	Army Crusaders	lost	0-3
Oct 10th 1928	RMC Sandhurst	won	3-1 (Craddock, Spencer, Jeavons)
Oct 13th 1928	The HAC	won	7-2 (Craddock 3, Fletcher 3, Jeavons)
Oct 20th 1928	Toc H	lost	1-3 (Cohen)
Oct 27th 1928	Lancing	won	9-0 (Spencer 2, Cohen, Craddock 3, Jeavons, Fletcher 2)
Oct 31st 1928	Cambridge Falcons	drew	2-2 (Jeavons, Spencer)
Nov 3rd 1928	Old Bradfieldians	lost	1-5 (Craddock)
Nov 8th 1928	Repton	lost	1-2 (Craddock)
Nov 14th 1928	Bradfield	won	5-0 (Cohen, Craddock, Jeavons 3)
Nov 17th 1928	Westminster	lost	2-4 (Craddock, Cohen)
Dec 1st 1928	Old Carthusians	lost	1-4 (Jeavons)
Dec 18th 1928	Shrewsbury	abnd	1-2 (Spencer) *played at Crystal Palace*
Jan 31st 1929	Casuals	lost	1-3 (Jeavons)
Feb 2nd 1929	Old Westminsters	won	5-1 (Fletcher 2, Jeavons 2, Spencer)
Feb 6th 1929	Cambridge OCs	won	6-2 (Fletcher 3, Cohen 2, Jeavons)
Feb 23rd 1928	OU Centaurs	lost	1-10 (Jeavons)
Mar 7th 1929	Winchester	lost	0-2
Sept 28th 1929	Rev EM Jameson's XI	lost	0-5
Oct 2nd 1929	Army Crusaders	lost	3-5 (Abrams, Stock, Matthews)
Oct 9th 1929	RMC Sandhurst	drew	2-2 (Middleton, o.g.)
Oct 12th 1929	The HAC	drew	2-2 (o.g., Hulton)
Oct 19th 1929	Toc H	won	4-1 (Stock 2, Hulton, Greening)
Oct 26th 1929	Lancing	won	4-0 (Jeavons 2, Wreford Brown, Hulton)
Nov 2nd 1929	Old Bradfieldians	lost	1-2 (Hulton)
Nov 7th 1929	Repton	lost	2-4 (Greening, Jeavons)
Nov 16th 1929	Westminster	won	4-0 (Jeavons 2, Moss, Greening)
Nov 27th 1929	Bradfield	drew	0-0
Nov 30th 1929	Old Carthusians	lost	2-4 (Greening, Moss)
Dec 18th 1929	Shrewsbury	lost	1-2 (Hulton) *played at Crystal Palace*
Jan 29th 1930	Casuals	won	6-5 (Pope, Jeavons 5)
Feb 1st 1930	Old Westminsters	won	5-1 (Hulton 3, Middleton, o.g.)
Feb 5th 1930	Cambridge OCs	lost	0-5
Feb 8th 1930	Oxford OCs	won	2-0 (Middleton, Pope)
Feb 15th 1930	Old Malvernians	drew	2-2 (o.g., Greening)
Feb 19th 1930	Corinthians	lost	1-3 (Pope)
Feb 22nd 1930	OU Centaurs	lost	1-3 (Jeavons)
Mar 6th 1930	Winchester	won	3-1 (Moss, Middleton 2)
Sept 27th 1930	Rev EM Jameson's XI	lost	0-1
Oct 1st 1930	Army Crusaders	won	4-2 (Greening 2, Samuelson, Paver)
Oct 4th 1930	RMC Sandhurst	drew	0-0
Oct 11th 1930	The HAC	won	8-2 (Samuelson 4, Pope 2, Moss, Paver)
Oct 18th 1930	Toc H	drew	3-3 (Greening, Pope, Samuelson)
Oct 25th 1930	Old Reptonians	drew	3-3 (Pope 2, Samuelson)
Nov 1st 1930	Lancing	drew	0-0
Nov 6th 1930	Repton	lost	3-4 (Samuelson, Paver, Pope)
Nov 8th 1930	Old Bradfieldians	lost	2-4 (Hunt, Watson)
Nov 12th 1930	Bradfield	won	3-1 (Paver, Moss 2)
Nov 15th 1930	Westminster	won	4-2 (Moss, Greening 2, Pope)
Dec 3rd 1930	London FA	lost	1-12 (Greening)
Dec 19th 1930	Shrewsbury	lost	3-6 (Samuelson, Pope, Greening)
Jan 28th 1931	Casuals	lost	2-5 (Matthews, Greening)
Jan 31st 1931	Old Westminsters	lost	1-3 (Greening)
Feb 4th 1931	Cambridge OCs	lost	1-3 (Moss)
Feb 7th 1931	Old Malvernians	lost	4-10 (Moss 2, Nicholl-Carne, Greening)
Feb 11th 1931	Old Carthusians	lost	1-3 (Moss)
Feb 18th 1931	Corinthians	lost	0-7
Feb 21st 1931	OU Centaurs	drew	2-2 (Watson, Moss)
Mar 5th 1931	Winchester	lost	0-2
Sept 26th 1931	Rev EM Jameson's XI	lost	1-2 (Samuelson)
Sept 30th 1931	Army Crusaders	lost	2-4 (Samuelson, Hunt)
Oct 7th 1931	RMC Sandhurst	lost	1-6 (JC Moss)
Oct 10th 1931	The HAC	won	2-1 (JC Moss, WF Moss)
Oct 17th 1931	Toc H	won	3-1 (WF Moss 2, Field)
Oct 24th 1931	Lancing	drew	1-1 (Cardew)
Oct 31st 1931	Old Bradfieldians	lost	0-5
Nov 12th 1931	Repton	lost	0-6
Nov 18th 1931	London FA	lost	1-8 (JC Moss)
Nov 21st 1931	Bradfield	drew	1-1 (Dunbar)
Nov 28th 1931	Westminster	won	4-1 (Dunbar 2, WF Moss)
Dec 5th 1931	Old Reptonians	lost	0-9
Dec 17th 1931	Shrewsbury	drew	4-4 (WF Moss, JC Moss 3)
Jan 23rd 1932	Cambridge OCs	lost	2-4 (WF Moss)
Jan 27th 1932	Casuals	lost	2-6 (Dunbar, JC Moss)
Jan 30th 1932	Old Westminsters	won	5-1 (Dunbar 3, WF Moss 2)
Feb 6th 1932	Old Malvernians	lost	3-6 (WF Moss, JC Moss, Dunbar)
Feb 17th 1932	Corinthians	won	3-2 (WF Moss 2, Samuelson)
Feb 20th 1932	OU Centaurs	lost	1-2 (WF Moss)
Feb 24th 1932	C Middleton's XI	lost	2-6 (Dunbar, JC Moss)
Mar 2nd 1932	Winchester	won	2-0 (Dunbar, WF Moss)
Mar 5th 1932	Old Carthusians	won	2-0 (JC Moss, Dunbar)
Sept 28th 1932	Army Crusaders	lost	1-2 (H Field)
Oct 1st 1932	Old Wykehamists	lost	1-5 (Carson)
Oct 5th 1932	RMC Sandhurst	lost	2-3 (J Field, Moss)
Oct 8th 1932	The HAC	won	2-1 (J Field 2)
Oct 15th 1932	Toc H	lost	1-2 (Hartland-Mahon)
Oct 19th 1932	London FA	lost	1-8 (Moss)
Oct 22nd 1932	Lancing	lost	1-2 (Moss)
Oct 29th 1932	Old Bradfieldians	lost	1-4 (H Field)
Nov 5th 1932	Repton	lost	3-5 (Gillchrest, Moss, J Field)
Nov 9th 1932	Bradfield	won	2-1 (Moss, Gillchrest)
Nov 19th 1932	Westminster	won	3-2 (H Field, J Field, Moss)
Dec 3rd 1932	Shrewsbury	lost	3-6 (J Field, H Field, Moss)
Feb 4th 1933	Old Malvernians	drew	4-4 (Moss, Hartland-Mahon 2, J Field)
Feb 8th 1933	Devon Regt	lost	1-3 (Moss)
Feb 11th 1933	Old Carthusians	lost	2-3 (H Field, Moss)
Feb 15th 1933	OU Centaurs	lost	1-4 (Caldwell)
Feb 22nd 1933	Oxford OCs	lost	0-3
Mar 2nd 1933	Winchester	lost	3-6 (Moss, Gillchrest 2)
Mar 4th 1933	Corinthians	lost	1-7
Sept 27th 1933	Army Crusaders	lost	0-5
Sept 30th 1933	Toc H	won	3-2 (Trapman, Frith, Field)
Oct 4th 1933	RMC Sandhurst	won	6-4 (Trapman, Tuckwell 4, Frith)
Oct 7th 1933	Old Bradfieldians	won	2-1 (Gillchrest, Tuckwell)
Oct 14th 1933	The HAC	won	3-1 (Trapman, Field 2)
Oct 18th 1933	London FA	lost	0-8
Oct 21st 1933	Lancing	won	6-1 (o.g., Gillchrest 2, Frith 3)
Oct 28th 1933	Old Wykehamists	won	2-0 (Swinbank, Dowding)
Nov 4th 1933	Bradfield	drew	2-2 (Trapman, Frith)
Nov 9th 1933	Repton	lost	0-2
Nov 18th 1933	Westminster	won	3-0 (Tuckwell 2, Frith)
Nov 22nd 1933	Cambridge OCs	won	5-1 (Hartland-Mahon, Gillchrest, Dunbar 2, Field)
Nov 25th 1933	2nd Devonshire Regt	lost	2-6 (Trapman, Tuckwell)
Dec 2nd 1933	Godalming	won	3-2 (Frith, Field 2)
Dec 16th 1933	Shrewsbury	won	3-1 (Trapman, Frith, Gillchrest)
Jan 27th 1934	Old Westminsters	lost	1-3 (Gillchrest)
Jan 31st 1934	Casuals	lost	3-4 (Gillchrest, Dunbar, Powell)
Feb 3rd 1934	Old Malvernians	lost	2-3 (o.g., Gillchrest)
Feb 7th 1934	Oxford OCs	won	5-3 (Dowding 3, Tuckwell 2)
Feb 10th 1934	Old Carthusians	lost	1-2 (Dowding)
Feb 14th 1934	OU Centaurs	won	3-1 (Powell 2, Tuckwell)
Feb 21st 1934	Corinthians	lost	1-2
Feb 24th 1934	Old Reptonians	drew	0-0
Mar 1st 1934	Winchester	won	3-1 (Richards, Gillchrest, Dowding)
Sept 29th 1934	Army Crusaders	won	4-2 (Yule, Daukes 2, Dunbar)
Oct 3rd 1934	RMC Sandhurst	won	4-2 (Dowding, Dunbar 2, Daukes)
Oct 6th 1934	Toc H	won	6-1 (Dowding, Daukes 3, Dunbar 2)
Oct 13th 1934	The HAC	won	5-1 (Daukes 2, Briggs 2, Dunbar)
Oct 17th 1934	London FA	lost	1-7 (Hodgson)
Oct 20th 1934	Lancing	lost	1-2 (Daukes)
Oct 27th 1934	Old Wykehamists	drew	2-2 ()
Nov 3rd 1934	Bradfield	won	3-1 (Hodgson, Lomas, Daukes)
Nov 8th 1934	Repton	won	2-1 (Guest, Dowding)
Nov 10th 1934	Old Bradfieldians	lost	0-9
Nov 17th 1934	Westminster	won	1-0 (Dunbar)
Nov 24th 1934	Godalming	lost	0-2
Dec 1st 1934	Shrewsbury	drew	2-2 (Daukes, Hodgson)
Jan 26th 1935	Old Westminsters	won	6-2 (Daukes 2, Dunbar 2, Hodgson, Ades)
Jan 30th 1935	Casuals	drew	2-2 (Dunbar, Hodgson)
Feb 2nd 1935	Corinthians	drew	3-3 (Daukes, Dowding)
Feb 9th 1935	Old Carthusians	lost	1-4 (Ades)

Date	Opponent	Result	Score
Feb 13th 1935	OU Centaurs	won	6-2 (Daukes 2, Ades 3, Hodgson)
Feb 16th 1935	Old Malvernians	drew	4-4 (Dunbar 2, Daukes 2)
Feb 23rd 1935	Old Reptonians	won	5-0 (Hodgson 4, Rhodes)
Feb 28th 1935	Winchester	won	2-1 (Hodgson, Dunbar)
Mar 2nd 1935	Surrey Senior League XI	lost	1-3
Sept 28th 1935	Army Crusaders	won	4-0 (Ades, Lomas, Hayes 2)
Oct 2nd 1935	RMC Sandhurst	lost	1-3 (Lomas)
Oct 5th 1935	Toc H	won	5-2 (Merz 2, Dunbar 2, Greene)
Oct 1935	London FA	lost	0-14
Oct 1935	The HAC	won	8-0 (Hayes, Dunbar 4, Greene, Dowding 2)
Oct 19th 1935	Lancing	won	5-1 (Ades, Greene 2, Dunbar, o.g.)
Nov 2nd 1935	Bradfield	lost	2-3 (Ades, Dowding)
Nov 7th 1935	Repton	lost	1-2 (Hayes)
Nov 16th 1935	Westminster	drew	0-0
Nov 23rd 1935	Shrewsbury	won	7-1 (Lomas 2, Greene 2, Dowding, Hayes, Crompton)
Nov 30th 1935	Godalming		
Dec 1935	Old Carthusians	won	6-0
LQ 1936	Winchester	lost	3-6
LQ 1936	Casuals	won	5-2
LQ 1936	Old Malvernians	won	2-1
LQ 1936	Old Reptonians	good effort	
LQ 1936	Old Westminsters	lost	1-5
LQ 1936	OU Authentics	lost	2-4
Incomplete			
Sept 26th 1936	Army Crusaders	won	4-3 (Lomas 4)
Oct 3rd 1936	Toc H	won	4-0 (Lomas 4)
Oct 7th 1936	RMC Sandhurst	lost	1-2 (Lomas)
Oct 10th 1936	The HAC	won	6-2 (Lomas 4, MacCunn 2)
Oct 14th 1936	London FA	lost	1-7 (Orton)
Oct 17th 1936	Lancing	won	3-2 (Hughes 2, Lomas)
Oct 24th 1936	Old Wykehamists	lost	0-2
Oct 31st 1936	Bradfield	won	4-1 (Stone, Lomas)
Nov 5th 1936	Repton	won	7-2 (Lomas 4, MacCunn, Hughes, Orton)
Nov 14th 1936	Westminster	won	2-0 (Hughes 2)
Nov 21st 1936	Shrewsbury	lost	1-2 (Hughes)
Nov 28th 1936	Godalming	lost	3-7 (Tanner)
Dec 12th 1936	Chouse-in-Southwark	lost	2-3 (Benké)
Jan 30th 1937	Old Westminsters	lost	1-5 (Page)
Feb 6th 1937	Casuals	won	5-2 (Lomas 4, MacCunn)
Feb 10th 1937	OU Authentics	lost	2-4 (Hughes, Lomas)
Feb 13th 1937	Old Malvernians	won	2-1 (Benké, Hughes)
Feb 20th 1937	Corinthians	lost	0-7
Feb 27th 1937	Old Carthusians	lost	1-4 (Benké)
Mar 4th 1937	Winchester	lost	1-2 (Benké)
Mar 11th 1937	Oranienstein-Stuhm	won	1-0

Trip to Paris April 4th 1937 – two matches played vs Lycée Lakanal – won 3-2, 5-3 (not 1st XI)

Date	Opponent	Result	Score
Oct 16th 1937	Lancing	lost	1-3 (Swinbank)
Oct 30th 1037	Bradfield	drew	1-1 (Geppert)
Nov 5th 1937	Repton	drew	1-1 (Stone)
Nov 20th 1937	Shrewsbury	won	2-1 (Stone, Larking)
Nov 27th 1937	Westminster	drew	1-1 (MacCunn)
Jan 1938	Old Westminsters	won	6-2
Jan 1938	Corinthians	lost	2-4 (Larking, McMillan)
Feb 1938	OU Centaurs	lost	1-2
LQ 1938	Casuals	lost	2-4
Feb 19th 1938	Old Carthusians	lost	1-6 (Stone)
Mar 3rd 1938	Winchester	lost	1-4 (Holme-Sumner)
Oct 15th 1938	Lancing	won	6-0 (Larking, Beattie, Tanner 3, Swinbank)
Oct 29th 1938	Bradfield	won	3-0 (Tanner 3)
Nov 3rd 1938	Repton	lost	0-3
Nov 19th 1938	Shrewsbury	lost	1-10
Nov 26th 1938	Westminster	won	3-1 (Larking, Tanner, Cunningham)
Feb 18th 1939	Old Carthusians	lost	1-2 (Larking)
Feb 23rd 1939	Winchester	drew	2-2 (*rushed* 2)
Sept 30th 1939	Occasionals	won	7-0
Oct 7th 1939	RMC Sandhurst	lost	1-2
Oct 11th 1939	Royal Engineers	drew	3-3
Oct 14th 1939	Lancing	lost	0-1
Oct 21st 1939	Royal Engineers	won	3-0
Oct 28th 1939	Bradfield	drew	2-2 (Tanner, Finlayson)
Nov 11th 1939	Godalming	won	4-1
Nov 18th 1939	Malvern	won	3-2 (Figg, Larking, Tanner)
Nov 25th 1939	Army PT School	won	4-1 (Larking, Finlayson, Tanner, Figg)
Dec 9th 1939	Chouse in Southwark	won	6-3
Feb 7th 1940	OU Centaurs	lost	2-3 (Tanner 2)
Feb 10th 1940	Occasionals	drew	1-1
Feb 22nd 1940	Winchester	lost	0-1
Oct 5th 1940	Royal Engineers	won	9-0 (Hawley 3, Spencer 6)
Oct 19th 1940	Old Wykehamists	won	4-2 (Spencer 3, Vlasto)
Oct 26th 1940	Bradfield	won	4-0 (Spencer 3, Evans)
Nov 2nd 1940	Queen's Btn	won	3-2 (Spencer 2, Hawley)
Nov 6th 1940	Wellingborough	won	6-2 (Evans 2, Spencer 2, Lovett, Figg)
Nov 16th 1940	Bradfield	won	5-2 (Figg 4, Hawley)
Nov 20th 1940	RASC Training Btn	won	3-2 (Spencer, Figg, Evans)
Nov 23rd 1940	RASC Dorking	won	2-1 (Milne, Figg)
Nov 30th 1940	Royal Engineers	won	3-1 (Hawley 2, Spencer)
Dec 4th 1940	OCTU Sandhurst	won	4-0 (Spencer, Evans 2)
Dec 7th 1940	Cambridge Czechs	drew	5-5 (Hawley, Figg 2, Lovett, Davidson)
Jan 25th 1941	London Yeomanry	won	3-1 (Lahaye, Figg, Lovett)
Feb 1st 1941	RASC Training Btn	won	9-3 (Evans 5, Figg, Hawley, Nesbitt, Lahaye)
Feb 8th 1941	Queen's Royal Regt	drew	2-2 (Lovett 2)
Feb 12th 1941	RAF Gatwick	lost	1-4 (Lovett)
Feb 15th 1941	Corinthian Casuals	lost	2-4 (Davidson, Hawley)
Feb 22nd 1941	RASC Aldershot	lost	3-6 (Lahaye 2, Lovett)
Feb 27th 1941	Winchester	won	2-1 (Lovett, Larking)
Oct 4th 1941	RASC Dorking	won	2-1 (Lovett, Larking)
Oct 8th 1941	Sherwood Foresters	drew	1-1 (Evans)
Oct 11th 1941	Coldstream Guards	lost	0-6
Oct 15th 1941	St Thomas's Hospital	won	3-0 (Evans 2, Lahaye)
Oct 18th 1941	Corinthian Casuals	won	1-0 (Larking)
Oct 25th 1941	Bradfield	won	2-1 (Evans, Lahaye)
Nov 1st 1941	RAF Horley	won	3-2 (Lomas, Evans 2)
Nov 8th 1941	OCTU Sandhurst	lost	1-5 (Hogg)
Nov 15th 1941	Bradfield	won	4-0 (Evans 3, Lahaye)
Nov 22nd 1941	Oxford XI	drew	1-1 (Lahaye)
Nov 26th 1941	Wellingborough	won	7-2 (Lahaye 4, Evans, Larking, Lovett)
Dec 3rd 1941	Cambridge Czechs	won	3-2
Dec 6th 1941	Navy XI	lost	1-7 (Evans)
Dec 17th 1941	Coldstream Guards	drew	3-3
Jan 31st 1942	Queen's Regt	drew	0-0
Feb 11th 1942	OCTU Sandhurst	drew	0-0
Feb 14th 1942	Medical Students' Union	won	6-0 (Larking, Seager 2, Lovett, Evans)
Feb 18th 1942	Royal Horse Artillery	lost	0-3
Feb 21st 1942	Royal Engineers	lost	0-2
Oct 3rd 1942	Headmaster's XI	won	1-0
Oct 10th 1942	RASC Aldershot	lost	1-7 (Dalgety)
Oct 17th 1942	Corinthian Casuals	lost	2-3 (Dalgety, Seager)
Oct 24th 1942	Bradfield	drew	1-1 (Crole-Rees)
Oct 31st 1942	OCTU Sandhurst	lost	0-4
Nov 7th 1942	Coldstream Guards	won	5-3 (Godden 2, Spratt, Dalgety, Sword)
Nov 21st 1942	RASC Aldershot	drew	3-3 (Stevenson 2, Sword)
Nov 24th 1942	Bradfield	drew	0-0
Nov 28th 1942	Malvern	won	5-0 (Godden, Spratt 2, Dalgety, o.g)(at Harrow)
OQ 1942	Malvern	won	6-1
Dec 5th 1942	Royal Engineers	won	3-1
Dec 12th 1942	Westminster Tech. Coll	won	3-2
Dec 19th 1942	Coldstream Guards	lost	0-1
Feb 2nd 1943	Westminster	won	7-1 (Godden 4, Dalgety, Stevenson, Spratt)
Feb 6th 1943	Queen's Regt	won	3-1 (Crole-Rees 2, Wells)
Feb 11th 1943	Univ Coll London	won	2-0 (Spratt, Godden)
Feb 18th 1943	Eton	won	4-3 (Spratt, Edwards, Dalgety 2)
Feb 20th 1943	St Mary's College	drew	1-1 (Spratt)
Feb 25th 1943	Winchester	won	2-1 (Dalgety, Godden)
Oct 2nd 1943	RAC Blackdown	drew	2-2 (Godden 2)
Oct 9th 1943	OCTU Sandhurst	lost	0-6
Oct 16th 1943	Corinthian Casuals	lost	1-4 (Crole-Rees)
Oct 27th 1943	Bradfield	drew	0-0
Nov 6th 1943	RASC Aldershot	lost	3-8 (Spratt 2, Pollock)
Nov 13th 1943	Chelsea Sea Cadets	lost	0-2
Nov 18th 1943	Bradfield	won	1-0 (Crole-Rees)
Nov 27th 1943	Royal Engineers	lost	0-3
Dec 1st 1943	Malvern	lost	0-3
Jan 8th 1944	Westminster	won	4-0 (Godden 3, Spratt) *at Bank of England Ground*
Jan 22nd 1944	RAC Blackdown	won	4-2 (Crole-Rees 2, Godden mi, Spratt)
Jan 29th 1944	St Mary's College	drew	2-2 (Crole-Rees, Price)
Feb 10th 1944	Eton	won	3-1 (Rimell, Spratt, Crole-Rees)
Feb 12th 1944	RMC Sandhurst	lost	1-5 (Crole-Rees)
Feb 19th 1944	St Thomas's Hosp	won	3-0 (Cranstoun 2, Price)
Feb 24th 1944	Winchester	won	3-0 (Spratt, Crole-Rees 2)
Oct 7th 1944	Chelsea Sea Cadets	drew	0-0
Oct 14th 1944	Corinthian Casuals	lost	4-5 (Godden)
Oct 21st 1944	RASC	lost	2-6 (Vlasto, Wilson)
Oct 28th 1944	Bradfield	won	4-0 (Godden 2, Wilson, M Rimell)
Nov 10th 1944	Chelsea Sea Cadets	drew	2-2 (Spratt, Whettem)
Nov 18th 1944	Bradfield	won	3-2 (Spratt 2, Godden)
Nov 25th 1944	Laleham	won	10-0 (Godden 4, Spratt 3, Price, Vlasto, Fenwick)

Date	Opponent	Result	Score
Nov 29th 1944	Malvern	lost	0-4
OQ 1944	Eton	won	3-1
Dec 2nd 1944	St Mary's College	lost	1-2 (Spratt)
Dec 9th 1944	OCTU Sandhurst	won	7-6 (Spratt 3, Godden 2, Price 2)
Dec 16th 1944	Lancing	won	8-0 (Spratt 5, Godden 2, Bishop)
Jan 6th 1945	Westminster	won	1-0 (Price) *played at Roehampton*
Jan 20th 1945	RASC	lost	0-1
Feb 3rd 1945	St Thomas's Hospital	drew	6-6 (Spratt 3, Wilson 2, Pollock)
Feb 10th 1945	Eton	drew	1-1 (Pollock)
Feb 17th 1945	Corinthian Casuals	lost	1-3 (Wilson)
Feb 22nd 1945	Winchester	won	2-0 (Spratt, Price)
Mar 31st 1945	Winchester	won	2-1 (Godden, Spratt) *at Redhill*
Oct 6th 1945	London Medical College	won	4-1 (Savill, Price, Meyer 2)
Oct 13th 1945	Corinthian Casuals	lost	3-4 (Savill, o.g., Wilson)
Oct 20th 1945	Lancing	won	2-1 (Wilson 2)
Oct 27th 1945	Bradfield	won	4-0 (Howard 2, May, Wilson)
Nov 1st 1945	Repton	lost	0-2
Nov 7th 1945	Shrewsbury	drew	2-2 (Howard, Wilson)
Nov 17th 1945	St Thomas's Hospital	lost	0-2
Nov 21st 1945	Malvern	won	3-1 (May 2, Howard)
Dec 1st 1945	Westminster	won	7-0 (May 3, Howard 2, Savill 2)
Jan 26th 1946	OCTU	lost	0-4
Feb 2nd 1946	St Thomas's Hospital	lost	2-3 (Marrot, Wilson)
Feb 9th 1946	AJ Wreford Brown's XI	won	2-0 (May, Savill)
Feb 14th 1946	Eton	won	10-1 (Wilson 4, May 3, Savill 2, Price)
Feb 16th 1946	8th Rifles	lost	3-7 (Howard, Wilson, Savill)
Feb 21st 1946	Winchester	lost	1-2 (Wilson)
Oct 5th 1946	St Thomas's Hospital	won	6-2 (May 2, Marrot 2, Mills, Gemmel)
Oct 12th 1946	Corinthian Casuals	drew	2-2 (Savill, Gemmel)
Oct 19th 1946	St Bartholomew's Hosp	lost	2-4 (Anthony, Sher)
Oct 23rd 1946	Brasenose College	won	3-1 (Savill)
Oct 26th 1946	Bradfield	won	6-0 (Savill 2, May 2, Mills, Gemmel)
Nov 2nd 1946	Old Bradfieldians	lost	1-3 (May)
Nov 6th 1946	Shrewsbury	lost	1-4 (Mills)
Nov 12th 1946	Repton	won	2-1 (May 2)
Nov 16th 1946	Oxford Centaurs	won	2-1 (Mills 2)
OQ 1946	Old Westminsters	won	2-1
Nov 23rd 1946	Lancing	won	8-2 (May 4, Savill 3, Seaman)
Nov 30th 1946	Old Westminsters	won	3-0 (Savill 2, Seaman)
Dec 7th 1946	Westminster	won	10-1 (Savill 4, Marrot 2, Mills 2, May 2) *at Grove Park*
Dec 18th 1946	Highgate	won	4-0 (Savill 2, May 2) *at Stamford Bridge*

Snow all through the LQ (winter of 1947)

Date	Opponent	Result	Score
Sept 27th 1947	AJ Wreford Brown's XI	lost	2-9 (Janes, Burt)
Oct 1st 1947	RMA Sandhurst	lost	0-2
Oct 4th 1947	St Thomas's Hospital	won	5-0 (Hastings 2, Divett 2, Millar)
Oct 8th 1947	London FA	lost	0-11
Oct 11th 1947	Old Westminsters	lost	1-3 (Whinney)
Oct 18th 1947	Lancing	drew	1-1 (Hastings)
Oct 22nd 1947	Oxford Centaurs	lost	0-1
Oct 25th 1947	Bradfield	won	3-1 (Burt, Whinney, Janes)
Nov 1st 1947	Old Bradfieldians	drew	1-1 (Burt)
Nov 5th 1947	Brasenose College	won	3-0 (Whinney 2, Burt)
Nov 11th 1947	Repton	won	1-0 (Whinney)
Nov 29th 1947	Corinthian Casuals	drew	2-2 (Burt 2)
Dec 6th 1947	Westminster	won	5-1 (Burt 2, Whinney, Divett, o.g.)
Dec 15th 1947	Shrewsbury	drew	2-2 (Nathan, o.g.)
Dec 17th 1947	Highgate	won	3-0 (Whinney 2, Hastings) at Stamford Bridge
Jan 28th 1948	AJ Wreford Brown's XI	lost	3-8 (Janes, Burt, Whinney)
Jan 31st 1948	Corinthian Casuals	lost	0-3
Feb 7th 1948	Old Cholmeleians	lost	2-4 (Burt 2)
Feb 9th 1948	Eton	won	3-0 (Divett 2, Whinney)
Feb 14th 1948	Old Carthusians	lost	1-2 (Archibald)
Feb 19th 1948	Winchester	drew	1-1 (Archibald)
Sept 25th 1948	AJ Wreford Brown's XI	lost	1-2 (Smithson)
Sept 29th 1948	Sandhurst 'A'	lost	0-3
Oct 2nd 1948	St Thomas's Hospital	won	1-0 (Smithson)
Oct 6th 1948	London FA	lost	0-17
Oct 9th 1948	Old Westminsters	lost	2-5 (Jordan, Atkinson)
Oct 16th 1948	Lancing	won	3-1 (Atkinson, Whinney, o.g.)
Oct 20th 1948	Oxford Centaurs	lost	0-3
Oct 23rd 1948	Bradfield	lost	0-1
Oct 30th 1948	Old Bradfieldians	won	2-1 (Gibbon 2)
Nov 3rd 1948	Brasenose College	lost	2-3 (Whinney 2)
Nov 10th 1948	Shrewsbury	won	2-1 (Goodliffe, Kay)
Nov 20th 1948	Repton	won	3-1 (Kay, Goodliffe, Spargo)
Nov 24th 1948	Trinity, Oxford	drew	3-3 (Gibbon, Kay, Whinney)
Nov 27th 1948	Corinthian Casuals	lost	2-6 (Gibbon, Ritchie)
Dec 4th 1948	Westminster	won	3-1 (Whinney, Atkinson, Gibbon)
Jan 29th 1949	Corinthian Casuals	lost	2-4 (Atkinson, Goodliffe)
Feb 5th 1949	Old Cholmeleians	won	4-2 (May, Jenks, Goodliffe, Jordan)
Feb 10th 1949	Eton	won	2-0 (Goodliffe, Kay)
Feb 12th 1949	Old Carthusians	lost	0-6
Feb 19th 1949	AJ Wreford Brown's XI	won	3-1 (Goodliffe, May, Pickersgill)
Feb 25th 1949	Winchester	won	3-2 (Kay, Ritchie, Spargo)
Sept 24th 1949	AJ Wreford Brown's XI	lost	0-2
Sept 28th 1949	RMA Sandhurst	drew	1-1 (Frankland)
Oct 1st 1949	St Thomas's Hospital	won	3-1 (Smithson 2, Vansittart)
Oct 5th 1949	London FA	lost	0-4
Oct 8th 1949	Corinthian Casuals	drew	1-1 (Edwards)
Oct 15th 1949	Lancing	won	1-0 (Smithson)
Oct 22nd 1949	Bradfield	lost	3-4 (Jenks, Gladstone, o.g.)
Oct 29th 1949	Old Bradfieldians	lost	0-4
Nov 2nd 1949	Brasenose College	won	2-1 (Vansittart 2)
Nov 9th 1949	Shrewsbury	drew	1-1 (May)
Nov 12th 1949	Oxford Centaurs	lost	1-6 (Edwards)
OQ 1949	OU Centaurs	won	2-1
Nov 19th 1949	Repton	lost	0-1
Nov 23rd 1949	Trinity Oxford	drew	1-1 (Agate)
Nov 26th 1949	Old Westminsters	won	4-2 (Agate 2, May, Edwards)
Dec 3rd 1949	Westminster	won	3-1 (Vansittart, May, Agate)
Jan 21st 1950	AJ Wreford Brown's XI	lost	3-4 (Young 2, Carver)
Jan 28th 1950	Corinthian Casuals	lost	2-3 (May, Carver)
LQ 1950	Liverpool Ramblers	won	1-0
LQ 1950	Balliol College	won	4-0
Feb 9th 1950	Eton	drew	2-2 (Vansittart, Young)
Feb 11th 1950	Old Carthusians	lost	0-3
Feb 23rd 1950	Winchester	lost	2-3 (Frankland, Jenks)
Sept 27th 1950	Sandhurst	won	3-0 (Gladstone 2, Yannaghas)
Sept 30th 1950	St Thomas's Hospital	won	5-2 (Gladstone 2, Young 2, Barclay)
Oct 4th 1950	London FA	lost	1-6 (Gladstone)
Oct 7th 1950	Corinthian Casuals	lost	2-4 (Bayman 2)
Oct 14th 1950	Lancing	won	6-0 (Monk 3, Pegler 2, Bayman)
Oct 18th 1950	Oxford Centaurs	lost	0-2
Oct 21st 1950	Old Bradfieldians	drew	2-2 (Young)
Oct 28th 1950	Bradfield	won	3-1 (Pegler 2, Yannaghas)
Nov 1st 1950	Brasenose College	drew	2-2 (Young, Pegler)
Nov 8th 1950	Trinity Oxford	drew	2-2 (Pegler 2)
Nov 15th 1950	Shrewsbury	drew	0-0
Nov 18th 1950	Old Westminsters	won	4-0 (Pegler 3, Gladstone)
Nov 25th 1950	Repton	won	3-0 (Monk, Gladstone 2)
Dec 2nd 1950	Westminster	drew	2-2 (May, Barclay)
Dec 9th 1950	Army Crusaders	drew	2-2 (Pegler, Gladstone)
Jan 27th 1951	Corinthian Casuals	lost	1-3 (Barclay)
Feb 3rd 1951	Liverpool Ramblers	lost	0-7
Feb 8th 1951	Eton	won	8-2 (Pegler 5, Barclay, Yannaghas, Monk)
Feb 10th 1951	Old Carthusians	lost	0-7
Feb 17th 1951	Brooke Hall	drew	2-2 (Young 2)
Feb 22nd 1951	Winchester	lost	0-1
Sept 26th 1951	Sandhurst	lost	0-3
Sept 29th 1951	St Thomas's Hospital	won	3-2 (Pegler, Duits, Barclay)
Oct 3rd 1951	London FA	lost	1-7 (Miller)
Oct 6th 1951	Corinthian Casuals	lost	1-3 (o.g.)
Oct 13th 1951	Lancing	won	3-0 (Spurrell, Miller 2)
Oct 17th 1951	Old Etonians	drew	2-2 (Gladstone, Pegler)
Oct 20th 1951	Old Bradfieldians	lost	2-4 (Tuck 2)
Oct 27th 1951	Bradfield	won	5-2 (Miller 3, Tuck, Pegler)
Oct 31st 1951	Cambridge Falcons	lost	0-7
Nov 7th 1951	Oxford Centaurs	won	4-2 (Pegler, Miller, Gladstone, Barclay)
Nov 10th 1951	Victoria College	drew	1-1 (Whinney)
Nov 14th 1951	Shrewsbury	won	7-0 (Barclay 2, Miller 2, Pegler, Spurrell, o.g.)
Nov 17th 1951	Norsemen	won	3-2 (Miller 2, Pegler)
Nov 24th 1951	Repton	lost	1-6 (Gladstone)
Dec 1st 1951	Westminster	won	7-1 (Gladstone 3, Pegler 2, Tuck 2)
Dec 5th 1951	Trinity Oxford	won	3-1 (Tuck 2, Miller)
Dec 8th 1951	Army Crusaders	lost	1-2 (Miller)
Jan 26th 1952	Corinthian Casuals	lost	0-4
Feb 7th 1952	Eton	won	3-2 (Parker, Pegler, Miller)
Feb 9th 1952	Old Carthusians	drew	2-2 (Tuck, Pegler)
Feb 13th 1952	Old Cholmeleians	won	4-3 (Pegler 2, Miller 2)
Feb 16th 1952	Brooke Hall	won	4-1 (Pegler, Miller 2, Tuck)
Feb 21st 1952	Winchester	lost	1-2 (Pegler)
Sept 24th 1952	RMA Sandhurst	drew	2-2 (White, Miller)
Sept 27th 1952	RMA Sandhurst	won	3-2 (Knox, Arnsby-Wilson 2)
Oct 1st 1952	London FA	lost	0-5
Oct 4th 1952	Corinthian Casuals	lost	1-2 (Cupitt)
Oct 11th 1952	Lancing	won	7-1 (Miller 3, Pratt 3, White)
Oct 15th 1952	RASC	lost	2-3 (Miller, White)
Oct 18th 1952	Old Bradfieldians	lost	0-3
Oct 25th 1952	Bradfield	drew	1-1 (Miller)
Oct 28th 1952	Cambridge Falcons	lost	2-8 (White, Cupitt)
Nov 5th 1952	Oxford Centaurs	lost	2-5 (Miller, Surman)
Nov 8th 1952	Godalming FC	won	8-0 (White 3, Miller 2, Pratt, o.g. 2)
Nov 12th 1952	Shrewsbury	lost	1-5 (Miller)

Date	Opponent	Result	Score
Nov 15th 1952	Old Wykehamists	lost	2-4 (Miller, Bright)
Nov 22nd 1952	Repton	lost	1-2 (Knox)
Nov 29th 1952	Westminster	drew	3-3 (Miller, Knox, White)
Dec 3rd 1952	Trinity, Oxford	lost	2-3 (White, Miller)
Jan 24th 1953	Corinthian Casuals	lost	3-4 (Pratt, White, Hardcastle)
Jan 28th 1953	1st Trg Batt RASC	won	5-0 (Miller 3, Pratt, Knox)
Jan 31st 1953	Old Carthusians	won	2-0 (Pratt, Knox)
Feb 5th 1953	Eton	won	3-2 (Hardcastle 2, White)
Feb 7th 1953	Liverpool Ramblers	lost	1-2 (White)
Feb 11th 1953	Old Cholmeleians	drew	0-0
Feb 14th 1953	Brooke Hall	lost	2-3 (White, Knox)
Feb 19th 1953	Winchester	won	2-1 (White, Pratt)
Sept 26th 1953	St Thomas's Hospital	won	9-2 (Mace 4, Wilkinson 3, Pratt, Buckley)
Sept 30th 1953	London FA	lost	1-6 (Wilkinson)
Oct 3rd 1953	Corinthian Casuals	lost	0-5
Oct 10th 1953	Lancing	drew	2-2 (Wilkinson, Mace)
Oct 14th 1953	RMA Sandhurst	lost	1-2 (Buckley)
Oct 17th 1953	Old Bradfieldians	won	4-0 (Gemmel, Mace, Percival, Buckley)
Oct 24th 1953	Bradfield	lost	0-1
Oct 28th 1953	Norsemen	lost	1-5 (Gemmel)
Nov 4th 1953	OU Centaurs	lost	1-3 (O'Brien)
Nov 7th 1953	Old Westminsters	won	3-0 (Lees 2, O'Brien)
Nov 11th 1953	Shrewsbury	lost	0-1
Nov 14th 1953	Old Wykehamists	lost	2-5 (Pratt 2)
Nov 21st 1953	Repton	lost	2-3 (Ruddock 2)
Nov 28th 1953	Westminster	won	3-0 (Buckley 2, Cairns)
Dec 2nd 1953	Trinity, Oxford	won	3-1 (O'Brien, Lees, Pratt)
Dec 5th 1953	Army Crusaders	lost	1-2 (Lees)
Jan 23rd 1954	Corinthian Casuals	lost	0-5
Feb 4th 1954	Eton	lost	0-4
Feb 10th 1954	Old Cholmeleians	won	2-0 (Pratt, Ruddock)
Feb 13th 1954	Brooke Hall	drew	2-2 (Buckley, Ruddock)
Feb 18th 1954	Winchester	won	5-4 (Lees 2, Ruddock 3)
Sept 25th 1954	Bank of England	lost	3-4 (Ruddock, Hornett, o.g.)
Sept 29th 1954	London FA	lost	0-11
Oct 2nd 1954	Corinthian Casuals	drew	4-4 (Ruddock 2, Lees, Percival)
Oct 9th 1954	Lancing	lost	1-2 (Ruddock)
Oct 13th 1954	RMA Sandhurst	drew	1-1 (Ruddock)
Oct 16th 1954	Old Bradfieldians	drew	2-2 (Ruddock 2)
Oct 23rd 1954	Bradfield	drew	1-1 (Ruddock)
Oct 27th 1954	Norsemen	drew	3-3 (Ruddock, Lees, Buckley)
Nov 3rd 1954	OU Centaurs	lost	3-7 (Lees 3)
Nov 6th 1954	Old Westminsters	won	7-3 (Lees 4, Jakobson, Buckley, Seth-Smith)
Nov 10th 1954	Shrewsbury	drew	1-1 (Buckley)
Nov 13th 1954	Old Wykehamists	won	6-1 (Jakobson 3, Lees, Percival, Seth-Smith)
Nov 20th 1954	Repton	lost	1-4 (Percival)
Nov 27th 1954	Westminster	won	2-0 (Ruddock 2)
Dec 1st 1954	Trinity, Oxford	lost	2-5 (Percival 2)
Dec 4th 1954	Army Crusaders	drew	2-2 (Ruddock 2)
Jan 22nd 1955	Corinthian Casuals	lost	1-6 (Jakobson)
Jan 26th 1955	Cambridge Falcons	lost	1-6 (Percival)
Jan 29th 1955	Old Cholmeleians	won	1-0 (Hornett)
Feb 3rd 1955	Eton	drew	2-2 (Buckley, o.g.)
Feb 5th 1955	Old Carthusians	lost	1-3 (Buckley)
Feb 9th 1955	Mons OCTS	lost	2-5 (Forsyth, Tunnock)
Feb 12th 1955	Brooke Hall	won	4-0 (Forsyth, Lees, Percival, Buckley)
Feb 17th 1955	Winchester	lost	1-2 (Forsyth)
Sept 24th 1955	1st Trg Btn RASC	lost	1-6 (Steed)
Oct 1st 1955	Corinthian Casuals	won	7-5 (Forsyth 4, Burrows 2, Jakobson)
Oct 5th 1955	London FA	lost	0-3
Oct 8th 1955	Lancing	won	3-1 (Jakobson, Forsyth 2)
Oct 12th 1955	RMA Sandhurst	lost	0-4
Oct 15th 1955	Old Bradfieldians	drew	1-1 (Jakobson)
Oct 22nd 1955	Bradfield	drew	3-3 (Burrows, Tunnock, Sparshatt)
Oct 26th 1955	Norsemen	won	3-1 (Hornett 2, Sparshatt)
Nov 2nd 1955	Oxford Centaurs	lost	0-6
Nov 5th 1955	Old Westminsters	won	2-0 (Hornett, Jakobson)
Nov 9th 1955	Shrewsbury	won	2-0 (Steed, Tunnock)
Nov 12th 1955	Old Wykehamists	won	4-3 (Steed 3, Tomlinson)
Nov 19th 1955	Repton	drew	1-1 (Forsyth)
Nov 26th 1955	Westminster	lost	1-3 (o.g.)
Nov 30th 1955	Trinity, Oxford	lost	2-3 (Burrows, o.g.)
Dec 3rd 1955	Army Crusaders	lost	1-3 (Steed)
Dec 7th 1955	Brooke Hall	lost	2-3 (Burrows, Tunnock)
Jan 25th 1956	Cambridge Falcons	lost	1-5 (Tunnock)
Jan 28th 1956	Liverpool Ramblers	won	6-0 (Jakobson 2, Burrows, Tunnock, Hornett, Forsyth)
Feb 9th 1956	Eton	won	6-2 (Steed 2, Forsyth, Jakobson, Tunnock, o.g.)
Feb 11th 1956	Corinthian Casuals	lost	1-3 (Hornett)
Feb 23rd 1956	Winchester	won	3-2 (Jakobson, Burrows, o.g.)
Sept 29th 1956	Corinthian Casuals	won	5-0 (Burrows, Agace 2, Steed, Sparshatt)
Oct 3rd 1956	London FA Minors	lost	0-7
Oct 10th 1956	RMA Sandhurst	won	2-1 (Burrows, Sparshatt)
Oct 13th 1956	Lancing	won	2-1 (Sparshatt, White)
Oct 20th 1956	Old Bradfieldians	won	3-1 (Sparshatt 2, White)
Oct 24th 1956	Army Crusaders	lost	1-2 (Sparshatt)
Oct 27th 1956	Bradfield	drew	2-2 (White, Sparshatt)
Nov 7th 1956	OU Centaurs	lost	0-3
Nov 10th 1956	Old Westminsters	won	4-2 (Steed, Hughesdon, Sparshatt, Foster-Brown)
Nov 14th 1956	Shrewsbury	drew	1-1 (Burrows)
Nov 17th 1956	Old Wykehamists	lost	0-7
Nov 24th 1956	Repton	lost	1-3 (Steed)
Dec 1st 1956	Westminster	won	1-0 (Burrows)
Dec 15th 1956	Brooke Hall	won	1-0 (Burrows)
Jan 26th 1957	Old Cholmeleians	won	3-2 (Visser, Gordon, White)
Jan 30th 1957	Cambridge Falcons	drew	0-0
Feb 2nd 1957	Old Carthusians	lost	0-2
Feb 7th 1957	Eton	won	2-1 (o.g., Visser)
Feb 9th 1957	Corinthian Casuals	lost	1-2 (Visser)
Feb 16th 1957	Bank of England	lost	1-3 (Visser)
Feb 21st 1957	Winchester	won	1-0 (Gibb)
Sept 28th 1957	Corinthian Casuals	lost	0-2
Oct 2nd 1957	London FA Minors	lost	0-4
Oct 9th 1957	RMA Sandhurst	lost	0-5
Oct 19th 1957	Old Bradfieldians	lost	2-3 (Sclater, Visser)
Oct 23rd 1957	Army Crusaders	lost	1-5 (Agace)
Oct 26th 1957	Bradfield	lost	0-3
Nov 6th 1957	OU Centaurs	lost	0-5
Nov 7th 1957	Old Westminsters	lost	1-2 (Tham)
Nov 13th 1957	Shrewsbury	drew	0-0
Nov 16th 1957	Old Wykehamists	lost	2-5 (White, Harrison)
Nov 23rd 1957	Repton	lost	2-6 (Harrison, o.g.)
Nov 27th 1957	Westminster	won	2-1 (Harrison, Topham)
Nov 30th 1957	Lancing	won	4-1 (Harrison, Agace, White, Gardiner)
Dec 13th 1957	Brooke Hall	won	3-0 (Gibb 2, Gardiner)
Jan 25th 1958	Liverpool Ramblers	lost	1-2 (Visser)
Jan 29th 1958	Cambridge Falcons	lost	1-4 (White)
Feb 1st 1958	Old Carthusians	won	7-2 (Agace 2, Gibb 2, White, Visser, Harrison)
Feb 6th 1958	Eton	drew	1-1 (Agace)
Feb 8th 1958	Corinthian Casuals	lost	2-6 (Harrison, o.g.)
Feb 12th 1958	Hampton GS	won	2-1 (Gibb, Visser)
Feb 15th 1958	Bank of England	won	3-2 (White 2, Gibb)
Feb 20th 1958	Winchester	won	2-1 (Harrison, Agace)
Sept 27th 1958	Corinthian Casuals	lost	2-6 (Topham, Gibb)
Oct 1st 1958	London FA Minors	lost	0-11
Oct 8th 1958	RMA Sandhurst	lost	1-4 (Topham)
Oct 11th 1958	Lancing	won	4-3 (Gibb 2, Topham 2)
Oct 18th 1958	Old Carthusians	lost	1-9 (Gibb)
Oct 22nd 1958	Army Crusaders	lost	4-6 (Gibb 2, Visser, Craig)
Oct 25th 1958	Bradfield	drew	0-0
Nov 5th 1958	OU Centaurs	lost	2-5 (Gibb 2)
Nov 8th 1958	Old Westminsters	lost	1-3 (Faulkner)
Nov 12th 1958	Shrewsbury	lost	0-2
Nov 15th 1958	Old Wykehamists	lost	2-4 (Gibb, Taylor)
Nov 22nd 1958	Repton	lost	1-3 (Strathern)
Nov 29th 1958	Westminster	won	2-0 (o.g., Gibb)
Dec 17th 1958	Brooke Hall	drew	1-1 (Gwyn Rees)
Jan 24th 1959	Old Cholmeleians	lost	1-2 (Taylor)
Jan 28th 1959	CU Falcons	lost	3-6 (Visser, Gibb, Faulkner)
Jan 31st 1959	Army Crusaders	drew	4-4 (Gibb 2, Topham 2)
Feb 5th 1959	Eton	won	5-1 (Gibb, Faulkner, Topham, Taylor 2)
Feb 7th 1959	Corinthian Casuals	lost	2-3 (Faulkner, Visser)
Feb 14th 1959	RMA Sandhurst	lost	1-2 (Womersley)
Feb 19th 1959	Winchester	lost	2-5 (Taylor, Visser)
Sept 30th 1959	Mons OCS	lost	0-2
Oct 3rd 1959	Corinthian Casuals	lost	0-5
Oct 7th 1959	RMA Sandhurst	lost	0-3
Oct 10th 1959	Lancing	lost	1-5 (Topham)
Oct 17th 1959	Old Carthusians	lost	0-11
Oct 21st 1959	Army Crusaders	lost	1-3 (Lamaison)
Oct 24th 1959	Bradfield	drew	1-1 (o.g.)
Nov 4th 1959	OU Centaurs	lost	1-5 (Taylor)
Nov 7th 1959	Old Wykehamists	lost	2-3 (Topham, Taylor)
Nov 11th 1959	Shrewsbury	won	2-1 (Blumer, Willcocks)
Nov 18th 1959	London FA Minors	lost	1-9 (Taylor)
Nov 21st 1959	Repton	lost	0-4
Nov 28th 1959	Westminster	lost	0-1
Dec 9th 1959	Brooke Hall	won	1-0 (Taylor)
Jan 23rd 1960	Liverpool Ramblers	lost	2-12 (Craig, Taylor)
Jan 27th 1960	Cambridge Falcons	lost	3-12 (Pilch, Craig, Taylor)
Jan 30th 1960	Corinthian Casuals	lost	2-4 (Taylor, Lorenz)
Feb 4th 1960	Eton	drew	1-1 (Taylor)
Feb 10th 1960	Middlesex GS	lost	1-9 (Craig)
Feb 13th 1960	Old Bradfieldians	lost	2-3 (Taylor, Knight)
Feb 18th 1960	Winchester	lost	2-4 (Pilch, Topham)

Oct 1st 1960	Mons OCS	won	4-0 (Powell 4)
Oct 5th 1960	Corinthian Casuals	lost	2-6 (Powell 2)
Oct 8th 1960	Old Carthusians	won	3-2 (Garrow 2, Pilch)
Oct 12th 1960	RMA Sandhurst	lost	2-3 (Powell 2)
Oct 15th 1960	Lancing	lost	1-5 (Powell)
Oct 19th 1960	Army Crusaders	lost	1-3 (Arnold)
Oct 22nd 1960	Bradfield	lost	0-2
Nov 2nd 1960	OU Centaurs	lost	0-2
Nov 5th 1960	Old Wykehamists	lost	1-6 (Powell)
Nov 9th 1960	Shrewsbury	drew	0-0
Nov 16th 1960	Hampton	lost	2-3 (Powell, Garrow)
Nov 19th 1960	Repton	lost	0-2
Nov 26th 1960	Westminster	lost	1-4 (Arnold)
Dec 7th 1960	Brooke Hall	drew	2-2 (Arnold, Garrow)
Jan 28th 1961	Old Cholmeleians	lost	0-4
Feb 1st 1961	Trinity, Oxford	won	1-0 (Lorenz)
Feb 4th 1961	Corinthian Casuals	lost	1-6 (Lorenz)
Feb 9th 1961	Eton	lost	2-3 (Powell, Gilliat)
Feb 15th 1961	Cambridge Falcons	lost	2-8 (Powell 2)
Feb 18th 1961	Old Bradfieldians	won	3-0 (Lorenz, Powell 2)
Feb 23rd 1961	Winchester	lost	0-1
Sept 30th 1961	Old Carthusians	won	3-2 (Gilliat, de Grunwald 2)
Oct 7th 1961	Corinthian Casuals	lost	0-2
Oct 11th 1961	RMA Sandhurst	drew	2-2 (Hopkins, de Grunwald)
Oct 14th 1961	Lancing	won	2-1 (Powell, Arnold)
Oct 21st 1961	Old Wykehamists	won	5-3 (de Grunwald, Arnold, Marks, Powell, Hopkins)
Oct 25th 1961	Army Crusaders	won	3-2 (Arnold, o.g.2)
Oct 28th 1961	Bradfield	drew	2-2 (Gilliat 2)
Nov 8th 1961	OU Centaurs	lost	1-5 (Gilliat)
Nov 11th 1961	Hampton GS	won	6-2 (Gilliat 4, Arnold, Bailhache)
Nov 15th 1961	Shrewsbury	won	2-0 (Arnold, de Grunwald)
Nov 22nd 1961	Highgate	lost	2-4 (Gilliat 2)
Nov 25th 1961	Repton	lost	0-1
Dec 2nd 1961	Westminster	won	3-0 (Martin, o.g., Gilliat)
Jan 27th 1962	Liverpool Ramblers	lost	0-1
Feb 3rd 1962	Corinthian Casuals	won	4-1 (Powell 2, Gilliat, Petrides)
Feb 8th 1962	Eton	won	3-0 (Gilliat 3)
Feb 14th 1962	Cambridge Falcons	lost	1-3 (de Grunwald)
Feb 17th 1962	Old Bradfieldians	won	3-0 (Powell 2, Bailhache)
Feb 22nd 1962	Winchester	won	1-0 (de Grunwald)
Sept 29th 1962	Old Carthusians	lost	1-5 (Gilliat)
Oct 6th 1962	Corinthian Casuals	lost	0-3
Oct 10th 1962	RMA Sandhurst	won	4-2 (Proud 3, Gilliat)
Oct 13th 1962	Lancing	won	2-0 (Gilliat, Hopkins)
Oct 20th 1962	Old Wykehamists	won	4-2 (Proud 2, Gilliat 2)
Oct 24th 1962	Army Crusaders	won	3-1 (Gilliat 2, Proud)
Oct 27th 1962	Bradfield	won	6-1 (Gilliat 4, Hooper, Martin)
Nov 7th 1962	OU Centaurs	lost	1-5 (Hooper)
Nov 10th 1962	Hampton GS	won	2-0 (Gilliat 2)
Nov 14th 1962	Shrewsbury	lost	1-2 (Marks)
Nov 21st 1962	Highgate	lost	1-3 (de Grunwald)
Nov 24th 1962	Repton	won	5-1 (Gilliat 3, Martin, Powell)
Dec 1st 1962	Westminster	won	2-0 (Gilliat, de Grunwald)
Sept 28th 1963	Old Carthusians	lost	0-3
Oct 5th 1963	Corinthian Casuals	lost	1-3 (Bailhache)
Oct 9th 1963	RMA Sandhurst	lost	1-5 (Drayson)
Oct 12th 1963	Lancing	lost	1-2 (Weir)
Oct 19th 1963	Old Wykehamists	won	6-4 (Drayson 2, Hooper 2, Hill, Bailhache)
Oct 23rd 1963	Army Crusaders	won	3-2 (Drayson, Hooper, Weir)
Oct 26th 1963	Bradfield	lost	1-4 (Hooper)
Nov 6th 1963	OU Centaurs	won	4-2 (Randel 2, Hill, Weir)
Nov 9th 1963	Hampton GS	lost	0-1
Nov 13th 1963	Shrewsbury	won	3-1 (Hill, Hooper, Weir)
Nov 20th 1963	Highgate	lost	2-8 (Randel, Bailhache)
Nov 23rd 1963	Repton	lost	2-7 (Randel, Bailhache)
Nov 30th 1963	Westminster	won	1-0 (Weir)
Jan 25th 1964	Liverpool Ramblers	lost	1-2 (Weir)
Jan 29th 1964	Trinity, Oxford	won	6-0 (Hooper 2, Weir 2, Bailhache, o.g.)
Feb 1st 1964	Corinthian Casuals	lost	1-4 (Hooper)
Feb 6th 1964	Eton	won	3-0 (Weir 2, Hooper)
Feb 12th 1964	CU Falcons	won	2-0 (Hooper 2)
Feb 15th 1964	Old Bradfieldians	won	3-2 (Hooper 2, Weir)
Feb 20th 1964	Winchester	won	2-1 (Weir, Hill)
Sept 26th 1964	Old Carthusians	lost	0-4
Oct 3rd 1964	Corinthian Casuals	lost	0-6
Oct 7th 1964	RMA Sandhurst	won	1-0 (Weir)
Oct 10th 1964	Lancing	drew	1-1 (Weir)
Oct 17th 1964	Old Wykehamists	won	5-2 (Samuelson 2, Weir 2, Hooper)
Oct 21st 1964	Army Crusaders	won	6-2 (Weir 3, Easton, Hooper, Samuelson)
Oct 24th 1964	Bradfield	won	3-0 (Hooper, Weir 2)
Nov 4th 1964	OU Centaurs	lost	1-6 (Hooper)
Nov 7th 1964	Hampton GS	drew	1-1 (Davis)
Nov 11th 1964	Shrewsbury	lost	2-3 (Weir 2)
Nov 18th 1964	Highgate	drew	1-1 (Weir)
Nov 21st 1964	Repton	lost	3-4 (Hooper 2, Weir)
Nov 28th 1964	Westminster	won	4-0 (Rolls, Hooper 3)
Jan 23rd 1965	Old Cholmeleians	lost	2-3 (Hooper, Weir)
Jan 27th 1965	Woking CGS	lost	0-1
Jan 30th 1965	Corinthian Casuals	drew	1-1 (Bidwell)
Feb 4th 1965	Eton	won	4-1 (Easton, Weir, Hooper 2)
Feb 10th 1965	CU Falcons	lost	0-4
Feb 13th 1965	Old Bradfieldians	lost	0-1
Feb 18th 1965	Winchester	won	5-3 (Hooper 3, Weir 2)
Sept 25th 1965	Old Malvernians	drew	2-2 (Rolls, Bennett)
Oct 2nd 1965	Old Carthusians	lost	0-5
Oct 6th 1965	RMA Sandhurst	lost	0-2
Oct 9th 1965	Lancing	lost	0-3
Oct 16th 1965	Old Wykehamists	lost	0-2
Oct 20th 1965	Army Crusaders	drew	1-1 (Easton)
OQ 1965	Hampton	lost	0-4
Oct 23rd 1965	Bradfield	lost	0-2
Nov 3rd 1965	OU Centaurs	lost	1-4 (Easton)
Nov 10th 1965	Shrewsbury	won	3-1 (Cohn, Bennett, Easton)
Nov 17th 1965	Highgate	won	1-0 (Bennett)
Nov 20th 1965	Repton	drew	3-3 (Gray, Deans, Easton)
Nov 27th 1965	Winchester	lost	1-4 (Deans)
Jan 29th 1966	Liverpool Ramblers	lost	1-9 (Howard)
Feb 2nd 1966	Woking CGS	won	7-2 (Howard 2, Cohn 2, Deans 3)
Feb 10th 1966	Eton	won	2-0 (Bennett, Gimson)
Feb 16th 1966	Old Bradfieldians	lost	3-5 (Bennett, Howard 2)
Feb 19th 1966	Westminster	won	5-0 (Howard 2, Deans 2, Simmons)
Oct 1st 1966	Old Carthusians	lost	1-7 (Bennett)
Oct 5th 1966	RMA Sandhurst	won	1-0 (Bennett)
Oct 8th 1966	Lancing	lost	0-2
Oct 15th 1966	Old Wykehamists	lost	2-5 (Bennett 2)
Oct 19th 1966	Army Crusaders	won	2-0 (Bennett, Provis)
Oct 22nd 1966	Bradfield	won	2-1 (Bennett)
Nov 9th 1966	OU Centaurs	lost	0-9
Nov 12th 1966	Hampton GS	lost	1-2 (Cohn)
Nov 16th 1966	Shrewsbury	lost	4-7 (Kennedy 2, Provis, Deans)
Nov 23rd 1966	Winchester	won	1-0 (Cohn)
Dec 3rd 1966	Highgate	lost	0-1
Dec 7th 1966	Repton	drew	0-0
Jan 28th 1967	Old Cholmeleians	lost	0-3
Feb 1st 1967	Woking CGS	lost	3-4 (Bennett 3)
Feb 4th 1967	Corinthian Casuals	lost	0-6
Feb 9th 1967	Eton	won	3-0 (Deans 2, Provis)
Feb 15th 1967	Old Bradfieldians	won	3-2 (Bennett 2, Provis)
Feb 18th 1967	Westminster	won	8-1 (Deans 3, Bennett 4, Provis)
Sept 23rd 1967	Old Malvernians	lost	0-2
Sept 30th 1967	Old Carthusians	lost	2-4 (Bennett, Deans)
Oct 4th 1967	RMA Sandhurst	drew	2-2 (Bennett, Deans)
Oct 7th 1967	Lancing	lost	1-2 (Bennett)
Oct 14th 1967	Old Wykehamists	lost	1-3 (Deans)
Oct 18th 1967	Army Crusaders	won	6-1 (Bennett 3, Deans, Provis, Cohn)
Oct 28th 1967	Bradfield	lost	1-2 (Gieve)
Nov 11th 1967	Hampton GS	lost	1-2 (Rintoul)
Nov 15th 1967	Shrewsbury	won	4-1 (Bennett 3, Cohn)
Nov 22nd 1967	Highgate	won	2-1 (Bennett, Provis)
Nov 25th 1967	Winchester	lost	1-3 (Deans)
Dec 2nd 1967	Repton	lost	1-8 (Cohn)
Jan 20th 1968	Liverpool Ramblers	won	2-1 (Bennett, Foster)
Jan 24th 1968	Woking CGS	won	2-1 (Bennett, Foster)
Jan 27th 1968	Corinthian Casuals	lost	1-5 (Foster)
Feb 1st 1968	Westminster	won	3-1 (Deans, Foster 2)
Feb 7th 1968	Old Bradfieldians	drew	3-3 (Carter 2, Bennett)
Feb 10th 1968	Eton	won	7-0 (o.g., Carter 2, Bennett 2, Deans, Rintoul)
Sept 21st 1968	Old Malvernians	won	5-3
Sept 25th 1968	RMA Sandhurst	lost	1-2
Sept 28th 1968	Old Carthusians	drew	1-1 (Foster)
Oct 5th 1968	Lancing	lost	0-3
Oct 12th 1968	Old Wykehamists	lost	4-8
Oct 16th 1968	Army Crusaders	drew	3-3
Oct 23rd 1968	Arsenal AFC	lost	0-2
Oct 26th 1968	Bradfield	lost	0-1
Nov 6th 1968	OU Centaurs	lost	2-3 (Foster, Grizelle)
Nov 9th 1968	Hampton GS	lost	1-4 (Foster)
Nov 13th 1968	Shrewsbury	lost	0-5
Nov 20th 1968	Highgate	won	6-0 (Foster 3, Carter, Walton, Ritchie)
Nov 23rd 1968	Winchester	won	1-0 (Foster)
Nov 30th 1968	Repton	lost	2-5 (Carter, Hannyngton)
Jan 18th 1969	Liverpool Ramblers	lost	3-4 (Grizelle 2, Foster)
Jan 22nd 1969	Woking GS	lost	0-2
Jan 25th 1969	Corinthian Casuals	lost	0-1
Jan 29th 1969	Old Bradfieldians	lost	1-3 (Foster)
Feb 1st 1969	Westminster	won	1-0 (Walton)
Feb 6th 1969	Eton	won	2-0 (Foster 2)
Sept 20th 1969	Old Carthusians	drew	1-1 (Walton)

Sept 24th 1969	RMA Sandhurst	lost	0-3
Oct 1st 1969	Camberley & Frimley	lost	0-2
Oct 4th 1969	Lancing	won	3-1 (Stewart, Walton 2)
Oct 11th 1969	Old Wykehamists	won	3-2 (Walton 2, Stewart)
Oct 15th 1969	Ardingly	drew	1-1 (Walton)
Oct 22nd 1969	KES Witley	won	3-0 (Walton, o.g. 2)
Oct 25th 1969	Bradfield	won	2-0 (Walton, Grizelle)
Nov 5th 1969	OU Centaurs	lost	0-1
Nov 8th 1969	Hampton GS	won	1-0 (Walton)
Nov 12th 1969	Shrewsbury	won	2-1 (Stewart, Walton)
Nov 19th 1969	Highgate	won	1-0 (Walton)
Nov 22nd 1969	Winchester	won	4-0 (Holder, Stewart, Lyle, Walton)
Nov 29th 1969	Repton	won	4-1 (Stewart 2, Holder, Walton)
Jan 17th 1970	Liverpool Ramblers	lost	0-1
Jan 24th 1970	Corinthian Casuals	lost	0-4
Jan 28th 1970	Old Bradfieldians	drew	1-1 (Hughes)
Jan 31st 1970	Westminster	drew	2-2 (Stewart, Holder)
Feb 5th 1970	Eton	drew	1-1
Sept 19th 1970	Old Carthusians	lost	1-3 (Walton)
Sept 23rd 1970	RMA Sandhurst	lost	1-4 (Walton)
Sept 26th 1970	Old Malvernians	lost	2-4 (Gibson, Walton)
Sept 29th 1970	Camberley & Frimley	lost	0-1
Oct 3rd 1970	Lancing	won	2-1 Wallis, Godby)
Oct 10th 1970	Old Wykehamists	won	1-0 (Holder)
Oct 14th 1970	Ardingly	drew	1-1 (Godby)
Oct 21st 1970	KES Witley	drew	0-0
Oct 24th 1970	Bradfield	won	2-1 (Godby, Hughes)
Nov 4th 1970	OU Centaurs	lost	2-4 (Stewart, Walton)
Nov 7th 1970	Hampton GS	won	3-1 (Stewart, Walton, Wallis)
Nov 11th 1970	Shrewsbury	drew	3-3 (Walton 2, Wisdom)
Nov 18th 1970	Highgate	lost	0-3
Nov 21st 1970	Winchester	won	3-0 (Godby, Stewart, Walton)
Nov 28th 1970	Repton	lost	1-2 (Walton)
Jan 16th 1971	Liverpool Ramblers	lost	0-1
Jan 20th 1971	Guildford TC	won	4-0 (Godby 2, Stewart, Gibson)
Jan 23rd 1971	Corinthian Casuals	lost	1-9 (Stewart)
Jan 27th 1971	Old Bradfieldians	won	2-0 (Godby, Gibson)
Jan 30th 1971	Westminster	won	4-0 (Godby, Stewart 2, Holder)
Feb 4th 1971	Eton	won	5-0 (Godby, Holder, Gibson, Stewart 2)
Sept 18th 1971	Old Carthusians	won	2-0 (Williams, o.g.)
Sept 22nd 1971	RMA Sandhurst	lost	3-4
Sept 25th 1971	Old Malvernians	won	2-0 (Doggart, Stewart)
Spet 28th 1971	Collingwood	lost	1-2
Oct 2nd 1971	Lancing	lost	1-4
Oct 9th 1971	Old Wykehamists	lost	3-4
Oct 13th 1971	Ardingly	won	5-2 (Godby 3, Stewart, Holder)
Oct 16th 1971	Eton	won	2-1 (Godby 2)
Oct 20th 1971	KES Witley	drew	2-2
Oct 23rd 1971	Bradfield	lost	0-4
Nov 3rd 1971	OU Centaurs	won	1-0 (Godby)
Nov 6th 1971	Hampton GS	won	6-0 (Godby 2, Stewart, Holder, Williams)
Nov 10th 1971	Shrewsbury	drew	1-1 (Godby)
Nov 17th 1971	Highgate	won	3-0 (Godby, Holder, Faull)
Nov 20th 1971	Winchester	drew	3-3 (Williams, Stewart, Faulkl)
Nov 27th 1971	Repton	won	3-1 (Godby, Stewart 2)
Jan 22nd 1972	Liverpool Ramblers	lost	1-2 (Stewart)
Jan 26th 1972	Old Bradfieldians	drew	2-2 (Stewart 2)
Jan 29th 1972	Millfield	won	3-2 (Doggart, Cragg, Adomakoh)
Feb 5th 1972	Westminster	won	6-2 (Stewart 2, Williams 2, Faull, Adomakoh)
Sept 23rd 1972	Old Carthusians	lost	2-3 (Oundjian 2)
Sept 30th 1972	Old Wykehamists	drew	2-2 (Williams)
Oct 7th 1972	Lancing	won	1-0 (Doggart)
Oct 11th 1972	Ardingly	won	1-0 (Doggart)
Oct 14th 1972	Eton	lost	1-3 (
Oct 18th 1972	KES Witley	won	4-2 (Doggart, Faull, Gibson, o.g.)
Oct 21st 1972	Bradfield	won	3-0 (Doggart, Stone, Parker)
Oct 28th 1972	Malvern	drew	0-0

Tour of Luxembourg 1972 (Nov 2nd -8th 1972)

Nov 3rd 1972	Diekirch	lost	1-2 (Oundjian)
Nov 5th 1972	Wiltz	won	3-1 (Parker, Stone)
Nov 7th 1972	Luxembourg Schools XI	drew	0-0
Nov 11th 1972	Shrewsbury	lost	0-2
Nov 15th 1972	Highgate	won	1-0 (Parker)
Nov 18th 1972	Winchester	lost	0-2
Nov 25th 1972	Repton	lost	2-3 (Williams, Doggart)
Jan 20th 1973	Liverpool Ramblers	won	2-0
Jan 24th 1973	Old Bradfieldians	won	6-3
Jan 27th 1973	Millfield	lost	0-6
Jan 31st 1973	Bedales	won	3-0
Feb 3rd 1973	Westminster	won	3-2
Sept 22nd 1973	Old Carthusians	won	2-0 (Adomakoh, Scholfield)
Sept 27th 1973	Malvern	drew	1-1 (Doggart)
Sept 29th 1973	Old Wykehamists	won	1-0 (Adomakoh)
Oct 3rd 1973	RMA Sandhurst	lost	0-1
Oct 6th 1973	Brooke Hall	won	6-0 (Adomakoh 2, Scholfield,

			Middleton, Grizelle, North)
Oct 6th 1973	Lancing	cancelled due to illness	
Oct 10th 1973	Ardingly	won	4-1 (Scholfield 2, Adomakoh, Middleton)
Oct 13th 1973	Eton	drew	0-0
Oct 17th 1973	KES Witley	lost	1-2 (Adomakoh)
Oct 20th 1973	Bradfield	lost	1-2 (
Oct 27th 1973	Bedales	won	5-0 (Williams, Middleton, Faull, Adomakoh, Napolitano)
Oct 31st 1973	OU Centaurs	won	5-0 (Adomakoh 2)
Nov 10th 1973	Shrewsbury	won	2-1 (Ecob, Adomakoh)

Visit from Chelsea FC (full squad) to give a demonstration training session and a match v Select XI

Nov 14th 1973	Highgate	won	3-1 (Faull, o.g., Adomakoh)
Nov 17th 1973	Winchester	won	2-1 (Adomakoh)
Nov 24th 1973	Repton	won	3-0 (Adomakoh 3)

Tour of Jamaica 1973 (Dec 27th – Jan)

Dec 1973	Vere Technical College	won	3-1 (Adomakoh, Williams, Doggart)
Jan 1974	Woolmers HS	drew	0-0
Jan 1974	Cornwall College	lost	1-2 (Adomakoh)
Jan 1974	Kingston College	lost	0-2
Jan 1974	Calabar HS	won	1-0 (Faull)
Jan 19th 1974	Liverpool Ramblers	won	2-1 (Adomakoh 2)
Jan 23rd 1974	Old Bradfieldians	won	4-0 (Adomakoh, Walker 2, North)
Jan 26th 1974	Bedales	won	3-0 (Adomakoh, North, Scholfield)
Jan 30th 1974	Oratory	won	4-1 (Adomakoh 3, Walker)
Feb 2nd 1974	Westminster	drew	1-1 (Adomakoh)
Sept 21st 1974	Old Carthusians	drew	1-1 (North)
Sept 25th 1974	Brooke Hall	won	3-0 (North, Middleton 2)
Sept 28th 1974	Old Wykehamists	won	5-4 (Walker 3, Williams, Adomakoh)
Oct 2nd 1974	Collyer's, Horsham	won	3-2 (Walker)
Oct 5th 1974	Lancing	won	5-2 (Middleton 3, Walker, Gibson)
Oct 9th 1974	Ardingly	won	5-0 (Adomakoh, Walker 2, Middleton 2)
Oct 12th 1974	Eton	lost	0-2
Oct 16th 1974	Hampton GS	won	2-1 (Adomakoh 2)
Oct 19th 1974	Bradfield	lost	1-3 (Adomakoh)
Oct 22nd 1974	Victoria College	won	5-1 (Walker 2, Middleton, Adomakoh, Belchamber)
Oct 26th 1974	Malvern	won	4-0 (Walker 2, Middleton, Adomakoh)
Oct 30th 1974	OU Centaurs	drew	2-2 (Walker, Adomakoh)
Nov 9th 1974	Shrewsbury	won	4-0 (Oulton, Middleton 2, Williams)
Nov 16th 1974	Winchester	won	2-0 (Walker, Adomakoh)
Nov 23rd 1974	Repton	lost	0-2
Nov 27th 1974	KES Witley	won	6-0 (Walker 4, Adomakoh, Middleton)
Jan 25th 1975	Bedales	won	2-1 (North, Phillips)
Feb 1st 1975	Westminster	won	5-0 (Gibson, Oulton 3, Phillips)
Sept 20th 1975	Old Carthusians		
Sept 27th 1975	Old Wykehamists		
Oct 1st 1975	Collyer's, Horsham		
Oct 4th 1975	Lancing	drew	0-0
Oct 8th 1975	Ardingly	lost	0-1
Oct 11th 1975	Eton	won	1-0 (Hayllar)
Oct 15th 1975	Hampton GS		
Oct 18th 1975	Bradfield	drew	1-1
Oct 25th 1975	Malvern	drew	0-0
OQ 1975	Victoria College	won	3-1 (Phillips, Ostrer, Cunningham)
Nov 8th 1975	Shrewsbury	lost	0-3
Nov 12th 1975	Highgate	drew	0-0
Nov 15th 1975	Winchester	drew	1-1 (Peet)
Nov 29th 1975	Royal Russell	won	7-0 (Belchamber 2, Phillips 2, Parker 2, Ostrer)
Jan 17th 1976	Liverpool Ramblers	won	3-2 (Cummins, Shepherd, Cunningham)
Jan 21st 1976	Old Bradfieldians	drew	1-1 (Phillips)
Jan 24th 1976	Bedales	won	1-0 (Cunningham)
Jan 28th 1976	Oratory		
Jan 31st 1976	Westminster	drew	0-0
Sept 11th 1976	Old Carthusians		
Sept 25th 1976	Old Wykehamists	won	3-1 (Cummins 2, Phillips)
Sept 29th 1976	Collyer's, Horsham		
Oct 2nd 1976	Lancing	drew	1-1 (Cummins)
Oct 6th 1976	Ardingly	won	3-1 (Reynolds, Cummins, Shepherd)
Oct 9th 1976	Eton	lost	1-4
Oct 13th 1976	Shrewsbury	lost	0-2
Oct 16th 1976	Bradfield	won	2-1 (Belchamber, Ostrer)
Oct 20th 1976	Salesian College		
Oct 23rd 1976	Malvern	lost	1-3
Oct 25th 1976	Victoria College	won	4-1 (Ostrer 2, Shepherd, Phillips)
Nov 10th 1976	Highgate	lost	2-8
Nov 13th 1976	Winchester	won	4-0 (Mole 3)
Nov 17th 1976	OU Centaurs	won	1-0 (Cummins)

Date	Opponent	Result	Score
Nov 20th 1976	**Brooke Hall**	won	4-1 (Ostrer 2, Belchamber, Shepherd)
Nov 24th 1976	Bedales		
Nov 27th 1976	**Old Carthusians**		
Jan 15th 1977	**Liverpool Ramblers**		
Jan 19th 1977	**Old Bradfieldians**	drew	1-1 (Shepherd)
Jan 22nd 1977	**Haileybury**	won	3-0 (Foley-Brickley, Whalley, Ostrer)
Jan 26th 1977	**Oratory**	won	4-0 (Whalley 2, Kirkbride, Shepherd)
Jan 29th 1977	**Westminster**	drew	1-1 (Wilson)
Sept 24th 1977	**Old Wykehamists**		
Sept 29th 1977	**Reigate GS**	won	5-0 (Adomahoh, Mole 2, Shepherd, Whalley)
Oct 1st 1977	**Old Carthusians**		
Oct 5th 1977	**Ardingly**	drew	2-2 (Adomahoh, Shepherd)
Oct 8th 1977	**Eton**	drew	0-0
Oct 11th 1977	**Malvern**		
Oct 15th 1977	**Bradfield**	drew	0-0
Oct 20th 1977	**Victoria College**	drew	1-1
Oct 22nd 1977	**Lancing**	lost	1-3 (Shepherd)
Oct 25th 1977	**Elizabeth College**	lost	2-4 (Mole, Doggart)
Nov 9th 1977	**Highgate**	won	3-0 (Mole, Shepherd 2)
Nov 12th 1977	**Winchester**	won	1-0 (Shepherd)
Nov 15th 1977	**Aldenham**	won	1-0 (Mole)
Nov 19th 1977	**Brooke Hall**	won	8-0 (Shepherd 3, Cummins 2, Kirkbride, Doggart, Mole)
Nov 23rd 1977	**Collyer's, Horsham**	won	3-1 (Shepherd, Kirkbride, Doggart)
Nov 26th 1977	**Shrewsbury**	lost	0-1
Dec 3rd 1977	**Repton**	lost	1-2
Jan 18th 1978	**Old Bradfieldians**	won	2-0 (Whalley, Doggart)
Jan 28th 1978	**Westminster**	won	5-1 (Mole 2, Mole, Whalley, Adomahoh)
Sept 23rd 1978	**Old Carthusians**	lost	0-2
Sept 28th 1978	**Reigate GS**	won	3-0 (Cummins, Farrow, Miller)
Sept 30th 1978	**Old Wykehamists**		
Oct 4th 1978	**Ardingly**	won	3-1 (Piper, Cummins, Haynes)
Oct 7th 1978	**Lancing**	won	3-0 (Piper 2, Farrow)
Oct 10th 1978	**Malvern**	drew	0-0
Oct 14th 1978	**Bradfield**	won	1-0 (Farrow)
Oct 21st 1978	**Eton**	lost	0-2
Oct 26th 1978	**Victoria College**	won	2-1 (Mole, Bishop)
Oct 27th 1978	**Hautlieu GS**	won	3-0 (Mole 2, Piper)
Nov 4th 1978	**Winchester**	drew	0-0
Nov 8th 1978	**Highgate**	drew	1-1 (Mole)
Nov 14th 1978	**Aldenham**	won	1-0 (Pride)
Nov 16th 1978	**OU Centaurs**		
Nov 18th 1978	**Brooke Hall**	won	5-0 (o.g., Pride 2, Piper 2)
Nov 25th 1978	**Shrewsbury**	drew	1-1 (Piper)
Nov 30th 1978	**Victoria College**	won	2-0 (Piper 2)
Dec 2nd 1978	**Repton**		
Dec 6th 1978	**Royal Russell**		
Jan 17th 1979	**Select XI**	won	4-3 (Frankland 2, Pratt, Farrow)
Jan 20th 1979	**Liverpool Ramblers**	drew	1-1 (Frankland)
Jan 27th 1979	**Westminster**	cancelled-weather	

Pre-season tour to Jersey

Date	Opponent	Result	Score
Sept 8th 1979	**De la Salle, Jersey**	won	2-0 (Haynes)
Sept 10th 1979	**Victoria College**	lost	0-4
Sept 19th 1979	**Reigate GS**	won	4-1 (Haynes 2, Kirkbride, Doggart)
Sept 22nd 1979	**Old Carthusians**	lost	2-4 (Doggart, Kirkbride)
Sept 25th 1979	**David Miller's XI**	lost	0-2
Sept 29th 1979	**Forest**	drew	1-1 (Gard)
Oct 3rd 1979	**Ardingly**	lost	1-2 (Haynes)
Oct 6th 1979	**Lancing**	lost	0-1
Oct 9th 1979	**Malvern**	drew	1-1 (Bowers)
Oct 13th 1979	**Bradfield**	won	2-1 (Raymonde 2)
Oct 20th 1979	**Eton**	won	2-0 (Haynes, Bishop)
Oct 23rd 1979	**Victoria College**	won	3-0 (Bishop 2, Raymonde)
Nov 7th 1979	**Highgate**	won	1-0 (Haynes)
Nov 10th 1979	**Winchester**	won	3-0 (Pratt, Haynes 2)
Nov 17th 1979	**Aldenham**	won	4-0 (Haynes 2, Raymonde, Lathwood)
Nov 24th 1979	**Shrewsbury**	lost	0-1
Dec 1st 1979	**Repton**	drew	1-1 (Bishop)
Dec 13th 1979	**Collyer's Horsham**	drew	2-2 (Raymonde, Haynes)
Dec 14th 1979	**Brooke Hall**	won	4-2 (Raymonde, Haynes, Doggart, Bishop)
Jan 19th 1980	**Liverpool Ramblers**	lost	1-3 (Gard)
Jan 23rd 1980	**Oratory**	drew	0-0
Jan 26th 1980	**Westminster**	drew	1-1 (Bowers)

Pre-season tour to Guernsey

Date	Opponent	Result	Score
Sept 8th 1980	**Winchester**	won	7-1 (Myers 5, Maddison, McCourt)
Sept 9th 1980	**Elizabeth College**	drew	2-2 (Cuff, o.g.)
Sept 17th 1980	**Godalming College**	drew	2-2 (Cuff 2)
Sept 20th 1980	**Old Carthusians**	lost	1-4 (Cuff)
Sept 23rd 1980	**David Miller's XI**	lost	0-1

Date	Opponent	Result	Score
Sept 27th 1980	**Forest**	lost	0-1
Oct 1st 1980	**Ardingly**	won	5-0 (Gard 2, Cuff 2, Myers)
Oct 4th 1980	**Lancing**	won	2-1 (May 2)
Oct 7th 1980	**Malvern**	won	3-1 (Gard, McCourt, Bonham-Carter)
Oct 11th 1980	**Bradfield**	lost	1-2 (McCourt)
Oct 18th 1980	**Eton**	drew	0-0
Oct 22nd 1980	**Elizabeth College**	lost	1-3 (Spooner)
Nov 5th 1980	**Highgate**	drew	1-1 (Gard)
Nov 8th 1980	**Winchester**	lost	0-1
Nov 11th 1980	**Aldenham**	won	2-1 (Cuff 2)
Nov 22nd 1980	**Shrewsbury**	lost	1-2 (May)
Nov 25th 1980	**Westminster**	won	3-2 (Myers 2, Mellstrom)
Nov 29th 1980	**Repton**	lost	0-3
Dec 13th 1980	**Brooke Hall**	lost	2-3 (Gard, Spooner)

LQ Football team now known as "A" XI

Date	Opponent	Result	Score
Sept 13th 1981	**Gibraltar Barracks**	lost	3-4 (Gard, Davis, Challen)
Sept 16th 1981	**Godalming College**	won	4-2 (Gard 2, Davis 2)
Sept 19th 1981	**Old Carthusians**	drew	1-1 (Fordham)
Sept 22nd 1981	**David Miller's XI**	lost	1-4
Sept 26th 1981	**Forest**	won	3-1 (McCourt, Fordham, Gard)
Sept 29th 1981	**Ardingly**	lost	1-3 (Challen)
Oct 3rd 1981	**Lancing**	won	1-0 (Gard)
Oct 6th 1981	**Malvern**	drew	0-0
Oct 10th 1981	**Bradfield**	lost	0-4
Oct 17th 1981	**Eton**	drew	0-0
Oct 22nd 1981	**Victoria College**	won	1-0 (Myers)
Oct 24th 1981	**Highgate**	drew	0-0
Nov 7th 1981	**Winchester**	lost	0-3
Nov 10th 1981	**Aldenham**	lost	1-2 (McCourt)
Nov 21st 1981	**Shrewsbury**	drew	1-1 (Bonham-Carter)
Nov 28th 1981	**Repton**	drew	2-2 (Myers, Bonham-Carter)
Mar 9th 1982	**Westminster**	lost	0-2

Pre-season tour to Derbyshire

Date	Opponent	Result	Score
Sept 7th 1982	**Bolton GS**	lost	1-4 (o.g.)
Sept 9th 1982	**King Edward VII**	won	3-2 (Ibru, Proctor, Frearson)
Sept 12th 1982	Gibraltar Barracks	drew	2-2 (Proctor, Ibru)
Sept 15th 1982	Godalming College	lost	1-2 (Newman)
Sept 18th 1982	**Old Carthusians**	lost	2-4 (Waters, Ibru)
Sept 21st 1982	**David Miller's XI**	lost	2-5 (Newman 2)
Sept 25th 1982	**Forest**	drew	4-4 (Proctor, Waters, Frearson, Aubrey)
Sept 28th 1982	**Ardingly**	won	2-1 (Waters 2)
Oct 2nd 1982	**Lancing**	won	3-1 (o.g., Newman, Frearson)
Oct 5th 1982	**Malvern**	lost	0-1
Oct 9th 1982	**Bradfield**	won	3-0 (Proctor 2, Newman)
Oct 16th 1982	**Eton**	lost	0-1
Oct 23rd 1982	**Highgate**	won	1-0 (Ibru)
Nov 6th 1982	**Winchester**	won	3-1 (Newman, Ibru 2)
Nov 9th 1982	**Aldenham**	lost	1-3 (Proctor)
Nov 20th 1982	**Shrewsbury**	lost	1-2 (Frearson)
Nov 27th 1982	**Repton**	drew	0-0
Dec 7th 1982	**Westminster**	won	5-0 (Newman 3, Frearson, Ibru)

Pre-season tour to Derbyshire

Date	Opponent	Result	Score
Sept 7th 1983	**Bolton GS**	lost	3-6 (Griffiths, Meesman, Haghighi)
Sept 8th 1983	**King Edward VII**	lost	0-2
Sept 14th 1983	**Steyning GS**	won	6-0 (Davis 2, Pennant, Ibru, Frearson, Haghighi)
Sept 17th 1983	**Old Carthusians**	lost	0-1
Sept 21st 1983	**Godalming College**	won	1-0 (Pennant)
Sept 24th 1983	**Forest**	won	3-2 (Frearson 2, Davis)
Sept 27th 1983	**Ardingly**	won	3-0 (Davis 2, Ibru)
Oct 1st 1983	**Lancing**	won	3-1 (Davis 2, Faulkner)
Oct 4th 1983	**Malvern**	lost	0-2
Oct 8th 1983	**Bradfield**	won	3-1 (Faulkner, Davis, Pennant)
Oct 15th 1983	**Eton**	drew	0-0
Oct 22nd 1983	**Highgate**	won	2-0 (Davis 2)
Nov 5th 1983	**Winchester**	drew	1-1 (Pennant)
Nov 15th 1983	**Aldenham**	won	4-1 (Davis 2, Ibru, Pennant)
Nov 26th 1983	**Shrewsbury**	won	6-3 (Ibru 3, Davis, Pennant, Faulkner)
Dec 3rd 1983	**Repton**	won	7-0 (Ibru 3, Davis, Pratt, Pennant, Griffiths)
Dec 6th 1983	**Westminster**	drew	2-2 (Griffiths, Pennant)

Tour to Bermuda 1984

Date	Opponent	Result	Score
Mar 28th 1984	**Bermuda Nat Youth**	lost	1-4 (Pride)
Mar 30th 1984	**Saltus GS**	won	1-0 (Haghighi)
Apr 2nd 1984	**Warwick Secondary**	won	4-1 (Waters, Wattar 2)
Apr 4th 1984	**Bermuda Youth**	lost	0-5
Apr 6th 1984	**Devonshire Colts**	won	4-2
Apr 8th 1984	**Somerset Youth**	won	3-1
Sept 19th 1984	**Steyning GS**	won	7-2 (Wattar 3, Kerevan 2)
Sept 22nd 1984	**Old Carthusians**	lost	1-3
Sept 26th 1984	**Godalming College**	won	6-1 (Wattar 3, Baker 2)
Sept 29th 1984	**Forest**	won	2-0

Date	Opponent	Result	Score (scorers)
Oct 2nd 1984	**Ardingly**	won	6-0 (Baker 3)
Oct 6th 1984	Lancing	lost	1-2
Oct 9th 1984	Malvern	lost	0-2
Oct 13th 1984	**Bradfield**	won	2-1 (Gough)
Oct 20th 1984	Eton	drew	2-2
Nov 10th 1984	**Winchester**	won	4-2 (Golder, Wattar)
Nov 13th 1984	Aldenham	drew	0-0
Nov 17th 1984	Highgate	lost	1-3
Nov 24th 1984	Shrewsbury	lost	0-1
Dec 1st 1984	**Repton**	won	3-1 (Golder, Baker 2)
Dec 4th 1984	Westminster	won	5-1 (Baker 2, Golder)

Pre-season tour to Holland

Date	Opponent	Result	Score (scorers)
Sept 5th 1985	FC Quick 'C'	won	6-0 (Faulkner, Bedford)
Sept 6th 1985	FC Quick 'B'	won	3-1
Sept 18th 1985	**Steyning GS**	won	3-2 (Jenkins 3)
Sept 21st 1985	Old Carthusians	lost	2-7 (Jenkins, Viall)
Sept 25th 1985	**Godalming College**	won	4-0 (Spiegel, Baker 2, Kerevan)
Sept 28th 1985	Forest	drew	2-2 (Spiegel, Abdali)
Oct 1st 1985	**Ardingly**	won	2-1 (Kerevan, Abdali)
Oct 5th 1985	Lancing	drew	0-0
Oct 8th 1985	Malvern	lost	0-1
Oct 12th 1985	**Bradfield**	won	1-0 (Baker)
Oct 19th 1985	Eton	lost	2-3 (Jenkins, Neill)
Nov 9th 1985	**Winchester**	won	4-3 (Jenkins 2, Kerevan, Faulkner)
Nov 12th 1985	Aldenham	lost	1-4 (Faulkner)
Nov 16th 1985	**Highgate**	won	3-1 (Kerevan 2, Jenkins)
Nov 23rd 1985	Shrewsbury	lost	0-1
Dec 1st 1985	Repton	lost	2-3 (Kerevan, Spiegel)
Dec 4th 1985	**Westminster**	won	3-1 (Kerevan, Neill)

Pre-season tour to Holland

Date	Opponent	Result	Score (scorers)
Sept 2nd 1986	FC Quick	drew	1-1 (Cowling)
Sept 3rd 1986	ADO	lost	3-4 (Mellstrom 2, Leale)
Sept 17th 1986	**Steyning GS**	won	4-3 (Leale 3, Jenkins)
Sept 20th 1986	Old Carthusians	lost	0-3
Sept 24th 1986	**Godalming College**	won	2-1 (Zervos 2)
Sept 27th 1986	**Forest**	won	3-2 (Zervos, Dow, Jenkins)
Sept 30th 1986	**Ardingly**	won	1-0 (Jenkins)
Oct 4th 1986	Lancing	lost	1-2 (Gray)
Oct 7th 1986	Malvern	lost	1-5 (Jenkins)
Oct 11th 1986	**Bradfield**	lost	0-1
Oct 18th 1986	Eton	drew	1-1 (Jenkins)
Nov 8th 1986	**Winchester**	won	4-0 (Jenkins, Gray, Payne, Bedford)
Nov 11th 1986	**Aldenham**	won	2-1 (Jenkins, o.g.)
Nov 15th 1986	Highgate	drew	0-0
Nov 22nd 1986	Shrewsbury	drew	1-1 (Ivermee)
Nov 29th 1986	Repton	lost	0-2
Dec 2nd 1986	**Westminster**	won	5-1 (Leale, Stevens 4)

Tour to Mayen OQ 1987

Date	Opponent	Result	Score (scorers)
Sept 1st 1987	Mayen FC	lost	1-3
Sept 3rd 1987	**Mayen Gymnasium**	won	1-0
Sept 15th 1987	Steyning GS	lost	1-2 (Gray)
Sept 19th 1987	Old Carthusians	lost	0-4
Sept 23rd 1987	**Godalming College**	won	4-3 (Leale 2, Gray, Strecker)
Sept 26th 1987	**Forest**	won	3-1 (Leale 2, Gray)
Sept 29th 1987	Ardingly	drew	1-1 (Hare)
Oct 3rd 1987	**Lancing**	won	1-0 (Gray)
Oct 6th 1987	**Malvern**	won	2-1 (Leale, Scott)
Oct 10th 1987	Bradfield	drew	1-1 (Gray)
Oct 14th 1987	**Richmond College**	won	1-0 [Surrey Cup]
Oct 17th 1987	Eton	drew	0-0
Oct 22nd 1987	**Elizabeth College**	won	4-2 (Gray 3, Leale)
Nov 4th 1987	St Joseph's College	lost	1-3 (Gray) [aet] [Surrey Cup]
Nov 7th 1987	Winchester	drew	2-2 (Gray, Stone)
Nov 10th 1987	**Aldenham**	won	3-0 (Leale 2, Henkes)
Nov 14th 1987	Highgate	drew	0-0
Nov 21st 1987	Shrewsbury	drew	1-1 (Gorman)
Nov 28th 1987	Repton	drew	1-1 (Strecker)
Dec 1st 1987	**Westminster**	won	3-1 (Leale 2, Henkes)

Tour to Mayen 1988

Date	Opponent	Result	Score (scorers)
Aug 25th 1988	FC Mayen	lost	1-3
Aug 26th 1988	**Alzheim**	won	2-1 (Clarke)
Aug 28th 1988	Rheinlander FC	lost	0-4
Sept 14th 1988	**Steyning GS**	won	2-1 (Austin, Benham)
Sept 17th 1988	Old Carthusians	lost	0-2
Sept 20th 1988	**Godalming College**	won	3-1 (Brooke 2, Gorman)
Sept 24th 1988	Forest	drew	1-1 (Sale)
Sept 27th 1988	Ardingly	drew	2-2 (Henkes, Scholefield)
Oct 1st 1988	Lancing	lost	0-2
Oct 8th 1988	Bradfield	drew	1-1 (Brooke)
Oct 11th 1988	**Malvern**	won	1-0 (Henkes)
Oct 15th 1988	Eton	drew	0-0
Oct 19th 1988	Richmond College	lost	1-2 (Gorman) [Surrey Cup]
Nov 5th 1988	Winchester	lost	1-3 (Benham)
Nov 8th 1988	**Aldenham**	won	3-0 (Scholefield 2, Ashby)

Date	Opponent	Result	Score (scorers)
Nov 12th 1988	**Highgate**	won	2-0 (Benham, Austin)
Nov 19th 1988	**Shrewsbury**	won	1-0 (Brooke)
Nov 26th 1988	Repton	drew	2-2 (Sale, Merrick)
Nov 29th 1988	Westminster	lost	1-4 (Brooke)
Sept 13th 1989	**Steyning GS**	won	4-0 (Clark 2, Sale 2)
Sept 16th 1989	Old Carthusians	lost	2-4 (E Ashby, Sale)
Sept 20th 1989	**Godalming College**	won	2-0 (Sale, Clark)
Sept 23rd 1989	Forest	drew	1-1 (Sale)
Sept 26th 1989	Ardingly	drew	0-0
Sept 30th 1989	Lancing	lost	0-2
Oct 7th 1989	Bradfield	lost	0-1
Oct 10th 1989	**Malvern**	won	4-2 (Rees, Hodson, o.g., Sale)
Oct 14th 1989	Eton	lost	0-2
Nov 1st 1989	**Reynalds**	won	3-0 (Sale 2, Wallace) [Surrey Cup]
Nov 4th 1989	**Winchester**	won	3-0 (Merrick, Butler, Mitten)
Nov 7th 1989	Aldenham	drew	1-1 (E Ashby)
Nov 9th 1989	**Salesian College**	won	4-2 (R Ashby, Fraser, Mitten 2) [Surrey Cup]
Nov 11th 1989	**Highgate**	won	3-0 (Sale, R Ashby, Mitten)
Nov 18th 1989	**Shrewsbury**	won	1-0 (Wallace)
Nov 23rd 1989	Heath Park	lost	1-6 (E Ashby) [Surrey Cup semi-final]
Nov 25th 1989	Repton	lost	1-3 (Sale)
Nov 28th 1989	**Westminster**	won	4-0 (Clark 2, Sale, Mitten)
Sept 12th 1990	**Steyning GS**	won	1-0 (Mitten)
Sept 15th 1990	Old Carthusians	lost	1-8 (Wallace)
Sept 19th 1990	Godalming College	lost	0-3
Sept 22nd 1990	Forest	drew	0-0
Sept 25th 1990	**Ardingly**	won	7-2 (Gompertz 3, Daly, Wallace, Mitten, o.g.)
Sept 29th 1990	Lancing	drew	0-0
Oct 6th 1990	**Bradfield**	drew	1-1 (Gompertz)
Oct 9th 1990	**Malvern**	won	2-1 (Mitten 2)
Oct 11th 1990	**Merton**	won	4-2 (Mitten 2, Gompertz 2) [Surrey Cup]
Oct 13th 1990	Eton	lost	0-2
Oct 18th 1990	**QE Guernsey**	won	3-2 (Gompertz 2, Rees)
Oct 31st 1990	**Spelthorne**	won	2-1 (Gompertz, Ashby) [Surrey Cup]
Nov 3rd 1990	Winchester	lost	0-1
Nov 6th 1990	**Aldenham**	won	2-1 (Mitten, Kidd)
Nov 10th 1990	Highgate	lost	2-3 (Wallace, Gompertz)
Nov 17th 1990	Shrewsbury	lost	1-2 (Rees)
Nov 19th 1990	Croydon College	lost	1-2 (Bower) [Surrey Cup Quarter Final]
Nov 24th 1990	Repton	lost	0-2
Dec 4th 1990	**Westminster**	won	3-2 (Ashby, Mitten, Rees)
Sept 11th 1991	Godalming College	lost	2-4 (Daly, Ashby)
Sept 14th 1991	Old Carthusians	lost	0-5
Sept 18th 1991	**Steyning GS**	won	2-1 (McCourtie, Peters)
Sept 21st 1991	Forest	lost	0-3
Sept 24th 1991	**Ardingly**	won	5-2 (McCourtie 3, Kidd 2)
Sept 28th 1991	Lancing	drew	0-0
Oct 2nd 1991	**Richard Challoner's**	won	3-2 (Bennett, McCourtie, Ashby) [Surrey Cup]
Oct 5th 1991	Bradfield	lost	0-2
Oct 8th 1991	**Malvern**	won	2-0 (Gompertz, Ashby)
Oct 12th 1991	Eton	drew	1-1 (Ashby)
Oct 16th 1991	**Esher College**	won	5-0 (Ashby 3, McCourtie, Pegler) [Surrey Cup]
Nov 2nd 1991	**Winchester**	won	3-0 (Gompertz 2, Pegler)
Nov 5th 1991	**Aldenham**	won	3-0 (Pegler, Ashby, Gompertz)
Nov 9th 1991	**Highgate**	won	3-0 (Ashby, Gompertz, Pegler)
Nov 11th 1991	Godalming College	lost	0-2 [Surrey Cup Quarter Final]
Nov 16th 1991	Shrewsbury	lost	1-2 (Gompertz)
Nov 23rd 1991	Repton	lost	0-1
Nov 27th 1991	**Hampton**	won	3-2 (Ashby, Gompertz, Pegler)
Dec 3rd 1991	**Westminster**	won	4-3 (Ashby 2, Gompertz, Pegler)

July 1992	U16 team played in the Gothia Cup for first time		
	IFK Gothenburg	won	2-1
	Mantorps	lost	0-2
	Lindholmens	lost	0-2
	Jagiellonia	lost	0-2
	Tilburg	won	2-0
Sept 16th 1992	**KES Witley**	won	3-0 (Webb, o.g.2)
Sept 19th 1992	Old Carthusians	lost	1-5 (Wakeham)
Sept 23rd 1992	Steyning GS	drew	3-3 (McCourtie 2, Wakeham)
Sept 26th 1992	**Forest**	won	3-0 (Webb 2, o.g.)
Sept 29th 1992	**Ardingly**	won	3-0 (McCourtie 3)
Oct 1st 1992	**John Lyon**	won	5-1 (McCourtie2, Webb, Wakeham, CunninghamBrown) [ISFA Cup 1]
Oct 3rd 1992	Lancing	lost	0-2
Oct 7th 1992	Malvern	lost	0-2
Oct 8th 1992	**Purley College**	won	3-2 (Webb 3) [Surrey Cup]
Oct 10th 1992	**Bradfield**	won	2-0 (Webb 2)
Oct 13th 1992	**Westminster**	won	5-1 (Webb 3, Younie, Wakeham) [ISFA Cup]

Date	Opponent	Result	Score
Oct 17th 1992	Eton	drew	1-1 (Webb)
Nov 7th 1992	**Winchester**	won	6-1 (Webb2, Wakeham, Wiegand, McCourtie, CunninghamBrown)
Nov 11th 1992	**St Joseph's**	won	3-1 (McCourtie 2, Webb) [Surrey Cup]
Nov 14th 1992	Aldenham	lost	2-3 (McCourtie 2)
Nov 19th 1992	Bradfield	won	2-1 (Jarvis, Wakeham) [ISFA Cup 3]
Nov 21st 1992	Shrewsbury	won	2-0 (McCourtie 2)
Nov 28th 1992	**Repton**	drew	0-0
Dec 1st 1992	Westminster	won	3-2 (McCourtie, Aldridge 2)
Dec 2nd 1992	**Richmond College**	won	6-4 (McCourtie 4, Jarvis, Aldridge) [Surrey Cup]
Jan 18th 1993	Taunton College	lost	1-2 (McCourtie) [ESFA Cup]
Feb 1st 1993	Shrewsbury	won	4-2 (Green, Webb, McCourtie, Jarvis) [ISFA Cup (semi-final)] aet
Mar 4th 1993	Wilson's	lost	0-1 [Surrey Cup Final] at Carshalton FC
Mar 16th 1993	Forest	drew	2-2(McCourtie, Jarvis)[ISFA Cup Final] aet *lost 0-3 on pens* *(played at Craven Cottage, Fulham FC)*
Sept 15th 1993	KES Witley	drew	2-2 (Wakeham, Sadler)
Sept 18th 1993	**Old Carthusians**	lost	1-5 (Younie)
Sept 23rd 1993	Kimbolton	won	4-1 (Younie, Wakeham, Guy 2) [ISFA Cup 1]
Sept 25th 1993	Forest	won	5-0 (Webb 5)
Sept 28th 1993	Ardingly	lost	1-5 (Drayson)
Oct 2nd 1993	**Lancing**	won	4-3 (Guy 2, Wakeham, Cunningham-Brown)
Oct 6th 1993	**Malvern**	won	3-2 (Wakeham, Webb, Cunningham-Brown)
Oct 9th 1993	Bradfield	lost	1-2 (o.g.)
Oct 13th 1993	**Hampton**	won	6-1(Wakeham2 Cunningham-Brown2 Webb 2) [Surrey Cup]
Oct 16th 1993	Eton	won	1-0 (Webb)
Oct 23rd 1993	Repton	won	2-1 (Webb 2) [ISFA Cup 2]
Nov 1st 1993	Farnham College	won	5-4 (Webb 3, Wakeham, Stern) [Surrey Cup]
Nov 6th 1993	Winchester	won	8-0 (Webb 3, Younie 2, Cunningham-Brown 2, Guy)
Nov 13th 1993	**Aldenham**	won	4-2 (Younie 2, Webb, o.g.)
Nov 16th 1993	**Ardingly**	lost	0-3 [ISFA Cup 3]
Nov 20th 1993	Shrewsbury	lost	0-3
Nov 27th 1993	Repton	lost	1-2 (Wakeham)
Nov 29th 1993	**Coulsdon College**	lost	2-3 (Webb, Aldridge) [Surrey Cup]
Nov 30th 1993	Westminster	won	6-2 (Younie 4, Webb, Tassell)

Pre-season tour to Holland

Date	Opponent	Result	Score
Sept 2nd 1994	E Hoensbroche C	drew	2-2 (Frendo, Dyson)
Sept 3rd 1994	Becherveld	drew	0-0
Sept 14th 1994	**KES Witley**	won	5-0 (Frendo 2, Smith 3)
Sept 17th 1994	**Old Carthusians**	lost	1-5 (Conn)
Sept 21st 1994	**Steyning GS**	won	1-0 (Frendo)
Sept 22nd 1994	Ashcombe Dorking	won	4-3 (Frendo, Waller, Dyson, Robertson) [Surrey Cup]
Sept 24th 1994	Forest	lost	1-3 (Frendo)
Sept 27th 1994	Ardingly	lost	1-5 (Robertson)
Sept 29th 1994	St Bede's, Manchester	lost	0-4 [ISFA Cup (1)]
Oct 1st 1994	Lancing	lost	1-2 (Waller)
Oct 4th 1994	Malvern	drew	1-1 (Frendo)
Oct 8th 1994	**Bradfield**	lost	0-1
Oct 15th 1994	Eton	won	2-0 (Frendo, Dolman)
Nov 2nd 1994	**Oxted**	won	2-0 (Robertson, Dyson) [Surrey Cup]
Nov 5th 1994	**Winchester**	won	2-0 (Waller, Brazier)
Nov 12th 1994	Aldenham	drew	2-2 (Brazier, Raven)
Nov 16th 1994	**Wilson's**	lost	0-4 [Surrey Cup]
Nov 19th 1994	Shrewsbury	lost	0-1
Nov 23rd 1994	**Hampton**	won	2-0 (Frendo, Waller)
Nov 26th 1994	Repton	lost	0-6
Nov 29th 1994	Westminster	lost	0-3

Pre-season tour to Holland

Date	Opponent	Result	Score
Aug 29th 1995	Casticum AFC	won	5-0 (Adie 2, Frendo, Hamblin, Carmichael)
Aug 31st 1995	Watersgraafmere AFC	drew	2-2 (Adie 2)
Sept 13th 1995	KES Witley	won	1-0 (Frendo)
Sept 16th 1995	**Old Carthusians**	lost	2-3 (Frendo, Raven)
Sept 20th 1995	Steyning GS	won	3-0 (Frendo, A Smith, Raven)
Sept 23rd 1995	Forest	drew	0-0
Sept 28th 1995	Westminster	lost	0-1 [ISFA (1)]
Sept 30th 1995	Lancing	lost	1-3 (Streatfeild)
Oct 2nd 1995	**St Andrew's, L'head**	won	4-3 (Lidstone, Hayes 2, Hamblin) [Surrey Cup] aet
Oct 4th 1995	Malvern	won	2-0 (Frendo 2)
Oct 7th 1995	Bradfield	won	3-2 (Frendo, A Smith, Lidstone)
Oct 14th 1995	Eton	lost	0-1
Oct 18th 1995	**Fulbrook College**	drew	1-1 (Savage) [Surrey Cup] *won on penalties aet*

Date	Opponent	Result	Score
Nov 4th 1995	Winchester	won	3-2 (Frendo 2, A Smith)
Nov 7th 1995	Ardingly	lost	3-4 (Frendo 3)
Nov 11th 1995	Aldenham	won	1-0 (Raven)
Nov 18th 1995	Shrewsbury	lost	1-5 (Hollingsworth)
Nov 23rd 1995	**Wimbledon College**	lost	0-2 [Surrey Cup Quarter Final]
Nov 25th 1995	Repton	lost	1-3 (Westcott)
Nov 28th 1995	Westminster	drew	1-1 (Westcott)

Pre-season tour of Holland

Date	Opponent	Result	Score
Sept 1st 1996	Standaard	won	5-1 (Smith 2, Westcott, Adie, Streatfeild)
Sept 2nd 1996	Roosteren	won	2-0 (Adie, Westcott)
Sept 14th 1996	**Old Carthusians**	lost	1-4 (Smith)
Sept 18th 1996	KES Witley	won	4-2 (Hollingsworth, Savage, Westcott, Smith)
Sept 21st 1996	**Forest**	drew	1-1 (Smith)
Sept 25th 1996	Malvern	won	2-1 (Adie 2) [ISFA Cup (1)]
Sept 28th 1996	Lancing	lost	0-3
Oct 2nd 1996	**Steyning GS**	won	3-1 (Adie 2, Hollingsworth)
Oct 5th 1996	Bradfield	won	2-1 (Saunders, Hollingsworth)
Oct 12th 1996	Eton	won	3-0 (Hollingsworth 2, Westcott)
Oct 15th 1996	Lancing	lost	0-3 [ISFA Cup (2)]
Oct 17th 1996	Epsom & Ewell	won	4-2 (Savage, Adie, Westcott, Saunders) [Surrey Cup]
Oct 19th 1996	**Winchester**	won	3-1 (Westcott 2, Smith)
Nov 9th 1996	Chichester HS	won	7-1 (Adie 3, Savage 2, Hollingsworth, o.g.)
Nov 12th 1996	**Ardingly**	lost	0-2
Nov 16th 1996	Aldenham	won	4-3 (Adie 2, Savage 2)
Nov 20th 1996	Wimbledon HS	won	5-3 (Adie, Westcott, Savage, Smith, Browne)[Surrey Cup] aet
Nov 23rd 1996	Shrewsbury	lost	1-2 (Smith)
Nov 26th 1996	Westminster	won	1-0 (Hollingsworth)
Nov 27th 1996	Richard Challenor's	lost	0-1 [Surrey Cup Semi Final] aet
Nov 29th 1996	Victoria College	won	1-0 (Saunders)
Dec 3rd 1996	Repton	lost	2-6 (Britten, Smith)

Pre-season tour to Holland

Date	Opponent	Result	Score
Sept 4th 1997	BMC	won	5-1 (Toulson, Burke-Murphy, Gay, Hollingsworth, Wallis)
Sept 5th 1997	RKVVSt Michiels	won	4-1 (Gay 3, Burke-Murphy)
Sept 13th 1997	**Old Carthusians**	lost	2-8 (Nash, Hollingsworth)
Sept 17th 1997	KES Witley	won	5-1 (Gay 3, Hollingsworth, Burke-Murphy)
Sept 20th 1997	Forest	won	5-3 (Hollingsworth 3, Gay, Leal)
Sept 24th 1997	St Bede's, Manchester	drew	3-3 (Hollingsworth 2, Nash) [ISFA Cup (1)] lost on pens aet
Sept 27th 1997	**Lancing**	won	4-1 (Gay, leal 2, Hollingsworth)
Oct 1st 1997	Fulbrook College	won	9-1 (Nash3, Gay, Hollingsworth, Leal, Savage, Burke-Murphy, o.g.)
Oct 4th 1997	Bradfield	won	7-0 (Gay 3, Hollingsworth 2, Nash, Beaumont)
Oct 7th 1997	Malvern	won	2-0 (Gay, o.g.)
Oct 11th 1997	Eton	won	4-2 (Toulson, o.g., Savage, Gay)
Oct 14th 1997	Ardingly	drew	3-3 (Hollingsworth, Gay 2)
Oct 18th 1997	Winchester	won	5-1 (Toulson, Burke-Murphy, Gay 2, o.g.)
Nov 5th 1997	**Victoria College**	drew	4-4 (Gay 4)
Nov 8th 1997	**St Bede's Hailsham**	won	6-1 (Leal 2, Hollingsworth 2, Beaumont, Savage)
Nov 11th 1997	**Fairfields**	lost	1-2 (Burke-Murphy) [Surrey Cup Quarter final]
Nov 15th 1997	Aldenham	won	1-0 (Savage)
Nov 19th 1997	Steyning GS	drew	0-0
Nov 21st 1997	**Shrewsbury**	won	1-0 (Gay)
Nov 25th 1997	**Westminster**	won	1-0 (o.g.)
Nov 29th 1997	Repton	lost	3-6 (Hollingsworth, Gay, Nash)

Pre-season tour to Holland

Date	Opponent	Result	Score
Sept 3rd 1998	Beaufays	won	4-1 (Schneider, Gay2, Wallis)
Sept 4th 1998	Maarheeves	won	8-0 (Beaumont, Schneider, o.g., Leal, Richardson 3, Wallis)
Sept 5th 1998	Garleen Zuig	won	9-0 (Gay 4, Jackson 2, Leal, Schneider, Poulsen)
Sept 12th 1998	Old Carthusians	lost	0-5
Sept 19th 1998	Forest	won	4-2 (Jackson, Leal 2, Wallis)
Sept 23rd 1998	Latymer Upper	lost	2-3 (Bailey, Jackson) [ISFA Cup (1)]
Sept 27th 1998	Surrey U16	won	3-2 (Burke-Murphy, Schneider, Gay)
Sept 29th 1998	Lancing	won	2-0 (Leal, Wallis)
Oct 3rd 1998	**Bradfield**	drew	1-1 (Burke-Murphy)
Oct 7th 1998	Malvern	won	6-0 (Jackson 2, Gay 2, Bailey, Beaumont)
Oct 10th 1998	Eton	lost	0-3
Oct 17th 1998	Winchester	drew	0-0
Nov 7th 1998	St Bede's Hailsham	won	2-1 (Beaumont, Wallis)
Nov 11th 1998	KES Witley	won	1-0 (Leal)
Nov 14th 1998	Aldenham	won	3-0 (Bailey, Burke-Murphy, Beaumont)

Date	Opponent	Result	Score
Nov 17th 1998	**Repton**	won	1-0 (Goodrich)
Nov 20th 1998	Shrewsbury	lost	0-3
Nov 24th 1998	**Westminster**	won	5-1 (Jackson, Wallis, Leal 2, Gay)
Nov 28th 1998	**Ardingly**	lost	0-1
Sept 11th 1999	**Old Carthusians**	lost	0-3
Sept 18th 1999	Forest	won	2-1 (Clark 2)
Sept 25th 1999	**Lancing**	won	3-0 (Bailey, Clark 2)
Sept 30th 1999	**Winchester**	won	2-0 (Byrne, Clark) [ISFA Cup (2)]
Oct 5th 1999	Malvern	won	3-1 (Clark 2, Jackson)
Oct 9th 1999	Eton	won	4-1 (Clark, Byrne, Bailey, Toller)
Oct 16th 1999	Winchester	won	2-0 (Bailey 2)
Oct 21st 1999	QEGS Blackburn	drew	2-2 (MacAuslan, Bailey) [ISFA Cup (3)] *won on penalties aet*
Nov 6th 1999	**St Bede's Hailsham**	won	3-0 (Toller, Bailey 2)
Nov 10th 1999	KES Witley	won	4-0 (Clark, Blake, Goodrich, Jackson)
Nov 13th 1999	**Aldenham**	won	4-0 (Bailey 2, Byrne, Shelton)
Nov 16th 1999	Repton	lost	0-3
Nov 19th 1999	**Shrewsbury**	won	2-0 (Clark, Byrne)
Nov 23rd 1999	**Westminster**	won	4-0 (Toller, Byrne, Shelton, Bailey)
Nov 27th 1999	Ardingly	won	6-0 (Bailey 2, Clark 2, Jackson, Toller)
Dec 4th 1999	Bury GS	won	2-1 (Bailey, Jackson) [ISFA Cup (4)]
Jan 25th 1999	Brentwood	won	2-0 (Jackson, Shelton) [ISFA Cup (Semi-final)]
Mar 20th 1999	Shrewsbury	lost	0-1 [ISFA Cup (final)] *played at Filbert Street, Leicester City*
Sept 9th 2000	**Old Carthusians**	lost	0-3
Sept 12th 2000	Hants U16	drew	4-4 (Burke-Murphy 2, Cook, Clark)
Sept 16th 2000	Forest	won	2-1 (Mezzetti, Williams)
Sept 19th 2000	Kimbolton	won	1-0 (Mezzetti) [ISFA 1]
Sept 23rd 2000	Lancing	won	1-0 (Burke-Murphy)
Sept 27th 2000	Alleyn's	won	2-0 (Clark 2) [ISFA 2]
Oct 4th 2000	Malvern	won	5-1 (Clark, Burke-Murphy, Mezzetti 2, Shelton)
Oct 7th 2000	Eton	won	2-0 (Williams 2)
Oct 14th 2000	**Winchester**	won	5-1 (Burke-Murphy, Clark, Shelton, Deschampsneufs, Mezzetti)
Oct 17th 2000	Brentwood	lost	3-4 (Clark 2, Mulligan) [ISFA Cup (3)]
Oct 19th 2000	**Bradfield**	won	3-0 (Deschampsneufs, Clark, Williams)
Nov 4th 2000	**St Bede's Hailsham**	won	4-1 (Clark 3, Burke-Murphy)
Nov 7th 2000	**KES Witley**	drew	1-1 (Clark)
Nov 11th 2000	Aldenham	won	5-0 (Burke-Murphy, Holmes, o.g., Mulligan, Clark)
Nov 14th 2000	**Repton**	won	3-2 (Clark 2, Deschampsneufs)
Nov 17th 2000	Shrewsbury	drew	1-1 (Cook)
Nov 21st 2000	**Westminster**	won	3-0 (Clark 2, Sogbetun)
Nov 25th 2000	**Ardingly**	won	2-0 (Clark, Mulligan)
Sept 8th 2001	**Old Carthusians**	lost	0-4
Sept 11th 2001	**Hants U16**	drew	1-1 (Sogbetun)
Sept 15th 2001	Forest	won	2-1 (Watson, Williams)
Sept 22nd 2001	**Lancing**	lost	1-2 (Griston)
Sept 27th 2001	Brentwood	lost	0-4 [ISFA Cup (1)]
Oct 2nd 2001	Malvern	won	3-1 (Sogbetun, Palley, Watson)
Oct 6th 2001	Eton	won	7-1 (Bunstead 2, Watson 3, Palley, Cook)
Oct 13th 2001	Winchester	won	2-0 (Sogbetun, Watson)
Oct 18th 2001	Bradfield	won	2-0 (Watson, Brennan)
Nov 3rd 2001	**St Bede's Hailsham**	won	4-0 (Marsden, Armstrong, N Bunstead 2)
Nov 10th 2001	**Aldenham**	won	7-0 (C Bunstead, Watson 2, Brennan 2, Williams, Palley)
Nov 13th 2001	Repton	lost	0-1
Nov 16th 2001	**Shrewsbury**	won	3-2 (Brennan, Armstrong 2)
Nov 20th 2001	**Westminster**	won	4-0 (o.g., N Bunstead, Brennan, Watson)
Nov 24th 2001	Ardingly	won	1-0 (Williams)
Sept 7th 2002	**Old Carthusians**	lost	0-1
Sept 10th 2002	Hants U16	won	3-0 (Hooper, Hunter, Barnett)
Sept 14th 2002	Forest	lost	1-2 (Ingham)
Sept 21st 2002	Lancing	won	2-0 (Barnett, Marsden)
Oct 2nd 2002	**Malvern**	drew	2-2 (Brennan, Katté)
Oct 5th 2002	Eton	drew	1-1 (Brennan)
Oct 9th 2002	St Bede's, Manchester	drew	5-5 (Bunstead 3, Ball, Millington Buck) [ISFA (2)] *won on penalties aet*
Oct 12th 2002	**Winchester**	drew	2-2 (Millington Buck 2)
Oct 17th 2002	**Bradfield**	drew	2-2 (Bunstead, Millington Buck)
Oct 19th 2002	Shrewsbury	lost	1-2 (Palley)
Nov 9th 2002	St Bede's, Hailsham	drew	3-3 (Bunstead, Barnett, Palley) [ISFA (3)] *won on penalties aet*
Nov 13th 2002	**Hampton**	won	4-0 (Marsden 2, Brennan, Katté)
Nov 19th 2002	Westminster	won	3-1 (Barnett 2, Palley)
Nov 23rd 2002	Ardingly	won	3-2 (Bunstead, Millington Buck, Barnett)
Nov 26th 2002	**Repton**	won	3-1 (Millington Buck, Palley, Katté)
Nov 30th 2002	Aldenham	won	5-2 (Bunstead, Marsden, Palley, Millington Buck, o.g.)
Dec 3rd 2002	Winchester	won	2-1 (Barnett, Millington Buck) [ISFA Cup (4)]
Feb 3rd 2003	Bolton	lost	0-5 [ISFA Cup (Semi-final)]
Sept 6th 2003	**Old Carthusians**	lost	0-3
Sept 9th 2003	Hants U16	lost	1-2 (Bourne)
Sept 13th 2003	Forest	won	4-2 (Ingham, Yabe, Hunter, Bourne)
Sept 20th 2003	**Lancing**	won	4-0 (Jenner, Yabe, Walker, Bardot)
Sept 30th 2003	Malvern	won	2-0 (o.g., Walker)
Oct 4th 2003	Eton	drew	0-0
Oct 7th 2003	Manchester GS	won	1-0 (Jenner) [ISFA Cup (2)]
Oct 11th 2003	Winchester	won	4-0 (Bourne, Hooper, Millington Buck, Walker)
Oct 16th 2003	Bradfield	lost	0-3
Oct 18th 2003	Shrewsbury	lost	1-2 (Bourne)
Nov 4th 2003	Eton	lost	1-2 (Bourne) [ISFA Cup (3)]
Nov 8th 2003	**St Bede's**	drew	2-2 (Hunter, Millington Buck)
Nov 12th 2003	Hampton	won	2-0 (Hunter, Millington Buck)
Nov 18th 2003	**Westminster**	drew	0-0
Nov 25th 2003	Repton	won	3-0 (Bourne 2, Millington Buck)
Nov 29th 2003	**Aldenham**	won	2-0 (Millington Buck, Ezekiel)
Sept 11th 2004	**Old Carthusians**	won	2-0 (Delaiglesia 2)
Sept 14th 2004	Hants U16	drew	1-1 (Holder)
Sept 18th 2004	Forest	won	3-1 (Yabe, Delaiglesia, Lucas)
Sept 25th 2004	Lancing	won	4-2 (Clinton, Millington Back, Holder, Cameron)
Sept 28th 2004	Brentwood	lost	1-2 (Paes) [ISFA Cup (1)]
Oct 10th 2004	Malvern	won	4-0 (Holder 2, Delaiglesia, Walker)
Oct 9th 2004	Eton	lost	2-3 (Clinton, Holder)
Oct 16th 2004	Winchester	won	3-1 (Walker, Holder, Paes)
Nov 2nd 2004	**Bradfield**	drew	3-3 (Clinton, Holder, Yabe)
Nov 6th 2004	St Bede's	won	1-0 (Millington Buck)
Nov 10th 2004	**Latymer Upper**	won	2-1 (Holder 2)
Nov 13th 2004	Brentwood	drew	1-1 (Cameron)
Nov 17th 2004	Westminster	won	5-1 (Nash 3, Yabe, O'Brien)
Nov 19th 2004	Shrewsbury	lost	0-3
Nov 23rd 2004	Repton	won	2-1 (Nash, Lucas)
Nov 27th 2004	Aldenham	won	3-1 (Lucas, Walker, Millington Buck)
Dec 4th 2004	Ardingly	won	4-0 (Clinton 2, Millington Buck, Yabe)
Sept 3rd 2005	**Old Carthusians**	lost	1-2 (Delaiglesia)
Sept 10th 2005	Highgate	won	3-1 (Delaiglesia, Clinton. Nash)
Sept 13th 2005	Hants U16	won	2-1 (Walford, Fyler)
Sept 17th 2005	Forest	won	6-0 (Delaiglesia, Cameron, Fyler 3, Holder)
Sept 24th 2005	Lancing	won	1-0 (Beddows)
Sept 28th 2005	St Mary's Crosby	won	10-1 (Nash, Holder 2, Clinton 2, Walford, Delaiglesia 3, Beddows) [ISFA Cup (1)]
Oct 4th 2005	Malvern	won	3-0 (Holder, Delaiglesia 2)
Oct 8th 2005	Eton	won	1-0 (Cameron)
Oct 11th 2005	St Bede's Hailsham	won	3-0 (Delaiglesia, Cameron, Clinton) [ISFA Cup (2)]
Oct 15th 2005	Winchester	drew	1-1 (Cameron)
Oct 20th 2005	Bradfield	won	2-0 (Holder, Delaiglesia)
Nov 10th 2005	Lancing	lost	1-2 (Holder) [ISFA Cup (3)]
Nov 12th 2005	St Bede's Hailsham	drew	2-2 (Delaiglesia 2)
Nov 15th 2005	**Westminster**	won	2-2 (Walford, Cameron)
Nov 19th 2005	Aldenham	won	1-0 (Cameron)
Nov 22nd 2005	Repton	won	3-1 (Cameron 2, Holder)
Dec 3rd 2005	Ardingly	won	2-1 (Cameron, Delaiglesia)
Sept 2nd 2006	**Old Carthusians**	drew	1-1 (Satterthwaite)
Sept 5th 2006	Hants U16	won	4-2 (Mason, Beddows, Nash 2)
Sept 9th 2006	Highgate	won	2-0 (Nash, Parsons)
Sept 13th 2006	Malvern	won	5-0 (Beddows 2, Clinton 3)
Sept 16th 2006	Forest	won	7-0 (Beddows, Rubinstein, Clinton 2, Nash, Evans, Cussins)
Sept 23rd 2006	Lancing	won	3-0 (Beddows, Mason, Satterthwaite)
Oct 3rd 2006	**Bankstown City FC**	lost	1-2 (Mason)
Oct 7th 2006	Eton	won	4-1 (Satterthwaite, Black, Cussins, Carter)
Oct 11th 2006	St Mary's, Crosby	won	2-1 (Rubinstein, Parsons) [ISFA Cup (2)]
Oct 14th 2006	Winchester	won	2-1 (Satterthwaite, Carter)
Oct 19th 2006	**Bradfield**	won	3-0 (Rubinstein, Parsons, Carter)
Oct 21st 2006	KES Witley	won	5-1 (Clinton 2, Carter, Parsons, Mason)
Nov 8th 2006	Hampton	drew	1-1 (o.g.)
Nov 11th 2006	St Bede's, Hailsham	lost	0-1
Nov 15th 2006	Latymer Upper	won	3-1 (Carter, Parsons, Clinton) [ISFA Cup (3)]
Nov 18th 2006	Aldenham	drew	1-1 (o.g.)
Nov 21st 2006	**Repton**	won	4-2 (Carter 3, Clinton)
Nov 24th 2006	Shrewsbury	won	1-0 (Rubinstein)

Nov 28th 2006	**Manchester GS**	won	2-1 (Beddows, Nash) [ISFA Cup (4)]
Nov 30th 2006	Westminster	drew	1-1 (Bowman)
Dec 3rd 2006	**Ardingly**	won	3-0 (Rubinstein 2, Satterthwaite)
Jan 29th 2007	Bury GS	won	2-0 (Carter, Rubinstein)[ISFA Cup (Semi-final)]
Apr 27th 2007	Hampton	drew*	1-1 (Nash) [ISFA Cup Final] *lost 2-4 on penalties* aet
	(played at Walkers Stadium, Leicester City)		
Sept 1st 2007	**Old Carthusians**	lost	0-1
Sept 4th 2007	**Hants U16**	drew	3-3 (Rogers, Watson, Hall)
Sept 8th 2007	Highgate	won	2-0 (Hall, Jamieson)
Sept 11th 2007	**Lancing**	won	1-0 (Rogers)
Sept 15th 2007	**Forest**	won	4-0 (Kimmins, Beddows, Hall 2)
Sept 22nd 2007	St Bede's Hailsham	won	2-1 (Hall, Black)
Oct 2nd 2007	Alleyn's	won	1-0 (Beddows)
Oct 6th 2007	**Eton**	drew	0-0
Oct 10th 2007	QEGS Blackburn	won	4-0 (Rogers, Beddows 2, Watson)[ISFA Cup (2)]

Oct 13th 2007	Winchester	drew	0-0
Oct 18th 2007	Bradfield	drew	0-0
Oct 20th 2007	**KES Witley**	won	1-0 (Rogers)
Nov 7th 2007	RGS Newcastle	won	1-0 (Beddows)[ISFA Cup (3)] *played at Whitley Bay FC*
Nov 10th 2007	Repton	won	3-1 (Hall 2, Jamieson)
Nov 14th 2007	**Hampton**	won	2-0 (Rogers, Kimmins)
Nov 17th 2007	**Aldenham**	won	3-1 (Jamieson 2, Beddows)
Nov 27th 2007	**Westminster**	won	1-0 (Jamieson)
Dec 1st 2007	Ardingly	won	6-0 (Beddows 2, Walker, Hall, Peat, Parsons)
Dec 4th 2007	Shrewsbury	drew	2-2 (Watson, Kimmins) [ISFA Cup (4)] *won on penalties 8-7* aet
Jan 23rd 2008	King's, Chester	won	1-0 (Hall) [ISFA Cup (Semi-final)]
Jan 28th 2008	Bradfield	won	3-0 (Rogers, Adolphus, Hall) [SIS Final]*at C-Casuals*
Mar 12th 2008	**Millfield at Charterhouse**	drew	0-0 [ISFA Cup Final] *won on penalties 8-7* aet

IX Boodles ISFA Cup Results

1992-3
Rd 1	Bye	
Rd 2	John Lyon, Harrow a	5-1
Rd 3	Bradfield a	2-1
S-f	Shrewsbury a	3-2 aet
Final	Forest	2-2 aet
	at Fulham FC	0-3 pens

1993-4
Rd 1	Kimbolton a	4-1
Rd 2	Repton a	2-1
Rd 3	Ardingly	0-3

1994-5
Rd 1	St Bede's	0-4
	Manchester a	

1995-6
Rd 1	Westminster	0-1

1996-7
Rd 1	Malvern	2-1
Rd 2	Lancing a	0-3

1997-8
Rd 1	St Bede's Manchester a	3-3 aet
		2-4 pens

1998-9
Rd 1	Latymer Upper	2-3

99-2000
Rd 1	Winchester	2-0
Rd 2	QEGS Blackburn a	2-2 aet
		5-4 pens
Rd 3	Bury GS a	1-2
S-f	Brentwood a	0-2
Final	Shrewsbury	0-1
	at Leicester FC	

2000-01
Rd 1	Kimbolton a	1-0
Rd 2	Alleyn's a	2-0
Rd 3	Brentwood	3-4

2001-02
Rd 1	Brentwood	0-4

2002-03
Rd 1	St Bede's Manchester a	5-5 aet
		5-4 pens
Rd 2	St Bede's Hailsham a	3-3 aet
		4-1 pens
Rd 3	Winchester	2-1
S-f	Bolton	0-5

2003-4
Rd 2	Manchester GS	1-0
Rd 3	Eton a	1-2

2004-5
Rd 1	Brentwood	1-2

2005-6
Rd 1	St Mary's Cosby a	10-1
Rd 2	St Bede's Hailsham	3-0
Rd 3	Lancing a	1-2

2006-7
Rd 2	St Mary's Crosby a	2-1
Rd 3	Latymer Upper	3-1
Rd 4	Manchester GS	2-1
S-f	Bury GS a	2-0 S-F
Final	Hampton	1-1 aet
	at Leicester FC	2-4 pens

2007-8
Rd 2	QEGS Blackburn a	4-0
Rd 3	RGS Newcastle a	1-0
Rd 4	Shrewsbury a	2-2 aet
		8-7 pens
S-f	King's Chester a	1-0
Final	Millfield	0-0 aet
	at Charterhouse	8-7 pens

Index